International Financial Reporting Standards and New Directions in Earnings Management

Jonas da Silva Oliveira
Instituto Universitário de Lisboa (ISCTE-IUL), Portugal

Graça Maria do Carmo Azevedo
University of Aveiro, Portugal

Augusta da Conceição Santos Ferreira
University of Aveiro, Portugal

A volume in the Advances in Finance, Accounting, and Economics (AFAE) Book Series

IGI Global
DISSEMINATOR OF KNOWLEDGE

Published in the United States of America by
IGI Global
Business Science Reference (an imprint of IGI Global)
701 E. Chocolate Avenue
Hershey PA, USA 17033
Tel: 717-533-8845
Fax: 717-533-8661
E-mail: cust@igi-global.com
Web site: http://www.igi-global.com

Library of Congress Cataloging-in-Publication Data

Names: Oliveira, Jonas da Silva, editor. | Azevedo, Graca Maria do Carmo, editor. | Ferreira, Augusta da Conceicao Santos, 1966- editor.
Title: International financial reporting standards and new directions in earnings management / Jonas da Silva Oliveira, Graca Maria do Carmo Azevedo, and Augusta da Conceicao Santos Ferreira, editors.
Description: Hershey, PA : Business Science Reference, [2019]
Identifiers: LCCN 2018037200| ISBN 9781522578178 (hardcover) | ISBN 9781522578185 (ebook)
Subjects: LCSH: Financial statements--Standards. | Accounting--Standards. | International business enterprises--Accounting.
Classification: LCC HF5681.B2 I57858 2019 | DDC 657/.30218--dc23 LC record available at https://lccn.loc.gov/2018037200

This book is published in the IGI Global book series Advances in Finance, Accounting, and Economics (AFAE) (ISSN: 2327-5677; eISSN: 2327-5685)

British Cataloguing in Publication Data
A Cataloguing in Publication record for this book is available from the British Library.

For electronic access to this publication, please contact: eresources@igi-global.com.

Advances in Finance, Accounting, and Economics (AFAE) Book Series

Ahmed Driouchi
Al Akhawayn University, Morocco

ISSN:2327-5677
EISSN:2327-5685

Mission

In our changing economic and business environment, it is important to consider the financial changes occurring internationally as well as within individual organizations and business environments. Understanding these changes as well as the factors that influence them is crucial in preparing for our financial future and ensuring economic sustainability and growth.

The **Advances in Finance, Accounting, and Economics** (**AFAE**) book series aims to publish comprehensive and informative titles in all areas of economics and economic theory, finance, and accounting to assist in advancing the available knowledge and providing for further research development in these dynamic fields.

Coverage

- Theoretical Issues in Economics, Finance, and Accounting
- Economics of Agriculture and Biotechnology
- Applied Accounting
- Economics Geography
- Economics of Natural and Environmental Resources
- Microfinance
- Statistical Analysis
- Interest Rates and Annuities
- Health economics
- Economics of Migration and Spatial Mobility

IGI Global is currently accepting manuscripts for publication within this series. To submit a proposal for a volume in this series, please contact our Acquisition Editors at Acquisitions@igi-global.com or visit: http://www.igi-global.com/publish/.

The Advances in Finance, Accounting, and Economics (AFAE) Book Series (ISSN 2327-5677) is published by IGI Global, 701 E. Chocolate Avenue, Hershey, PA 17033-1240, USA, www.igi-global.com. This series is composed of titles available for purchase individually; each title is edited to be contextually exclusive from any other title within the series. For pricing and ordering information please visit http://www.igi-global.com/book-series/advances-finance-accounting-economics/73685. Postmaster: Send all address changes to above address.

Titles in this Series

For a list of additional titles in this series, please visit: www.igi-global.com/book-series

Planning and Analyzing Foreign Direct Investment Projects Emerging Research and Opportunities
Halil Sarıaslan (Başkent University, Turkey)
Business Science Reference • copyright 2019 • 338pp • H/C (ISBN: 9781522576969) • US $215.00 (our price)

Maintaining Financial Stability in Times of Risk and Uncertainty
Abhishek Behl (Indian Institute of Technology Bombay, India) and Sushma Nayak (Symbiosis International University (Deemed), India)
Business Science Reference • copyright 2019 • 377pp • H/C (ISBN: 9781522572084) • US $265.00 (our price)

Global Trends of Modernization in Budgeting and Finance
Denis Ushakov (Suan Sunandha Rajabhat University, Thailand)
Business Science Reference • copyright 2019 • 354pp • H/C (ISBN: 9781522577607) • US $215.00 (our price)

Corporate Insolvency Law and Bankruptcy Reforms in the Global Economy
Amit Kashyap (Nirma University, India)
Business Science Reference • copyright 2019 • 261pp • H/C (ISBN: 9781522555414) • US $185.00 (our price)

Time Bank as a Complementary Economic System Emerging Research and Opportunities
Lukas Valek (University of Hradec Kralove, Czech Republic) and Vladimir Bures (University of Hradec Kralove, Czech Republic)
Business Science Reference • copyright 2019 • 208pp • H/C (ISBN: 9781522569749) • US $175.00 (our price)

Economic Dynamics of Global Energy Geopolitics
Ahmet Salih Ikiz (Muğla Sıtkı Koçman University, Turkey)
Engineering Science Reference • copyright 2019 • 305pp • H/C (ISBN: 9781522542032) • US $195.00 (our price)

Co-Manufacturing and New Economic Paradigms
Giulio Focardi (Osun WES, Italy) and Lorenza Salati (Osun WES, Italy)
Business Science Reference • copyright 2019 • 217pp • H/C (ISBN: 9781522570899) • US $185.00 (our price)

Handbook of Research on Microfinancial Impacts on Women Empowerment, Poverty, and Inequality
Ramesh Chandra Das (Katwa College, India)
Business Science Reference • copyright 2019 • 452pp • H/C (ISBN: 9781522552406) • US $275.00 (our price)

IGI Global
DISSEMINATOR OF KNOWLEDGE

701 East Chocolate Avenue, Hershey, PA 17033, USA
Tel: 717-533-8845 x100 • Fax: 717-533-8661
E-Mail: cust@igi-global.com • www.igi-global.com

Editorial Advisory Board

List of Reviewers

Cláudia Roberta de Araújo Alves Pinto, *Polytechnic Institute of Viana Castelo, Portugal*
Maria José Pires Carvalho da Silva, *University of Aveiro, Portugal*
Maria da Conceição da Costa Tavares, *University of Aveiro, Portugal*
Flora Hermengarda de Pinho e Cunha Lobo, *University of Aveiro, Portugal*
Maria Fátima Ribeiro Borges, *University of Aveiro, Portugal*

Table of Contents

Detailed Table of Contents

The quality of earnings is a summary metric in firm performance evaluation and a focal question to assess the quality of accounting information. A high-quality earnings figure will reflect a firm's current operating performance, being a good indicator of future operating performance; it also accurately annuitizes the intrinsic value of the firm. The multidimensional nature of the earnings quality (EQ) concept has given form to a multiplicity of constructs and measures. This chapter offers a systematic literature review on EQ and its implication on firm value. On the one hand, it discusses the different existent definitions of EQ and the multidimensional nature of the concept; on the other hand, it highlights a "new" EQ perspective taking into account the virtuosities of the residual income model. An empirical model is proposed that reinterprets rebuilding the linear information dynamics in relation to market value added and captures, in a composite measure, the three-dimensional facet of the EQ concept: persistence, predictability, and informativeness of earnings.

This chapter aims to analyze if and the extent to which earnings management activities are detected by market participants. For that purpose, this chapter reviews prior literature on stock market reaction to earnings management and earnings quality. A main conclusion obtained with this approach is that stock market participants are to some extent misled by earnings management activities consistent with those activities making the firm's information environment more opaque, thus increasing the difficulty for investors to interpret financial statements. Both the theoretical and empirical contributions provided in such works are relevant given the potential negative consequences of earnings management for stakeholders, firms, and even for the entire economy. In addition, it must be emphasized that accounting regulation is fundamental to balance the trade-off between more informative financial statements and reducing the level of managers' opportunistic choices.

This chapter provides insights on earnings management (EM) explanatory factors. These factors are analyzed within the framework of a specific strategy of EM: income smoothing (IS). This strategy is often used to report earnings with an artificially reduced variability. Thereby, the purpose of the chapter is to explore the motivations, the determinants (anticipated by the positive accounting theory), and some firm-specific factors that might explain IS practices. The relevance of this chapter is justified essentially by two reasons. First, it highlights the contemporary importance of this research line. The academic community, professionals, and regulatory bodies have expressed publicly the concern about the quality of financial reporting. Consequently, a deep knowledge of the factors that possibly explain these accounting discretionary practices is crucial. Second, the extensive literature on EM also justifies this chapter. Thereby, the systematization of the literature on the IS explanatory factors can help researchers and increase future empirical research focused on this area.

This chapter investigates whether Italian-listed companies involved in mergers and acquisitions (M&A) during the period 2009–2017 manipulated earnings through recourse to discretionary accruals in response to financial market competition. Interest in the possible effects of competition on earnings management practices follows the considerable attention attracted by the effects of business combinations on disclosure quality and reliability. M&A represents an opportunity for managers to manipulate financial reports and to deliver misleading market information in order to enhance company reputation and attract funds from investors. This empirical analysis demonstrates that Italian-listed companies involved in M&A used goodwill as a discretionary accrual for managing earnings. The findings indicate that the increasing level of financial market competition between Italian-listed companies prompted major recourse to earnings management practices based on discretionary accruals.

Although small and medium-sized enterprises (SMEs) are represented on a large scale around the world, the literature on earnings management (EM) has focused mainly on listed firms. In this sense, this chapter provides important insights on the determinants and main incentives for EM in the context of Portuguese and Spanish SMEs, over a period of 10 years, also considering two relevant macroeconomic events (financial crisis and entry into force of harmonized accounting regulations). The results obtained are

Inventories are the base element for the manufacturing (industrial) companies. The inclusion of discretionary in the inventory management processes of production leads to changes in the value of the companies. The accounting system produces information used in predictions and for management decision. The usefulness and opportunity of information are considered indispensable. If managers use their discretionarily, in the accounting system and in real activities, to achieve the firm value and earnings forecast, they will influence and modify the financial information quality. Ferrer and Ferrer said that a simple decision can enrich one company from one moment to another, and a small accounting change allows a great loss of results. The question arises: Do managers use their discretionarily and modify the financial information quality? Using adjusted models to capture discretionary accounting management and real activity management, it is possible to conclude that there is a strong evidence of discretionary management of the inventory in manufacturing Portuguese SME.

This chapter assesses the influence of organizational performance in the adoption of impression management strategies in the Chairmen's statements of the Portuguese financial companies. It also evaluates the impact of the financial crisis on the adoption of impression management strategies. To this end, and using the content analysis of the Chairmen's statements included in the individual annual reports for 2006-2012 of 27 financial institutions, the authors conclude that even throughout the financial crisis period, Portuguese financial companies did not tend to adopt more impression management strategies. However, they have seen that in some years there is some evidence of its adoption.

The chapter intends to determine if managers make use of impression management strategies to hide or obfuscate risk disclosures through the analyses of the risk information disclosed by Portuguese non-financial listed companies. A content analysis of the management reports, notes to the financial statements, and corporate governance reports of companies listed at Euronext Lisbon, in the years 2007, 2010, and 2013 was carried out. Findings indicate that the understandability of the risk information is positively associated with the company's size. Results also indicate that there is a negative association between the readability of risk information disclosed and the company's size and industry.

Preface

ABOUT THE SUBJECT

The topic of earnings management has gained a huge international relevance. According to Healy and Wahlen (1999) "earnings management occurs when managers use judgment in financial reporting and in structuring transactions to alter financial reports to either mislead some stakeholders about the underlying economic performance of the company or to influence contractual outcomes that depend on reported accounting numbers" (p. 368). According to Schipper (1989) and Bouchareb et al. (2014), earnings management is pursued with the intention of obtaining some of its own benefits associated with opportunistic actions to increase or decrease net earnings. Thus, the concept of earnings management deals with maximization, minimization, and smoothing of earnings (Copeland & Wojdak, 1969). Research on earnings management allows us to predict future manager behavior. Basically, because helps identifying managers' behavioral patterns and how they use accounting policies in different opportunistic circumstances.

Research on these topics has been focused in the accounting quality. However, earnings management continues to face news challenges. Earnings management may be difficult for individual investors to detect due to the complexity of accounting rules, the characteristics of corporate governance structures, the kind of linguistics used by managers, and the inability of auditing some sets of disclosures. In fact, theoretically, firms with large accruals and weak governance structures are more likely to engage in earnings management. Developments in social psychology have suggested that some linguistics-based methods can detect financial manipulation. In a simpler way, accounting irregularities, deceptive restatements and financial reporting aggressiveness are associated with the tone at the top (Patteli & Pedrini, 2015) either in the CEO letters or in the conference calls. Some of these documents include voluntary information that is not audited, intrinsically linked with forward-looking information on earnings announcements, future performance and its forecasting ability. Consequently, if these pieces of information are associated with earnings management behaviors, this will affect investors' ability to predict future earnings accurately.

Therefore, it would be fruitful to investigate and disseminate the results of theoretical and empirical studies that reveal different aspects of earnings management phenomenon in order to obtain insightful knowledge on how to promote effectively the financial reporting transparency.

This book gathers several coherent chapters which allow, on a scientific basis, to discuss at an international level the new directions in earnings management upgraded and refocused, mainly, in issues such as the International Financial Reporting Standards, Corporate Governance, Auditing, Public Sector, and Ethics.

EXPECTATIONS

The editors intend this book to be useful for regulatory authorities and researchers in the field of financial accounting, corporate governance, finance, impression management, and auditing. Through dissemination of the research findings on the rigor of accounting quality this publication could also be valuable to develop and inspire further studies by researchers and students in postgraduate courses, whose research interests are related to earnings management.

This book aims to achieve the following main objectives:

- Disseminate methodologies that would ensure the quality of financial information;
- Document the earnings management that are being used by public institutions to increase their quality of financial reports;
- Review processes/governance models that promote better earnings management;
- Analyze if the earnings management involves changes in financial reports and make a critical reflection on other theoretical perspectives grounded on social psychology to explain managers' behavior;
- Discuss and disseminate the level of earnings management in less developed countries;
- Analyze if the voluntary adoption of International Financial Reporting Standards (IFRS) is associated with lower earnings management;
- Analyze the evidence about the effectiveness of mandatory audits to improve earnings quality.

ORGANIZATION OF THE BOOK

This book is organized into 13 chapters. The first three chapters are focused on literature review of earnings management phenomenon. Thus:

- Chapter 1, "Earnings Quality and Firm Valuation: A "New" Perspective Deriving From the Literature," offers a systematic literature review on earnings quality and its implication on firm value. It discusses the different existent definitions of earnings quality, the multidimensional nature of the concept, and highlights a "new" earnings quality perspective taking into account the virtuosities of the residual income model.
- Chapter 2, "Earnings Management and Stock Market Reaction," reviews prior literature on stock market reaction to earnings management and earnings quality in order to analyze if and the extent to which earnings management activities are detected by market participants.
- Chapter 3, "An Overall Perspective of Income Smoothing as a Strategy of Earnings Management," provides a systematization of the literature on the income smoothing explanatory factors that can help researchers and increase future empirical research focused on this research field.

The next two following chapters provide reflections on the association between earnings management and the International Financial Accounting Standards. In this way:

- Chapter 4, "Earnings Management and Mergers and Acquisitions: Empirical Evidence From Italian-Listed Companies," investigates whether Italian-listed companies involved in mergers and acquisitions used goodwill as a discretionary accrual for managing earnings in response to financial market competition.
- Chapter 5, "Earnings Management in SMEs: Evidence From Portugal and Spain," provides important insights on the influence of the recent financial crisis and the adoption of adapted International Financial Accounting Standards on the incentives for EM in the context of Portuguese and Spanish SMEs.

The following three chapters cover issues on the influence of corporate governance, auditing, and inventories on earnings management. Thus:

- Chapter 6, "Earnings Management and Corporate Governance in Family Firms: Evidence From a Small Market," examines the relationship between earnings management and corporate governance among Portuguese listed family firms.
- Chapter 7, "Earnings Management and Audit in Private Firms: The Effect of Financial Recuperation," investigates the relationship between the level of earnings management and the audit in private firms under the influence of financial crisis recuperation, using a sample of Ireland and Portuguese firms from 2008 to 2016.
- Chapter 8, "The Relationship Between the Quality of Financial Information in Industrial Companies and Discretionary Inventory Management," analyses the effect of earnings management on inventories fluctuation among manufacturing firms.

Chapters 9 to 11 provide some knowledge about how linguistics and graphic manipulation are associated with financial manipulation. Thus:

- Chapter 9, "Impression Management Strategies in the Chairmen's Statements: Evidence From the Portuguese Banking Industry," assesses the influence of organizational performance in the adoption of impression management strategies in the Chairmen's statements of the Portuguese financial companies. It also evaluates the impact of the financial crisis on the adoption of impression management strategies.
- Chapter 10, "Determinants of the Readability and Comprehensibility of Risk Disclosures: Evidence From Portuguese Listed Companies," determines if managers use impression management strategies to hide or obfuscate risk disclosures, through the analyses of the risk information disclosed by Portuguese non-financial listed companies.
- Chapter 11, "The Use of Financial Graphics as an Impression Management Tool: Evidence of Portuguese Listed Companies," analyzes which factors can actually influence the graphical discrepancy index, based on the strategies of impression management.

Finally, the last two chapters address issues concerning earnings management in emerging economies. Thus:

- Chapter 12, "Convergence of Accounting Standards to International Standards and Earnings Management in Brazilian Companies," sought to highlight the main challenges of the initial adoption of accounting standards converged to international standards applied to public companies and treasury-dependent companies and how the results of economic agents in public and private companies in Brazil are managed.
- Chapter 13, "Developments in Earnings Management Practices in the IFRS Perspective: An Application in a Public Company," examines the examples of a public company that is traded on the Istanbul Stock Exchange for the purpose of determining earnings management practices under International Financial Reporting Standards (IFRS).

Jonas da Silva Oliveira
Instituto Universitário de Lisboa (ISCTE-IUL), Portugal

Graça Maria do Carmo Azevedo
University of Aveiro, Portugal

Augusta da Conceição Santos Ferreira
University of Aveiro, Portugal

REFERENCES

Bouchareb, M., Ajina, A., & Souid, S. (2014). Does the adoption of ias/ifrs with a strong governance mechanism can deter earnings management? *International Journal of Academic Research in Economics and Management Sciences*, *3*(1), 264–282. doi:10.6007/IJAREMS/v3-i1/645

Copeland, R. M., & Wojdak, J. F. (1969). Income manipulation and the purchase-pooling choice. *Journal of Accounting Research*, *7*(2), 188–195. doi:10.2307/2489964

Healy, P. M., & Wahlen, J. M. (1999). A review of the earnings management literature and its implications for standard setting. *Accounting Horizons*, *13*(4), 365–383. doi:10.2308/acch.1999.13.4.365

Patelli, L., & Pedrini, M. (2015). Is tone at the top associated with financial reporting aggressiveness? *Journal of Business Ethics*, *126*(1), 3–19. doi:10.100710551-013-1994-6

Schipper, K. (1989). Commentary on earnings management. *Accounting Horizons*, *3*(4), 91–102.

Acknowledgment

The editors would like to acknowledge the help of all the people involved in this project and, more specifically, the authors and reviewers who took part in the review process. Their effort was an excellent and relevant contribution to this publication process. Without their support, this book would not have become a reality.

First, the editors would like to thank each of the chapters' authors who contributed with their time and expertise to this book.

Second, the editors wish to acknowledge the excellent and valuable work of the Editorial Advisory Board members regarding the improvement of quality, coherence, and content presentation of chapters which ensured the highest accuracy in the double-blinded review process. Most of the authors also served as referees; we highly appreciate their double task.

Jonas da Silva Oliveira
Instituto Universitário de Lisboa (ISCTE-IUL), Portugal

Graça Maria do Carmo Azevedo
University of Aveiro, Portugal

Augusta da Conceição Santos Ferreira
University of Aveiro, Portugal

Chapter 1
Earnings Quality and Firm Valuation:
A "New" Perspective Deriving From the Literature

Liliana Marques Pimentel
University of Coimbra, Portugal

Susana Jorge
https://orcid.org/0000-0003-4850-2387
University of Coimbra, Portugal

ABSTRACT

The quality of earnings is a summary metric in firm performance evaluation and a focal question to assess the quality of accounting information. A high-quality earnings figure will reflect a firm's current operating performance, being a good indicator of future operating performance; it also accurately annuitizes the intrinsic value of the firm. The multidimensional nature of the earnings quality (EQ) concept has given form to a multiplicity of constructs and measures. This chapter offers a systematic literature review on EQ and its implication on firm value. On the one hand, it discusses the different existent definitions of EQ and the multidimensional nature of the concept; on the other hand, it highlights a "new" EQ perspective taking into account the virtuosities of the residual income model. An empirical model is proposed that reinterprets rebuilding the linear information dynamics in relation to market value added and captures, in a composite measure, the three-dimensional facet of the EQ concept: persistence, predictability, and informativeness of earnings.

DOI: 10.4018/978-1-5225-7817-8.ch001

1. INTRODUCTION

The subject of earnings quality (EQ) is a complex area and no researcher has this far been able to provide a unique definition of EQ, neither to find an adequate measure for it.

However, there is an overall agreement that EQ is a summary measure in firm performance evaluation and a crucial question to assess the quality of accounting information. A high-quality earnings figure will reflect firm's current operating performance, being a good indicator of future operating performance. Although EQ is a useful summary measure for assessing firm value, determining EQ and its implications for firm value, is rather difficult.

Knowing that earnings are important for evaluation effects and investors see in the earnings management a valuable information source to assess firm value, valuation models based on earnings, and based on book value, are viewed typically as an alternative approach to assess firm value. The use of earnings in various valuation models can be theoretically justified. The higher EQ, the more useful the earnings data are as a forecasting metric and the more accurate the firm valuation. Ohlson's (1995) model, and its subsequent refinements by Feltham and Ohlson (1995). Ohlson (1999) and Barth et al. (1999, 2005), offer a formal link between valuation and accounting numbers, being cited frequently as the theoretical foundation of such research.

This chapter offers a systematic literature review on EQ and its implications on firm value. On the one hand, it discusses the different EQ definitions and, on the other hand, it presents the relevant literature on studies about the relationship between financial statement data and firm value.

The discussion on these models allows to conclude that, determining the value of a company on the basis of accounting and financial variables in a framework of nonlinear relationships, presents a high potential for future research. Therefore, the chapter summarizes a theoretical basis for future researches on what determines a firm's value, starting from the accounting and financial statements figures.

Finally, the chapter also highlights a "new" EQ perspective taking in account the virtuosities of the residual income model. An empirical model is proposed, which reinterprets rebuilding the linear information dynamics in relation to market value added and captures, in a composite measure, the three-dimensional facet of the EQ concept: persistence, predictability and *informativeness* of earnings.

Henceforth, the chapter is organized as follows. Section 2 offers an overview of the relevance of the EQ concept and its multidimensional nature. Section 3 starts by highlighting the relationship between financial statement data and firm value, followed by a review of the relevant models in the literature that addressed that relationship. Section 4 continues the literature on models that started to evidence the importance of looking at the earnings components. Section 5, finally proposes a model on a "new" EQ perspective. The chapter finalizes with a short summary and conclusions.

2. DEFINING EARNINGS QUALITY

The subject of EQ is a complex area of research. So far, theoretical literature and empirical studies have not been able to provide a consensual definition of EQ, neither to find an adequate measure for it.

In what concerns the definition, some of the most important definitions, constructs and measures of EQ relate with persistence, predictability and variability (time-series properties) of earnings. Another stream of knowledge relates EQ with the relationship between income, accruals and cash, taking the view that earnings that map more closely into cash are more desirable (e.g. Penman, 2001). Others, in turn, consider that EQ is "conditional on the decision-relevance of the information", hence considering that EQ is defined only in the context of a specific decision model (Dechow *et al.*, 2010: 344).

Many studies give a definition on EQ. All of them agree that the concept is complex and nebulous, there is not a unique definition, neither an adequate measure for it. Although the concept is of common use, there is no consensus between academics and practitioners on its content, that is, there is no single definition of EQ. In fact, as mentioned, namely, by Bernstein (1996: 749) "virtually, there is no general agreement as regard to the definitions or assumptions on this term (earnings quality)". Or, as stated by Ghosh *et al.* (2005: 34) "the earnings quality is a nebulous concept".

Earnings are of high quality when the earnings number accurately annuitizes the intrinsic value of the firm. Such earnings are referred to as "permanent earnings" in the accounting literature (*e.g.*, Black, 1980; Beaver, 1998; Ohlson and Zhang, 1998).

Beaver (1999: 41) explains that "earnings are of high quality if they are sustainable", thus they are a good indicator of future earnings. Or, according to Penman and Zhang (2002: 237), "earnings can be regarded as good quality if it is a good indicator of future earnings".

EQ and, more generally, financial reporting quality, are of interest to those who use financial reports for contracting purpose and for investments decision making (Schipper and Vincent, 2003).

Some of the most important definitions, constructs and measures are related with the persistence, predictability and variability of earnings (time-series properties of earnings). Persistence has to be understood in the sense that current earnings provide a good indication of future earnings, capturing the extent to which a given innovation remains in future realizations. Predictability is a function of the distribution (especially the variance) of the innovation series: "the ability of past earnings to predict future earnings" (Lipe, 1990). Variability measures the time-series variance of innovations directly (Leuz *et al.*, 2003). Hermanns (2006) considers an additional measure derived from time-series properties of earnings – *informativeness* of earnings: the capacity to explain stock returns (Warfield *et al.*, 1995) or the information content with respect to future earnings (Ahmed *et al.*, 2004).

Others relate EQ to the relation between income, accruals and cash, taking the view that earnings that map more closely into cash are more desirable (*e.g.*, Penman, 2001). According to several authors (*e.g.*, Sloan, 1996; Graham *et al.*, 2005; Richardson *et al.*, 2005 and 2006), one can assess EQ considering the relation between accruals and cash flows. In line with this point of view, the results of Graham *et al.* (2005) indicate that financial officers believe that earnings, not cash flows, are the key metric to outsiders. Managers are focused on short-term earnings benchmarks, especially the seasonally lagged quarterly earnings number and the analyst consensus estimate. Managers also work to maintain predictability in earnings and financial disclosures. This finding could reflect superior informational content in earnings over the other metrics.

In fact, several studies document the benefits of the accruals process, finding that earnings are a better measure of performance than the underlying cash flows (*e.g.*, Dechow *et al.,* 1998; Dechow and Dichev, 2002; Dechow and Schrand, 2004), that earnings explain more of the cross-sectional variation in stock returns or stock prices relative to operating cash flows (*e.g.*, Bernard and Stober, 1989; Dechow, 1994; Barth *et al.*, 2001b; Liu *et al.*, 2002). Being the accrual accounting more ambitious than a "cash-flow-oriented accounting system" (Beaver and Demski, 1979: 43). Dechow (1994) finds that accruals improve earnings' ability to measure performance relative to cash flows.

Sloan (1996) finds that the accruals portion of earnings is less persistent than the cash flow portion. This suggests that firms with high levels of accruals have low quality of earnings. Dechow and Dichev (2002), analysing the interrelations between accrual quality, level of accruals, and earnings persistence suggests a reconciliation of the findings of Dechow (1994) and Sloan (1996). Their reconciliation is based on the observation that a high level of accruals signifies both earnings that are a greater improvement over underlying cash flows, and low-quality earnings.

This emphasis on earnings, indicating that they have more information content about firm value than cash flow is noteworthy, because cash flows continue to be the measure emphasized in the finance literature.

In the path of Sloan (1996), academic researchers focused on the development of simple empirical models that objectively assess EQ in order to predict future return performance (see, for example, Penman and Zang, 2002; Richardson *et al.*, 2005 and 2006; Chan *et al.*, 2006). For Richardson *et al.* (2005 and 2006) EQ is the degree to which earnings performance persists into the next period.

Another EQ dimension is derived from qualitative concepts in the IASB/FASB's conceptual framework. The conceptual framework focuses on decision usefulness, defined in terms of relevance, reliability, and comparability, as the criterion for assessing quality. Some authors, namely Schipper and Vicent (2003) and Hermans (2006), consider another EQ category, which is derived from implementation decisions. EQ is seen as the accurate representation of underlying economic transactions and events as in Penman and Zhang (2002).

Schipper and Vicent (2003: 98) view EQ in relation to Hicksian income[1], more precisely, they see it as the extent to which reported earnings faithfully represent Hicksian income. The term "faithfully representing" means the "correspondence or agreement between a measure or description and the phenomenon that it purports to represent".

Dechow *et al.* (2010: 344) consider that EQ is "conditional on the decision-relevance of the information", so, in this sense the authors consider that the term "earnings quality" alone is meaningless; EQ is defined only in the context of a specific decision model. The quality of earnings could be evaluated with respect to *any* decision that depends on an informative representation of financial performance and it depends on many aspects, which are unobservable.

Table 1 summarizes some main EQ definitions found in literature.

In the view of the authors of this chapter, following particularly Dechow and Schrand (2004), the quality of earnings is a summary metric in performance evaluation and a central question to assess the quality of accounting information. A high-quality earnings figure will reflect current operating performance, being a good indicator of future operating performance, and it accurately annuitizes the intrinsic value of the firm.

In order to explore the determining of EQ and its implications for firm value, we present in the next section the relevant literature on studies about the relationship between financial statement data and firm value based on valuation models (*e.g.*, Ohlson, 1995; Feltham and Ohlson, 1995; Ohlson, 1999).

3. THE RELATIONSHIP BETWEEN FINANCIAL STATEMENT DATA AND FIRM VALUE

The quality of accounting information is a function of its relevance, which means of its predictive, *informativeness* and confirmatory value. Information has predictive value if it has value as an input to predictive processes used by investors to form their own expectations about the future.

The accounting model communicates an asset-based view of the organizational reality, which is consistent with the assertion that the "primary focus of financial reporting is information about a com-

Table 1. Definitions on earnings quality

Author	Definition
Bernstein and Siegel (1979: 73)	"Earnings figures should have integrity – that is, they should not be the product of manipulations designed purely to increase the reported income of the company. Earnings figures should also be reliable, in the sense that they provide a good indication of the firm's earning power. But it is important to keep in mind that the notion of 'quality', in the context of earnings evaluation, is one of *comparative*, integrity, reliability and predictability. There are no absolute elements of earnings quality".
Bernstein (1996: 749)	"Virtually, there is no general agreement as regard to the definitions or assumptions on this term (earnings quality)".
Penman and Zhang (2002: 237)	"(...) earnings can be regarded as good quality if it is a good indicator of future earnings".
Schipper and Vicent (2003: 98)	"We define earnings quality as the extent to which reported earnings faithfully represent Hicksian income, where representational faithfulness means correspondence or agreement between a measure or description and the phenomenon that it purports to represent".
Dechow and Schrand (2004: Preface)	"A high-quality earnings number, as we define it, will do three things: it will reflect current operating performance; it will be a good indicator of future operating performance; and it will accurately annuitize the intrinsic value of the firm. Not all earnings are created equal. Earnings quality depends on the composition of the earnings, the stage of the company's life cycle, the time period, and the industry."
Ghosh *et al.* (2005: 33)	"With respect to earnings quality, firms with revenue-supported increases in earnings have more persistent earnings, exhibit less susceptibility to earnings management, and have higher future operating performance."
Dechow *et al.* (2010: 344)	"Higher quality earnings provide more information about the features of a firm's financial performance that is relevant to a specific decision made by a specific decision-maker".

pany's performance provided by measures of comprehensive income and its components. Earnings and its components measured by accrual accounting generally provide a better indication of enterprise performance than information about current cash receipts and payments" (FASB, 1978, §43). The FASB position finds support in the empirical evidence documenting that earnings constitute a more relevant proxy of the future cash flows comparatively to the contemporaneous values of cash flows (Barth *et al.*, 2001b; Dechow *et al.*, 1998). It is also important to add that in the medium and long term, firm earnings and cash flows tend to be synchronic.

The financial and economic models establish relationships between earnings or cash-flows of the companies and their market value (*e.g.*, Fama and Miller, 1972: Chapter 2). The earnings role, as well as the one of other financial variables, in many of these models consists of supplying investors with information on stock returns (*e.g.*, Ohlson, 1988). In that context, the quality of the company's performance is assessed by its contribution to predict future stock returns.

Earnings are important for evaluation effects; in other words, the investors see in earnings a valuable information source to assess the firm's value, and, in this sense, the EQ concept is a way to assess the relevance and reliability of earnings, in short, the *informativeness* of earnings, in terms of value relevance.

The link between accounting values and contemporaneous equity values have been extensively studied. Valuation models based on earnings, and based on book value, are viewed typically as an alternative approach to assess the firm's value. When market assumptions are more realistic and markets are imperfect, book values and earnings act as complementary indicators of equity values (*e.g.*, Feltham and Ohlson, 1995; Ohlson, 1995; Penman, 1998). Ohlson's (1995) model, which offers a formal link between valuation and accounting numbers, is cited frequently as the theoretical foundation of such research. In fact, Ohlson's (1995) paper became a classic (Lo and Lys, 2000), being the paper most cited in the last decades, into this research area[2].

The next subsections move backwards in time and in terms of relevant literature, to look at studies about the relationship between financial statement data and firm value.

3.1 The Feltham-Ohlson Framework

The Ohlson (1995) and Feltham and Ohlson (1995) studies stand among the most important developments in capital markets research in the last several years (Beaver, 2002)[3]. These studies provide a foundation for redefining the appropriate objective of research on the relation between financial statement data and firm value. At the same time, they provide some structure for modelling in a field where structure has been sorely lacking.

Ohlson's model (Ohlson, 1995) derives of the Residual Income Valuation Model (hereafter RIV) or Edwards-Bell Model (hereafter EB) (Edwards and Bell, 1961). Those models are already thoroughly recognized in the literature. It is important to highlight that the initial theoretical framework is the neoclassical model of the present value of future expected dividends (hereafter PVED) and well-known for the Gordon Model[4], which assumes an economy where the agents beliefs are homogeneous and individuals are risk-neutral. Note that RIV is a specific case of PVED model.

Ohlson' (1995) and Feltham and Ohlson's (1995) studies provide a logically consistent framework for thinking about the value relevance of accounting numbers. They show how:

- To link the market value of equity (MVE_t) with the past and future financial information of the firm, that is: i) with the contemporaneous and future net income; ii) with the book value and how to use book value and income together in the same valuation model; and iii) with dividends;
- The valuation model can be used to capture different properties of different asset classes, such as operating and financial assets, and different value relevance of earnings components;
- To illustrate the effect of conservative accounting on the relation between equity value, accounting book value, and future earnings.

Feltham and Ohlson (1995: 726) said that "one can view abnormal earnings as a contraction of "above normal earnings", where normal earnings equal the risk-free interest rate times the book value of firm's equity". Table 2 presents some definitions about "abnormal earnings". However, the accounting literature typically refers to it as "residual income".

Given the competition effect, it is expected that the abnormal earnings follow a mean reverting process, that is, it is expected that abnormal earnings quickly revert for the sector/industry mean. Thus under unbiased accounting, in the medium and long period, the book value of the common equity (BVE_t) constitutes an unbiased estimator of the firm market value of equity (MVE_t).

Knowing that Feltham-Ohlson (1995) framework came through the Ohlson (1995) model, adding some complexity, one will begin by presenting the Ohlson's (1995) model (assumptions and definitions based on residual income valuation model) in the next sub-section (3.2), the linear information dynamics and the "other information" will be presented in sub-section 3.3, and finally the linear information dynamics extensions based on Feltham and Ohlson (1995) in sub-section 3.4.

Table 2. Definitions on abnormal earnings

Author	Definition
Canning (1929) and Preinreich (1938)[5]	These authors refer to "abnormal earnings" as "excess earnings".
Edey (1957)[6]	Refers to abnormal earnings or abnormal profits as "super-profits".
Edwards and Bell[7] (1961)	Refers to abnormal earnings as "excess realizable profit".
Ohlson (1995: 663)	"(...) this variable (abnormal earnings) is defined as current earnings minus the risk-free rate times the beginning of period book value, that is, earnings minus a charge for the use of capital".
Feltham and Ohlson (1995: 691)	"(...) abnormal earnings are defined to equal reported earnings minus the risk-free interest rate times the book value of the firm's equity".
Myers (1999)	Throughout the paper, the author uses the term "residual income" (RI) rather than the standard "abnormal earnings" because readers tend to relate abnormal earnings with abnormal stock market returns or unexpected earnings. Residual income (RI) may be completely anticipated. In fact, RI valuation depends on the anticipation of future RI.
Barth *et al.* (2005)	Abnormal earnings are based on the definition provided in Ohlson (1995).

3.2 The Ohlson's (1995) Model

The analytical model of Ohlson (1995) proposes an approach consistent with a measurement perspective, revealing that the fundamental value of a company can be expressed by the fundamental components of balance sheet and profit and loss account. Ohlson (1995) does not explicitly consider the uncertainty, assuming a neutral position towards the risk, the absence of information asymmetry, non-stochastic interest rates and a term structure of horizontal interest rates, the cost of capital being given by the risk free interest rate. In other words, connected to the Ohlson's framework is the concept of an ideal market functioning, which does not accept the existence of information asymmetry between companies and investors, and of a set of assumptions that secure the consistency with the basic principles of the financial theory.

There are three crucial assumptions in the Ohlson's model, displayed in Table 3, all based on Residual Income Valuation Model (RIV).

Analysing the mathematical expressions [1.1], [1.3] and [1.5], one can found that Ohlson's framework is a direct descendant of the research done in the 1960s (*e.g.,* Edwards and Bell, 1961; Modigliani and Miller, 1958; Miller and Modigliani 1961) and also Preinreich (1938). In fact, the valuation expression of accounting data writing succinctly as the sum of book value and the present value of future abnormal earnings is not new; it can be found in Preinreich (1938), and in Edwards and Bell (1961). Its revival constitutes a major contribution to modern financial accounting. By using earnings, book value, and the clean surplus equation to carry the dividend information, one can rewrite the discounted dividend valuation as a discounting of accounting figures.

In mathematical expression [1.5]:

$$MVE_t = BVE_t + \sum_{\tau=1}^{\infty} \frac{E_t\left[x_{t+\tau}^a\right]}{\left(1+r_f\right)^{\tau}}$$

Table 3. The residual income valuation model development: Ohlson's model assumptions

Crucial Assumptions	Analytic Formulation
Assumption A_1 is the **equilibrium condition**: the market value of the firm in time t (MVE_t) is equal to the present value of expected dividends. By reference to Ohlson (1995), it actually follows a more primitive assumption about the economy. In particular, assumption A_1 is the no intertemporal arbitrage price that results when: – Interests rates are nonstochastic; – Beliefs are homogeneous; – Individuals are risk-neutral. Ohlson's formulation requires a valuation assumption based on the present value of expected future dividends, on the irrelevancy of dividends politics for the determination of the firm value (Modigliani and Miller, 1958 and 1961).	**[1.1]** $MVE_t = \sum_{\tau=1}^{\infty} \frac{E_t\left[\tilde{d}_{t+\tau}\right]}{\left(1+r_f\right)^{\tau}}$ Where: MVE_t - price of the firm's equity at time t ; d_t - net dividends paid at time t ; R_f - risk-free return, $R_f = 1 + r_f$. r_f is a risk-free discount rate, which is an intertemporal constant rate; and $E_t\left[\ldots\right]$ - expected value operator conditioned on date t information.
Assumption A_2 defines the clean-surplus relation as: this year's book value equals last year's book value plus income minus dividends (and, therefore, a capital contribution corresponds to a negative dividend). This assumption allows future dividends to be expressed in terms of future earnings and book values.	**[1.2]** $BVE_t = BVE_{t-1} + x_t - d_t$ Denote that: BVE_t - book value of equity at time t ; x_t - earnings for the period from $t-1$ to t ; and d_t - net dividends paid at time t .
With these two assumptions (**A_1** and **A_2**) and with simple algebraic manipulation, Ohlson derives the following relation between price and accounting information.	[1.3] $MVE_t = BVE_t + \sum_{\tau=1}^{\infty} \frac{E_t\left[x_{t+\tau} - r_f BVE_{t+\tau-1}\right]}{\left(1+r_f\right)^{\tau}} - \frac{E_t\left[BVE_{t+\infty}\right]}{\left(1+r_f\right)^{\infty}}$
The "residual income" or "abnormal earnings" is defined as the amount the firm earns in excess of the risk-free rate of interest on the book value.	**[1.4]** $x^a_{t+\tau} \equiv x_{t+\tau} - r \times BVE_{t+\tau-1}$
With this definition the valuation expression can be written even more succinctly as the sum of book value and the present value of future abnormal earnings: Equation [1.5] presents the company's fundamental value defined in terms of accounting variables.	**[1.5]** $MVE_t = BVE_t + \sum_{\tau=1}^{\infty} \frac{E_t\left[x^a_{t+\tau}\right]}{\left(1+r_f\right)^{\tau}}$
Assumption A_3 is a final assumption in Ohlson's paper referred as the "linear information model". This third assumption provides the additional structure necessary to yield dividends irrelevancy. It defines the stochastic process for abnormal earnings and non-accounting information (v_t) as:	[1.6] $x^a_{t+1} = \omega\, x^a_t + v_t + \varepsilon_{1t+1}$ $v_{t+1} = \gamma v_t + \varepsilon_{2t+1}$ Where ω and γ are fixed and known parameters between zero and one, and ε s are mean zero and uncorrelated with other variables in the model[8]. Assumption **A_3** says that both abnormal earnings and non-accounting information are autoregressive. In *lato sensus*, these exogenous parameters to the model are determined by the environmental context that characterizes the firm.

"A firm's value equals its book value adjusted for the present value of anticipated abnormal earnings" (Ohlson, 1995: 667). This value is a function of book value of equity, with unit coefficient, and infinite geometric series of expected abnormal earnings, "unrecorded goodwill" in the authors' terminology, or the "market valued added", for the proposers of EVA™ terminology. The goodwill equals the current value of the expected abnormal earnings, and the firm's value or the firm's evaluation can be centred on the prediction of these. In other words, behind this formula there is a connection that can be summarised in the following way:

$$MVE_t = BVE_t + g\omega_t$$

Considering $g\omega_t$ the value of the company's goodwill, in other words, the intangible assets value not expressed on the balance sheet, measured from the abnormal earnings that the company will generate in the future. The value of the company's goodwill ($g\omega_t$) becomes the component that corrects the asset value (BVE_t) in order to obtain the company's fundamental value.

The transformation of the expression [1.5] in others, which include only contemporaneous accounting information, requires the definition of an evaluation process of the future abnormal earnings (x_t^a). This is the third assumption considered in Table 3, **Assumption A$_3$**.

3.3 Linear Information Model (LIM) and *Other Information*

Ohlson assumes that the abnormal earnings of the period $t+1$ $\left(x_{t+1}^a\right)$ are dependent of the earnings observed in the previous period $\left(x_t^a\right)$ and of the *other information* $\left(v_t\right)$ that may affect the prediction of x_{t+1}^a and is not reflected in x_t^a. The relationship between these components completes the following stochastic process.

$$\begin{aligned} x_{t+1}^a &= \omega\, x_t^a + v_t + \varepsilon_{1t+1} \\ v_{t+1} &= \gamma v_t + \varepsilon_{2t+1} \end{aligned} \qquad [1.6]$$

This **assumption A$_3$** (see Table 3) is a final assumption in Ohlson's model, referred as the "linear information dynamics". This third assumption provides the additional structure necessary to yield dividends irrelevancy.

The parameters ω and γ are fixed and known, they assume values between zero and one, and ε's are mean zero variables and uncorrelated with other variables in the model. These parameters are exogenous to the model and are determined by the environmental context that characterises the firm[9]. The only restriction to which they are subjected is that they are inferior to the unit, which means that the process will converge to zero. The prediction of the *other information* (v_{t+1}) is not a function of the earnings, considering that it synthesises the information not yet reflected in the financial statements.

Ohlson's (1995) innovation in relation to the Residual Income Valuation Model (RIV) or Edwards-Bell Model consists in the treatment that he gives to the structure of the abnormal earnings time-series (x_t^a). In order to define the stochastic process that follows the x_t^a variable, Ohlson (1995) introduces the v_t variable – *other information*: a variable that captures important events in terms of informative content and that affect the market prices (market value of equity – MVE_t), but that are not yet reflected in the financial statements. This means that *other information* variable captures the extent to which the accounting variables do not explain market value of equity. This is a time *lag* that mediates the occurrence of certain events important for the formulation of economic agents' expectations, and its inclusion in the financial statements conveys information for the beliefs formulation on the firm abnormal earnings growth. *Other information* is one of the limitations pointed out to the financial statements, or better, to its capacity in disclosing all the important information and in opportune time – *lack of timeliness* (Beaver, 2002). Non-accounting information (or *other information*) is an "additive shock to next period's abnormal earnings". In order to correct this *gap*, Ohlson (1995) used the dynamics of information to characterise the abnormal earnings dynamics: a first-order autoregressive process (AR(1)).

Table 4 presents the main definitions of *other information*.

Kothari (2001) notes that the current performance of a firm (as represented in accounting reports) is an important information source but not the only for assessing the firm market value. Dechow *et al.* (1999) point out that academic literature recognizes that stock prices reflect information about future earnings that are not contained in current earnings. Such information "cannot be observed directly" (Ohlson, 2001: 112). In operational terms, candidates for these *other information* (v_t) are new patent, laws to approve a new product in pharmaceutical firms, long-term contracts, among others (Myers, 1999).

Ohlson (1995) defines *other information* as a scalar variable, but not specifically establishes its analytical content. Ohlson (2001: 112) referred to v_t as a "mysterious variable". The fuzzy and abstract character of this idea, *other information*, has led that some empirical applications, based on Ohlson's model, use this variable in an *ad hoc* form or simply neglect it. Hand (2001) notes that, until 1998, almost all empirical research on Ohlson's model neglected the information content of this variable (*other in-*

Table 4. Definitions on other information

Author	Definition
Ohlson (1995: 668)	"(...) *other information* (v_t) as capturing all nonaccounting information used in the prediction of future abnormal earnings".
Feltham and Ohlson (1995: 702 and 703)	"(...) nonaccounting data, provide the basis for predicting future abnormal operating earnings". "(...) The *other information* acts as serially correlated, but convergent, noise in the prediction of abnormal earnings and operating assets".
Barth *et al.* (2005: 315)	"(...) *other information*, v_t, is defined as $MVE_{t-1} - \overline{MVE_{t-1}}$, where $\overline{MVE_{t-1}}$ is the fitted value of MVE_{t-1} on the equation: $MVE_{it} = \alpha_0 + \alpha_1 NI^a_{it} + \alpha_2 BV_{it} + \alpha_3 v_{it} + \mu_{it}$ that does not include v_t. MVE is market value of equity, NI[a] is abnormal earnings, defined as earnings minus the normal return on equity book value, BVE, μ_{it} is the error term and i and t subscripts denote firm and year".

formation). The few papers that not neglected the *other information* variable chose an intuitive way rather than a formal construction (*e.g.*, Myers, 1999; Barth *et al.*, 2005).

Ohlson (2001) states that, although there may be an analytical interest in not specify the value of v_t, such procedure reduces the empirical content of the Ohlson's model. It is highlighted that, for example, the financial analysts' predictions constitute a reasonable tool to measure the expected future profits and that there is no reason to eliminate v_t of the model, since the variable can be supported in observable data. Hand (2001) adds that to consider v_t equal to zero is to assume that the accounting data publicly available are sufficient to explain the behaviour of the stock prices.

Table 5 summarises some important aspects in order to correctly understand the model, and finally, the intrinsic value of the company is also presented, as well as the linear solution of the model's coefficients.

So, the current intrinsic value of the company, defined by the expression [1.7], can be attained based on the current values of the book value equity, the abnormal earnings and the *other information*, considering the above specification of the linear information dynamic (expression [1.6]). The impact on the company's value of these variables will depend on the persistence of earnings and on the discount rate of future profitability flows[10].

"Larger values of ω and γ make MVE_t more sensitive to $\left(x_t^a, v_t\right)$ realisations" (Ohlson, 1995: 669). However, the bigger the "persistence parameters" are, ω and γ, the faster the decline process will be. Anyway, these two parameters are enough in this context to characterise the earnings persistence. "The function $\alpha_1\left(\omega\right)$ and $\alpha_2\left(\omega, \gamma\right)$ are increasing in their arguments. The property reflects that ω and γ act as persistence parameters in the $\left(x_t^a, v_t\right)$ process" (Ohlson, 1995: 669).

3.4 Extensions to the LIM Based on Feltham and Ohlson (1995)

Feltham and Ohlson (1995) extend the Ohlson's model (Ohlson, 1995) introducing two new effects: "conservatism accounting effect" and the "growth in the operating assets".

The "conservatism accounting effect" reflects the persistence of the difference between the market value of equity (MVE_t) and book value of common equity (BVE_t), which originates the "unrecorded goodwill", in the authors' terminology or the "market valued added". This "unrecorded goodwill" can result of an undervaluation of assets and/or of an overestimate expected abnormal earnings.

Taking into consideration that "conservatism accounting effect" results in goodwill, Feltham and Ohlson (1995) admit that the current accounting value offers information about future abnormal earnings and they introduce the distinction between the value of operating assets (oa_t) and financial assets (fa_t). In this way, in order to consider the abnormal earnings persistence effect, the conservatism accounting effect, as well as the growth in both operating assets (oa_t) and operating earnings (ox_t), Feltham and Ohlson (1995) redefine the information dynamics initially specified on the Ohlson's model (1995). Thus, the linear information model (LIM) is now defined as in Table 6.

In this context, and based on the mathematical expression [1.9], the goodwill ($g\omega_t$) is identified as:

$$MVE_t - BVE_t = g\omega_t = \alpha_1 ox_t^a + \alpha_2 oa_t + \beta \bullet v_t \qquad [1.10]$$

Table 5. Linear information model (LIM) and other information: key issues

Key Issues	Explanations
1) Linear information model (LIM)	[1.6] $x^a_{t+1} = \omega\, x^a_t + v_t + \varepsilon_{1t+1}$ $v_{t+1} = \gamma v_t + \varepsilon_{2t+1}$
2) *Other information* (v_t)	– The *other information* is incorporated in the residual income with a discrepancy, having a gradual impact on the earnings; in other words, v_t follows a first order auto-regressive process; – Ohlson (1995) defines v_t as a scalar variable, independent from x^a_t, which should be considered as summarising the relevant events in terms of value which did not yet have an impact on the financial statements.
3) Random terms $(\varepsilon_{1t+1}\ ;\ \varepsilon_{2t+1})$	All the components of the model introduced are known. The only sources of uncertainty are the random terms $(\varepsilon_{1t+1}\ ;\ \varepsilon_{2t+1})$, which can be associated to new information (not expected), which is translated into equally in unexpected earnings.
4) Parameters $(\omega\ ;\ \gamma)$	– They are determined by the entity's economic environment and by the accounting principles; – They are positive and lower than one, $0 \leq \omega < 1$ and $0 \leq \gamma < 1$. The model introduces in the theory the concept of earnings persistence, represented by the parameter ω. The persistence reflects the degree in which the current abnormal earnings are reproduced in the next period: - If $\omega = 0$ there is no earnings persistence. In each period these would be only function of the other information and of the new information (unexpected). The events that affect the current earnings are transitory; - If $\omega = 1$, current earnings would be fully reproduced in the next period, which means that the growth opportunities persisted indefinitely; this is not consistent with the empirical evidence; - If $0 \leq \omega < 1$, as predicted in the model, the earnings persistence is not total and current events that affect the current earnings tend to have a decreasing impact on future earnings.
5) The linear solution – the intrinsic value	The combination of the earnings' dynamic [1.6] with the model introduced in [1.5] allows to obtain a model in which the intrinsic value depends only on the contemporaneous accounting information: [1.7] $MVE_t = BVE_t + \alpha_1 x^a_t + \alpha_2 v_t$ Being: $\alpha_1 = \frac{\omega}{1 + r_f - \omega} \geq 0$ and $\alpha_2 = \frac{1 + r_f}{(1 + r_f - \omega)(1 + r_f - \gamma)} > 0$

This is, the goodwill is a growing function of the abnormal operating earnings, whose persistence is measured by parameter ω_{11} (the higher ω_{11} is, the greater α_1 will be), of the operating assets (oa_t) only if these are under evaluated, due to the fact that the necessary condition to $\alpha_2 > 0$ is that $\omega_{12} > 0$ and of the variable v_t. Note also that in both models (Ohlson' model and Feltham and Ohlson's model) the tax effect is ignored.

However, and since both models assume a perfect capital market (for which costs derived from information asymmetry, agency and transaction are not equally admitted), the Feltham and Ohlson's model also assumes that financing decisions do not create value. The tax effect will not have relevant consequences on the evaluation function.

Table 6. Linear information model extensions (Fetham and Ohlson, 1995)

Key Issues	Explanations
Linear information model extensions by (Feltham and Ohlson, 1995)	[1.8] $\begin{cases} ox^a_{t+1} = \omega_{11} ox^a_t + \omega_{12} oa_t + v_{1t} + \varepsilon_{1,t+1} \\ oa_{t+1} = + \omega_{22} oa_t + v_{2t} + \varepsilon_{2,t+1} \\ v_{1,t+1} = \gamma_1 v_{1t} + \varepsilon_{3,t+1} \\ v_{2,t+1} = \gamma_2 v_{2t} + \varepsilon_{4,t+1} \end{cases}$ Where: $ox^a_t \left(= x_{t+1} - r_f * oa_{t+1}\right)$ - operating abnormal earnings after taxes at time t; r_f is a discount rate, which is an intertemporal constant rate; oa_t - operating assets at time t; v_{1t}; v_{2t} - *other information*; ε_{1t+1}; ε_{2t+1}; ε_{3t+1}; ε_{4t+1} - random terms. With: $0 \leq \omega_{11} < 1, \quad 0 \leq \gamma_k < 1\ (k = 1; 2), \quad \omega_{12} \geq 0$ and $1 \leq \omega_{22} < (1 + r_f)$.
ω_{12} coefficient	The parameter ω_{12} allows to introduce the dichotomy in the analysis "unbiased accounting" *versus* "conservative accounting", that is, the problem of the operating assets understatement (the problematic of subvaluation of the operating assets): – If $\omega_{12} > 0$, there is conservatism in accounting (undervaluation of the operating assets). More conservatism indicates that bigger abnormal earnings are expected.
ω_{22} coefficient	The parameter ω_{22} reflects the operating assets growth effect. It assumes values belonging to the interval $\left[1, R_f\right[$, with $R_f = (1 + r_f)$. R_f is the risk-free return and r_f is a discount rate, which is an intertemporal constant rate. Accordingly, restrictions to the operating assets long term growth are introduced to ensure the convergence on the calculus of the abnormal operating earnings present value (ox^a_t).

continued on following page

Table 6. Continued

Key Issues	Explanations
The linear solution – the intrinsic value	Considering: $BVE_t = oa_t + fa_t$ Note that: bv_t - book value of equity at time t; oa_t - operating assets at time t; fa_t - financial assets at time t; [1.9] $MVE_t = BVE_t + \alpha_1 ox_t^a + \alpha_2 oa_t + \beta_1 v_{1,t} + \beta_2 v_{2,t}$ With: $\alpha_1 = \frac{\omega_{11}}{1 + r_f - \omega_{11}} \geq 0$, $\alpha_2 = \frac{\omega_{12}(1 + r_f)}{\left(1 + r_f - \omega_{11}\right)\left(1 + r_f - \omega_{22}\right)} \geq 0$ And, $\beta_1 = \frac{1 + r_f}{(1 + r_f - \omega_{11})(1 + r_f - \gamma_1)} > 0$, $\beta_2 = \frac{\alpha_2}{1 + r_f - \gamma_2} \geq 0$

Earnings persistence or the EQ is not just a function of the "conservatism accounting effect", but also a function of the different value relevance of the different earnings components. The different value relevance of the different earnings components leads Ohlson (1999) to extend Ohlson (1995) by modelling the earnings components. In this way, Ohlson's (1999) model incorporates a x_2 variable, defined as transitory earnings, which can be any earnings components (cash flows or accruals), that evidences an incremental explanatory power on the prediction of future abnormal earnings.

In the next section, a very brief presentation of the Ohlson's (1999) model is done, followed by the generalized version used by Barth *et al.* (1999 and 2005).

4. THE DIFFERENT VALUE RELEVANCE OF THE DIFFERENT EARNINGS COMPONENTS

Ohlson (1999) considers concepts of "transitory earnings", and analyses how this source of earnings differs from other income items.

The Ohlson (1999) modelling follows Ohlson's (1995), but with an extension to permit two earnings components: "core" earnings (x_{1t}) and "transitory" earnings (x_{2t}). In Table 7, Ohlson's (1999) model is presented, as well as its assumptions and definitions:

Considering the linear solution introduced by Ohlson (1999):

$$MVE_t = BVE_t + \alpha_1 x_t^a + \alpha_2 x_{2t} + \beta \cdot v_t \qquad [1.13]$$

The value-irrelevance occurs if $\alpha_1 + \alpha_2 = 0$. This condition implies that core abnormal earnings alone, rather than a combination of core abnormal earnings and transitory earnings, determine the goodwill.

4.1 Barth *et al.*'s (1999 and 2005) Models

As said before, in the next section, the authors propose a model, which is based on the generalized version of the Ohlson's (1999) model, in turn extending the Ohlson's and Feltham-Ohlson's framework (Ohlson, 1995; Feltham and Ohlson, 1995). This proposed model allows modelling earnings components, just as in Barth *et al.*'s (1999 and 2005). Accordingly, it seems important to offer a very brief presentation of the Barth *et al.*'s (1999 and 2005) models.

In developing predictions on how the accruals and cash flows components of earnings relate to equity value, Barth *et al.* (1999) consider a generalized version of the Ohlson's (1999) model. The basic

Table 7. Ohlson's (1999) model: assumptions and definitions

Crucial Assumptions	Analytic Formulation
Equations [1.1] and [1.2] correspond to the first two assumptions of the Ohlson's (1999) model, which are standard of the residual income model and are used in Ohlson's (1995) model, explained previously in Table 3. According to Ohlson (1999: 148), "in words, the present value of expected dividends determines value, and regular owners' equity accounting applies. One can think of x_t as including any dirty surplus items which have bypassed the "official" income statement. Alternatively, one can think of equation [1.2] as a definition rather than as an assumption". Equations [1.1] and [1.2] imply the well-known residual earnings valuation formula: equation [1.5].	[1.1] $MVE_t = \sum_{\tau=1}^{\infty} \frac{E_t\left[\tilde{d}_{t+\tau}\right]}{\left(1+r_f\right)^{\tau}}$ [1.2] $BVE_t = BVE_{t-1} + x_t - d_t$ Where: MVE_t - price of the firm's equity at time t; d_t - net dividends paid at time t; R_f - risk-free return, $R_f = 1 + r_f$. r_f is a discount rate, which is an intertemporal constant rate; $E_t\left[\ldots\right]$ - expected value operator conditioned on date t information. BVE_t - book value of equity at time t; x_t - earnings for the period from $t-1$ to t. [1.5] $MVE_t = BVE_t + \sum_{\tau=1}^{\infty} \frac{E_t\left[x_{t+\tau}^a\right]}{\left(1+r_f\right)^{\tau}}$

continued on following page

Table 7. Continued

Crucial Assumptions	Analytic Formulation
Equation [1.11] is the critical assumption introduced by Ohlson (1999). It specifies the forecasting of the sequence of expected abnormal earnings in terms of the current information. Some important comments are: – It may seems inevitable that ω_{22} should be zero if one wants to label x_{2t} transitory earnings. $\omega_{22} = 0$ means transitory earnings unpredictability, that is, an attribute of transitory earnings. – If $0 < \omega_{22} < 1$ is interesting because it leads to serially correlated transitory earnings whose long run average equals zero. – The second sub-equation of the main equation [1.11] excludes a term $\omega_{21} x_t^a$, which means that $\omega_{21} = 0$. Core earnings and book value do not influence the evolution of transitory earnings (Ohslon 1999). This assumption may appear somewhat restrictive, but it is, in fact, merely an assumption of analytical convenience. - $\omega_{12} \neq 0$ is an essential model ingredient since the concurrent predictor variable x_t^a includes transitory earnings. The real issue concerns the condition $\omega_{11} + \omega_{12} = 0$, as an assumption or conclusion – the forecasting-irrelevance.	[1.11] $\begin{array}{l} x_{t+1}^a = \omega_{11}\; x_t^a + \omega_{12} x_{2t} + \varepsilon_{1t+1} \\ x_{2t+1} = \qquad\qquad \omega_{22} x_{2t} + \varepsilon_{2t+1} \end{array}$ Where x_{2t} are transitory earnings.
To generalize equation [1.11], consider the dynamic equations	[1.12] $\begin{cases} x_{t+1}^a = \omega_{11}\; x_t^a + \omega_{12} x_{2t} + \gamma_1 \cdot v_t + \varepsilon_{1t+1} \\ x_{2t+1} = \qquad \omega_{22} x_{2t} + \gamma_2 \cdot v_t + \varepsilon_{2t+1} \\ v_{t+1} = \qquad\qquad G \cdot v_t + \varepsilon_{3t+1} \end{cases}$ Where v_t is a vector of K random variables representing "other information"; γ_1 and γ_2 are two K-dimensional vectors of fixed constants, and G is a square matrix of size $K \times K$.
The linear solution – the intrinsic value	Applying the dynamic equation [1.12] to the residual income valuation formula [1.5], one obtains: [1.13] $MVE_t = BVE_t + \alpha_1 x_t^a + \alpha_2 x_{2t} + \beta \cdot v_t$ Where β is a K-dimensional vector. It can be shown that the parameters γ_1, γ_2, G do not affect α_1 and α_2, they still are: $\alpha_1 = \dfrac{\omega_{11}}{1 + r_f - \omega_{11}} \geq 0$, $\alpha_2 = \dfrac{\omega_{12}(1 + r_f)}{(1 + r_f - \omega_{11})(1 + r_f - \omega_{22})} \geq 0$ The elements in the vector β depend generally on ω_{11}, ω_{12} and ω_{22}, as well as γ_1, γ_2, G, but the related mathematical expressions are of no interest here. Thus one can think of $\beta \cdot v_t$ as "background" information that influences value without violating the idea that accounting data provide kernel information. Ohlson (1999: 156) explain that "to be sure, this feature works only because the information dynamics has a triangular structure".

structure of the Barth *et al.*'s (1999) model is analogous to the *other information* model of Ohlson (1995) and of the linear information dynamics of Myers (1999). The model of Barth *et al.* (1999) comprises four equations, as follows:

$$\begin{cases} (1.14a) & x_{t+1}^{a} = \omega_{11}x_{t}^{a} + \omega_{12}x_{2t} + \omega_{13}BVE_{t} + \varepsilon_{1t+1} \\ (1.14b) & x_{2t+1} = \omega_{22}x_{2t} + \omega_{23}BVE_{t} + \varepsilon_{2t+1} \\ (1.14c) & BVE_{t+1} = + \omega_{33}BVE_{t} + \varepsilon_{3t+1} \\ (1.14d) & MVE_{t} = BVE_{t} + \alpha_{1}x_{t}^{a} + \alpha_{2}x_{2t} + \mu_{t} \end{cases} \quad [1.14]$$

Equation [1.14a] is the abnormal earnings prediction equation, where abnormal earnings, x_t^a, are defined in the usual way as earnings less a normal return on equity book value. Although x_2 in Ohlson (1999) is modelled as transitory earnings, the model applies to any component of earnings. In Barth *et al.* (1999), x_2 is either accruals or cash flows. If all earnings components have the same ability to forecast abnormal earnings, x_2 will equals zero, and thus knowing that component of earnings does not aid in forecasting abnormal earnings; as in Ohlson (1999), this assumption is considered the "forecasting-irrelevance".

Barth *et al.* (1999) conclude empirically that accruals are a less persistent component of the abnormal earnings in comparison with the cash flows. Sloan (1996) also documents that the high levels of accruals are associated with systematic reductions of future earnings.

Barth *et al.* (1999) additionally conclude that there is a significant variation in the importance of the abnormal earnings coefficients among industries. Anyway, these components being less persistent, or more transitory, are relevant in terms of value. However, they would not be so, as Ohlson (1999) demonstrates, if they would not be relevant in the future earnings prediction or if the "forecasting-irrelevance assumption" would not be predictable.

Equation [1.14b] describes the autocorrelation of each earnings component.

Equation [1.14a] and equation [1.14b] include equity book value (BVE). According to Feltham and Ohlson (1995 and 1996), "including equity book value allows for the effects of conservatism to manifest themselves and partially relaxes the assumption that the cost of capital associated with calculating abnormal earnings is a predetermined cross-sectional constant" (Barth *et al.*, 1999: 208).

In Barth *et al.* (1999 and 2005), equation [1.14c] permits to preserve the triangular information structure of the generalized version of Ohlson's (1999) model. In theory, this triangular structure ensures that parameters relating to equity book value have no effect on the valuation multiples on abnormal earnings and the earnings components in equation [1.14d].

Finally, equation [1.14d] is the valuation equation based on the information dynamics in equations [1.14a] through [1.14c].

Later, Barth *et al.* (2005) extended the previous model, considering three levels of earnings disaggregation based on the Feltham-Ohlson framework: aggregate earnings, cash flows and total accruals, and cash flows and four major components of accruals. At each level of earnings disaggregation, Barth *et al.* (2005) called three linear information models (LIMs), respectively.

The first linear information model, LIM1, is based on Ohlson (1995), and comprises four equations, as follows:

$$\begin{cases} (1.15a) & NI_t^a = \omega_{10} + \omega_{11} NI_{t-1}^a + \omega_{12} BVE_{t-1} + \omega_{13} v_{t-1} + \varepsilon_{1t} \\ (1.15b) & BVE_t = \omega_{20} \qquad\qquad + \omega_{22} BVE_{t-1} + \varepsilon_{2t} \\ (1.15c) & v_{it} = \omega_{30} + \omega_{33} v_{it-1} + \varepsilon_{3t} \\ (1.15d) & MVE_t = \alpha_0 + \alpha_1 NI_t^a + \alpha_2 BVE_t + \alpha_3 v_{it} + \mu_t \end{cases} \quad [1.15]$$

MVE is market value of equity; NI^a is abnormal earnings, defined as earnings minus the normal return on equity book value, BVE; the ε_k and μ are error terms.

Equation [1.15a], equation [1.15b] and equation [1.15c] are forecasting equations, and equation [1.15d] is the valuation equation implied by the linear information dynamics of the forecasting equations.

In relation to the previous model, Barth *et al.* (2005) also added the *other information* variable (v_{it}). For these authors, the *other information* (v_{it}) is defined as $MVE_{t-1} - \overline{MVE_{t-1}}$, where $\overline{MVE_{t-1}}$ is the fitted value of MVE_{t-1} (market value equity), based on a version of equation [1.15d] that does not include v_{it}.

The second linear information model, LIM2, is based on Bart *et al.* (1999). It relaxes the assumption that the total accruals, ACC, and cash flows components of earnings have the same model parameters. LIM2 comprises five equations, as follows:

$$\begin{cases} (1.16a) & NI_t^a = \omega_{10} + \omega_{11} NI_{t-1}^a + \omega_{12} ACC_{t-1} + \omega_{13} BVE_{t-1} + \omega_{14} v_{t-1} + \varepsilon_{1t} \\ (1.16b) & ACC_t = \omega_{20} + \omega_{22} ACC_{t-1} + \omega_{23} BVE_{t-1} + \varepsilon_{2t} \\ (1.16c) & BVE_t = \omega_{30} + \omega_{33} BVE_{t-1} + \varepsilon_{3t} \\ (1.16d) & v_{it} = \omega_{40} + \omega_{44} v_{it-1} + \varepsilon_{4t} \\ (1.16e) & MVE_t = \alpha_0 + \alpha_1 NI_t^a + \alpha_2 ACC_t + \alpha_3 BVE_t + \alpha_4 v_{it} + \mu_t \end{cases} \quad [1.16]$$

In LIM2, equations [1.16a] through [1.16d] are forecasting equations, and equation [1.16e] is the valuation equation implied by the linear information dynamics of the forecasting equations.

Finally, the third linear information model, LIM3, further relaxes the assumption relating to earnings components by permitting the model parameters for four major accrual components to differ from one another as well as from those for other components of earnings, including cash flow. LIM3 comprises the following eight equations:

$$
\begin{cases}
(1.17a) & NI_t^a = \omega_{10} + \omega_{11} NI_{t-1}^a + \omega_{12}\Delta REC_{t-1} + \omega_{13}\Delta INV_{t-1} + \omega_{14}\Delta PAY_{t-1} + \\
& \quad + \omega_{15} DEP_{t-1} + \omega_{16} BVE_{t-1} + \omega_{17} v_{t-1} + \varepsilon_{1t} \\
(1.17b) & \Delta REC_t = \omega_{20} + \omega_{22}\Delta REC_{t-1} + \omega_{23}\Delta INV_{t-1} + \omega_{25} DEP_{t-1} + \omega_{26} BVE_{t-1} + \\
& \quad + \omega_{27} v_{t-1} + \varepsilon_{2t} \\
(1.17c) & \Delta INV_t = \omega_{30} + \omega_{32}\Delta REC_{t-1} + \omega_{33}\Delta INV_{t-1} + \omega_{34}\Delta PAY_{t-1} + \omega_{35} DEP_{t-1} + \\
& \quad + \omega_{36} BVE_{t-1} + \varepsilon_{3t} \\
(1.17d) & \Delta PAY_t = \omega_{40} + \omega_{43}\Delta INV_{t-1} + \omega_{44}\Delta PAY_{t-1} + \omega_{46} BVE_{t-1} + \varepsilon_{4t} \\
(1.17e) & DEP_t = \omega_{50} + \omega_{55} DEP_{t-1} + \omega_{56} BVE_{t-1} + \varepsilon_{5t} \\
(1.17f) & BVE_t = \omega_{60} + \omega_{66} BVE_{t-1} + \varepsilon_{6t} \\
(1.17g) & v_{it} = \omega_{70} + \omega_{77} v_{it-1} + \varepsilon_{7t} \\
(1.17h) & MVE_t = \alpha_0 + \alpha_1 NI_t^a + \alpha_2\Delta REC_t + \alpha_3\Delta INV_t + \alpha_4\Delta PAY_t + \alpha_5 DEP_t + \\
& \quad + \alpha_6 BVE_t + \alpha_7 v_t + \mu_t
\end{cases}
\qquad [1.17]
$$

ΔREC is the annual change in receivables, ΔINV is the annual change in inventory, ΔPAY is the annual change in payables and DEP is the annual depreciation and amortization expense.

For LIM3, equations [1.17a] through [1.17g] are forecasting equations, and equation [1.17h] is the valuation equation implied by the linear information dynamics of the forecasting equations.

In the next section the authors of this chapter propose an empirical model (based on Ohlson, 1995; Feltham and Ohlson, 1995; Ohlson, 1999; and Barth *et al.*, 1999 and 2005), which reinterprets rebuilding the linear information model (LIM) in relation to the market value added, and captures, in a composite measure, the three EQ constructs: persistence, predictability and *informativeness* of earnings.

5. A PROPOSAL FOR AN ACCOUNTING-BASED VALUATION MODEL AND EARNINGS QUALITY

The evaluation is always based, direct and indirectly, on earnings predictions and the earnings predictions are an important information source both as an evaluation element for management and, as well as for investors, i.e., for the capitals market.

As starting point to the proposed model it is acknowledged that:

- "Ohlson's model incorporates the earnings prediction; however, this prediction must be placed in a theoretical duality that underlines the model – evaluating and signalling. That is, firm intrinsic value contains information about earnings quality" (Canadas, 2004: 241).
- The unrecorded goodwill is defined as the excess of the intrinsic value (market value of equity - MVE_t) in relation to the accounting value (book value of equity - BVE_t), that is, $MVE_t - BVE_t$. In these terms, the goodwill presents itself as a measure for the abnormal earnings generation. As such, the goodwill captures all the "hidden assets", as well as the difference between the sum of the cost value of the assets shown on the balance sheet, individually considered, and their market value or the intrinsic value.

In the following, the linear information model (LIM) structure is explained, as well as its link with the composite measure of EQ, namely the proxies to persistence, predictability and informativeness of the earnings components – the EQ measures. As said, the proposed model is based on the generalized version of the Ohlson's (1999) model, which extends the Ohlson's and Feltham-Ohlson's framework (Ohlson, 1995; Feltham and Ohlson, 1995), allowing for modelling earnings components, just as in Barth *et al.* (1999, 2005).

5.1 Earnings Quality: The Proposed Rebuilding LIM

It should be noteworthy that the authors reinterpret rebuilding the base models (Ohlson, 1995; Feltham and Ohlson, 1995; Ohlson, 1999), analysing them and introducing some modifications, taking into consideration their fundamental lines. More specifically:

1. Considering the "conservatism accounting effect", introduced by Feltham and Ohlson (1995), which reflects the persistence of the difference between the market value of equity (MVE_t) and the book value of common equity (BVE_t), originating the "unrecorded goodwill", and knowing that this "unrecorded goodwill" can result of an undervaluation of assets and/or of an overestimate of expected abnormal earnings;
2. The model examines the EQ in terms of value relevance, namely because it can contemplate the distinction between the permanent and transitory earnings components and the different weighing among them;
3. The information dynamics can be expressed in terms of the profitability rates and it should highlight not the expected earnings for the next period but its permanent component, i.e., the one which has relevance in what concerns value;
4. On the linear information dynamics, it is highlighted the role of *other information*, i.e., the fact that the accounting values predictions depend on information not present in the current accounting data. The apparently vague and abstract essence of this idea can lead some empirical applications of the model to treat it in an *ad hoc* manner or to neglect it (Barth *et al.*, 1999; Lara *et al.*, 2009; just to mention some studies). However, the potential of this idea is stressed by many authors, so the *other information* variable cannot just be equal to zero. If the *other information* is ignored, the model according to Ohlson's hypothesis (1995) must produce similar results to the mere capitalization of the accounting price-value or price-earnings ratios, as stated by Lee *et al.* (1999);
5. The *other information* variable is not directly observed but it can be calculated from the earnings predictions for the next period, as Ohlson (2001) suggests.

In the rebuilt linear information model (LIM), **three main aspects** were retained.

A. First of all, and knowing that "firm's value equals its book value adjusted for the present value of anticipated abnormal earnings"(Ohlson, 1995: 667) and that, such value is a function of the equity accounting value, with unitary coefficient, in the proposed model the dependent variable of the valuation equations is the market value added ($Dif_{MBV} = MVE_{it} - BV_{it}$), which means the difference between the current market and book values of common equity. Therefore, the valuation function is expressed in terms of *goodwill*.

If one considers the valuation formula in line with earnings response coefficient (ERC) literature, one can also (re)interpret the β *coefficients* of the valuation equations as a *score*. As such, they can be a *proxy* of the *informativeness* of market value added, with LIM structure β *coefficients* providing a composite measure of EQ that simultaneously captures the persistence (ω_{11}, γ_{22}), the predictability (ω_{12}) and the *informativeness* of earnings (β) and its components, building a composite and three-dimensional measure of EQ. Accordingly, the valuation formula is written in terms of market value added, in order to capture in the β *coefficients* the *informativeness* of earnings. In section 5.2, further and better explanation will be provided regarding the coefficients ω_{11}, ω_{12}, γ_{22} and β.

B. In the linear information dynamic formulation, the role of the *other information* (v_{it}) is underlined. In spite of the vagueness and fuzzy nature of this variable, its potentialities are pointed out by many authors that recognize its importance in the industry-specific or entity-specific treatment of the model. Accordingly, and knowing that *other information* (v_{it}) is reflected in abnormal earnings, it is not defined as a first-order autoregressive process AR(1), but instead as difference between abnormal earnings (x_{it}^{a}) and the fitted value of abnormal earnings equation that does not include v_{it}, that is, $x_{it}^{a} - \overline{x_{it}^{a}}$, where $\overline{x_{it}^{a}}$ is the fitted value of MVE_{t-1} based on a version of abnormal earnings equation that does not include $\frac{1}{2}_{t}$..

According to Feltham and Ohlson (1995) and Ohlson (1995), v_{it} captures the extent to which the accounting variables do not explain market value added. Therefore, v_{it} is the difference between two residual income values for the next period. Being certain that the difference between two earnings variables is an earning variable, in the model's context, v_{it} is not just a difference between two earnings variables; it is by itself a earning variable (Canadas, 2004: 237).

C. Third, one also redesign the linear information model (LIM) in order to examine whether differences between the market and book value of common equity (market value added) can be explained by the different value relevance of earnings components: accruals and cash flows. A test was run on whether the disaggregation of earnings into cash flow and total accruals (or in the major components of accruals) results in different predictive ability of accounting numbers and the composite measure of EQ towards market value added, this means, this disaggregation was tested to check whether it has a different impact in β *coefficients* information content.

5.2 The Development of the Proposed Model

According to Ohlson (1995), market value of equity, MVE_{it}, is defined as the sum of current equity book value, BVE_{it}, and expected future abnormal earnings, x_{it}^{a}, discounted at a constant rate, r_f (mathematical expression [1.5] already presented above):

$$MVE_t = BVE_t + \sum_{\tau=1}^{\infty} \frac{E_t\left[x_{t+\tau}^a\right]}{\left(1+r_f\right)^{\tau}} \quad [1.5]$$

In order to determine whether and to what extent, disaggregating earnings provides a composite measure of EQ, the relation between MVE_{it}, BVE_{it} and x_{it}^a was rebuilt, considering the persistence, in terms of earnings sustainability, the predictability and the *informativeness* of earnings, which means taking into account the EQ concept.

To achieve the intended objective, the valuation formula is written in terms of market value added [$\underbrace{\left(MVE_t - BVE_t\right)}_{Dif_{MBV}}$], in order to capture in the β *coefficient* (see the following equation 2.2c) the *informativeness* of earnings:

$$\underbrace{\left(MVE_t - BV\right)}_{Dif_{MBV}} = E_t\left|\sum_{t=1}^{\infty} \frac{x_{t+\tau}^a}{\left(1+r\right)^{\tau}}\right|. \quad [2.1]$$

As one of the objectives is to obtain a composite measure of EQ, one have to isolate the earnings variables (x_{it}^a), in one of the sides of the equation. In this context, the dependent variable will be a measure of the excess between the market value of equity, MVE_{it}, and the equity book value, BVE_{it}.

Subsequently, the proposed general model comprises three main equations:

$$\begin{cases} (2.2a) & x_{t+1}^a = \omega_{10} + \omega_{11}x_t^a + \omega_{12}x_t + \omega_{13}v_t + \varepsilon_{1t+1} \\ (2.2b) & x_{t+1} = \gamma_{20} + \gamma_{22}x_t + \varepsilon_{2t+1} \\ (2.2c) & \underbrace{\left(MVE_t - BVE_t\right)}_{DifMBV} = \beta_0 + \beta_1 x_t^a + \beta_2 x_t + \beta_3 v_{it} + \mu_t \end{cases} \quad [2.2]$$

Equation [2.2a] is the abnormal earnings prediction equation, where abnormal earnings, x_{it}^a, are defined in the usual way as earnings less a normal return on equity book value (BVE_t). In the context of the proposed model, as in Barth *et al.* (2005), x_{it} is either accruals or cash flows or four major components of the total accruals.

Equations [2.2a] through [2.2b] are forecasting equations, and equation [2.2c] is the valuation equation: market value added equation as a function of contemporaneous abnormal earnings, any component of earnings (cash flows, total accruals, or four major components of the total accruals) and *other information* imposing LIM structure, that is:

$$\beta_1 = \frac{\omega_{11}}{R_f - \omega_{11}},$$

$$\beta_2 = \frac{\omega_{12} \times R_f}{\left(\omega_{11} - R_f\right)\left(\omega_{22} - R_f\right)}$$

With $R_f = (1 + r_f)$, R_f is the risk-free return and r_f is a discount rate, which is an intertemporal constant rate.

As in Barth *et al.* (2005), three levels of earnings disaggregation are considered based on the Feltham-Ohlson's framewok: aggregate earnings, cash flows and total accruals, and cash flows and four major components of accruals.

The signs and magnitudes of the β_j in [2.2c] depend on the ω in equations [2.2a] through [2.2b]. The relations between the β_j and the ω are complex because of the number of explanatory variables in equation [2.2c], each of which has its own forecasting equation. The signs of β_j are determined by the signs of ω. For example, the sign of ω_{12} determines the sign of β_2. Also, the higher the predictive ability of the component for future abnormal earnings, the larger, in absolute value, will be β_2.

Abnormal Earnings Equation: Persistence (ω_{11}) and Predictability (ω_{12}) Coefficients

Equation [2.2a], allows us to measure the persistence of abnormal earnings. The autoregressive coefficient (ω_{11}) reflects the persistence of abnormal earnings. Prior research (*e.g.*, Dechow *et al.*, 1999; Barth *et al.*, 1999, 2005) leads us to predict that ω_{11} is positive. So, the autoregressive coefficient (ω_{11}) is an EQ construct that captures the persistence of earnings (earnings sustainability).

The coefficient of the earnings component (x_t), ω_{12}, reflects the incremental effect on the forecast of abnormal earnings of knowing x_t. As said before, x_t is either accruals or cash flows or four major components of the total accruals, i.e., different components of earnings. If all earnings components have the same ability to forecast abnormal earnings, ω_{12} will equals zero, and thus that component of earnings does not aid in forecasting abnormal earnings. Accordingly, in the proposed model, similarly with Barth *et al.* (1999, 2005), the coefficient ω_{12} measures the predictability of earnings components. In this context, predictive ability is the ability of current earnings components to predict future earnings.

Barth *et al.* (1999: 208), citing Sloan (1996), argue that "accruals possess less predictive ability with respect to future earnings. The reason is that accruals involve a higher degree of subjectivity than cash flows, are more likely the object of management discretion, and are more apt to contain unusual accruals that are less likely to recur in future periods. Sloan's evidence supports lower predictability of accruals with respect to future earnings". So, in particular, the authors would predict $\omega_{12} < 0$ for accruals, and $\omega_{12} > 0$ for cash flows.

Earnings Component Autoregressive Equations: Persistence (ω_{22}) Coefficients

Equation [2.2b] describes the autocorrelation, or persistence, of each earnings component[11]. Transitory earnings can be characterised as a process in which $\omega_{22} = 0$, as in Ohlson (1999). For earnings components those are not entirely transitory; the higher ω_{22} is, the more predictable the component will be because one expects accruals and cash flows to be positively auto correlated. One predicts $\omega_{22} > 0$ for each component.

Valuation Equations: Informativeness or Valuation (β) Coefficients

Finally, equation [2.2c] is the valuation equation based on the information dynamics in equations [2.2a] through [2.2b]. The goodwill (market value added – Dif_{MBV}) is a growing function of abnormal earnings, whose persistence is measured by the parameter ω_{11}: the bigger ω_{11} is, the bigger β_1 will be. β_2 is the valuation multiple on x_{it}, i.e., accruals or cash flows or four major components of accruals. Analogous to the interpretation of ω_{12} in equation [2.2a], β_2 reflects the incremental effect on valuation from knowing x_t. If both earnings components have the same relation with the market value added, β_2 will equal zero, knowing that component of earnings does not aid in explaining market value added. Thus, if $\beta_1 + \beta_2 = 0$, x_t is irrelevant for valuation. Ohlson (1999) labels this condition as "value irrelevance". Conversely, if $\beta_1 + \beta_2 \neq 0$, then x_t is "value relevant".

Barth *et al.* (1999: 209) explain that, "this positive relation between persistence and value relevance is consistent with predictions made and tested in prior research (*e.g.*, Lipe (1986), Kormendi and Lipe (1987) and Barth *et al.* (1992))". β_2 is similarly dependent on the persistence of abnormal earnings ω_{11}, *i.e.*, the higher the persistence of abnormal earnings, the higher β_2 is.

The "β *Coefficient*" can be seen, simultaneously, as a type of earnings response coefficient (ERC), which can be used as a measure of earnings information content and as a *proxy* of reported EQ. Prior research demonstrates that firms with sustained increases in earnings have higher ERCs than other firms (Barth *et al.*, 1999). EQ concept, in terms of informative content, is a way of assessing the relevance and reliability of earnings, to explain future earnings (Ahmed *et al.*, 2004) or to explain stock returns (Warfield *et al.*, 1995), as one will see on EQ constructs derived from time-series properties.

6. SUMMARY AND CONCLUSION

The quality of earnings is a summary metric in performance evaluation and a fundamental question to assess the quality of accounting information.

The literature on EQ currently embraces various aspects of this nebulous concept. No unique definition of EQ can be found. On the contrary, several definitions are suggested, as it was presented in this chapter. Aspects often mentioned are the persistence, predictability, variability of earnings (time-series properties of earnings) and the *informativeness* of earnings. Different studies focus on just one aspect of EQ. In several studies, accruals and cash flows have been established as indicators of EQ. Moreover, many authors have used abnormal or unexpected accruals to measure EQ.

Despite such diversity, it is overall acknowledged that a high-quality earnings figure will reflect firm's current operating performance, being a good indicator of future operating performance; it accurately annuitizes the intrinsic value of the firm.

Understanding that earnings are important for firm's evaluation effects and that investors recognise earnings management as relevant for their assessment and decisions, firm valuation models based on earnings, and based on book value, have been developed. Ohlson´s (1995) model and its subsequent refinements by Feltham and Ohlson (1995) and Ohlson (1999), are perhaps the paramount works, offering a formal link between valuation and accounting figures.

In summary, the fundamental lines of the models presented in this chapter (Ohlson, 1995; Feltham and Ohlson, 1995; Ohlson, 1999; Barth *et al.*, 1999 and 2005) are:

– The model is centred on the two base accounting variables, book value equity (BVE_t) and earnings. It respects the accounting system properties, namely the clean surplus accounting relation, which being just a mere identity, is the identity that gives unity to the system.

- The earnings persistence or EQ is not only a function of the "conservatism accounting effect", but also a function of the different value relevance of the different earnings components.
- Earnings components have a different value relevance, being accruals component less persistent than cash flows component. In other terms, for the future earnings predictions accruals are less persistent than cash flows (Beaver, 2002).
- "Firm's value equals its book value adjusted for the present value of anticipated abnormal earnings" (Ohlson, 1995: 667). Such value is a function of the accounting value of equity, with unitary coefficient, and of the infinite geometric series of expected abnormal earnings, "unrecorded goodwill" in the authors' terminology, or the "market value added" in the proposers of EVA™ terminology.
- The "goodwill equals the present value of the future expected abnormal earnings" and the evaluation can be centred on their prediction (Ohlson, 1995: 662).
- The "unrecorded goodwill" is defined as the excess of the intrinsic value (market value of equity – MVE_t) in relation to the accounting value (book value of equity – BVE_t), i.e., $MVE_t - BVE_t$. In these terms, the goodwill presents itself as a measure for the abnormal earnings generation. As such, the goodwill captures all the "hidden assets", as well as the difference between the sum of the cost value of the assets shown on the balance sheet, individually considered, and their market value or the intrinsic value.

The description points to the fact that, determining the value of the company using accounting and financial variables in a framework of nonlinear relationships, presents a high potential for future research. Indeed, Bernard (1995: 735) noted that:

The Ohlson model represents the base of a branch (for) capital market research ... Ohlson (1995) and Feltham and Ohlson (1995) return to "step one" and attempt to build a more solid foundation for further work. Our challenge is clear.

Knowing that firm intrinsic value contains information about EQ, earnings persistence or EQ is a function of the different value relevance of earnings components, and earnings or earnings components are important for evaluation effects, this chapter also proposed a model which reinterprets rebuilding the link between contemporaneous and future earnings, taking into account the three-dimensional facet of the EQ concept: persistence, predictability and *informativeness*.

This model is based on the models by Feltham and Ohlson (1995) and Ohlson (1999), which in turn were an extension of the one by Ohlson (1995), and it models earnings components just as in Barth *et al.*

(2005). It contributes to the literature because it highlights a "new" EQ perspective taking into account the virtuosities of the residual income model. The empirical model proposed reinterprets rebuilding the linear information dynamics in relation to market value added, and captures, in a composite measure, the three-dimensional facet of the EQ concept, referred above.

Given that investors see in earnings a valuable information source to assess the firm value, the EQ concept raises as significant as a way to assess the relevance, the reliability and the *informativeness* of earnings, in terms of value relevance. The evaluation is always based on earnings predictions and the model proposed in this chapter, as Ohlson's (1995, 1999) model, incorporates this aspect.

REFERENCES

Ahmed, A., Billings, B., & Morton, R. (2004). *Extreme Accruals, Earnings Quality, and Investor Mispricing*. Working paper, Florida State University.

Barth, M., Beaver, W., Hand, J., & Landsman, W. (1999). Accruals, Cash Flows and Equity Values. *Review of Accounting Studies*, *3*(3/4), 205–229. doi:10.1023/A:1009630100586

Barth, M., Beaver, W., Hand, J., & Landsman, W. (2005). Accruals, Accounting-Based Valuation Models, and the Prediction of Equity Values. *Journal of Accounting, Auditing & Finance*, *3*(4), 311–345. doi:10.1177/0148558X0502000401

Barth, M., Beaver, W., & Landsman, W. (1992). The Market Valuations Implications of Net Periodic Pension Costs. *Journal of Accounting and Economics*, *15*(1), 27–62. doi:10.1016/0165-4101(92)90011-P

Barth, M., Cram, D., & Nelson, K. (2001b). Accruals and Prediction of Future Cash Flows. *The Accounting Review*, *76*(1), 27–58. doi:10.2308/accr.2001.76.1.27

Beaver, W. (1998). *Financial Reporting: An Accounting Revolution* (3rd ed.). Prentice Hall.

Beaver, W. (1999). Comments on "An Empirical Assessment of the Residual Income Valuation Model". *Journal of Accounting and Economics*, *26*(1-3), 35–42. doi:10.1016/S0165-4101(98)00042-1

Beaver, W. (2002). Perspectives on Recent Capital Research. *The Accounting Review*, *77*(2), 453–474. doi:10.2308/accr.2002.77.2.453

Beaver, W., & Demski, J. (1979, January). The Nature of Income Measurement. *The Accounting Review*, 38–46.

Bernard, V. (1995). The Feltham–Ohlson Framework: Implications for Empiricists. *Contemporary Accounting Research*, *11*(2), 733–747. doi:10.1111/j.1911-3846.1995.tb00463.x

Bernard, V., & Stober, T. (1989). The Nature and Amount of Information in Cash Flows and Accruals. *The Accounting Review*, *64*(4), 624–652.

Bernstein, L. (1996). *Análisis de Estados Financeiros. Teoría, Aplicación e Interpretación*. Madrid: Ed. IRWIN.

Bernstein, L., & Siegel, J. (1979). The Concept of Earnings Quality. *Financial Analysts Journal, 35*, 72–75. doi:10.2469/faj.v35.n4.72

Black, F. (1980). The Magic in Earnings: Economic Earnings versus Accounting Earnings. *Financial Analysts Journal, 36*(6), 19–24. doi:10.2469/faj.v36.n6.19

Brown, L. (1996). Influencial Accounting Articles, Individuals, Ph.D. Granting Institutions and Faculties: A Citation Analysis. *Accounting, Organizations and Society, 21*(7-8), 723–754. doi:10.1016/0361-3682(96)00012-8

Canadas, N. (2004). *Um Modelo Dual de Análise, Avaliação e Relato do Valor Intangível: O Caso das Telecomunicações Móveis em Portugal. Tese de doutoramento*. Universidade do Minho.

Canning, J. (1929). *The Economics of Accountancy*. New York: The Ronald Press Company.

Chan, K., Chan, L., Jegadeesh, N., & Lakonishok, J. (2006). Earnings Quality and Stock Returns. *The Journal of Business, 79*(3), 1041–1082. doi:10.1086/500669

Dechow, P. (1994). Accounting Earnings and Cash Flows as Measure of Firm Performance: The Role of Accounting Accruals. *Journal of Accounting and Economics, 18*, 3–42. doi:10.1016/0165-4101(94)90016-7

Dechow, P., & Dichev, I. (2002). The Quality of Accruals and Earnings: The Role of Accrual Estimation Errors. *The Accounting Review, 77*(s-1), 35–59. doi:10.2308/accr.2002.77.s-1.35

Dechow, P., Ge, W., & Schrand, C. (2010). Understanding Earnings Quality: A Review of the Proxies, their Determinants and their Consequences. *Journal of Accounting and Economics, 50*(2-3), 344–401. doi:10.1016/j.jacceco.2010.09.001

Dechow, P., Hutton, A., & Sloan, R. (1999). An Empirical Assessment of the Residual Income Valuation Model. *Journal of Accounting and Economics, 26*(1-3), 1–34. doi:10.1016/S0165-4101(98)00049-4

Dechow, P., Kothari, S., & Watts, R. (1998). The Relation Between Earnings and Cash Flows. *Journal of Accounting and Economics, 25*, 133–168. doi:10.1016/S0165-4101(98)00020-2

Dechow, P., & Schrand, C. (2004). *Earnings Quality*. Research Foundation of CFA Institute.

Edey, H. (1957, January). Business Valuation, Goodwill and the Super-Profit Method. *Accountancy*.

Edwards and Bell (1961). *The Theory and Measurement of Business Income*. Author.

Fama, E., & Miller, M. (1972). *The Theory of Finance*. New York: Rinehand S. Winston.

FASB. (1978). *Statements of Financial Accounting Concepts, n.º 1, Objectives of Financial Reporting by Business Enterprises*. Stanford, CT: Financial Accounting Standard Board (FASB).

Feltham, G., & Ohlson, J. (1995). Valuation and Clean Surplus Accounting for Operating and Financial Activities. *Contemporary Accounting Research, 11*(2), 689–732. doi:10.1111/j.1911-3846.1995.tb00462.x

Feltham, G., & Ohlson, J. (1996). Uncertainty Resolution and the Theory of Depreciation Measurement. *Journal of Accounting Research, 34*(2), 209–234. doi:10.2307/2491500

Ghosh, A., Gu, Z., & Jain, P. (2005). Sustained Earnings and Revenue Growth, Earnings Quality, and Earnings Response Coefficients. *Review of Accounting Studies*, *10*(1), 33–57. doi:10.100711142-004-6339-3

Gordon, M., & Shapiro, E. (1956). Capital Equipment Analysis: The Required Rate of Profit. *Management Science*, *3*(1), 102–110. doi:10.1287/mnsc.3.1.102

Graham, J., Harvey, C., & Rajgopal, S. (2005). The Economic Implications of Corporate Financial Reporting. *Journal of Accounting and Economics*, *40*(1–3), 3–73. doi:10.1016/j.jacceco.2005.01.002

Hand, J. (2001). Discussion of Earnings, Book Values, and Dividends in Equity Valuation: An Empirical Perspective. *Contemporary Accounting Research*, *18*(1), 121–130. doi:10.1506/6A7C-74ML-TGBD-DYBW

Hermanns, S. (2006). *Financial Information and Earnings Quality.* Working paper, Facultes Universitaires Notre-Dame de la Paix.

Hicks, J. (1939). *Value and Capital.* Oxford University Press.

Kormendi, R., & Lipe, R. (1987). Earnings Innovations, Earnings Persistence, and Stock Returns. *The Journal of Business*, *60*(3), 323–345. doi:10.1086/296400

Kothari, S. (1992). Price-Earnings Regressions in the Presence of Prices Leading Earnings. *Journal of Accounting and Economics*, *15*(2-3), 173–202. doi:10.1016/0165-4101(92)90017-V

Lara, J., Grambovas, C., & Walker, M. (2009). *On the Development of an Efficient Deflator for the Estimation of Accounting-Based Valuation Models.* Working paper.

Lee, C., Myers, J., & Swaminathan, B. (1999). What Is the Intrinsic Value of the Dow? *The Journal of Finance*, *54*(5), 1693–1741. doi:10.1111/0022-1082.00164

Leuz, C., Nanda, D., & Wisocki, P. (2003). Investor Protection and Earnings Management: An International Comparison. *Journal of Financial Economics*, *69*, 505–527. doi:10.1016/S0304-405X(03)00121-1

Lipe, R. (1990). The Relation Between Stock Returns and Accounting Earnings Given Alternative Information. *The Accounting Review*, *65*, 49–71.

Lipe, R. (1990). The Relation Between Stock Returns and Accounting Earnings Given Alternative Information. *The Accounting Review*, *65*, 49–71.

Liu, J., Nissim, D., & Thomas, J. (2002). Equity Valuation Using Multiples. *Journal of Accounting Research*, *40*(1), 135–172. doi:10.1111/1475-679X.00042

Lo, K., & Lys, T. (2001). The Ohlson Model: Contribution to Valuation Theory, Limitations, and Empirical Applications. *Journal of Accounting, Auditing & Finance*, *15*(3), 337–367. doi:10.1177/0148558X0001500311

Miller, M., & Modigliani, F. (1961). Dividend Policy, Growth and the Valuation of Shares. *The Journal of Business*, *34*(4), 411–433. doi:10.1086/294442

Modigliani, F., & Miller, M. (1958). The Cost of Capital, Corporate Finance and the Theory of Investment. *The American Economic Review*, *48*(3), 261–297.

Mota, G., Nunes, J., & Ferreira, M. (2004). *Finanças Empresariais – Teoria e Prática*. Team.

Myers, J. (1999). Implementing Residual Income Valuation with Linear Information Dynamics. *The Accounting Review*, *74*(1), 1–28. doi:10.2308/accr.1999.74.1.1

Ohlson, J. (1988). *Accounting Earnings, Book Value and Dividends. The Theory of the Clean Surplus Equation*. Working paper, Columbia University.

Ohlson, J. (1995). Earnings, Book Values and Dividends in Equity Valuation. *Contemporary Accounting Research*, *11*(2), 661–687. doi:10.1111/j.1911-3846.1995.tb00461.x

Ohlson, J. (1999). On Transitory Earnings. *Review of Accounting Studies*, *3*(3/4), 145–162. doi:10.1023/A:1009653114699

Ohlson, J. (2001). Earnings, Book Values and Dividends in Equity Valuation: An Empirical Perspective. *Contemporary Accounting Research*, *3*(1), 107–120. doi:10.1506/7TPJ-RXQN-TQC7-FFAE

Ohlson, J., & Zhang, X. (1998). Accrual Accounting and Equity Valuation. *Journal of Accounting Research*, *36*(Supplement), 85–111. doi:10.2307/2491308

Penman, S. (1998). Combining Earnings and Book Value in Equity Valuation. *Contemporary Accounting Research*, *15*(3), 291–324. doi:10.1111/j.1911-3846.1998.tb00562.x

Penman, S. (2001). *Financial Statement Analysis and Security Valuation*. New York: McGraw Hill/Irwin.

Penman, S., & Zhang, X. (2002). Accounting Conservatism, the Quality of Earnings, and Stock Returns. *The Accounting Review*, *77*(2), 237–264. doi:10.2308/accr.2002.77.2.237

Preinreich, G. (1938). Annual Survey of Economic Theory: The Theory of Depreciation. *Econometrica*, *6*(3), 219–231. doi:10.2307/1907053

Richardson, S., Sloan, R., Soliman, M., & Tuna, I. (2005). Accrual Reliability, Earnings Persistence and Stock Prices. *Journal of Accounting and Economics*, *39*(3), 437–485. doi:10.1016/j.jacceco.2005.04.005

Richardson, S., Sloan, R., Soliman, M., & Tuna, I. (2006). The Implications of Accounting Distortions and Growth for Accruals and Profitability. *The Accounting Review*, *81*(3), 713–743. doi:10.2308/accr.2006.81.3.713

Schipper, K., & Vincent, L. (2003). Earnings Quality. *Accounting Horizons*, *17*(s-1supplement), 97–110. doi:10.2308/acch.2003.17.s-1.97

Sloan, R. (1996). Do Stock Prices Fully Reflect Information in Accruals and Cash Flows about Future Earnings? *The Accounting Review*, *71*, 289–315.

Warfield, T., Wild, J., & Wild, K. (1995). Managerial Ownership, Accounting Choices, and Informativeness of Earnings. *Journal of Accounting and Economics*, *20*(1), 61–91. doi:10.1016/0165-4101(94)00393-J

KEY TERMS AND DEFINITIONS

Abnormal Earnings: Current earnings minus the risk-free rate, times the book value at the beginning of period (i.e., earnings minus a charge for the use of capital). Abnormal earnings are defined to equal reported earnings minus the risk-free interest rate times the book value of the firm's equity. The accounting literature typically refers to it as "residual income," excess earnings, or super-profits.

Earnings Quality (EQ): A complex and nebulous concept with a multidimensional nature. EQ is a summary measure in firm performance evaluation and a crucial issue to assess the quality of accounting information. A high-quality earnings figure will reflect firm's current operating performance, being a good indicator of future operating performance; it also accurately annuitizes the intrinsic value of the firm. The multidimensional nature of the EQ concept has given form to a multiplicity of constructs and measures.

Firm Valuation: To assess and to evaluate the firm' value. There are different methodological approaches to evaluate companies. This work highlights that earnings are important for firm evaluation effects. Investors recognize earnings management as relevant for their assessment and decisions; accordingly, firm valuation models based on earnings, and based on book value, have been developed.

Linear Information Model: Determining the value of the company using accounting and financial variables in a framework of nonlinear relationships.

Market Value Added: The excess of the intrinsic value (market value of equity) in relation to the accounting value (book value of equity). It is also known as "unrecorded goodwill." In these terms, the goodwill presents itself as a measure for the abnormal earnings generation. As such, the goodwill captures all the "hidden assets," as well as the difference between the sum of the cost value of the assets shown on the balance sheet, individually considered, and their market value or the intrinsic value.

Other Information Variable: A variable that captures important events in terms of informative content, which affect the market prices (market value of equity), but that are not yet reflected in the financial statements. This variable captures the extent to which the accounting variables do not explain the market value of equity.

Residual Income Model: Is an approach to equity valuation that formally accounts for the cost of equity capital. Here, "residual" means in excess of any opportunity costs measured relative to the book value of shareholders' equity; residual income is then the income generated by a firm after accounting for the true cost of capital.

ENDNOTES

1. Hicksian income (Hicks, 1939) corresponds to the amount that can be consumed (that is, paid out as dividends) during a period, while leaving the firm equally well off at the beginning and the end of the period, that is, the maximum amount that can be consumed consistent with the maintenance of wealth.
2. Brown (1996) characterizes the papers cited in the SCCI – Social Sciences Citation Index, as been a classic, when the mean quotation is situated, at least between 4.00 and 8.35. According to Lo and Lys (2001), in 1999, and with reference to the Ohlson's model (1995), the citations mean was already superior to 9.

3 Beaver (2002: 457): "The F-O approach [Ohlson, 1995 and Feltham and Ohlson, 1995] is, in my opinion, one of the most important research developments in the last ten years".

4 Gordon and Shapiro (1956) rewrite the initial model, admitting the assumption that the growth rate for the dividends is constant.

5 *Apud* in Feltham and Ohlson (1995: 726).

6 *Apud* in Feltham and Ohlson (1995: 728).

7 *Apud* in Feltham and Ohlson (1995: 728).

8 ω and γ parameters assume values bigger than zero, due to economic conditions and values inferior to the unit in order to guarantee the model's stability/stationarity. This condition implies that $E_t\left(x^a_{t+\tau}\right) \to 0$ and $E_t\left(v_{t+\tau}\right) \to 0$ with $\tau \to \infty$. If indeed $\omega = 1$, this means that the growing opportunities persisted indefinitely, which is not consistent with the empirical evidence.

9 As referred by Mota et al. (2004), the value of a company depends of multiple factors that involve the detailed analysis of a set of variables associated to the company (market position, profitability, financial structure, management characteristics, human resources quality, etc.), as well as an analysis of the environment in which the company operates (macro-economic, political, activity sector, competition variables, among others.).

10 It is important to highlight that the company's value does not depend on the dividend policy, consistent with the assumption adopted regarding its irrelevance.

11 Ohlson labels "predictability" as the autocorrelation, or persistence, of each earnings component expressed in equation [2.2b], but the model proposed here considers the autocorrelation of each earnings component, as persistence. The autoregressive coefficients (MVE_t, BVE_t) are earnings quality constructs that capture the persistence of earnings or the earnings components persistence. In the proposed model, similarly with Barth *et al.* (1999, 2005), the coefficient ω_{12} measures the predictability of earnings components, being predictive ability, the ability of current earnings components to predict future earnings.

Chapter 2
Earnings Management and Stock Market Reaction

Antonio Melo Cerqueira
University of Porto, Portugal

Claudia Ferreira Pereira
Porto Polytechnic, Portugal

ABSTRACT

This chapter aims to analyze if and the extent to which earnings management activities are detected by market participants. For that purpose, this chapter reviews prior literature on stock market reaction to earnings management and earnings quality. A main conclusion obtained with this approach is that stock market participants are to some extent misled by earnings management activities consistent with those activities making the firm's information environment more opaque, thus increasing the difficulty for investors to interpret financial statements. Both the theoretical and empirical contributions provided in such works are relevant given the potential negative consequences of earnings management for stakeholders, firms, and even for the entire economy. In addition, it must be emphasized that accounting regulation is fundamental to balance the trade-off between more informative financial statements and reducing the level of managers' opportunistic choices.

INTRODUCTION

The main objective of this chapter is to analyze whether earnings management practices developed by managers are fully detected or not by market participants, relying on stock market reaction.

To understand the relevance of studying earnings management researchers may begin by recalling some extreme events where companies allegedly developed actions with the main purpose of misleading investors, Desai (2005), Zang (2012) and Agrawal & Cooper (2015). This is the case of a number of corporate financial scandals occurring over the first decade of the 21st century. Such corporate scandals uncover a hidden reality in a number of publicly held firms which misreported earnings to capital markets and they had a widespread negative and long-lasting impact on the real economy and on the financial sector. For example, in 2000 Xerox revealed that it had overstated profits by $1.4 billion over a 4-year

DOI: 10.4018/978-1-5225-7817-8.ch002

period. Diverse rules used to report earnings to capital markets and to fiscal authorities allowed Enron to engage in transactions designed to report financial accounting benefits immediately, while the corresponding income tax benefits would only occur into the future, Desai (2005).

What is puzzling in those scandals is how it was possible for the companies to get into such a dramatic situation despite the obligation to disclose financial information under the scrutiny of audit firms, financial analysts, international rating agencies and regulatory institutions. From the above evidence, sometimes reported earnings may not reflect the true performance of the firm, therefore to study the quality of earnings is fundamental. Leuz et al. (2003) argue that managers have incentives to misrepresent firm performance through earnings management due to the conflict of interest between insiders and outsiders.

The methodology used to develop this study is essentially based on a literature review. In more general terms, the problematic of earnings management can be analysed within theoretical frameworks such as the agency theory and the stakeholder theory. Stakeholder theory tends to be more extensive than the agency theory by viewing cash flows of a firm as a pie divided among stakeholders, as dividends to shareholders, taxes to governments, and bonuses to managers and perhaps employees, Ball et al. (2000). Both discretionary accounting choices and deliberate managerial strategies can be used to exploit information asymmetries and differences in stakeholder power, Roberts & Mahoney (2004). Such earnings management practices may be explained for example by managers' incentives to engage in income-increasing earnings because of the links between their reputation and reported earnings.

In prior literature the fundamental role of earnings relies on their use both for contracting purposes or to make investment decisions, Schipper & Vincent (2003). In the case of the contracting perspective, compensation contracts and debt agreements are usually based on accounting earnings. In the case of investment decisions, earnings are the basis for predicting future cash-flows and for risk assessment. In line with the above arguments, Francis et al. (2004) refer that earnings are a premier source of firm-specific information and that investors rely on earnings more than any other summary measure of performance, such as dividends, cash flows and EBITDA.

Once earnings are important, sometimes managers may have incentives to exercise discretion when preparing financial statements. In the case of the formal contracting perspective incentives result, for example, when managers pursue some target numbers that are specified in formal contracts, Healy & Wahlen (1999). Concerning the decision making perspective, which relates to implicit contracts between the firm and stakeholders, managers may be motivated to overstate or understate earnings relative to the normal level of discretion anticipated by stakeholders.

While in accounting standards is recognized that managers need a certain degree of flexibility when reporting financial information in order to communicate the true and fair value of the firm, it may be used by managers for diverse purposes, Healy & Wahlen (1999). Sometimes they take advantage of the accounting choice to signal their private information to investors. But, they may choose an accounting treatment that is expected to maximize the utility of management or that is economically efficient in the perspective of the company. In more extreme situations they may develop practices with the only purpose of misrepresenting or reduce the transparency of financial reports.

There is a branch in literature, named earnings management, which analyzes the discretionary use of the flexibility allowed by accounting standards in order to influence contractual outcomes or to mislead some stakeholders, Dechow & Dichev (2002), Francis et al. (2005) and Kothari et al. (2005). Nevertheless, the same objectives can be achieved through real activities manipulation, which deviate from normal business practices, in order to meet certain earnings targets, Zang (2012) and Kothari et al.

(2016). The former strand in literature is known as accrual-based earnings management, and the latter as real earnings management. In this study it is followed the accrual-based earnings management approach.

Given that earnings management is a broad and unobservable concept there is not a single and precise definition of the concept. Probably, the most often cited definition of earnings management is *"Earnings management occurs when managers use judgment in financial reporting and in structuring transactions to alter financial reports to either mislead some stakeholders about the underlying economic performance of the company or to influence contractual outcomes that depend on reported accounting numbers."* (Healy and Wahlen, 1999, p. 368). This definition relies on the incentives to manage earnings, such as the expected impact on capital markets, contracts written in terms of accounting numbers and antitrust or other government regulation. The definition also indicates two techniques to manage earnings: the first technique is to alter reported data; the other refers to the structuring of transactions in order to influence reported earnings.

As mentioned above, this chapter focus on earnings management activities based on accounting choices. If managers are aware that the association between the quality of reported earnings and stock market reaction exists, then they may be influenced towards earnings management. Prior literature examines whether some measures frequently used to represent the quality of earnings are actually interpreted by the stock market as indicators of the quality of the firm's information environment.

To deepen the understanding about financial reporting practices this study begins to focus on the International Financial Reporting Standards (IFRS). While the adoption of IFRS relies on the assumption that the use of these standards provides superior information to market participants, there are several concerns namely IFRS are based on principles rather than rules, leading to different interpretations which may be the reason for a higher level of flexibility in financial reporting, Nobes (2006) and Kvaal & Nobes (2010). Besides, Ball (2006) develops the argument that the fair value orientation of IFRS could add volatility to financial statements and thus increase the potential for managers' discretion.

In contrast with the above perspective that IFRS might increase opportunistic financial reporting, there is a growing body of evidence which suggests that principles-based standards tend to increase the quality of reported earnings. Agoglia et al. (2011) conduct two experiments to investigate if financial reporting under principles-based accounting standards leads to more aggressive reporting as compared to reporting under more rules-based accounting standards. Their results provide evidence that principles-based accounting standards lead preparers to issue higher-quality financial reports. Cohen et al. (2013) find that auditors are more likely to constrain aggressive reporting under principles-based accounting standards than under rules-based standards implying that principles-based standards lead to higher quality earnings.

From the presumed level of flexibility allowed by accounting standards and in order to understand its impact on earnings quality it is important to consider the incentives underlying managers' decisions when preparing a firm's financial statements. For most of prior research, the level of discretion exercised by managers is reflected in accounting accruals, Jones (1991), Dechow et al. (1995), Dechow & Dichev (2002), Francis et al. (2005) and Kothari et al. (2005). In order to deepen the understanding of the quality of reported information and to test the performance of commonly used indicators of earnings quality, market-based methods have been used to examine the statistical association between them and stock market variables such as information asymmetry, Bhattacharya et al. (2013) and Cerqueira & Pereira (2015, 2017), idiosyncratic volatility, Rajgopal & Venkatachalam (2011), Aabo et al. (2017), cost of capital, Francis et al. (2004, 2005), Bhattacharya et al. (2012).

The remaining of this chapter is organized as follows: section 2 describes accounting-based measures of earnings quality used in prior studies, section 3 details some approaches that reflect the market reaction to earnings management and section 4 presents some concluding remarks.

ACCOUNTING-BASED MEASURES OF EARNINGS QUALITY

Once earnings quality is negatively affected by earnings management activities it has been widely examined in literature. However, earnings quality is a broad concept that is related to the usefulness of financial statements to a number of parties contracting with the firm, Ball & Shivakumar (2005). Therefore, earnings quality cannot be assessed directly and several proxies have been used in prior literature for the quality of earnings as can be seen in Schipper & Vincent (2003), Dechow et al. (2010) and Ewert & Wagenhofer (2011). A group of measures is based on the time-series characteristics of reported earnings, such as persistence, smoothness and timely loss recognition. Another group of measures assesses the extent to which earnings map into cash flows, such as discretionary accruals and accruals quality. The relevance of each measure must be evaluated in the context of a specific decision model (Dechow et al., 2010). For example, Francis et al. (2004) find evidence that accrual quality is the most powerful measure to capture the effect of earnings attributes on the cost of equity capital.

Earnings Persistence

Persistence is a desirable attribute of earnings because it captures sustainability, and sustainability enhances the performance of earnings as a summary metric of expected cash flows used for equity valuation. In short, earnings persistence is measured as the slope coefficient (beta) from a regression of current earnings on lagged earnings,

$$Earnings_t = \alpha + \beta Earnings_{t-1} + \varepsilon_{t-1}$$

The rationale behind the usefulness of earnings persistence as a metric of earnings quality is that if a firm has a more persistent series of earnings then current earnings is a more accurate measure of future performance leading to small error in estimated firm value. Consistently, persistent earnings tend be related to a larger investors' response to reported earnings. In addition, persistence increases the usability of earnings in multiple valuations, for example price-to-earnings multiple.

When using persistence as an indicator of earnings quality, there are some issues that need to be taken into. Firstly, persistence depends both on the firm's fundamental performance and on the accounting measurement system. Secondly, another potential problem with using earnings persistence is that earnings are decomposed into cash flow and accruals and it is not enough to account for accrual management because cash flows can also be managed through real earnings management.

However, empirical findings suggest that accruals are less persistent than operating cash flows in predicting 1-year-ahead operating income, consistent with earnings performance attributable to the accrual component of earnings exhibiting lower persistence than earnings performance attributable to the cash flow component of earning. Besides, Sloan (1996) report that firms with high levels of current accruals tend to exhibit negative future abnormal stock returns and that investors do not anticipate such decline as if they were unable to separate cash flow and accruals component of earnings.

Earnings Smoothness

Another measure of earnings quality is smoothness that consists in reducing earnings variability by increasing low reported earnings and reducing high reported earnings relative to economic earnings. The accounting choices involved in smoothing does not necessarily mean that managers have the intention to mislead investors. When the accounting treatment is neutral then, in the long run, the average reported earnings equals average economic earnings. To measure smoothness by capturing the relative absence of variability it is applied the ratio between the standard deviation of operating earnings to the standard deviation of cash from operations, Dechow et al. (2010) and Leuz et al. (2003).

$$smoothness = \frac{\sigma\left(earnings\right)}{\sigma\left(cash\,flows\right)}$$

Leuz et al. (2003) use a number of measures of earnings management, including earnings smoothness to analyze differences in earnings management across 31 countries. These authors find evidence on the impact of investors' protection in reducing the level of earnings management. They argue that managers may use accounting discretion to conceal economic shocks to operating cash flows. In the case of poor current performance managers may accelerate the reporting of future revenues or delay the report of current costs.

A number of reasons have been presented to explain why smoothness is a desirable attribute of earnings, namely because such earnings are perceived by investors as less risky thus reducing the required return and make easier for investors to predict future earnings. In addition, because smoother earnings are less volatile they allow for better forecasting. For example, managers can use their private information to smooth nonrecurring effects. Conversely, when smoothing is used to manipulate firm performance it leads to a reduced information content and less timely earnings, Dechow et al. (2010), Ewert & Wagenhofer (2011) and Ewert & Wagenhofer (2015). The former view considers smoother earnings as having higher quality while the later view associates smoother earnings with more earnings management.

Timely Loss Recognition

Timely loss recognition is a measure of earnings quality usually related to conditional conservatism because it reflects a tendency to require a higher degree of verification to recognize good news relative to bad news. In general, timely loss recognition is said to make managers less likely to invest in projects with negative net present value, then reducing agency costs. In addition, when earnings reflect bad news quickly than good news then more quickly are triggered debt covenants violations, increasing the efficiency of debt contracting. This definition contrasts the argument that managers have an asymmetric incentive to reveal their private information, namely because of their preference to disclose timely information about expected future gains is greater than to disclose timely information about future loses (Ball and Shivakumar, 2005). Additionally, in the case of losses, managers are likely to have incentives to differ loss recognitions to future periods, when the corresponding loss recognition is passed on to a subsequent generation of manager. Therefore, timely loss recognition is expected to mitigate agency problems by reporting losses around the time expectations are revised downward. In short, timely loss recognition increases earnings quality by making financial statements more useful for a number of stakeholders.

To deepen the understanding of timely loss recognition as a measure of earnings quality some insights about the construction of this measure provided by Ball & Shivakumar (2005) are analyzed. These authors examine whether financial reporting quality, as measured by timely loss recognition, differs between private and public firms for the UK. As explained in detail by the authors, an important contribution of the study results from the predominance of private firms in the UK economy, while the regulatory context is similar for public and private firms.

These authors provide an interesting perspective to measure earnings quality based on timely loss recognition. They build on the prior study of Basu (1997) that analyses the asymmetric timeliness of earnings, where reported earnings respond more quickly to bad news than to good news. In his study, Basu (1997) uses negative and positive unexpected stock returns as a measure for bad news and for good news, respectively. This author regresses annual earnings on annual unexpected returns to test the hypothesis that the slope coefficient and R squared are higher for negative unexpected returns than for positive unexpected returns.

$$\frac{X_{i,t}}{P_{i,t-1}} = \alpha_0 + \alpha_1 DR_{i,t} + \beta_0 R_{i,t} + \beta_1 R_{i,t} \times DR_{i,t} + \varepsilon_t$$

Where, X represents earnings per share; P is the share price; DR is a dummy variable which is set to one for negative stock returns and zero otherwise and R is the stock return. A higher estimated coefficient of the interaction term β_1 implies more timely recognition of losses.

Ball & Shivakumar (2005) assess the timeliness of gains and losses by measuring the tendency for increases and decreases in reported income to reverse. For that purpose they estimate a new version of Basu's equation, specified by,

$$\Delta NI_t = \alpha_0 + \alpha_1 D\Delta NI_{t-1} + \alpha_2 \Delta NI_{t-1} + \alpha_3 D\Delta NI_{t-1} \times \Delta NI_{t-1} + \varepsilon_t \mathfrak{M}$$

Where, ΔNI is the change in reported income and $D\Delta NI$ is a dummy variable which is set to one for negative values of ΔNI. In order to understand the expected signs of the estimated coefficients let us assume that the incorporation of gains is deferred until the corresponding cash flow is realized, meaning that gains are persistent and tend not to reverse. In this case, the estimated coefficient $\alpha_2 = 0$. In the case of timely recognition of losses, because they are recognized has a transitory income decrease, they are expected to reverse in the following period thus implying $\alpha_2 + \alpha_3 < 0$. By assuming a certain degree of reversion in reported gains then $\alpha_2 < 0$. The hypothesis that loses are recognized in a more timely way than gains implies $\alpha_3 < 0$.

Discretionary Accruals

To explain how to construct discretionary accruals measure, it must be said that accruals represent the difference between reported earnings and the corresponding cash flows. Such difference arises due to accounting conventions in relation to when and how much to recognize as income and expenses. Discretionary accruals measure the part of the variation in working capital not explained by the variation in the company's economic conditions, such as the level of investment and the variation in sales. This proxy was first developed by Jones (1991), modified by Dechow et al. (1995) and Kothary et al. (2005). To obtain discretionary accruals based on the modified Jones model with lagged return-on-assets proposed by Kothari et al. (2005), it is usual to begin with total accruals for firm i in year t defined as,

$$TA_{i,t} = \Delta CA_{i,t} - \Delta CL_{i,t} - \Delta Cash_{i,t} + \Delta STDEBT_{i,t} - DEPN_{i,t}$$

Where ΔCA is the change in current assets, ΔCL is the change in current liabilities, $\Delta Cash$ is the change in cash, $\Delta STDEBT$ represents the change in short term debt and $DEPN$ is the depreciation and amortization expense.

Using firm-year observations on total accruals, cross-sectional regressions at the industry level are estimated.

$$TAcc_{i,t} = \alpha_0 + \alpha_1 \left(\frac{1}{Assets_{i,t-1}} \right) + \alpha_2 \left(\Delta Sales_{i,t} - \Delta AR_{i,t} \right) + \alpha_3 PPE_{i,t} + \alpha_4 ROA_{i,t-1} + \varepsilon_{i,t}$$

Where $TAcc_{i,t}$ is the total accruals scaled by lagged total assets, $\Delta Sales$ is the change in sales scaled by lagged total assets ($Assets_{i,t-1}$), ΔAR is the change in accounts receivable scaled by lagged total assets, PPE is net property, plant and equipment scaled by lagged total assets and ROA represents return on assets in period t-1.

As in the modified Jones model with the Kothari contribution, discretionary accruals are defined as the residuals of equation above. These residuals represent the component of accruals left after controlling for firm performance, firm economic activity and investment in Plant, Property and Equipment. Such component of accruals is likely to be associated with manager's discretionary choices.

Accruals Quality

Now it is explained the construction of the accruals quality metric developed by Dechow & Dichev (2002), as modified by McNichols (2002) and used in prior literature, for example Francis et al. (2005). Dechow & Dichev (2002) measure the quality of accruals by the extent to which current accruals map into past, current and future cash flows, more specifically by the standard deviation of the residuals of the regression of currents accruals on cash flows (estimated at the firm level or at the sector level). McNichols (2002) include in the estimation of residuals the variables current year property, plant and equipment and change in net sales, which are the fundamental variables in the Jones (1991) model. Francis et al. (2005)

investigate the impact of this measure on the cost of capital. Specifically, they estimate the regression residuals cross-sectionally, by year, within each of the Fama & French (1997) 48 industry classification.

To measure accruals quality requires computing total current accruals as the change in noncash working capital,

$$TCA_{i,t} = \Delta CA_{i,t} - \Delta CL_{i,t} - \Delta Cash_{i,t} + \Delta STDebt_{i,t}$$

Where ΔCA is the change in current assets, ΔCL is the change in current liabilities, $\Delta Cash$ is the change in cash, $\Delta STDebt$ represents the change in short term debt.

Accruals quality is measured by the standard deviation of the residuals obtained by regressing total current accruals on operating cash flow in the current period, prior period and future period, change in revenues and gross value of property plant and equipment.

$$TCA_{i,t} = \alpha_0 + \alpha_1 CFO_{i,t-1} + \alpha_2 CFO_{i,t} + \alpha_3 CFO_{i,t+1} + \alpha_4 PPE_{i,t} + \alpha_5 Rev_{i,t} + \varepsilon_{i,t}$$

All variables are scaled by average total assets.

Cash flow from operations are estimated as the difference between net income before extraordinary items and total accruals (TA),

$$CFO_{i,t} = NIBE_{i,t} - TA_{i,t}$$

Where TA is defined as the change in noncash working capital minus depreciation and amortization expense,

$$TA_{i,t} = \Delta CA_{i,t} - \Delta CL_{i,t} - \Delta Cash_{i,t} + \Delta STDEBT_{i,t} - DEPN_{i,t}$$

In order to obtain the residuals $\varepsilon_{i,t}$ for firm i and year t, the last regression is cross-sectionally estimated in year t at the Fama & French's (1997) industry level. Accruals quality in year t refers to the standard deviation of a firm's residuals calculated over year t-4 through t.

A further development, consists in decomposing the accruals quality metric into an innate component and a discretionary component following the Francis et al. (2005) approach and applied by Lobo et al. 2012. For that purpose, the authors estimate cross-sectional regressions of accruals quality on a number of explanatory variables that are measures for operating uncertainty.

$$Innate_{i,t} =$$
$$\alpha_0 + \alpha_1 Size_{t-1} + \alpha_2 \sigma\left(CFO\right)_{i,t} + \alpha_3 \sigma\left(Sales\right)_{i,t} + \alpha_4 OperCycle_{i,t} + \alpha_5 NumNegEarn_{i,t} + \varepsilon_t$$

Where Size is the log of total assets, $\sigma\left(CFO\right)$ is the standard deviation of cash flow from operations (scaled by the average total assets) over the 10 years ending in year t, $\sigma\left(Sales\right)$ is the standard deviation of Sales (scaled by average total assets) over the 10 years ending in year t, $NumNegEarn$ is the proportion of reported negative net income before extraordinary items over the past 10 years and $OperCycle$ is the log of operating cycle, where the operating cycle is calculated as follows:

$$OperCycle = 360 \times \frac{\text{Average Accounts Receivable}}{\text{Sales}} + 360 \times \frac{\text{Average inventory}}{\text{COGS}}$$

EARNINGS QUALITY AND STOCK MARKET REACTION

This section focus on whether stock markets react to earnings management activities. By studying the association between an indicator of information quality and a variable representative of stock market performance allows to assess the usefulness of the indicator in the perspective of stock market investors. This approach depends on the performance of the indicator to capture information quality and in particular earnings quality.

At this point it is essential to imbed this issue into a more general perspective. Accounting earnings is the most common way to assess a firm's underlying economic earnings. In fact, economic earnings are not directly observable, but accounting earnings is likely to differ from economic earnings namely because of the rules used to recognize current gains and losses. For example, Ball et al. (2000) use change in stock value as a proxy for current economic earnings and define timeliness as the extent to which current accounting earnings incorporate current economic income. Their study analyzes the association between a market variable and an accounting variable which is assumed to capture the non-observable economic earnings.

Once earnings management activities erode earnings quality (Dechow et al., 2010) prior studies employ a number of measures of earnings quality to assess the level of earnings management. Therefore, it is fundamental to assess whether the market is indeed misled by earnings management activities or, in a slightly different way, if such activities make the firm's information environment more opaque, thus increasing the difficulty for investors to interpret financial statements. A common procedure is to analyze the market reaction to earnings management through a number of characteristics that are stock prices, cost of capital, information asymmetry and idiosyncratic return volatility.

Earnings Quality and Stock Prices

This section begins with stock prices, specifically reporting some evidence obtained in prior studies that sometimes managers succeed in misleading investors in situations where they are likely to have incentives in maintaining stock prices high. As examples of situations in which managers have allegedly manipulated stock prices upward include mergers and acquisitions, initial public offerings and seasoned equity offerings.

In the case of mergers and acquisitions, when a merger or acquisition is conducted, there are several ways the shareholders of the target company can be paid for their assets. The acquirer can pay a specified amount in cash for each share. Alternatively, in the case of a stock-for-stock merger, the acquirer provides its own shares to the shareholders of the target company according to a specified conversion ratio. In stock-for-stock mergers and acquisitions, where the shareholders of the target firm are paid in stocks of the acquiring firm, managers of the latter have incentives to increase their stock price in order to reduce the cost of the merger to their own shareholders. Specifically, managers of the acquiring entity may exercise discretion to increase reported earnings prior to the acquisition, so that the market price of its shares would also increase. Thus the acquiring entity may negotiate an arrangement in which it would provide less shares, taking advantage of the higher price of its stock. This increase in reported earnings has two main characteristics. Firstly, it is likely to have a short-time effect and secondly this effect is likely to be subsequently reversed.

Accordingly, Louis (2004) finds evidence that acquirer firms succeed in managing earnings in order the increase stock prices in stock-for-stock acquisitions.

Describing in more details, the results document positive abnormal returns, consistent with upward earnings management, in the quarter preceding the merger announcement. However, those results do not provide evidence of market reaction over the three day- window around the event. Moreover, the author finds a significant negative correlation between the discretionary accrual measure of earnings quality and the long-term performance of stock-for-stock acquirers, suggesting that the long-term poor performance of acquiring firms reported in the extant literature is partly attributable to the reversal of the effect of prior earnings management. Besides, the reversal of the effects of earnings management in a stock-for-stock acquisition is not fully anticipated by financial analysts in the month immediately following the merger announcement. This means that the market is aware of the earnings management activity but apparently cannot assess its exact magnitude, consistent with the market anticipating earnings management only imperfectly.

Other examples of studies that analyse the relation between stock-for-stock mergers and acquisitions and earnings management by the acquirer are Erickson & Wang (1999) who provide evidence that acquiring firms manage earnings upward in the periods prior to the merger agreement and Gong et al. (2008) that find a positive association between stock-for-stock pre-merger abnormal accruals and post-merger lawsuits.

So far in this section it has been analysed the side of acquiring firms in mergers and acquisitions. Given the extant empirical evidence that acquiring firms tend to underperform in the post-merger period some justifications may be advanced in addition to the above mentioned imperfect assessment of the magnitude of earnings management. For example, Campa & Hajbaba (2016) provide evidence that target firms manage earnings upward in order to increase stock price. However, incentives for target firms to manipulate earnings may not be a major concern once its value depends crucially on anticipated synergies. Therefore, most of studies on target firms tend to examine related issues such as payment method, type of earnings management (Campa & Hajbaba, 2016). Specifically, in that study the authors provide evidence that target companies manage earnings upwards through sales manipulation over the year prior to the merger. However, their results show that such behaviour is restricted to cash-financed mergers and acquisitions. Their results also suggest a long-term reversal of the effects of the manipulations prior to the announcement date. Others studies relate earnings quality to the preference for negotiated takeovers, Raman et al. (2013) and Marquardt & Zur (2015). Raman et al. (2013) show that acquires prefer negotiated takeovers in deals involving targets with poor earnings quality. In addition, their study documents a negative relation between earnings quality and takeovers premiums in the case of negotiated takeovers. Marquardt & Zur (2015) reports that the quality of accounting earnings is positively associated with the use of negotiations, the speed of the process, and with the likelihood of deal completion.

Another operation that seems to be appropriate to examine the relationship between earnings management and changes in stock prices is the initial public offering (IPO). In an IPO, a private corporation rises capital by offering its stock to the public for the first time. Usually, the corporation uses the services of an investment bank to determine the offering price, the number of shares to issue and the timing of the operation. During the IPO, managers usually hold private information about future cash flows, while investors are uncertain about the prospects of the firm. In this context of information asymmetry managers may have incentives to disclose information that leads to higher stock prices. In addition, it is more risky to buy the shares of new listed firms because there is no historical data related to the stock trading process.

Consistent with this view, Teoh et al. (1998) documents that managers opportunistically increase earnings to influence IPO pricing. Specifically, they argue that issuers can report high earnings by adjusting aggressively accounting accruals in order to increase share price. In a context of information asymmetry where investors make their pricing decisions based on earnings, buyers may be unware that earnings are artificially increased by the use of accruals and could pay too much for the shares of the firm.

After the operation, as new information about the firm is disclosed by the media, financial analysts' reports, and subsequent financial statements, investors may find that prior earnings were overstated and adjust their beliefs about firm value. It's likely that the greater the level of earnings management at the time of the operation, the larger the subsequent price correction will be.

In contrast, Ball et al. (2008) find evidence that firms report more conservatively because higher quality reporting is demanded for public firms by financial statement users. Another reason contradicting the hypothesis of substantial earnings management by IPO firms is that the IPO would attract increased scrutiny from financial analysts, potential underwriters, auditors, regulators and the press. In addition, there is a risk of subsequent detection that would increase the cost of capital, which is particularly relevant because the firm is likely to anticipate more needs of external financing.

In fact, stock prices are expected to change as a result of new information arrivals. A corporate event that is of particular interest to study the actual impact of earnings management on stock prices is the seasoned equity offering.

The case of Seasoned Equity Offerings (SEO) represents a proper setting for assessing the stock market reaction to potential earnings manipulations. Managers clearly have incentives to manage earnings upward, since by increasing stock price at the time of the seasoned equity offering results in more wealth being transferred from the participants in the operation to the company and its current shareholders. However, to mislead potential buyers may not be too easy, because around this well-identified operation there is a significantly increased emphasis on a firm's operations and its stock price. Therefore, any potential overvaluation at the time of the event is more likely when managers engage in real earnings management which is assumed to be a more opaque method to manage earnings relative to accrual-based earnings management. An important question is how to detect if investors are actually misled by earnings manipulations. An approach used by Cohen & Zarowin (2010) and Kothari et al. (2016) relies on the assumption that if earnings are artificially overstated then reversals would be observed in the future when investors learn the true stock value. In line with this argument Cohen & Zarowin (2010) and Kothari et al. (2016) provide empirical results revealing that earnings management is most consistently related to market underperformance when it is driven by real earnings management; in particular, through the reduction of expenditures on R&D and selling, general, and administrative activities.

Earnings Quality and the Cost of Capital

After analysing the relation between earnings management activities and stock prices, the focus now is on whether the cost of equity capital is affected by the quality of accounting information. To examine whether and to what extent earnings quality affects investors' investment decisions is an important way to understand stock market reaction to the quality of accounting information.

Now some studies are analysed that provide the theoretical framework for such association. For example, Easley & O'Hara (2004) develop a model showing that in equilibrium, stock returns include a risk premium that depends upon the information structure of each stock, consistent with investors demanding compensation related to idiosyncratic factors, in contrast with common asset pricing models. In particular, required returns are affected by information risk, captured both by the quantity of private information and by the precision of both public and private information. Investors require higher returns for holding stock of firms with more private information and less precise information (both public and private). Another example is Lambert et al. (2007) where the quality of accounting information affects both directly and indirectly the cost of equity capital. The direct effect manifests through the firm's assessed covariances with other firms' cash flows. The indirect effect manifests through the changes in the firm's real decisions.

Once theoretical models predict a risk premium related to the quality of reported information, several empirical studies have analysed whether poor information quality is associated with a higher cost of equity capital.

Francis et al. (2004) examines the association between seven attributes of reported earnings and the cost of equity capital with the intent of determining which attributes matter for investors. The idea underlying that analysis is to use the cost of capital as a benchmark to assess the intensity of the market reaction to each particular attribute. After classifying the attributes into accounting-based attributes (accruals quality, persistence, predictability, and smoothness) and market-based attributes (value relevance, timeliness, and conservatism) they provide evidence that the effects associated with the former group of attributes generally exceeds the effects associated with the later. In particular, the authors find that among accounting-based attributes, accruals quality has the strongest effect on the cost of equity capital.

Therefore, most of recent studies, that use accounting-based measures of earnings quality, tend to rely predominantly on the accruals quality metric. In those studies, a relevant research question is whether investors differentiate between the innate and discretionary component of accruals quality. The study of Francis et al. (2005) examines if the innate and discretionary components of accruals quality have different impacts on the cost of capital. Their finding indicates that investors assign more importance to the innate component of accrual quality than to the discretionary component. Such results suggest that investors are less concerned about managers' discretionary choices than about the innate features of the firm's business model and operating environment.

Earnings Quality and Information Asymmetry

Previous literature theoretically and empirically documents several links between the quality of reported earnings and information asymmetry in stock markets. The definition expressed herein of information asymmetry is the difference in information precision between informed and uninformed investors, Lambert et al. (2012). Information asymmetry can be seen, at first glance, as a vague theoretical concept with no serious practical consequences for the operation of stock markets. However, information asymmetry is a concept widely used in many economic and financial areas. Information asymmetry is expected to increase the cost of capital because in microstructure models asymmetric information between buyers and sellers tends to reduce liquidity in the market for firm shares, implying that firms must issue capital at a discount (Leuz and Verrecchia, 2000). In addition, recent research suggests that, except for perfect capital markets, information asymmetry is positively related to the cost of capital (Armstrong et al., 2011; Lambert et al., 2012; Bhattacharya et al., 2012).

Based on Market Microstructure theory, stock market investors trade in an information asymmetry context where traders with superior information profit from their informational advantage. In a microstructure setting there are two types of participants commonly referred to as informed and uninformed. Informed participants base their trading on private information, while uninformed participants trade on public information or for liquidity reasons. Informed participants have an informational advantage because they hold private information about the performance of the firm or because of their superior ability to process public information.

Information asymmetries among market participants create an adverse selection problem because participants with superior information about the performance of the firm will selectively participate in trades which benefit them at the expense of the other market participants. When markets makers set their price quotations, they address the adverse selection problem they face by adjusting the adverse selection component of the spread in order to take into account their expected losses with informed participants. In practical terms, larger spreads tend to reduce liquidity and increase the cost of capital.

Based on the above arguments, earnings management practices are likely to inflate information asymmetry among market participants. Firstly, earnings management makes more difficult to market participants to interpret financial statements and if they do not have private information they tend to trade on public information. Secondly such increased opacity may offer to more sophisticated participants an opportunity to profit from their private information, therefore they may be interested in increasing their trading in the stock of firms with high levels of earnings management practices.

Therefore, to understand the aggregation of information into stock prices is fundamental to study the relation between information quality and information asymmetry. Several studies empirically address this relation, such as that of Brown & Hillegeist (2007) where better information quality tends to reduce information asymmetry because of the increase in trading by uninformed investors and the lower likelihood that investors trade based on private information. Another study is that of Bhattacharya et al. (2012) analysing the association between earnings quality and the cost of equity mediated by information asymmetry. Both studies suggest that poor earnings quality tends to increase information asymmetry. These findings are consistent with the results of Easley & O´Hara (2004) that poor public information implies an information advantage for informed investors because of their private information. Further empirical evidence based on U.S. data shows that accrual-based earnings management is associated with higher information asymmetry and reductions in market liquidity, leading to a higher cost of capital (e.g. Bhattacharya et al., 2013; Jayaraman, 2008; Rajgopal and Venkatachalam, 2011). Results of empirical studies, examining information quality, are likely to be affected by a number of institutional factors such as market forces, ownership, governance structure and accounting standards used. Therefore, it is important to test the robustness of the results to changes in the institutional context, for example by investigating diverse markets, such as European markets, as is the case of the work of Cerqueira & Pereira (2015) providing evidence consistent with poor public information implying more information asymmetry.

The above empirical evidence requires the construction of measures to capture information asymmetry. Therefore, some measures commonly applied in empirical studies are presented.

A simple way to measure information asymmetry is to use the closing bid-ask spread that is available for listed stocks. This spread consists of the difference between the prices quoted by a market maker for an immediate sale and for an immediate purchase. In most of empirical studies the relative spread, measured as the ratio between the absolute spread and the mean value of ask price and bid price, is used instead of the absolute spread.

Market Microstructure Models propose three components of the spread: order processing costs, inventory costs and adverse selection. Once the adverse selection component is needed to represent the information asymmetry the remaining components must be removed. Following the approach of Jayaraman (2008) and Cerqueira & Pereira (2015) to take into account the order processing costs component is used turnover based on Bollen et al. (2004) and Acker et al. (2002). Turnover is defined as the ratio of shares traded over the year, divided by the total number of shares outstanding. To account for the inventory holding component is used a measure of illiquidity proposed by Amihud (2002) and Hasbrouck (2009).

An alternative proxy for information asymmetry is the relative effective spread. The effective spread captures the three components of the spread (order processing costs, inventory costs, adverse selection). Following Bhattacharya et al. (2013) the relative effective spread is given by:

$$Relative\,effective\,spread = 2 \times D \times \frac{Price - Mid}{Mid}$$

Where, D is a binary variable that is set to one for market buy orders and -1 for market sell orders, Price is the transaction price and Mid represents the midpoint of the ask price and bid price.

Another measure of information asymmetry is the probability of informed trading (PIN) used for example by Jayaraman (2008). The construction of this measure requires using trade data, more specifically the arrival rates of informed and uninformed traders and the probability of an information event. This variable is expected to assess the likelihood that the market maker transacts with an informed investor. The higher the ratio of informed to uninformed investors, the higher the PIN.

Some of the measures described above used to capture information asymmetry are estimated at the transaction level, relying on high frequency data. For example, Easley et al. (2002) and Bhattacharya et al. (2012) use intraday information on trades to capture the adverse selection component of spread.

However, for most of the European markets high frequency data is not available on the form of organized databases. In this case the Corwin & Schultz (2012) high-low spread estimator can be used. These authors argue that the estimator can be used both with daily or intraday data and found empirical evidence of a similar performance of the spread estimator as compared to alternative measures based on high-frequency data for U.S. markets. This measure is applied as a proxy for information asymmetry by Cerqueira & Pereira (2015) and Cerqueira & Pereira (2017) to analyze the stock market reaction to the firm's informational context in Europe, as measured by accruals quality and the dispersion in analysts' forecasts.

Earnings Quality and Idiosyncratic Return Volatility

An alternative form to assess market reaction is to investigate the association between accrual-based measures of earnings quality and idiosyncratic volatility. To study this association matters because idiosyncratic volatility represents the major component of stock return volatility and volatility reflects uncertainty, risk and higher transaction costs. In particular, idiosyncratic volatility has been associated with stock mispricing and more risk. However, opposite to that expected such risk is not related to higher future returns but to lower future returns.

Building on asset pricing theory, idiosyncratic volatility is the part of the variation in stock returns after controlling for non-diversifiable risk factors. For example, idiosyncratic volatility is given by the volatility of the residuals of an equation based on the Capital Asset Pricing Model (CAPM). Another well-known proposition in Asset Pricing Theory asserts that only systematic risk is priced in equilibrium, because in theory idiosyncratic risk can be eliminated by portfolio diversification. However, recent literature claims that investors hold poorly diversified portfolios due to transaction costs, taxes or other institutional restrictions, Angelidis & Tessaromatis (2008).

In line with the above arguments, previous studies have argued that idiosyncratic volatility can reflect either the capitalization of firm-specific information into stock prices, Morck et al. (2000), Ferreira & Laux (2007) and Hutton et al. (2009) or noise, namely poor earnings quality, Rajgopal & Venkatachalam (2011) and Chen et al. (2012) or noise trading, Aabo et al. (2017) and Kelly (2014).

The most recent trend in the literature supports the noise hypothesis of idiosyncratic volatility claiming that idiosyncratic volatility tends to capture noise trading instead of the aggregation of firm-specific information. In this context a positive association is expected between poor earnings quality and idiosyncratic volatility.

Two approaches can be used to estimate the idiosyncratic volatility: direct decomposition method and indirect decomposition method, Xu & Malkiel (2003). The direct decomposition method estimates idiosyncratic volatility as the variance of the residuals of an asset pricing model, such as the CAPM or the Fama and French Three-Factor Model. The indirect decomposition Method developed by Campbell et al. (2001) yields a weighted average of firm-level volatility across firms.

To explain the direct method, for each firm and year, requires obtaining the residuals from the regression of a firm's daily returns on the variables included in the Capital Asset Pricing Model:

$$r_{i,t} = r_{f,t} + \beta_i \times \left(r_{m,t} - r_{f,t}\right) + e_{i,t}$$

Where $r_{i,t}$, $r_{m,t}$ and $r_{f,t}$ represent, respectively, the daily return of the stock, of the market and the risk free rate. The beta of the stock i, β_i, is obtained on an annual basis given by the average of monthly betas. Furthermore, it is assumed that the daily risk-free rate is given by the three-month government bond return divided by the number of trading days.

The indirect method, which provides an aggregate measure of idiosyncratic volatility and was proposed by Campbell et al. (2001), consists in a decomposition of the volatility that does not require the estimation of covariances or betas for industries or firms.

As a final development, given that accrual-based measures may be noisy indicators of earnings quality, researchers can analyze the association between market measures (information asymmetry, idiosyncratic volatility) and accrual-based measure of earnings quality, but including other variables capturing complementary dimensions of the quality of the firm's information environment.

CONCLUSION

This chapter analyzes a number of studies that investigate the market reaction to the quality of reported earnings, assuming that those earnings are affected by the level of earnings management.

Both the theoretical and empirical contributions provided in such works are relevant given the potential negative consequences of earnings management for stakeholders, firms and even for the entire economy. Therefore such research may assist economic agents to understand the nature of earnings management practices and to what extent they affect the market and stakeholders.

Based on prior literature, it is explained in some detail a number of measures of earnings quality, either those based on the time-series characteristics of reported earnings, such as persistence, smoothness and timely loss recognition, or measures assessing the extent to which earnings map into cash flows, such as discretionary accruals and accruals quality.

After this study analyzes the main results reported in prior studies on the association between the measures of earnings quality and variables representing stock market performance. This approach suggests that stock market is to some extent misled by earnings management activities or, in a slightly different way, that such activities make the firm's information environment more opaque, thus increasing the difficulty for investors to interpret financial statements.

As a final remark, some caution is required when interpreting the results of empirical studies relying on accrual-based measures of earnings quality. Besides other limitations, one important point discussed in this chapter is to assess managers' incentives when making their accounting choices, for example accruals can be used either to communicate manager's private information to the market or to opportunistically manage earnings. Regarding this last point, regulation plays a crucial role because accounting standards are expected to balance the trade-off between more informative financial statements and reducing the level of managers' opportunistic choices.

ACKNOWLEDGMENT

The authors thank anonymous reviewers for their useful comments and suggestions, which have improved this chapter greatly.

REFERENCES

Aabo, T., Pantzalis, C., & Park, J. (2017). Idiosyncratic Volatility: An Indicator of Noise Trading? *Journal of Banking & Finance*, *75*, 136–151. doi:10.1016/j.jbankfin.2016.11.003

Acker, D., Stalker, M., & Tonks, I. (2002). Daily Closing Inside Spreads and Trading Volumes Around Earnings Announcements. *Journal of Business Finance & Accounting*, *29*(9/10), 1149–1179. doi:10.1111/1468-5957.00465

Agoglia, C., Doupnik, T., & Tsakumis, G. (2011). Principles-Based versus Rules-Based Accounting Standards: The Influence of Standard Precision and Audit Committee Strength on Financial Reporting Decisions. *The Accounting Review*, *86*(3), 747–767. doi:10.2308/accr.00000045

Agrawal, A., & Cooper, T. (2015). Insider Trading before Accounting Scandals. *Journal of Corporate Finance*, *34*, 169–190. doi:10.1016/j.jcorpfin.2015.07.005

Amihud, Y. (2002). Illiquidity and Stock Returns: Cross-Section and Time-Series Effects. *Journal of Financial Markets*, *5*(1), 31–56. doi:10.1016/S1386-4181(01)00024-6

Angelidis, T., & Tessaromatis, N. (2008). Idiosyncratic Volatility and Equity Returns: UK Evidence. *International Review of Financial Analysis*, *17*(3), 539–556. doi:10.1016/j.irfa.2006.10.006

Armstrong, C., Core, J., Taylor, D., & Verrecchia, R. (2011). When Does Information Asymmetry Affect the Cost of Capital? *Journal of Accounting Research*, *49*(1), 1–40. doi:10.1111/j.1475-679X.2010.00391.x

Ball, R. (2006). *International Financial Reporting Standards (IFRS): Pros and Cons for Investors*. Accounting and Business Research, International Accounting Policy Forum. 10.1080/00014788.2006.9730040

Ball, R., Kothari, S., & Robin, A. (2000). The Effect of International Institutional Factors on Properties of Accounting Earnings. *Journal of Accounting and Economics*, *29*(1), 1–51. doi:10.1016/S0165-4101(00)00012-4

Ball, R., & Shivakumar, L. (2005). Earnings Quality in UK Private Firms: Comparative Loss Recognition Timeliness. *Journal of Accounting and Economics*, *39*(1), 83–128. doi:10.1016/j.jacceco.2004.04.001

Ball, R., & Shivakumar, L. (2008). Earnings Quality at Initial Public Offerings. *Journal of Accounting and Economics*, *45*(2-3), 324–349. doi:10.1016/j.jacceco.2007.12.001

Basu, S. (1997). The Conservatism Principle and the Asymmetric Timeliness of Earnings. *Journal of Accounting and Economics*, *24*(2-3), 3–37. doi:10.1016/S0165-4101(97)00014-1

Bhattacharya, N., Desai, H., & Venkataraman, K. (2013). Does Earnings Quality Affect Information Asymmetry? Evidence from Trading Costs. *Contemporary Accounting Research*, *30*(2), 482–516. doi:10.1111/j.1911-3846.2012.01161.x

Bhattacharya, N., Ecker, F., Olsson, P., & Schipper, K. (2012). Direct and Mediated Associations among Earnings Quality, Information Asymmetry, and the Cost of Equity. *The Accounting Review*, *87*(2), 449–482. doi:10.2308/accr-10200

Bollen, N., Smith, T., & Whaley, R. (2004). Modeling the Bid/Ask Spread: Measuring the Inventory-Holding Premium. *Journal of Financial Economics*, *72*(1), 97–141. doi:10.1016/S0304-405X(03)00169-7

Brown, S., & Hillegeist, S. (2007). How Disclosure Quality Affects the Level of Information Asymmetry. *Review of Accounting Studies*, *12*(2/3), 443–477. doi:10.100711142-007-9032-5

Campa, D., & Hajbaba, A. (2016). Do Targets Grab the Cash in Takeovers: The Role of Earnings Management. *JInternational Review of Financial Analysis*, *44*, 56–64. doi:10.1016/j.irfa.2016.01.008

Campbell, J., Lettau, M., Malkiel, B., & Xu, Y. (2001). Have Individual Stocks Become More Volatile? An Empirical Exploration of Idiosyncratic Risk. *The Journal of Finance*, *56*(1), 1–43. doi:10.1111/0022-1082.00318

Cerqueira, A., & Pereira, C. (2015). Accounting Accruals and Information Asymmetry in Europe. *Prague Economic Papers*, *24*(6), 638–661. doi:10.18267/j.pep.528

Cerqueira, A., & Pereira, C. (2017). Accruals Quality, Managers' Incentives and Stock Market Reaction: Evidence from Europe. *Applied Economics*, *49*(16), 1606–1626. doi:10.1080/00036846.2016.1221047

Chen, C., Huang, A., & Jha, R. (2012). Idiosyncratic Return Volatility and the Information Quality Underlying Managerial Discretion. *Journal of Financial and Quantitative Analysis*, *47*(4), 873–899. doi:10.1017/S002210901200018X

Cohen, D., & Zarowin, P. (2010). Accrual-based and Real Earnings Management Activities around Seasoned Equity Offerings. *Journal of Accounting and Economics*, *50*(1), 2–19. doi:10.1016/j.jacceco.2010.01.002

Cohen, J., Krishnamoorthy, G., & Peytchevaand, M. (2013). How Does the Strength of the Financial Regulatory Regime Influence Auditors' Judgments to Constrain Aggressive Reporting in a Principles-Based Versus Rules-Based Accounting Environment? *Accounting Horizons*, *27*(3), 579–601. doi:10.2308/acch-50502

Corwin, S., & Schultz, P. (2012). A Simple Way to Estimate Bid-Ask Spreads from Daily High and Low Prices. *The Journal of Finance*, *67*(2), 719–759. doi:10.1111/j.1540-6261.2012.01729.x

Dechow, P., & Dichev, I. (2002). The Quality of Accruals and Earnings: The Role of Accrual Estimation Errors. *The Accounting Review*, *77*(s-1), 35–59. doi:10.2308/accr.2002.77.s-1.35

Dechow, P., Ge, W., & Schrand, C. (2010). Understanding Earnings Quality: A Review of the Proxies, their Determinants and their Consequences. *Journal of Accounting and Economics*, *50*(2-3), 344–401. doi:10.1016/j.jacceco.2010.09.001

Dechow, P., Sloan, R., & Sweeney, A. (1995). Detecting Earnings Management. *The Accounting Review*, *70*(2), 193–225.

Desai, M. (2005). The Degradation of Reported Corporate Profits. *The Journal of Economic Perspectives*, *19*(4), 171–192. doi:10.1257/089533005775196705

Easley, D., Hvidkjaer, S., & O'Hara, M. (2002). Is Information Risk a Determinant of Asset Returns? *The Journal of Finance*, *57*(5), 2185–2221. doi:10.1111/1540-6261.00493

Easley, D., & O'Hara, M. (2004). Information and the Cost of Capital. *The Journal of Finance*, *59*(4), 1553–1583. doi:10.1111/j.1540-6261.2004.00672.x

Erickson, M., & Wang, S. (1999). Earnings Management by Acquiring Firms in Stock for Stock Mergers. *Journal of Accounting and Economics*, *27*(2), 149–176. doi:10.1016/S0165-4101(99)00008-7

Ewert, R., & Wagenhofer, A. (2011). *Earnings Quality Metrics and What They Measure*. Working Paper, August. University of Graz.

Ewert, R., & Wagenhofer, A. (2015). Economic Relations Among Earnings Quality Measures. *Abacus, 51*(3), 311–355. doi:10.1111/abac.12054

Fama, E., & French, K. (1997). Industry Costs of Equity. *Journal of Financial Economics, 43*(2), 153–193. doi:10.1016/S0304-405X(96)00896-3

Ferreira, M., & Laux, P. (2007). Corporate Governance, Idiosyncratic Risk, and Information Flow. *The Journal of Finance, 62*(2), 951–989. doi:10.1111/j.1540-6261.2007.01228.x

Francis, J., LaFond, R., Olsson, P., & Schipper, K. (2004). Cost of Equity and Earnings Attributes. *The Accounting Review, 79*(4), 967–1010. doi:10.2308/accr.2004.79.4.967

Francis, J., LaFond, R., Olsson, P., & Schipper, K. (2005). The Market Pricing of Accruals Quality. *Journal of Accounting and Economics, 39*(2), 295–327. doi:10.1016/j.jacceco.2004.06.003

Gong, G., Louis, H., & Sun, X. (2008). Earnings Management, Lawsuits, and Stock-for-Stock Acquirers' Market Performance. *Journal of Accounting and Economics, 46*(1), 62–77. doi:10.1016/j.jacceco.2008.03.001

Hasbrouck, J. (2009). Trading Costs and Returns for U.S. Equities: Estimating Effective Costs from Daily Data. *The Journal of Finance, 64*(3), 1445–1477. doi:10.1111/j.1540-6261.2009.01469.x

Healy, P., & Wahlen, J. (1999). A Review of the Earnings Management Literature and Its Implications for Standard Setting. *Accounting Horizons, 13*(4), 365–383. doi:10.2308/acch.1999.13.4.365

Hutton, A., Marcus, A., & Tehranian, H. (2009). Opaque Financial Reports R^2. *Journal of Financial Economics, 49*(1), 67–86. doi:10.1016/j.jfineco.2008.10.003

Jayaraman, S. (2008). Earnings Volatility, Cash Flow Volatility and Informed Trading. *Journal of Accounting Research, 46*(4), 809–851. doi:10.1111/j.1475-679X.2008.00293.x

Jones, J. (1991). Earnings Management During Import Relief Investigation. *Journal of Accounting Research, 29*(2), 193–228. doi:10.2307/2491047

Kelly, P. (2014). Information Efficiency and Firm-Specific Return Variation. *Quarterly Journal of Finance, 4*(4), 1–44. doi:. doi:10.1142/S2010139214500189

Kothari, S., Leone, A., & Wasley, C. (2005). Performance Matched Discretionary Accrual Measures. *Journal of Accounting and Economics, 39*(1), 163–197. doi:10.1016/j.jacceco.2004.11.002

Kothari, S., Mizik, N., & Roychowdhury, S. (2016). Managing for the Moment: The Role of Earnings Management via Real Activities versus Accruals in SEO Valuation. *The Accounting Review, 91*(2), 559–586. doi:10.2308/accr-51153

Kvaal, P., & Nobes, C. (2010). International Differences in IFRS Policy Choice: A Research Note. *Accounting and Business Research, 40*(2), 173–187. doi:10.1080/00014788.2010.9663390

Lambert, R., Leuz, C., & Verrecchia, R. (2007). Accounting Information, Disclosure, and the Cost of Capital. *Journal of Accounting Research*, *45*(2), 385–420. doi:10.1111/j.1475-679X.2007.00238.x

Lambert, R., Leuz, C., & Verrecchia, R. (2012). Information Asymmetry, Information Precision, and the Cost of Capital. *Review of Finance*, *16*(1), 1–29. doi:10.1093/rof/rfr014

Leuz, C., Dhananjay, N., & Wysocki, P. (2003). Earnings Management and Investor Protection: An International Comparison. *Journal of Financial Economics*, *69*(3), 505–527. doi:10.1016/S0304-405X(03)00121-1

Leuz, C., & Verrecchia, R. (2000). The Economic Consequences of Increased Disclosure: Evidence from International Cross-Listings. *Studies on Accounting Information and the Economics of the Firm. Supplement to the Journal of Accounting Research*, *38*, 91–124. doi:10.2307/2672910

Lobo, G., Song, M., & Stanford, M. (2012). Accruals Quality and Analyst Coverage. *Journal of Banking & Finance*, *36*(2), 497–508. doi:10.1016/j.jbankfin.2011.08.006

Louis, H. (2004). Earnings Management and the Market Performance of Acquiring Firms. *Journal of Financial Economics*, *74*(1), 121–148. doi:10.1016/j.jfineco.2003.08.004

Marquardt, C., & Zur, E. (2015). The Role of Accounting Quality in the M&A Market. *Management Science*, *61*(3), 604–623. doi:10.1287/mnsc.2013.1873

McNichols, M. (2002). Discussion of the Quality of Accruals and Earnings: The Role of Accrual Estimation Errors. *The Accounting Review*, *77*(s-1), 61–69. doi:10.2308/accr.2002.77.s-1.61

Morck, R., Yeung, B. & Yu, W. (2000). The Information Content of Stock Markets: Why Do Emerging Markets Have Synchronous Stock Price Movements? *Journal of Financial Economics, 58d*(1-2), 215-260. doi:. doi:10.1016/S0304-405X(00)0007d1-d4

Nobes, C. (2006). The Survival of International Differences under IFRS: Towards a Research Agenda. *Accounting and Business Research*, *36*(3), 233–245. doi:10.1080/00014788.2006.9730023

Rajgopal, S., & Venkatachalam, M. (2011). Financial Reporting Quality and Idiosyncratic Return Volatility. *Journal of Accounting and Economics*, *51*(1-2), 1–20. doi:10.1016/j.jacceco.2010.06.001

Raman, K., Shivakumar, L., & Tamayo, A. (2013). Target's Earnings Quality and Bidders' Takeover Decisions. *Review of Accounting Studies*, *18*(4), 1050–1087. doi:10.100711142-013-9224-0

Roberts, R., & Mahoney, L. (2004). Stakeholder Conceptions of the Corporation: Their Meaning and Influence in Accounting Research. *Business Ethics Quarterly*, *14*(3), 339–431. doi:10.5840/beq200414326

Schipper, K., & Vincent, L. (2003). Earnings Quality. *Accounting Horizons*, *17*(s-1Supplement), 97–110. doi:10.2308/acch.2003.17.s-1.97

Sloan, R. (1996). Do Stock Prices Fully Reflect Information in Accruals and Cash Flows about Future Earnings? *The Accounting Review*, *71*(3), 289–315.

Teoh, S., Welch, I., & Wong, T. (1998). Earnings Management and the Long-run Market Performance of Initial Public Offerings. *The Journal of Finance*, *53*(6), 1935–1974. doi:10.1111/0022-1082.00079

Xu, Y., & Malkiel, B. (2003). Investigating the Behavior of Idiosyncratic Volatility. *The Journal of Business*, *76*(4), 613–644. doi:10.1086/377033

Zang, A. (2012). Evidence on the Trade-Off between Real Activities Manipulation and Accrual-Based Earnings Management. *The Accounting Review*, *87*(2), 675–703. doi:10.2308/accr-10196

Chapter 3
An Overall Perspective of Income Smoothing as a Strategy of Earnings Management

Cláudia Araújo Mendes
Polytechnic Institute of Cávado and Ave, Portugal

Lúcia Lima Rodrigues
University of Minho, Portugal

Laura Parte
Universidad Nacional de Educación a Distancia (UNED), Spain

ABSTRACT

This chapter provides insights on earnings management (EM) explanatory factors. These factors are analyzed within the framework of a specific strategy of EM: income smoothing (IS). This strategy is often used to report earnings with an artificially reduced variability. Thereby, the purpose of the chapter is to explore the motivations, the determinants (anticipated by the positive accounting theory), and some firm-specific factors that might explain IS practices. The relevance of this chapter is justified essentially by two reasons. First, it highlights the contemporary importance of this research line. The academic community, professionals, and regulatory bodies have expressed publicly the concern about the quality of financial reporting. Consequently, a deep knowledge of the factors that possibly explain these accounting discretionary practices is crucial. Second, the extensive literature on EM also justifies this chapter. Thereby, the systematization of the literature on the IS explanatory factors can help researchers and increase future empirical research focused on this area.

DOI: 10.4018/978-1-5225-7817-8.ch003

INTRODUCTION

Stakeholders in general (e.g. academic community, professionals, regulatory bodies) have expressed publicly the concern about the quality of financial reporting. Investors and other accounting information users only can make more accurate decisions if financial reporting has certain quality levels.

Generally, according to the literature (e.g. Monterrey, 1998; Albornoz, 2003), it is possible to identify three earnings management strategies:

- Aggressive accounting policies, aimed at improving income;
- Conservative accounting policies, aimed at reducing income; and
- Income smoothing policies, aimed at increasing income in some fiscal exercises and at decreasing it in others, in order to minimize its long-term fluctuations.

Unlike the other hypotheses of earnings management, income smoothing is a general strategy that can be tested in samples of heterogeneous companies, without requiring the presence of strong incentives to manipulate income in a specific direction (e.g. Porciau, 1993; Perry & Williams, 1994; Teoh et al., 1998). Income smoothing seems, thereby, more rational on the long-term (Chaney et al., 1998), being, also for these reasons, the object of this chapter.

Although, income smoothing is a topic widely analysed in the literature since the 1970s, there is still a long-run debate about the positive or negative effects of income smoothing in the academia. One stream of research suggests that income smoothing is an efficient vehicle for managers to provide private information and, consequently, it is positive for both managers and investors (Ronen & Sadan, 1981; Chaney & Lewis, 1995; Kirschenheiter & Melumad, 2002; Gassen & Fuelbier, 2015; Li & Richie, 2016; Demerjian et al., 2018). However, other stream considers that managers opportunistically smooth income and, as a result, this practice is a vehicle to mislead investors and other users (Fudenberg & Tirole, 1995; Leuz et al., 2003).

The chapter provides insights on income smoothing explanatory factors and its relevance is justified essentially by two reasons. Firstly, it highlights the contemporary importance of this research line, and, consequently, offers a deep knowledge of the factors that possibly explain income smoothing discretionary practices. Second, there is an extensive literature on income smoothing explanatory factors, since its systematization can help researchers and increase future empirical research focused on this subject. Finally, the chapter provides the conclusions and future avenues.

MAIN GENERAL MOTIVATIONS ANTICIPATED IN THE LITERATURE

Income Smoothing and Company Risk

In their survey of 400 financial executives, Graham et al. (2005) reported that, for about 97% of respondents, an income smoothing path is preferred because it is perceived as less risky by investors, and it would therefore be expected to be associated with lower stock return volatility.

Indeed, multiple authors (e.g. Iñiguez & Poveda, 2004; Habib, 2005; Tseng & Lai, 2007; Markarian & Gill, 2012) suggested that management would be motivated to reduce income and cash flows variability as an attempt to reduce the company's perceived risk.

However, there is still scarce evidence concerning the central belief that appeared to motivate Graham et al.'s (2005) respondents. Namely, there is scarce research on the economic effects of income smoothing, insofar as whether income smoothing is associated with any measurable reduction in stock price volatility or any increase in the firm market value (the latter analysed in the next section).

Beidleman (1973), one of the first authors to express the hypothesis that income smoothing reduces the company's risk, argued that smoothing aims to reduce the cyclical nature of the reported earnings and, as such, tends to reduce the covariance between the company's expected returns and the market returns, leading, thus, to an increase in the shares price. This suggests, as stressed by Lev & Kunitzky (1974), Moses (1987) and Chalayer (1994), that market risk measures are associated with the accounting measures of the income variability. Accordingly, Lev & Kunitzky (1974) and Chalayer (1994) admit that a negative association between the smoothing proportion and systematic risk is expected to emerge.[1]

Subsequently, Lev & Kunitzky (1974) found empirical support for the hypothesis put forward by Beidleman (1973) that income smoothing may raise the securities price by reducing their systematic risk. Indeed, the authors were the first to seek to empirically demonstrate that one of the motivations for income smoothing is to reduce the company's risk. To that end, Lev & Kunitzky (1974) suggested that companies actively perform smoothing of various input and output series (real smoothing), such as sales and capital expenditures, so as to reduce environmental uncertainty. This argument being valid, the authors expected to observe an association between the smoothing proportion of the company's series and the market risk measures, which reflect, among other things, the features of the company's business risk. Thus, management success in reducing the uncertainty associated with the company's operations through various smoothing activities should be reflected in the perceived risk of the company from the investor's point of view.

In this field, and adopting a different perspective, Amihud et al. (1983) developed a study where they tested the hypothesis of differences between manager-controlled companies and owner-controlled companies with respect to their risk. The results of their empirical research suggest that manager-controlled companies develop income smoothing practices to a greater extent than owner-controlled companies, also presenting a unique risk of the company and a systematic risk relatively lower. These results are consistent with the authors' standpoint that managers seek to reduce their employment risk internally through the selection of policies aimed at stabilising a given income stream of the company.

Considering Beidleman´s (1973) arguments, Beattie et al. (1994) also argued that income smoothing emerges as a rational behaviour, inasmuch that they assume, among other aspects, that fluctuations in earnings and their unpredictability are the main determinants of market risk measures.

Wang & Williams (1994), in a study that analyses the relationship between income smoothing and shareholders' wealth, obtained consistent evidence demonstrating that income smoothing is seen favourably by markets and that companies with smoothed income streams are perceived as being less risky. The empirical results are consistent with the authors' theoretical arguments. In fact, the authors argue that the proportion in which managers can perform income smoothing is a function of the accuracy of the private company management's knowledge and that failing to smooth the reported income is indicative of the lack of ability to anticipate future events. Hence, companies with less smoothed reported income series were expected to be perceived as being riskier. Therefore, a negative relationship was suggested between the company's perceived risk and the ability to smooth the reported income, which was confirmed by their empirical results.

Moreover, Chalayer (1994) and Michelson et al. (1995) obtained empirical evidence supporting the hypothesis that companies that perform income smoothing have lower market betas (systematic risk) than companies that do not engage in such behaviour. In turn, Booth et al. (1996), who also sought to infer Michelson et al.'s (1995) assertion, obtained divergent results, justifying them on the basis of biases in the calculation of betas.

In the context of the banking sector, Bhat (1996) argues that there are several reasons for banks to stabilise their earnings, giving as examples the fact that income smoothing improves investors' and regulators' perception of the bank's risk, as well as the fact that it improves the stability of the securities price by reducing the perceived income volatility. Similarly, Carlson & Bathala (1997) argue that reducing the income streams variability can increase the attractiveness of the company to investors by reducing the company's risk perceived by them.

More recently, and following the study published in 1995, Michelson et al. (2000), in order to assess the capital market reaction to income smoothing, used risk-adjusted returns to test whether the response of the stock market to accounting performance measures is related to smoothed earnings. The results of the study suggest that companies that engage in income smoothing have higher abnormal average returns than companies that do not adhere to such practices. Furthermore, Iñiguez & Poveda (2004) obtained similar results in the Spanish context, also concluding that income smoothing exerts influence on securities risk, which is why companies performing it reduce the investors' risk perception. In a more recent study, Markarian & Gill (2012) made a direct extension of Rajgopal & Venkatachalam's (2011) work, who analyse the relationship between several proxies of income quality and idiosyncratic risk, by examining income smoothing as a special case of earnings management. Markarian & Gill's (2012) results reveal a negative association between income smoothing and idiosyncratic risk, which they interpret as evidence that income smoothing practices contribute to reducing stock price idiosyncratic volatility.

Thereby, on the one hand, the literature generally agrees that income smoothing reduces the uncertainty associated with the company's future cash flows by mitigating fluctuations in the company's income due to the evolution of general economic conditions. On the other hand, authors such as Lev & Kunitzky (1974), Chalayer (1994) and Markarian & Gill (2012) considered it reasonable to admit that income smoothing is also a function of the non-systematic risk level, a component of company risk that is not associated with general economic conditions. In fact, as previously stated, it is a component of risk that is closely related to specific factors of the company or the sector in which it operates, affecting only it and, possibly, its closer competitors. Thus, the authors admit, for example, that smoothing activities can reduce the company's sensitivity to the economic fluctuations of the sector to which it belongs (such as oscillations in demand) or also mitigate different conflicts. This is the case of labour conflicts, given that significant income fluctuations can generate wage demands or indicate crisis situations (if these oscillations are upward or downward, respectively), which can lead to a halt or a slowdown in activity, with consequent fluctuations in productivity (e.g. Hepworth, 1953; Benston & Krasney, 1978; Liberty & Zimmerman, 1986; Moses, 1987; Godfrey & Jones, 1999). Also, Markarian & Gill's (2012) results indicate that managers facing a higher probability of dismissal, and so having potentially higher benefits from smoothing, are more likely to alter earnings volatility (see Gordon, 1964; Fudenberg & Tirole, 1995; DeFond & Park, 1997; Ahmed et al., 2000; Albornoz & Alcarria, 2003; Elgers et al., 2003; Kanagaretnam et al., 2003; Bushman et al., 2010, for a related discussion). Moreover, in line with the signalling property of smoothing, prior research shows that income smoothing succeeds in conveying information about future profitability (Turcker & Zarowin, 2006; Dichev & Tang, 2009), and Pastor & Veronesi (2003) argue that stock return volatility is positively related to uncertainty about future profitability. Consequently, we consider that it is also appropriate to determine whether income smoothing is negatively related to total risk.

In light of some of the arguments put forward in the literature, we can, therefore, conclude that there is an understanding that risk negatively influences the shares price and that it even has a direct effect on investors, inasmuch that it is considered a factor influencing investment decisions. As such, it seems rational that those entities with higher risk are more motivated to use smoothing in order to sidestep its effects.

Finally, it should be stressed that, notwithstanding the existence of supporters of the premise that smoothing reduces investors' perception of risk, some authors point out that this is not compatible with a market efficiency situation.

In a context of market efficiency, which rejects all information asymmetry, investors are rational about accounting information, inasmuch that access to information does not involve costs. As such, accounting income smoothing is a behaviour that is difficult to admit because sophisticated investors can correct without costs the company's income in the light of the different accounting methods used to calculate it. Indeed, rational investors are aware of the effects of accounting manipulations aimed at reporting an artificially reduced variance of the income level. Consequently, assuming market efficiency, income smoothing should not, *ceteris paribus*, have any influence on the company's risk (Chalayer, 1994).

As stressed by Fern et al. (1994), several studies have suggested that capital markets are efficient and that investors would not be mislead by mere accounting schemes (e.g. Copeland, 1968; Imhoff, 1981). Imhoff (1981), for instance, claims that shareholders, investors and analysts would not be deceived by income manipulations carried out by internal elements of organisations.

Moses (1987) also expressed some considerations about the issue of the market efficiency hypothesis, arguing that there has been considerable criticism about the possibility that income smoothing can be practiced so as to directly reduce market risk (e.g. Ronen & Sadan, 1981), since, in an efficient market, the relationship between accounting figures and market parameters may not be mechanistic (i.e., there may not be a direct relationship between both) and the use of visible accounting practices to affect the risk may not be effective. Nevertheless, the author admits that there is a reason to, at least, question the complete market efficiency with regard to accounting methods (Lev & Ohlson, 1982) and, more importantly, to the management's belief in market efficiency (Mayer-Sommer, 1979). Furthermore, the author believes that it is possible to accept market efficiency and yet believe that the processing costs for users, in order to adjust the effects of accounting techniques, outweigh the perceived benefits, specifically when using past income series to assess risk.

Contrary to the view of market efficiency, which Moses (1987), in certain manner, also questions, is assuming that investors suffer from functional fixation. Indeed, as pointed out by Chalayer (1994), in order to explain managers' accounting decisions, the behavioural accounting, which studies the treatment of accounting information by its users, has put forward the hypothesis of functional fixation (or the hypothesis of the naive investor). According to the aforementioned author, this paradigm introduced in accounting (i.e., market efficiency *versus* functional fixation hypotheses) postulates that simple investors focus their attention on any items published by the accounting system, that is, they only take into account the income reported by the company without considering the different accounting methods used to determine it and possibly modify its level. As such, according to the functional fixation hypothesis, an investor is *a priori* unable of modifying his/her decision-making process on the basis of the accounting procedures adopted by the company, given the way in which the accounting information is provided, which is why it also seems reasonable to admit that investors can be systematically misled by the choices that companies make in terms of accounting policy.

Consequently, this leads us to believe that income smoothing may translate into less risk perception if investors suffer from functional fixation, whereas in a context of market efficiency, where investors are rational, smoothing should not affect the company's risk level. Thereby, testing whether companies that engage in artificial income smoothing have a lower risk level than companies that do not adhere to such practices allows us, at the same time, to test investors' rationality *versus* functional fixation, that is, to determine whether they are aware of the accounting manipulations performed by companies and their artificial consequences on the income variability.

Income Smoothing and Company Value

Numerous research studies in the field of income smoothing suggest that smoothing translates into a better assessment of the company by investors. For instance, as shareholders will feel more confident if a company reports stable earnings (Hepworth, 1953), smoothing income should have a favourable effect on share value and cost of capital (Beidleman, 1973; Trueman & Titman, 1988; Li & Richie, 2016), or shareholders will obtain more information from earnings announcements (Easton & Zmijewski, 1989).

Although there is some consensus that one of the goals of income smoothing is to increase the value of the company to shareholders, the reasons given for this expected increase in value differ, not being restricted to the aspects previously stated.

In fact, as emphasised by Chalayer (1994), several research studies on income smoothing generally agree that income smoothing increases the value of the company. In the author's view, since the value of an asset is equal to the current value of the set of cash flows that it will generate, income smoothing may affect the value of the company if it affects the level of its future cash flows or if it reduces the risk associated with these cash flows and, consequently, if it decreases the return rate required by investors.

Gordon (1964), for example, suggests that a smoothed income stream allows for a higher dividend ratio and, subsequently, higher stock prices. In turn, Trueman & Titman (1988) proposed that income smoothing can increase the company's market value through its effect on the cost of the company's debt level. According to the authors, lower earnings volatility reduces the assessment of the possibility of the company's bankruptcy and, as such, reduces the cost in obtaining loans by the company. Lower debt costs, in turn, should have a positive effect on the company's market value. Similarly, Li & Richie (2016) show that a smoothed pattern of earnings reduces the cost of debt and, subsequently, is desired for both managers and investors.

On the other hand, Gibbins et al. (1990) provide an intriguing discussion about the organisational behaviour of reporting financial information that helps explaining an investor's preference for companies with smoothed earnings. The authors sustain that an organisation builds a financial reputation and that the consistency and credibility of its publications are vital to that reputation. As a result, investors place more value on companies with consistent (smoothed) financial publications than on companies with floating financial statements. Similarly, but in the banking sector, Bhat (1996) sustains that, since it is difficult for investors to assess the quality of a bank's management, income smoothing is an excellent alternative for a poor management to project an image of high quality.

In line with these arguments, several authors consider that certain accounting practices may be a signalling instrument to the market of the company's good quality. For example, Ronen & Sadan (1981) find that income smoothing is a signal to investors. Also, Chaney & Lewis (1995) developed a model that shows that companies smooth income in order to signal the company's value to investors. This positive view is also supported by Tucker & Zarowin (2006), Li & Richie (2016), Demerjian et al. (2018), among others.

Following the arguments presented by the accounting literature regarding the company's value towards smoothing activities, it appears that companies with smoothed earnings are more attractive to investors than companies with widely fluctuating earnings. Notwithstanding, it should also be stressed that the considerations made in terms of risk concerning the market efficiency *versus* functional fixation hypotheses and, therefore, whether investors are rational or not, are equally valid with regard to the hypothesis that income smoothing translates into a better assessment of the company by investors. Chalayer (1994), for example, in a study on the motivations to develop smoothing practices, in order to evaluate the differences in market value between the companies that smooth their earnings and those that do not, integrated in the logistic regression the Tobin's Q and the PER (Price Earnings Ratio) to measure the company's market value. However, contrary to the trend widely reported in the literature, the author concluded that companies that smooth their earnings do not hold a higher market value than companies that do not adhere to such practices, thus validating the hypothesis of investors' rationality. Recent studies highlight the importance of firm-factors and cross-country studies to infer conclusions about income smoothing and firm value. For example, Gao & Zhan (2015) suggest that income smoothing enhances firm value but only for social responsibility companies.

Income Smoothing and Communication of Private Information and Projections Support

Contrary to what happens with the remaining earnings management strategies, many scholars consider that income smoothing practices provide private information for investors (e.g. Barnea et al., 1976; Ronen & Sadan, 1981; Chaney & Lewis, 1995; Li & Richie, 2016). This school of thought, underpinned by a positive view of income smoothing, informational and predictive objectives, support these practices. In this case, smoothing is perceived as a tool that is available to management to convey additional information, expectations, which conventional accounting practices do not allow disclosing. In this sense, it is considered that smoothing can be used as a tool to communicate the persistence of earnings when it cannot be conveyed directly to users.

From early on, Hepworth (1953) adopted this content by suggesting that managers are motivated to smooth income to improve the relationships with creditors, employees and investors. Reinforcing this idea, Gordon (1964) suggested that shareholders satisfaction increases with the growth ratio of a company's income and with the stability of its income.

A clearer position in this regard was offered by Barnea et al. (1976). According to the authors, income smoothing can be developed to convey relevant information that allows stakeholders to predict future earnings, insofar that the management expresses its expectations about the company's future earnings through smoothed earnings. Thus, from the authors' standpoint, the intention of management is not to try to deceive the market through income smoothing, but rather to report additional information, in particular its expectations about future earnings. Thereby, the authors sustain that smoothing is used as a vehicle for management to convey its expectations under GAAP, which do not allow for direct forecasts.

Later, Ronen & Sadan (1981) again emphasised this aspect, arguing that income smoothing is a signalling technique, since by this means the managers convey private information on the company's future earning, which, in turn, reinforce the ability of external users to predict earnings. Likewise, Hand

(1989) mentions that managers are likely to smooth earnings to align their expectations of earnings with market expectations and even to increase the persistence of earnings.

Furthermore, Easton & Zmijewski (1989) also suggested that smoothing allows shareholders obtaining more information from reported earnings. Also, Wang & Williams (1994), in a study analysing the relationship between income smoothing and shareholders' wealth, showed that, contrary to the belief that smoothing is a misleading action on the part of the management, income smoothing reinforces the informative value of the reported earnings. Specifically, they suggest that the income smoothing process necessarily incorporates managers' private knowledge in terms of the company's future performance. In addition, the analysis demonstrates that the extent to which the manager is able to smooth the company's reported earnings reflects the accuracy of the manager's knowledge about future performance. Hence, the authors expect investors benefiting from this private knowledge to respond favourably to more informative earnings, which, in turn, tend to favour shareholder's wealth. They obtained empirical support for their theory.

Still in this domain, and in their study of financial analysts' reports, Bricker et al. (1995) provided evidence that analysts associate the quality of earnings with the ability of managers of a company to manage earnings in order to avoid negative earnings surprises. Similarly, Jaggi & Sannella (1995) suggest that the management's incentive to manage earnings consists of improving the accuracy of its earnings' predictions. In addition, Subramanyam (1996) detected significant evidence of income smoothing and that it improves earnings' persistence and predictability. He also concluded that management uses discretionary accruals to convey information about the company's future earnings.

Similarly, Turcker & Zarowin (2006) and Dichev & Tang (2009), in research studies that test whether income smoothing is associated with more informative stock prices, gather evidence that validates their hypothesis, which, according to the authors, again suggests that managers use income smoothing to reveal their private information about the company's future profitability.

Following the above considerations, according to this current of thought, income smoothing is not a reprehensible conduct, as it does not violate the basic objective of accounting and does not disregard the applicable accounting principles and standards. Rather, it is an instrument that increases the usefulness of the information presented in the financial statements, insofar that it helps conveying additional information, assists the decisions making process and make projections easier, since it anticipates future earnings and management plans. It should be noted that, in a context of information asymmetry between external financial users and managers, this positioning of facing smoothing as an additional information conveyer and with a predictive nature was also advocated by other authors, such as, for instance, Koch (1981), Chaney & Lewis (1995, 1998), Booth et al. (1996), Kirschenheiter & Melumad (2002).

Income Smoothing and Employees Relationship Improvement

As an intrinsic objective of the income smoothing phenomenon, the literature also comes up with the possibility that managers are motivated by the desire to maintain a good relationship with the company's employees. Hepworth (1953) suggests that stable earnings benefit relationships with employees. A similar positioning was taken by Benston & Krasney (1978) when they discussed the attempt to avoid labour costs as a possible motivation to engage in smoothing practices. According to the authors, the demands of employees or labour unions are sensitive to earnings fluctuations: large increases may generate a demand for wage increases; large reductions may generate the fear of financial difficulties.

In this field, but in empirical terms, Liberty & Zimmerman (1986) sought to obtain evidence that management carried out accounting decisions aimed at reducing income during the period of negotiation of employment contracts, in order to avoid wage and social claims by employees. Nevertheless, their results did not corroborate this premise.

Subsequently, in a study that aimed to analyse the relationship between income smoothing and the existence of strong labour unions, Moses (1987) predicted that considerable increases in a company's earnings could lead to a demand for wage increases by such labour unions and that significant reductions would have adverse labour effects, such as poor employees' morale, resulting reductions in productivity and reduced retention ratios, as employees seek high job stability and better conditions. Thus, the author maintained that concerns about labour costs (e.g. wages, productivity) motivates management to reduce earnings fluctuations, so one would expect that the smoothing behaviour was more strongly associated to companies with strong labour union organisations. Indeed, these labour unions tend to facilitate the dissemination of the information contained in the financial statements among employees, and, therefore, collective actions to seek wage increases or other improved employment conditions are more common when labour unions are involved. However, as happened with the aforementioned authors, Moses' prediction was not supported by evidence in the United States. Conversely, Godfrey & Jones (1999), keeping with Moses' (1987) arguments, obtained empirical support that validated the hypothesis that companies with a high degree of unionisation are more likely to smooth income, in particular through classificatory smoothing.

On the basis of these considerations, we believe that it is plausible to assume the possibility that income smoothing strengthens management relationships with its employees and, at the same time, avoid its exposure to labour-related political costs.

Income Smoothing and Job Security Achievement

Research on the smoothing field indicates that earnings variability can affect the stability of the managers' position in the company and, therefore, their personal wealth. Once again, Gordon (1964) was one of the first authors to draw a parallel between maximising the management's utility or well-being and its job security, paving the way for the smoothing research line to address this possible motivation for income smoothing.

Through the development of a theory suggesting that concerns about job security create incentives for managers to smooth current and future earnings, Fudenberg & Tirole (1995) showed analytically that income smoothing increases job security on the basis of three premises. First, management obtains monetary and non-monetary benefits and, additionally, is risk-averse. Second, the company cannot commit to a long-term incentive contract, as poor management performance, measured by the earnings of the period, can lead to its dismissal. Third, the accounting earnings for the current period are more informative than earnings of previous periods in management performance assessment. Hence, poor earnings in a given year increase the likelihood of dismissal, whereas good earnings in a given year do not outweigh poor performance in coming periods. According to the authors, combining the three hypotheses mentioned above, managers tend to smooth income in two related ways: (1) in bad periods, they promote or stimulate earnings to guarantee their permanence in the company; (2) in good periods, they save earnings for future bad periods, given that they know at the outset that these will not compensate for a future poor performance.

DeFond & Park (1997) found empirical support for this theory, showing that managers smooth income by considering current and future relative performance. Specifically, the authors concluded that managers of companies that experience poor (good) performance in the current period and expect good (poor) performance in the following period use discretionary accruals that increase (reduce) current earnings, in order to reduce the threat of being dismissed in the present period (in the following period). Thus, similar to the premise of Fudenberg & Tirole's (1995) theory, these results suggest that managers "save" earnings of good years for their possible use in the future.

More recently, Ahmed et al. (2000) again analysed the hypothesis put forward by Fudenberg & Tirole (1995) that the proportion of income smoothing behaviour is greater when concerns about job security are more severe, arguing that they would provide more direct evidence about this relationship than Defond & Park (1997) had done. To do so, they used three business features as proxies for job security concerns: the degree of competition in industry, product durability, and capital intensity. Consistent with the hypotheses formulated, they concluded that managers of companies in more competitive industries and industries of durable goods exhibit higher levels of income smoothing (since job insecurity is also higher).

Similar results were subsequently obtained within the scope of research studies by Albornoz & Alcarria (2003), Elgers et al. (2003), Kanagaretnam et al. (2003), Markarian & Gill (2012).

From the above, it is clear that there is strong evidence supporting the hypothesis that one of the manager's objectives when using income smoothing is to secure his/her current and future job position, inasmuch that variations in the company's performance may result in the intervention by the owners to replace him/her.

Income Smoothing and Tax Purposes

It is also common in accounting theory to argue that income smoothing practices allow mitigating tax payment. Hepworth (1953), for example, suggested that managers are motivated to smooth income to obtain tax advantages. Likewise, Chenok (1976, cited by Buckmaster, 2001) and, later on, Foster (1986) also mentioned the reduction of the tax bill as a powerful incentive for smoothing the reported income. Subsequently, Dhaliwal et al. (1994) showed that companies use LIFO to smooth income and obtain direct tax benefits (accounting method currently eliminated from standards). In fact, the literature agrees to recognize that the adoption of the LIFO method in the valuation of stocks leads, in inflationary periods, to the emergence of lower profits, given the higher cost of sales, which determines a lower tax weight. Concurrently, Bhat (1996) also invoked this motivation for income smoothing (attainment of tax advantages) in the context of the banking sector. Coppens & Peek (2005) also demonstrate that tax accounting conditioned earnings management in private companies setting.

Thus, smoothing behaviour is a good positioning in the control of the relationship with the tax authorities, since it avoids reporting too high earnings with the inherent increase of the tax bill, as well as too low earnings, to the point of giving rise to undesirable inspections.

DETERMINANTS ANTICIPATED BY THE POSITIVE ACCOUNTING THEORY

Income Smoothing and the Political Costs Hypothesis

One of the hypotheses traditionally put forward by the Positive Accounting Theory is the assumption of the existence of political costs. According to what the theory postulates, some companies have greater political visibility than others, so they attract greater attention from the public authorities. Thus, companies that are subject to public scrutiny may call for government or public interventions that may involve costs. In line with this argument, this visibility and the resulting costs are variables that explain companies' accounting choices (Watts & Zimmerman, 1978, 1990).

Moses (1987) was the first author to assume and test the idea that managers of companies which are politically visible and therefore likely to bear political costs are encouraged to smooth reported accounting earnings. Indeed, according to the author, fluctuations in earnings attract the attention of public authorities: significant increasing earnings fluctuations can be perceived as a sign of monopolistic practices and significant decreasing oscillations may indicate a crisis situation, and both cases may prompt public authorities to act. Thus, in light of the author's standpoint, in the case of companies that are subject to possible interventions by public authorities, the more rational conduct seems to be earnings stabilisation, thus minimising the likelihood of an adverse intervention.

However, researchers in this field are faced with the difficulty of operationalising the concept of political costs, that is, of finding a measure that is able to empirically test the hypothesis of political costs. Hence, different types of measures have been proposed, although the size of the company is the most often used substitution variable (or proxy) to reflect the company's political visibility and the resulting costs.

Large companies have a greater incentive for income smoothing than small companies, since they attract more scrutiny from government and the general public, and, thus, the management of such companies is motivated to minimise the expected costs of a potential external intervention through income smoothing practices. As examples of studies that have assumed and corroborated the hypothesis that there is more incentive for large companies to smooth their income we can state the ones by Moses (1987), Craig & Walsh (1989), Chalayer (1994), Michelson et al. (1995, 2000), and Iñiguez & Poveda (2004). Further researches, that focus also on the differences between private *versus* public companies, listed *versus* non-listed companies or family *versus* non-family companies, to engage in earnings smoothing are driven by Coppens & Peek (2005), Ball & Shivakumar (2006), Burgstahler et al. (2006), Prencipe et al. (2011), Dou et al. (2013), Liu & Skerratt (2018), among others.

Even though the size of the company is the most frequently used proxy, usually measured by total assets, sales, trade volume or market capitalisation, other measures of political costs have been anticipated in the literature. The company's market share, the company's degree of unionisation, the industry concentration are examples of proxies that have also been suggested to capture political costs (e.g. Moses, 1987; Hagerman & Zmijewski, 1979; Zmijewski & Hagerman, 1981; Godfrey & Jones, 1999).

Following the previous considerations, it is noted that the propensity for adverse political attention (political costs) determines the accounting choices of a company. In particular, it is understandable that the propensity for large fluctuations in earnings to attract public scrutiny is eliminated through income smoothing, although this conclusion depends on the relevance of the substitution variables used to operationalise political costs, which have varied considerably in the studies that have addressed this topic.

Income Smoothing and the Bonus Plan Hypothesis

According to Chalayer (1994), given that the manager is mandated by the equity holders, shareholders, to manage the company on their behalf, this may result in conflicts. In fact, the manager can take actions that maximise his/her own utility, which may not be compatible with the shareholders' interests. Furthermore, he/she usually has information that shareholders are unaware of. Consequently, it is possible that the manager manipulates reported information for purely personal purposes. In order to drive the manager to act in accordance with the equity holders' interests, shareholders may define remuneration contracts that encourage the manager to maximise the company's value by indexing part of his/her remuneration, directly or indirectly, to the company's accounting earnings. Nevertheless, the manager may, however, to the extent allowed by GAAP, manipulate the accounting information disclosed to shareholders in order to maximise his/her wealth.

In this context, the Positive Accounting Theory stresses the importance of assessing the extent to which the managers' remunerations that are established by reference to accounting figures determine the companies' accounting choices (Watts & Zimmerman, 1990).

Empirical tests allow, in general, concluding that there is an influence of the remuneration schemes on the companies' accounting choices. In particular, several studies in the accounting field have tested and, in part, empirically validated the hypothesis that managers of companies where remuneration is indexed to earnings tend to choose accounting methods that maximise the reported income (e.g. Hagerman & Zmijewski, 1979; Zmijewski & Hagerman, 1981; Hunt, 1985).

However, although it seems consistent to establish the premise that companies whose management is remunerated by reference to accounting figures will have a strong incentive to attain the desired income, this may not necessarily mean that, so as to maximise its wealth, the management bodies are encouraged to select accounting methods that increase earnings. On the contrary, many authors have also argued that the optimal policy is the stabilisation of the income streams, rather than its maximisation.

Watts & Zimmerman (1978) and Ronan & Sadan (1981) were the first authors to argue that earnings-based remuneration plans can lead to smoothing behaviours. Subsequently, Lambert (1984) used the agency theory to construct a simple economic model able of describing the shareholder (principal) – manager (agent) relationship. The author shows that, since the manager's actions are not observable, smoothing can be an optimal equilibrium behaviour.

Moses (1987) empirically supported this theory by validating the hypothesis that managers' remuneration contracts based on bonus (over earnings), and especially those that incorporate maximum and minimum remuneration thresholds, encourage managers to develop income smoothing practices. Moses justified his analysis from the considerations developed in a study by Healy (1985), which has been considered by the academia as one of the most important references regarding income-based rewards. In fact, the latter argues that the companies' accounting choices must be studied in the context of the details of remuneration contracts' clauses. According to the author, most of these contracts have a minimum and maximum threshold associated with them, so the manager's incentives to increase income seem to vary with the income level. In line with this argument, Moses (1987) reiterates that if earnings are above the maximum threshold, it may be beneficial for the manager to try to reduce them so as to produce "reserves" that can be used in difficult periods, given that an additional increase in earnings would not provide any additional bonus. Moreover, when earnings are very high, even if it falls within the two thresholds, the increasing marginal tax rates and the decreasing marginal utility for this type of remuneration may encourage managers to not increase earnings again. Thus, according to the author, decreasing earnings probably involves fewer costs for the manager when earnings (and bonus) are relatively high. Finally, Moses mentions another argument in favour of the income smoothing hypothesis: the objective in terms of income to be reached in future periods is often determined by reference to current income, which may encourage managers to not report earnings that cannot be reached in the future. As a result, the manager will avoid poor earnings as it significantly affects the part of his/her remuneration that is earnings-based and, in turn, will avoid very high earnings, inasmuch that it increases the levels of performance that he/she should achieve in the future. Thus, considers that the combination of all these aspects should lead to a reduction of reported earnings when they are high and to an increase when they are low, that is, the manager's goal is to achieve smoothed earnings, which, as we have mentioned, Moses proves empirically.

Gaver et al. (1995) obtained similar evidence in their study, despite having used a different methodology. In particular, they concluded that when earnings before discretionary accruals are below the minimum threshold established in the contract, managers select discretionary accruals that increase earnings and *vice versa*, which is consistent with the smoothing hypothesis.

Later, Carlson & Bathala (1997), in a study where they try to determine possible explanatory variables of the smoothing behaviour, introduce in the analysis, as management incentive mechanisms, the remuneration structure (cash-based remuneration *versus* securities performance-based remuneration). Their results have proved consistent with previous observations, that is, when the managers' remuneration is related to the securities performance, managers are more likely to smooth income than in the absence of this kind of remuneration.

Similarly, Godfrey & Jones (1999) also studied whether the existence of bonus explains the incidence of classificatory smoothing, although they have tested it indirectly, given that Australian companies do not disclose management remuneration plans. Thus, they assumed that in a multi-period context, managers of companies with disperse ownership tend to smooth the reported operating earnings so as to avoid that their remuneration plans are revised. The results obtained provided evidence that a less concentrated capital ownership structure is associated with higher smoothing.

Given the above, the existence of a positive relationship between the manager's remuneration plans and his/her income smoothing behaviour seems to make sense. It should be noted, however, that the conclusions of the empirical studies on this hypothesis may raise some controversy due to the operationalisation of concepts, insofar as the use of a dummy variable can be considered as somewhat reductive.

Income Smoothing and the Debt Covenant Hypothesis

The Positive Accounting Theory also considers the influence of the relationships between shareholders and creditors in explaining the accounting methods adopted in a company. Thus, the debt contracts and their restrictive clauses are another possible explanation for the companies' accounting choices (Watts & Zimmerman, 1990).

Typically, companies are faced with problems related to information asymmetry and agency conflicts (Jensen & Meckling, 1976). Hence, regarding the agency relationship between shareholders (through management) and creditors, the latter often chose to set out restrictive clauses in debt contracts to control management actions, thus mitigating the risk of wealth transfer in favour of shareholders and to the detriment of creditors (Carlson & Bathala, 1997). However, as the clauses of these contracts are generally defined on the basis of the accounting figures, the manager can be led into manipulating the financial information, within the latitude allowed by GAAP, so as to mitigate the restrictions imposed by this type of contracts.

In line with these arguments, the Positive Accounting Theory puts forward the hypothesis that companies, where debt contracts have restrictive clauses defined by reference to accounting figures, prefer accounting methods that increase reported earnings (Watts & Zimmerman, 1990).

Several studies have validated this hypothesis regarding the restrictive clauses of debt contracts, in particular, that the more the level of the company debt, the more its manager tends to make accounting choices that increase the reported income (e.g. Dhaliwal, 1980; Zmijewski & Hagerman, 1981; Zimmer, 1986).

Nevertheless, some authors who have analysed the shareholder/creditors agency relationship have proposed hypotheses where they do not return to this traditional Positive Accounting Theory hypothesis, arguing that debt level may favour practices that smooth the reported income and not necessarily its maximisation. In this regard, the work by Trueman & Titman (1988) stands out as the main driver of this premise, as they introduce the debt level into their agency model, shareholders/creditors, as a variable that explains income smoothing.

Trueman & Titman (1988) developed a theory where they provide an explanation for the managers' smoothing behaviour: the lower the creditors' assessment of the probability of variance of the company's economic earnings, the lower the estimation of the probability of bankruptcy and, consequently, the lower the interest rate required for the debt issued. As a result, the current value of cash flows for shareholders also increases; hence, in such a context, the shareholders of companies that smooth their earnings are benefited in comparison with the shareholders of companies that do not smooth their earnings.

Chalayer (1994) empirically tested this theory, specifically the extent to which the probability of bankruptcy associated with the debt level is different as the company smooth or does not smooth its earnings and the extent to which income smoothing translates into a weaker interest weight. However, the results indicate that the debt level rate, the probability of bankruptcy and the amount of interest incurred in the two groups of companies (smoothers and non-smoothers) are similar, which, in the author's view, suggests that creditors are rational, inasmuch that they take into account the influence of the earnings smoothing practices on their variance, which leads them to demand similar interest rates if the levels of debt and the likelihood of bankruptcy are similar.

However, Carlson & Bathala (1997), in a study where they sought to identify some of the possible explanatory factors of smoothing behaviour, gathered evidence that the debt level is an incentive for companies to smooth their earnings, which was consistent with their argument that managers with high debt ratios are likely to smooth income in order to minimise the risk perceived by creditors or to respect debt covenants.

More recently, Gassen & Fuelbier (2015) using a sample of private European companies, investigate the relationship between earnings smoothness and creditors preferences. They document that the earnings smoothness is associated with lower cost of debt but only in weak debt contracting environments. Demerjian et al. (2018) also show that income smoothing is useful in monitoring borrowers because it is able to reduce the effects of transient shocks. More important, it seems that income smoothing could help to predict spurious technical default.

Regarding the substitution variables chosen to operationalise the hypothesis concerning the impact on the accounting choices of debt contracts established by reference to accounting, studies have generally used the company's debt ratio (e.g. Zmijewski & Hagerman, 1981; Chalayer, 1994). Indeed, it is generally acknowledged that the debt ratio is a representative variable of such contracts, insofar that its increase leads creditors to include restrictions on loan contracts referring to the accounting figures (Begley, 1990; Duke & Hunt, 1990).

In sum, the accounting literature seems to favour the premise that the debt level may be an incentive for an income smoothing policy, despite empirical evidence is mixed with regard to the impact of this determinant of smoothing, since some studies have gather evidence on the rationality of creditors regarding artificially reduced variations in reported earnings.

FIRM-SPECIFIC FACTORS

Income Smoothing and Company Ownership Structure

Companies' development and growth have made a contribution to a clear and effective separation between the equity holders (principal) and the manager (agent). In fact, shareholders have slighter capacity and opportunity to influence the administration of the company and transfer this function to the manager, which gives the latter a considerable power in decision-making.

Aware of this reality, Hunt (1986) emphasises the importance of considering capital and its control in explaining a company's accounting choices. Thus, in companies with concentrated ownership (whose control is ensured by equity holders) managers are expected to maximise the company's value, since the owners perform the management function. However, this does not appear to occur in the case of companies with diffused capital ownership, where the decision-making and ownership functions are separated (manager-controlled companies). Hence, it is possible that the managers of these sort of companies prefer firstly to maximise their own utility and wealth before maximising the company's economic value and, consequently, the wealth of shareholders who have mandated them to make decisions on their behalf.

A number of factors may be on the basis of the possible divergences of interests between the shareholders and the manager. On the one hand, labour market constraints are greater for managers of manager-controlled companies, given that, in this case, job security is not guaranteed. In turn, in owner-controlled companies, the need to preserve employment is not so pressing, given that owners, as managers, have the control of the company (Smith, 1976; Salamon & Smith, 1979; Koch, 1981; Carlson & Bathala, 1997). In this context, Monsen & Downs (1965) and Baumol (1967, cited by Amihud et al., 1983) developed business management theories where they admit that the income streams in manager-controlled companies are less variable than in owner-controlled companies, that is, the former make decisions that stabilise income instead of promoting its maximisation. In particular, Monsen & Downs (1965), admitting that the manager of this kind of companies acts in order to maximise the current value of all his/her monetary and non-monetary revenues and that a part of his/her salary is a function of his/her performance, assessed by the accounting earnings or by the stock market value of the company, considered that it would be beneficial to maintain a regular and steady earnings growth. In turn, the manager of owner-controlled companies, since he/she is him/herself the dominant shareholder, does not depend on these remuneration contracts.

This prediction was later tested in the empirical studies carried out by Monsen et al. (1968), Palmer (1973), Smith (1976), and Salamon & Smith (1979). Such studies have assumed that the degree of control that the manager has over the conduct of the company may influence its propensity for income smoothing, providing, for the most part, evidence that manager-controlled companies report relatively smoother income streams than owner-controlled companies. This hypothesis has continued to be the subject of numerous empirical tests, being notably recognized the works by Kamin & Ronen (1978),

Koch (1981), Amihud et al. (1983), Moses (1987), Beattie et al. (1994), Chalayer (1994), Carlson & Bathala (1997), and Godfrey & Jones (1999).

Given the above, empirical works have documented evidence where an association between the company's ownership structure and its propensity for income smoothing is noticeable. In fact, on the one hand, these studies allow concluding that when the company ownership and its administration fall upon the same individuals (concentrated ownership), that is, when the company shareholders (equity holders) are those that manage, there is a lower incentive for income smoothing. On the other hand, empirical evidence suggests that when the ownership structure is diversified, that is, when there is a separation between ownership and control, the manager is encouraged to adopt an income smoothing behaviour.

Income Smoothing and Company Profitability

Some studies that have analysed the possible explanatory factors of the smoothing phenomenon included and also tested in their investigations the hypothesis that the companies' profitable propensity may influence the choice of income standardisation techniques, although the arguments and results obtained have not always been fully coincident.

In fact, on the one hand, we find studies providing evidence that the incidence of smoothing is greater in less profitable companies. Ashari et al. (1994), for example, in a study where they seek to identify factors associated with the incidence of income smoothing, assume and corroborate their premise that fluctuations in income streams have a more severe impact on low-profit companies, so they have a greater motivation to smooth reported earnings. Ashari et al.'s (1994) tests and arguments emerged from the conclusions drawn in previous studies by Archibald (1967) and White (1970). According to the latter, the variability in negative income streams may be less beneficial for the management than the variability in positive streams, leading to a more concerted effort to use accounting alternatives that stabilise income, inasmuch that, through the negative performance standardisation, the management can convey the notion of a controlled decline, whereas an uncontrolled variability of negative performance may lead investors and creditors to perceive greater risk and lose confidence in the management.

On the other hand, Carlson & Bathala (1997), contrary to the previous studies, concluded that more profitable companies are more likely to be classified as income smoothers than less profitable companies. This conclusion has proved to be consistent with their argument that the manager's ability to smooth income is largely limited by the company's potential for generating profits. Thus, according to them, companies that experience successive years of poor performance (that is, negative earnings) tend to find fewer available instruments with which they can smooth income.

In view of these arguments and the results of the previous studies, it seems coherent to establish the hypothesis of a possible impact of the company's profitability on its smoothing behaviour, notwithstanding the fact that there are two opposing stances regarding its influence on income smoothing.

CONCLUSION

Following what has been discussed throughout this chapter, we consider that most of the reasons mentioned for adhering to income smoothing practices stem from the need felt by management to neutralise environmental uncertainty and reduce wide fluctuations in the company's operating performance that is subject to an intermittent cycle of good and bad moments.

Some authors advocate that the distortion of financial information may be driven by the management's personal interests achievement (e.g. job security, remuneration objectives) or by the attempt to satisfy the expectations of the financial information users (e.g. investors, creditors, analysts).

Regarding the determinants of the smoothing behaviour, we also placed particular emphasis on the hypotheses put forward by the Positive Accounting Theory to justify the companies' accounting choices and, in parallel, to understand the income smoothing practices. The Positive Accounting Theory explains the companies' accounting policy through the manager's opportunistic behaviour, given that it assumes that the accounting choices are driven by the objective of maximising his/her utility. Specifically, this theory allows for a better understanding of the companies' accounting policy, by explaining how contractual relationships within the company and the political costs can influence managers' accounting choices.

Despite the existence of different contracts established with the purpose of reducing agency costs, the manager has a certain latitude to act in accordance with his/her interests, since the contracts or objectives set out in those contracts are often defined by reference to the accounting figures, which he/she can, to some extent, manipulate. Thus, from a contractual point of view, accounting research has essentially focused its analysis on the contracts negotiated within the company and their consequences on the behaviour of the different contracting parties. In this context, the remuneration contracts that link the manager to the shareholders, as well as the contracts that reflect the shareholders'/creditors' relationships, can be an explanatory element of the income smoothing practices. Likewise, the relationships that involve the company with the public authorities may encourage the manager to pursue an income smoothing goal.

However, this theory, classified as positivist by Watts and Zimmerman (1978), is the subject of some controversies, one of which refers to the proxies used to empirically validate the postulates of the theory, and, hence, the conclusions must be interpreted with caution.

In addition to these determinants, some empirical studies have emphasised the importance of also taking into account the company's capital structure and its control, the company's profitability, the sector in which it is inserted, whether the company is audited or not by a Big4, the corporate governance measures adopted, among others, as possible explanatory factors of the phenomenon under analysis.

The relevance of this chapter is justified essentially by two reasons. First, it highlights the contemporary importance of this research line and the concern about financial information quality. Consequently, a deep knowledge of the factors that possibly explain these accounting discretionary practices is crucial. Second, the extensive literature on earnings management also justifies this chapter. Thereby, the systematisation of the literature on the income smoothing explanatory factors can help researchers and increase future empirical research focused on this area.

As future research, it would be interesting keep still analysing the incidence of income smoothing in the mandatory IFRS adoption period (Capkun et al., 2016), as well as the impact on income smoothing after the international financial crises, where, to the best of our knowledge, there is still little empirical detailed research.

REFERENCES

Ahmed, A. S., Lobo, G. J., & Zhou, J. (2000). Job security and income smoothing: An empirical test of the Fudenberg and Tirole (1995) model. *SSRN Working Paper Series*, October version.

Albornoz, B. G. (2003). *Alisamiento del beneficio y manipulación de ajustes por devengo: Análisis empírico en el contexto español. In Accounting Research Award "José M.ª Fernández Pirla" (XI Edition)*. Madrid: ICAC.

Albornoz, B. G., & Alcarria, J. J. (2003). Analysis and diagnosis of income smoothing in Spain. *European Accounting Review*, *12*(3), 443–463. doi:10.1080/0963818022000001154

Amihud, Y., Kamin, J. Y., & Ronen, J. (1983). 'Managerialism', 'ownerism' and risk. *Journal of Banking & Finance*, *7*(2), 189–196. doi:10.1016/0378-4266(83)90031-6

Archibald, T. R. (1967). The return to straight-line depreciation: An analysis of a change in accounting method. *Journal of Accounting Research*, *5*(Supplement), 164–180. doi:10.2307/2489918

Ashari, N., Koh, H. C., Tan, S. L., & Wong, W. H. (1994). Factors affecting income smoothing among listed companies in Singapore. *Accounting and Business Research*, *24*(96), 291–301. doi:10.1080/00014788.1994.9729488

Ball, R., & Shivakumar, L. (2006). The role of accruals in asymmetrically timely gain and loss recognition. *Journal of Accounting Research*, *44*(2), 207–242. doi:10.1111/j.1475-679X.2006.00198.x

Barnea, A., Ronen, J., & Sadan, S. (1976). Classificatory smoothing of income with extraordinary items. *The Accounting Review*, *51*(1), 110–122.

Beattie, V., Brown, S., Ewers, D., John, B., Manson, S., Thomas, D., & Turner, M. (1994). Extraordinary items and income smoothing: A positive accounting approach. *Journal of Business Finance & Accounting*, *21*(6), 791–811. doi:10.1111/j.1468-5957.1994.tb00349.x

Begley, J. (1990). Debt covenants and accounting choice. *Journal of Accounting and Economics*, *12*(1-3), 125–139. doi:10.1016/0165-4101(90)90044-5

Beidleman, C. R. (1973). Income smoothing: The role of management. *The Accounting Review*, *48*(4), 653–667.

Benston, G., & Krasney, M. (1978). The economic consequences of financial accounting statements. In *Economic Consequences of Financial Standards: Selected Papers* (pp. 159–252). Financial Accounting Standards Board.

Bhat, V. N. (1996). Banks and income smoothing: An empirical analysis. *Applied Financial Economics*, *6*(6), 505–510. doi:10.1080/096031096333953

Booth, G. G., Kallunki, J. P., & Martikainen, T. (1996). Post-announcement drift and income smoothing: Finnish evidence. *Journal of Business Finance & Accounting*, *23*(8), 1197–1211. doi:10.1111/j.1468-5957.1996.tb01165.x

Brealey, R. A., & Myers, S. C. (1998). *Princípios de finanças empresariais*. Lisbon: McGraw-Hill.

Bricker, R., Previts, G., Robinson, T., & Young, S. (1995). Financial analyst assessment of company earnings quality. *Journal of Accounting, Auditing & Finance*, *10*(3), 541–544. doi:10.1177/0148558X9501000307

Buckmaster, D. (2001). *Development of the income smoothing literature 1893-1998: A focus on the United States*. JAI.

Burgstahler, D. C., Hail, L., & Leuz, C. (2006). The importance of reporting incentives: Earnings management in european private and public firms. *The Accounting Review*, *81*(5), 983–1016. doi:10.2308/accr.2006.81.5.983

Bushman, R., Dai, Z., & Wang, X. (2010). Risk and CEO turnover. *Journal of Financial Economics*, *96*(3), 381–398. doi:10.1016/j.jfineco.2010.03.001

Capkun, V., Collins, D., & Jeanjean, T. (2016). The effect of IAS/IFRS adoption on earnings management (smoothing): A closer look at competing explanations. *Journal of Accounting and Public Policy*, *35*(4), 352–394. doi:10.1016/j.jaccpubpol.2016.04.002

Carlson, S. J., & Bathala, C. T. (1997). Ownership differences and firms' income smoothing behaviour. *Journal of Business Finance & Accounting*, *24*(2), 179–196. doi:10.1111/1468-5957.00101

Chalayer, S. (1994). *Identification et motivations des pratiques de lissage des résultats comptables des entreprises françaises cotées en Bourse* (Doctoral dissertation). Saint-Etienne University, France.

Chaney, P. K., Jeter, D. C., & Lewis, C. M. (1998). The use of accruals in income smoothing: A permanent earnings hypothesis. *Advances in Quantitative Analysis of Finance and Accounting*, *6*, 103–135.

Chaney, P. K., & Lewis, C. M. (1995). Earnings management and firm valuation under asymmetric information. *Journal of Corporate Finance*, *1*(1), 319–345. doi:10.1016/0929-1199(94)00008-I

Chaney, P. K., & Lewis, C. M. (1998). Income smoothing and underperformance in initial public offerings. *Journal of Corporate Finance*, *4*(1), 1–29. doi:10.1016/S0929-1199(97)00007-2

Copeland, R. M. (1968). Income smoothing. *Journal of Accounting Research*, *6*, 101–116. doi:10.2307/2490073

Coppens, L., & Peek, E. (2005). An analysis of earnings management by European private firms. *Journal of International Accounting, Auditing & Taxation*, *14*(1), 1–17. doi:10.1016/j.intaccaudtax.2005.01.002

Craig, R., & Walsh, P. (1989). Adjustments for 'extraordinary items' in smoothing reported profits of listed Australian companies: Some empirical evidence. *Journal of Business Finance & Accounting*, *16*(2), 229–245. doi:10.1111/j.1468-5957.1989.tb00015.x

DeFond, M. L., & Park, C. W. (1997). Smoothing income in anticipation of future earnings. *Journal of Accounting and Economics*, *23*(2), 115–139. doi:10.1016/S0165-4101(97)00004-9

Demerjian, P. R., Donovan, J., & Lewis-Western, M. F. (2018). Income smoothing and the usefulness of earnings for monitoring in debt. *SSRN Working Paper Series*, April version.

Dhaliwal, D. S. (1980). The effect of the firm's capital structure on the choice of accounting methods. *The Accounting Review*, *55*(1), 78–85.

Dhaliwal, D. S., Frankel, M., & Trezevant, R. (1994). The taxable and book income motivation for a LIFO layer liquidation. *Journal of Accounting Research*, *32*(2), 278–289. doi:10.2307/2491286

Dichev, I. D., & Tang, W. (2009). Earnings volatility and earnings predictability. *Journal of Accounting and Economics*, *47*(1-2), 160–181. doi:10.1016/j.jacceco.2008.09.005

Dou, Y., Hope, O., & Thomas, W. (2013). Relationship-specificity, contract enforceability, and income smoothing. *The Accounting Review*, *88*(5), 1629–1656. doi:10.2308/accr-50489

Duke, J., & Hunt, H. III. (1990). An empirical examination of debt covenant restrictions and accounting-related debt proxies. *Journal of Accounting and Economics*, *12*(1-3), 43–63. doi:10.1016/0165-4101(90)90041-2

Easton, P. D., & Zmijewski, M. E. (1989). Cross-sectional variation in the stock market response to accounting earnings announcements. *Journal of Accounting and Economics*, *11*(2-3), 117–141. doi:10.1016/0165-4101(89)90003-7

Elgers, P. T., Pfeiffer, R. J. Jr, & Porter, S. L. (2003). Anticipatory income smoothing: A re-examination. *Journal of Accounting and Economics*, *35*(3), 405–422. doi:10.1016/S0165-4101(03)00039-9

Foster, G. (1986). *Financial statement analysis*. Prentice-Hall, Inc.

Fudenberg, D., & Tirole, J. (1995). A theory of income and dividend smoothing based on incumbency rents. *Journal of Political Economy*, *103*(1), 75–93. doi:10.1086/261976

Gao, L., & Zhan, J. (2015). Firms' earnings smoothing, corporate social responsibility, and valuation. *Journal of Corporate Finance*, *32*, 108–127. doi:10.1016/j.jcorpfin.2015.03.004

Gassen, J., & Fuelbier, R. U. (2015). Do Creditors prefer smooth earnings? Evidence from European Private Firms. *Journal of International Accounting Research*, *14*(2), 151–180. doi:10.2308/jiar-51130

Gaver, J. J., Gaver, K. M., & Austin, J. R. (1995). Additional evidence on bonus plans and income management. *Journal of Accounting and Economics*, *19*(1), 3–28. doi:10.1016/0165-4101(94)00358-C

Gibbins, M., Richardson, A., & Waterhouse, J. (1990). The management of corporate financial disclosure: Opportunism, ritualism, policies, and process. *Journal of Accounting Research*, *28*(1), 121–143. doi:10.2307/2491219

Godfrey, J. M., & Jones, K. L. (1999). Political cost influences on income smoothing via extraordinary item classification. *Accounting and Finance*, *39*(3), 229–254. doi:10.1111/1467-629X.00025

Gordon, M. J. (1964). Postulates, principles and research in accounting. *The Accounting Review*, *39*(2), 251–263.

Graham, J. R., Harvey, C. R., & Rajgopal, S. (2005). The Economic Implications of Corporate Financial Reporting. *Journal of Accounting and Economics*, *40*(1-3), 3–73. doi:10.1016/j.jacceco.2005.01.002

Habib, A. (2005). Firm-specific determinants of income smoothing in Bangladesh: An empirical evaluation. *Advances in International Accounting*, *18*, 53–71. doi:10.1016/S0897-3660(05)18003-9

Hagerman, R. L., & Zmijewski, M. E. (1979). Some economic determinants of accounting policy choice. *Journal of Accounting and Economics*, *1*(2), 141–161. doi:10.1016/0165-4101(79)90004-1

Healy, P. M. (1985). The effect of bonus schemes on accounting decisions. *Journal of Accounting and Economics*, *7*(1-3), 85–107. doi:10.1016/0165-4101(85)90029-1

Hepworth, S. R. (1953). Smoothing periodic income. *The Accounting Review*, *28*(1), 32–39.

Hunt, H. (1985). Potential determinants of corporate inventory accounting decisions. *Journal of Accounting Research*, *23*(2), 448–467. doi:10.2307/2490820

Hunt, H. (1986). The separation of corporate ownership and control: Theory, evidence and implications. *Journal of Accounting Literature*, *5*, 85–124.

Imhoff, E. A. (1981). Income smoothing: An analysis of critical issues. *The Quarterly Review of Economics and Business*, *21*(3), 23–42.

Iñiguez, R., & Poveda, F. (2004). Long-run abnormal returns and income smoothing in the spanish stock market. *European Accounting Review*, *13*(1), 105–130. doi:10.1080/0963818032000138224

Jaggi, B., & Sannella, A. (1995). The association between the accuracy of management earnings forecasts and discretionary accounting changes. *Journal of Accounting, Auditing & Finance*, *10*(1), 1–21. doi:10.1177/0148558X9501000101

Jensen, M. C., & Meckling, W. H. (1976). Theory of the firm: Managerial behavior, agency costs and ownership structure. *Journal of Financial Economics*, *3*(4), 305–360. doi:10.1016/0304-405X(76)90026-X

Kamin, J. Y., & Ronen, J. (1978). The smoothing of income numbers: Some empirical evidence on systematic differences among management-controlled and owner-controlled firms. *Accounting, Organizations and Society*, *3*(2), 141–157. doi:10.1016/0361-3682(78)90022-3

Kanagaretnam, K., Lobo, G. J., & Mathieu, R. (2003). Managerial incentives for income smoothing through bank loan loss provisions. *Review of Quantitative Finance and Accounting*, *20*(1), 63–80. doi:10.1023/A:1022187622780

Kirschenheiter, M., & Melumad, N. D. (2002). Can 'big bath' and earnings smoothing co-exist as equilibrium financial reporting strategies? *Journal of Accounting Research*, *40*(3), 761–796. doi:10.1111/1475-679X.00070

Koch, B. S. (1981). Income smoothing: An experiment. *The Accounting Review*, *56*(3), 574–586.

Lambert, R. A. (1984). Income smoothing as rational equilibrium behaviour. *The Accounting Review*, *59*(4), 604–618.

Leuz, C., Nanda, D., & Wysocki, P. D. (2003). Earnings management and investor protection: An international comparison. *Journal of Financial Economics*, *69*(3), 505–527. doi:10.1016/S0304-405X(03)00121-1

Lev, B., & Kunitzky, S. (1974). On the association between smoothing measures and the risk of common stocks. *The Accounting Review*, *49*(2), 259–270.

Lev, B., & Ohlson, J. (1982). Market-based empirical research in accounting: A review, interpretations and extension. *Journal of Accounting Research*, *20*(Supplement), 249–331. doi:10.2307/2674685

Li, S., & Richie, N. (2016). Income smoothing and the cost of debt. *China Journal of Accounting Research*, *9*(3), 175–190. doi:10.1016/j.cjar.2016.03.001

Liberty, S. E., & Zimmerman, J. L. (1986). Labor union, contract negotiations and accounting choices. *The Accounting Review*, *61*(4), 692–712.

Liu, S., & Skerratt, L. (2018). Earnings quality across different reporting regimes: Listed, large private, medium-sized, small and micro companies in the UK. *Journal of Applied Accounting Research*, *19*(1), 2–19. doi:10.1108/JAAR-02-2015-0009

Markarian, G., & Gill, B. (2012). Income smoothing and idiosyncratic volatility, *SSRN Working Paper Series*, February version.

Mayer-Sommer, A. (1979). Understanding and acceptance of the efficient markets hypothesis and its accounting implications. *The Accounting Review*, *54*(1), 88–106.

Michelson, S. E., Jordan-Wagner, J., & Wootton, C. W. (1995). A market based analysis of income smoothing. *Journal of Business Finance & Accounting*, *22*(8), 1179–1193. doi:10.1111/j.1468-5957.1995.tb00900.x

Michelson, S. E., Jordan-Wagner, J., & Wootton, C. W. (2000). The relationship between the smoothing of reported income and risk-adjusted returns. *Journal of Economics and Finance*, *24*(2), 141–159. doi:10.1007/BF02752709

Monsen, R. J., Chiu, J. S., & Cooley, D. E. (1968). The effect of separation of ownership and control on the performance of the large firm. *The Quarterly Journal of Economics*, *82*(3), 435–451. doi:10.2307/1879516

Monsen, R. J. Jr, & Downs, A. (1965). A theory of large managerial firms. *Journal of Political Economy*, *73*(3), 221–236. doi:10.1086/259012

Monterrey, J. (1998). Un recorrido por la contabilidad positiva. *Revista Española de Financiación y Contabilidad*, *27*(95), 427–467.

Moses, O. D. (1987). Income smoothing and incentives: Empirical tests using accounting changes. *The Accounting Review*, *62*(2), 358–377.

Palmer, J. (1973). The profit performance effects of the separation of ownership from control in large U.S. industrial corporations. *The Bell Journal of Economics and Management Science*, *4*(1), 293–303. doi:10.2307/3003151

Pastor, L., & Veronesi, P. (2003). Stock valuation and learning about profitability. *The Journal of Finance*, *58*(5), 1749–1789. doi:10.1111/1540-6261.00587

Perry, S. E., & Williams, T. H. (1994). Earnings management preceding management buyout offers. *Journal of Accounting and Economics*, *18*(2), 157–179. doi:10.1016/0165-4101(94)00362-9

Porciau, S. (1993). Earnings management and non-routine executive changes. *Journal of Accounting and Economics*, *16*(1-3), 317–336. doi:10.1016/0165-4101(93)90015-8

Prencipe, A., Bar-Yosef, S., Mazzola, P., & Pozza, L. (2011). Income smoothing in family-controlled companies: Evidence from Italy. *Corporate Governance*, *19*(6), 529–546. doi:10.1111/j.1467-8683.2011.00856.x

Rajgopal, S., & Venkatachalam, M. (2011). Financial reporting quality and idiosyncratic return volatility. *Journal of Accounting and Economics*, *51*(1-2), 1–20. doi:10.1016/j.jacceco.2010.06.001

Ronen, J., & Sadan, S. (1981). *Smoothing income numbers: Objectives, means, and implications*. Addison-Wesley Publishing Company.

Salamon, G. L., & Smith, E. D. (1979). Corporate control and managerial misrepresentation of firm performance. *The Bell Journal of Economics*, *10*(1), 319–328. doi:10.2307/3003333

Smith, E. D. (1976). The effect of the separation of ownership from control on accounting policy decisions. *The Accounting Review*, *51*(4), 707–723.

Subramanyam, K. R. (1996). The pricing of discretionary accruals. *Journal of Accounting and Economics*, *22*(1-3), 249–281. doi:10.1016/S0165-4101(96)00434-X

Teoh, S. H., Welch, I., & Wong, T. J. (1998). Earnings management and the long-run market performance of initial public offerings. *The Journal of Finance*, *53*(6), 1935–1974. doi:10.1111/0022-1082.00079

Trueman, B., & Titman, S. (1988). An explanation for accounting income smoothing. *Journal of Accounting Research*, *26*, 127–139. doi:10.2307/2491184

Tseng, L. J., & Lai, C. W. (2007). The relationship between income smoothing and company profitability: An empirical study. *International Journal of Management*, *24*(4), 727–733.

Tucker, J. W., & Zarowin, P. A. (2006). Does income smoothing improve earnings informativeness? *The Accounting Review*, *81*(1), 251–270. doi:10.2308/accr.2006.81.1.251

Wang, Z., & Williams, T. H. (1994). Accounting income smoothing and stockholder wealth. *Journal of Applied Business Research*, *10*(3), 96–110. doi:10.19030/jabr.v10i3.5929

Watts, R. L., & Zimmerman, J. L. (1978). Towards a positive theory of the determination of accounting standards. *The Accounting Review*, *53*(1), 112–134.

Watts, R. L., & Zimmerman, J. L. (1990). Positive Accounting Theory: A ten year perspective. *The Accounting Review*, *65*(1), 131–156.

White, G. E. (1970). Discretionary accounting decisions and income normalization. *Journal of Accounting Research*, *8*, 260–273. doi:10.2307/2490111

Zimmer, I. (1986). Accounting for interest by real estate developers. *Journal of Accounting and Economics*, *8*(1), 37–51. doi:10.1016/0165-4101(86)90009-1

Zmijewski, M. E., & Hagerman, R. L. (1981). An income strategy approach to the positive theory of accounting standard setting/choice. *Journal of Accounting and Economics*, *3*(2), 129–149. doi:10.1016/0165-4101(81)90010-0

KEY TERMS AND DEFINITIONS

Earnings Management: Any practice undertaken deliberately by managers to alter reported earnings, with the purpose of obtaining some specific gain.

Income Smoothing: Practices aimed at increasing income in some fiscal years and at decreasing it in others, in order to minimize its long-term fluctuations.

Income Smoothing Determinants: Motivations anticipated by the positive accounting theory which can lead managers to engage in income smoothing practices.

Income Smoothing Firm-Specific Factors: Firm features that might explain the adoption of income smoothing practices.

Income Smoothing Motivations: General motivations which lead managers to engage in income smoothing practices.

Positive Accounting Theory: Hypotheses developed by Watts and Zimmerman to justify the companies' accounting choices and, in parallel, to understand the earnings management strategies undertaken deliberately by managers.

ENDNOTES

1 So as to clarify some of the aspects mentioned, there is the need for some considerations on risk decomposition. According to Brealey & Myers (1998), total risk is subdivided into two components: on the one hand, unsystematic risk (also known as specific risk, residual risk, unique risk or idiosyncratic risk), and, on the other hand, systematic risk or market risk. The former usually involves a specific company and, possibly, its direct competitors, and can be reduced *via* diversification. Market risk, in turn, affects all companies because it depends on general economic conditions (e.g. uncertainty of inflation, monetary, exchange rate and other policies) and cannot be diminished by the diversification strategy. The latter is measured using beta (β).

Chapter 4
Earnings Management and Mergers and Acquisitions:
Empirical Evidence From Italian-Listed Companies

Raffaela Casciello
University of Naples Federico II, Italy

Adele Caldarelli
University of Naples Federico II, Italy

Marco Maffei
University of Naples Federico II, Italy

ABSTRACT

This chapter investigates whether Italian-listed companies involved in mergers and acquisitions (M&A) during the period 2009–2017 manipulated earnings through recourse to discretionary accruals in response to financial market competition. Interest in the possible effects of competition on earnings management practices follows the considerable attention attracted by the effects of business combinations on disclosure quality and reliability. M&A represents an opportunity for managers to manipulate financial reports and to deliver misleading market information in order to enhance company reputation and attract funds from investors. This empirical analysis demonstrates that Italian-listed companies involved in M&A used goodwill as a discretionary accrual for managing earnings. The findings indicate that the increasing level of financial market competition between Italian-listed companies prompted major recourse to earnings management practices based on discretionary accruals.

DOI: 10.4018/978-1-5225-7817-8.ch004

INTRODUCTION

In recent decades, numerous empirical accounting studies have discussed the determinants and consequences of financial disclosure quality, which are often linked to earnings quality (e.g. Schipper & Vincent, 2003; Dechow, Weili, & Schrand, 2010; Kothari, 2001). Managers' decisions concerning the appropriate level of disclosure involve a trade-off between the benefits of informing the capital market about the firm's value and the costs of aiding its rivals (Cheng, Man, & Yi, 2013, p. 140). On the other hand, the demand for financial disclosure arises from an asymmetry between the quantity and quality of business information held by firm insiders and what external stakeholders effectively perceive through disclosure (e.g. Lang & Lundholm, 1996; Healy & Palepu, 2001).

Many areas of the accounting literature on earnings quality address the potential influence of governance, fiscal, ethical and auditing variables on strategic earnings management choices while ignoring environmental macroeconomic factors (e.g. Jiang, Zhu, & Huang, 2013; Sundvik, 2017; Shleifer, 2004; Badolato, Donelson, & Ege, 2014). These analyses offer only a partial view because they assume that the economic background remains the same and does not influence either accounting choices or the stability of financial markets (Filip & Raffournier, 2014).

Analyses of the effects of macroeconomic features on earnings quality have yielded mixed empirical results in relation to how they influence managerial accounting behaviour. In certain circumstances, such macroeconomic features have been found to incentivize strategic manipulation of earnings (Burgstahler, Hail, & Leuz, 2004; Bushman & Piotroski, 2006; Filip & Raffournier, 2014; Persakis & Iatridis, 2014). Some of the most investigated environmental proxies are linked to financial market trends. For example, Kane, Richardson and Graybeal (1996) and Richardson, Kane and Lobinger (1998) proved that both quantity and quality of financial disclosure are profoundly influenced by economic recession. In contrast, a more recent study by Filip and Raffouriner (2014) provided evidence that earnings management practices decreased in those countries impacted by the global financial crisis. There is also evidence that key characteristics of business cycles, such as periods of expansion and contraction, influence disclosure quality (Johnson, 1999; Jenkins, Kane, & Velury, 2009). However, more research is needed to fully understand the effects of macro-economic features on earnings and disclosure quality.

Despite the risk of reputational damage, recourse to earnings manipulations have been identified even when stakeholders are fully focused on the information contained in financial reports. Business combinations (corporate strategic decisions involving plural economic identities) are strategic market operations implemented to change relevant market situations and strategic positioning. While some empirical studies have investigated the determinants of unethical managerial accounting practices in takeover and merger settings (Easterwood, 1998; Erickson & Wang, 1999), there is little evidence in relation to the effects of a given macroeconomic proxy (such as financial market competition) on recourse to earnings management during mergers and acquisitions (M&A) business combinations.

The objective of the present study is to investigate whether Italian-listed companies involved in M&A during the period 2009–2017 manipulated reported earnings through the use of discretionary accruals in response to financial market competition, focusing in particular on goodwill recognition and impairment. Our interest in investigating the role of competition in earnings manipulations during business combinations derives from stakeholders' focus on the quality of information disclosures by companies involved in such operations (e.g. Bens, Goodman, & Neamtiu, 2012). M&A present an opportunity for managers to manipulate financial reports by adopting earnings management policies such as income smoothing and disclosing to market only information that enhances the company's reputation and attracts funds from investors.

The Italian case is of interest to an international audience for the following reasons. First, the Italian stock exchange is now suffering the effects of the global financial crisis of 2008 in terms of a reduced ratio of real business investment to value added in Italy as compared to the long-term Euro area average (European Central Bank, 2017). Additionally, Italy's political system is inherently weak and unstable, especially in recent decades (Banca d'Italia, 2018). Nevertheless, the Italian financial market has maintained its attractiveness for investors, encouraging M&A and an optimistic growth dynamic, although at a lower absolute level than in the pre-crisis period (KPMG, 2018).

Managers of Italian-listed firms have shown increased trust in the convenience of business combinations, as they enhance stock value and improve company profitability. The particular features of the Italian setting created the right conditions for an increasing focus on potentially unethical and opportunistic accounting behaviours in accounting treatment of business combinations between 2009 and 2017. In 2008, IASB updated the IFRS 3 regarding business combinations; in Italy, the changes were first applied by listed companies in 2009. Specially, the updated edition of the IFRS 3 introduced the accounting rule of *full goodwill*, altering how goodwill should be accounted during M&A operations. As the role of operations of M&A in promoting unethical accounting behaviour in the Italian context through exploitation of the discretionary accounting space arising from international regulation has not yet been comprehensively investigated, this paper aims to bridge that gap.

The findings which come from this empirical examination confirm that Italian-listed companies involved in M&A between 2009 and 2017 used goodwill recognition and impairment as discretionary accruals to manage earnings, despite business combinations capture the attention of market participants on information disclosed in financial reports. Although accounting research field is characterized by some studies about the main determinants of unethical accounting strategies during takeovers and mergers, there is still little evidence about the effects of some macroeconomic conditions of market, such as financial market competition, could exert on earnings manipulations. For this purpose, the paper aims to contribute to fill the gap inside the extent literature by investigating whether goodwill could be used for managing disclosure informativeness. Moreover, the present study can help stakeholders and practitioners to address issues of financial disclosure quality and transparency and how to deal with atypical levels of goodwill recognition and impairment. The findings can drive regulators toward an implementation and strengthening of international accounting rules (such as IFRS) to provide a better reliability of financial disclosure.

The rest of the paper is organized as follows. **Section 2** outlines some key characteristics of the Italian financial market. **Section 3** reviews the existing literature on the relationship between earnings management and financial market competition and formulates a number of hypotheses. **Section 4** describes the dataset and explains the research method. **Section 5** reports results and discusses the study findings, and **Section 6** presents some conclusions.

INSTITUTIONAL BACKGROUND

Despite the negative effects of the global financial crisis on market stability worldwide, conditions in the Italian financial market have improved over time (Banca d'Italia, 2018). Europe's adoption of an expansionary monetary policy and the positive effects of the European Economic Recovery Plan increased trust among market participants such as investors and financiers and boosted Italian stock market trading (Banca d'Italia, 2018). Analysts' expectations and forecasts were exceeded, helping to strengthen the stock prices of Italian banks and alleviating the credit crunch. The general improvement in financial activities has also seen major recourse to business combinations such as M&A (e.g. KPMG, 2018). Companies resorted to M&A to avoid bankruptcy or to implement business and production activities; as a consequence, many groups registered non-recurring revenues, as they were linked to goodwill recognition based on the positive difference between the purchase price and fair value of target firm net activities.

In Italy, the M&A market is experiencing growth in terms of both counter value and volume. Over time, these activities have continued to increase because of major recourse to corporate restructuring operations and cross-border, Sovereign Wealth, Initial Public Offering (IPO) and private equity funds (e.g. Arletta et al. 2015). From 2009 to 2014, the Italian M&A market registered increasing operations and counter value (Arletta et al., 2015, p. 26) and this evolutionary trend has been confirmed even in recent years for listed companies and banks (KPMG, 2017; KPMG, 2018). Italy's regulated market is helping to boost business combinations, and the associated risk of resorting to unethical accounting practices such as earnings manipulation to gain corporate or personal advantage remains high, not least because of the flexibility of the IFRS regulatory system. For that reason, an empirical analysis of the possible effects of financial market competition on recourse to accrual-based earnings management practices among Italian-listed companies involved in M&A is of undoubted interest.

There is a growing tendency in the accounting literature to assume that IFRS adoption may provide the necessary (and in some cases sufficient) conditions for good accounting quality (Levitt, 1998). Many countries decided to adopt the new international accounting standards developed by IASB to harmonize European accounting practices, to eliminate differences in bookkeeping (e.g. Van Hulle, 2004) and to ensure transparent comparability of financial statements. Italy is among those ones choosing to pursue accounting homogenization by adopting the IFRS framework. After the transposition of European Regulation 1606/2002 and issuance of Legislative Decree No. 38/2005, all publicly listed companies in Italy were required (from January 1, 2006; optionally, from January 1, 2005) to draw up financial statements and consolidated financial statements that complied with the new accounting standards. In the Italian context, the consolidated financial statement serves an informative purpose while the financial statement has legal significance in determining both income taxes and distribution of dividends. To ensure equal accounting treatment for firms obliged to comply with IFRS regulations and others that are not subject to international guidelines, Italian legislators adopted Legislative Decree No. 38/2005 art. 11, representing the pure twin-track approach.

The introduction of a new accounting regulatory system in Italy from 2006 and the consequent obligation to prepare annual and consolidated financial statements marked a huge change in company esteems and valuations. While IFRS adopts a fair value criterion, the code-related regulation compels the use of historical values. As international standards can amplify the effects of market macroeconomic conditions on financial statements in the Italian accounting context, managers might be incentivized to intervene in reports to manipulate financial information for their own ends. In these circumstances, managers might be motivated to exploit the discretionary space within the IFRS provisions by manipulating reports to increase or decrease information quality for internal or external, personal or corporate, and corrupt or ethical ends. For example, during periods of crisis, financial reports tend to show weaker performance, which reflects on credit ratings and stock value and can damage a company's reputation. The need to protect competitive and strategic positioning might prompt managers to manipulate earnings, exploiting the discretionary space left within the IFRS regulatory system to give managers a margin of discretion in their accounting choices. Even in situations where managers are under pressure from the expectations of market participants because of M&A, this flexibility facilitates discretionary accounting choices and illegal safeguarding of corporate and individual interests.

Despite the common belief that disclosure quality and transparency could benefit from the IASB's renewed accounting system (Barth, Landsman, & Lang, 2008), empirical evidence showed that regulatory adoption of IFRS in the financial reports of Italian-listed companies could in some cases reduce earnings quality, especially in those business combinations where market participants are focused on the financial statements of companies involved in M&A. IFRS 3 Business Combinations provides guidance on how to account for M&A operations between firms; strategic decisions of this kind affect not only capital structure and governance characteristics but also the composition and value of patrimonial assets. As aggregations of distinct business entities into a single entity, business combinations are responsible for preparing the consolidating financial statement in line with the update of IFRS 3 in 2008. This introduced a modification of goodwill valuation and recording criteria, contributing to the creation of large areas of discretion in relation to accounting treatment of intangible assets. Goodwill is itself an intangible asset that expresses the target firm's sustainability as a "going concern" and the benefits of combining the acquiree's net assets with those of the acquirer. In the same way, goodwill can reflect the possibility of an error in the appreciation of the target firm's real value during M&A because of an overpayment by the acquirer or a mistake in assessing the fair value of either the cost of the business combination or the acquiree's identifiable net assets (e.g. IFRS, 2015). The IFRS 3 revision relates to a new way of assessing goodwill as "full goodwill", where the full amount is recorded in the acquirer's financial statement.

This differs from the previous "traditional goodwill" methodology, in which goodwill was recorded only for the pertinent share. In other words, while goodwill was previously calculated as the difference between the price paid for a portion of the firm as object of business combination and a portion of the firm's overall fair value, the introduction of IFRS 3 2008 significantly widened the scope of goodwill, where "*discretion regarding the valuation of assets and informational asymmetry culminates in the amount of goodwill the acquirer recognizes since goodwill remains as a residual after deducting the fair value of acquired net assets from the price paid for the target*" (Detzen & Zulch, 2012, p. 107). As a consequence of the IFRS 3 renewal in 2008, the amount of goodwill that the acquirer can record during M&A became much wider, as even the non-controlling interest is now included in the target firm's goodwill. In the same way, managers could exploit the flexibility of this discretionary accrual through earnings management practices in order to increase financial year income, representing a deterioration of information asymmetry.

Moreover, according to IFRS 3, goodwill is not subject to amortization but only to a yearly (at least) impairment test. This means that managers who wish to disclose a high level of income may be more likely to compensate for the loss of goodwill value by adopting unethical accounting policies. They might include increasing goodwill initial value (Detzen & Zulch, 2012) or reducing fair depreciation and amortization. In this way, IFRS 3 contributes to a system of accounting regulation that leaves room for extensive discretionary choices, which could be exploited by managers to gain a personal advantage over third parties such as investors and financiers (Landsman, 2007), as "*discretionary valuation of intangible assets translates into discretion regarding the recognition of goodwill*" (Detzen & Zulch, 2012, p. 107). This paper therefore attempts to analyse whether financial market competition may have incentivized managers to engage in earnings management practices involving goodwill recognition and other discretionary accruals during the decade immediately following the 2008 updating of IFRS 3 in relation to the accounting treatment of Business Combinations as in M&A.

LITERATURE REVIEW AND HYPOTHESIS DEVELOPMENT

Competition

Within the accounting literature, competition has always attracted considerable interest, as it can be determined by many factors and exerts a significant influence on national economic well-being. Numerous accounts of the relationship between competition and firm performance (Caves, 1980; Porter, 1990; Green & Mayes, 1991; Nickell, 1996) note the opposition between two analytical perspectives. While some of these studies suggest that product market competition promotes efficient allocation of resources (Caves, 1980; Porter, 1990; Nickell, 1996), others assert the exact contrary, attributing firms' economic inefficiency and ethical crises to competitive pressures from marketplace structures and competitors (Green & Mayes, 1991). Given this profound divergence of findings in relation to the consequences of competition for strategic business and accounting choices, there is clearly a need to extend the scope of such research. A high level of market competition creates the conditions for improvement of firms' production processes and profitability, reducing costs and differentiating the offering system (Porter, 1990).

However, other findings suggest new negative interpretations of the potential effects of market competition, encompassing issues of information asymmetry and moral hazard (Milgrom & Roberts, 1992). On this view, managers are more likely to exploit the discretionary space for accounting and business decisions where there is strong external competitive pressure (Christie, Joye, & Watts, 2006). According to this interpretation, competition promotes greater managerial discretion. For example, Shleifer (2004) claimed that market competition between firms causes unethical management practices in the short term, including the use of child labour, corruption and accounting manipulation. Managers of competitive firms facing high market expectations have strong incentives to increase share prices through misrepresentation of real earnings results, and "*these accounting tricks in fact represent a conscious attempt to manipulate shareholder beliefs*" (Shleifer, 2004, p. 416). These unethical creative accounting practices serve to reduce the cost of capital; managers' compensation increases and companies ultimately endure. In fact, "*without creative accounting, their cost of capital might have been too high for them to survive*" (Shleifer, 2004, p. 416). The potential cost of enduring in a challenging context, in which financial results define a firm's success or lack of success, is the damage that managers may inflict on accounting quality and disclosure informativeness by resorting to earnings management. Cummins and Nyman (2005) found support for the thesis that perceived competitive pressure can lead managers to make inefficient business and accounting decisions, reflected in the quality of information disclosure. As one of the effects of competition is increasing volatility of cash flows (Irvine & Pontiff, 2009) because of precarious income capacity, managers seek to protect the firm's reputation and market value by manipulating earnings to smooth income.

While much of the existing research focuses on the negative effects of competition on market efficiency and managerial conduct, it remains a possibility that competition may have positive long-term consequences. Shleifer (2004) considered the possibility that competition over time might promote market efficiency and growth, and that managers might not therefore feel compelled to resort to unethical behaviours. In the same manner, Li (2010) found support for the hypothesized double impact of product market competition. As competition is seen to be an important determinant of corporate decisions and disclosure strategies, Li (2010) suggested that, depending on the nature of competition from entrants or existing rivals, managers might or might not be motivated to manipulate financial informativeness. Ultimately, the empirical evidence is that competition generally increases disclosure quality, but the heterogeneity of research approaches and results highlights the need for further research on the consequences of product market competition, especially in relation to types and modalities of strategic accounting decisions.

Over time, the global financial crisis provided empirical evidence of managers' deliberate attempts to manipulate financial information to convince market participants about the economic performance of auspicious firms. The stream of research investigating determinants of earnings management has illuminated the potential relationship between product market competition and earnings manipulation inside firms (Balakrishnan & Cohen, 2009; Cheng, Man, & Yi, 2013; Markarian & Santalò, 2014, Laksmana & Yang 2014; Karuna, Subramanyam, & Tian, 2015; Kordestani & Mohammadi, 2016; Shi, Sun, & Zhang, 2017). Earnings management can be defined as the "*process of taking deliberate actions within the constraints of general accepted accounting principles (GAAP) so as to bring about a desired level of reported earnings*" (Koumanakos, Siriopoulos, & Georgopoulos, 2005, p. 663). On this perspective, all accounting choices that infringe regulatory accounting systems in order to deliberately manipulate the information content of financial reports can be linked to earnings management practices.

Throughout the existing literature, there is as yet no agreed interpretation of the role of competition in strategic choices related to earnings manipulation and disclosure, and there are two competing perspectives on the association between product market competition and earnings management. Some argue that when the level of product market competition between firms is high, more companies tend to compete to acquire limited capital funds (Balakrishnan & Cohen, 2009), and managers resort to earnings manipulation in order to exceed market expectations and forecasts. In this way, competition impacts negatively on accounting quality by prompting recourse to accrual-based earnings management (e.g. Hermalin & Weisback, 2007; Karuna, 2007; Bagnoli & Watts 2010; Karuna, Subramanyam, & Tian 2012; Karuna, Subramanyam, & Tian, 2015; Kordestani & Mohammadi, 2016). According to this perspective, managers may be more likely to manipulate financial disclosure of income capacity for the fiscal year in order to secure the attention of market participants and sources of finance, as financiers and investors decide to allocate money to economic activities characterized by positive prospective income capacity.

On the other hand, others have argued that competition can enhance the legibility and transparency of financial disclosure by disciplining managers to act in the interests of shareholders (e.g. Grullon & Michaely, 2007; Balakrishnan & Cohen, 2009; Marciukaityte & Park, 2009; Guadalupe & Perez-Gonzalez, 2010; Li, 2010; Cheng, Man, & Yi, 2013; Laksmana & Yang, 2014). On this view, the desire to protect the firm's reputation and market share value disincentivizes manipulation of accounting items, as the damage caused by unethical accounting behaviour in a competitive industry may exceed any advantage of earnings manipulation.

Competition in the listed market, attracting funds from investors, advising stakeholders on the profitability of a business combination and exceeding shareholders' high expectations are among the most common explanations of earnings manipulation during M&A. The present study finds support for the idea that managers of companies involved in M&A are more likely to resort to earnings management practices involving discretionary accruals when market competition is high. In particular, it is assumed that discretionary accruals manipulations (such as goodwill) are designed to misrepresent economic performance as better than it actually is.

Goodwill: A Discretionary Accrual to Manage Earnings During M&A

Business combinations are strategic operations of economic relevance to both acquirer and acquiree companies as "*corporate events that often have a considerable impact on an acquirer's financial posi-*

tion and on the public's perception of the merging companies" (Detzen & Zulch, 2012, p. 107). Business combinations represent critical situations for an accurate accounting practice.

Because the transforming effects of M&A on shareholding structure, corporate identity and governance mechanisms can destabilize a company's economic and financial balance, such as future earnings and cash flows, disclosure quality is crucial for market participants in these transactions. The ancient "disclosure theory" (Verrecchia, 1983; Dye, 1985) is among the most widely used models of the quality and depth of financial information provided to the market. This advocates that managers are much more likely to reveal good news, as this may impact positively on stock price, and to hide bad news by reducing disclosure transparency, even engaging in accounting misrepresentations to avoid negative market reaction. The focus on this particular item reflects a view of goodwill (or badwill) as a mandatory economic consequence of the M&A process, as well as the subjectivity of any such evaluation.

Some recent accounting researches documented that business combinations could be exploited by managers for making accounting manipulations. During the accounting stages of business combinations, the fair value- based evaluation of assets and liabilities of target firm could create enough discretional space for a precise accounting strategy of income up warding or down warding, for example through the goodwill recognition. Coherently with this assumption, the assets book value of target firm tends to increase during M&A, since the target's transaction-implied value, composed of fair value of net assets plus goodwill, typically exceeds its pre-merger book value (Custodio, 2014). In fact, empirical evidence demonstrated that in a period of widespread reduction in market value Italian companies recurred to goodwill-based accounting strategies inside financial statements (Onesti & Romano, 2012; Caruso, Ferrari & Pisano, 2016). Moreover, the passage under IAS 36 rule from the accounting practice of goodwill amortization to goodwill impairment determined an increasing level of discretional space when defining the goodwill residual value, encouraging directors to use goodwill impairment testing for manipulating earnings.

The present paper takes the view that manipulating an increase in goodwill as a form of earnings management can be seen as a strategic (and unethical) choice to disclose good news in order to improve a firm's reputation and to attract funds from investors. It follows that unethical practices of recognition and upward evaluation of goodwill may reflect executives' desire to reassure the market about the economic convenience or profitability of a given business combination and to communicate the solidity of firm income capacity despite changes in governance and proprietary structures.

In short, while motivations for unethical earnings management behaviour of this kind may differ, they share the objective of dishonestly protecting corporate or CEO interests (Detzen & Zulch, 2012; Shalev, Zhang, & Zhang, 2013). Benefits derived from accounting recording of higher goodwill may relate not only to the administrative period of business combination but also to income in future years. According to Shalev, Zhang and Zhang's (2013) empirical findings, executive compensation packages involving earnings-based bonuses make it more likely that managers will manipulate earnings by over-allocating goodwill to the purchase price. As tangible and intangible assets serve to reduce earnings through depreciation and amortization, and goodwill cannot be amortized but only tested periodically for impairment, managers can conceal goodwill impairment and increase post-acquisition earnings (Hayn & Hughes, 2006; Ramanna & Watts, 2012; Shalev, Zhang, & Zhang, 2013).

The empirical evidence suggests that there is sometimes a correspondence between the disclosed portion of the purchase price allocated to goodwill and the real amount of unexpressed income capacity, along with the impact of goodwill on economic results for the year. In this way, goodwill can be used as a discretionary accrual to increase earnings and exceed analysts' expectations.

This paper posits that managers of M&A acquirers may be more likely to overestimate goodwill in order to manipulate net profit for the year upward in highly competitive financial market. In the literature, upward manipulation of goodwill is not always interpreted as a positive consequence for M&A or as an accounting item that will encourage financiers. For example, in his empirical analyses of the causes and consequences of disclosure level, Shalev (2009) found that "*the level of disclosure on business combinations decreases with abnormal portions of the purchase price allocated to goodwill*" because "*abnormal portions of the purchase price allocated to goodwill could, on average, be associated with (1) overpayment and/or, (2) overstatement of goodwill in the allocation to avoid amortization expense, both of which could be considered bad news for investors*" (p. 240). As there is as yet no definitive interpretation of the effectiveness of managing goodwill to manipulate earnings or to communicate reliable information to the market, the present paper investigates whether managers in Italian-listed companies involved in M&A operations between 2009 and 2017 used goodwill as a discretionary accrual to manipulate earnings.

Hypothesis One: Companies involved in M&A use goodwill as a discretionary accrual to manage earnings.

Financial Market Competition and Accrual-Based Earnings Management During M&A

According to the literature, there is a strong link between legal and market macroeconomic conditions and listed companies' recourse to M&A strategies (Bergstresser, Desai, & Rauh, 2003; Shleifer & Vishny, 2003; Shleifer, 2004; Rossi & Volpin, 2004; Bens, Goodman, & Neamtiu, 2012). In an empirical investigation of the determinants of M&A choices across countries, Rossi and Volpin (2004) reported evidence of the role of legal and regulatory proxies in the reallocation of control and funds. They found that there is a higher volume of M&A activity in countries with stronger shareholder protection and better accounting standards because efficient accounting regulation can improve the quality and reliability of information disclosure. In markets characterized by strong protection of shareholders rights, managers are more likely to resort to M&A, as radical changes in proprietary and governance structure do not frighten market investors or minority shareholders (Rossi & Volpin, 2004). Firms from countries with weak legal protection for minority shareholders are less likely to resort to M&A and are more likely to list abroad (Pagano, Roelle, & Zechner, 2002; Reese & Weisbach, 2002).

The perspective adopted here follows Bergstresser, Desai and Rauh (2003), Shleifer and Vishny (2003) and Shleifer (2004). When competitive pressure is intense and market participants are strongly focused on stock price because of a forthcoming or current M&A, managers are more likely to manipulate earnings by using discretionary accruals in disclosures to external stakeholders such as investors and financiers to exaggerate economic performance and so achieve the best possible results for the M&A (Bergstresser, Desai, & Rauh, 2003). As "'*excessively' high levels of incentives to increase stock prices could create too much pressure, which results in misreporting*" (Bens, Goodman, & Neamtiu, 2012, p. 842), this attitude degrades both ethical values and overall accounting quality. According to Shleifer and Vishny (2003), the negative effects of competition on earnings quality occur not only when executing a merger or acquisition but also during the planning stage: "*for many mature firms a high equity valuation was the matter of survival as an independent company, rather than being acquired for stock by company with a higher valuation*" (Shleifer, 2004, p. 416). The motivations for manipulating informativeness of disclosure during M&A may relate both to corporate interests and to personal incentives. Bens, Goodman and Neamtiu (2012) reported that managers misrepresent financial statements through earnings management in the post-investment period as a way of handling investment-related pressure, which might be interpreted as the increased pressure on managers trying to retain their jobs after M&A.

According to Shalev, Zhang and Zhang (2013), "*mergers and acquisitions are critical corporate events, affecting both future business activities and financial reporting*" (p. 819). The most recent research questions made efforts of abstraction and looked for empirical confirmation regarding the possibility that the determinants of managerial goodwill-based strategic accounting choices could be brought back not only to the individual company characteristics, but also to the dynamics of the whole sector. Stenheim and Madsen (2016) have found that goodwill manipulation occurs much more frequently in companies that operate in those sectors with a downward trend of ROAs, in companies that record low returns and in companies that have high book to market ratios in the period prior managing of goodwill. The present paper augments the scarce current literature on determinants of misrepresentation in financial reports during business combinations by illuminating the role of financial market competition among Italian-listed companies involved in strategic M&A operations between 2009 and 2017 in earnings management practices based on discretionary accruals manipulation.

Hypothesis Two: The level of financial market competition exerts a positive and direct influence on recourse to earnings management practices employing discretionary accruals among companies involved in M&A.

METHOD

Sampling and Data Description

To test the above hypotheses, the sampling started from the collection of all active Italian-listed companies from January 1, 2009 and December 31, 2017 for a total amount of 327 companies object of observation. We refined the sample by removing 70 companies from the finance and banking sectors, as their accounting regulatory system follows different rules. In the end, we extracted only those 197 companies that announced and completed operations of M&A (acquirers and targets) during the period under investigation, eliminating cases in which M&A activity was only rumoured. This cross-sectional procedure produced a sample of 197 active Italian-listed companies. Financial data and ratios were extracted from AIDA, a comprehensive database of accounting information on Italian companies.

Data Analysis

Accrual-based earnings management practices are measured using a cross-sectional statistical model based on discretionary accruals. Discretionary accruals are calculated as the difference between total accruals and predicted non-discretionary accruals, which are estimated using the cross-sectional modified Jones model with the changing cash flows from operations (Jones, 1991; Dechow, Sloan, & Sweeney, 1995; Kasznik, 1999; Siregar & Utama, 2008). The empirical analysis is grounded on the assumption that the discretionary component of total accruals expresses a manager's recourse to earnings manipulation, and that this practice damages disclosure quality and reliability. The earlier Jones model (Jones, 1991) estimated non-discretionary accruals by introducing both changing revenues (ΔREV_t) and property, plant and equipment (PPE_t). However, it was limited by the assumption that changing revenues could be interpreted as non-discretionary accruals without earnings management practices. Instead, many studies have shown that revenues are useful tools of manipulating earnings and disclosure informativeness (Turner et al., 2001; Dechow & Schrand, 2004; Stubben, 2010). In the Jones model, some non-discretionary accruals may be influenced by earnings management practices rather than by production decisions, with consequent contamination of the analysis. Excluding the hypothesis that revenues are immune from unethical accounting strategies, Dechow, Sloan and Sweeney (1995) estimated non-discretionary accruals in the event period using a new regression function containing the changing receivables (ΔREC_t). The modified Jones model (Dechow, Sloan and Sweeney, 1995) is widely used in accounting research and performs better than others in terms of significance of results (McNichols, 2000). Nevertheless, it imposes some restrictions in detecting earnings management, as it does not consider the effect that changing cash flows from the firm's operating activities ($\Delta CFO_{t)}$ may have on strategic decisions to manipulate earnings (Kasznik, 1999; Siregar & Utama, 2008). Because cash flows have direct monetary implications for income, they cannot be used for income smoothing purposes. According to Kasznik (1997, p.14), "*to the extent that the temporary component of cash flows has a nondiscretionary effect on total accruals, some of this nondiscretionary component can be extracted by orthogonalizing total accruals with respect to changes in cash flow from operations*"; it follows that ΔCFO_t should be introduced in the model that detects total accruals (1). In the accounting literature, this is preferred to many other accrual-based models because of its high explanatory power in terms of adjusted R^2 (Siregar & Utama, 2008). To facilitate accurate detection of discretionary accruals, the present analysis adopted the cross-sectional modified Jones model (Jones, 1991; Dechow, Sloan & Sweeney, 1995) with ΔCFO_t as described in Kasznik (1999) and Siregar and Utama (2008) and sometimes known as "Kasznik's Model":

$$TA_t / A_{t-1} = \alpha + \beta_1 1/ A_{t-1} + \beta_2 (\Delta REV_t - \Delta REC_t) / A_{t-1} + \beta_3 (PPE_t) / A_{t-1} + \beta_4 \Delta CFO_{t+} \varepsilon_{t\,(1)}$$

Total accruals (TA_t) are expressed as the difference between accounting earnings and operating cash flows ($TA_t = EARN_t\text{-}CFO_t$). Earnings proxy ($EARN_t$) is expressed as net income before extraordinary items, and cash flows from operation proxy (CFO_t) is the net cash flow from the firm's operating activities. Change in net revenues proxy $^{(\Delta REV}t)$ is the difference between revenues in year t and those in year t-1. Change in accounts receivable proxy $(^{\Delta REC}t)$ is the difference between receivables in year t and those in year t-1. Property, plant and equipment (PPE_t) is incorporated to control for normal depreciation expenses. $^{\Delta CFO}t$ is the difference between cash flows from operations in year t and those in year t-1. To reduce heteroscedasticity in the data, all variables in the regression model are scaled by the lagged value of their assets (A_{t-1}). According to the general approach adopted in estimating discretionary accruals by means of a regression model, non-discretionary accruals are the unexplained part of total accruals in equation (1). Non-discretionary accruals (NDAt) are the fitted values (estimated values) from the above model as expressed in equation (2) (Shi, Sun, & Zhang, 2017). Discretionary accruals are the difference between total accruals and estimated non-discretionary accruals as in equation (3). They are defined as "residuals".

$$NDA_t = \varepsilon_{t=} TA_t/A_{t-1} - [\alpha + \beta_1 1/A_{t-1} + \beta_2 (\Delta REV_t - \Delta REC_t) /A_{t-1} + \beta_3 (PPE_t) /A_{t-1} + \beta_4 \Delta CFO_t] \quad (2)$$

$$_{DAt=} TA_t / A_{t-1} - NDA_t \quad (3)$$

In line with the existing literature (Balsam, Krishnan & Yang, 2003; Jenkins, Kane, & Velury, 2006; Ding & Jia, 2012), the absolute value of discretionary accruals is used to highlight the magnitude of accruals and recourse to income smoothing strategies rather than the direction of such manipulation; that is, the search does not take account of the aims of overstating or understating income.

The two hypotheses are tested using the following linear regression model.

$$|DA_t| = \alpha + \beta_{1GWt+} \beta_{2HHIt+} \beta_{3MTBt+} \beta_{4EARNt+} \beta_{5CFOt+} \beta_{6ROAt+} \beta_7 NOA_t + \beta_{8ATAt} + \beta_{9EBTt} + \varepsilon_t$$

where DA_t is the absolute value of discretionary accruals to total assets of the year t; GW_t is the natural logarithm of goodwill for year t; HHI_t is the Herfindhal-Hirschman Index for year t; MTB_t is the market-to-book ratio for year t; $EARN_t$ is the profit (or loss) to total assets for year t; CFO_t is the cash flow from operations to total assets for year t; ROA_t is the ratio of return on assets to total assets for year t; NOA_t is the net operating assets ratio for year t; ATA_t is the natural logarithm of total accruals to total assets; and EBT_t is the index of earnings before interest and tax to total assets for year t.

Table 1 presents the descriptive statistics for variables introduced in the model and observed cross-sectionally for the period 2009–2017.

In the following linear regression model (OLS), the dependent variable is the absolute value of discretionary accruals to total assets, a measure of recourse to accrual-based earnings management practices. In this way, the investigation of discretionary accruals does not take into consideration the direction of income smoothing strategies (Balsam, Krishnan, & Yang, 2003; Jenkins, Kane & Velury, 2006; Ding & Jia, 2012). The possibility that companies involved in M&A between 2009 and 2017 resorted to goodwill recognition and impairment as a strategy for managing earnings has been investigated empirically by reference to the goodwill level for year t (GW_t). On this view, managers can exploit the vulnerability of accounting practices in M&A by using goodwill recognition and impairment for opportunistic manipulation of earnings and disclosure informativeness. As attributing a high value to goodwill from M&A operations means increasing the level of income, and vice versa, the paper expects a positive coefficient for GW_t. According to IFRS 3, goodwill is not subject to amortization but only to a yearly impairment test, and managers who wish to disclose better economic results could attribute a smaller goodwill impairment to fiscal year t, in financial statements incorporating high levels of goodwill. Managers would also be more likely to compensate for the potential loss of goodwill value by resorting to unethi-

Table 1. Descriptive statistics

Variable	*Obs*	*Mean*	*Std. Dev.*	*Min*	*Max*
DA	1704	*0.0000154*	*0.0002789*	*0*	*0.0111404*
HHI	*1971*	*0.0000173*	*0.000399*	*0*	*0.0170881*
MTB	*1653*	*0.0016173*	*0.0036996*	*-0.1060615*	*0.0269809*
EARN	*1673*	*0.0001397*	*0.4197496*	*-15.97325*	*2.569838*
CFO	*1673*	*0.0239591*	*0.3784345*	*-14.18114*	*2.688853*
ROA	*1674*	*-0.00001*	*0.00047*	*-0.0190309*	*0.0021912*
NOA	*1674*	*0.4396356*	*0.2536324*	*-1.987757*	*1.018906*
ATA	*1704*	*0.0001858*	*0.002255*	*-0.0840414*	*0.0241011*
EBT	*1673*	*0.0189363*	*0.1145332*	*-0.9896328*	*2.975639*

cal accounting policies such as increasing initial goodwill value as a consequence of M&A (Detzen & Zulch, 2012) or reducing the amount of fair depreciation and amortization for year t. As high goodwill or reduction of impaired value could both serve as strategies to manage earnings, the expected result is a positive coefficient for (GW_t).

Analysis of the positive or negative direct influence of competition between Italian-listed companies on recourse to earnings management through discretionary accruals is conducted by introducing regression model variables measuring market competition, including $_{HHI}$, $_{MTBt}$ and (indirectly) $_{EARNt}$ and ROA_t. The empirical data confirm that, in international listed markets, M&A announcements can engender a negative reaction if investors believe that managers have made suboptimal strategic decisions. The first proxy used to measure financial market competition is the Herfindahl-Hirschman Index (HHI). Although the HHI is a direct measure of industry concentration (Cheng, Man, Yi, 2013; Fosu, 2013; Datta, Iskandar-Datta, & Singh, 2013), it is also widely used to assess the level of competition between companies (Berger, Klapper, & Turk-Ariss, 2008; Li, 2010; Karuna, Subramanyam, & Tian, 2012; Karuna, Subramanyam, & Tian, 2015; Laksmana & Yang, 2014) because it can capture single-firm competitive pressure in the market. HHI is calculated as the square of market share of each company, where market share is the ratio of a firm's sales to the sum of sales of all firms in the same market. A low HHI corresponds to low industry concentration and high market competition; according to economic theory, when there are few companies in the market (high market concentration), competition is more likely to be weak. HHI is a measure of market concentration and is inversely related to market competition (Laksmana & Yang, 2014). For present purposes, HHI is constructed using annual data for Italian-listed companies across a broad spectrum of industries (other than financial and insurance). Although there is some empirical evidence that competition has positive effects on market efficiency and earnings quality (Laksmana & Yang, 2014; Marciukaityte & Park, 2009), strengthening financial market competition is expected to deter managers from managing earnings and overstating performance, as a competitive context highlights the differences between efficient and non-efficient companies (Markarian & Santalò, 2014). It follows that the coefficient of HHI is expected to be negative.

Another proxy for market competition between Italian-listed companies is Market-to-Book ratio (or Price-to-Book ratio) for year t, which is a financial metric of a company's current market value in relation to its book value. As this measures the extent to which a company is underestimated or overestimated in the market, it is one of the most widely used methods of assessing a company's stock value. Based on how much equity investors pay for each euro in net assets, it is adopted to measure investors' perception of a company's stock value. A firm's competitive positioning in the financial market is influenced by market-to-book ratio because "*firms with higher market-to-book ratio are, on average, more profitable and face lower borrowing costs*" (Chen & Zhao, 2006, p. 254). During business combinations, firms that come to market as high performing (high levels of MTB_t and $EARN_t$, firm profit for year t) may be exposed to higher competitive pressure and may be more likely to resort to earnings manipulation practices in order to preserve shareholders' positive expectations and attract funds from investors. The coefficient of MTB_t is therefore expected to be positive.

Recognition and impairment of goodwill and market competition are not the only factors that can influence recourse to accrual-based earnings management practices. For that reason, some control variables have been introduced to the regression model in order to isolate proxies that might prompt managers to adopt unethical accounting decisions (e.g. $EARN_t$, CFO_t, ROA_t, NOA_t, EBT_t and ATA_t).

In the financial market, level of earnings disclosed ($EARN_t$) exerts a direct influence on investment decision-making among market participants and has been developed as a tool for measuring a firm's stock value (e.g. Ohlson, 1995). This paper adopts the $EARN_t$ proxy to investigate the effect of performance and competition in the financial market on earnings management. As significant profits strengthen investors' perceptions of listed companies in terms of prospective income capacity and potential profitability of investment, it is generally expected that weak economic performance will deter managers from adopting unethical accounting strategies to increase or smooth income level for corporate or personal purposes. A negative coefficient is expected for $EARN_t$.

CFO_t (cash flow from operations for year t) is a measure of the amount of money that a company can bring in through its core business activities. As operating cash flow is the result of incoming and outgoing monetary manifestations linked to characteristic business activities, it can be tracked and is not easily manipulated. A higher level of cash flow means lower recourse to earnings manipulation (Kasznik, 1999; Chen, Firth, Gao, & Rui, 2006; Dechow, Sloan, & Sweeney, 1995; DeFond & Jiambalvo 1994; Yang, Lai, & Tan, 2008). The coefficient of CFO_t is expected to be negatively related to discretionary accruals.

ROA_t (return on assets for year t) measures individual company financial performance (Li, 2010; Karuna, Subramanyam, & Tian, 2012; Bens, Goodman, & Neamtiu, 2012; Laksmana & Yang, 2014; Shi, Sun, & Zhang, 2017). According to previous accounting research, firms that disclose weak economic performance at the end of the year are more likely to resort to earnings manipulation strategies such as depreciation and amortization in order to manage financial informativeness and influence stakeholder decision-making (Chen, Firth, Gao, & Rui, 2006). In line with most of the accounting literature, then, the coefficient of ROA_t is expected to be negative.

NOA_t is the proxy that measures a firm's net operating assets for year t and is a useful comparison tool when examining firms' financial structures and self-financing capacity. As a high level of NOA_t is good information to deliver to market, the expected result is a positive coefficient. EBT_t is the firm's profit before tax and interest for year t and indicates the relationship between managers' use of discretionary accruals and economic performance deriving from non-extraordinary activities. Finally, ATA_t (total accruals for year t) indicates whether major total accruals determine the prevalence of discretionary accruals relative to those that are non-discretionary.

RESEARCH RESULTS AND DISCUSSION

Tables 2, **3** and **4** show the results of linear regression.

The empirical evidence supports the thesis that managers of listed firms involved in business combinations such as M&A adopt discretionary accrual-based strategies based on recognition and impairment of goodwill in order to manipulate earnings. The positive coefficient of GW_t indicates that an increasing level of goodwill is associated with greater recourse to discretionary accruals. The decision to report a high level of goodwill after concluding a business combination may reflect a willingness to overstate performance in order to attract funds from investors and reassure the market about the profitability of such a business combination. If the level of goodwill remains relatively (and abnormally) constant, this may mean that appropriate impairment politics have not been implemented over time to avoid loading income with too many operating costs, as they can depress economic performance. The empirical results confirm that Italian-listed companies involved in M&A may be more likely to overstate goodwill to indicate the positive effects of M&A strategies and to reduce amortization charges in subsequent years. Moreover, this creates the right accounting conditions for showing better actual and prospective economic performance to market participants, especially shareholders. Lending empirical support to

Table 2. Results of linear regression (1)

DA	Coef.	Std. Err.	t	P>|t|	[95% Conf. Interval]	
GW	2.52e-06	3.46e-07	7.29	0.000	1.84e-06	3.20e-06
HHI	-0.0055466	0.000037	-0.97	0.330	-0.0167317	0.0056386
MTB	0.0006333	0.0000215	3.20	0.001	0.0002447	0.001022
EARN	0.000208	0.0000413	5.03	0.000	0.0001269	0.0002892
CFO	-0.0001873	0.000037	-5.06	0.000	-0.00026	-0.0001146
ROA	2.045214	0.0972814	21.02	0.000	1.854132	2.236296
NOA	9.03e-06	5.82e-06	1.55	0.121	-2.40e-06	0.0000205
ATA	0.1309674	0.0031285	41.86	0.000	0.1248224	0.1371124
EBT	-0.0000733	0.0000215	-3.40	0.001	-0.0001155	-0.000031
ε_t	-0.0000297	4.35e-06	-6.82	0.000	-0.0000383	-0.0000212

Note to Table 2.

DA_t is the absolute value of discretionary accruals to total assets for year t; GW_t is the natural logarithm of goodwill for year t; HHI_t is the Herfindhal-Hirschman Index for year t, MTB_t is the market-to-book ratio for year t, $EARN_t$ is the profit (or loss) to total assets for year t; CFO_t is the cash flow from operations to total assets for year t; ROA_t is the return on assets ratio for year t, NOA_t is the net operating assets ratio for year t; ATA_t is natural logarithm of total accruals to total assets; and EBT_t is the index of earnings before interest and tax to total asset for year t.

Table 3. Results of linear regression (2)

Number of obs	569
F(9, 559)	561.11
Prob > F	0.0000
R-squared	0.9003
Adj R-squared	0.8987
Root MSE	2.3e-05

Table 4. Results of hypothesis testing

Hypothesis 1	**Companies Involved in M&A Use Goodwill as a Discretionary Accrual to Manage Earnings.**	**Supported**	$\beta_{1} > 0$	***P = 0.000***
Hypothesis 2	The level of financial market competition exerts a positive and direct influence on recourse to earnings management practices employing discretionary accruals among companies involved in M&A.	**Supported**	$\beta_{2} < 0$ $\beta_{3} > 0$	***P = 0.330*** ***P = 0.001***

some earlier studies (Detzen & Zulch, 2012), the present findings confirm that managers can exploit IFRS 3 regulatory flexibility to use goodwill recognition and impairment as a discretionary accrual to manipulate earnings during M&A.

There is also evidence of a direct relationship between the level of financial market competition as perceived by Italian-listed companies during M&A and recourse to accrual-based earnings manipulation strategies. This view finds empirical support in the negative coefficient of HHI_t and the positive coefficient of MTB_t. The former indicates the potential negative effects of strengthening competition on financial disclosure quality and reliability; when HHI_t diminishes as a result of a company's small market share, market concentration reduces and competition increases (Laksmana & Yang, 2014). As a direct consequence, managers are more likely to use accrual-based manipulation strategies to disclose better economic performance and attract funds from investors, especially during business combinations where market participants are focusing on profitable outcomes (Bergstresser, Desai, & Rauh, 2003). The positive coefficient of MTB_t supports the same conclusion; when a company registers an increasing price-to-book ratio, this raises stakeholders' expectations in relation to future gains and income capacity. The consequent exacerbation of financial competition among listed companies for external grants creates the right conditions for recourse to opportunistic earnings manipulation practices.

The positive coefficient of the $EARN_t$ proxy indicates that when Italian-listed companies report good economic performance at year end during M&A operations, they are more likely to manage earnings through recourse to discretionary accruals. The results of this linear regression are not as expected. While previous studies have explored deep and hidden influences on managerial decisions to manage earnings upward or downward in cases of poor outcomes, the present findings indicate that good economic performance in the Italian listed market burdens managers with the weight of shareholders' expectations. This in turn leads to unethical accounting practices such as adjusting the last line of the income statement to meet or exceed earnings targets. Contrary to expectations, weak economic performance does not serve to deter earnings manipulation of income capacity; indeed, the positive $EARN_t$ coefficient could be seen to indicate major recourse to earnings manipulation due to strengthening of stock market competition and the increasing attractiveness of financing activities in such companies.

The negative coefficient of CFO_t confirms that monetary components of income reduce the accounting margin for earnings manipulation, as cash flows are strictly traceable and cannot easily be used for income smoothing. Higher levels of cash flow lead to minor recourse to manipulation of discretionary accruals among Italian-listed companies involved in M&A.

Although diverging from expectations concerning the positive effect of strong performance on earnings quality, the positive coefficient of ROA_t accords exactly with the interpretation of the $EARNt_t$ coefficient. Disclosing good economic performance to market participants (in terms of a high return on assets ratio and profit) both intensifies competition between listed firms in the financial market and creates strong expectations for future results to be exceeded, if necessary by misstatements in financial reports. The results of statistical modelling demonstrate that good performance has deleterious effects on earnings quality among Italian-listed companies involved in M&A during the period 2009–2017. The positive coefficient of NOA_t confirms the same view.

The positive coefficient of ATA_t means that strong recourse to total accruals in financial disclosure may indicate an increase in earnings management practices through discretionary accruals.

The negative coefficient of EBT_t contrasts with previous performance proxies ($EARN_t$, ROA_t) but does not invalidate the empirically supported interpretations of the above variables.

The results of this analysis of all Italian-listed companies involved in M&A during 2009–2017 align with the authors' expectations. Goodwill is effectively a discretionary tool that can be used to manipulate earnings (Detzen & Zulch, 2012; Shalev, Zhang, & Zhang, 2013), as goodwill recognition and impairment can be used to manipulate financial statements (Hayn & Hughes, 2006; Ramanna & Watts, 2012; Shalev, Zhang, & Zhang, 2013). The present findings do not clarify whether such earnings manipulations seek opportunistic personal economic advantage or improvement of a company's stock market reputation to attract funds from investors (Shalev, Zhang, & Zhang, 2013; Detzen & Zulch, 2012). These results conflict with the view expressed by some researchers that high goodwill recognition should not be used for earnings management purposes because this can damage company prestige in the eyes of stakeholders (Shalev, 2009).

As mentioned above, while there are many studies of how business combinations can affect disclosure quality in relation to goodwill, the possibility that specific macroeconomic conditions such as competition might impact directly on the quality and reliability of accounting practices has not yet been examined in depth. Some previous studies have posited a connection between earnings management and competition among companies involved in M&A (Bergstresser, Desai, & Rauh, 2003; Shleifer & Vishny, 2003; Shleifer, 2004). In this regard, the present paper expands the scope of existing research. Specifically, the empirical results support the thesis that the level of financial market competition between Italian-listed companies exerts a positive and direct influence on recourse to earnings manipulation practices during business combinations; the more competition intensifies, the more managers smooth income for specific personal and corporate economic purposes. While such behaviour aligns in part with expectations (Bergstresser, Desai, & Rauh, 2003; Bens, Goodman, & Neamtiu, 2012), the additional component is that managers adopt discretionary accrual-based strategies to achieve these aims.

CONCLUSION

The aim of the present study is to investigate whether Italian-listed companies involved in M&A during the period 2009 – 2017 manipulated reported earnings through recourse to discretionary accruals as a response to financial market competition, with particular reference to goodwill recognition and impairment. This interest in how competition might influence earnings management practices in the financial market follows considerable research interest in disclosure quality and reliability in business combinations (e.g. Bens, Goodman, & Neamtiu, 2012). These strategic operations tend to create accounting conditions that prompt managers to pursue unethical manipulation practices because of pressures to reassure shareholders and financiers about the successful execution of such business combinations and the profitability of their investment.

The empirical findings confirmed that Italian-listed companies involved in M&A between 2009 and 2017 used goodwill recognition and impairment as discretionary accruals to manage earnings despite the updated IFRS 3 accounting regulations. The results also indicate that increasing financial market competition between Italian-listed companies prompted major recourse to earnings management through discretionary accruals.

Business combinations involve strategic decisions that are likely to modify business and corporate structure, impacting directly on disclosure quality. Although some studies have investigated the determinants of unethical managerial accounting practices during takeovers and mergers, there is still little evidence in relation to the potential positive or negative effects of financial market competition on earnings management. The paper contributes to the literature by bridging that gap, investigating the role of M&A in promoting earnings manipulation in the Italian listed market by using goodwill recognition and impairment to smooth income opportunistically. As this field of accounting research is still developing, the present findings contribute to its expansion by highlighting the potential relevance of macroeconomic conditions such as financial market competition in managers' discretionary accounting choices during M&A. In this way, the study can help stakeholders, shareholders and practitioners to address issues of disclosure quality and reliability during business combinations and how the discretionary space around goodwill recognition and impairment can be used to manipulate earnings.

The present paper has also some limitations. As the sample is confined to companies listed on the Italian stock market, it would be interesting to test the same research hypotheses among other European listed companies. Further studies might also usefully investigate any differences in earnings manipulation practices in pre-M&A and post-M&A accounting strategies, perhaps introducing some country-specific contextual variables. In conclusion, the present findings invite reflection on how IFRS regulation can be monitored and deployed to improve the overall quality and reliability of financial disclosure.

REFERENCES

Arletta, C., Coda Negozio, E., Di Diego, S., Fantoni, M., Fici, L., Imparato, A., …Zucca M. (2015). *PMI e M&A in Italia. Una strada sicura per la crescita.* Economia & Management, Milano, FrancoAngeli.

Badolato, P. G., Donelson, D. C., & Ege, M. (2014). Audit committee financial expertise and earnings management: The role of status. *Journal of Accounting and Economics*, *58*(2–3), 208–230. doi:10.1016/j.jacceco.2014.08.006

Bagnoli, M., & Watts, S. (2010). Oligopoly, disclosure, and earnings management. *The Accounting Review*, *85*(4), 1191–1214. doi:10.2308/accr.2010.85.4.1191

Balakrishnan, K., & Cohen, D. A. (2009). *Product market competition, financial accounting misreporting and corporate governance: Evidence from accounting restatements* (Working Paper). New York University.

Balsam, S., Krishnan, J., & Yang, J. S. (2003). Auditor industry specialization and earnings quality. *Auditing*, *22*(2), 71–97. doi:10.2308/aud.2003.22.2.71

Barth, M. E., Landsman, W. R., & Lang, M. H. (2008). International accounting standards and accounting quality. *Journal of Accounting Research*, *46*(3), 467–498. doi:10.1111/j.1475-679X.2008.00287.x

Bens, D. A., Goodman, T. H., & Neamtiu, M. (2012). Does investment-related pressure lead to misreporting? An analysis of reporting following M&A transactions. *The Accounting Review*, *87*(3), 839–865. doi:10.2308/accr-10210

Berger, A. N., Klapper, L. F., & Turk-Ariss, R. (2008). *Bank competition and financial stability*. Policy Research Working Paper No. 4696. World Bank.

Bergstresser, D., Desai, M., & Rauh, J. (2003). *The Gerstner Effect: managerial motivations and earnings manipulations*. Working Paper, Harvard Business School.

Burgstahler, D., Hail, L., & Leuz, C. (2004). *The importance of reporting incentives: Earnings management in European private and public firms* (Working Paper). Wharton Financial Institutions Center.

Bushman, R. D., & Piotroski, J. D. (2006). Financial reporting incentives for conservative accounting: The influence of legal and political institutions. *Journal of Accounting and Economics*, *42*(1–2), 107–148. doi:10.1016/j.jacceco.2005.10.005

Caruso, G. D., Ferrari, E. R., & Pisano, V. (2016). Earnings management and goodwill impairment: An empirical analysis in the Italian M&A context. *Journal of Intellectual Capital*, *17*(1), 120–147. doi:10.1108/JIC-09-2015-0081

Caves, R. E. (1980). Industrial organization, corporate strategy and structure. *Journal of Economic Literature*, *18*(1), 64–92.

Chen, L., Firth, M., Gao, D. N., & Rui, O. M. (2006). Ownership structure, corporate governance, and fraud: Evidence from China. *Journal of Corporate Finance*, *12*(3), 424–448. doi:10.1016/j.jcorpfin.2005.09.002

Chen, L., & Zhao, X. (2006). On the relation between the market-to-book ratio, growth opportunity, and leverage ratio. *Finance Research Letters*, *3*(4), 254. doi:10.1016/j.frl.2006.06.003

Cheng, P., Man, P., & Yi, C. H. (2013). The impact of product market competition on earnings quality. *Accounting and Finance*, *53*(1), 4. doi:10.1111/j.1467-629X.2011.00457.x

Christie, A., Joye, M., & Watts, R. L. (1989). *Organization of the firm: Theory and evidence*. Rochester, NY: Simon Graduate School of Business Administration. University of Rochester.

Cummins, J. G., & Nyman, I. (2005). The dark side of competitive pressure. *The Rand Journal of Economics*, *36*(2), 361–377.

Custodio, C. (2014). Mergers and Acquisitions Accounting and the Diversification Discount. *The Journal of Finance*, *69*(1), 219–240. doi:10.1111/jofi.12108

d'Italia, B. (2018). *Relazione annuale 2017*. Retrieved from http://www.bancaditalia.it/pubblicazioni/relazione-annuale/2017/rel_2017.pdf

Datta, S., Iskandar-Datta, M., & Singh, V. (2013). Product market power, industry structure, and corporate earnings management. *Journal of Banking & Finance*, *37*(8), 3273–3285. doi:10.1016/j.jbankfin.2013.03.012

Dechow, P., & Schrand, C. (2004). *Earnings quality*. Charlottesville, VA: CFA Institute Research Foundation.

Dechow, P. M., Sloan, R. G., & Sweeney, A. P. (1995). Detecting earnings management. *The Accounting Review*, *70*(2), 199.

Dechow, P. M., Weili, G., & Schrand, C. M. (2010). Understanding earnings quality: A review of proxies, their determinants and their consequences. *Journal of Accounting and Economics*, *50*(2–3), 344–401. doi:10.1016/j.jacceco.2010.09.001

DeFond, M. L., & Jiambalvo, J. (1994). Debt covenant violation and manipulation of accruals. *Journal of Accounting and Economics*, *17*(1–2), 145–176. doi:10.1016/0165-4101(94)90008-6

Detzen, D., & Zulch, H. (2012). Executive compensation and goodwill recognition under IFRS: Evidence from European mergers. *Journal of International Accounting, Auditing & Taxation*, *21*(2), 106–126. doi:10.1016/j.intaccaudtax.2012.07.002

Ding, R., & Jia, Y. (2012). Auditor mergers, audit quality and audit fees: Evidence from the PricewaterhouseCoopers merger in the UK. *Journal of Accounting and Public Policy*, *31*(1), 69–85. doi:10.1016/j.jaccpubpol.2011.08.002

Dye, R. A. (1985). Disclosure of nonproprietary information. *Journal of Accounting Research*, *23*(1), 123–145. doi:10.2307/2490910

Easterwood, C. M. (1998). Takeovers and incentives for earnings management: An empirical analysis. *Journal of Applied Business Research*, *14*(1), 29–47. doi:10.19030/jabr.v14i1.5726

Erickson, M., & Wang, S. (1999). Earnings management by acquiring firms in stock-for-stock mergers. *Journal of Accounting and Economics*, *27*(2), 149–176. doi:10.1016/S0165-4101(99)00008-7

European Central Bank. (2009). *Does it pay to have the Euro? Italy's politics and financial markets under the Lira and the Euro.* Working Paper Series, No. 1064, 1–41.

European Central Bank. (2017). *Business investment developments in the euro area since the crisis.* Retrieved from https://www.ecb.europa.eu/pub/pdf/other/eb201607_article02.en.pdf?e917ba5e5156495c3a382abf942e9e53

Filip, A., & Raffournier, B. (2014). Financial crisis and earnings management: The European evidence. *The International Journal of Accounting*, *49*(4), 455–478. doi:10.1016/j.intacc.2014.10.004

Fosu, S. (2013). Capital structure, product market competition, and firm performance: Evidence from South Africa. *The Quarterly Review of Economics and Finance*, *53*(2), 140–151. doi:10.1016/j.qref.2013.02.004

Green, A., & Mayes, D. (1991). Technical inefficiency in manufacturing industries. *Economic Journal (London)*, *101*(406), 523–538. doi:10.2307/2233557

Grullon, G., & Michaely, R. (2007). *Corporate payout policy and product market competition.* Working Paper. Retrieved from http://ssrn.com/abstract=972221

Guadalupe, M., & Perez-Gonzalez, F. (2010). *Competition and private benefits of control.* Working Paper. Retrieved from http://ssrn.com/abstract=890814

Hayn, C., & Hughes, P. J. (2006). Leading indicators of goodwill impairment. *Journal of Accounting, Auditing & Finance*, *21*(3), 223–265. doi:10.1177/0148558X0602100303

Healy, P. M., & Palepu, K. G. (2001). Information asymmetry, corporate disclosure, and the capital markets: A review of the empirical disclosure literature. *Journal of Accounting and Economics*, *31*(1–3), 405–440. doi:10.1016/S0165-4101(01)00018-0

Hermalin, B., & Weisback, M. (2007). *Transparency and corporate governance.* NBER working paper No. 12875.

IFRS. (2015). *Post-implementation Review of Review of IFRS 3 Business Combinations. Report and Feedback Statement.* IFRS.

Irvine, P., & Pontiff, J. (2009). Idiosyncratic return volatility, cash flows, and product market competition. *Review of Financial Studies*, *22*(3), 1149–1177. doi:10.1093/rfs/hhn039

Jenkins, D. S., Kane, G. D., & Velury, U. (2006). Earnings quality decline and the effect of industry specialist auditors: An analysis of the late 1990s. *Journal of Accounting and Public Policy*, *25*(1), 71–90. doi:10.1016/j.jaccpubpol.2005.11.003

Jiang, F., Zhu, B., & Huang, J. (2013). CEO's financial experience and earnings management. *Journal of Multinational Financial Management*, *23*(3), 134–145. doi:10.1016/j.mulfin.2013.03.005

Johnson, M. F. (1999). Business cycles and the relation between security returns and earnings. *Review of Accounting Studies*, *14*(2), 93–117. doi:10.1023/A:1009649018325

Jones, J. F. (1991). Earnings management during import relief investigations. *Journal of Accounting Research*, *29*(2), 193–228. doi:10.2307/2491047

Kane, G. D., Richardson, F., & Graybeal, P. (1996). Recession-induced stress and the prediction of corporate failure. *Contemporary Accounting Research*, *13*(2), 631–650. doi:10.1111/j.1911-3846.1996.tb00517.x

Karuna, C. (2007). Industry product market competition and managerial incentives. *Journal of Accounting and Economics*, *43*(2–3), 275–297. doi:10.1016/j.jacceco.2007.02.004

Karuna, C., Subramanyam, K. R., & Tian, F. (2012). *Industry product market competition and earnings management*. Paper presented at American Accounting Association Financial Accounting and Reporting Section Mid-Year Conference.

Karuna, C., Subramanyam, K. R., & Tian, F. (2015). *Competition and earnings management*. Working Paper.

Kasznik, R. (1997). *On the association between voluntary disclosure and earnings management*. Research Paper No. 1401, University of Stanford.

Kasznik, R. (1999). On the association between voluntary disclosure and earnings management. *Journal of Accounting Research*, *37*(1), 57–81. doi:10.2307/2491396

Kordestani, G. R., & Mohammadi, M. R. (2016). A study of the relationship between product market competition and earnings management. *Procedia Economics and Finance*, *36*, 266–273. doi:10.1016/S2212-5671(16)30037-5

Kothari, S. P. (2001). Capital markets research in accounting. *Journal of Acçounting and Economics*, *31*(1–3), 105–231. doi:10.1016/S0165-4101(01)00030-1

Koumanakos, E., Siriopoulos, C., & Georgopoulos, A. (2005). Firm acquisitions and earnings management: Evidence from Greece. *Managerial Auditing Journal*, *20*(7), 663–678. doi:10.1108/02686900510611212

KPMG. (2017). *Mercato M&A in Italia: nei primi 9 mesi chiuse operazioni per 27 miliardi di euro*. Retrieved from: https://home.kpmg.com/it/it/home/media/press-releases/2017/10/m-a-in-italia-primi-9-mesi-2017.html

KPMG. (2018). *Continuing to climb. Global Banking M&A trends 2018*. Retrieved from https://assets.kpmg.com/content/dam/kpmg/xx/pdf/2018/04/2018-banking-m-and-a-trends.pdf

Laksmana, I., & Yang, Y. (2014). Product market competition and earnings management: Evidence from discretionary accruals and real activity manipulation. *Advances in Accounting*, *30*(2), 264. doi:10.1016/j.adiac.2014.09.003

Landsman, W. R. (2007). Is fair value accounting information relevant and reliable? Evidence from capital market research. *Accounting and Business Research*, *37*(SI), 19–30. doi:10.1080/00014788.2007.9730081

Lang, M. H., & Lundholm, R. J. (1996). Corporate disclosure policy and analyst behavior. *The Accounting Review*, *71*(4), 467–492.

Levitt, A. (1998). The importance of high quality accounting standards. *Accounting Horizons*, *12*(2), 79–82.

Li, X. (2010). The impacts of product market competition on the quantity and quality of voluntary disclosures. *Review of Accounting Studies*, *15*(3), 663–711. doi:10.100711142-010-9129-0

Marciukaityte, D., & Park, J. C. (2009). *Market competition and earnings management.* Retrieved from https://papers.ssrn.com/sol3/papers.cfm?abstract_id=1361905

Markarian, G., & Santalò, J. (2014). Product market competition, information and earnings management. *Journal of Business Finance & Accounting*, *41*(5–6), 574.

McNichols, M. F. (2000). Research design issues in earnings management studies. *Journal of Accounting and Public Policy*, *19*(4-5), 313–345. doi:10.1016/S0278-4254(00)00018-1

Milgrom, P., & Roberts, J. (1992). *Economics, organization and management*. Englewood Cliffs, NJ: Prentice Hall.

Nickell, S. J. (1996). Competition and corporate performance. *Journal of Political Economy*, *104*(4), 724–746. doi:10.1086/262040

Ohlson, J. A. (1995). Earnings, book values, and dividends in equity valuation. *Contemporary Accounting Research*, *11*(2), 661–687. doi:10.1111/j.1911-3846.1995.tb00461.x

Onesti, T., & Romano, M. (2012). *Earnings Management and Goodwill Accounting: Implication on Dividend Policy in Italian Listed Companies*. Retrieved from https://ssrn.com/abstract=2179159

Pagano, M., Roelle, A., & Zechner, J. (2002). The geography of equity listing: Why do companies list abroad? *The Journal of Finance*, *57*(6), 2651–2694. doi:10.1111/1540-6261.00509

Persakis, A., & Iatridis, G. E. (2015). Earnings quality under financial crisis: A global empirical investigation. *Journal of Multinational Financial Management*, *30*(c), 1–35. doi:10.1016/j.mulfin.2014.12.002

Porter, M. E. (1990). The competitive advantage of nations. *Harvard Business Review*, 77–93.

Ramanna, K., & Watts, R. (2012). Evidence on the effects of unverifiable fair-value accounting. *Review of Accounting Studies*, *17*, 749–780. doi:10.100711142-012-9188-5

Reese, W., & Weisback, M. (2002). Protection of minority shareholder interests, cross-listing in the United States, and subsequent equity offerings. *Journal of Financial Economics*, *66*(1), 65–104. doi:10.1016/S0304-405X(02)00151-4

Richardson, F. M., Kane, G. D., & Lobinger, P. (1998). The impact of recession on the prediction of corporate failure. *Journal of Business Finance & Accounting*, *25*(1/2), 167–186. doi:10.1111/1468-5957.00182

Rossi, S., & Volpin, P. F. (2004). Cross-country determinants of mergers and acquisitions. *Journal of Financial Economics*, *74*(2), 277–304. doi:10.1016/j.jfineco.2003.10.001

Schipper, K., & Vincent, L. (2003). Earnings quality. *Accounting Horizons*, *17*(Supplement), 97–110. doi:10.2308/acch.2003.17.s-1.97

Shalev, R. (2009). The information content of business combination disclosure level. *The Accounting Review*, *84*(1), 240. doi:10.2308/accr.2009.84.1.239

Shalev, R., Zhang, I. X., & Zhang, Y. (2013). CEO compensation and fair value accounting: Evidence from purchase price allocation. *Journal of Accounting Research*, *51*(4), 819–854. doi:10.1111/1475-679X.12015

Shi, G., Sun, J., & Zhang, L. (2017). Product market competition and earnings management: A firm-level analysis. *Journal of Business Finance & Accounting*, 1–21.

Shleifer, A. (2004). Does competition destroy ethical behavior? *The American Economic Review*, *92*(2), 414–418. doi:10.1257/0002828041301498

Shleifer, A., & Vishny, R. W. (2003). Stock market driven acquisitions. *Journal of Financial Economics*, *70*(3), 295–311. doi:10.1016/S0304-405X(03)00211-3

Siregar, S. V., & Utama, S. (2008). Type of earnings management and the effect of ownership structure, firm size, and corporate-governance practices: Evidence from Indonesia. *The International Journal of Accounting*, *43*(1), 1–27. doi:10.1016/j.intacc.2008.01.001

Stenheim, T., & Madsen, D. O. (2016). Goodwill Impairment Losses, Economic Impairment, Earnings Management and Corporate Governance. *Journal of Accounting and Finance*, *16*(2), 11–30.

Stubben, S. R. (2010). Discretionary revenues as a measure of earnings management. *The Accounting Review*, *85*(2), 695–717. doi:10.2308/accr.2010.85.2.695

Sundvik, D. (2017). Book-tax conformity and earnings management in response to tax rate cuts. *Journal of International Accounting, Auditing & Taxation*, *28*, 31–42. doi:10.1016/j.intaccaudtax.2016.12.003

Turner, L., Dietrich, J. R., Anderson, K., & Bailey, A. (2001). *Accounting restatements*. Working paper, United States Securities and Exchange Commission.

Van Hulle, K. (2004). From accounting directives to International Accounting Standards. In C. Leuz, D. Pfaff, & A. Hopwood (Eds.), *International perspectives on research trends, policy and practices*. Oxford, UK: Oxford University Press. doi:10.1093/0199260621.003.0014

Verrecchia, R. E. (1983). Discretionary disclosure. *Journal of Accounting and Economics*, *5*(1), 179–194. doi:10.1016/0165-4101(83)90011-3

Yang, C. Y., Lai, H. N., & Tan, B. L. (2008). Managerial ownership structure and earnings management. *Journal of Financial Reporting and Accounting*, *6*(1), 35–53. doi:10.1108/19852510880000634

KEY TERMS AND DEFINITIONS

Discretionary Accruals: Accounting items which are documented inside financial statements according to the accrual basis principle, in spite of the absence of any financial manifestation. Because of their discretionary identification they could be manipulated by managers according to a particular legal or illegal policy of reporting. Discretionary accruals represent that part of total accruals which mainly impact on earnings quality.

Earnings Management: Accounting practices adopted by managers who, acting in an opportunistic manner, tend to apply accounting principles in order to misrepresent real patrimonial state, financial position, and fiscal year result, for obtaining personal advantages. Earnings management explicates even through strategic policies such as income smoothing in order to disclose to market only information that enhances the company's reputation and attracts funds from investors.

Earnings Quality: The ability of the economic result to describe the current income capacity of a company and provides reliable information about its long-term economic performances. According to this perspective, income is an "accounting measure" whose quality is defined in relation to the usefulness of information for stakeholders' decision making process. The notion of Earnings Quality is a strategic investigation tool about reliability of financial reports.

Goodwill: An accounting item which arises from business combination strategies. It is based on the positive difference between the purchase price and fair value of target firm net activities during an operation of merger or acquisition. Goodwill is itself an intangible asset that expresses the target firm's sustainability as a "going concern" and the benefits of combining the acquiree's net assets with those of the acquirer.

Income Smoothing: An accounting policy which aims to reduce the variability of economic results coming from adjacent fiscal years. Income smoothing strategies bring forward or postpone the identification of revenues and costs in order to increase or decrease the level of income. The recourse to Income smoothing as an Earnings management policy can exert a direct impact on Earnings quality.

Mergers and Acquisitions: Strategic decisions of business combinations which determine aggregations of distinct business entities into a single entity. Mergers and acquisitions affect not only capital structure and governance characteristics but also the composition and value of patrimonial assets of entities involved.

Chapter 5
Earnings Management in SMEs: Evidence From Portugal and Spain

Andreia Sousa
Polytechnic Institute of Coimbra, Portugal

Cristina Gonçalves Góis
https://orcid.org/0000-0003-1724-9411
Polytechnic Institute of Coimbra, Portugal

Clara Viseu
Polytechnic Institute of Coimbra, Portugal

ABSTRACT

Although small and medium-sized enterprises (SMEs) are represented on a large scale around the world, the literature on earnings management (EM) has focused mainly on listed firms. In this sense, this chapter provides important insights on the determinants and main incentives for EM in the context of Portuguese and Spanish SMEs, over a period of 10 years, also considering two relevant macroeconomic events (financial crisis and entry into force of harmonized accounting regulations). The results obtained are similar for both countries and are intended to underline the possible positive effects of reducing these practices after the entry into force of a harmonized accounting standard with the International Accounting Standards Board (IASB) standards and also to warn against the possible negative effects of managers' opportunistic behavior during a period of financial crisis. The close association between accounting and taxation, since the calculation of the tax income depends partly on the accounting income, remains an incentive to engage in EM practices.

INTRODUCTION

In the endless world of research on earnings management (EM), much has already been written about various topics: several authors have focused on the concept and its legality (e.g. Healy & Wahlen, 1999; Howard, 1996; Naser, 1993; Schipper, 1989; Skinner & Dechow, 2000), some aimed to detect EM (e.g. Beneish, 1997; Burgstahler & Dichev, 1997; Healy, 1985; Jones, 1991), others focused on their incen-

DOI: 10.4018/978-1-5225-7817-8.ch005

tives (e.g. Dechow & Schrand, 2004; Healy & Wahlen, 1999; Othman & Zeghal, 2006; Sweeney, 1994; Watts & Zimmerman, 1978), others researched the effect of several variables, such as Anglo-Saxon vs Continental countries (e.g. Ball & Shivakumar, 2005; Lisboa & Kacharava, 2018; Othman & Zeghal, 2006). Other authors addressed post accounting regulation change (e.g. Ames, 2013; Christensen, Lee, Walker, & Zeng, 2015; E.Dimitropoulos, Asteriou, Dimitrios Kousenidis, & Leventis, 2013; Karampinis & Hevas, 2013; Păşcan, 2015; Pereira & Alves, 2017; Zeghal, Chtourou, & Fourati, 2012), and financial crisis (e.g. Argilés-Bosch, García-Blandón, & Martínez-Blasco, 2012; Cimini, 2015; Kousenidis, Ladas, & Negakis, 2013; Lisboa, 2017; Lisboa & Kacharava, 2018; Persakis & Iatridis, 2015), among others.

The common factor of all prior research is the sample. These studies are focused in EM that occurs in listed firms. However, the question that arises is: in smaller private firms (therefore, non-listed ones) is there an absence of EM? Is not it important to study them? Around the world, small and medium-sized enterprises (SMEs) come to represent more than 95% of firms worldwide and more than 65% of employment (Bonito & Pais, 2018). In this way, the SMEs sector is the most crucial sector and the backbone of many developed and developing economies around the world (Alp & Ustundag, 2009; Perera & Chand, 2015). Even though in both the EU and the US economies these firms have no value (Allee & Yohn, 2009), in other countries, such as Portugal and Spain, private SMEs represent 99.9% of their business environment and, for that reason, their importance is higher (European Comission, 2017a, 2017b).

So, if listed firms from Portugal and Spain manage their earnings as shown by the studies of Argilés-Bosch *et al.* (2012) and also Pereira and Alves (2017), the authors have enough motivations to believe that non-listed SMEs also engage in these practices, although with different incentives.

Portugal and Spain, besides being composed of an absolute majority of SMEs, have very similar economic-legal contexts. Both countries are included in a *code law* legal system, belonging to the European continental system (Arnedo, Lizarraga, & Sánchez, 2007; Callao Gastón, Ferrer García, Jarne Jarne, & Laínez Gadea, 2010; Callao Gastón & Jarne Jarne, 1995; Jarne Jarne, 2000; Parker & Nobes, 2004), in which political and economic ties were influenced by France. Accounting is closely related to taxation, the financing system is based on the credit of financial institutions (banks), and the main concerns are the pursuit of the true image of accounting information, strict compliance with the law and protection of creditors. In addition to its geographical proximity, business contexts of both countries tend to have a largely family-owned corporate structure, where ownership and management are mixed. This implies that the interests of the firm are those of its manager (Moreira, 2009, 2010), where entrepreneurs/managers have academic and financial qualifications considered weak (Moreira, 2009) and firms' external financing is obtained through the banking system (Arnedo *et al.*, 2007; Cenni, Monferrà, Salotti, Sangiorgi, & Torluccio, 2015). These firms are not affected by the pressure in the capital markets to report results that meet investors' and analysts' expectations (Healy & Wahlen, 1999; Höglund & Sundvik, 2016; Moreira, 2009, 2010), and are less subject to monitoring by the supervisory entities than their public firms (Höglund & Sundvik, 2016). Furthermore, both countries became interesting case studies because they have recently harmonized their accounting standards and because both were forced to implement harsh austerity measures under financial supervision by the international financial authorities due to the strong impact of the financial crisis (Kousenidis *et al.*, 2013).

This study differs from prior literature because it is directed towards a reality that is still little explored (Belot & Serve, 2018). Thus, this research seeks to mitigate this gap through empirical analysis by investigating whether EM practices occur at the level of SMEs, in countries whose representation is high. It also aims to research the determinants that induce them to incur in these practices, considering the period of financial crisis and the change in the accounting standards framework. To achieve these goals, discretionary accruals were calculated for measuring EM from 12,265 Portuguese and 33,253 Spanish SMEs' observations, and the results were obtained on the basis of the estimation of an econometric model with panel data for a period of ten years (2005 to 2015), where several determinants were taken into account. The long period under analysis will allow considering the economic and legal changes that have taken place in these countries, namely the financial crisis (CRIS) and the recent harmonization in accounting regulations in line with IASB standards (IASB). Additionally, it was possible to examine several factors supported by the literature that can influence EM practices, such as income taxation (TAX), leverage (LEV), financial accounting audited (AUD), firm size (SIZ), firm growth (GRW), profitability (ROA), and location of firms in special tax regimes (STR).

The findings of the study indicate that the main incentives to manipulate earnings in SMEs are intrinsically related to the intention to pay lower taxes and to obtain bank financing. However, the firms' behaviour is not constant, and changes according to macroeconomic events. During the period of the financial crisis, these practices were more intense. However, the entry into force of the accounting regulation in line with the international standards of the IASB seems to be decisive for the reduction of these practices.

The results obtained will provide new insights on EM practices in the present time, since the few existing studies are already outdated, as is the case of studies by Marques, Rodrigues and Craig (2011), Monterrey Mayoral and Sánchez-Segura (2009) and Moreira (2009), and, therefore, it is not possible to extend the results to the present day, since the economical-business and legal conditions have changed.

LITERATURE REVIEW

As a privileged source for obtaining information on corporate financial health, accounting should be prepared in an unbiased manner, depicting the firm's real situation, in order to provide true information to all users of financial information. Yet, unfortunately, this often does not happen. This was when, at the beginning of the 21st century, there were consecutive worldwide accounting scandals, such as Enron, Xerox, WorldCom and Adelphia in the United States, and Parmalat, Royal Ahold and Volkswagen in Europe. These firms, considered to be manipulative, presented financial information that had been juggled, in a more or less significant extent, so as to meet certain benefits that the firm intended to achieve, mirroring a reality that does not exist. For these reasons, EM has gained importance and enhanced relevance in terms of scientific research, which sought to understand, firstly, what is "earnings management", to identify the incentives that lead firms to incur in such practices, and these incentives are influenced by several factors, such as cultural factors in the countries in which they operate.

Prior accounting research about this topic proposes two theories associated with EM: the positive accounting theory (PAT) and the agency theory, as being able to explain the accounting decisions made by managers, reinforcing the clear existence of incentives to the practice of EM (Missonier-Piera, 2004). Regarding the PAT proposed by Watts and Zimmerman (1978), it is part of the positive investigation of accounting, which argues that the economic man moves in his own interest, with a view to maximizing his own wealth or that of the firms he manages, minimizing any contractual costs. The authors formulated a set of three hypotheses related to EM incentives, in particular with regard to the manager's remuneration plans dependent on accounting figures (bonus plan hypothesis), as regards the related restrictive clauses with debt agreements (debt covenant hypothesis), and, finally, regarding the firm's political visibility (political costs hypothesis), where these contracts are directly indexed to accounting variables, thus impelling the manager to incur management to meet their needs (Mendes & Rodrigues, 2007). Regarding the agency theory, when the manager is also the owner of the firm, he will always make decisions that maximize his interest, which is not the case when there are two actors – manager and owner – with different interests. In addition to this relationship, there is still a conflict of interests between owners and creditors (Cenni *et al.*, 2015; Meckling & Jensen, 1976), and between the firm and the State (Coppens & Peek, 2005; Moreira, 2009), since interests between the two are not coincidental, and often, are even opposite.

The motivations for managers to incur in EM are also dependent on the economic and institutional environment in which firms are inserted (Baralexis, 2004; Coppens & Peek, 2005; Jones, 1991; Moreira, 2006; Rodrigues, 2013). In the Anglo-Saxon countries, the incentives that lead managers to implement EM focus on the capital market considered the main source of financing, wage remuneration, debt contracts and political costs (Healy & Wahlen, 1999). On the other hand, in Continental countries, the incentives that lead managers to implement EM are focused on reducing the tax payable and obtaining external financing (Arnedo *et al.*, 2007; Baralexis, 2004; Coppens & Peek, 2005; Eilifsen, Knivsfla IV, & Saettem, 1999; Othman & Zeghal, 2006).

As Portugal and Spain belong to Continental countries, and their accounting systems are characterized by their intrinsic relationship with the tax system, where accounting serves as a basis for calculating the payable income tax, firms can take advantage of the flexibility of accounting standards in order to see their results decrease and, consequently, pay lower taxes. Thus, the first incentive results from a tax motive, the minimization of payable tax. The second incentive relates to the need for bank financing. If, in the first incentive, the intention is to reduce the earnings (accounting-tax) to pay a lower tax, in this second this attitude can create the inverse effect in obtaining bank financing. Moreira (2006) found that obtaining financing is generally conditional on the amounts presented in the financial statements by Portuguese firms holding financial debts. In these cases, it is possible to sustain that these are the main motivations for EM, in opposite directions (Baralexis, 2004; Coppens & Peek, 2005; Fernández-Rodríguez & Martínez-Arias, 2015; Martins & Moreira, 2009; Monterrey Mayoral & Sánchez-Segura, 2009, 2017; Moreira, 2006; Sousa, Góis, & Viseu, 2017). Others studies emphasize that, in addition, SMEs manage their earnings downwards to avoid income taxes (Höglund & Sundvik; 2016; 2018) because the financial reporting objectives of these are largely influenced by taxation (Höglund & Sundvik, 2016).

As Persakis and Iatridis (2015) maintain, "in the last decade, there is an extensive attention from researchers to investigate the determinants and consequences of earnings management. However, they pay more attention on examining the earnings manipulation due to the incentives of managers individually and pay little attention in the economic environment of the firm" (p. 2). For this reason, it is important to study not only the individual incentives to EM practices but also to assess the impacts of the various macroeconomic events on these practices.

In recent years, most of the world was hit by the financial crisis with huge impacts on their economies. Consistent with this, several articles show that EM is sensitive to the occurrence of a bad economic environment (Iatridis & Dimitras, 2013; Kousenidis *et al.*, 2013; Persakis & Iatridis, 2015). During a crisis, firms have enormous financial difficulties and pressure, and so on they have incentives to manage their reported performance and survive the economic downturn (Arthur, Tang, & Lin, 2015). It is expected that the quality of financial reporting would be low during a period of economic recession because a firm's financial performance generally would be poor during a crisis (Arthur *et al.*, 2015), as their managers tend to mask true firm performance (Ball & Brown, 1968). Two distinct situations may arise: managers have an incentive to EM, choosing a more aggressive conservatism during the financial crisis to try to deal with bad news (Persakis & Iatridis, 2015) and taking advantage of the expected pessimistic scenarios; or managers tend to engage more in EM in their effort to improve firms' lower profitability and liquidity during the financial crisis (Iatridis & Dimitras, 2013). In this last study, the authors found some evidence that Portuguese firms tend to have this type of behaviour, while the results about Spanish firms are somewhat conflicting.

Another important event that can have major effects on EM is related to the accounting harmonization process that has emerged with the increasing internationalization of firms, the globalization of capital markets and the complexity of business transactions (Ali, Akbar, Ormrod, & Shah, 2016). There is the need to develop a process of harmonizing international accounting information by making comparable, consistent, relevant and timely information between the various regulatory systems (Frankel & Li, 2004), facilitating the entire process of producing accounting information, so that firms do not have to draw up various financial statements in light of the different accounting regulations in force in each country (Amaral, 2001). It is consensual among the literature that harmonized standards improve the quality of financial information, and also increase the quality of accounting (Soderstrom & Sun, 2007).

The starting point for this process of accounting reform with a view to international harmonization of accounting practices began in March 2000 at the Lisbon European Council, where a plan was "put in place" to improve the comparability of firms' financial information (Doadrio, Alvarado, & Carrera, 2015, p. 203) "as one of the ways to make capital markets more transparent and efficient" (Costa, 2007, p. 29).

The European Commission, with the approval of Regulation (CE) no. 1606/2002, established the obligation to apply the International Accounting Standards / International Financial Reporting Standards (IAS / IFRS) by firms with listed securities in the preparation of their consolidated accounts, as from January 1, 2005, for Member-States of the European Union. It also allowed for the possibility of applying these standards to the individual and consolidated accounts of other firms. In Portugal, "the need for a new accounting standardization system arises from the acknowledged insufficiency of POC [Accounting Official Plan] (Marques & Silva, 2010), for entities with a higher qualitative requirement, in terms of financial reporting, technical criteria, concepts of assets, liabilities and results, since the standards of the IASB and POC were not consistent with each other" (Alves, Saraiva, & Gabriel, 2015, p. 7). Thus, in order to bring Portugal closer to the international accounting reality, the Portuguese Commission of Accounting Standards (CNC) prepared an accounting model inspired in the IASB model adopted by the European Union, named *Sistema de Normalização Contabilística* (SNC), based on principles rather than rules (Cruz *et al.*, 2013; Marques & Silva, 2010), which came into force in January 1, 2010. Subsequently, through Decree-Law no. 36-A / 2011 of March 9, an autonomous accounting system directed to micro-entities was approved, named Accounting Standard for Micro-entities (NCM), inspired by SNC. More recently, with Decree-Law no. 98/2015 of June 2, the 4th and 7th Directives were repealed, transposing into the Portuguese law the European Union's Directive no. 2013/34 / EU of June 26, where SNC is reviewed, redefining the limits of the categories of entities, simplifying some accounting obligations for smaller firms and inserting NCM freelance as an integral part of SNC. These obligations were soon extended to other firms so that all entities were governed by a single set of accounting standards. As regards Spain, an accounting reform was carried out in 2008, in which accounting legislation was adapted in accordance with international harmonization with the approval of Royal Decree 1514/2007, which gave rise to the *Plan General de Contabilidad 2007* (PGC-07), creating a simplified regulation for SMEs, approved by Royal Decree 1515/2007, which established the *Plan General de Contabilidad de Pequeñas y Medianas Empresas (PGC-PYMES)* (Gracia-Sarubbi, San Juan-Pajares, & Rodríguez-López, 2014). More recently, Royal Decree 602/2016 of December 2 amends PGC-07 and PGC-PYMES, as a result of the need to adapt the Directive 3013/34 / EC, whose main purpose is to extend the scope of the rules and simplify the accounting obligations which firms are subject to.

Regarding EM, Guimarães, Lima, Ocejo and Gonçalves (1998), in a comparative study on accounting alternatives in Portugal and Spain, noted that, before the adoption of a harmonized accounting standards, there was room for management of accounting information through the various "gaps and possible interpretations and principles" (p. 1078).

Pope and McLeay (2011) argued that the introduction of accounting standards in line with international practices entails a greater transparency and comparability of accounting information within the European Union, by establishing a set of common standards and the consequent elimination accounting diversity, thus increasing the quality of the financial reporting produced.

Approaching and adapting the accounting rules to IASB is an improvement in firms' financial reporting, with the introduction of a conceptual framework (Gonzalo Angulo, 2014; Guimarães, 2010), which is a "more closed" rule for the management of accounts (Rodrigues, 2013, p. 279). Moreover, these standards are presented as being high-quality ones (Rodrigues, 2013), insofar as they are based on internationally advocated accounting principles, reflecting better the firms' economic reality. These rules are based on principles and not on rules, they embody a complete change of philosophy, as they provide a better quality information to the users and imply that the professionals who produce this information "are ethical, honest and of good formation and that are able to make judgments and estimates that lead to a better picture of the entity's financial position" (Niyama *et al.*, 2015, p. 84).

However, "accounting policies and standards cannot cover all aspects of business transactions, there is considerable scope for entities to use alternatives, interpretations, judgments and estimates in the measurement of assets and liabilities, and in some cases, the subjectivity and complexity of standards contributes to the use of practices harmful to good accounting known as creative accounting or earnings management" (Niyama *et al.*, 2015, p. 84).

Barth, Landsman and Lang (2008) showed that the firms that adopted IAS managed less of their earnings compared to firms that did not adopt international standards.

As for the studies that attempt to verify whether these accounting changes increase or decrease the scope of results' management, Chen, Tang, Jiang and Lin (2010) found, in a study of 15 EU countries, Portugal and Spain included, evidence that the implementation of IAS / IFRS reduced results' management, limiting the opportunistic management of accounting figures" (p. 223). Ali *et al.* (2016) validated their hypothesis wherein "the adoption of IFRS is intended to improve reporting quality by providing less flexibility and discretion in the measurement of assets, liabilities and profits" (p. 362).

Furthermore, Păşcan (2015), Zeghal, Chtourou and Fourati (2012), Christensen *et al.* (2015), Morais and Curto (2008), Dayanandan, Donker, Ivanof and Karahan (2016), Ames (2013) and E.Dimitropoulos, Asteriou, Dimitrios Kousenidis and Leventis (2013) demonstrated in their studies an improvement in the quality of financial information when adopting IASB standards, by reducing EM.

Following the arguments presented, next section addresses the design of the hypothesis under analysis and the methodology used in the research study.

METHODOLOGY, DATA, AND VARIABLES

The thesis that the new harmonized accounting standard will reduce the possibility of managing earnings is based on the fact that IASB standards are internationally acknowledged for their high-quality because they contain fewer options and less regulatory gaps, thus reducing management's options (Rodrigues, 2013). Therefore, the main purpose of this study is to determine whether the most recent accounting standards are relevant to EM, and whether the quality of the financial information has increased with the adoption of these standards. Accordingly, the following research hypothesis is presented:

Hypothesis 1: The adoption of the recent accounting standards (SNC for Portugal, PGC-07 for Spain), contributes to the reduction of the earnings management, thus increasing the quality of financial information.

ECONOMETRIC CHOICES

Several empirical studies that attempt to measure and detect the practice of EM use methods based on the variation of working capital, a variation known as accruals (Healy & Wahlen, 1999; Pereira & Alves, 2017). In our work, we use the latter methodology. Accruals are the part of revenues and expenses that have not yet been translated into receipts or payments (Callao Gastón *et al.*, 2010; Pellicer & Blasco, 2004), and can be indirectly calculated through cash flows[1] or through the balance[2] sheet (Dechow, Richardson, & Tuna, 2003). In this case, total accruals (att) are calculated by the formula:

$$ATT_{i,t} = \left[\Delta CA_{i,t} - \Delta CX_{i,t}\right] - \left[\Delta CL_{i,t} - \Delta ML_{i,t}\right] - DEPR_{i,t}{}^{3}, \tag{1}$$

Jones's (1991) model, used to determine the discretionary and non-discretionary component of the accruals, has undergone successive changes and attempts to be improved. Some examples are the models by Dechow *et al.* (1995) and Kothari, Leone and Wasley (2005). In Jones's model, modified by Dechow *et al.* (1995), the discretionary accruals (the proxy of EM) are obtained as follows:

$$ATT_{i,t} = AND_{i,t} + ADA_{i,t} AND_{i,t} ADA_{i,t} \tag{2}$$

All the variables are divided by the value of the total assets of the beginning of the year (end of year t-1), in order to avoid problems of heteroscedasticity and to allow the comparison between firms (Beneish, 2001; Dechow *et al.*, 1995; Jones, 1991), between sectors and between different countries (Coppens & Peek, 2005; Goncharov & Zimmermann, 2006).

$$\frac{ATT_{i,t}}{AT_{i,t-1}} = \alpha_0 + \alpha_1 \frac{1}{AT_{i,t-1}} + \alpha_2 \frac{\left(\Delta REV_{i,t} - \Delta REC_{i,t}\right)}{AT_{i,t-1}} + \alpha_3 \frac{PPE_{i,t}}{AT_{i,t-1}} + \varepsilon_{i,t} \mathrm{AT}_{i,t-1} \Delta \mathrm{REV}_{i,t} \Delta \mathrm{REC}_{i,t} \mathrm{PPE}_{i,t} \mu_{i,t i,t} \tag{3}$$

Equation (3) was estimated to obtain non-discretionary accruals, with residuals (εi) being the discretionary or abnormal accruals. All the results were obtained using the *EViews* 7. Thus,

$$\frac{ADA_{i,t}}{AT_{i,t-1}} = \varepsilon_{i,t}, \quad (4)$$

that is

$$\frac{ADA_{i,t}}{AT_{i,t-1}} = \frac{ATT_{i,t}}{AT_{i,t-1}} - \left[\alpha_0 + \alpha_1 \frac{1}{AT_{i,t-1}} + \alpha_2 \frac{\left(\Delta REV_{i,t} - \Delta REC_{i,t}\right)}{AT_{i,t-1}} + \alpha_3 \frac{PPE_{i,t}}{AT_{i,t-1}}\right] \quad (5)$$

Our sample consists of available firm-years; therefore, the methodology used was the panel data models, more specifically, the fixed effects model[4].

Greene (2008) states that the problems related to the omission of variables and multicollinearity between them decrease when using the panel data, as it incorporates the cross-section and time-series components. The use of panel data also allows controlling the effects of unobserved variables; in this case, the panel data models control the cultural and political differences between countries. Hsiao (2004) emphasizes that another advantage of using panel data is that they control the heterogeneity present in individuals. In addition, panel data are also able to identify and measure effects that are not possible to detect by cross-sectional data analysis or time series alone.

In order to evaluate the research hypothesis, that is, to determine the extent to which harmonized accounting regulations have affected EM and, in turn, the quality of financial information, the absolute value of discretionary accruals is used, insofar as it does not concern its signal, but its greatness (Heras, Cañibano, & Moreira, 2012; Lopes, Cerqueira, & Brandão, 2010; Othman & Zeghal, 2006). The model used to analyse the hypothesis proposes a linear relationship between the dependent variable and the explanatory variables, since it is widely accepted that it is the best way to describe the relationship between accounting variables (Martins & Moreira, 2009) and is formalized as follows:

$$\begin{aligned}\left|ADA_{i,t}\right| &= \beta_0 + \beta_1 TAX_{i,t} + \beta_2 LEV_{i,t} + \beta_3 AUD_{i,t} + \beta_4 SIZ_{i,t} + \beta_5 GRW_{i,t} + \\ &\beta_6 ROA_{i,t} + \beta_7 STR_{i,t} + \beta_8 CRIS_{i,t} + \beta_9 IASB_{i,t} + \varepsilon_{i,t}\end{aligned} \quad (6)$$

$\left|\boldsymbol{ADA}_{i,t}\right|$ – Absolute value (module) of the discretionary accruals, for firm i, in year t; $\boldsymbol{TAX}_{i,t}$ – corporate tax for firm i, in year t; $\boldsymbol{LEV}_{i,t}$ – indebtedness for firm i, in year t; $\boldsymbol{AUD}_{i,t}$ – presence of the auditor for firm i, in year t; $\boldsymbol{SIZ}_{i,t}$ – size for firm i in year t; $\boldsymbol{GRW}_{i,t}$ – growth for firm i in year t; $\boldsymbol{ROA}_{i,t}$ – profitability of the asset, for firm i, in year t; $\boldsymbol{STR}_{i,t}$ – location in a special tax regime, for firm i, in year t; $\boldsymbol{CRIS}_{i,t}$ – period of financial crisis (years 2008 to 2012); $\boldsymbol{IASB}_{i,t}$ – period in which the recent accounting standard became effective (iasb = 1 for the period 2008-2015 for spain, and 2010-2015 for portugal); $\varepsilon_{i,t}$ – model resids.

DATA, VARIABLES, AND SUMMARY STATISTICS

The common denominator of the diverse research on EM focuses on the sample, mainly composed of large firms with listed securities, whose accounts are subject to legal certification of accounts, and are thus subject to market scrutiny; SMEs, as well as smaller countries, are neglected (Baralexis, 2004; Belot & Serve, 2018). For this reason, many studies carried out internationally are not applicable to smaller firms operating in a different economic and fiscal context, such as Portugal and Spain (Baralexis, 2004). This chapter intends to contribute to the literature about EM in small and SMEs, based in Portugal and Spain. These firms have a significant weight (99.9%) in the business structures of these countries, and their main incentive for EM is tax savings (Amat Salas & Blake, 1999; Baralexis, 2004; Moreira, 2006).

The financial and non-financial information required of all Portuguese and Spanish firms with unlisted securities was gathered from the Iberian Balance Sheet Analysis System database (SABI). Subsequently, financial entities and insurers (Peasnell, Pope, & Young 2000), firms with incomplete data and entities not considered SMEs were excluded from this universe in light of the common European definition. As in the work of Burgstahler *et al.* (2006), only the sectors with at least ten observations for the final sample were considered, in order to efficiently estimate discretionary accrual parameters for each firm (Dechow *et al.*, 1995).

The sample period starts in 2005 and ends in 2015, allowing to assess the impact in both countries of the entry into force of a new accounting standard, comparing reliably the studies carried out in previous years. Table 1 shows the sample construction process.

The final sample for Portugal contains 1,115 firms/year with a total of 12,265 observations, while for Spain, there are 3,023 firms/year with a total of 33,253 observations. Table 2 presents some indicators of these firms.

It is noteworthy that this is a diversified sample, including firms with a very high turnover, net profit for the period and total assets. Compared to Portugal, Spain has firms with twice the average turnover and total assets.

Table 1. Sample construction process

	Portugal		Spain	
Criteria	*Firms / year*	*Observations (2005-2015)*	*Firms/ year*	*Observations (2005-2015)*
All firms, with unlisted securities, with complete data available for the years 2004 to 2015	1,260	13,860	5,874	64,614
Excluded were: enterprises not considered SMEs according to criteria defined by the European Union in Recommendation 2003/361/CE	(129)	(1,419)	(2,768)	(30,448)
Excluded: entities engaged in financial and insurance activities	0	0	(17)	(187)
Excluded: sectors with less than ten firms/year	(16)	(176)	(66)	(726)
Final sample	**1,115**	**12,265**	**3,023**	**33,253**

Table 2. Sample indicators

	Portugal			Spain		
	$\bar{x}$	*Med*	σ	$\bar{x}$	*Med*	σ
Total Revenues	9,559,570	5,572,419	12,169,933	18,878,901	13,191,136	28,533,787
Net Income for the period	-30,877	59,624	8,266,583	477,182	215,980	9,046,008
Total Assets	14,721,236	6,132,071	76,175,961	24,441,885	12,346,231	79,571,863

$\bar{x}$ *– average; Med – median; σ – standard deviation.*

In this model, two major incentives to EM are considered: income taxation and leverage, as proposed by the literature. The control variables that determine these practices, related to size, growth, profitability, auditor presence and the location of firms in special tax regimes are included, with the purpose of increasing the explanatory capacity of the model, increasing its consistency (Martins & Moreira, 2009; Monterrey Mayoral & Sánchez-Segura, 2006; Monterrey Mayoral & Sánchez Segura, 2010).

Taxation income (TAX) results from the amount between the tax on income and total assets. A positive sign is expected, since this charge contributes positively to EM (Chaney & Lewis, 1995; Coppens & Peek, 2005; Eilifsen *et al.*, 1999; Frank, Lynch, & Rego, 2009; Goncharov & Zimmermann, 2006; Hepworth, 1953; Martins & Moreira, 2009; Monterrey Mayoral & Sánchez-Segura, 2009; Stolowy & Breton, 2000). Leverage (LEV) results from the quotient between total liabilities and total assets, and a positive relationship between debt and EM is expected (Burgstahler *et al.*, 2006; Dias, 2015; DeFond & Jiambalvo, 1994; Martins & Moreira, 2009; Monterrey Mayoral & Sánchez-Segura, 2006, 2009; Stolowy & Breton, 2000; Sweeney, 1994). As for the presence of an auditor in the firms (AUD), it is represented in the form of a dummy variable (1 for the firm with an auditor, 0 otherwise), and it is not possible to predict its signal, due to the incongruities in the literature (Burgstahler *et al.*, 2006; Costa & Moreira, 2010; Heras *et al.*, 2012; Huguet & Gandía, 2016; Martins & Moreira, 2009; Monterrey Mayoral & Sánchez-Segura, 2006). The firm size (SIZ) is calculated through the natural logarithm of the total assets (Martins & Moreira, 2009). In this case, a negative relationship between this variable and the discretionary accruals is expected (Albornoz Noguer & Munõz, 2007; Carmo, Moreira, & Miranda, 2016; Dias, 2015; Martins & Moreira, 2009; Othman & Zeghal, 2006;). For firm growth (GRW), measured as the annual percentage change in total assets; a negative relationship is predicted (Burgstahler *et al.*, 2006; Monterrey Mayoral & Sánchez-Segura, 2009). The firm profitability (ROA) is measured by the ratio between the net result of the period and the total assets, not establishing a forecast of its signal. For the location of the firm under a special tax regime (STR), a dummy variable was created that identifies whether the firms are located in a region with a special tax regime (Portugal: = 1 if it belongs to the Madeira Free Trade Zone; and Spain: = 1 if it belongs to the Autonomous Community of the Canaries, = 0 otherwise).

To characterize the relevant macroeconomic events two other variables were created. As regards the period of crisis, Cimini (2015) and Persakis and Iatridis (2015) considered that the period of financial crisis occurred between 2008 and 2012. The former author identified, in this period, a decrease in EM in Portugal; however, this decrease did not occur in Spain. Dimitras, Kyriakou and Iatridis (2015) and Iatridis and Dimitras (2013) prove the exact opposite. Callao Gastón and Jarne (2011) demonstrated that firms listed in the Spanish market increased management during the crisis period. For the above, the CRIS dummy variable identifies the period of financial crisis that both countries experienced (=1 if the period between 2008 and 2012; = 0 otherwise), whose impact is not clear, according to Parte-Esteban and Ferrer García (2014); the IASB dummy variable was created to identify the period from which the latest accounting regulations harmonized with IASB standards were applied. For Portugal, the variable takes the value 1 if the period is between 2010 and 2015 and takes the value 0 for the remaining cases, while for Spain the variable takes the value 1 if the period is between 2008 and 2015, taking the value 0 otherwise. To the extent that high-quality financial information constrains results' management (Goncharov & Zimmermann, 2006), it is expected that, with the adoption of the new accounting standard that bases its standards on the IASB, considered as high quality standards (Dayanandan *et al.*, 2016; Morais & Curto, 2008), the relationship between this variable and EM is negative (Amat Salas, 2010; Chen *et al.*, 2010; Christensen *et al.*, 2015; Dias, 2015; Zeghal *et al.*, 2012).

Table 3 summarizes the study variables and their expected signals.

Regarding the outliers of the variables under study, for the subject in question, we considered their non-exclusion as relevant. We are studying the phenomenon of results' management carried out by firms and by eliminating them we may be losing pertinent cases of study. In this sense, we performed a pre-test and eliminated the outliers of the leverage variable. The results obtained did not differ significantly, so we chose to include all the cases under study for the different levels of indebtedness. Thus, in our view, we can verify that all firms with different levels of leverage (even those overindebted) incur or not in practical EM. This position is in line with what Pestana and Gageiro (2014, p. 676), who suggested that "outliers that do not result from data entry errors allow us to know unique characteristics or new valid segments of the population, that otherwise would not be found; they should only be excluded if there is evidence that they are not valid members of the population. Excluding outliers, although it may improve the quality of the analysis, there is a risk of limiting the generalization of studies to the population in which they are inserted".

In this case, the model in question presents a coefficient of determination around 13.5% for Portugal and 11.0% for Spain, which is in line with the value of R^2 obtained by previous studies (Dias, 2015).

Table 3. Variables and expected signals

	Portugal	**Spain**
Variables	*Expected Signal*	*Expected Signal*
Taxation Income – TAX	+	+
Leverage – LEV	+	+
Presence of an auditor – AUD	?	?
Firm size – SIZ	-	-
Firm growth – GRW	-	-
Firm profitability – ROA	?	?
Location in a special tax regime – STR	?	?
Financial crisis – CRIS	?	?
Accounting harmonization – IASB	-	-

EMPIRICAL RESULTS

Table 4 reports descriptive statistics for the variables under study, for Portugal and Spain, between 2005 and 2015.

Discretionary accruals, in their broad sense (|ADA|), have a mean value of 0.079 for Portugal, and 0.076 for Spain. Regarding the fiscal variable, IMP has an average of 0.007 for Portugal and 0.010 for Spain, a median of 0.004 for Portugal and 0.006 for Spain. The firms have an average leverage level of 67.9% for Portugal and 59.6% for Spain, with more leverage in Portugal than in Spain. In the Portuguese SMEs observations, the auditor is present in 70.9% of the cases (AUD = 1, in 9,492 observations). None of the SMEs of the sample is located in an area with a special tax regime (STR = 1, in 0 observations), as is the case in the Madeira Free Trade Zone. 98.8% of the observations concerning Spanish SMEs are audited (AUD = 1, 35,832 observations). In the case of SMEs located in the special tax regime, 2.5% are in the Autonomous Community of the Canaries (STR = 1, 912 observations).

It is expected that accounting rules will influence the quality of financial information, and therefore, will be able to change the incentives for EM (Amat Salas, 2010; Christensen *et al.*, 2015). For this reason, the descriptive statistics for two periods corresponding to the pre-normative and post-normative accounting are presented, as Table 5 and 6 show.

The year of transition of accounting regulations was excluded from the analysis, 2010 in the case of Portugal and 2008 in the case of Spain, according to DeFond, Hu, Hung, and Li (2011), Peasnell *et al.* (2000), and Zeghal *et al.* (2012), since the adjustments resulting from these changes are reflected in the firms' accounts.

From the analysis of the descriptive statistics by periods, it is possible to verify that, in Portugal, from the pre-normative accounting period to the post-normative accounting period, all variables, with the exception of variable SIZ, show a decrease in their mean values. This common event can be justified by the fact that, in the post-harmonization period, Portugal has also adopted a new accounting standard. Furthermore, it is experiencing a financial crisis that has affected its macroeconomic and microeconomic structure, with a great impact on profitability and growth. It is also pertinent to point out that there is a decrease in the mean value of discretionary accruals, which may be related to both the events described.

Table 4. Descriptive statistics (2005-2015)

	Portugal					Spain				
	$\bar{x}$	M_d	σ	m	M	$\bar{x}$	M_d	σ	m	M
$\lvert ADA \rvert$	0.079	0.053	0.100	0.000	4.576	0.076	0.052	0.085	0.000	3.331
TAX	0.007	0.004	0.012	-0.102	0.140	0.010	0.006	0.022	-0.381	0.436
LEV	0.679	0.685	0.209	0.015	5.004	0.596	0.613	0.200	0.005	2.466
SIZ	15.667	15.629	1.128	12.239	21.597	16.410	16.329	0.903	13.696	22.226
GRW	0.020	0.019	0.180	-3.923	0.861	0.012	0.016	0.180	-7.084	0.824
ROA	0.013	0.011	0.079	-3.585	3.426	0.025	0.019	0.066	-4.640	1.471

$\bar{x}$ – average; Md – median; σ – standard deviation; m – minimum; M – maximum.

Table 5. Descriptive statistics pre- versus post normative accounting – Portugal

	2005-2009					2011-2015				
	$\bar{x}$	M_d	σ	*m*	*M*	$\bar{x}$	M_d	σ	*m*	*M*
$\|ADA\|$	0.082	0.056	0.100	0.000	2.358	0.072	0.049	0.099	0.000	4.576
TAX	0.008	0.005	0.012	-0.101	0.099	0.006	0.004	0.012	-0.085	0.140
LEV	0.692	0.704	0.152	0.108	2.366	0.667	0.664	0.259	0.015	5.004
SIZ	15.575	15.529	1.117	12.292	21.504	15.741	15.729	1.134	12.239	21.597
GRW	0.051	0.045	0.160	-1.57	0.772	-0.017	-0.008	0.191	-3.923	0.861
ROA	0.02	0.014	0.049	-0.711	0.614	0.006	0.008	0.104	-3.585	3.426

$\bar{x}$ – average; Md – median; σ – standard deviation; m – minimum; M – maximum.

Table 6. Descriptive statistics pre- versus post normative accounting – Spain

	2005-2007					2009-2015				
	$\bar{x}$	M_d	σ	*m*	*M*	$\bar{x}$	M_d	σ	*m*	*M*
$\|ADA\|$	0.082	0.057	0.096	0.000	3.331	0.070	0.048	0.078	0.000	2.095
TAX	0.017	0.012	0.023	-0.281	0.436	0.007	0.004	0.020	-0.381	0.344
LEV	0.644	0.668	0.178	0.032	1.475	0.572	0.583	0.208	0.005	2.466
SIZ	16.358	16.255	0.890	13.847	22.226	16.427	16.360	0.907	13.696	21.931
GRW	0.081	0.078	0.155	-1.697	0.822	-0.013	-0.002	0.178	-7.084	0.824
ROA	0.041	0.031	0.055	-0.766	-0.766	0.018	0.014	0.063	-1.480	1.471

$\bar{x}$ – average; Md – median; σ – standard deviation; m – minimum; M – maximum.

Also in Spain, the descriptive statistics indicate that, from the pre-normative accounting period to the accounting post-normative period, the mean values of all variables, except for variable SIZ, decreased. The strong impact on profitability (which has turned negative) and growth may be indicative of the effect that the financial crisis has had on them. Moreover, the decrease in the average value of discretionary accruals may also be related to changes in accounting standards.

In general, the variations of the variables under study, for both Portuguese and Spanish firms, prove to be similar.

Table 7 depicts Pearson's correlations between the study variables, which the literature shows to be more relevant in terms of EM for Portugal.

From the analysis of the Pearson's correlation matrix, there is a positive correlation between taxes, leverage and growth of firms with EM. These results reveal preliminary evidence of a positive association between these variables and increased EM. However, the firm's size and profitability may be associated with a decrease in EM, given its negative correlation with the dependent variable |ADA|, and consequently

Table 7. Pearson correlations between variables – Portugal (2005 to 2015)

	$\lvert ADA_{i,t} \rvert$	TAX	*LEV*	*SIZ*	*GRW*	*ROA*
$\lvert ADA_{i,t} \rvert$	1					
TAX	0.029***	1				
LEV	0.132***	-0.153***	1			
SIZ	-0.028***	-0.121***	-0.104***	1		
GRW	0.067***	0.111***	-0.094***	0.074***	1	
ROA	-0.072***	0.388***	-0.386***	0.026***	0.342***	1

*, **, *** for significance levels of 10%, 5% and 1%, respectively.

with the increase in the quality of financial information in Portuguese SMEs. It also verified that the higher correlation coefficients are related to the ROA variable. The highest coefficient is 0.388 and it can be verified that the problem of perfect multicollinearity is not present, since this value is less than 0.8, meaning a weak correlation (Judge *et al.*, 1988; Firth, 1997; Carmona & Momparler, 2011; *apud* Huguet & Gandía, 2016). In a theoretical-practical sense, this higher correlation between profitability and the tax variable makes sense, because as profitability increases, the tax burden also tends to increase.

Table 8 shows the Pearson correlation matrix for the variables of Spanish SMEs.

In the case of Spanish SMEs, there is a correlation table that is quite similar to that of Portugal. There is a positive association between all the quantitative variables and the dependent variable, thus anticipating that all variables contribute to an increase in EM. The correlation between the ROA variable and the TAX variable is 0.63, the highest coefficient. The problem of perfect multicollinearity is removed because it is considered a weak to moderate correlation (Judge *et al.*, 1988; Firth, 1997; Carmona & Momparler, 2011; *apud* Huguet & Gandía, 2016). As in Portugal, the correlation between profitability and the variable representative of the tax burden makes sense, because as profitability increases, the tax burden also tends to increase.

Table 8. Pearson correlations between variables – Spain (2005 to 2015)

	$\lvert ADA_{i,t} \rvert$	TAX	*LEV*	*SIZ*	*GRW*	*ROA*
$\lvert ADA_{i,t} \rvert$	1					
TAX	0.035***	1				
LEV	0.113***	-0.184***	1			
SIZ	0.032***	-0.013**	-0.012**	1		
GRW	0.016***	0.132***	0.053***	0.072***	1	
ROA	0.015***	0.630***	-0.237***	0.018***	0.266***	1

The quality of the financial information, which is the subject of analysis on the first hypothesis, is influenced by the existence or absence of em, that is, by proving the management of the accounts, financial information loses quality, given their inverse relationship (albornoz noguer & munõz, 2007; carmo *et al.*, 2010; dechow & schrand, 2004; martins & moreira, 2009; pineda gonzález, 2000). Table 9 reports the results of the model estimation for the iberian countries – portugal and spain[5].

First of all, our evidence suggests that the variable iasb, which represents the adoption of the most recent accounting standards harmonized with the iasb standards, has contributed to the reduction of em, increasing the quality of the financial information provided by the entities, which is in accordance with the results obtained by Amat Salas (2010), Chen, Tang, Jiang and Lin (2010), Christensen *et al.* (2015) and Zeghal *et al.* (2012). Also Klann and Beuren (2018) showed reduction in earnings management levels in british companies with the adoption of iasb standards. We may conclude that this evidence occurs "because the accounting and financial reporting are more in line with the European and international standards, and there is, therefore, a greater uniformity and homogeneity of accounting practices at the spatial level" (Marques & Silva, 2010, p. 276). This denotes greater cohesion and internationalization of the accounting profession, in addition to the development and modernization of accounting matters, "representing an added value to accounting science" (Marques & Silva, 2010, p. 276)[6]. Thus, our research hypothesis 1 is validated by empirical evidence. It should be noted that the results indicate that the iasb variable is more significant in spain than in portugal. However, such evidence can be justified by the fact that the period contemplated in the variable with respect to Spain is wider than in Portugal and may thus reflect a more significant impact.

The coefficients associated with the variables TAX and LEV are positive and significant. This indicates that the tax burden and the level of corporate indebtedness are the determinants that induce the increase in EM, and, consequently, the decrease in the quality of the financial information for both countries. It is

Table 9. Model results: Portugal and Spain

	Portugal			Spain		
	Coef.	***t***	***Sig.***	***Coef.***	***t***	***Sig.***
C	-0.030	-0.560		0.049	1.514	
TAX	0.176	1.838	*	0.047	1.832	*
LEV	0.061	8.640	***	0.069	13.987	***
AUD	MP	MP	MP	MP	MP	MP
SIZ	-	-		-	-	
GRW	0.068	12.739	***	0.016	5.726	***
ROA	-0.124	-8.913	***	-	-	
STR	S/O	S/O	S/O	MP	MP	MP
CRIS	0.005	2.820	***	0.010	9.158	***
IASB	-0.003	-1.728	*	-0.008	-6.086	***
	$R^2 = 26\%$		***	$R^2 = 24\%$		***

*, **, *** for significance levels of 10%, 5% and 1%, respectively.
- was not relevant in this period.
S / O – without observations.
MP – perfect multicollinearity problems.

concluded that these are the main incentives for EM, as expected (Amat Salas & Gowthorpe, 2004; Amat Salas *et al.*, 1996; Burgstahler *et al.*, 2006; Carmo *et al.*, 2010; Chaney & Lewis, 1995; Coppens & Peek, 2005; Eilifsen, 1996; Eilifsen *et al.*, 1999; Guenther, 1994; Hepworth, 1953; Martins & Moreira, 2009; Maydew, 1997; Monterrey Mayoral & Sánchez-Segura, 2009; Moreira, 2006; Stolowy & Breton, 2000).

Relative to TAX, the managers intend to incur in practices of reducing the firm's accounting income, in order to simultaneously reduce its taxable income, reducing the resulting tax payable. On the other hand, the LEV variable acts as an incentive for the practice of EM, because SMEs in these countries are governed by managers who are simultaneously the owners of SMEs, and when bank financing is required to manage their activity, they tend to present their creditors with increased accounting income in order to benefit from access to credit and a more reasonable cost.

The results obtained also show evidence that the variable GRW is positively related to EM, in accordance with the results of the study carried out by Heras, Cañibano and Moreira (2012). Relative to the variable SIZ, it was expected to negatively influence EM and positively influence the quality of the financial information. According to Martins and Moreira (2009, p. 225), "the larger firms tend to be more visible abroad, and therefore, their information tends to be subject to greater scrutiny". However, the size of the firms has shown to be of little relevance to explain EM in the broad sense for both countries (Amat Salas *et al.*, 1996; Moreira, 2006). In addition, the ROA variable only influences – negatively – the financial information in Portugal, thus contributing to the improvement of the quality of financial information. The variables AUD (in Portugal and Spain) and STR (Spain only) could not be estimated due to the existence of a perfect multicollinearity problem.

Additionally, we found evidence that, in the period of the financial crisis, EM increased, contributing to the deterioration of the quality of financial information. These results are in line with those obtained by Persakis and Iatridis (2015), according to which managers have an incentive to choose a more aggressive conservatism during the financial crisis, to try to deal with bad news. Some authors, such as Reguera Alvarado, Laffarga Briones and Fuentes Ruiz (2012), confirm that in Spain, during the crisis, financial accounting reports were more manipulated, where managers took advantage of the crisis to behave opportunistically. Lisboa (2017) verified that, in the period of financial crisis, EM also increased in Portugal. Entrepreneurs may be taking advantage of pessimistic scenarios, which may explain this result.

Furthermore, the results obtained are similar in almost all variables for the two countries, which seems reasonable considering their similarities in the economic-legal and accounting-tax contexts.

CONCLUSION

One of the most popular topics in accounting research is EM. In this study, our focus was to determine the factors that induce SMEs to engage in EM practices and to determine the impact of these practices on the recent events that have taken place all over the world: the financial crisis and the normalization and harmonization of accounting standards in line with IASB standards.

According to Baralexis (2004, p. 440), "the research undertaken refers mainly to large firms located in large, developed countries. Small firms, or firms located in developing countries have received little attention". In this way, this chapter contributes to the literature about EM and the quality of financial information in the following ways: first at all, it extends the few existing literature about EM to the SMEs context, bridging this gap. Novel and important features of the study are that the sample covers a wide variety of micro, small and medium-sized firms, which have not been analysed previously. Unlike the other studies that analyse the factors separately, our proposal analyses, in a single study, several factors capable of influencing EM practices. Second, the results obtained for both countries are similar, which can be explained by similarities in the business, accounting and fiscal contexts of both countries. Furthermore, since these countries belong to the continental system, the results attained enrich the literature on this area. Third, these results suggest that the manager has many incentives to incur in EM, where the trade-off in reporting to lower the cost of capital or to reduce the tax is verified (Chaney & Lewis, 1995). Fourth, it was also suggested that the period of the financial crisis was used by managers to present even lower earnings camouflaged by the period of recession that the countries crossed. Fifth, our evidence suggests that the implementation of accounting standards harmonized with IASB standards has reduced EM practices, thus proving that the goal of increasing the reliability and quality of financial information is being achieved. Finally, our findings have important implications for understanding why SMEs engage in EM practices. They also allow us to understand the reality and the comparability of SMEs between countries, since our results can be applied to countries that basically resemble the Portuguese and Spanish settings.

The results obtained from the Portuguese and Spanish cases can also clarify the problem of the strong dependence between accounting and taxation, since taxation depends on the accounting income for the calculation of the income taxes to be paid to the State. They also allow us to shed light on simplified financial information reported by SMEs which, overall, apply simpler and flexible accounting standards than the original IFRS, which can be intentionally managed to achieve a particular purpose and, for that reason, they can influence users of financial information to make misallocated economic decisions. These findings are relevant for standards setters, policymakers and supervisory authorities, alerting them to this relevant problem in the SMEs context, so that they can restrict the managerial discretion in reporting earnings, increasing the reliability and the quality of financial information for all stakeholders.

It would be interesting to evaluate the behavioural differences in relation to EM by sectoring the firms by size groups (micro, small and medium-sized enterprises). The results obtained can also be estimated under alternative measures and different estimation approaches. Evidence has also grown about the relevance of corporate governance in SMEs (Al-Najjar, 2018). Study the corporate governance in Portugal and Spain context can provide important knowledge for the literature.

In 2018 there are still some important questions to be answered. "It is not clear to me that we can eradicate earnings management, or that we should" (Barth, 2018, p. 11). The main problem stems from the use of judgment in accounting, which creates a margin to manage earnings. Professional judgment cannot be excluded, inasmuch as this is the only way to "measure" and determine the relevant financial information to convey to stakeholders in the financial report. The real question is whether there is an acceptable and "tolerable amount of earnings management, and how we should determine the trade-off between the costs of earnings management with the benefits of allowing judgment" (Barth, 2018, p. 11).

REFERENCES

Al-Najjar, B. (2018). Corporate governance and audit features: SMEs evidence. *Journal of Small Business and Enterprise Development, 25*(1), 163–179. doi:10.1108/JSBED-08-2017-0243

Ali, A., Akbar, S., Ormrod, P., & Shah, S. Z. A. (2016). The impact and implications of international financial reporting standards in the United Kingdom: Evidence from the alternative investment market. *Australian Accounting Review, 26*(4), 360–375. doi:10.1111/auar.12140

Allee, K. D., & Yohn, T. L. (2009). The demand for financial statements in an unregulated environment: An examination of the production and use of financial statements by privately held small businesses. *The Accounting Review, 84*(1), 1–25. doi:10.2308/accr.2009.84.1.1

Alp, A., & Ustundag, S. (2009). Financial reporting transformation: The experience of Turkey. *Critical Perspectives on Accounting, 20*(5), 680–699. doi:10.1016/j.cpa.2007.12.005

Alves, M. do C. G., Saraiva, H. I. B., & Gabriel, V. M. de S. (2015). Normalização contabilística em Portugal : a sua evolução e situação atual. In *V Congresso dos TOC* (pp. 1–19). Retrieved from http://www.occ.pt/news/trabalhoscongv/pdf/32.pdf

Amaral, C. X. (2001). Processo de harmonização contabilística internacional : Tendências actuais. *Gestao e Desenvolvimento, 10*, 33–58.

Amat, O., & Blake, J. (1996). Contabilidad creativa. *Gestion.*

Amat, O., & Gowthorpe, C. (2004). Creative accounting: Nature, incidence and ethical issues. *Journal of Economic Literature*, 1–19. doi:10.2139srn.563364

Amat Salas, O. (2010). Fiabilidad de la nueva normativa contable (PGC y NIIF) y detección de maquillajes contables. *Boletin de Estudios Economicos, 65*(199), 93–105.

Ames, D. (2013). IFRS adoption and accounting quality: The case of South Africa. *Journal of Applied Economics & Business Research, 3*(3), 154–165. doi:10.2308/accr-50494

Argilés-Bosch, J. M., García-Blandón, J., & Martínez-Blasco, M. (2012). Earnings management behaviour under the recent economic downturn in Spain. *International Finance Review, 13*, 231–255. doi:10.1108/S1569-3767(2012)0000013011

Arnedo, L., Lizarraga, F., & Sánchez, S. (2007). Does public/private status affect the level of earnings management in code-law contexts outside the United States? a study based on the Spanish case. *The International Journal of Accounting, 42*(3), 305–328. doi:10.1016/j.intacc.2007.06.004

Arthur, N., Tang, Q., & Lin, Z. (2015). Corporate accruals quality during the 2008–2010 global financial crisis. *Journal of International Accounting, Auditing & Taxation, 25*, 1–15. doi:10.1016/j.intaccaudtax.2015.10.004

Ball, R., & Shivakumar, L. (2005). Earnings quality in U.K. private firms: Comparative loss recognition timeless. *Journal of Accounting and Economics, 39*(1), 83–128. doi:10.1016/j.jacceco.2004.04.001

Baralexis, S. (2004). Creative accounting in small advancing countries. *Managerial Auditing Journal, 19*(3), 440–461. doi:10.1108/02686900410524427

Barth, M. E. (2018). The future of financial reporting: Insights from research. *Abacus, 54*(1), 66–78. doi:10.1111/abac.12124

Barth, M. E., Landsman, W. R., & Lang, M. H. (2008). International accounting standards and accounting quality. *Journal of Accounting Research, 46*(3), 467–498. doi:10.1111/j.1475-679X.2008.00287.x

Belot, F., & Serve, S. (2018). Earnings quality in private SMEs: do CEO demographics matter? *Journal of Small Business Management, 56*, 323–344. doi:10.1111/jsbm.12375

Ben Othman, H., & Zeghal, D. (2006). A study of earnings-management motives in the Anglo-American and Euro-Continental accounting models: The Canadian and French cases. *The International Journal of Accounting, 41*(4), 406–435. doi:10.1016/j.intacc.2006.09.004

Beneish, M. D. (1997). Detecting GAAP violation: Implications for assessing earnings management among firms with extreme financial performance. *Journal of Accounting and Public Policy, 16*(3), 271–309. doi:10.1016/S0278-4254(97)00023-9

Beneish, M. D. (2001). Earnings management: A perspective. *Managerial Finance, 27*(12), 3–17. doi:10.1108/03074350110767411

Bonito, A., & Pais, C. (2018). *The macroeconomic determinants of the adoption of IFRS for SMEs.* Revista de Contabilidad. doi:10.1016/j.rcsar.2018.03.001

Burgstahler, D., & Dichev, I. (1997). Earnings management to avoid earnings decreases and losses. *Journal of Accounting and Economics, 24*(1), 99–126. doi:10.1016/S0165-4101(97)00017-7

Burgstahler, D. C., Hail, L., & Leuz, C. (2006). The importance of reporting incentives: Earnings management in European private and public firms. *The Accounting Review, 81*(5), 983–1016. doi:10.2308/accr.2006.81.5.983

Callao Gastón, S., Ferrer García, C., Jarne Jarne, J. I., & Laínez Gadea, J. A. (2010). IFRS adoption in Spain and the United Kingdom : Effects on accounting numbers and relevance. *Advances in Accounting*. doi:10.1016/j.adiac.2010.08.003

Callao Gastón, S., & Jarne Jarne, J. I. (1995). La informacion financiera en el contexto internacional: analisis descriptivo. *Revista Espanola de Financiacion y Contabilidad1, 24*(85), 937–969.

Callao Gastón, S., & Jarne Jarne, J. I. (2011). El impacto de la crisis en la manipulación contable. *Revista de Contabilidad, 14*(2), 59–85. doi:10.1016/S1138-4891(11)70028-0

Cenni, S., Monferrà, S., Salotti, V., Sangiorgi, M., & Torluccio, G. (2015). Credit rationing and relationship lending. Does firm size matter? *Journal of Banking & Finance, 53*, 249–265. doi:10.1016/j.jbankfin.2014.12.010

Chaney, P. K., & Lewis, C. M. (1995). Earnings management and firm valuation under asymmetric information. *Journal of Corporate Finance: Contracting. Governance and Organization, 1*(3–4), 319–345.

Chen, H., Tang, Q., Jiang, Y., & Lin, Z. (2010). The role of international financial reporting standards in accounting quality : Evidence from the European Union. *Journal of International Financial Management & Accounting, 21*(3), 220–278. doi:10.1111/j.1467-646X.2010.01041.x

Christensen, H. B., Lee, E., Walker, M., & Zeng, C. (2015). Incentives or standards: What determines accounting quality changes around IFRS adoption? *European Accounting Review, 24*(1), 31–61. doi:10.1080/09638180.2015.1009144

Cimini, R. (2015). How has the financial crisis affected earnings management? a European study. *Applied Economics, 47*(3), 302–317. doi:10.1080/00036846.2014.969828

Coppens, L., & Peek, E. (2005). An analysis of earnings management by European private firms. *Journal of International Accounting, Auditing & Taxation, 14*(1), 1–17. doi:10.1016/j.intaccaudtax.2005.01.002

Costa, M., & Moreira, J. A. (2010). A experiência do auditor como determinante da qualidade da auditoria: uma análise para o caso português. *Contabilidade & Gestão*, (9).

Cruz, S. N. da S. R. A., Azevedo, G. M. do C., & Pinheiro, C. F. R. (2013). Do POC ao SNC : evolução e aspetos diferenciadores. *Revista Portuguesa de Contabilidade, 3*(10).

da Costa, S. F. (2007). *A Ley 16/2007, de 4 de Julho e a reforma do direito contabilístico Espanhol* (pp. 29–34). Revista TOC.

Dayanandan, A., Donker, H., Ivanof, M., & Karahan, G. (2016). IFRS and accounting quality: Legal origin, regional, and disclosure impacts. *International Journal of Accounting & Information Management, 24*(3), 296–316. doi:10.1108/IJAIM-11-2015-0075

de las Heras, E., Cañibano, L., & Moreira, J. A. (2012). The Impact of the Spanish financial act on audit quality. *Revista Española de Financiación y Contabilidad, 41*(156), 521–546. doi:10.1080/02102412.2012.10779734

de Noguer, B. G., & Munõz, M. (2007). La calidad de los ajustes por devengo no afecta al coste de la deuda de las PYMES españolas. *Investigacion Economica, 31*(1), 79–117.

de Sousa, A. S. N., Góis, C. M. G. G., & Viseu, C. M. P. (2017). A relação dos impostos com as necessidades de financiamento na manipulação de resultados. *XVI Congresso Internacional de Contabilidade e Auditoria*.

Dechow, P., & Schrand, C. (2004). *Earnings quality*. The Research Foundation of CFA Institute; doi:10.1016/j.jacceco.2010.09.001

Dechow, P., Sloan, R., & Sweeney, A. (1995). Detecting earnings management. *The Accounting Review, 70*(2), 193–225.

Dechow, P. M., & Dichev, I. (2002). The quality of accruals and earnings : The role of accrual estimation errors. *The Accounting Review, 77*(s-1), 35–59. doi:10.2308/accr.2002.77.s-1.35

Dechow, P. M., Richardson, S., & Tuna, I. (2003). Why are earnings kinky? An examination of the earnings management explanation. *Review of Accounting Studies, 8*(2–3), 355–384. doi:10.1023/A:1024481916719

DeFond, M., Hu, X., Hung, M., & Li, S. (2011). The impact of mandatory IFRS adoption on foreign mutual fund ownership: The role of comparability. *Journal of Accounting and Economics*, *51*(3), 240–258. doi:10.1016/j.jacceco.2011.02.001

DeFond, M., & Jiambalvo, J. (1994). Debt covenant violation and manipulation of accruals. *Journal of Accounting and Economics*, *17*(1–2), 145–176. doi:10.1016/0165-4101(94)90008-6

Dias, P. (2015). *As diferenças entre o resultado contabilístico e o fiscal e a gestão dos resultados Evidência empírica de empresas privadas portuguesas (Tese de Doutoramento)*. Lisboa: ISCTE-IUL.

Dimitras, A. I., Kyriakou, M. I., & Iatridis, G. (2015). Financial crisis, GDP variation and earnings management in Europe. *Research in International Business and Finance*, *34*, 338–354. doi:10.1016/j.ribaf.2015.02.017

Dimitropoulos, E., Asteriou, P., Dimitrios Kousenidis, D., & Leventis, S. (2013). The impact of IFRS on accounting quality: Evidence from Greece. *Advances in Accounting*, *29*(1), 108–123. doi:10.1016/j.adiac.2013.03.004

do Carmo, C. R., Moreira, J. A., & Miranda, M. C. (2010). A qualidade dos accruals e o custo do financiamento nas empresas portuguesas: uma análise por grupos de dimensão. In XVI Encuentro AECA (pp. 1–31). Leiria.

do Carmo, C. R., Moreira, J. A., & Miranda, M. C. (2016). Earnings quality and cost of debt: Evidence from Portuguese private companies. *Journal of Financial Reporting and Accounting*, *14*(2), 178–197. doi:10.1108/JFRA-08-2014-0065

Doadrio, L., Alvarado, M., & Carrera, N. (2015). Reforma de la normativa contable española: Análisis de su entramado institucional. *Spanish Accounting Review*, *18*(2), 200–216. doi:10.1016/j.rcsar.2015.02.002

Eilifsen, A. (1996). The relationship between accounting and taxation in Norway. *European Accounting Review*, *5*(sup1), 835–844. doi:10.1080/09638189600000061

Eilifsen, A., Knivsfla, K. H. IV, & Saettem, F. (1999). Earnings manipulation : Cost of capital versus tax. *European Accounting Review*, *8*(3), 481–491. doi:10.1080/096381899335899

European Commission. (2003). Commission Recommendation of 6 May 2003 concerning the definition of micro, small and medium-sized enterprises. *Official Journal of the European Union*, 36–41. Retrieved from https://eur-lex.europa.eu/legal-content/EN/TXT/PDF/?uri=CELEX:32003H0361&from=EN

European Commission. (2017a). *2017 SBA fact sheet Portugal*. Author.

European Commission. (2017b). *2017 SBA fact sheet Spain*. Author.

Fernández-Rodríguez, E., & Martínez-Arias, A. (2015). La discrecionalidad en las diferencias temporarias entre Contabilidad y Fiscalidad. *Spanish Journal of Finance and Accounting*, *44*(2), 180–207. doi:10.1080/02102412.2015.1006427

Francis, J., Lafond, R., Olsson, P., & Schipper, K. (2005). The market pricing of accruals quality. *Journal of Accounting and Economics*, *39*(2), 295–327. doi:10.1016/j.jacceco.2004.06.003

Frank, M. M., Lynch, L. J., & Rego, S. O. (2009). Tax reporting aggressiveness to aggressive and its relation financial reporting. *The Accounting Review*, *84*(2), 467–496. doi:10.2308/accr.2009.84.2.467

Frankel, R., & Li, X. (2004). Characteristics of a firm's information environment and the information asymmetry between insiders and outsiders. *Journal of Accounting and Economics*, *37*(2), 229–259. doi:10.1016/j.jacceco.2003.09.004

Goncharov, I., & Zimmermann, J. (2006). Earnings management when incentives compete: The role of tax accounting in Russia. *Journal of International Accounting Research*, *5*(1), 41–65. doi:10.2308/jiar.2006.5.1.41

Gonzalo Angulo, J. A. (2014). La reforma contable española de 2007: Um balance. *Revista de Contabilidad: Spanish Accounting Review*, *17*(2), 183–200. doi:10.1016/j.rcsar.2014.09.001

Gracia-Sarubbi, F., San Juan-Pajares, C. A., & Rodríguez-López, Á. (2014). Evolución del proceso de armonización contable en España y Brasil en el período 1973-2013. *Cuadernos de Contabilidad*, *15*(38), 397–425. doi:10.11144/Javeriana.cc15-38.epac

Greene, W. H. (2008). *Econometric Analysis*. Pearson.

Guenther, D. A. (1994). The relation between tax rates and pre-tax returns direct evidence from the 1981 and 1986 tax rate reductions. *Journal of Accounting and Economics*, *18*(3), 379–393. doi:10.1016/0165-4101(94)90027-2

Guimarães, J. (2010). Reflexões sobre o SNC. *Contabilidade & Empresas*, *2*, 22–27.

Guimarães, R., Lima, L., Ocejo, J. L. S., & Gonçalves, P. (1998). Alternativas contabilísticas: estudo comparativo entre Portugal e Espanha. VII Jornadas de Contabilidade e Auditoria.

Healy, P. M. (1985). The effect of bonus schemes on accounting choices. *Journal of Accounting and Economics*, *7*(1–3), 85–107. doi:10.1016/0165-4101(85)90029-1

Healy, P. M., & Wahlen, J. M. (1999). A Review of the earnings management literature and its implications for standard setting. *Accounting Horizons*, *13*(4), 365–383. doi:10.2308/acch.1999.13.4.365

Hepworth, S. R. (1953). periodic income smoothing. *The Accounting Review*, *28*(1), 32–39.

Höglund, H., & Sundvik, D. (2016). Outsourcing of accounting tasks and tax management: Evidence from a corporate tax rate change. *Applied Economics Letters*, *23*(7), 482–485. doi:10.1080/13504851.2015.1083074

Höglund, H., & Sundvik, D. (2018). Do auditors constrain intertemporal income shifting in private companies? *Accounting and Business Research*, 1–26. doi:10.1080/00014788.2018.1490166

Howard, M. (1996). Downsizing to destruction. *Management Accounting: Magazine for Chartered Management Accountants*, *74*, 66.

Hsiao, C. (2004). *Analysis of panel data* (Vol. 47). Computers & Mathematics with Applications; doi:10.1016/S0898-1221(04)90099-5

Huguet, D., & Gandía, J. L. (2016). Audit and earnings management in Spanish SMEs. *BRQ Business Research Quarterly*, *19*(3), 171–187. doi:10.1016/j.brq.2015.12.001

Iatridis, G., & Dimitras, A. I. (2013). Financial crisis and accounting quality: Evidence from five European countries. *Advances in Accounting*, *29*(1), 154–160. doi:10.1016/j.adiac.2013.03.001

Jarne Jarne, J. I. (2000). *Clasificación y evolución internacional de los sistemas contables*. Associación Española de Contabilidad y Administración de Empresas.

Jones, J. (1991). Earnings Management during import relief investigations. *Journal of Accounting Research*, *29*(2), 193. doi:10.2307/2491047

Karampinis, N. I., & Hevas, D. L. (2013). Effects of IFRS adoption on tax-induced incentives for financial earnings management: Evidence from Greece. *The International Journal of Accounting*, *48*(2), 218–247. doi:10.1016/j.intacc.2013.04.003

Klann, R. C., & Beuren, I. M. (2018). Earnings management IFRS adoption in Brazilian and British companies. *International Journal of Disclosure and Governance*, *15*(1), 13–28. doi:10.105741310-018-0032-4

Kothari, S. P., Leone, A. J., & Wasley, C. E. (2005). Performance matched discretionary accrual measures. *Journal of Accounting and Economics*, *39*(1), 163–197. doi:10.1016/j.jacceco.2004.11.002

Kousenidis, D. V., Ladas, A. C., & Negakis, C. I. (2013). The effects of the European debt crisis on earnings quality. *International Review of Financial Analysis*, *30*, 351–362. doi:10.1016/j.irfa.2013.03.004

Lisboa, I. (2017). Impact of financial crisis and family control on earning management of Portuguese listed firms. *European Journal of Family Business*, *6*(2), 118–131. doi:10.1016/j.ejfb.2017.06.002

Lisboa, I., & Kacharava, A. (2018). Does financial crisis impact earnings management: Evidence from Portuguese and UK. *European Journal of Applied Business and Management*, *4*(1), 80–100.

Lopes, C., Cerqueira, A., & Brandão, E. (2010). Impact of IFRS adoption on accounting quality in European firms. *Journal of Modern Accounting and Auditing*, *6*(9), 20–31.

Marques, A., & Silva, N. (2010). A contabilidade criativa e o Sistema de Normalização Contabilística. Sistema de Normalização Contabilística - Jornadas de Contabilidade e Fiscalidade.

Marques, M., Rodrigues, L. L., & Craig, R. (2011). Earnings management induced by tax planning: The case of Portuguese private firms. *Journal of International Accounting, Auditing & Taxation*, *20*(2), 83–96. doi:10.1016/j.intaccaudtax.2011.06.003

Martins, O., & Moreira, J. A. (2009). Endividamento bancário e qualidade da informação financeira: um estudo para o caso Português. *Jornal de Contabilidade, 388*, 217–231.

Maydew, E. L. (1997). Tax-induced earnings management by firms with net operating losses. *Journal of Accounting Research*, *35*(1), 83–96. doi:10.2307/2491468

Mcnichols, M. F. (2002). Discussion of the quality of accruals and earnings : The role of accrual estimation errors. *The Accounting Review*, *77*(s-1), 61–69. doi:10.2308/accr.2002.77.s-1.61

Meckling, W. H., & Jensen, M. C. (1976). Theory of the firm: Managerial behavior, agency costs and ownership structure. *Journal of Financial Economics, 3*(4), 305–360. doi:10.1016/0304-405X(76)90026-X

Mendes, C. A., & Rodrigues, L. L. (2007). Determinantes da manipulação contabilística. *Revista de Estudos Politécnicos, 4*(7), 189–210.

Missonier-Piera, F. (2004). Economic determinants of multiple accounting method choices in a Swiss context. *Journal of International Financial Management & Accounting, 15*(2), 118–144. doi:10.1111/j.1467-646X.2004.00104.x

Monterrey Mayoral, J., & Sánchez-Segura, A. (2006). Las características socioeconómicas como incentivos para la información financiera: evidencia empírica Española. *Investigaciones Economicas, 30*(3), 611–634. Retrieved from http://www.scopus.com/inward/record.url?eid=2-s2.0-38849199573&partnerID=tZOtx3y1

Monterrey Mayoral, J., & Sánchez-Segura, A. (2009). Como afectan los impuestos a la calidad del resultado? evidencia empirica en las empresas españolas no cotizadas. *Spanish Accounting Review, 12*, 117–138. doi:10.1016/S1138-4891(09)70004-4

Monterrey Mayoral, J., & Sánchez Segura, A. (2010). Diferencias en agresividad fiscal entre empresas familiares y no familiares. *Revista Española de Financiación y Contabilidad, 39*(145), 65–97. doi:10.1080/02102412.2010.10779679

Monterrey Mayoral, J., & Sánchez-Segura, A. (2017). Los impuestos como determinantes de la inversión empresarial. evidencia empírica en empresas españolas que no cotizan en bolsa. *Spanish Accounting Review*, 1–15. doi:10.1016/j.rcsar.2017.04.001

Morais, A. I., & Curto, J. D. (2008). Accounting quality and the adoption of IASB standards – Portuguese evidence. *Revista Contabilidade & Finanças, 19*(48), 103–111. doi:10.1590/S1519-70772008000300009

Moreira, J. (2006). *Are financing needs a constraint to earnings management? evidence for private Portuguese firms* (Working paper). Porto.

Moreira, J. A. (2009). O PEC e outros "sinais" fiscais: impacto sobre a manipulação dos resultados. *Jornal de Contabilidade, 386*, 155–169.

Moreira, J. A. (2010). O SNC – Sistema de Normalização Contabilística e a qualidade da informação financeira: consequências (esperadas) do uso do justo valor. Sistema de Normalização Contabilística - Jornadas de Contabilidade e Fiscalidade.

Naser, K. (1993). *Creative Financial Accounting: Its Nature and Use*. Prentice Hall.

Niyama, J., Rodrigues, A. M., & Rodrigues, J. (2015). Some thoughts on creative accounting and international accounting standards. *Revista Universo Contábil*, (1), 69–87. doi:10.4270/ruc.2015104

Parker, R., & Nobes, C. (2004). *Comparative international accounting*. Pearson.

Parte-Esteban, L., & Ferrer García, C. (2014). The influence of firm characteristics on earnings quality. *International Journal of Hospitality Management, 42*, 50–60. doi:10.1016/j.ijhm.2014.06.008

Păşcan, I.-D. (2015). Measuring the effects of IFRS adoption on accounting quality: A review. *Procedia Economics and Finance*, *32*(15), 580–587. doi:10.1016/S2212-5671(15)01435-5

Peasnell, K. V., Pope, P. F., & Young, S. (2000). Detecting earnings management using cross-sectional abnormal accruals models. *Accounting and Business Research*, *30*(4), 313–326. doi:10.1080/00014788.2000.9728949

Pellicer, M. J. A., & Blasco, M. A. V. (2004). Actuación discrecional sobre el resultado ante un cambio en la normativa fiscal. *Revista Española de Financiación y Contabilidad*, *33*(122), 603–636. doi:10.1080/02102412.2004.10779527

Pereira, A., & Alves, M. do C. G. (2017). Earnings management and European Regulation 1606/2002: Evidence from non-financial Portuguese companies listed in Euronext. *Spanish Accounting Review*, *20*(2), 107–117. doi:10.1016/j.rcsar.2017.05.002

Perera, D., & Chand, P. (2015). Issues in the adoption of international financial reporting standards (IFRS) for small and medium-sized enterprises (SMES). *Advances in Accounting*, *31*(1), 165–178. doi:10.1016/j.adiac.2015.03.012

Persakis, A., & Iatridis, G. E. (2015). Earnings quality under financial crisis: A global empirical investigation. *Journal of Multinational Financial Management*, *30*, 1–35. doi:10.1016/j.mulfin.2014.12.002

Pestana, M. H., & Gageiro, J. N. (2014). *Análise de dados para as ciências sociais* (6th ed.). Edições Sílabo.

Pineda González, C. (2000). Determinantes de la calidad del resultado. *Revista de Contabilidad*, *3*(5), 149–182.

Pope, P. F., & McLeay, S. J. (2011). The European IFRS experiment: Objectives, research challenges and some early evidence. *Accounting and Business Research*, *41*(3), 233–266. doi:10.1080/00014788.2011.575002

Reguera Alvarado, N., Laffarga Briones, J., & Fuentes Ruiz, P. de. (2012). Afecta la crisis a la gestión de reultados? *Revista de La Asociación Española de Contabilidad y Administración de Empresas*, (97), 22–23.

Rodrigues, L. L. (2013). Manipulação de contas ou marketing das percepções? In A. M. Rodrigues & T. Tavares (Eds.), *O SNC e os juízos de valor: uma perspectiva crítica e multidisciplinar* (pp. 265–285). Almedina.

Schipper, K. (1989). Commentary on earnings management. *Accounting Horizons*, 91–102. doi:10.1016/0361-3682(86)90013-9

Skinner, D. J., & Dechow, P. M. (2000). Earnings management: Reconciling the Views of accounting academics, practitioners, and regulators. *Accounting Horizons*, *14*(2), 235–250. doi:10.2308/acch.2000.14.2.235

Soderstrom, N. S., & Sun, K. J. (2007). IFRS adoption and accounting quality: A review. *European Accounting Review*, *16*(4), 675–702. doi:10.1080/09638180701706732

Stolowy, H., & Breton, G. (2000). *A framework for the classification of accounts manipulations*. Working paper.

Sweeney, A. P. (1994). Debt-covenant violations and managers' accounting responses. *Journal of Accounting and Economics*, *17*(3), 281–308. doi:10.1016/0165-4101(94)90030-2

Watts, R. L., & Zimmerman, J. L. (1978). Towards a positive theory of the determination of accounting standards. *The Accounting Review*, *53*, 112–134.

Zeghal, D., Chtourou, S. M., & Fourati, Y. M. (2012). The effect of mandatory adoption of ifrs on earnings quality: Evidence from the European Union. *Journal of International Accounting Research*, *11*(2), 1–25. doi:10.2308/jiar-10221

KEY TERMS AND DEFINITIONS

Earnings Management: Legal management of earnings obtained by firms, where, according to accounting principles, some accounting options are made in order to achieve a certain level of earnings, so as to obtain a benefit or reduce/avoid a cost.

SMEs: Firms employing less than 250 persons whose annual turnover does not exceed EUR 50 million or whose annual balance sheet total does not exceed EUR 43 million.

ENDNOTES

1. *E.g.* Dechow & Dichev (2002); Francis, Lafond, Olsson, & Schipper (2005); Mcnichols (2002).
2. *E.g.* Dechow *et al.* (1995); Jones (1991); Kothari, Leone, & Wasley (2005).
3. $ATT_{i,t}$ – total acrruals for firm i, in year t; CA – Current Assets; CX – Cash; CL – Current Liabilities; ML – Current Maturities of Long-Term Debt; DEPR – Depreciation and Amortization Expense; where the change (Δ) is computed between time t and time t - 1.
4. The Hausman test was used to evaluate the consistency of the estimator compared to another alternative estimator, through the difference between the coefficients of the regression by fixed effects and random effects. If the difference is statistically significant, the fixed effects model must be used; otherwise, the random effects model is used.
5. In the deviation of the residues no outliers were found, and for Portugal and Spain the residue modulus is less than 2.5, which is considered an acceptable value.
6. About this topic, the recent revision of the Directive no. 2013/34/UE are not examined due to insufficient data.

Chapter 6
Earnings Management and Corporate Governance in Family Firms:
Evidence From a Small Market

Elisabete Vieira
https://orcid.org/0000-0003-3593-368X
GOVCOPP Unit Research, Portugal

Mara Madaleno
https://orcid.org/0000-0002-4905-2771
GOVCOPP Unit Research, Portugal

ABSTRACT

Earnings management and corporate governance relationships are examined for a sample of 49 Portuguese listed firms considering an unbalanced panel for the period 2002-2017, using panel corrected standard errors models and considering the family ownership effect. Empirical findings reveal that there is a positive relationship between corporate board independence and earnings management and that the presence of women on board decreases earnings management practices. Results are consistent with the hypothesis that earnings management practices are lower in family firms than in non-family firms. Size, being audited by the Big 4 companies, return on assets, loss, and the existence of an audit committee on board influence positively earnings management, but leverage, age, and ownership control are negatively related to earnings management. Results indicate that further auditing and control is necessary for Portuguese listed companies leading to strict recommendations to be followed by policymakers regarding control of these firms.

DOI: 10.4018/978-1-5225-7817-8.ch006

INTRODUCTION

The main objective of this study is to investigate the relationship between earnings management and corporate governance, since it is a new direction in research about earnings management. We intend to analyze this relationship in the context of family firms, to see their motivation to implement earnings management practices. Furthermore, we will analyze whether family firms differ from their counterparts in what concerns the association between earnings management practices and corporate governance.

Previous literature document that firms with independent boards are more likely to have less earnings management (Dechow & Dichev, 2002). Jaggi, Leung, and Gul (2009), using a sample of Hong Kong firms, document that corporate board independence is important to ensure high-quality financial reporting. In spite of the studies that document earnings management, there are other studies finding no evidence of significant earnings management practices, such as Ball and Shivakumar (2005), in the UK. Although there are some studies analyzing the relationship between corporate governance and earnings management in these two countries, it is a scarce topic studied in other countries. Consequently, we would like to study this relationship in the Portuguese market. As far as we know, no other study attempt to study this relationship in Portugal.

We extend the existing research on the relationship between earnings management and corporate governance in several ways. First, Portugal is a country of interest because it differs from the main studied markets in some features, such as the USA and the UK, namely because it has a weak legal protection for shareholders (La Porta, Lopez-de-Silanes, & Shleifer, 1999; Setia-Atmaja, Tanewsky, & Skully, 2009), it has a high level of ownership concentration, and it is influenced by the civil law. This characteristics can cause differences among countries, namely with regard to corporate governance, ownership and control (Jaggi et al., 2009). Thus, the results may differ from the ones obtained in countries where outside investors are well protected by the legal system, the level of transparency is high and the equity ownership is relatively dispersed (González & García-Meca, 2014). Some studies indicate that the institutional arrangements of a country have a significant impact on the earnings management practices and, consequently, on earnings quality. Leuz, Nanda, and Wysocki (2003) find higher earnings management in countries with lower investor protection and with undeveloped capital markets, and Ball, Robin, and Wu (2003) maintain that institutional factors have a significant influence on the managerial incentives for financial reporting[1].

Second, we investigate the specific case of family firms, and, indeed, a significant number of family businesses characterizes Portugal. Family businesses are usual among listed firms around the world (La Porta et al., 1999; Anderson & Reeb, 2003; Prencipe, Bar-Yosef, & Dekker, 2014). Specifically, Faccio and Lang (2002) document that 60.34% of Portuguese firms are family businesses. Portuguese family firms (FF) are mainly small and medium firms, with managers having low levels of training, and having problems of succession. Although their relevant contribution to the employment (about 60%) and to the Gross Domestic Product (around 50%), studies on Portuguese family businesses are very rare, so, we think this type of firms is in need of research.

In what concerns studies about earnings management practices and family firms, some authors document that family ownership concentration influences earnings quality, such as Anderson and Reeb (2004), Ali, Chen, and Radhakrishnan (2007), and Siregar and Utama (2008). Hence, the issue of the impact of corporate governance on earnings management in family firms in an environment of weaker investor protection merits empirical investigation.

Finally, the relationship between corporate governance mechanisms and earnings management in the context of listed family firms is an important topic for researchers and practitioners[2]. Indeed, there has been extensive research on earnings management. However, literature regarding the association between corporate governance and earnings management in the context of family firms is inexistent, as the best of our knowledge, or quite rare. According to Ferramosca and Allegrini (2018), the effect of family involvement on earnings management is a complex issue, and cannot be studied in isolation without considering other variables, such as corporate governance variables. Moreover, investors are interested to know whether corporate governance characteristics improves earnings quality, namely the board independence.

In this context, we analyze a sample of non-financial Portuguese firms listed on the Euronext Lisbon, using Panel Corrected Standard Errors (PCSE) estimations. Our results, when considering family firms, reveal that the role of independent non-executive directors is not limited but that of women on board is, showing a higher and lower use of manipulative practices, respectively. Moreover, they point for the existence of non-linear relationships between independent non-executive directors and earnings management in the form of an inverted U-shape, while curvilinear effects of the U-shape form between women on board and earnings management. The findings have important policy implications regarding control and stricter account audit needs, since this is to the best of our knowledge, the first study to analyze the relationship between the effectiveness of independent non-executive directors, women on board and earnings management considering family firms in Portuguese publically listed firms.

Ussman (2004) reports that, in Portugal, many of the business' founders are male who have a low academic level. However he evidences they are very entrepreneurial, self-confident and intuitive, centralizing the power in themselves and developing paternalistic relations with their family and employees. In Marques and Couto (2017) it is possible to retain that family-owned businesses (overwhelmingly SMEs, even though they may comprise large economic groups), in general, are arguably important agents for the creation of employment, wealth, as well as for territorial and social cohesion. European Union reports (European Commission, 2009) present evidence that FF account for over 60% of enterprises in various sectors of activities. In Portugal, it is estimated that 70% to 80% of national businesses are family owned, taking up 50% of the labour force and accounting for 2/3 of the GDP (Marques and Couto, 2017; Portuguese Family Businesses Association, 2011, 2015). However, it is still not possible to determine exactly how many are, in fact, family businesses and when that is the case, their dynamics and (potential) contribution to the national and international markets remain unknown, turning Portugal an interesting case study for earnings management and corporate governance.

The remainder of the chapter is organized as follows: Section 2 contains the literature review and formulates the hypotheses. Section 3 presents the research design, including the sample selection procedures, the variables, and the research methodology. The results are provided in Section 4, and, finally, Section 5 presents the conclusions.

LITERATURE REVIEW AND HYPOTHESES

In what concerns earnings management, there is empirical evidence that manager's use accounting policies to smooth earnings or to reach a target in the earnings level (e.g., Leuz et al. 2003). According to previous literature, managers tend to adopt earnings management practices for two main reasons. On one hand, managers tend to escape to significant fluctuations in reported earnings, avoiding positive or negative extremes in profitability and a negative market reaction to earnings decreases, inspired by investors' preference for earnings smooth. On the other hand, managers tend to avoid the violation of debt-covenants in their contracts (Abeyratna & Power 2002). Healy and Wahlen (1999) review the academic evidence on earnings management, concluding that this practice occurs for several reasons, including: i) capital market motivations, to influence stock market perceptions; ii) contracting motivations, in order to increase management's compensation and to reduce the likelihood of violating lending agreements, and; iii) regulatory motivations, avoiding regulatory intervention.

Dechow and Skinner (2000) argue that, besides the different reasons that can motivate earnings management (the managers' incentives to meet earnings benchmarks, avoiding losses, reporting increases in seasonally adjusted earnings, meeting analysts' expectations for earnings and share offerings), academics' research efforts should focus more on capital market incentives for earnings management, as well as on managerial incentives.

Nelson et al. (2003) and Cheong et al. (2015) suggest that earnings management are usually implemented by manipulating some specific costs, such as provisions, amortizations, cost capitalization, impairment of assets and depreciations. Dechow et al. (2010) mention six classes of earnings quality causes, which are: i) external factors; ii) equity market incentives; iii) governance and controls, iv) firm characteristics, v) financial reporting practices, and; vi) auditors.

However, the agency conflict might be more towards rent extraction, or managerial-family compensation.

The main theories related to corporate governance and family businesses are the agency theory (Jensen & Meckling, 1976) and the stewardship theory (Davis, Schoorman, & Donaldson, 1997).

Family firms are likely to face agency problems differently from non-family firms (Jaggi et al., 2009). For family businesses, the conflict between family owners and minority shareholders fits into the majority-minority shareholder agency framework, namely because family owners have incentives to report financial accounting information in good faith, aligning their interests with the ones of minority shareholders, i.e., because of the alignment effect (Wang, 2006).

Because of the presence of majority and minority shareholders in family firms, they are more prone to suffer from agency conflicts between majority and minority shareholders (Type II agency problem) than conflicts between managers and shareholders (Type I agency problems) (Anderson & Reeb, 2004; Ali et al., 2007). Controlling shareholders may be motivated to maximize their private benefits by expropriating minority shareholders (Cheung, Rau, & Stouraitis, 2006). Consequently, some managerial decisions in family firms may not be in the best interest of minority shareholders. The global effect of family control on earnings management depends on the type of agency problem that dominates, the Type I or Type II agency problem.

The stewardship theory suggests that managers tend to make decisions that benefit firms' shareholders, and not themselves, acting with altruism (Davis et al., 1997; Siebels & Knyphausen-Aufseß, 2012). According to Miller and Le Breton-Miller (2006), this theory will be particularly prevalent in family businesses because managers are family members or have emotional connections to the families.

Overall, there is no consensus on which effect is prevalent in the context of family businesses. Higher control rights are associated with lower market valuation, which suggests expropriation of minority shareholders by controlling shareholders. However, Jaggi et al. (2009) find that concentrated ownership is associated with low earnings quality, which is consistent with the entrenchment effect.

Board Independence

There are several empirical studies finding evidence that independent directors on the board leads to better monitoring of management decisions (Fama & Jensen, 1983) and reduce the agency conflicts between large and minority shareholders (Anderson & Reeb, 2004), promoting the interests of other stakeholders (Chen & Roberts, 2010). According to Jaggi et al. (2009), independent corporate boards are more likely to provide severer monitoring of managerial behavior in what concerns earnings management, which will result in better earnings quality.

Some studies have examined the impact of board independence on earnings management on the USA and the UK (Dechow, Sloan, & Sweeney, 1996; Beasley, 1996; Xie, Davidson, & DaDalt, 2003).

Dechow et al. (1996) conclude that firms with greater earnings manipulation are more likely to have a board dominated by insiders and Beasley (1996) argue that inclusion of a larger proportion of outside directors on boards reduces the likelihood of financial statement fraud. Xie et al. (2003) find a negative relationship between corporate board independence and discretionary accruals, using a sample of USA and UK firms, respectively.

In the last decade, some studies have emerged, considering samples from countries other than the US and the UK. For example, Jaggi et al. (2009) analyze a sample based on all firms traded on the Hong Kong Stock Exchange during the period between 1998 and 2000, finding a negative relationship between earnings management and board independence, concluding that a higher proportion of independent members on corporate boards results in more effective monitoring of earnings management, which increases earnings quality. Moreover, Jaggi et al. (2009) find that the negative association between earnings management and board independence is weak for family-controlled firms, suggesting that board independence does not improve earnings quality in family-controlled firms. According the authors, a possible explanation for this result could be that independent directors and family control are substitutes for controlling earnings management.

Studying a sample of Portuguese listed firms, Alves (2014) find evidence that independent board members improve earnings quality by reducing earnings management practices. Based on the conceptual arguments presented in the literature, as well as in the previous empirical evidence, we formulate the first hypothesis as follows:

H_1: *There is a negative relationship between corporate board independence and earnings management.*

Gender Diversity

Previous literature argue that female directors are less prone to take high risks and tend to be more ethical than male directors, suggesting that female executive members could increase the firm's transparency (e.g., Betz, O'Connell, & Shepard, 1989).

There is empirical evidence that women have a positive impact on earnings quality. Krishman and Parsons (2007) explore the relationship between gender and earnings management, finding evidence that earnings quality is positively associated with gender diversity in senior management. Gul, Srinidhi, and Ng (2011) find that the higher the proportion of female directors in board members, the lower the firm's earnings manipulation and the better the quality of the financial information. Consistently, Xingqiang, Shaoyuan, and Hongmei (2017) argue that female executives can better participate in the firm's decision-making, reducing the earnings manipulation motivation. More recently, Zalata, Tauringana, and Tingbani (2018) examine the relationship between gender and earnings management, using data from a sample of USA firms, and find evidence that the proportion of female financial experts is significantly related with less earnings management. This evidence is consistent with previous results (Srinidhi, Gul, & Tsui, 2011).

There are some studies which evidence is not so clear. Huili, Ran, and Jingyi (2010) find that female executives did not have a significant impact on earnings quality and Abdullah and Ku (2016) find that the representation of women on the boards is not related to a decline in the earnings management practices.

Peni and Vähämaa (2010) find evidence that firms with female chief financial officers (CFO) are associated with income decreasing discretionary accruals, suggesting that women are following more conservative earnings management strategies. The results of Vähämma (2014) indicate that firms who employ a female CFO after a male tend to present more conservative practices of financial reporting, and the discretionary accruals tend to become more negative.

According to Na and Hong (2017), since the board of directors are responsible for making decisions for a firm, the gender of board may affect the firms' earnings management. Indeed, the authors find that firms manage earnings by accruals and real activities to avoid losses or earnings decreases when the CEO is male, but disappears when the CEO is female. Gull, Nekhili, Nagati, and Chtioui (2018) investigate also how female directors influence earnings management, considering a sample of French listed firms. The authors find that the presence of female directors prevents managers from managing earnings. However, this influence require particular competencies and skills, such as business expertise and audit committee memberships.

In Portugal, the women on board vary from 5.9% to 9.5%, from 2010 to 2014, showing that the management body consisted mainly of men (CMVM, 2014).

Based on previous literature, we state the next hypothesis as follows:

H_2: *The presence of women on board decreases earnings management practices.*

Family Control

We expect earnings management to be lower in family firms than in non-family firms by several reasons. First, family firms tend to monitor managerial decision-making process, which reduces the opportunities to participate in manage earnings actions. Second, according to the stewardship theory, families' interests are aligned with the firms' wealth (e.g., Davis et al., 1997). Third, family firms have a long-term business orientation (Anderson, Mansi, & Reeb, 2003; Jiraporn and DaDalt, 2009; Cascino, Pugliese, Mussolino, & Sansone, 2010) and a desire to protect firms wealth for later generations (Achleitner, Günter, Kaserer, & Siciliano, 2014), which decreases the pressure to manage earnings in order to meet short-term earnings expectations (Jaggi et al., 2009).

According to Fama and Jensen (1983), family-controlled firms should be more efficient than publicly owned firms because monitoring costs are lower in family firms. However, family shareholders might expropriate minority shareholders to benefit family members (Villalonga & Amit, 2006), resulting in Type II agency problems. In this context, the controlling shareholders may use earnings management to disguise the reported earnings and hide expropriation from minority shareholders. Some empirical studies document that the owners of family firms extract private benefits to the detriment of minority shareholders (e.g., DeAngelo & DeAngelo, 2000). In addition, there is evidence that earnings management actions are higher in countries with lower investor protection (Leuz et al., 2003), suggesting that earnings management may be used to maximize the private benefits of majority shareholders (Jaggi et al., 2009).

There is large evidence that family firms are less likely to manage earnings than non-family firms, such as Wang (2006), Ali et al. (2007) and Jiraporn and DaDalt (2009), in the USA, Prencipe, Bar-Yosef, and Dekker (2008) in Italy, Siregar and Utama (2008), in Indonesia, Ghabdian, Attaran, and Froutan (2012) in Tehran, and Achleitner et al. (2014), in Germany.

However, some studies have provided evidence that public family firms do not differ from their non-family counterparts in what concerns earnings management (González & García-Meca, 2013; Vieira, 2016). Using a sample of American firms, Liu, Shi, Wilson, and Wu (2017) analyse how family involvement in the ownership and management affects its engagement in earnings management, finding evidence that family firms engage in less accrual-based earnings management, although they are indistinguishable from non-family firms in what concerns of real earnings management.

More recently, Gottardo and Moisello (2019) analyze the value relevance of earnings management practices, using a sample of non-financial listed firms. The results show a negative effect on non-family firms' market value at the same time as they do not affect family firms' value in a significant way. In addition, the results suggest that the influence used by families in terms of founder presence in management, family CEO and family members on the board does not have significant impact on firms' market value.

Diregar and Utama (2008) investigate the effect of ownership structure and corporate governance practices on earnings management in Indonesia, finding evidence that firms with a high proportion of family ownership are more likely to choose efficient earnings management than other types of firms. However, the authors find results that are not consistent with the evidence that institutional ownership, firm size, and corporate governance practices have important influence on earnings-management type.

Other authors find a nonlinear relationship between family ownership and earnings management. Razzaque, Ali, and Mather (2016) examine this association in Bangladesh, finding evidence of existence of curvilinear relationships between family ownership and earnings management, and Ferramosca and Allegrini (2018) consider a sample of Italian firms, which results show an inverted U-shaped relationship between discretionary accruals and family involvement in firm's management and control.

Based on the assumptions of the stewardship theory, the long-term perspectives of family firms and the desire to pass firms to future generations, we formulate the following hypothesis:

H_3: *The earnings management practices are lower in family firms than in non-family firms.*

RESEARCH DESIGN

Variables

Dependent Variable

To estimate a firm's earnings management (EM), we use the accruals management, proxied by the abnormal accruals estimated from the modified Jones (1991) model, suggested by Dechow, Sloan, and Sweeney (1995), and used after by several authors, such as González and García-Meca (2014) and Na and Hong (2017). The Dechow et al. (1995) model is used to estimate the accrual component of earnings:

$$Total\ Accruals_{i,t} = (\Delta CA_{i,t} - \Delta Cash_{i,t}) - (\Delta CL_{i,t} - \Delta STD_{i,t}) - Dep_{i,t} \qquad (1)$$

where, for firm i and year t, ΔCAi,t is the change in total current assets; ΔCashi,t is the change in cash and cash equivalents; ΔCLi,t is the change in total current liabilities; ΔSTDi,t is the change in long-term debt included in current liabilities; and Depi,t is the depreciation and amortization expense.

Following González and García-Meca (2014), we use the cross-sectional version of the modified Jones' (1991) model to estimate the non-discretionary component of total accruals, regressing total accruals (TAC) as follows:

$$\frac{TAC_{i,t}}{TA_{i,t-1}} = \alpha + \beta_1 \frac{\Delta REV_{i,t}}{TA_{i,t-1}} + \beta_2 \frac{PPE_{i,t}}{TA_{i,t-1}} + \varepsilon_{i,t} \qquad (2)$$

where, for firm i and year t, ΔREVi,t is the change in revenues; and PPEi,t is the level of gross property, plant and equipment. The variables are scaled by lagged total assets (TAi,t-1), in order to mitigate the residuals heteroscedasticity (Kothari, Leone, & Wasley, 2005).

In order to estimate each sample firm's non-discretionary accruals component (NDAC), we use the estimated parameters of regression (2), adjusting the change in sales for the change in accounts receivable (ΔAR), which allows for the possibility that firms could have manipulated sales by changing credit terms (Dechow et al., 1995):

$$NDAC_{i,t} = \hat{\alpha} + \hat{\beta}_1 \frac{\Delta REV_{i,t} - \Delta AR_{i,t}}{TA_{i,t-1}} + \hat{\beta}_2 \frac{PPE_{i,t}}{TA_{i,t-1}} \qquad (3)$$

Discretionary accruals component (DAC) are defined as the remaining portion of total accruals:

$$DAC_{i,t} = \frac{TAC_{i,t}}{TA_{i,t-1}} - NDAC_{i,t} \qquad (4)$$

We consider the absolute value of discretionary accruals $\left|DAC_{i,t}\right|$ as the proxy for earnings management (EM), since the quality of earnings does not impose any direction or sign on the earnings management expectations (Jiraporn & DaDalt, 2009; González & García-Meca, 2014). Variables are described in table 1 and data descriptive statistics is presented in table 2.

Independent Variables

To test the formulated hypotheses, we use as independent variables the independence of non-executive directors, gender diversity (women on board) and family firms.

Following Siregar and Utama (2008) and Jaggi et al. (2009), we use the proportion of independent non-executive directors (INED) on corporate boards to measure the corporate board independence, calculated from the number of independent members divided by the number of members on the board.

Gender diversity, measured by the women on board (WOB) is the number of women on the board divided to the total number of directors (Shukeri, Shin, & Shaari, 2012).

There are several definitions of family firms (FF), as opposed to non-family firms (NFF), which do not facilitate a generalized accepted concept of FF (e.g., Prencipe et al. 2014). Based on La Porta, Lopez-de-Silanes, Shleifer, and Vishny (2000) and Setia-Atmaja et al. (2009), we identify FF as companies in which the founding family or a family member is involved in the top management of the firm and control twenty per cent or more of the equity. Thus, we consider FF as a dummy variable, which takes the value of one if a firm is considered as a FF, and zero otherwise. Recently, Ferramosca and Allegrini (2018) investigated family firms' behaviors in terms of their earning management strategies, to conclude for the existence of an inverted U-shaped relationship between discretionary accruals and family involvement in firm management and control, considering Italian firms for the 2007-2015 period.

We have also included the interaction terms INEDFF (Interaction term between Independent non-executive directors and family firms) and WOBFF (Interaction term between women on board and family firms) as well as their squared values (to capture non-linear effects) to validate the findings related to H1 and H2, but considering only the FF effect both with respect to independence of non-executive directors and women on board.

Control Variables

We evaluate the relationship between the independent variables and earnings management, after monitoring for the impact of control variables, considering their relevance to earnings management. In this context, we use the following control variables: the audit firm, firm size, growth opportunities, profitability, leverage and losses.

We include a dummy variable for Big 4 auditors (BIG4). Several studies find evidence that earnings management in firms audited by Big 6 auditors is smaller than in firms audited by non-Big 6 auditors (e.g., Francis, Maydew, & Spark, 1999). BIG4 is used to measure audit quality, considering one for firms audited by Big 4 auditors (high audit quality) and zero for firms audited by non-Big 4 auditors (low audit quality) (Siregar & Utama, 2008).

We use firm size (SIZE) as a control variable. Lee and Choi (2002) find evidence that small firms are more likely to manage earnings than large firms are, namely to avoid losses. Consequently, it is expected that larger firms are engage in less opportunistic earnings management than the smaller companies (Siregar & Utama, 2008). We measure the SIZE as the natural logarithm of the book value of total assets (Prencipe, Markarian, & Pozza, 2008).

Firms with higher growth opportunities are more likely to manage earnings in order to meet investors' expectations (e.g., Skinner & Sloan, 2002). Thus, we control for future growth opportunities, considering the market-to-book ratio (MB), computed as the market value to the book value of the equity (Ali et al., 2007; Prencipe et al., 2008). Moreover, higher growth opportunities are directly related to age (Muritala, 2012). Muritala (2012) results, from Panel Least Square (PLS) model applied in the Nigerian context, confirm that asset turnover, size, firm's age and firm's asset tangibility are positively related to firm's performance. As such, we also use age (AGE) as a control variable since prior literature suggest that earnings management might depend on firm age, measured as the natural log of the number of years since its founding (Ferramosca and Allegrini, 2018).

Prencipe et al. (2008) find evidence that profitability is negatively related to earnings management procedures. Thus, we expect that managers are less likely to manage earnings in profitable firms. We

Table 1. Definition and operationalization of variables

Variable Label	Definition	Role
EM	Earnings Management = absolute value of discretionary accruals	Dependent variable
INED	Independent non-executive directors = number of independent members divided by the number of members on the board	Independent variable
INED2	Independent non-executive directors squared	Independent variable
WOB	Women on board = number of women on the board divided to the total number of directors	Independent variable
WOB2	Women on board squared	Independent variable
FF	Dummy, 1 if classified as Family Firm	Independent variable
INEDFF	Interaction term between Independent non-executive directors and family firms	Independent variable
WOBFF	Interaction term between women on board and family firms	Independent variable
INEDFF2	Interaction term between Independent non-executive directors and family firms squared	Independent variable
WOBFF2	Interaction term between women on board and family firms squared	Independent variable
BIG4	Big 4 auditors = Dummy, 1 for firms audited by Big 4 auditors	Control variable
SIZE	Natural logarithm of the book value of total assets	Control variable
AGE	Natural logarithm of the difference between the constituion date and year t	Control variable
MB	Market-to-book ratio = market value to the book value of the equity	Control variable
ROA	Return on assets ratio = operating income divided by the total assets	Control variable
LEV	Leverage = total liabilities divided by total assets	Control variable
LOSS	Dummy, 1 if the firm incurred in a loss in the previous period	Control variable
BS	Board size = log of the total number of directors in the firm	Control variable
AC	Audit committee = Dummy, 1 if an audit committee exists	Control variable
OC	Ownership concentration = percentage of cumulative shareholdings by the ten top shareholders	Control variable
IND	Dummy, 1 if the firm belongs to the industry sector	Control variable
YEAR	Dummy, 1 if the year corresponds to year t (2017 until 2002)	Control variable

measure profitability by the return on assets ratio (ROA), calculated by the operating income divided by the total assets (Prencipe et al., 2008). Prencipe et al. (2008) also find that family firms manage earnings in order to avoid debt-covenants violations. Consequently, we expect that the incentive to manage earnings is stronger for most indebt firms. Following Wang (2006) and Prencipe et al. (2008), we calculate leverage (LEV) as the total liabilities divided by total assets.

Houqe, Dunstan, Waresul, and Van (2010) argue that firms with a poor financial situation are more likely to incur in earnings management practices. Thus, we include a dummy variable loss (LOSS), which takes the value of one if the firm incurred a loss in the previous period, and zero otherwise (González & García-Meca 2014; Razzaque et al., 2016).

As in Waweru and Prot (2018), we control for Board Size (BS) measured as the natural log of the total number of directors in the firm, for the presence of an audit committee (AC), including a dummy which takes the value of one if an audit committee exists and zero otherwise, and for ownership concentration (OC), being the percentage of cumulative shareholdings by the ten top shareholders.

Finally, we control for the effect of industry (IND) and year (YEAR), considering dummy variables. Table 1 describes the variables used in this study.

Sample

The sample is comprised of all non-financial firms listed on Euronext Lisbon, from the period 2002-2017. Because not all firms had data available for the entire period, we have an unbalanced panel. Financial firms were excluded because they have distinct regulations and disclosures, turning more complex the determination of accruals (Waweru & Prot, 2018). Of the 55 Portuguese firms available in the database, we use in the sample 49 (some were excluded for being financial firms but others due to missing data). Our sample of 49 is composed of 24 NFF and 30 FF, considering that 5 of them were initially FF and turned into NFF at the end of the analysis period. The 49 companies are considered a good representative of the population as they constitute 88.09% of the listed companies. Since 5 turned to be NFF in the middle of the period we have in the final sample 24 NFF and 25 FF, representative of the weight of FF in the stock exchange in Portugal, which is consistent with the evidence of Faccio and Lang (2002), that FF are predominant in Portugal.

Data were collected from a private database provided by Bureau van Dijk, the SABI. In addition, we needed to collect manually some data concerning corporate governance and family control from the annual reports of sample firms. The sample period was conditioned by the data availability on SABI. The final sample consists of 49 firms and 637 firm-years observations, from these 352 correspond to FF and 285 to NFF.

We study the Portuguese firms for several reasons. First, Portugal is a small and medium-sized financial markets with a growing importance in the world financial market. There are around 50 Portuguese publicly trading firms As compared to the U.S. market, where the number of firms in the Nasdaq or in the NYSE index totals more than 3000, turns Portugal an interesting case study even when compared to those firms publically listed in other European countries. Second, this country takes the shape of family firms, where the most dominant companies are owned and/or managed by the family. When analyzing the listed firms, the relevance of family firms is also evident, since around half of the Portuguese listed firms are family firms. Third, there are significant differences between Portuguese publicly traded firms and those of Anglo-Saxon economies, which is what the majority of studies focus on, starting with the very different financial market when compared to that Anglo-Saxon economies (different dimensions and also in terms of financial market liquidity[3]). Firm's market size is also too distinct, since the number of firms traded in the markets is also different. These differences make it relevant to analyze Portugal, not only to expand international evidence, but also to compare the results and to determine whether the conclusions are international evidence. These reasoning's and others have also been presented by Miralles-Marcelo et al. (2014) while studying the impact of family control on firm performance in both Portugal and Spain.

Estimation Model

To analyze the relationship between corporate governance and earnings management, we used the following regression model, and adaptations for robustness check.

$$| EM_{i,t} | = \alpha + \beta_1 INED + \beta_2 WOB_{i,t} + \beta_3 FF_{i,t} + \beta_4 INEDFF_{i,t} + \beta_5 WOBFF_{i,t} + \beta_6 BIG4_{i,t} + \beta_7 SIZE_{i,t} + \beta_8 MB_{i,t} + \beta_9 ROA_{i,t} + \beta_{10} LEV_{i,t} + \beta_{11} LOSS_{i,t} + \beta_{12} IND_{i,t} + \beta_{13} YEAR_{i,t} + \beta_{14} AGE_{it} + \beta_{15} BS_{it} + \beta_{16} AC_{it} + \beta_{17} OC_{it} + \varepsilon_{i,t} \quad (5)$$

INEDFF and WOBFF are interaction terms, in order to see if the effects of INED and WOB variables are statistically different between FF and NFF. We also use in estimations the interactions terms INEDFF and WOBFF squared to see if there exists a U-shaped relationship, as well as the independent variables INED2 and WOB2 meaning Independent non-executive directors and women on board both squared, following Ferramosca and Allegrini (2018) which also use INED2 for a sample of Italian firms. Different model specifications were used for robustness check, including and excluding independent and control variables to observe if results change to different variables inclusion into estimations.

Previous test (Pesaran's test) results revealed the presence of cross sectional independence and the Modified Wald test for group wise heteroscedasticity showed the presence of heteroscedasticity. While, serial correlation has long been recognized as a potential problem for panel data, cross-sectional dependence has recently received renewed attention. This is a problem, because most common panel data estimators are unable to simultaneously handle both serial correlation and cross sectional dependence. One estimator that can is Parks' Feasible Generalized Least Squares (FGLS) estimator, but it can only be implemented when the number of time periods (T) is greater than or equal to the number of cross-sections (N), being also known to underestimate standard errors in finite samples. Beck and Katz (1995) report that a two-step, modified version of 'inefficient' Ordinary Least Squares (OLS) – known as 'Panel Corrected Standard Error' (PCSE) estimation – performs substantially better than the asymptotically efficient FGLS estimator in many circumstances, being used in diverse contexts (Reed & Ye, 2009; Muritala, 2012).

Following Reed and Ye (2009), we presented Beck and Katz's (1995) Panel Corrected Standard Errors (PCSE) because they are robust to contemporaneous correlation besides heteroskedasticity, and because they perform well in finite sample and panel with time dimension (T) greater than cross-section (N). PCSE preserves the weighting of observations for autocorrelation, using a sandwich estimator to incorporate cross-sectional dependence when calculating standard errors. In the present work we apply PCSE using Durbin-Watson autocorrelation and errors considering panel-level heteroscedastic and correlated across panels.

Table 2 reports descriptive statistics of the variables included in the regression analysis. The results show that EM ranges from a minimum of 0 and a maximum of 49.9 with a mean of 0 when considering all firms in the sample. The last column of table 2 shows the significant differences in means between the sub-samples of FF and NFF. We observe that NFF are on average more indebted, being the difference significant. Additionally, on average, FF perform significantly better than NFF, as opposed to the sample of Italian firms of Ferramosca and Allegrini (2018), having a mean ROA higher. It should also be expected a higher mean MB in FF, which is proven by the mean values present in table 2. Size is similar for both NFF and FF on average, being age also similar between both types. While the size difference is significant, age is not. EM is higher in FF on average, having also higher volatility as measured by standard deviation, when compared to NFF, however this difference is not significant. On average the presence of WOB, BS and the presence of an AC is more likely in FF, although standard deviation values are higher in NFF.

Table 2. Descriptive statistics

	All					FF					NFF					Diff. in Mean
Variable	Obs	Mean	Std. Dev.	Min	Max	Obs	Mean	Std. Dev.	Min	Max	Obs	Mean	Std. Dev.	Min	Max	t-test
EM	637	0.0	0.1	0.0	49.9	352	0.1	0.13	0.0	49.9	285	0.0	0.8	0.0	7.53	-1.0
AGE	637	3.2	0.8	0.0	4.8	352	3.2	0.9	0.0	4.6	285	3.2	0.8	0.0	4.8	-0.4
INED	637	0.4	0.1	0.0	0.7	352	0.4	0.1	0.0	0.6	285	0.3	0.2	0.0	0.7	-1.5*
WOB	637	0.2	0.1	0.0	0.5	352	0.2	0.1	0.0	0.5	285	0.2	0.2	0.0	0.5	-4.3***
BS	637	2.6	0.4	1.4	3.6	352	2.7	0.3	2.1	3.3	285	2.6	0.5	1.4	3.6	-2.0**
AC	637	0.5	0.5	0.0	1.0	352	0.5	0.5	0.0	1.0	285	0.5	0.5	0.0	1.0	-2.1**
OC	637	0.9	0.1	0.5	1.0	352	0.9	0.1	0.6	1.0	285	0.9	0.2	0.5	1.0	-1.2
BIG4	637	0.5	0.5	0.0	1.0	352	0.6	0.5	0.0	1.0	285	0.5	0.5	0.0	1.0	-3.5***
SIZE	637	19.3	1.8	10.8	23.9	352	19.4	1.7	10.8	22.4	285	19.1	2.0	14.3	23.9	-1.6*
MB	637	981.8	24,509.3	-11.4	61,8573.2	352	1,759.4	32,970.0	-11.4	61,8573.2	285	21.4	320.8	-6.4	5,416.6	-1.0
ROA	637	0.0	0.2	-2.9	1.7	352	0.0	0.1	-0.5	0.4	285	-0.0	0.3	-2.9	1.7	-0.9
LEV	637	0.5	0.3	0.0	2.5	352	0.5	0.2	0.0	1.6	285	0.6	0.4	0.0	2.5	4.1***
LOSS	637	0.3	0.5	0.0	1.0	352	0.3	0.5	0.0	1.0	285	0.3	0.5	0.0	1.0	0.0
IND	637	0.2	0.4	0.0	1.0	352	0.2	0.4	0.0	1.0	285	0.1	0.3	0.0	1.0	-3.6***

*, **, *** represent statistical significance at 10%, 5% and 1% levels, respectively. Variables are defined and explained in Table 1.

Pearson correlation values were also computed and presented in Table 3. The dependent variable EM is not highly correlated with any of the other independent nor control variables and only significant considering age. Age and size are both highly correlated with the rest of the variables in the study.

Considering the independent variables, INED is significantly and positively correlated with BS, OC, BIG4 and SIZE, whereas WOB is positively and significantly correlated with BS and ROA, being negatively and significantly correlated with BIG4, Leverage and LOSS. The presence of an AC is significantly correlated with all the other variables except with MB. While SIZE is negatively correlated with MB, AGE has a positive correlation. LEV and MB are also negatively and significantly correlated, whereas ROA and LOSS also have a negative and significant correlation between them. From all the values presented in this table 3 we cannot say that variables evidence multicollinearity issues, but previous test results reveal that we should take into account heteroscedasticity and cross-sectional dependence, evidencing also that simple panel models (both fixed or random effects) are not the most appropriate to perform the estimation results. Thus, we have adopted the PCSE as also explained in the methodology section.

We assessed collinearity problems by determining the variance inflation factors (VIFs). All the dependent variables are greater than the level of 10, being the highest one that of women's on board. As such, one can be the linear transformation of the other and we have removed some of the variables in question from the subsequent analysis for robustness check also.

EMPIRICAL RESULTS

Table 4 presents the multivariate regression results considering all firms without distinguishing FF from NFF (Panel A), and considering the presence of FF and NFF (Panel B). In Table 4 we do not consider the possibility of curvilinear relationships with earnings management of INED and WOB. It is observable from the results that when significant the INED coefficient has a negative influence over EM, variable which loses significance when we consider the variables AGE, BS, AC and OC into estimations.

By opposition, WOB has a positive and significant influence over EM, independently of the inclusion of age, board size, the presence of an audit committee and ownership concentration, confirming robustness of results, provided the fact that it is verified when including the family ownership effect (FF). As such, considering FF into the analysis we are able to confirm hypothesis 1 that there is a negative relationship between corporate board independence and earnings management, if board size, audit committee and ownership concentration are not considered (validating the agency theory arguments).

Our results favour those of Jaggi et al. (2009) considering that the negative coefficient associated to INED is lower for the FF sample. As such, results seem to indicate that the negative association between earnings management and board independence is weaker for FF. Results also favour those of Gul et al. (2011), Krishman and Parsons (2007), Xingqiang et al. (2017) and Waweru and Prot (2018), among others, who found a positive relationship between gender and earnings management, independently of the variables considered into estimations, being that the effect is lower in FF considering coefficient values. Thus, female executives seem to have a significant impact on earnings quality in the sample of Portuguese firms, as in the US (Zalata et al., 2018), whose results remain valid considering board size, audit committee memberships (as in Gull et al., 2018) and ownership control. Thus table 4 results seem to turn invalid our hypothesis 2 that the presence of women on board decreases earnings management practices, being results robust to the inclusion of these variables.

Table 3. Pearson's correlation matrix

	EM	AGE	INED	WOB	BS	AC	OC	BIG4	SIZE	MB	ROA	LEV	LOSS	IND
EM	1													
AGE	-0.09**	1												
INED	-0.00	-0.02	1											
WOB	0.03	0.12***	-0.03	1										
BS	0.03	-0.16***	0.30***	0.15***	1									
AC	0.04	-0.05	0.03	0.04	0.28***	1								
OC	-0.05	0.10***	0.21***	0.06	-0.12***	-0.28***	1							
BIG4	0.04	-0.19***	0.41***	-0.07*	0.24***	0.26***	0.13***	1						
SIZE	0.04	-0.22***	0.15***	-0.01	0.58***	0.52***	-0.31***	0.38***	1					
MB	-0.00	-0.10**	-0.00	0.03	0.03	0.04	-0.05	0.04	-0.19***	1				
ROA	-0.00	0.10**	0.04	0.09**	-0.01	0.08**	0.06	0.06	0.04	-0.01	1			
LEV	-0.01	0.05	0.02	-0.24***	0.01	-0.30***	-0.06	-0.05	-0.14***	-0.07*	-0.04	1		
LOSS	0.06	0.04	-0.02	-0.19***	-0.21***	-0.23***	0.18***	-0.03	-0.28***	0.06	-0.22***	0.21***	1	
IND	-0.02	0.29***	-0.21***	0.12***	-0.01	-0.23***	0.28***	-0.05	-0.28***	-0.02	0.09**	0.14***	-0.02	1

*, **, *** represent statistical significance at 10%, 5% and 1% levels, respectively. Variables are defined and explained in Table 1.

Table 4. Panel correction standard errors initial results: dependent earnings management

Variable	Coefficient	z-Stat	Coefficient	z-Stat	Coefficient	z-Stat	Coefficient	z-Stat
INED	-62.05***	-2.91	17.63	1.38	-56.29***	-2.82	22.87	1.32
WOB	109.34***	4.39	136.45***	4.2	84.11***	5.53	54.18***	4.12
BIG4	27.19***	3.65	19.47***	2.94	25.91***	3.68	17.85***	2.83
SIZE	10.32***	4.94	4.22***	3.05	9.86***	4.96	3.16**	2.34
MB	-0.00	-0.01	-0.00	-1.26	-0.00	-0.10	-0.00	-1.33
ROA	28.18***	3.82	46.00***	4.67	28.38***	3.76	49.78***	4.98
LEV	-8.24**	-2.18	-16.33***	-3.08	-6.54**	-2.00	-19.42***	-4.13
LOSS	65.88***	9.19	78.82***	9.91	63.54***	9.28	75.10***	9.87
FF					10.41	1.57	-16.78*	-1.83
INED*FF					-20.69	-1.10	-21.89	-1.08
WOB*FF					39.20	1.58	149.89***	2.89
AGE			-35.29***	-4.26			-37.88***	-4.19
BS			-9.99*	-1.67			-6.87	-1.3
AC			15.97***	4.21			13.20***	4.27
OC			-173.92***	-4.62			-185.87***	-4.48
constant	-231.58***	-5.23	142.47***	2.97	-225.54***	-5.38	186.37***	3.15
IND	-10.34**	-2.44	30.06***	4.22	-13.11***	-2.70	32.53***	4.09
YEAR effects	included		included		included		included	
Wald chi2	4,7648.81		4,538.27		5,3271.42		3,725.1	
Prob > chi2	0.000		0.000		0.000		0.000	

*, **, *** represent statistical significance at 10%, 5% and 1% levels, respectively. Variables are defined and explained in Table 1.

The results of Table 2 show that in average FF have higher EM than NFF. In table 4 we observe a negative and statistically significant coefficient associated to FF influence over EM, where we have a positive and significant interaction term influence (WOBFF) over EM. Thus, we validate our hypothesis 3 and confirm the results of Wang (2006), Jiraporn and DaDalt (2009), Prencipe et al. (2008), and Ferramosca and Allegrini (2018), that family involvement is associated with reduced earnings management, also in Portuguese firms.

Age has a negative and significant impact over earnings management showing that EM decreases with AGE, whereas increases with SIZE. BS exerts a negative and statistical influence over EM, which is not verified considering FF. However, the negative and statistical significant effect of ownership control over EM is evident for the entire sample and being robust considering FF. This also happens considering the existence of an AC that has a positive influence over EM.

EM are also positively and significantly influenced by BIG4, ROA and LOSS, being negatively impacted by LEV, being these results robust to the consideration of FF and to the inclusion of other variables as control. As such, LEV and AGE seem to increase EM practices, while SIZE, being audited by the big 4 companies, ROA and having a LOSS in the previous period all decrease EM practices, where LOSS, Big4 and SIZE have lower coefficient values considering panel B in table 4 (FF), and ROA and AGE with higher coefficient values considering FF. Therefore, we may argue that the negative effect of

AGE over EM is higher in FF and the positive effect of ROA seems higher when considering FF. For robustness control and considering the possibility of non-linear relationships between firms' involvement and EM, we present further results through PCSE in Table 5.

Results point for a significant non-linear relationship between INED and EM and WOB and EM, of opposite sign. The INED term was significantly positive, while the squared INED term was significantly negative, denoting an inverse U-shaped relationship between independent non-executive directors and earnings management. However, results seem to favour a U-shaped relationship between gender (WOB) and earnings management. The relationship with family involvement seems robust favouring the curvilinear relationship between INED, WOB and EM (see last two columns in table 5). Thus, family firms with more INED involved have higher reciprocal control and less room for earnings management. The inverted U-shaped relationship between EM, family involvement and INED is also verified through interaction terms (INEDFF). Curiously, with respect to the interaction term WOBFF we also verify an inverted U-shaped relationship, whereas considering only FF and WOB results seem to point for a U-shaped relationship.

Our validated hypothesis 1 (validating the agency theory) through Table 4 is no longer valid when we include FF and non-linear effects into the analysis. The coefficient associated to INED (measuring board independence as in Waweru and Prot, 2018) is now positive, being inconsistent with the agency theory prediction, since results suggest that the high proportion of independent directors does not reduce EM in Portugal. Thus, these results could be due to the fact that boards may be independent in form or structure but not in present effectiveness. We also found a negative and significant relationship between WOB and EM, this turn contradicting Krishman and Parsons (2007) and Waweru and Prot (2018) when we considered the possibility of non-linear effects. However, in this case we reject our formulated H1 but are able to confirm H2. Thus, when accounting for possible curvilinear relationships, results suggest that the presence of women on Portuguese listed company boards help in constraining EM, whose value coefficients are higher considering the FF reality. It is worth to mention that H2 does not allows to validate neither the agency nor the stewardship theory, it simply evidences gender, related to risk aversion and personal skills, among others.

At mid-levels of board independence and family involvement, firms were more likely to resort to EM practices, whereas at both lower and higher levels of INED and family involvement, firms were more likely to use earnings management. The right opposite happens, considering the presence of WOB and FF (except for the interaction terms WOBFF and its square which are positive and negative, respectively). Finally, we should also mention that our results favour those of Jaggi et al. (2009) with respect to the positive and significant sign of INEDFF.

Family control in Portuguese firms moderates the negative association between women on board and earnings management provided that the coefficient on WOB is negative but that of WOBFF is positive, both statistically significant. So, an increase in manipulative practices happens with the presence of women's on board, but there is a decrease in manipulative practices considering the positive and negative values of INED and INED2, respectively.

Contrary to González and García-Meca (2014), who did not found any statistically significant relationship between FF and EM, our results indicate a negative and significant relationship between FF and EM which remains valid to different model specifications. FF would tend to maximize the firms wealth in the long term and are less likely to manage earnings (Wang, 2006; Ali et al., 2007; Achleitner et al., 2014).

We also found evidence in favour of a nonlinear relationship between family ownership and EM (through INED and WOB consideration as Razzaque et al., 2016). For the sample of Portuguese firms considered results point that being a FF reduces the opportunities to participate in manage earning actions, suggesting that families' interests are aligned with the firms' wealth (Davis et al., 1997), that they have a long-term business orientation (Cascino et al., 2010) and a desire to protect firms wealth for later generations (also favouring Achleitner et al., 2014, results), thus decreasing the pressure to manage earnings in order to meet short-term earnings expectations (as in Jaggi et al., 2009). If controlling FF tend to maximize the firms' wealth in the long term, there would be fewer incentives to obtain private benefits at the expense of minority shareholders, resulting in higher earning quality (González & García-Meca, 2014).

With a negative sign, being a FF entail lower incentives for controlling shareholders to obtain private benefits, thus decreasing EM. Thus, being a FF would not lead to the expropriation of the minority shareholders' interest due to the negative and statistical influence on earnings management. As such, we validate our H3 that earnings management practices are lower in FF than in NFF, based on the stewardship theory (long term perspectives of FF and the desire to pass firms to future generations).

Considering our control variables, we should expect a positive influence of BS over EM, but our results are not statistically significant, contrary to González and García-Meca (2014) results. Thus we cannot say that a larger board size results in a better supervision of the management team and in a higher quality of corporate decisions, considering or not FF.

Large shareholders play a key role in internal control of companies, leading to lower opportunistic behaviours' and greater tendencies to maximize firm value. However, when the level of ownership concentration (OC) is high it can lead to agency problems due to the expropriation of the minority shareholders' interests. The negative and statistically significant coefficient obtained for the sample of Portuguese firms support the efficient monitoring hypothesis. These results favour those of González and García-Meca (2014), but contradict the ones of Waweru and Prot (2018).

The existence of an AC reveals a positive and statistical influence over EM, as in Waweru and Prot (2018) results, which is not consistent (in statistical terms) to all models estimated. Thus results suggest that ACs play an important role in constraining EM among the Portuguese subject firm.

Firm size has a positive and significant coefficient but age has a negative and statistically significant influence over EM. As such, larger firms have higher levels of EM but older firms have lower levels of EM. Our results contradict those of Ferramosca and Allegrini (2018) although the authors did not found statistically significant results. They also contradict Lee and Choi (2002) findings, because in the Portuguese sample larger firms are more likely to manage earnings, namely to avoid losses, which is in part a surprise provided that the Portuguese entrepreneurial structure is mainly composed by small and medium enterprises (SME), although we are also considering in the sample robust and public listed companies. However, the higher the number of years operating in the market (AGE) it is expected that older firms engage in less opportunistic earnings management. Belonging to the industry also reveals to have a positive relationship with EM.

Considering growth opportunities, as measured by MB, we cannot conclude if firms with higher growth opportunities are more likely to manage earnings in order to meet investors' expectations since results are not statistically significant in any of the estimation results.

Provided there is evidence that EM in firms audited by BIG4 auditors is smaller than in firms audited by non-big 4 auditors (Siregar & Utama, 2008; Jaggi et al., 2009; González and García-Meca, 2014) we included BIG4 and results reveal a consistent positive and statistically significant coefficient. All the previous authors found non-significant and negative coefficients (the later, as expected). The Portuguese sample results seem to indicate that EM in firms audited by big 4 auditors is higher, revealing that policy

Table 5. Panel correction standard errors results – non-linear effects: dependent earnings management

Variable	Coefficient	z-Stat	Coefficient	z-Stat	Coefficient	z-Stat	Coefficient	z-Stat	Coefficient	z-Stat	Coefficient	Z-Stat	Coefficient	z-Stat	Coefficient	z-stat	Coefficient	z-Stat
INED			264.8***	3.56	349.2***	3.67	43.2	0.79	227.8***	2.91					61.7	1.14	211.1***	2.77
INED2			-346.8***	-3.22	-439.0***	-3.33	-132.7	-1.63	-270.8***	-2.65					-149.5*	-1.86	-235.4**	-2.37
WOB	-12.2	-0.34			-48.2	-1.27	-97.1**	-2.38			-244.7***	-3.37	-114.4**	-2.31			-196.0***	-3.47
WOB2	333.7***	3.35			446.9***	3.69	359.6***	3.46			726.8***	4.1	427.6***	3.39			589.5***	4.2
INEDFF							505.8***	4.01	97.9	1.53					276.5***	3.75	445.5***	3.55
WOBFF							321.7***	3.33			473.8***	3.82	431.4***	3.58			298.8***	3.36
INEDFF2							-688.7***	-3.93	-214.3**	-2.47					-354.0**	-3.67	-713.7***	-3.72
WOBFF2							-340.7***	-2.96			-787.2***	-4.04	-728.6***	-3.86			-228.2*	-1.84
FF							-119.0***	-3.78	7.8	0.53	-40.6***	-3.29	-33.5***	-2.99	-32.4**	-2.56	-100.6***	-3.44
BIG4	22.1***	3.36	20.7***	2.84	22.3***	3.04	13.9**	2.55	21.9***	2.96	18.2***	3.28	5.2*	1.73	12.6**	2.34	25.0***	3.21
SIZE	4.8***	3.05	2.3*	1.9	5.3***	3.39	8.9***	5.46	1.7	1.36	3.9***	2.75	9.4***	5.36	8.5***	5.26	4.1***	2.7
MB	-0.0	-1.24	0.0	-1.47	-0.0	-1.22	-0.0	-0.86	-0.0	-1.47	-0.0	-1.29	-0.0	-0.74	-0.0	-0.78	-0.0	-1.3
ROA	48.2***	4.71	52.4***	4.67	50.1***	4.32	43.3***	4.78	53.4***	4.98	48.9***	4.99	38.9***	4.63	43.0***	5.04	56.8***	4.62
LEV	-22.2***	-4.06	-30.7***	-5.26	-21.9***	-4.13	-11.5***	-2.79	-32.0***	-5.46	-22.8***	-4.18	-8.9**	-1.99	-18.1***	-4.1	-34.5***	-5.72
LOSS	78.8***	9.77	73.0***	9.79	80.0***	9.8	67.5***	9.12	71.2***	9.81	77.3***	9.78	68.0***	9.49	63.4***	9.36	76.6***	9.37
AGE	-35.1***	-4.21	-33.2***	-4.35	-37.4***	-4.3	-36.7***	-4.09	-31.8***	-4.31	-37.5***	-4.08	-35.8***	-4.04	-30.9***	-4.27	-38.7***	-4.17
BS	-1.9		6.3	1.43	-2.1	-0.39			4.8	1.07	4.1	0.87					-1.5	-0.25
AC	13.5		12.2***	3.42	11.1***	3.14			10.1***	2.94	10.0***	3.12					1.6	0.46
OC	-183.3		-173.3***	-4.6	-201.0***	-4.62			-178.9***	-4.53	-193.9***	-4.44					-225.2**	-4.58
constant	137.1***	2.92	128.9***	2.98	91.2**	2.28	-82.6***	-4.10	142.5***	3.11	175.7***	3.05	-94.4***	-4.64	-91.5***	-4.41	180.9***	3.15
IND	30.2***	3.97	31.7***	4.33	34.5***	4.24	16.8***	3.48	26.3***	4.35	29.8***	3.54	12.4***	2.88	13.9***	4.6	38.4***	3.89
YEAR effects	included		included		included		included		included		included		included		included		included	
Wald chi2	4,153.62		4,145.38		5,510.01		4,619.31		4,478.38		4,091.75		8,068.63		4,149.42		5,787.64	
Prob > chi2	0.000		0.000		0.000		0.000		0.000		0.000		0.000		0.000		0.000	

*, **, *** represent statistical significance at 10%, 5% and 1% levels, respectively. Variables are defined and explained in Table 1.

makers should be aware of the influence and management power, demanding higher surveillance for firms listed in the stock exchange.

ROA is positive and statistically significant as in González and García-Meca (2014), but by opposition to Jaggi et al. (2009) and Prencipe et al. (2008) results. As such, our findings seem to suggest that managers are more likely to manage earnings in profitable firms, a result that remains valid considering different model specifications. This result (ROA) and that of BIG4 provide further evidence for the need to better auditing and control of Portuguese listed firms, since the current audit and control is still not enough, leading to the possibility of EM manipulation.

Year effects also revealed to be statistically significant through the different model specifications. Finally, results point for a negative and significant effect of leverage over EM but for a positive effect of LOSS over EM. With respect to loss, our results are consistent with those of González and García-Meca (2014), despite that the authors did not achieve significance for this coefficient. However, we contradict the conclusions of the same authors considering debt since they found that debt increases EM. In the Portuguese sample, leverage seems to reduce EM, and this can be due to agency problems considering managers and creditors. More creditors, or more debt volume, thus, impose restrictions in EM, revealing that for Portuguese listed firms the incentive to manage earnings is weaker for more indebted firms, also contradicting Prencipe et al. (2008). Following Houqe et al. (2010), our results contradict the findings that firms with a poor financial situation (measured by ROA) are more likely to incur in earnings management practices. Therefore, a loss in the previous period conditions EM practices in Portuguese listed firms.

CONCLUSION

Current literature points that opportunistic earnings management activities may exist, turning relevant to infer which factors may constrain these actions. This study investigates the relationship between corporate governance and earnings management, in the context of family firms. To do so, we consider a sample of 49 non-financial Portuguese listed firms, analyzing an unbalanced panel for the period 2002-2017, using panel corrected standard errors models and considering the family ownership effect. Findings offer new insights into these relations in an entrepreneurial context, which differs greatly from the most commonly analyzed contexts such as the US.

When considering only simple effects, board independence decreases earnings management (EM), but the presence of women's on board increases EM. However, results are completely different when non-linear effects are considered since they reveal an inverted U-shaped relationship between independent non-executive directors and EM and a U-shaped relationship considering the presence of women on board. Thus, gender can be considered as a limiting factor of earnings management in Portuguese firms. Moreover, results seem to indicate that also for Portuguese firms, family involvement is associated with reduced earnings management. Considering the existence of non-linear effects it was possible to conclude that being a FF entails lower incentives for controlling shareholders to obtain private benefits, decreasing EM. Also, the high proportion of independent directors does not seem to reduce EM in public listed firms in Portugal, suggesting that boards may be independent in structure but not in present effectiveness. Jointly, when considering curvilinear effects, the presence of women on board helps to constrain EM practices.

Results further suggest that variables like leverage, age and ownership control help to reduce earnings management practices, but size, return on assets, the existence of a loss in the previous period, the presence of an audit committee on board and being audited by the BIG4 companies, all seem to increase EM practices, leading to higher opportunistic behaviors. Thus, we are able to conclude that even if family firms would tend to maximize firms wealth in the long run (due to future generation pass through), there are additional conditioning factors that would lead FF in Portugal to be more prone to manage earnings. These conclusions should alert policy makers and the need to control EM practices which are still evident and may impact the balance between performance, control, EM and private benefit gains. This is a concern since it may be harmful for the entire financial and business system.

We are aware that one of the greatest limitations in this study is the availability of data in terms of years and number of firms in Portugal. Another issue is related to estimation procedures which had to be limited in the context of panel data, since there is no way to apply time-series models, with the data available. This could be one of the reasons able to justify why in the present study we are able to contradict previous findings that firms with a poor financial situation are more likely to incur in earnings management practices, since with the Portuguese sample we conclude the right opposite (considering that return on assets are able to increase EM practices, as results seem to indicate). Also, being in a loss situation in the previous period would make Portuguese public listed firms to be more prone to manage earnings.

Future research can be expanded from several topics. We would like to analyze earnings management from the perspective of managers' risk preference, according to the measurement method of manager's risk preference. In addition, based on the theory of behavioral finance and overconfidence, it will be interesting to study the impact of managerial overconfidence on earnings management.

REFERENCES

Abdullah, S. N., & Ku, I. N. (2016). Women directors, family ownership and earnings management in Malaysia. *Asian Review of Accounting*, *24*(4), 525–550. doi:10.1108/ARA-07-2015-0067

Abeyratna, G., & Power, D. (2002). The post-announcement performance of dividend-changing companies: The dividend-signalling hypothesis revisited. *Accounting and Finance*, *42*(2), 131–151. doi:10.1111/1467-629X.00071

Achleitner, A., Günther, N., Kaserer, C., & Siciliano, G. (2014). Real earnings management and accrual based earnings management in family firms. *European Accounting Review*, *23*(3), 431–461. doi:10.1080/09638180.2014.895620

AEP (Portuguese Entrepreneurial Association) (2011). *Livro Branco da Sucessão Empresarial. O desafio da sucessão empresarial em Portugal*. Associação Empresarial de Portugal.

Ali, A., Chen, T. Y., & Radhakrishnan, S. (2007). Corporate disclosures by family firms. *Journal of Accounting and Economics*, *44*(1-2), 238–286. doi:10.1016/j.jacceco.2007.01.006

Alves, S. (2014). The Effect of Board Independence on the Earnings Quality: Evidence from Portuguese Listed Companies. *Australasian Accounting. Business and Finance Journal*, *8*(3), 23–44.

Anderson, R. C., Mansi, S. A., & Reeb, D. M. (2003). Founding family ownership and the agency cost of debt. *Journal of Financial Economics*, *68*(2), 263–285. doi:10.1016/S0304-405X(03)00067-9

Anderson, R. C., & Reeb, D. M. (2003). Founding family ownership and firm performance: Evidence from the S&P 500. *The Journal of Finance*, *58*(3), 1301–1328. doi:10.1111/1540-6261.00567

Anderson, R. C., & Reeb, D. M. (2004). Board composition: Balancing family influence in S&P 500 Firms. *Administrative Science Quarterly*, *49*, 1301–1328.

Ball, R., Robin, A., & Wu, J. (2003). Incentives versus standards: Properties of accounting income in four East Asian countries. *Journal of Accounting and Economics*, *36*(1-3), 235–270. doi:10.1016/j.jacceco.2003.10.003

Ball, R., & Shivakumar, L. (2005). Earnings quality in UK private firms: Comparative loss recognition timeless. *Journal of Accounting and Economics*, *39*(1), 83–128. doi:10.1016/j.jacceco.2004.04.001

Beasley, M. (1996). An empirical analysis of the relation between the board of director composition and financial statement fraud. *The Accounting Review*, *71*(4), 443–464.

Beck, N., & Katz, J. N. (1995). What to do (and not to do) with time series cross-section data. *The American Political Science Review*, *89*(03), 634–647. doi:10.2307/2082979

Betz, M., O'Connell, L., & Shepard, J. M. (1989). Gender differences in proclivity for unethical behavior. *Journal of Business Ethics*, *8*(5), 321–324. doi:10.1007/BF00381722

Cascino, S., Pugliese, A., Mussolino, D., & Sansone, C. (2010). The influence of family ownership on the quality of accounting information. *Family Business Review*, *23*(3), 246–265. doi:10.1177/0894486510374302

Chen, J. C., & Roberts, R. W. (2010). Toward a more coherent understanding of the organization-society relationship: A theoretical consideration for social and environmental accounting research. *Journal of Business Ethics*, *97*(4), 651–665. doi:10.100710551-010-0531-0

Cheong, P. C., Teh, B. H., Ong, T. S., & Hong, Y. H. (2015). The relationship among audit quality, earnings management and financial performance of Malaysian Public Listed companies. *International Journal of Economics and Management*, *9*(1), 209–229.

Cheung, Y. L., Rau, P. R., & Stouraitis, A. (2006). Tunneling, propping, and expropriation: Evidence from connected party transactions in Hong Kong. *Journal of Financial Economics*, *82*(2), 341–386. doi:10.1016/j.jfineco.2004.08.012

CMVM. (1999). *Recommendations of CMVM about corporate governance of Portuguese listed companies*. Available at www.cmvm.pt

CMVM. (2013). *CMVM corporate governance code*. Available at www.cmvm.pt

CMVM. (2014). *Report on corporate governance of Portuguese listed companies*. Annual Report. Available at www.cmvm.pt

Davis, J., Schoorman, R., & Donaldson, L. (1997). Towards a stewardship theory of management. *Academy of Management Review*, *22*(1), 20–47. doi:10.5465/amr.1997.9707180258

DeAngelo, H., & DeAngelo, L. (2000). Controlling stockholders and the disciplinary role of corporate payout policy: A study of the time mirror company. *Journal of Financial Economics*, *56*(2), 153–207. doi:10.1016/S0304-405X(00)00039-8

Dechow, P., & Dichev, D. (2002). The quality of accruals and earnings: The role of accrual estimation errors. *The Accounting Review*, *77*(s-1), 35–59. doi:10.2308/accr.2002.77.s-1.35

Dechow, P., & Skinner, D. (2000). Earnings Management: Reconciling the Views of Academics, Practitioners, and Regulators. *Accounting Horizons*, *14*(2), 235–250. doi:10.2308/acch.2000.14.2.235

Dechow, P., Sloan, R., & Sweeney, A. (1995). Detecting earnings management. *The Accounting Review*, *70*, 193–225.

Dechow, P., Sloan, R., & Sweeney, A. (1996). Causes and consequences of earnings manipulation: An analysis of firms subject to enforcement actions by the SEC. *Contemporary Accounting Research*, *13*(1), 1–36. doi:10.1111/j.1911-3846.1996.tb00489.x

Dechow, P., Weili, G., & Schrand, C. (2010). Understanding earnings quality: A review of the proxies, their determinants and their consequences. *Journal of Accounting and Economics*, *50*(2-3), 344–401. doi:10.1016/j.jacceco.2010.09.001

Diregar, S. V., & Utama, S. (2008). Type of earnings management and the effect of ownership structure, firm size, and corporate-governance practices: Evidence from Indonesia. *The International Journal of Accounting*, *43*(1), 1–27. doi:10.1016/j.intacc.2008.01.001

European Commission. (2009). *Final Report of the Expert Group – Overview of Family-Business-Relevant Issues: Research, Networks, Policy Measures and Existing Studies.* Directorate-Generale for Entreprise and Industry. Available online at: http://ec.europa.eu/entreprise/policies/sms/index_en.htm

Faccio, M., & Lang, L. (2002). The ultimate ownership of Western European corporations. *Journal of Financial Economics*, *65*(3), 365–395. doi:10.1016/S0304-405X(02)00146-0

Fama, E., & Jensen, M. (1983). Separation of ownership and control. *The Journal of Law & Economics*, *26*(2), 301–325. doi:10.1086/467037

Ferramosca, S., & Allegrini, M. (2018). The complex role of family involvement in earnings management. *Journal of Family Business Strategy*, *9*(2), 128–141. doi:10.1016/j.jfbs.2018.01.001

Francis, J. R., Maydew, E. L., & Spark, H. C. (1999). The role of Big 6 auditors in the credible reporting of accruals. *Auditing*, *18*(2), 17–34. doi:10.2308/aud.1999.18.2.17

Ghabdian, B., Attaran, N., & Froutan, O. (2012). Ownership structure and earnings management: Evidence from Iran. *International Journal of Business and Management*, *7*(15), 88–97. doi:10.5539/ijbm.v7n15p88

González, J. S., & García-Meca, E. (2013). Does corporate governance influence earnings management in Latin American markets? *Journal of Business Ethics*, *121*(3), 419–440. doi:10.100710551-013-1700-8

Gottardo, P., & Moisello, A. M. (2019). Earnings Management, Issues and Firm Market Value. In *Capital Structure, Earnings Management, and Risk of Financial Distress.* Cham: Springer. doi:10.1007/978-3-030-00344-9_5

Gul, F., Srinidhi, B., & Ng, A. (2011). Does board gender diversity improve the in formativeness of stock prices. *Journal of Accounting and Economics*, *51*(3), 314–338. doi:10.1016/j.jacceco.2011.01.005

Gull, A. A., Nekhili, M., Nagati, H., & Chtioui, T. (2018). Beyond gender diversity: How specific attributes of female directors affect earnings management. *The British Accounting Review*, *50*(3), 255–274. doi:10.1016/j.bar.2017.09.001

Healy, P., & Wahlen, J. (1999). A Review of the Earnings Management Literature and Its Implications for Standard Setting. *Accounting Horizons*, *13*(4), 365–383. doi:10.2308/acch.1999.13.4.365

Houqe, M. N., Dunstan, K., Waresul, A., & Van, Z. (2010). *Board ethics and auditor choice: International evidence*. Working Paper n.º 72, Centre for Accounting, Governance and Taxation Research.

Huili, Z., Ran, Z., & Jingyi, L. (2010). Does female senior management affect earnings quality: A large sample analysis of Chinese listed firms. *The Theory and Practice of Finance and Economics*, *6*, 62–66.

Jaggi, B., Leung, S., & Gul, F. (2009). Family control, board independence and earnings management: Evidence based on Hong Kong firms. *Journal of Accounting and Public Policy*, *28*(4), 281–300. doi:10.1016/j.jaccpubpol.2009.06.002

Jensen, M., & Meckling, W. (1976). Theory of the firm: Managerial behavior, agency cost and ownership structure. *Journal of Financial Economics*, *3*(4), 305–360. doi:10.1016/0304-405X(76)90026-X

Jiraporn, P., & DaDalt, P. (2009). Does founding family control affect earnings management? *Applied Economics Letters*, *16*(2), 113–119. doi:10.1080/17446540701720592

Jones, J. (1991). Earnings management during import relief investigation. *Journal of Accounting Research*, *29*(2), 193–228. doi:10.2307/2491047

Kothari, S. P., Leone, A. J., & Wasley, C. E. (2005). Performance matched discretionary accrual measures. *Journal of Accounting and Economics*, *39*(1), 163–197. doi:10.1016/j.jacceco.2004.11.002

Krishman, G. V., & Parsons, L. M. (2007). Getting to the bottom line: An exploration of gender and earnings quality. *Journal of Business Ethics*, *78*(1-2), 65–76. doi:10.100710551-006-9314-z

La Porta, R., Lopez-de-Silanes, F., & Shleifer, A. (1999). Corporate ownership around the World. *The Journal of Finance*, *LIV*(2), 471–517. doi:10.1111/0022-1082.00115

La Porta, R., Lopez-de-Silanes, F., Shleifer, A., & Vishny, R. W. (2000). Agency problems and dividend policies around the World. *The Journal of Finance*, *55*(1), 1–33. doi:10.1111/0022-1082.00199

Lee, B. B., & Choi, B. (2002). Company size, auditor type, and earnings management. *Journal of Forensic Accounting*, *III*, 27–50.

Leuz, C., Nanda, D., & Wysocki, D. (2003). Earnings management and investor protection: An international comparison. *Journal of Financial Economics*, *69*(3), 505–527. doi:10.1016/S0304-405X(03)00121-1

Liu, M., Shi, Y., Wilson, C., & Wu, Z. (2017). Does family involvement explain why corporate social responsibility affects earnings management? *Journal of Business Research*, *75*, 8–16. doi:10.1016/j.jbusres.2017.02.001

Marques, A. P., & Couto, A. I. (2017). SMEs and Family Smes: Specificities from the Portuguese Socio-Business Context. *European Journal of Economics and Business Studies*, *3*(2), 190–199. doi:10.26417/ejes.v8i1.p190-199

Miralles-Marcelo, J. L., Miralles-Quirós, M. del M., & Lisboa, I. (2014). The impact of family control on firm performance: Evidence from Portugal and Spain. *Journal of Family Business Strategy*, *5*(2), 156–168. doi:10.1016/j.jfbs.2014.03.002

Muritala, T. A. (2012). An Empirical Analysis of Capital Structure on Firms' Performance in Nigeria. *International Journal of Advances in Management and Economics*, *1*(5), 116–124.

Na, K., & Hong, J. (2017). CEO gender and earnings management. *Journal of Applied Business Research*, *33*(2), 297–308. doi:10.19030/jabr.v33i2.9902

Nelson, M. W., Elliott, J. A., & Tarpley, R. L. (2003). How are earnings managed: Example from auditors. *Accounting Horizons*, *17*(Supplement), 17–35. doi:10.2308/acch.2003.17.s-1.17

Peni, E., & Vähämaa, S. (2010). Female executives and earnings management. *Managerial Finance*, *36*(7), 629–645. doi:10.1108/03074351011050343

Prencipe, A., Bar-Yosef, S., & Dekker, H. (2014). Accounting research in family firms: Theoretical and empirical challenges. *European Accounting Review*, *23*(3), 361–385. doi:10.1080/09638180.2014.895621

Prencipe, A., Markarian, G., & Pozza, L. (2008). Earnings management in family-firms: Evidence from R&D cost capitalization in Italy. *Family Business Review*, *21*(1), 71–88. doi:10.1111/j.1741-6248.2007.00112.x

Razzaque, R. M., Ali, M. J., & Mather, P. R. (2016). Real earnings management in family firms: Evidence from an emerging economy. *Pacific-Basin Finance Journal*, *40*, 237–250. doi:10.1016/j.pacfin.2015.12.005

Reed, W., & Ye, H. (2009). Which panel data estimator should I use? *Applied Economics*, *43*(8), 985–1000. doi:10.1080/00036840802600087

Setia-Atmaja, L. S., Tanewski, G. A., & Skully, M. (2009). The role of dividends, debt and board structure in the governance of family-controlled firms. *Journal of Business Finance & Accounting*, *36*(7&8), 863–898. doi:10.1111/j.1468-5957.2009.02151.x

Shukeri, S. N., Shin, O. W., & Shaari, M. S. (2012). Does board of director's characteristics affect firm performance? Evidence from Malaysian public listed companies. *International Business Research*, *5*(9), 120–127. doi:10.5539/ibr.v5n9p120

Siebels, J. F., & zu Knyphausen-Aufseß, D. (2012). A review of theory in family business research: The implications for corporate governance. *International Journal of Management Reviews*, *14*(3), 280–304. doi:10.1111/j.1468-2370.2011.00317.x

Siregar, S. V., & Utama, S. (2008). Type of earnings management and the effect of ownership structure, firm size, and corporate-governance practices: Evidence from Indonesia. *The International Journal of Accounting*, *43*(1), 1–27. doi:10.1016/j.intacc.2008.01.001

Skinner, D. J., & Sloan, R. G. (2002). Earnings surprises, growth expectations and stock returns or don't let an earnings torpedo sink your portfolio. *Review of Accounting Studies*, *7*(2-3), 289–310. doi:10.1023/A:1020294523516

Srinidhi, B., Gul, F. A., & Tsui, J. (2011). Female directors and earnings quality. *Contemporary Accounting Research*, *28*(5), 1610–1644. doi:10.1111/j.1911-3846.2011.01071.x

Ussman, A. M. (2004). *Empresas Familiares* [Family business]. Lisboa: Edições Sílabo. (in Portuguese)

Vähämma, E. (2014). Executive turnover, gender, and earnings management: An exploratory analysis. *Accounting Perspectives*, *13*(2), 103–122. doi:10.1111/1911-3838.12029

Vieira, E. S. (2016). Earnings management in public family firms under economic adversity. *Australian Accounting Review*, *26*(2), 190–207. doi:10.1111/auar.12096

Wang, D. (2006). Founding family ownership and earnings quality. *Journal of Accounting Research*, *44*(3), 19–656. doi:10.1111/j.1475-679X.2006.00213.x

Waweru, N. M., & Prot, N. P. (2018). Corporate governance compliance and accrual earnings management is eastern Africa: Evidence from Kenya and Tanzania. *Managerial Auditing Journal*, *33*(2), 171–191. doi:10.1108/MAJ-09-2016-1438

Xie, B., Davidson, W. N. III, & DaDalt, P. J. (2003). Earnings management and corporate governance: The roles of the board and the audit committee. *Journal of Corporate Finance*, *9*(3), 295–316. doi:10.1016/S0929-1199(02)00006-8

Xingqiang, D., Shaoyuan, L., & Hongmei, P. (2017). Do women top managers always mitigate earnings management? Evidence from China. *Accountability in Research*, *1*, 39–45.

Zalata, A. M., Tauringana, V., & Tingbani, I. (2018). Audit committee financial expertise, gender, and earnings management: Does gender of the financial expert matter? *International Review of Financial Analysis*, *55*, 170–183. doi:10.1016/j.irfa.2017.11.002

KEY TERMS AND DEFINITIONS

Accruals: Earned revenues and incurred expenses that have an overall impact on an income statement (including accounts payable, accounts receivable, goodwill, future tax liabilities, and future interest expenses).

Assets Turnover: Value of a company's sales generated divided by the value of assets, used as an indicator of the efficiency with which a company is deploying its assets in generating revenue.

Board Independence: Proportion of independent non-executive directors on corporate boards, calculated from the number of independent members divided by the number of members on the board.

Corporate Governance: System of rules, practices, and processes by which a firm is directed and controlled.

Earnings Management: Accruals management, where the proxy considered are the abnormal accruals.

Family Firms: Companies in which the founding family or a family member is involved in the top management of the firm and control twenty per cent or more of the equity.

Gender Diversity: Measured by the number of women on the board divided to the total number of directors.

ENDNOTES

1 Portugal adopted the Official Accounting Plan (POC), published by the Law n.º 47/77, from February, 7. On November 21, 1989, the revised POC was published, satisfying the requirements resulting from the admission of Portugal to the then European Economic Community. As a member state of the European Union, Portugal adopted the International Financial Reporting Standards (IFRS) in 2005, for the listed firms.

2 In what concerns corporate governance (CG), Portugal published, for the first time, in 1999, a set of recommendations, principles and guides, through the Portuguese Securities Market Commission (CMVM, 1999). In 2007, the document change its name from "Recommendations of the CMVM on Corporate Governance of Listed Companies" to "Code on the Governance of CMVM Companies". These recommendations were revised several times, being the last version published in 2013 (CMVM, 2013), which were into force since January 2014 to the end of 2017. The code of CG of the CMVM (2013) was repealed on December 31, 2017, and the code of CG of the Portuguese Corporate Governance Institute (IPCG) has entered into force on January 1, 2018.

3 For instance, only 20 companies are more liquid and are present in the Portuguese index, compared to 500 of the S&P and 100 of Nasdaq.

Chapter 7

Earnings Management and Audit in Private Firms:
The Effect of Financial Recuperation

Inna Sousa Paiva
Instituto Universitário de Lisboa (ISCTE-IUL), Portugal

Paulo Varela Dias
https://orcid.org/0000-0002-0351-9751
Instituto Universitário de Lisboa (ISCTE-IUL), Portugal

ABSTRACT

This chapter examines the relationship between the level of earnings management and the audit in private firms under the influence of financial crisis recuperation, using a sample of Ireland and Portuguese firms from 2008 to 2016. The authors use accruals methodology, namely four earnings management measures to capture earnings management in private firms. Multivariate statistical analysis was applied using the traditional multiple regression technique. Empirical results show that private firms with audited financial statements have powerful incentives to expropriate wealth from minority shareholders, pursuing their own interests at the expense of non-controlling shareholders. They also find that the private firms with audited financial statements in years under adjustment programs demonstrated lower level of earnings management. This study contributes to the accounting literature by providing empirical evidence for the effects of audit and earnings management in private firms in a financial recuperation context.

INTRODUCTION

Earnings management and its role in the economy have been widely studied in the academic literature with main highlights in worldwide listed firms and have often been linked to accounting practice with objectives that potentially affect managers' discretionary behaviour (Bharath, Sunder, & Sunder, 2008; Doyle, Ge, & McVay, 2007; Zhao & Chen, 2008). Some previous literature aim do detect earnings management (Beneish, 1999; Dechow, Sloan, & Sweeney, 1995; Jones, 1991), others focus on numerous

DOI: 10.4018/978-1-5225-7817-8.ch007

incentives for earnings management in listed companies (Aharony, Lin, & Loeb, 1993; Teoh, Welch, & Wong, 1998; Teoh & Wong, 2002; Healy, 1985; Holthausen, Larcker, & Sloan, 1995; Beneish & Vargus, 2002; Warfield, Wild, & Wild, 1995; Cheng & Warfield, 2005; Gabrielsen, Gramlich, & Plenborg, 2002; DeFond, Hu, Hung, & Li, 2012; Sweeney, 1994; Cahan, 1992; Francis, Khurana, & Pereira, 2005).

The trend of research on earnings management has focussed on the private firms and audit (Burkart, Panunzi, & Shleifer, 2003; Faccio & Lang, 2002; La Porta, Lopez-de-Silanes, & Shleifer, 1999; Wang, 2006). Prior research on auditor choice and audit fees in private firms presents two possible scenarios. Due to lower conflict of interest between owners and managers agency problems in private firms, it is expected that private firms will have lower demand for audit quality (Ho & Kang, 2013; Burgstahler, Hail, & Leuz, 2006). On the other hand, the presence of strong incentives in private firms to engage in fraudulent activities may increase audit risk (Cano-Rodriguez, 2010). The presence of such conflicting arguments makes auditor choice in private firms an interesting research area. The private companies suffered significant impact which struck both their performance and their auditor options, forcing adjustments in the latter, imposed by the rise of financing conditions.

The programmes of macroeconomic adjustment induce processes which seek not only the change of politics but also of behaviours which should be adopted by the countries, acting over variables such as consumption, investment and imports, to increase competition after periods of great shock (Alcidi et al., 2016). From November 2010 Ireland would be the first country to seek the adjustment programme, leaving it successfully in December 2013. Portugal would follow a similar programme in the first semester of 2011, marking its exit, also successfully, in May 2014 (European Stability Mechanism, 2014).

The objective of this study is to analyse the relationship between the level of earnings management and the auditor choice of private unlisted firms in Portugal and Ireland, two countries liable to economic adjustment programmes between 2008 and 2016. In a sample of 970 private firms from both countries, and according to the method of accruals, whose discretionary component was obtained by four models originated in Jones (1991), we found evidence that there is a positive relationship between the audit and the level of earnings management, which suggested that private firms with audited financial report have powerful incentives to expropriate wealth from minority shareholders, and pursue their own interests at the expense of non-controlling shareholders. We also found that the private firms with audited financial statements in years under adjustment programmes demonstrated lower level of earnings management. For instance, our results indicate that incentives for earnings management across private firms are not the same. At a more detailed level, we realised that the large private firms have higher incentives for earnings management when financial statements are audited, whereas for small private firms that is not the case. Additionally, the large private firms with audited financial statements in years under adjustment programmes demonstrated lower level of earnings management. Our findings are consistent with a number of statistical tests.

Prior literature has produced divergent conclusions as far as the relationship between the level of earnings management and audit is concerned. The present investigation contributes to previously published literature so as to understand if more recent data clearly distinguish one of those options. This study does not neglect that it is totally impossible to exclude the impact of many of the context variables that have suffered changes in the meantime. These context variables are the central banks' monetary policy decisions, accounting standards which stop the struggle of the strength of the economy, the experience accumulated by the financing entities and the consequent evolution of financing contracts.

This chapter is structured as follows: after the introduction, the second section presents the literature review and the development of the hypothesis. A subsequent section then discusses the methodology used in this paper and the models used to test the hypothesis. This is followed by a section that discusses the results. Finally, a concluding section summarises the findings and discusses possible implications.

LITERATURE REVIEW AND HYPOTHESIS

Earnings Management and Audit

The issue of information asymmetry related to the interaction of companies with their external partners, namely with investors, has recurrently been discussed. Previous studies found that asymmetry information will tend to grow once the quality of financial information decreases (Easley & O'Hara, 2014). The financial and accounting information thus undertake a crucial role in decisions of capital allocation (Bhattacharya, Guner, & Ventura, 2013). Schipper and Vincent (2003) add that that same allocation will be inefficient if it is done based on information of low level of quality.

The concept of earnings management is strongly linked to the concept of agency theory, suggesting that firms can mitigate or exacerbate the agency problem (La Porta et al., 1998). Although the traditional agency problem characterised by a conflict of interest between owners and managers is less of an issue for private firms, a growing body of literature (for example, Faccio & Lang, 2002; Villalonga & Amit, 2006) suggests that private firms where ownership and management is overlapped, have powerful incentives to expropriate wealth from minority shareholders, and pursue their own interests at the expense of non-controlling shareholders. Prior literature has produced divergent conclusions as far as the relationship between the level of earnings management and audit is concerned and presents two possible scenarios. Type I agency problem consists on the separation between ownership and control, which leads to a divergence between management and owner interests (Jensen & Meckling, 1976). These agency problems occur when asymmetric information coexists with divergent objectives between managers and shareholders. Due to type I agency problems, previous studies demonstrated that private firms will have lower demand for audit quality (Ho & Kang, 2013; Burstahler et al., 2006).

Type II agency problem arises from conflicts between controlling and non-controlling shareholders, which can result in executive entrenchment and high incentives for earnings management (Fama & Jensen, 1983; Shleifer & Vishny, 1997). The presence of strong incentives in private firms to engage in fraudulent activities may increase audit risk and consequently reduce the quality of financial reporting. The differences in the earnings management between private firms would depend on the difference in the severity of their type I and type II agency problems in private firms. Different arguments for these problems can be found in previous studies. Using a sample of small private firms in Finland, Niskanen, Karjalainen and Niskanen (2010) found that an increase in ownership decreases the likelihood of hiring a Big 4 auditor. This is consistent with the type I agency argument regarding the prevalence of lower information asymmetry between owners and managers in private firms.

Badolaro et al. (2014) realised that audit committees with financial expertise and high relative status are associated with lower levels of earnings management and the stakeholders believe that the auditors had the ability to discourage earnings management due to the influence of audit report (Barghathi et al., 2018).

Jaffer and Sohail (2007) reported that corporate governance structures are almost non-existent in the majority of family-owned firms in India. Consequently, only 15 percent of private owned businesses in India and Pakistan survive to the third generation. Frequent family disputes lead to the family firm's inability to implement a succession plan, which, in the absence of proper corporate governance mechanisms, poses a significant threat to a family firm's survival. Burstahler et al. (2006) concluded that audit quality for private European firms is unlikely to be the primary mechanism through which public markets reduce earnings management. Cano-Rodriguez (2010) provided evidence for Spanish firms that for high levels of litigation and reputation risk, big auditors tend to promote unconditional conservatism, which can reduce the quality of financial reports.

Based on the previous literature and agency theory problems, we expect that private audited firms provide higher level of earnings management, testing the following hypothesis:

H1: There is a positive relationship between the audit and earnings management.

Earnings Management and the Background of the Crisis

Crisis periods may influence the intention of changing results to lower or at least maintain the cost of debt, or to meet financial investors' expectations (Lisboa, 2017; Chia, Lapsley, & Lee 2007; Kim & Yi, 2006). In fact, previous studies found evidence that firms manage earnings in periods of crisis. Persakis and Iatridis (2016) revealed that earnings quality decreases during recession periods, especially in countries with weak investor protection.

Habib, Uddin, and Islam (2013) summarized that in more difficult economic times, there is more caution from investors, who, attentive to possible maneuvers of distortion of information, end up taking some emphasis from the financial statements. Therefore, the incentives for practice of results management are, of course, lower. Kousenidis, Ladas, and Negakis (2013) provided evidence that, for a variety of reasons, investor confidence in the quality of financial information declined during the crisis, although previous studies point to a reduction in the practice of results management with positive effects on the quality of financial reporting period.

A committee consisting of the European Commission (EC), the International Monetary Fund (IMF) and the European Central Bank (ECB) through the European Stability Mechanism (ESM), provided funding to economies in the context of financial assistance programmes, establishing conditions on countries, which were embodied in programmes of economic and financial adjustment (adjustment programmes), which prescribed severe austerity measures, with very significant economic and social consequences. From November 2010, Ireland would be the first country to seek the adjustment programme, leaving it successfully in December 2013. Portugal would follow a similar programme in the first semester of 2011, marking its exit, also successfully, in May 2014 (European Stability Mechanism, 2014).

The crisis that broke in the Irish economy in 2008 was rather similar to that in other European countries. A major property bubble had developed over the previous five years, which was financed by inflows of capital into the domestic banking system. The high expected returns from investment in housing in Ireland had evoked a huge supply response. When the crisis hit, the building and construction sector collapsed, resulting in a fall in GDP from peak-to-trough of just under 10 percent and a fall in GNP of over 15 percent. The unemployment rate rose very rapidly. Between 2007 and 2012 it had increased by 10 percentage points. As discussed in Fitzgerald (2012), the current account adjustment was particularly rapid in countries, such as Ireland, where there was a collapse in the construction sector, whereas in economies, such as Portugal and Greece, where there was no real estate bubble, the adjustment in the current account was slower, being driven by the fall in domestic consumption rather than the very rapid fall in domestic investment. In the Ireland the funding needs of the banking system placed the sovereign under such severe pressure that, without the support of its EU partners and the IMF, Ireland would not have been able to deal with the situation in the way it did (Duffy et al. 2013).

In 2010, Ireland asked the EU and the IMF for financial support and enter an assistance programme. The total support provided by creditors was €67.5 billion. It was the first assistance package for the European Financial Stability Facility (EFSF), which had been established months earlier. The EFSF provided €17.7 billion, with the rest supplied by the EU, individual EU Member States, and the IMF. Towards the end of this era of rapid growth, the economy started to overheat. Government spending increased swiftly, and tax revenues became less reliable. Wages were climbing too rapidly, making products expensive for buyers abroad. The booming economy was fed largely by aggressive bank lending. At the same time, financial regulation had become less restrictive.

During its three-year assistance programme, Ireland fixed many of these problems. Two major banks were shut down, while some of the remaining firms received a capital boost. A bad bank was set up to deal with problem loans and isolate them from the healthy banking business. The country reduced its fiscal deficit, and successfully exited its EFSF programme without the need for any further assistance in December 2013.

Portugal was the country to receive assistance during the euro crisis. Unlike some other programme countries, Portugal had suffered a long period of weak economic growth before the crisis. Low interest rates created an illusion of prosperity, because credit was easily available. This contributed to high debt levels for companies, households, and the government. Wage growth persistently above productivity gains contributed to Portuguese products becoming expensive abroad, which accelerated a decrease in exports.

There were also problems with the country's banks. Investors were worried that they were overly exposed to the weak economy and had stopped funding them. When the global crisis hit Europe in 2010, the country had little scope to support the economy or the banks.

Investors responded by demanding ever-higher returns on Portugal's bonds. Early in 2011, it became too expensive for the country to borrow money on financial markets. There was a risk it would default. By April 2011, Portugal requested assistance from the EFSF, the EU, and the IMF. A two-digit current account deficit was erased. The budget deficit shrank, and growth resumed. Portugal was able to issue bonds again, and successfully exited the programme in June 2014 (European Stability Mechanism, 2017).

It is expected that in context of economic crisis, recuperation may affect earnings management behaviours of firms. In crisis periods, governments are likely to provide support to firms in financial distress. In general, the studies about accounting information and financial crisis have attracted field of interest for various researches around Europe and Asian financial crisis. In this context, Davis-Friday, Eng and Liu (2006) in a study of Asian financial crisis in Indonesia, Malaysia and Thailand, concluded that the extent of the change in value relevance is related to the corporate-governance mechanisms and accounting system of these countries.

Choi, Kim, and Lee (2011) have investigated nine Asian countries during the Asian crisis and determined that the strength of a country's institutional infrastructure is related to aggravation in the information value of the discretionary earnings component. The role of the monitoring effect of auditors was explored by Chi, Lisic, and Pevzner (2011) in a study of Singapore firms, which provided evidence that the earnings management activities were reduced for the firms that were audited by the Big 6 as far as accounting and financial procedures are concerned, along with risk analysis empowerment by investors/creditors and research contributions have also had a crucial role in the decrease of the levels of earnings management.

H2: The positive relationship between audit and earnings management is attenuated in periods of economic adjustment programmes.

RESEARCH DESIGN

Sample

This study focusses on the analysis of unlisted private firms in countries which have successfully complied economic adjustment programmes (Portugal and Ireland). Portugal is a small-size country, with the predominance of small and medium enterprises, around 99% (Statistics of Portugal Portal INE, 2016). Moreover, around 80% of the firms and half of the Portuguese stock indexes are family firms (Miralles-Marcelo et al., 2014). Ireland is a small-size country with predominance of 99,8% of small and medium enterprises (Central Statistics Office, 2014). The data was taken from Amadeus database, which belongs to Bureau Van Dijk group (BvD), between 2008 and 2016. This research has determined a total of 35 547 companies. Afterwards, we have eliminated the companies which didn't provide enough information for the calculation of the pertinent variables, which reduced the sample to 1031 firms.

Then, we have removed the entities which belong to public administration, financial administration and insurances, because due to their specific systems and accounting standards, the method of estimating accruals is different from the companies of the remaining sectors. From this operation we found a total of 1025 firms.

Finally, in each of the remaining sectors we have eliminated the values considered extreme, correspondent to the data with quantities outside the range of the average more/less 3 times the standard deviation, thus closing the sample in 970 firms, which correspond to 8730 observations in the period from 2008 to 2016. Table 1 summarises up the distribution of the sample per country and activity sector.

Table 1 summarises the sample per activity sector, where the prevaling of Industry and Commerce sectors is obvious, more than half of the companies of our sample (51,4%), followed by the Consultancy sector with 13,2% of the companies involved. The sample is majorly build of Portuguese companies, due to lack of data from Ireland's analogous.

Dependent Variable

The dependent variable of our study is the level of earnings management (EM). The way to measure the level of EM has been a major issue shared by most authors throughout research dedicated to it. The method based on the accruals is one of the alternatives followed by many, among who we have included ourselves for the present study.

Accruals ensue from the economic or financial performance registered (expenses and incomes) which does not have permanent nor temporary equivalence with a corresponding cash-flow (cash receipts and payments). Together with the cash-flows, the accruals are the core of financial statements presented by the companies. Its calculation is possible, though indirectly, by the difference between the operational cash-flows and the earnings of a certain period (Healy, 1985).

The work of Callao and Jarne (2010) had Amadeus database (BvD) as the source for its data collection. The calculation of the total accruals (TA) was done according to the following equation:

Table 1. Distribution of the sample per country and activity sector

Sector		Portugal	Ireland	Total	%
A	Agriculture and Fishing	189	0	189	2.2
B	Extraction industries	18	0	18	0.2
C	Transformation industries	2061	54	2115	24.2
D	Energy	72	0	72	0.8
E	Water	27	0	27	0.3
F	Construction	657	9	666	7.6
G	Commerce	2322	54	2376	27.2
H	Transportation and storage	288	0	288	3.3
I	Accommodation and catering	486	0	486	5.6
J	Information and communication	63	27	90	1.0
L	Real-estate activities	216	27	243	2.8
M	Consultancy	1044	108	1152	13.2
N	Support services	144	63	207	2.44
P	Education	135	9	144	1.6
Q	Human health and social support	252	27	279	3.2
R	Culture	54	26	180	2.1
S	Other services	90	108	198	2.3
	Total	8118	612	8730	100

$$TA_{i,t} = \Delta AREC_{i,t} + \Delta INV_{i,t} - \Delta AP_{i,t} - DEP_{i,t} \quad (1)$$

In which:

$TA_{i,t}$. = Total Accruals of company i during period t
$\Delta AREC_{i,t}$. = Variation of the Recievables of company i during period t
$\Delta INV_{i,t}$. = Variation of Inventories of company i during period t
$\Delta AP_{i,t}$. = Variation of Payables of company i during period t
$DEP_{i,t}$. = Total of depreciations of company i during period t

Nevertheless, not all accruals are truly changeable, evidence which has found wide agreement amongst researchers in the past few years. As a result, in the literature it is almost certain that TA has two ways: one that comes from normal operational activity and investment, which corresponds to non-discretionary accruals (AND), and another one that occurs from accounting standards and managers' professional judgement, which assumes the discretionary way (AD) (Gorgan et al., 2012).

However, the latter may not be obtained nor calculated directly from the companies' financial statements. It can be done through estimation models, and in the context of this study we have chosen to follow the model suggested by Jones (1991), as well as the versions modified by Dechow et al. (1995), Kasznik (1999) and Kothari et al. (2005).

From the regression of the models mentioned above, we obtain the portion of AND present in TA, while AD will be the released residues (that is to say, the unexplained portion of the models) or, if we will, the difference between TA and AND.

Mathematically we reach:

$$TA_{i,t} = AND_{i,t} + AD_{i,t} \quad (2)$$

Readjusting according to AD:

$$AD_{i,t} = TA_{i,t} - AND_{i,t} \quad (3)$$

In which:

$AD_{i,t}$. = Discretionary Accruals of company i during t
$TA_{i,t}$. = Total Accruals of company i during t
$AND_{i,t}$. Non-Discretionary Accruals of company i during t

The measure of EM will be:

$$AD_{i,t} = \left|\varepsilon_{i,t}\right| \quad (4)$$

The more the level of EM, the greater the absolute value of AD, due to estimation models, individually applied to each sector as a way to decrease possible sectorial effects while finding the level of accruals.

The original model of Jones (1991) estimates the accruals according to the variation of the companies' turnover and the companies' tangible fixed assets. It is obvious that the turnover is a non discretionary caption, so it is not subjected to manipulation. This model, Original Jones Model (OJM), is embodied in the following phrase:

$$\frac{TA_{i,t}}{A_{i,t-1}} = \beta_0 + \beta_1 \frac{1}{A_{i,t-1}} + \beta_2 \frac{\left(\Delta Sales_{i,t}\right)}{A_{i,t-1}} + \beta_3 \frac{PPE_{i,t}}{A_{i,t-1}} + \varepsilon_{i,t} \quad (5)$$

Afterwards, in order to improve the original model, several changes of the original model were developed (Dechow et al., 1995; Kasznik, 1999; Kothari et al., 2005). In the present study, three additional models apart from the original model were followed: Modified Jones Model suggested by Dechow et al. (1995); Cash-Flow Jones Model developed by Kasznik (1999); and Performance Matched Model developed by Kothari et al.(2005).

Dechow et al. (1995) lead the first change of the previous model because they feel the turnover caption is highly influenced by managers' discretionary behaviour, which leads them to suggest the inclusion of the caption of receivables, subtracting it to the turnover, so that it is possible to decrease the effect of credit sales. The materialisation of this change is quite obvious in the Modified Jones Model (MJM), illustrated in the following equation:

$$\frac{TA_{i,t}}{A_{i,t-1}} = \beta_0 + \beta_1 \frac{1}{A_{i,t-1}} + \beta_2 \frac{\left(\Delta Sales_{i,t} - \Delta REC_{i,t}\right)}{A_{i,t-1}} + \beta_3 \frac{PPE_{i,t}}{A_{i,t-1}} + \varepsilon_{i,t} \quad (6)$$

A new adjustment was developed by Kasznik (1999), by adding Operational Cash-Flow (CFO). The author considered that this component had a non-discretionary effect on AT, and its inclusion is plausible to soften mistakes in measuring the accruals. Cash-Flow Jones Model (CFJM) is represented as follows:

$$\frac{TA_{i,t}}{A_{i,t-1}} = \beta_0 + \beta_1 \frac{1}{A_{i,t-1}} + \beta_2 \frac{\left(\Delta Sales_{i,t} - \Delta \operatorname{Re} c_{i,t}\right)}{A_{i,t-1}} + \beta_3 \frac{PPE_{i,t}}{A_{i,t-1}} + \beta_4 \frac{CFO_{i,t}}{A_{i,t-1}} + \varepsilon_{i,t} \quad (7)$$

The mathematical expression comes from the change operated by Dechow et al. (1995), in addition to the element ROA, Performance Matched Jones Model (PMJM):

$$\frac{TA_{i,t}}{A_{i,t-1}} = \beta_0 + \beta_1 \frac{1}{A_{i,t-1}} + \beta_2 \frac{\left(\Delta Sales_{i,t} - \Delta REC_{i,t}\right)}{A_{i,t-1}} + \beta_3 \frac{PPE_{i,t}}{A_{i,t-1}} + \beta_4 ROA_{i,t} + \varepsilon_{i,t} \quad (8)$$

In which:

$TA_{i,t}$ = Total Accruals of company i in year t
$\Delta Sales_{i,t}$ = Sales variation of company i in year t according to year t-1
$\Delta \operatorname{Re} c_{i,t}$ = Variation of the receivables of company i in year t according to year t-1
$PPE_{i,t}$ = Total of AFT (property, plant and equipment) of company i in year t
$CFO_{i,t}$ = Operational Cash-flow of company i in year t
$ROA_{i,t}$ = Return on Assets of company i in year t;
$A_{i,t-1}$ = Total Assets of company i in year t-1.

To close and make the estimation of AD possible in the equation (3) for the correspondent phrase in equation (4) which allows its calculation.

Original Jones - Jones (1991)

$$\frac{AD_{i,t}}{A_{i,t-1}} = \frac{TA_{i,t}}{A_{i,t-1}} - \left[\beta_0 + \beta_1 \frac{1}{A_{i,t-1}} + \beta_2 \frac{Sales_{i,t}}{A_{i,t-1}} + \beta_3 \frac{PPE_{i,t}}{A_{i,t-1}}\right] \quad (9)$$

The rest of the changed models were estimated according to the same method.

Independent Variables

According to previous studies, the main independent variable of this study is the audit (AUD). Audit is defined as a dummy variable that take value 1 if auditor is hired and 0 otherwise for firms.

A dummy variable was created, named ADJPR (Adjustment Programme), which allows to control the effects of the readjustment period earlier referred to, whose value equals to one for the years of adjustment and a value equal to zero for the rest of the years (Iatridis and Dimitras, 2013; Lin et al., 2015; Lisboa, 2016). To analyse whether the relationship between the use of earnings management and audit is softened during the economic adjustment programmes applied to Portugal and Ireland, an interaction variable was created, named ADJPR*AUD (Lin et al., 2015).

We have selected, as variables of control, some aspects of corporate reality which simultaneously influence the level of EM, and that have earlier been followed by many researchers, such as Watrin et al. (2014) and Gu et al. (2005), just to mention a few. They have found relationships in different ways between financial leverage (LEV), size (SIZE), profitability (PROF), growth (GROW) and earnings management. There are also those who add the level of tangible fixed actives as a preferable variable to measure EM (e.g., Harris & Raviv 1991), an option that we too have chosen to follow.

According to previous studies, the financial leverage variable (LEV) has differed, as there are those who prefer considering only the long term debt over the total active as a ratio (e.g., Bowen et al. 2008). Other studies, for instance, Watrin et al. (2014), divide the total of the financial debt (which consists of long and short term debt) by equity. In the present study we defined the debt variable according to Gu et al. (2005), by dividing the total passive for the total active.

The variable firm size (SIZE) goes beyond reflecting political sensitivity and its consequences (namely a more regular tool to EM by larger companies in order to control the inherent political costs which come from its size), mentioned by Watts and Zimmerman (1978), because larger companies tend to show specific behaviour in what indebtedness is concerned, according to their ability to access different sources of investment and growing to remain in higher financial leverage standards (Rajan & Zingales, 1995). Size is focussed on many studies (e.g., Doyle et al., 2007 and Ge & McVay, 2005) as a discouragement of EM, because of the higher level of exposure and scrutiny that companies in this condition are subjected to. The calculation of the variable SIZE is done through the natural logarithm of the total assets.

The ability to generate positive earnings, catalyst for self-financing, allows greater Independence in what external financing is concerned, and at the same time it places companies in more comfortable situations in accessing it, in terms of negotiating. Rajan & Zingales (1995) also prove that more profitable companies are more likely to be less leveraged. The same authors determine profitability (PROF) through the quotient EBITDA / Total Assets, option that we have also chosen for our research.

The level of tangible actives (TANG) is also essential, equally important, in the path for securing financing. One of the main reasons lay on the fact that these actives may easily be changed (Rajan & Zingales, 1995). The works of Titman and Wessels (1988), Frank and Goyal (2009) and Rajan and Zingales (1995) confirm these inferences. The ratio Tangible Fixed Assets / Total Assets was a factor to take into account for the calculation in TANG, as Cohen and Zarowin (2008) had noticed, among other authors.

We also added another variable of control, growth (GROW), which corresponds to the growth rate of the companies in the sample, calculated through the percentage variation of the total assets, copying Lee and Mande (2002). In addition to being a motivation for earnings management itself, this also allows to help the control of the effects of different performances between companies. Finally, according to previous studies, we also capture industry and country effect. We considered variable INDUSTRY for industry dummies, and to reflect differences of earnings management in two countries, we created dummy variables COUNTRY that defined as 1 for Ireland and 0 for Portugal.

The Model

As the main goal of this study is to analyse the relationship between the audit and the EM practice, we have developed the following model:

$$EM_{i,t} = \alpha_0 + \beta_1 AUD_{i,t} + \beta_2 ADJPR{*}AUD_{i,t} + \beta_3 LEV_{i,t} + \beta_4 SIZE_{i,t} + \beta_5 PROF_{i,t} + \beta_6 TANG_{i,t} + \beta_7 GROW_{i,t} + \beta_8 COUNTRY_{i,t} + +\beta_9 INDUSTRY_{i,t} \quad (1)$$

Where:

$EM_{i,t}$ = Level of Earnings Management of company i during t
$AUD_{i,t}$ = Dummy variable that take value 1 if auditor is hired and 0 otherwise for company i during t.
$ADJPR{*}AUD_{i,t}$ = Interaction variable that result from multiplication of ADJPR * AUD.
$LEV_{i,t}$ = Level of financial leverage of company i during t.
$SIZE_{i,t}$ = Logarithm natural of total of assets of company i during t.
$ROA_{i,t}$ = Net income deflated by total assets of company i during t.
$TANG^{i,t}$ = Tangible assets deflated by total assets of company i during t
$GROW_{i,t}$ = Change of sales from t to t- of company i during t.
$COUNTRY_{i,t}$ = Dummy variable that take value 1 for Ireland and 0 for Portugal.
$INDUSTRY_{i,t}$ = Dummy variable for each industries.

RESULTS

Descriptive Statistics

The average values for each of the variables present in the model, as well as other descriptive measures of statistic relevance, are shown in Table 2.

The level of EM measured by the four models presents averages around 9.9% which are similar to the values presented by Leuz et al. (2003) for Portuguese companies, with averages around approximately 7.5% and 12%, as foreseen by the study of Dias (2015). Such as in Gu et al. (2005), the main independent variable, which finds the financial leverage level, presents a relatively high average value, in our case even higher, with a value around 76%. The average profitability below 1% and the negative growth rate partially justify the difficult economic period of the years studied. The average level of tangible actives rested at 34.7%, in rough terms.

Regression Results

Table 3 reports the Ordinary Least Squares regression results of four absolute discretionary accruals models obtained on the estimation of the model (1) for the total of the sample. The results show, with

Table 2. Descriptive statistic of the variables present in the model

Variável	Medium	Median	Standard Deviation	Minimum		Maximum
EM-OJ	0.100	0.061	0.145	0.000		4.808
EM-MJ	0.099	0.060	0.147	0.000		4.733
EM-CFJ	0.097	0.060	0.143	0.000		4.593
EM-PMJ	0.098	0.060	0.144	0.000		4.864
AUD	0.243	0.000	0.429	0.000		1.000
LEV	0.760	0.691	0.875	-0.053		29.137
PROF	0.002	0.013	0.170	-5.9742		1.452
SIZE	6.561	6.364	1.739	1.799		12.166
TANG	0.347	0.287	0.277	0.000		0.999
GROW	0.005	0.002	0.223	-6.714		0.901
	EM-OJ is the absolute value of discretionary accruals calculated by Original Jones Model; EM-MJ is the absolute value of discretionary accruals calculated by Modified Jones Model; EM-CFJ is the absolute value of discretionary accruals calculated by Cash-Flow Jones Model; EM-PMJ is the absolute value of discretionary accruals calculated by Performance Matched Jones Model; AUD is the dummy variable that takes value 1 for firms auditor hired and 0 otherwise; LEV is the ratio between the total liabilities and the total assets; PROF is the ratio between EBITDA and the total assets; SIZE is the natural logarithm of the total assets; GROW is the annual percentage variation of the total active; Number of observation is 8730.					

statistical relevance (a level of 0.05), a positive relationship between the level of EM and the firm audit. We infer that this relationship show the same level of significance in all the other estimation models, that is to say, for the four variants of the EM variable (EM-OJ, EM-MJ, EM-CFJ, EM-PMJ). Our results indicate that audit of firms is positively related to levels of earnings management, suggested that private firms with audited financial report have powerful incentives to expropriate wealth from minority shareholders, and pursue their own interests at the expense of non-controlling shareholders. Our results confirm our first hypothesis of this study.

The second hypothesis of the study intends to analyse whether the relationship between the use of earnings management and firms audit is softened during the economic adjustment programmes applied to Portugal and Ireland. As it is indicated in Table 3, in all estimations of earnings management, the coefficient of interaction variable ADJPR*AUD is negative and significant at 1% and 5%, which allows the conclusion that the relationship between the level of EM and the audit is attenuated in the adjustment period. The second research hypothesis was validated, and indicates that external enforcement (i.e. adjustment programmes) is a more effective control for earnings management, which is confirmed by what was found by Habib et al. (2013) and Kousenidis et al. (2013), for periods of economic retraction.

Finally, our results indicate that the variable leverage (LEV) is significantly and positively associated with earnings management, which indicates that more debt companies revealed poorer earnings quality. The variable size (SIZE) is negatively associated to earnings management, which indicates that smaller companies tend to use EM more than larger companies. The same is proven in what the profitability variable (PROF) is concerned, indicating that less profitable companies use EM more than those which are more profitable. Furthermore, we have the growth rate variable (GROW) which presents a positive relationship with EM, meaning that companies with higher growth rates are more likely to manipulate their earnings, such as McNichols (2000), Skinner and Sloan (2002) and again Doyle et al. (2007) had

Table 3. Relationship between audit and earnings management

	EM-OJ	EM-MJ	EM-CFJ	EM-PMJ
AUD	0.015** (2.528)	0.015** (2.414)	0.015** (2.542)	0.016** (2.579)
ADJPR*AUD	-0.016** (-3.166)	-0.016*** (-3.155)	-0.017*** (-3.217)	-0.016*** (-3.171)
LEV	0.013*** (5.597)	0.013*** (5.422)	0.011*** (5.005)	0.013*** (5.734)
SIZE	-0.010*** (-7.310)	-0.009*** (-7.045)	-0.010*** (-7.537)	-0.010*** (-7.184)
TANG	-0.070*** (-11.167)	-0.069*** (-10.930)	-0.074*** (-11.886)	-0.070*** (-11.163)
GROW	0.110*** (13.551)	0.112*** (13.616)	0.101*** (12.622)	0.104*** (12.767)
PROF	-0.182*** (-13.055)	-0.185*** (-13.150)	-0.161*** (-11.655)	-0.145*** (-10.339)
COUNTRY	-0.019** (-2.553)	-0.018** (-2.313)	-0.015** (-2.067)	-0.011** (-2.770)
INDUSTRY	Yes	Yes	Yes	Yes
Adj R^2	0.095	0.092	0.087	0.070
N	8730	8730	8730	8730

*, **, e *** statistically significant for a level of significance of 0.1, 0.05 e 0.01 respectively. ; EM-OJ is the absolute value of discretionary accruals calculated by Original Jones Model; EM-MJ is the absolute value of discretionary accruals calculated by Modified Jones Model; EM-CFJ is the absolute value of discretionary accruals calculated by Cash-Flow Jones Model; EM-PMJ is the absolute value of discretionary accruals calculated by Performance Matched Jones Model; AUD is the dummy variable that takes value 1 for firms auditor hired and 0 otherwise; ADJPR*AUD is the interaction variable that result into multiplication of ADJPR and AUD; LEV is the ratio between the total liabilities and the total assets; PROF is the ratio between EBITDA and the total assets; SIZE is the natural logarithm of the total assets; GROW is the annual percentage variation of the total assets.

stated. Finally, the negative association between the level of fixed tangible actives (TANG) and EM found, is in accordance with Frank and Goyal (2009), Rajan and Zingales (1995), Harris and Raviv (1991) and Titman and Wessels (1988), and allows us to conclude that to a lower level of tangible fixed actives (AFT) corresponds a higher level of EM.

In order to observe the separate effect of private firms in different sized firms, we re-estimated our research model for two subsamples: large firms and small firms. The total sample was split into two subsamples in line with the medium level of firm size (large firm size >= 6.561, and small firm size <6.561). Table 4 reports the Ordinary Least Squares regression results of absolute discretionary accruals estimated for the subsample of large firms and small firms.

For subsample of small private firms, the results indicate that audit of firms (AUD) is negatively related to levels of earnings management, however, statistically it is not significant. For the interaction variable (ADJPR*AUD) we find the negative relation to earnings management however, statistically not significant. Our results indicate that small private audited firms have not incentives to earnings management. For the subsample of large private firms, we find that audit firms (AUD) are positively and significantly related to earnings management, which indicated that the large private firms have higher incentives for earnings management when financial statements are audited, whereas for small private firms that is not the case. Additionally, the large private firms with audited financial statements in years under adjustment programmes (ADJPR*AUD) demonstrated lower level of earnings management.

Table 4. Relationship between audit and earnings management in large and small firms

	Firms SIZE<6.561 EM-OJ	EM-MJ	Firms SIZE≥6.561 EM-OJ	EM-MJ
AUD ADJPR*AUD	-0.017 (-0.817) -0.014 (-0.501)	-0.013 (-0.490) -0.009 (-0.259)	0.015** (2.412) -0.014*** (-3.507)	0.010** (2.506) -0.015** (-2.274)
LEV	0.011*** (4.323)	0.011*** (3.897)	0.015* (1.805)	0.015* (1.832)
SIZE	-0.015*** (-4.751)	-0.016*** (-4.364)	-0.009*** (-3.592)	-0.006** (-2.819)
TANG	-0.068*** (-7.526)	-0.064*** (-6.521)	-0.070*** (-8.183)	-0.073*** (-8.963)
GROW	0.094*** (8.960)	0.102*** (9.275)	0.158*** (11.598)	0.137*** (10.611)
PROF	-0.184*** (-11.115)	-0.191*** (-11.001)	-0.107*** (-3.225)	-0.117*** (-3.580)
COUNTRY INDUSTRY Adj R^2	-0.005 (-0.218) Yes 0.10	-0.043** (-1.726) Yes 0.10	-0.016 (-1.101) Yes 0.087	-0.008 (-1.106) Yes 0.070
N	8730	8730	8730	8730

*, **, e *** statistically significant for a level of significance of 0.1, 0.05 e 0.01 respectively. ; EM-OJ is the absolute value of discretionary accruals calculated by Original Jones Model; EM-MJ is the absolute value of discretionary accruals calculated by Modified Jones Model; EM-CFJ is the absolute value of discretionary accruals calculated by Cash-Flow Jones Model; EM-PMJ is the absolute value of discretionary accruals calculated by Performance Matched Jones Model; AUD is the dummy variable that takes value 1 for firms auditor hired and 0 otherwise; ADJPR*AUD is the interaction variable that result into multiplication of ADJPR and AUD; LEV is the ratio between the total liabilities and the total assets; PROF is the ratio between EBITDA and the total assets; SIZE is the natural logarithm of the total assets; GROW is the annual percentage variation of the total assets.

Robustness Analysis

To confirm the robustness of our findings, we consider alternative definitions of audit variable. Specifically, we defined audit as dummy variables that take value one if private firms are audited by big four audited firms (BIG4) and zero otherwise.

The main findings of the different definition of audited firms (BIG4) are qualitatively the same as those reported in the previous Table 4 for all alternative definition of earnings management. The results presented confirm our findings that private firms audited by BIG 4 firms have higher level of earnings management. Additionally, in years of adjustment programmes (ADJPR*BIG4) the private firms presented lower level of earnings management, confirming our previous findings.

CONCLUSION

The present study analyses the relationship between the auditors of firms and the level of earnings management in Portuguese and Irish private firms between 2008 and 2016. The choice of these two countries lies on the fact that they both experienced strong financial adjustment programmes, and it is

Table 5. Relationship between auditors (BIG4) and earnings management

	EM-OJ	EM-MJ	EM-CFJ	EM-PMJ
BIG4 **ADJPR*BIG4**	**0.047***** **(3.922)** **-0.035***** **(-3.567)**	**0.049***** **(4.098)** **-0.043**** **(-1.967)**	**0.055***** **(4.634)** **-0.055***** **(-3.987)**	**0.050***** **(4.161)** **-0.035***** **(-3.645)**
LEV	0.012*** (5.478)	0.012*** (5.302)	0.011*** (4.873)	0.013*** (5.598)
SIZE	-0.009*** (-8.650)	-0.009*** (-8.3934)	-0.009*** (-9.007)	-0.009*** (-8.520)
TANG	-0.068*** (-10.832)	-0.067*** (-10.606)	-0.072*** (-9.007)	-0.068*** (-10.809)
GROW	0.110*** (13.615)	0.112*** (13.677)	0.102*** (12.679)	0.104*** (12.838)
PROF	-0.184*** (-13.169)	-0.187*** (-13.260)	-0.162*** (-11.778)	-0.146*** (-10.462)
COUNTRY INDUSTRY Adj R^2	-0.017** (-2.420) Yes 0.096	-0.016** (-2.207) Yes 0.094	-0.013** (-1.933) Yes 0.092	-0.008** (-1.176) Yes 0.081
N	8730	8730	8730	8730

*, **, e *** statistically significant for a level of significance of 0.1, 0.05 e 0.01 respectively; EM-OJ is the absolute value of discretionary accruals calculated by Original Jones Model; EM-MJ is the absolute value of discretionary accruals calculated by Modified Jones Model; EM-CFJ is the absolute value of discretionary accruals calculated by Cash-Flow Jones Model; EM-PMJ is the absolute value of discretionary accruals calculated by Performance Matched Jones Model; AUD is the dummy variable that takes value 1 for firms auditor hired and 0 otherwise; ADJPR*AUD is the interaction variable that result into multiplication of ADJPR and AUD; LEV is the ratio between the total liabilities and the total assets; PROF is the ratio between EBITDA and the total assets; SIZE is the natural logarithm of the total assets; GROW is the annual percentage variation of the total assets.

pertinent to assess the audit quality and earnings management phenomenon in this particularly economic harsh context.

Our results are consistent with the hypothesis. The main results of the study demonstrate that the fact of having an auditor in private companies is associated with stronger level of earnings management. Our results, consistent with Persakis and Iatridis (2015), suggested that private firms with audited financial report have powerful incentives to expropriate wealth from minority shareholders, and pursue their own interests at the expense of non-controlling shareholders. Additionally, the results show that earnings management is softened in the economic adjustment period, which is similar to what was found by Habib et al. (2013) and Kousenidis et al. (2013), for periods of economic retraction. Finally, we concluded that the large private firms with audited financial statements in years under adjustment programmes demonstrated lower level of earnings management. Firm size in previous literature is believed to influence the relationship between firms' ownership and earnings management. In private audited large firms, the visibility, reputation and better monitoring of managers suggest that earnings management in large private firms is likely to be lower than in small private firms (Fama and Jensen, 1983; Jensen and Meckling, 1976).

The limitations of this research are as follows. Firstly, the data have some limitations that preclude generalizations to the universe of private firms. We cover only private firms in the Portugal and Ireland firms between 2008 and 2016. These findings do not necessarily apply to firms that are publicly listed. Secondly, our sample does not include the firms from other countries that were exposed to greater vigilance from the European Union. For future studies it would be interesting to include other countries subjected to adjustment programmes in the sample. Greece and Spain would utterly be good candidates for that. Thirdly, the time period is another limitation of this study. The few years after the adjustment programmes are obviously insufficient to allow a post-adjustment analysis, which would be relevant to understand whether the conclusions expounded would be the same. Future studies may research those effects. Finally, the important concerns about the national context. The study's result might be specific to Ireland, where the relationship between firms and the financial recuperation is presumed to generate different incentives for earnings management from Portugal. For example, the legal rules covering shareholder protection and the quality of their enforcement vary considerably across countries (La Porta et al., 1998; 2000). Accordingly, the difference in the severity of agency problems and therefore the difference in the earnings management practice in private firms would vary across countries.

REFERENCES

Afshartous, D., & Preston, R. (2011). Key result of interaction models with centering. *Journal of Statistics Education: An International Journal on the Teaching and Learning of Statistics, 19*(3), 1–24. doi:10.1080/10691898.2011.11889620

Aharony, J., Lin, C., & Loeb, M. (1993). Initial public offerings, accounting choices, and earnings management. *Contemporary Accounting Research, 10*(1), 61–81. doi:10.1111/j.1911-3846.1993.tb00382.x

Alcidi, C., Belke, A., Giovannini, A., & Gros, D. (2016). Macroeconomic adjustment programmes in the euro area: An overall assessment. *International Economics and Economic Policy, 13*(3), 345–358. doi:10.100710368-016-0350-6

Allayannis, G., & Weston, J. P. (2006). *Earnings volatility, cash Flow volatility, and Firm value*. American Accounting Association, Annual Meeting.

Badolato, P. G., Donelson, D. C., & Ege, M. (2014). Audit committee financial expertise and earnings management: The role of status. *Journal of Accounting and Economics, 58*(2-3), 208–230. doi:10.1016/j.jacceco.2014.08.006

Baker, M., & Wurgler, J. (2002). Market Timing and Capital Structure. *The Journal of Finance, 57*(1), 1–32. doi:10.1111/1540-6261.00414

Ball, R., Kothari, S. P., & Robin, A. (2000). The effect of international institutional factors on properties of accounting earnings. *Journal of Accounting and Economics, 29*(1), 1–52. doi:10.1016/S0165-4101(00)00012-4

Baralexis, S. (2004). Creative accounting in small advancing countries. The Greek case. *Managerial Auditing Journal, 19*(3), 440–461. doi:10.1108/02686900410524427

Barghathi, Y., Collison, D., & Crawford, L. (2018). Earnings management and audit quality: Stakeholders' perceptions. *The Journal of Management and Governance, 22*(3), 629–659. doi:10.100710997-017-9396-2

Barth, M. R., Beaver, W. H., Hand, J. M., & Landsman, W. R. (1999). Accruals, cash flows, and equity values. *Review of Accounting Studies, 4*(3), 205–229. doi:10.1023/A:1009630100586

Beatty, A., & Weber, J. (2003). The effects of debt contracting on voluntary accounting method changes. *The Accounting Review*, *78*(1), 119–142. doi:10.2308/accr.2003.78.1.119

Belke, A., & Schnabl, G. (2013). Four Generations of Global Imbalances. *Review of International Economics*, *21*(1), 1–5. doi:10.1111/roie.12015

Ben Othman, H., & Zeghal, D. (2006). A study of earnings-management motives in the Anglo-American and Euro-Continental accounting models: The Canadian and French cases. *The International Journal of Accounting*, *41*(4), 406–435. doi:10.1016/j.intacc.2006.09.004

Beneish, D., & Vargus, E. (2002). Insider trading, earnings quality, and accrual mispricing. *The Accounting Review*, *77*(4), 755–791. doi:10.2308/accr.2002.77.4.755

Beneish, M. D. (1999). Incentives Earnings and Penalties Related to Overstatements that Violate. *The Accounting Review*, *74*(4), 425–457. doi:10.2308/accr.1999.74.4.425

Beneish, M. D. (2001). Earnings management : A perspective. *Managerial Finance*, *27*(12), 3–17. doi:10.1108/03074350110767411

Bharath, S., Sunder, J., & Sunder, S. (2008). Accounting quality and debt contracting. *The Accounting Review*, *83*(1), 1–28. doi:10.2308/accr.2008.83.1.1

Bhattacharya, D., Guner, N., & Ventura, G. (2012). Distortions, endogenous managerial skills and productivity differences. *Review of Economic Dynamics*, *13*, 11–25.

Bowen, R. M., Rajgopal, S., & Venkatachalam, M. (2008). Accounting Discretion, Corporate Governance, and Firm Performance. *Contemporary Accounting Research*, *25*(2), 351–405. doi:10.1506/car.25.2.3

Bradley, M., Jarrell, G., & Kim, H. (1984). On the Existence of an Optimal Capital Structure: Theory and Evidence. *The Journal of Finance*, *39*(3), 857–878. doi:10.1111/j.1540-6261.1984.tb03680.x

Brennan, M. J., & Schwartz, E. S. (1978). Corporate Income Taxes, Valuation, and the Problem of Optimal Capital Structure. *The Journal of Business*, *51*(1), 103–114. doi:10.1086/295987

Burgstahler, D., & Eames, M. J. (2003). Earnings Management to Avoid Losses and Earnings Decreases: Are Analysts Fooled? *Contemporary Accounting Research*, *20*(2), 253–294. doi:10.1506/BXXP-RGTD-H0PM-9XAL

Burgstahler, D. C., Hail, L., & Leuz, C. (2006). The Importance of Reporting Incentives: Earnings Management in European Private and Public Firms. *The Accounting Review*, *81*(5), 983–1016. doi:10.2308/accr.2006.81.5.983

Burkart, M., Panunzi, F., & Shleifer, A. (2003). Family firms. *The Journal of Finance*, *58*(5), 2167–2201. doi:10.1111/1540-6261.00601

Cahan, S. F. (1992). The Effect of Antitrust Investigations on Discretionary Accruals: A Refined Test of the Political-Cost Hypothesis. *The Accounting Review*, *67*(1), 77–95.

Callao, S., & Jarne, J. I. (2010). Have IFRS Affected Earnings Management in the European Union? *Accounting in Europe*, *7*(2), 159–189. doi:10.1080/17449480.2010.511896

Cano-Rodriguez, M. (2010). Big Auditors, Private Firms and Accounting Conservatism: Spanish evidence. *European Accounting Review*, *19*(1), 131–159. doi:10.1080/09638180902989426

Cheng, Q., & Warfield, T. (2005). Equity incentives and earnings management. *The Accounting Review*, *80*(2), 441–476. doi:10.2308/accr.2005.80.2.441

Chi, W., Lisic, L., & Pevzner, M. (2011). Is Enhanced Audit Quality Associated with Greater Real Earnings Management? *Accounting Horizons*, *25*(2), 315–335. doi:10.2308/acch-10025

Chia, Y., Lapsley, I., & Lee, H. (2007). Choice of auditors and earn-ings management during the Asian financial crisis. *Managerial Auditing Journal*, *22*(2), 177–196. doi:10.1108/02686900710718672

Choi, J., Kim, J., & Lee, J. (2011). Value relevance of discretionary accruals in the Asian financial crisis of 1997–1998. *Journal of Accounting and Public Policy*, *30*(2), 166–187. doi:10.1016/j.jaccpubpol.2010.09.002

Christie, A., & Zimmerman, J. L. (1994). Efficient and Opportunistic Choices of Accounting Procedures: Corporate Control Contests. *The Accounting Review*, *69*(4), 539–566.

Christie, A. A. (1990). Aggregation of test statistics. *Journal of Accounting and Economics*, *12*(1–3), 15–36. doi:10.1016/0165-4101(90)90039-7

Cohen, D. A., & Zarowin, P. (2008). *Economic Consequences of Real and Accrual-Based Earnings Management Activities.* Working Paper, New York University.

Coppens, L., & Peek, E. (2005). An analysis of earnings management by European private firms. *Journal of International Accounting, Auditing & Taxation*, *14*(1), 1–17. doi:10.1016/j.intaccaudtax.2005.01.002

Dai, R. (2012). *International Accounting Databases on WRDS: Comparative Analysis.* Wharton Research Data Services. University of Pennsylvania.

Davis-Friday, P., Eng, L., & Liu, C. (2006). The effects of the Asian crisis, corporate governance and accounting system on the valuation of book value and earnings. *The International Journal of Accounting*, *41*(1), 22–40. doi:10.1016/j.intacc.2005.12.002

Dechow, P., & Dichev, I. D. (2002). The Quality of Accruals and Earings: The Role of Accruals Estimation Errors. *The Accounting Review*, *77*(supplement), 35–59. doi:10.2308/accr.2002.77.s-1.35

Dechow, P. M. (1994). Accounting earnings and cash flows as measures of firm performance. The role of accounting accruals. *Journal of Accounting and Economics*, *18*(1), 3–42. doi:10.1016/0165-4101(94)90016-7

Dechow, P. M., Ge, W., Larson, C. R., & Sloan, R. G. (2011). Predicting Material Accounting Misstatements. *Contemporary Accounting Research*, *28*(1), 17–82. doi:10.1111/j.1911-3846.2010.01041.x

Dechow, P. M., & Skinner, D. J. (2000). Earnings management: Reconciling the views of accounting academics, practitioners, and regulators. *Accounting Horizons*, *14*(2), 235–250. doi:10.2308/acch.2000.14.2.235

Dechow, P. M., & Sloan, R. G. (1991). Executive incentives and the horizon problem: An empirical investigation. *Journal of Accounting and Economics*, *14*(1), 51–89. doi:10.1016/0167-7187(91)90058-S

Dechow, P. M., Sloan, R. G., & Sweeney, A. P. (1995). Detecting Earnings Management. *The Accounting Review*, *70*(2), 193–225.

Dechow, P. M., Sloan, R. G., & Sweeney, A. P. (1996). Causes and Consequences of Earnings Manipulation: An Analysis of Firms Subject to Enforcement Actions by the SEC. *Contemporary Accounting Research*, *13*(1), 37–47. doi:10.1111/j.1911-3846.1996.tb00489.x

DeFond, M., Hu, X., Hung, M., & Li, S. (2012). Has the widespread adoption of IFRS reduced US firms' attractiveness to foreign investors? *Journal of International Accounting Research*, *11*(2), 27–55. doi:10.2308/jiar-50205

DeFond, M. L., & Jiambalvo, J. (1994). Debt covenant violation and manipulation of accruals. *Journal of Accounting and Economics*, *17*(1–2), 145–176. doi:10.1016/0165-4101(94)90008-6

Dhaliwal, D. S. (1980). The Effect of the Firm's Capital Structure on the Choice of Accounting Methods. *The Accounting Review*, *55*(1), 78–84.

Dichev, I. D., & Skinner, D. J. (2002). Large-sample evidence on the debt covenant hypothesis. *Journal of Accounting Research*, *40*(4), 1091–1123. doi:10.1111/1475-679X.00083

Doyle, J., Ge, W., & McVay, S. (2007). Accruals and internal control over financial reporting. *The Accounting Review*, *82*(5), 1141–1170. doi:10.2308/accr.2007.82.5.1141

DuCharme, L. L., Malatesta, P. H., & Sefcik, S. E. (2001). Earnings Management: IPO Valuation and Subsequent Performance. *Journal of Accounting, Auditing & Finance*, *16*(4), 369–396. doi:10.1177/0148558X0101600409

Duffy, D., Fitzgerald, J., Byrne, D., & Timoney, K. (2013). *Quarterly Economic Commentary, Winter*. Dublin: ESRI.

Easley, D., & O'Hara, M. (2004). Information and the cost of capital. *The Journal of Finance*, *59*(4), 1553–1583. doi:10.1111/j.1540-6261.2004.00672.x

Easterwood, C. M. (1997). Takeovers and Incentives for Earnings Management: An Empirical Analysis. *Journal of Applied Business Research*, *14*(1), 29–48. doi:10.19030/jabr.v14i1.5726

Elliot, J., & Hanna, J. D. (1996). Repeated Accounting Write-Offs and the Information Content of Earnings. *Journal of Accounting Research*, *34*(Supplement), 135–155. doi:10.2307/2491430

European Stability Mechanism. (2014). *European Stability Mechanism Annual Report -2014*. Author.

Faccio, M., & Lang, L. (2002). The ultimate ownership of Western European corporations. *Journal of Financial Economics*, *65*(3), 365–395. doi:10.1016/S0304-405X(02)00146-0

Fama, E., & Jensen, M. (1983). Separation of ownership and control. *The Journal of Law & Economics*, *26*(2), 301–325. doi:10.1086/467037

Fischer, E. O., Heinkel, R., & Zechner, J. (1989). Dynamic Capital Structure Choice : Theory and Tests. *The Journal of Finance*, *44*(1), 19–40. doi:10.1111/j.1540-6261.1989.tb02402.x

Fitzgerald, J. (2012). Financial Crisis, Economic Adjustment and a Return to Growth in the EU. *Revue de l'OFCE, Debates and Policies*, 127.

Francis, J., Hanna, J. D., & Vincent, L. (1996). Causes and Effects of Discretionary Asset Write-Offs. *Journal of Accounting Research*, *34*, 117–134. doi:10.2307/2491429

Francis, J. R., Khurana, I. K., & Pereira, R. (2005). Disclosure incentives and effects on cost of capital around the world. *The Accounting Review*, *80*(4), 1125–1162. doi:10.2308/accr.2005.80.4.1125

Frank, M. Z., & Goyal, V. K. (2009). Capital Structure Decisions around the World: Which Factors Are Reliably Important? *Financial Management*, *38*(1), 1–37. doi:10.1111/j.1755-053X.2009.01026.x

Froot, K., Scharfstein, D., & Stein, J. (1993). Risk management Coordinating corporate investment and Financing Policies. *The Journal of Finance*, *48*(5), 1624–1658. doi:10.1111/j.1540-6261.1993.tb05123.x

Gabrielsen, G. J., Gramlich, J., & Plenborg, T. (2002). Managerial ownership, information content of earnings, and discretionary accruals in a non-US setting. *Journal of Business Finance & Accounting*, *29*(7/8), 967–988. doi:10.1111/1468-5957.00457

Gaio, C. (2010). The relative importance of firm and country characteristics for earnings quality around the world. *European Accounting Review*, *19*(4), 693–738. doi:10.1080/09638180903384643

Ge, V., & McVay, S. (2005). The diclosure of material weaknesses in internal control after the Sarbanes -Oxley Act. *Accounting Horizons*, *19*(3), 137–158. doi:10.2308/acch.2005.19.3.137

Giavazzi, F., & Spaventa, L. (2010). *Why the current account matters in a monetary union Lessons from the financial crisis in the Euro area*. Author.

Gorgan, C., Gorgan, V., Dumitru, V. F., & Pitulice, I. C. (2012). The Evolution of the Accounting Practices During the Recent Economic Crisis : Empirical Survey Regarding the Earning Management. *The Amfiteatru Economics Journal*, *14*(32), 550–563.

Gu, Z., Lee, C. W. J., & Rosett, J. G. (2005). What determines the variability of accounting accruals? *Review of Quantitative Finance and Accounting*, *24*(3), 313–334. doi:10.100711156-005-6869-1

Guidry, F., Leone, A. J., Rock, S., Simon, W. E., Beneish, D., Billings, B., & Stuart, N. (1999). Earnings-based bonus plans and earnings management by business-unit managers. *Journal of Accounting and Economics*, *26*, 113–142. doi:10.1016/S0165-4101(98)00037-8

Habib, A., Uddin, B. B., & Islam, A. (2013). Financial distress, earnings management and market pricing of accruals during the global financial crisis. *Managerial Finance*, *39*(2), 155–180. doi:10.1108/03074351311294007

Harris, M., & Raviv, A. (1991). The Theory of Capital Structure. *The Journal of Finance*, *46*(1), 297–355. doi:10.1111/j.1540-6261.1991.tb03753.x

Healy, P. M. (1985). The effect of bonus schemes on accounting decisions. *Journal of Accounting and Economics*, *7*(1–3), 85–107. doi:10.1016/0165-4101(85)90029-1

Healy, P. M., & Wahlen, J. M. (1999). A review of the earnings management literature and its implications for standard setting. *Accounting Horizons*, *13*(4), 365–383. doi:10.2308/acch.1999.13.4.365

Ho, L. J., & Kang, F. (2013). Auditor Choice and Audit Fees in Family Firms: Evidence from the S&P 1500. *Auditing*, *32*(4), 71–93. doi:10.2308/ajpt-50533

Holthausen, R. W., Larcker, D. F., & Sloan, R. G. (1995). Annual bonus schemes and the manipulation of earnings. *Journal of Accounting and Economics*, *19*(1), 29–74. doi:10.1016/0165-4101(94)00376-G

Jaffer, M. J., & Sohail, S. B. (2007). *Corporate Governance Issues in Family-Owned Enterprises*. Center for International Private Enterprise (CIPE), Economic Reform Feature Service. Available at http://www.cipe.org/publications/fs/pdf/042007.pdf

Jelinek, K. (2007). The effect of leverage increases on real earnings management. *The Journal of Business and Economic Studies*, *13*(Fall), 24–46.

Jensen, M. C., & Meckling, W. H. (1976). Theory of the firm: Managerial behavior, agency costs and ownership structure. *Journal of Financial Economics*, *3*(4), 305–360. doi:10.1016/0304-405X(76)90026-X

Jones, J. J. (1991). Earnings Management During Import Relief Investigations. *Journal of Accounting Research*, *29*(2), 193–228. doi:10.2307/2491047

Jones, M. J. (2011). *Creative accounting, fraud and international accounting scandals*. John Wiley & Sons.

Kasznik, R. (1999). On the Association between Voluntary Disclosure and Earnings Management. *Journal of Accounting Research*, *37*(1), 57–82. doi:10.2307/2491396

Kim, Y., & Yi, C. (2006). Ownership structure, business group affiliation, listing status, and earnings management: Evidence from Korea. *Contemporary Accounting Research*, *23*(2), 427–464. doi:10.1506/7T5B-72FV-MHJV-E697

Kothari, S. P., Leone, A. J., & Wasley, C. E. (2005). Performance matched discretionary accrual measures. *Journal of Accounting and Economics*, *39*(1), 163–197. doi:10.1016/j.jacceco.2004.11.002

Kousenidis, D. V., Ladas, A. C., & Negakis, C. I. (2013). The effects of the European debt crisis on earnings quality. *International Review of Financial Analysis*, *30*, 351–362. doi:10.1016/j.irfa.2013.03.004

Kraus, A., & Litzenberger, R. H. (1973). A State-Preference Model of Optimal Financial Leverage. *The Journal of Finance*, *28*(1), 911–922. doi:10.1111/j.1540-6261.1973.tb01415.x

La Porta, R., Lopes-de-Silanes, F., & Shleifer, A. (1999). Corporate ownership around the world. *The Journal of Finance*, *54*(2), 471–517. doi:10.1111/0022-1082.00115

La Porta, R., Lopes-de-Silanes, F., Shleifer, A., & Vishny, R. (1998). Law and Finance. *Journal of Political Economy*, *106*(6), 1113–1155. doi:10.1086/250042

Lee, H. Y., & Mande, V. (2002). The Effect of the Private Securities Litigation Reform Act of 1995 on Accounting Discretion of Client Managers of Big 6 and Non-Big 6 Auditors. *Auditing*, *22*(1), 93–108. doi:10.2308/aud.2003.22.1.93

Leland, H. E. (1994). Corporate Debt Value, Bond Covenants, and Optimal Capital Structure. *The Journal of Finance*, *49*(4), 1213–1252. doi:10.1111/j.1540-6261.1994.tb02452.x

Leland, H. E., & Pyle, D. H. (1977). Informational Asymmetries, Financial Structure, and Financial Intermediation. *The Journal of Finance*, *32*(2), 371–387. doi:10.2307/2326770

Leuz, C., Nanda, D., & Wysocki, P. D. (2003). Earnings management and investor protection: An international comparison. *Journal of Financial Economics*, *69*(3), 505–527. doi:10.1016/S0304-405X(03)00121-1

Lisboa, I. (2017). Impact of financial crisis and family control on earnings management of Portuguese listed firms. *European Journal of Family Business*, *6*(2), 118–131. doi:10.1016/j.ejfb.2017.06.002

McNichols, M. F. (2000). Research design issues in earnings management studies. *Journal of Accounting and Public Policy*, *19*(4–5), 313–345. doi:10.1016/S0278-4254(00)00018-1

Mendes, C. A., & Rodrigues, L. L. (2007). Determinantes da Manipulação Contabilística. *Revista de Estudos Politécnicos*, *IV*(7), 189–210.

Minton, B. A., & Schrand, C. (1999). The impact of cash flow volatility on discretionary investment and the costs of debt and equity financing. *Journal of Financial Economics*, *54*(3), 423–460. doi:10.1016/S0304-405X(99)00042-2

Modigliani, F., & Miller, M. H. (1963). Corporate Income Taxes and the Cost of Capital: A Correction. *The American Economic Review*, *53*(3), 433–443.

Mulford, C. W., & Comiskey, E. E. (2011). *The Financial Numbers Game : Detecting Creative Accounting Practices*. John Wiley & Sons.

Myers, S. (2001). Capital Structure. *The Journal of Economic Perspectives*, *15*(2), 81–102. doi:10.1257/jep.15.2.81

Myers, S., & Majluf, N. (1984). Corporate financing and investment decisions when firms have information that investors do not have. *Journal of Financial Economics*, *13*(2), 187–221. doi:10.1016/0304-405X(84)90023-0

Nardi, P. C. C., & Nakao, S. H. (2009). Gerenciamento de resultados e a relação com o custo da dívida das empresas brasileiras abertas. *Revista Contabilidade & Finanças*, *20*(51), 77–100. doi:10.1590/S1519-70772009000300006

Niskanen, M., Karjalainen, J., & Niskanen, J. (2010). The role of auditing in Small, Private Family Firms: Is it about Quality and Crebility? *Family Business Review*, *23*(3), 230–245. doi:10.1177/0894486510374456

Persakis, A., & Iatridis, G. (2016). Audit quality, investor protectionand earnings management during the financial crisis of 2008: An international perspective. *Journal of International Financial Markets, Institutions and Money*, *41*, 73–101. doi:10.1016/j.intfin.2015.12.006

Rajan, R. G., & Zingales, L. (1995). What Do We Know about Capital Structure? Some Evidence from International Data. *The Journal of Finance*, *50*(5), 1421–1460. doi:10.1111/j.1540-6261.1995.tb05184.x

Rangan, S. (1998). Earnings management and the performance of seasoned equity offerings. *Journal of Financial Economics*, *50*(1), 101–122. doi:10.1016/S0304-405X(98)00033-6

Ross, S. A. (1977). The Determination of Financial Structure: The Incentive Signalling Approach. *The Bell Journal of Economics*, *8*(1), 23–40. doi:10.2307/3003485

Schipper, K. (1989). Commentary on Earnings Management. *Accounting Horizons*, *3*, 91–102.

Schipper, K., & Vincent, L. (2003). Earnings Quality. *Accounting Horizons*, *85*(s-1), 97–110. doi:10.2308/acch.2003.17.s-1.97

Shivakumar, L. (2000). Do firms mislead investors by overstating earnings before seasoned equity offerings? *Journal of Accounting and Economics*, *29*(3), 339–371. doi:10.1016/S0165-4101(00)00026-4

Shleiefer, A., & Vishny, R. (1997). A survey of corporate governance. *The Journal of Finance*, *52*(2), 737–783. doi:10.1111/j.1540-6261.1997.tb04820.x

Skinner, D. J., & Sloan, R. G. (2002). Earnings Surprises, Growth Expectations, and Stock Returns or Don't Let an Earnings Torpedo Sink Your Portfolio. *Review of Accounting Studies*, *7*(2/3), 289–312. doi:10.1023/A:1020294523516

Subramanyam, K. R. (1996). The pricing of discretionary accruals. *Journal of Accounting and Economics*, *22*(1–3), 249–281. doi:10.1016/S0165-4101(96)00434-X

Sweeney, A. (1994). Debt-covenant violations and managers' accounting responses. *Journal of Accounting and Economics*, *17*(3), 281–308. doi:10.1016/0165-4101(94)90030-2

Teoh, S., & Wong, T. (2002). Why new issues and high-accrual firms underperform: The role of analysts' credulity. *Review of Financial Studies*, *15*(3), 869–900. doi:10.1093/rfs/15.3.869

Teoh, S. H., Welch, I., & Wong, T. J. (1998). Earnings management and the long-run market performance of initial public offerings. *The Journal of Finance*, *53*(6), 1935–1974. doi:10.1111/0022-1082.00079

Teoh, S. H., Welch, I., & Wong, T. J. (1998). Earnings Management and the Underperformance of Seasoned Equity Offerings. *Journal of Financial Economics*, *50*(1), 63–99. doi:10.1016/S0304-405X(98)00032-4

Titman, S., & Wessels, R. (1988). The Determinants of Capital Structure. *The Journal of Finance*, *43*(1), 1–19. doi:10.1111/j.1540-6261.1988.tb02585.x

Tucker, J. W., & Zarowin, P. A. (2006). Does Income Smoothing Improve Earnings Informativeness? *The Accounting Review*, *81*(1), 251–270. doi:10.2308/accr.2006.81.1.251

Villalonga, B., & Amit, R. (2006). How do family ownership, control and management affect firms value? *Journal of Financial Economics*, *80*(2), 385–417. doi:10.1016/j.jfineco.2004.12.005

Wang, D. (2006). Founding family ownership and earnings quality. *Journal of Accounting Research*, *44*(3), 619–656. doi:10.1111/j.1475-679X.2006.00213.x

Warfield, T., Wild, J., & Wild, K. (1995). Managerial ownership, accounting choices, and informativeness of earnings. *Journal of Accounting and Economics*, *20*(1), 61–91. doi:10.1016/0165-4101(94)00393-J

Watrin, C., Ebert, N., & Thomsen, M. (2014). Book-Tax Conformity and Earnings Management: Insights from European One-and Two-Book Systems. *The Journal of the American Taxation Association*, *36*(2), 55–89. doi:10.2308/atax-50769

Watts, R. L., & Zimmerman, J. L. (1978). Towards a Positive Theory of the Determination of Accounting Standards. *The Accounting Review*, *53*(1), 112–134.

Welch, I. (2011). Two common problems in capital structure research: The financial-debt-to-asset ratio and issuing activity versus leverage changes. *International Review of Finance*, *11*(1), 1–17. doi:10.1111/j.1468-2443.2010.01125.x

White, H. (1980). A Heteroskedasticity-Consistent Covariance Matrix Estimator and a Direct Test for Heteroskedasticity. *Econometrica*, *48*(4), 817. doi:10.2307/1912934

Zhao, Y., & Chen, K. (2008). The influence of takeover protection on earnings management. *Journal of Business Finance & Accounting*, *35*(3), 347–375. doi:10.1111/j.1468-5957.2008.02081.x

Zimmerman, J. L. (1983). Taxes and firm size. *Journal of Accounting and Economics*, *5*(C), 119–149. doi:10.1016/0165-4101(83)90008-3

KEY TERMS AND DEFINITIONS

Agency Theory: Agency theory is concerned with resolving problems that arise in agency relationships. An agency relationship is described as a situation in which one party (the principal) delegates work to another party (the agent). This principal-agent relationship exists between employers and employees, lawyers and clients, or buyers and suppliers. Agency theory attempts to explain two problems. The first is the agency problem that arises when the goals of the principal and the agent diverge, and it is difficult for the principal to verify the agent's actions. The second is the problem of risk sharing which occurs when the principal and the agent have different attitudes towards risk.

Big Four Accounting Firms: The Big Four (Ernst & Young [EY], Deloitte & Touche, KPMG, and PricewaterhouseCoopers [PwC]) accounting firms are the four biggest professional services networks in the world, offering audit, assurance services, taxation, management consulting, advisory, actuarial, corporate finance and legal services. They handle the vast majority of audits for public companies as well as many private companies.

Economic Adjustment Programme for Ireland: Usually referred to as the Bailout Programme, is a memorandum of understanding on financial assistance to the Republic of Ireland in order to cope with the Irish financial crisis.

Economic Adjustment Programme for Portugal: Usually referred to as the Bailout Programme, is a Memorandum of understanding on financial assistance to the Portuguese Republic in order to cope with the Portuguese financial crisis.

Financial Auditing: The process of examining an organization's (or individual's) financial statements to determine if they are accurate and in accordance with any applicable rules (including accounting standards), regulations, and laws.

Financial Crisis: The financial crisis of 2007–2008, also known as the global financial crisis and the 2008 financial crisis, is considered by many economists to have been the worst financial crisis since the Great Depression of the 1930s. It began in 2007 with a crisis in the subprime mortgage market in the United States, and developed into a full-blown international banking crisis with the collapse of the investment bank Lehman Brothers on September 15, 2008. In 2010, the Dodd–Frank Wall Street Reform and Consumer Protection Act was enacted in the US following the crisis to promote the financial stability of the United States. The Basel III capital and liquidity standards were adopted by countries around the world. The European sovereign debt crisis started in 2008 with the collapse of Iceland's banking system and spread primarily to Portugal, Italy, Ireland, Greece and Spain in 2009. The debt crisis has led to a loss of confidence in European businesses and economies.

Private Firms: A private firm can be a corporation, a limited liability company, a partnership, or a sole proprietorship, as long as the shares are privately held and not traded publicly. Although private companies are legally required to file certain documents with their state and follow required compliance laws for shareholders, public companies must follow strict government regulations.

Chapter 8
The Relationship Between the Quality of Financial Information in Industrial Companies and Discretionary Inventory Management

Maria Filipa Nogueira
Instituto Politécnico de Santarém, Portugal

ABSTRACT

Inventories are the base element for the manufacturing (industrial) companies. The inclusion of discretionary in the inventory management processes of production leads to changes in the value of the companies. The accounting system produces information used in predictions and for management decision. The usefulness and opportunity of information are considered indispensable. If managers use their discretionarily, in the accounting system and in real activities, to achieve the firm value and earnings forecast, they will influence and modify the financial information quality. Ferrer and Ferrer said that a simple decision can enrich one company from one moment to another, and a small accounting change allows a great loss of results. The question arises: Do managers use their discretionarily and modify the financial information quality? Using adjusted models to capture discretionary accounting management and real activity management, it is possible to conclude that there is a strong evidence of discretionary management of the inventory in manufacturing Portuguese SME.

INTRODUCTION

Inventories are the base element for the production. Inventory management causes changes in the company's patrimonial and economic value, through its processing, acquisition and sale. The inclusion of discretionary in the management processes that include inventories leads to changes of the company's value. The possibility of the occurrence of discretionary management is the motivation for the develop-

DOI: 10.4018/978-1-5225-7817-8.ch008

ment of this article. The focus will be inventories because manufacturing companies are one of the more inventory-dependent activity sectors (e.g. Bernard & Noel, 1991; Cannon, 2008; Aaker & Gjesdal, 2010; Cook, Huston, & Kinney, 2012; Nissim, 2017; Pustylnick, Temchenko, & Gubarkov, 2017).

All management acts are reflected in the financial statements of the companies (Ferrer & Ferrer, 2016). The preparation of financial information must be based on existing regulations to provide objective and reliable financial statements. However, the ambiguity of some norms allows subjective judgments and the exercise of discretion in the accounting of operations. This discretion results in accruals change of the financial statements (changing assets and liabilities as well as items of the income statement). There are several econometric models to study accruals (e.g. Jones, 1991; Dechow, Sloan, & Sweeney, 1995). The information provided by the accounting system is one of the focus of research in accounting to study the quality of information provided (Herath & Lu, 2017).

Accounting is a system that produces information. It is used to register and quantify the facts or events that occurred during a period, to inform about the company economic and financial situation and about the results achieved. This information is useful to make predictions and to base decision-making management. The financial information can be managed by using the flexibility of the accounting normative (Stolowy & Breton, 2003).

Manufacturing companies have, in the inventories, one of their preponderant items for the introduction management discretion in accounting and in real activities. For this reason, the quality of information will be studied based on accruals and on real activities.

All management acts cause change in the financial statements, but decisions related to the volume and time of purchase and sale (timing) are used in the discretion included in real earning management (Roychowdhury, 2006). One method of managing discretionarily results is to take decisions about the operational process, that is, about activities. Changing operational practices can lead to goals on the financial information, influencing the judgment of users and it can be studied using accrual models.

For those countries where there is a big dependence between accounting and taxation, i.e. between the accounting result and the fiscal result, taxes arise as an incentive to manage the results. In the countries of continental Europe, such as Portugal, managers have a strong incentive to manage the accounting results in the downward direction, with the objective of reducing the amount of tax payable (Eilifsen, Knivsflå, & Sættem, 2010). One of the main incentives for managing results as the decrease of the tax payable (Moreira, 2008).

This study involved 12.181 Portuguese manufacturing SME. The first part is about discricionarity of accounting practices and its link with inventory management. The second part is about the discritionarity of real activities and its link with inventory management. There is an evidence that both kinds of management are used in the companies of the sample. For the study were regressed adaptations of the models used in several studies corroborating their results (Dechow, Sloan, & Sweeney, 1995; Ferrer & Ferrer, 2016; Gao, Gao, & Wang, 2017; Gunny, Jacob, & Jorgensen, 2013; Roychowdhury, 2006; Roychowdhury, Kothari, & Mizik, 2012).

The reminder of this study is organized as follows. First is the review of related literature and development of hypotheses. Next is the explanation of the sample and show of the results. Finally, the conclusions are presented on the main findings and the limitation of the study is presented.

LITERATURE REVIEW

The positive accounting theory (PAT) describes explanatory assumptions for opportunistic choices of managers. It assumes that management objectives encourage the maximization of their wealth or the companies they manage. So the motivations of managers target specific results (Watts & Zimmerman, 1978). This theory was formulated after the formulation of the agency theory (Jensen & Meckling, 1976). PAT assumes that actors in discretionary management act for their own benefit by trying to obtain political visibility, better remuneration (when contracts are indexed to an accounting reference); trying to present results that do not collide with restrictive clauses of existing contracts (as is the example of debt contracts). In addition to these motivations there are still others related to the structure of ownership of the company. The theory developed by these authors also relates to the agency contract and the management characteristics and the consequent asymmetry of information.

To monitor business performance is used the data provided by the financial reporting and financial statements produced by the accounting system. Accounting should provide useful information, contributing to the reduction of informational asymmetry. The financial statements are expected to present the economic and financial reality of the company and provide support for decision-making. There are several social, economic, political and behavioral factors that interfere so that not all economic agents have the same information (Dechow, Ge, & Schrand, 2010) so the accounting information has being the most elementary tool for the management mechanism (Santos & Paulo, 2006).

In small- and medium-sized enterprises (SME) the management (actions and decisions) is made by the owner, who holds the position of manager. The owner works as if he were a single shareholder, making the decisions that he believes are best for the (good) development of his business. When companies are larger and more complex decisions are made by professional managers hired for the job (Bahri, St-Pierre & Sakka, 2017) who acts to improve their own richness.

Production is the main activity of manufacturing firms. When the products are sold, their production cost appears in the income statement as "Cost of goods sold" (CGS). This item, represent a significant percentage on the total expenditures (includes direct labor costs, raw materials consumed and production overheads such as depreciation of equipment and indirect labor) so it can be used to achieve the company value desirable (Bahri et al., 2017).

Discretionary management occurs when managers use judgment in financial reporting to alter financial reports to mislead stakeholders about the underlying economic performance of the company (Healy & Wahlen, 1999). Discretionary management could arise from accounting choices that are fraudulent or from choices that are aggressive, but acceptable by the use of accounting discretion (Dechow & Skinner, 2000).

Real earnings management result from choices such as overproduction, reduction in research and development expenditures, product price reductions to increase sales, and reduction in discretionary expenditures, and it entails allocation of resources (Gupta, Pevzner, & Seethamraju, 2010; Healy & Wahlen, 1999; Roychowdhury, 2006).

Discretionary Management Based on Accounting Choices (Accruals)

Dechow & Skinner (2000) presented a study on the management of accounting. They conclude that management of accounting can be divided into two large groups: the management of results resulting from "pure" accounting decisions and the result of decisions with influence on cash flows. "Pure" accounting standards and accounting principles the overvaluation of provisions, the acceleration of depreciation and depreciation of fixed assets and the recognition of income. The intention is to present few variations between the economic periods. There are situations where the accounting allows the choice between accounting processes or methods, without configuration of fraud.

The first empirical studies of earnings management were based on the modelling of accruals that are based on accounts included in the financial statements and can be used as a reference for the discretionary management. It is understood by discretionary accruals, all the associated accounting specialization of the economic year, which do not involve financial flows, and where the discretionary action of the manager is decisive for the recognition of an expense or income (e.g. Jones, 1991; Dechow, Sloan, & Sweeney, 1995).

There are some researchers who consider the use of discretionary measures of accruals does not provide a plausible detection of discretionary management. Ball (2013) claims that it is a form of arrogance of the researchers to assert that they can detect the management using larges data, when the auditors and the stakeholders unable to do so. To verify the management of net income and lack of accounting information quality, it's worth to make an interview to the managers (Dichev, Graham, Harvey, & Rajgopal, 2013). The specialization of the exercise and the timing are the two most important criteria to evaluate the quality of accounting reports. There are investigations that claim that there are sophisticated investors who uses discretionary accruals to analyze the results, however it is more likely that sophisticated investors analyze the difference between cash flows and additions. Accounting researchers use discretionary accruals for the study of the quality of information (Jackson, 2017).

Discretionary Management Based on Real Activities

Examples of decisions with influence on the cash flows practiced by managers are: slow sales; increase spending on advertising, training, research and development; and increase expenditure of non-operational nature. With these decisions' manager reduces the net cash flows. It is considered that the manager is having an influence on the actual activity of the company and not only on accounting management (e.g. Dechow & Skinner, 2000; Roychowdhury, 2006; Cohen, Cornett, Marcus, & Tehranian, 2014; Choi, Kim, & Zang, 2010).

Commerford, Hermanson, Houston, & Peters (2014) claim that companies generate results by using the system of accruals and accounting policies, which they call accounting-based results management and that this management can also be done through the management of real activities such as: strategic definition of the moment to make an investment, a financing or temporal definition of operational decisions to which. The authors said that the management of real activities is less subject to audit and regulation, so it is more attractive to the managers.

Quality of the Accounting Information

Accounting information is associated with its usefulness for decision-making, which depends on two qualitative characteristics: the relevance (predictive value and confirmatory value) and reliability (free from errors and prejudices). In quality of earnings analyses, one is generally concerned when growth in net operating assets exceeds growth in sales. This scenario suggests companies are inappropriately recording costs on the balance sheet instead of the income statement. The most popular proxy for earnings management is the estimated abnormal accruals. The first version is from Jones (1991).

Empirical studies use different proxies associated with the quality of the information. Licerán-Gutiérrez & Cano-Rodríguez (2017) use three categories of proxies. The first uses a set of characteristics of the financial statements that provide information to users. The second measure the investor's reaction to the published results. The third aggregates external indicators as negative opinions of auditors reviewing companies ' accounts. The investigation has mainly focused on the characteristics of the financial information.

One common way to measure the quality of accounting information is through accruals. Inventories and accounts receivable and payable are part of the models of accruals. Sudden or unexpected changes in these accounts allow discretionary behaviors because these accounts reflect the transactions that have occurred and a part of the balance sheet (Roychowdhury, 2006).

The verification of the influence of discretion on the inventory line and the quality of accounting information is a poorly analyzed area so far. However, manufacturing companies have in their inventories one of their preponderant items for the introduction of discretion in management either in accounting terms or through real activities. For this reason, the quality of information will be studied taking into account the specificity of the accruals and the actual activities focusing on the inventory heading in the manufacturing sector that is one of the sectors of activity most dependent on inventories (e.g.; Cannon, 2008; Aaker & Gjesdal, 2010; Kesavan & Mani, 2010 Basu, Nilanjan; Wang, 2011; Cook, Huston, & Kinney, 2012; Pustylnick, Temchenko, & Gubarkov, 2017).

Inventory

Inventory and accounts receivable are underestimated components in determining the degree of discretionary accruals. Unexpected or sudden changes in these accounts reflect possible discretionary behavior of activity (Roychowdhury, 2006). Discretionary management can be taken by varying level of activity. If a firm starts higher activity levels, that can be discretionary management. The activity ratios are altered and reflects those changes. The ratios capture daily operations and demonstrate the values of the current assets, particularly of inventories and of accounts of receivables. Sales is the primary target of the increase or decrease activity. Accruals are important when managers have a desired activity ratio for benchmarking operational factors. Activities "can be difficult to control while changes in accounting estimates provide a direct and controllable effect on the financial statement figures" (Ferrer & Ferrer, 2016).

Hypothesis

The information provided by the accounting system has been one of the focuses of research in accounting. It is intended to realize the quantity and the type information widespread (Herath & Lu, 2017). Accounting system serve to produce information for various purposes and different agents. It serves to quantify the facts or events that occurred during a given period and to inform about the economic and financial situation of a company and the results achieved. This information is useful to make predictions and to base decision-making management.

Based on the importance of financial information, this study analyses the economic truth of the transactions that enable the financial statements. The question arises: is there a way to detect discretionary information management through the study of financial statements? Prior and actual studies base the study of the information quality in the study of the accruals. The information provided can be amended by using the flexibility of the accounting normative (Stolowy & Breton, 2003), using real management activities (Roychowdhury, 2006) and fraudulent management (Dechow & Skinner, 2000).

Quality of Information Management

The preparation of financial information should be based on existing regulations to provide objective and reliable financial statements. However, the ambiguity of some norms allows subjective judgments and the exercise of discretion in the accounting of some facts. This discretion results in discretionary accruals that alter the financial statements (changing assets and liabilities as well as earnings and income-accounting form of results management). The quality of the accounting information depends on the management discretion the following assumptions of investigation are formulated:

Hypothesis One: Discretionary accruals have a positive relation with inventory fluctuation.

Using accruals as quality of accounting information indicator, it is expected to find evidence that discretionary accruals are influenced by the inventory and by the accounts receivable and payable. Sales and cost of the good sold are components of the income statement (not from the balance sheet), so they must have relation with discretionary management of real activities.

The results of the studies indicate that the influence of the discretion on the inventory line and the quality of the accounting information is an area with few studies. It is intended to investigate whether the managers of the companies in the manufacturing sector practice discretionary management on their inventories and the reflexes of this management on the accounting information. It is expected to obtain confirmation of the use of accounting discretion on inventories which will influence the results and the patrimonial value described in the financial statements.

Real Activities Management

All management acts cause change in the financial statements, but decisions related to the volume and time of purchase and sale (timing) are one of the most preponderant factors in the discretion included (Roychowdhury, 2006). One method of managing discretionarily results is to make decisions about the operational process, that is, about real activities. Changing operational practices can lead to goals on the financial information influencing the judgment of users. The question arises: is there a way to detect real earnings management through the study of financial statements?

Hypothesis Two: Discretionary management of real activities have a positive relation with inventory fluctuation.

Using discretional production cost and working capital as an indicator of discretionary management of real activities it is expected to find evidence that working capital and production are influenced by the management of real activities (Zang, 2012).

Production is the process of combining various material inputs and immaterial inputs to make an output. It is the act of creating output, a good or service which has value and contributes to the utility of individuals. Production is a function of the company sales. When the amount of outputs increases the production increases too. So, the production cost is the sum of cost of goods sold with change in inventory and depends on it (Roychowdhury et al., 2012).

Working capital is a of a company's liquidity, efficiency, and overall health. It includes cash, inventory, accounts receivable, accounts payable, the portion of debt due within one year, and other short-term accounts, a company's working capital reflects the results of a company activities, including inventory management, debt management, revenue collection, and payments to suppliers. Positive working capital indicates that a company can pay its short-term liabilities. Negative working capital indicates a company is unable to do so. One of the most significant uses of working capital is inventory. The longer inventory stays in the company, the longer the company's working capital is stopped (Ferrer & Ferrer, 2016).

In a turbulent and competitive environment, the survival of the companies depends on the sales. However, SMEs depend on a few numbers of costumers and supplier, making them vulnerable (Bahri et al., 2017). This is the reason to include accounts receivable and liabilities in the study of the discretionary management of real activities. Empirically researchers showed that sales are positively related with customer satisfaction.

RESEARCH

The data was collected in the data base *Amadeus* de *Bureau Van Dijk*. The base was the entire population of manufacturing industries of Portuguese SMEs between 2005 and 2015. This data base contains comparable financial data for European public and private companies.

The selected financial data were related to all active companies, from the manufacture sector. With the intention of ensuring that the companies in study were in operation, were imposed the following restrictions: have accounts available for each year; the total value of the assets, the value of the sales, the value of the fixed assets, the value of current assets, the value of current liabilities, the value of inventories and the value added is greater than 1 for all years of the sample.

The data collected was data from the financial statements of the companies, specifically the balance sheet, and the income statement of results, other data and accounting and financial information. The sample is 121,810 company-year observations.

Methodology

All variables used in the models are described in the Appendix.

Accruals Management

In general, an accruals model is run by regressing total accruals on variables that are associated with explaining those levels. Generally, these models are run on an industry-year basis using an OLS model:

$$y_i = \alpha + \sum_{k=1}^{n} \beta_k x_i + \varepsilon_i$$

The fitted values from equation are then generally classified as the "normal" level of accruals. The residual is the discretionary component of accruals. The success of discretionary accruals models depends on the assumption of homogeneity to estimate normal accruals (Jackson, 2017). The proxy for quality of information is based on discretionary accruals to study the accrual-based earnings management. Discretionary accruals are the difference between firms' actual accruals and the normal level of accruals. The estimation was based on the following adjusted Jones (1991) (Dechow et al., 1995):

$$\frac{Accruals_{it}}{TA_{it-1}} = \beta_1 + \beta_2 \frac{1}{TA_{it-1}} + \beta_3 \left[\frac{\Delta REV_{it}}{TA_{it-1}} - \frac{\Delta REC_{it}}{TA_{it-1}} \right] + \beta_4 \frac{FA_{it}}{TA_{it-1}} + \varepsilon_{it}$$

where accruals are working capital minus operating profit (net cash from operations) in year t; TA_{it-1} is total assets in year t – 1; ΔREV_{it} is the change in operating revenue from year t –1 to t; ΔREC_{it} is the change in accounts receivable from year t– 1to t and FA_{it} it is gross property, plant and equipment. The estimated residual captures discretionary accruals. It is used the absolute value of the residual as the proxy for accrual-based earnings management.

The results are presented in Table 1 – Estimation of accruals. The Model is adjusted, and all the variables are statically significant. All variables of the model have impact on total accruals. The increase of the value of each variable of the model leads to a decrease of the total accrual value. The variable ΔREV_{it} - ΔREC_{it} is related with the acquisition and with the sells because captures the accounts receivable and payable (AltintaŞ, Sari, & OtluoĞlu, 2017). This variable has an impact of 0,491 with a significance of *p*=0,000. This suggests that acquisitions and sales have a big impact on the accounts. The question arises: is the impact due to the discricionarity included? The answer is achieved by the studies of the residuals.

The decrease in the variation in operating revenue subtracted from accounts receivable causes a decrease in the value of accruals, as well as the variation of tangible fixed assets. In this type of management, discretionary management is not linked to the change in the company's economic activities, but rather to the accounting choices used for the preparation of the financial statements. The decrease in debtors ' values and the postponement of increasing the value of tangible fixed assets are some of the examples of management of results by accruals (Roychowdhury, 2006). An advantage of management by accruals is that it does not affect the cash flow of the current exercise and doesn't destroy company value. Another motivation for the use of this type of management is the possibility of recording the accruals at the end of the economic period, when managers already know the amount needed to be manipulated to achieve the objectives in relation to the results (Gunny et al., 2013).

With the coefficients obtained were estimated the normal level of accruals. The difference between the total accruals and normal accruals is the discretionary accruals. With the discretionary accruals estimated a new equation is regressed. Inventories is a component of the balance sheet and it is influenced by accounting choices. Like the study of real earnings management, in this paper is studied the influence of inventory stocks, debtors' sales and cost of the good sold.

$$\frac{AccrualsD_{it}}{TA_{it-1}} = \beta_1 + \beta_2 \frac{\Delta Stock_{it}}{TA_{it-1}} + \beta_3 \frac{\Delta REC_{it}}{TA_{it-1}} + \beta_4 \frac{\Delta S_{it}}{TA_{it-1}} + \beta_5 \frac{\Delta CGS_{it}}{TA_{it-1}}$$

where $AccrualsD_{it}$ are discretionary accruals estimated, $\Delta Stock_{it}$ is the change in inventory sock from year t −1 to t; ΔREC_{it} is the change in accounts receivable from year t− 1to t; ΔS_{it} is the change in sales from year t – 1 to t and ΔCGS_{it} is the change in cost of goods sold from year t – 1 to t.

The production activities influence fixed assets, current assets (cash, inventories and accounts receivable) and current liabilities reported in the balance sheet. A manufacturing firm invests in fixed assets (as equipment, machinery, systems, vehicles and buildings). Assets' depreciation, maintenance and provisions for renewal can represent a significant percentage of the firm's costs. In addition, quality of equipment has a direct impact on product quality and production costs. This clearly shows the importance of managing fixed assets properly, not only to ensure their best use but also to control their associated costs (Bahri et al., 2017).

The results are presented in Table 2 – Study of the influence of inventory in accruals. The model is adjusted, and all the variables are statically significant. The variables have impact on total accruals. The increase of the value of each variable in the balance sheet (stock and accounts receivable) of the model leads to an increase of the discretionary accrual. There is a strong evidence that the quality of accounting information is influenced by the management ability to introduce discretionarily in the judgement and in the actions. This is consistent with several studies about earnings quality. Discretionary accruals models have been widely used in the literature, and are often considered to be a proxy for earnings management, or earnings quality (Jackson, 2017).

Discretionary accruals have a positive relation with inventory fluctuation, is confirmed in this study. Stock (inventory stock) has 0.724 impact on measuring discretionary accrual and ΔREC_{it} has 0.086 impact so, it is possible to say that managers of Portuguese SMEs include discretionarily in the accounts using the variable inventory as well as accounts receivable.

Table 1. Estimation of Accruals

Model Summary						
Model	R	R Squared	Adjusted R Squared	Estimated standard error	Durbin-Watson	
	.495	.245	.245	.36608	1.296	
ANOVA						
		Sum of squares	gl	Medium square	F	Sig.
	Regression	5,309.403	3	1,769.801	13,206.220	.000
	Residual	16,323.549	121,806	.134		
	Total	21,632.952	121,809			
Coefficients						
		Non-standard coefficients		Standardized coefficients	t	Sig.
		B	Standard error	Beta		
	(Constant)	.426	.001		312.351	.000
	1/TA-1	-5.006	.119	-.112	-42.084	.000
	ΔREV- ΔREC	-.612	.003	-.491	-178.873	.000
	FA/TA1	-.277	.002	-.347	-131.560	.000
Dependent variable: Accruals/TA-1						

Table 2. Study of the influence of inventory in accruals

Model Summary						
Model	R	R Squared	Adjusted R Squared	Estimated standard error	Durbin-Watson	
	.636	.404	,4.4	.1617	1.514	
ANOVA						
		Sum of squares	gl	Medium square	F	Sig.
	Regression	2,146.013	4	536.503	20,653.379	.000
	Residual	3,164.072	121,805	.026		
	Total	5,310.085	121,809			
Coefficients						
		Non-standard coefficients		Standardized coefficients	t	Sig.
		B	Standard error	Beta		
	(Constant)	.313	.001		426.115	.000
	Stock/TA-1	.075	.002	.086	36.511	.000
	ΔREC /TA-1	.481	.002	.724	237.662	.000
	ΔS/TA-1	-.044	.001	-.171	-54.772	.000
	ΔCGS/at-1	-.080	.001	-.167	-71.424	.000
Dependent variable: AccrualD						

Real Activity Management

All activities may be subject to discretionary decisions that cause changes in the valuation of the company. Managers make decisions about business activities that bring them benefits. These may increase or decrease the values presented in the financial statements and lead to the presentation of economic and financial results favorable to the manager's intention (Ferrer & Ferrer, 2016).

In this paper will be studied two types of real activities earnings management: accelerating the timing of sales and/or generating additional unsustainable sales through increased price discounts or more lenient credit terms; increasing earnings by reducing cost of goods sold through overproduction (Roychowdhury et al., 2012). The first type is measured by the abnormal level of cash flow from operations. The second type is measured by the abnormal level of production cost (Gao et al., 2017).

To estimate the normal level of cash flow from operation is used following equation (Choi et al., 2010):

$$\frac{WC_{it}}{TA_{it-1}} = \beta_1 + \beta_2 \frac{1}{TA_{it-1}} + \beta_3 \frac{S_{it}}{TA_{it-1}} + \beta_4 \frac{\Delta S_{it}}{TA_{it-1}} + \beta_5 \frac{\Delta S_{it-1}}{TA_{it-1}} + \beta_6 \frac{Employees_{it}}{TA_{it-1}} + \beta_7 \frac{Tax_{it}}{TA_{it-1}} + \varepsilon_{it}$$

WC_{it} is working capital in year t; S_{it} is sales in year t; ΔS_{it} is the change in sales from year t to t –1; ΔS_{it-1} is the change in sales from year t –1 to t –2; $Employees_{it}$ is the cost of the employees in year t;

Tax_{it} is tax payments in year t. The discretionary working capital is estimated with the residual from the equation. The results, in Table 3- Estimation of Working Capital, show that the model is well adjusted, and all variables are significative. Sales and ΔS_{it-1} have a negative impact in working capital. The reason may be the credit conceded to buyers. The cost of employees and the payment of taxes have a positive influence in the working capital, that means the companies are trying to sell more to solve their obligations (Choi et al., 2010).

It is possible to suppose that the need of payment brings to the companies the need of collecting more money. The upward management of sales, using discounts and special credit conditions implies the increase of the results and at the same time the decrease of the working capital. In the sample used the working capital decrease slightly the increase in sales volume, which assumes that Portuguese companies do not use aggressive discount and credit policies to manage sales volume (Choi et al., 2010).

To estimate the normal level of production costs is used the following equation (Roychowdhury, 2006):

$$\frac{PROD_{it}}{TA_{it-1}} = \beta_1 + \beta_2 \frac{1}{TA_{it-1}} + \beta_3 \frac{S_{it}}{TA_{it-1}} + \beta_4 \frac{\Delta S_{it}}{TA_{it-1}} + \beta_5 \frac{\Delta S_{it-1}}{TA_{it-1}} + \varepsilon_{it}$$

where $PROD_{it}$ is the sum of cost of goods sold in year t and the change in inventory from year t – 1 to t. The abnormal level of production costs is measured as the estimated residual from the above equation.

Table 3. Estimation of working capital

Model Summary						
Model	R	R Squared	Adjusted R Squared	Estimated standard error	Durbin-Watson	
	.237	.056	.056	.39711	1.256	
ANOVA						
		Sum of squares	gl	Medium square	F	Sig.
	Regression	1,136.132	6	189.355	1,200.763	.000
	Residual	19,101.549	121.129	.158		
	Total	20,237.681	121.135			
Coefficients						
		Non-standard coefficients		Standardized coefficients	t	Sig.
		B	Standard error	Beta		
	(Constant)	.360	.002		182.379	.000
	1/TA-1	-6.395	.145	-.138	-44.037	.000
	S/TA-1	-.006	.002	-.017	-4.140	.000
	ΔSit-1/TA-1	.100	.002	.173	44.463	.000
	ΔSit-2	-.003	.001	-.010	-3.408	.001
	Employees/TA-1	.173	.008	.071	20.761	.000
	Tax/TA-1	.572	.061	.032	9.364	.000
Dependent variable: WC/TA-1						

The higher the residual, the larger the amount of inventory overproduction, and the greater increase in reported earnings through reducing cost of goods sold. In Table 4 – Estimation of Production Costs, is possible to read the results of the regression. The model is well adjusted, and all variables are significative. Sales and the growth of sales has a positive and significant impact in PROD, that means when the sales grow the cost of goods sold grows have influence in inventory.

Operational decisions to increase results can generate: abnormally low operating working capital and production costs abnormally high (Cohen & Frazzini, 2008). The values obtained for the discretionary working capital (WCD), discretionary production (PRODD) represent management of results by means of operational decisions (Cohen & Zarowin, 2010; Cohen & Frazzini, 2008; Rezaee, 2002; Roychowdhury, 2006; Roychowdhury et al., 2012; Zang, 2012).

Some Business practices can affect financial performance via operational performance (Bahri et al., 2017). It is important to add the income before taxes and taxes to measure the firm's performance. The variables defined in this study, which are subject to some type of discretionary management are: stock of inventories, represented by the variable St_{It}, accounts receivable represented by REC_{It}, accounts payable represented $LIAB_{It}$, income before taxes represented with $Incbefore_{It}$ and taxes payed represented by Tax_{It}. With the coefficients obtained, in the estimated models, the normal and discretionary values were calculated for each of the companies/year for working capital and for production. The real activities earnings management measures were aggregated into one proxy, RMit, by taking their sum (Zang, 2012): RMit = WCDit + PRODDit or the second hypotheses developed there are five independent variables: St_{It},(inventory sock), REC_{It},(accounts receivable), $LIAB_{It}$ (accounts payable), $Incbefore_{It}$ (income before taxes) and Tax_{It} (taxes payed).

Table 4. Estimation of production costs

Model Summary						
Model	R	R Squared	Adjusted R Squared	Estimated standard error	Durbin-Watson	
	.534	.285	.285	.40642	1.137	
ANOVA						
		Sum of squares	gl	Medium square	F	Sig.
	Regression	7,979.355	4	1,994.839	12,077.005	.000
.	Residual	20,008.009	121,131	.165		
	Total	27,987.364	121,135			
Coefficients						
		Non-standard coefficients		Standardized coefficients	t	Sig.
		B	Standard error	Beta		
	(Constant)	.283	.002		141.966	.000
	1/TA-1	-1.228	.146	-.023	-8.435	.000
	S/TA-1	.204	.002	.461	135.709	.000
	ΔS/TA-1	.086	.002	.126	38.060	.000
	ΔSit-1	-.010	.001	-.028	-10.817	.000
Dependent variable PROD						

The reduction of the tax may be one of the managers ' goals (Moreira, 2008). By lowering income, the taxable base became lower and so it is possible to ascertain a lower tax value. The results obtained in Table 5 show that companies manage inventories, receivables, payables, income before taxes and taxes, causing changes discretionary working capital and production. The values determined in the regression indicate there is a strong impact of the change in inventory values and fees payable on RM (production and working capital).

The coefficient obtained in real activities earnings management confirm hypothesis two: discretionary management of real activities have a positive relation with inventory fluctuation. Inventory have an impact of 0.547 in the discretionary managing and the only variable that has a negative signal is liabilities (this is a passive), this means when the company uses discricionarity the obligations increase, so the purchases are made on credit (this is consistent with other studies as Roychowdhury et al., 2012).

CONCLUSION

From reading the results of the regressions it is noted that companies continue to use discretionary power over the accounting policies and about the activities to benchmarking the company income. With the results obtained it is verified that companies in the manufacturing sector incur in practices of discretionary management of accruals confirming hypothesis 1 and of production confirming hypothesis 2.

Table 5. Real activities earnings management

			Model Summary			
Model	R	R Squared	Adjusted R Squared	Estimated standard error	Durbin-Watson	
	.539	.291	.291	.51596	1.229	
			ANOVA			
		Sum of squares	gl	Medium square	F	Sig.
	Regression	13,206.000	5	2,641.200	9,921.261	.000
	Residual	32,246.762	121.130	.266		
	Total	45,452.762	121.135			
			Coefficients			
		Non-standard coefficients		Standardized coefficients	t	Sig.
		B	Standard error	Beta		
1	(Constant)	-.213	.002		-89.505	.000
	St/TA-1	1.415	.007	.547	211.107	.000
	REC/TA-1	2.138E-5	.000	.026	10.657	.000
	LIAB /TA-1	-.228	.002	-.271	-100.411	.000
	Incbefore/TA-1	.208	.011	.059	19.412	.000
	Tax/TA-1	3.466	.083	.128	41.979	.000
Dependent variable RM						

Portuguese companies are included in a code law system, so the accounting is a mean of achieving the income desirable to avoid tax payable (Incbefore and Tax) and the amount of taxes to be paid. The results confirm the existence of a positive link between these two variables and the discretionary management of real activities.

Discretionary production costs cover a large part of the company's operational activity. It is confirmed that SME managers belonging to the manufacturing sector, use the increase of debt, decrease current liabilities and the increase of the value of inventories and accounts receivable to practice reach objectives.

Using Dechow et al (1995) model was found the quality of the information is affected. With the intention of perceiving the activities to which the companies suspected of manipulating results were calculated to normal and discretionary values for the working capital and production volume. Variables were introduced in the previous model that allowed to ascertain the characteristics and objectives of discretionary management and there is evidence that the inventory is a way of discricionarity.

The production and real activities are a target of the discricionarity (Ferrer & Ferrer, 2016; Gunny, 2005; Gunny et al., 2013; Roychowdhury, 2006; Roychowdhury et al., 2012; Whelan & Mcnamara, 2004; Zang, 2012). By reducing the sales flow, the working capital reduces too. Managers caused decreases in results through discricionarity attributed to the accounts, such as asset and liabilities measurement criteria and registration of imparity. The Portuguese manufacturing SME present evidence of managing discretionarily inventories. This evidence is valid either for accounting management or for management by real activities. It can be managed lowering the cash flows and the accrual.

The purpose of this study is to verify the existence of earnings management as well as real activities management that affects the information quality in Portuguese SME. It is possible to conclude there is an evidence of the discretionarily included in the accounts and in the activities and its influence in the information. It is also a concern the use of inventory discretionarily, and it was also showed in the models used. This study is consistent with other actual studies (Altinta et al., 2017; Ferrer & Ferrer, 2016).

This study contributes to literature by presenting evidence of discretionarily management in the manufacturing Portuguese SME based on the inventories. This discretionarily affect the value of the company and the relevance and reliability of the information given to the stakeholders.

REFERENCES

Aaker, H., & Gjesdal, F. (2010). *Do Models of Discretionary Accruals Detect Actual Earnings Management via Inventory? A Comparison of General and Specific Models*. Academic Press.

Altinta, Ş. A. T., Sari, E. S., & OtluoĞlu, E. (2017). The impact of earnings management on the value relevance of earnings: empirical evidence from Turkey. *The Journal of International Social Research, 10*(51), 885–891.

Bahri, M., St-Pierre, J., & Sakka, O. (2017). Performance measurement and management for manufacturing SMEs: A financial statement-based system. *Measuring Business Excellence*, *21*(1), 17–36. doi:10.1108/MBE-06-2015-0034

Ball, R. (2013). Accounting informs investors and earnings management is rife: Two questionable beliefs. *Accounting Horizons*, *27*(4), 847–853. doi:10.2308/acch-10366

Basu, N., & Wang, X. (2011). Evidence on the Relation Between Inventory Changes, Earnings, and Firm value. *The International Journal of Business and Finance Research*, *5*(3), 1–14.

Bernard, V., & Noel, J. (1991). Do Inventory Disclosures Predict Sales and Earnings? *Journal of Accounting, Auditing & Finance*, *6*(2), 145–181. doi:10.1177/0148558X9100600202

Cannon, A. R. (2008). Inventory improvement and financial performance. *International Journal of Production Economics*, *115*(2), 581–593. doi:10.1016/j.ijpe.2008.07.006

Choi, J. H., Kim, J. B., & Zang, Y. (2010). Do abnormally high audit fees impair audit quality? *Auditing*, *29*(2), 115–140. doi:10.2308/aud.2010.29.2.115

Cohen, D. A., & Zarowin, P. (2010). Accrual-based and real earnings management activities around seasoned equity offerings. *Journal of Accounting and Economics*, *50*(1), 2–19. doi:10.1016/j.jacceco.2010.01.002

Cohen, L., & Frazzini, A. (2008). Economic links and predictable returns. *The Journal of Finance*, *63*(4), 1977–2011. doi:10.1111/j.1540-6261.2008.01379.x

Cohen, L. J., Cornett, M. M., Marcus, A., & Tehranian, H. (2014). Bank Earnings Management and Tail Risk during the Financial Crisis. *Journal of Money, Credit & Banking, 46*(1), 171–197.

Commerford, B. P., Hermanson, D. R., Houston, R. W., & Peters, M. F. (2014). *Real Earnings Management: A Threat to Auditor Comfort?* Academic Press.

Cook, K. A., Huston, G. R., & Kinney, M. R. (2012). *Managing earnings by manipulating inventory: The effects of cost structure and valuation method.* Available at https://Ssrn.Com/Abstract=997437

Dechow, P., Ge, W., & Schrand, C. (2010). Understanding earnings quality: A review of the proxies, their determinants and their consequences. *Journal of Accounting and Economics*, *50*(2–3), 344–401. doi:10.1016/j.jacceco.2010.09.001

Dechow, P. M., & Skinner, D. J. (2000). Earnings Management: Reconciling the Views of Accounting Academics, Practitioners, and Regulators. *Accounting Horizons*, *14*(2), 235–250. doi:10.2308/acch.2000.14.2.235

Dechow, P. M., Sloan, R. G., & Sweeney, A. P. (1995). Detecting Earnings Management. *The Accounting Review*, *70*(2), 193–225. doi:10.2307/248303

Dechow, P. M., Sloan, R. G., & Sweeney, A. P. (1996). Causes and Consequences of Earnings Manipulation: An Analysis of Firms Subject to Enforcement Actions by SEC. *Contemporary Accounting Research*, *13*(1), 1–36. doi:10.1111/j.1911-3846.1996.tb00489.x

Dichev, I. D., Graham, J., Harvey, C. R., & Rajgopal, S. (2013). Earnings Quality: Evidence from the Field. *Journal of Accounting and Economics*, *56*(2–3), 1–33. doi:10.1016/j.jacceco.2013.05.004

Dos Santos, A., & Paulo, E. (2006). Diferimento das perdas cambiais como instrumento de gerenciamento de resultados. *Brazilian Business Review*, *3*(1), 15–31.

Eilifsen, A., Knivsflå, K. H., & Sættem, F. (2010). *European Accounting Review Earnings manipulation : cost of capital versus tax.* Academic Press. doi:10.1080/096381899335899

Ferrer, R. C., & Ferrer, G. J. (2016). Earnings management indicators and their impact on inventory turnover under food, beverage and tobacco sector: A thorough study using simultaneous equations model. *Academy of Accounting and Financial Studies Journal*, *20*(2), 93–103.

Gao, J., Gao, B., & Wang, X. (2017). Trade-off between real activities earnings management and accrual-based manipulation-evidence from China. *Journal of International Accounting, Auditing & Taxation*, *29*, 66–80. doi:10.1016/j.intaccaudtax.2017.08.001

Gunny, K. (2005). *What Are the Consequences of Real Earnings Management?* Working Paper, University of Colorado at Boulder.

Gunny, K. A., Jacob, J., & Jorgensen, B. N. (2013). Implications of the integral approach and earnings management for alternate annual reporting periods. *Review of Accounting Studies*, *18*(3), 868–891. doi:10.100711142-013-9235-x

Gupta, M., Pevzner, M., & Seethamraju, C. (2010). The implications of absorption cost accounting and prodution decisions for future firm performance and valuation. *Contemporary Accounting Research*, *27*(3), 889–922. doi:10.1111/j.1911-3846.2010.01030.x

Healy, P. M., & Wahlen, J. M. (1999). A review of Earnings Management Literature and its implications for Standard Setting. *Accounting Horizons*, *13*(4), 365–383. doi:10.2308/acch.1999.13.4.365

Herath, H. S. B., & Lu, X. (2017, September). Inference of economic truth from financial statements for detecting earnings management: Inventory costing methods from an information economics perspective. *Managerial and Decision Economics*, 1–14. doi:10.1002/mde.2912

Jackson, A. B. (2017). Discretionary Accruals: Earnings Management ... or Not? *Abacus*, *54*(2), 136–153. doi:10.1111/abac.12117

Jensen, C., & Meckling, H. (1976). Theory of the Firm: Managerial Behavior, Agency Costs and Ownership Structure. *Journal of Financial Economics*, *3*(4), 305–360. doi:10.1016/0304-405X(76)90026-X

Jones, J. J. (1991). Earnings Management During Import Relief Investigations. *Journal of Accounting Research*, *29*(2), 193–228. doi:10.2307/2491047

Kesavan, S., & Mani, V. (2010). *The predictive power of abnormal inventory growth : Application to earnings forecasting for retailers*. North.

Licerán-Gutiérrez, A., & Cano-Rodríguez, M. (2017). A Review on the multidimensional analysis of earnings quality. In *XIX Congresso AECA. Santiago de Compostela, Espanha.* (pp. 1–24). Academic Press. 10.2139srn.2998134

Moreira, J. A. C. (2008). *A Manipulação dos Resultados das Empresas: um contributo para o estudo do caso português*. Academic Press.

Nissim, D. (2017). *Overproduction and EBITDA*. Columbia Business School Research Paper, No. 17-102. doi:10.2139srn.3054282

Pustylnick, I., Temchenko, O., & Gubarkov, S. (2017). Estimating the influence of accounting variables change on earnings management detection. *Journal of International Studies*, *10*(1), 110–122. doi:10.14254/2071-8330.2017/10-1/7

Rezaee, Z. (2002). The Three Cs of Fraudulent Financial Reporting. *Internal Auditor*, 56–61. doi:10.3102/00346543067001043

Roychowdhury, S. (2006). Earnings management through real activities manipulation. *Journal of Accounting and Economics*, *42*(3), 335–370. doi:10.1016/j.jacceco.2006.01.002

Roychowdhury, S., Kothari, S. P., & Mizik, N. (2012). *Managing for the Moment: The Role of Real Activity Versus Accruals Earnings Management in SEO Valuation*. SSRN Electronic Journal. doi:10.2139srn.1982826

Stolowy, H., & Breton, G. (2003). La gestion des donnés comptables: une revue de la littérature. *Comptabilité-Contrôle-Audit, 9*(1), 125–152.

Watts, R. L., & Zimmerman, J. L. (1978). Towards a Positive Theory of Determination of Accounting Standards. *The Accounting Review*. doi:10.2307/245729

Whelan, C., & Mcnamara, R. (2004). *The Impact of Earnings Management on the Value-relevance of Financial Statement Information*. Academic Press.

Zang, A. Y. (2012). Evidence on the trade-off between real activities manipulation and accrual-based earnings management. *The Accounting Review*, *87*(2), 675–703. doi:10.2308/accr-10196

KEY TERMS AND DEFINITIONS

Accounting: Financial accounting is the process of recording, summarizing and reporting the transactions resulting from business operations over a period. The transactions are shown in financial statements, including the balance sheet, income statement and cash flow statement. Financial reporting occurs using financial statements. The financial statements present the classifications of financial data: revenues, expenses, assets, liabilities, and equity.

Accruals: Change of the financial statements (changing assets and liabilities as well as items of the income statement); all the associated accounting specialization of the economic year, which do not involve financial flows, and where the discretionary action of the manager is decisive for the recognition of an expense or income.

Inventory: Is an asset that is intended to be sold in the ordinary course of business. The inventory of a manufacturer should report the cost of its raw materials, work-in-process, and finished goods. The cost of inventory should include all costs necessary to acquire the items and to get them ready for sale. Inventory items can fall into one of the following three categories: held for sale in the ordinary course of business; or in the process of being produced for sale; or for consumption in the production process. Inventory is typically classified as a short-term asset, since it is usually liquidated within one year.

Inventory Management: Is the management of inventory and stock. As an element of supply chain management, inventory management includes aspects such as controlling and overseeing ordering inventory, storage of inventory, and controlling the amount of product for sale.

Quality of Accounting Information: The usefulness of accounting for decision-making, which depends on qualitative characteristics as the relevance (predictive value and confirmatory value) and reliability (free from errors and prejudices).

Real Activities Discretionary Management: Alteration of normal course operational practices, motivated by managers' desire to mislead some stakeholders to achieve financial reporting goals.

Real Activity: All the normal operational activities of a company.

APPENDIX

Table 6. Variable description

Variable	Description
$\frac{Accruals_{it}}{TA_{it-1}}$	Working capital minus operating profit of the company i for the year t deflated by total assets of the year t-1
$\frac{\Delta CGS_{it}}{TA_{it-1}}$	Change in cost of goods sold of the company i for the year t deflated by total assets of the year t-1
$\frac{\Delta REC_{it}}{TA_{it-1}}$	Change in accounts receivable of the company i for the year t deflated by total assets of the year t-1
$\frac{\Delta REV_{it}}{TA_{it-1}}$	Change in operating revenue of the company i for the year t deflated by total assets of the year t-1
$\frac{\Delta S_{it}}{TA_{it-1}}$	Change in sales of the company i for the year t deflated by total assets of the year t-1
$\frac{\Delta S_{it-1}}{TA_{it-2}}$	Change in sales of the company i for the year t-1 deflated by total assets of the year t-2
$\frac{\Delta Stock_{it}}{TA_{it-1}}$	Change in inventory stock of the company i for the year t deflated by total assets of the year t-1
$\frac{AccrualsD_{it}}{TA_{it-1}}$	Discretionary accruals estimated of the company i for the year t deflated by total assets of the year t-1
$\frac{Employees_{it}}{TA_{it-1}}$	Cost with employees of the company i for the year t deflated by total assets of the year t-1
$\frac{FA_{it}}{TA_{it-1}}$	Gross property, plant and equipment of the company i for the year t deflated by total assets of the year t-1
$\frac{Incbefore_{it}}{TA_{it-1}}$	Income before taxes of the company i for the year t deflated by total assets of the year t-1

continued on following page

Table 6. Continued

$\frac{LIAB_{it}}{TA_{it-1}}$	Liabilities of the company i for the year t deflated by total assets of the year t-1
$\frac{PROD_{it}}{TA_{it-1}}$	Production is the sum of cost of goods sold and inventory in the company i for the year t deflated by total assets of the year t-1
$\frac{REC_{it}}{TA_{it-1}}$	Accounts receivable of the company i for the year t deflated by total assets of the year t-1
$\frac{S_{it}}{TA_{it-1}}$	Sales of the company i for the year t deflated by total assets of the year t-1
$\frac{Tax_{it}}{TA_{it-1}}$	Tax payments of the company i for the year t deflated by total assets of the year t-1.
$\frac{WC_{it}}{TA_{it-1}}$	Working capital of the company i for the year t deflated by total assets of the year t-1
$PRODD_{it}$	Discretionary production estimated of the company i for the year t deflated by total of the year t-1
RM_{it}	$WCD_{it} + PRODD_{it}$
WCD_{it}	Discretionary working capital estimated of the company i for the year t deflated by total of the year t-1

Chapter 9
Impression Management Strategies in the Chairmen's Statements:
Evidence From the Portuguese Banking Industry

Jonas da Silva Oliveira
https://orcid.org/0000-0001-5374-1062
Instituto Universitário de Lisboa (ISCTE-IUL), Portugal

Graça Maria do Carmo Azevedo
https://orcid.org/0000-0002-6346-4035
University of Aveiro, Portugal

Stéphanie Fernandes Pinheiro
University of Aveiro, Portugal

Maria Fátima Ribeiro Borges
University of Aveiro, Portugal

ABSTRACT

This chapter assesses the influence of organizational performance in the adoption of impression management strategies in the Chairmen's statements of the Portuguese financial companies. It also evaluates the impact of the financial crisis on the adoption of impression management strategies. To this end, and using the content analysis of the Chairmen's statements included in the individual annual reports for 2006-2012 of 27 financial institutions, the authors conclude that even throughout the financial crisis period, Portuguese financial companies did not tend to adopt more impression management strategies. However, they have seen that in some years there is some evidence of its adoption.

DOI: 10.4018/978-1-5225-7817-8.ch009

INTRODUCTION

Impression Management has been defined as the "conscious or unconscious attempt to control images that are projected during actual or potential social interactions" (Schlenker, 1980, p.6). Hooghiemstra (2000, p.60) defines IM as "a branch of social psychology that studies how individuals present themselves to others in order to be perceived favourably by them."

In a context of financial reporting, IM strategies contemplate attempts "to control and manipulate users' perception of the financial information disclosed" (Clatworthy & Jones, 2001, p.311). The literature on the quality of financial reporting has indicated that these strategies take the form of subliminal, verbal and/or non-verbal messages through manipulation of the content and presentation of financial information (Hooghiemstra 2000, Merkl-Davies & Brennan 2007).

In the annual reports, voluntary information has been increasingly disclosed. However, this information is not audited (Clatworthy & Jones, 2006). In this type of voluntary information, the Chairman's statement (CS) has been an increasingly important component of these reports and a relevant indicator of firms' financial performance (Smith & Taffler, 1995). Smith and Taffler (2000) consider that both the keywords and the narrative themes in the CS are useful for discriminating between corrupt and healthy companies.

Much of the existing literature is based on an economic perspective, in which the adoption of IM strategies is related to negative organizational performance (Brennan et al., 2009; Merkl-Davies & Brennan, 2007, Merkl-Davies et al., 2011). According to this perspective, IM is seen as reflecting the opportunistic behaviour of managers to consciously disguise investors' perception of a company's performance (Merkl-Davies & Brennan, 2007). However, some studies use a social psychology perspective to try to explain the motivations for the adoption of IM strategies (Merkl-Davies et al., 2011). According to this perspective, IM may derive from the opportunistic behaviour of managers to consciously disguise the corporate image, or simply from the informational process, through which managers contextualize events favourably (Oliveira et al., 2016).

Most of the existing literature is based on samples from Anglo-Saxon companies (Brennan et al., 2009; Merkl-Davies & Brennan, 2007; Merkl-Davies et al., 2011). The literature on the adoption of IM strategies by Portuguese banks is scarce (Oliveira et al., 2016; Costa et al, 2011).

This study intends to analyze the CS of Portuguese financial companies, during a period in which these companies experienced a very unfavourable financial period. More specifically, we analyze the period from 2006 to 2012 in order to assess if, during periods of financial distress, Portuguese financial companies use more IM strategies to manipulate stakeholders' perception on companies' performance. In 2008, the global financial crisis had a negative impact on the Portuguese economy, which still resents today. The Portuguese government was bailed out by the International Monetary Fund and was forced to take extreme measures in order to cut public spending, increase market liquidity, basically through higher tax and lower wages. This article is structured as follows: it describes the literature review and develops a set of research hypotheses. Subsequently, it explains the research methodology, discusses results, and it finalizes with conclusions, limitations and proposals for future studies.

LITERATURE REVIEW

Impression Management Strategies in the President's Letter

There are several studies on IM strategies (Oliveira et al., 2006; Brennan et al., 2009; Clatworthy & Jones, 2006; Merkl-Davies et al., 2011). The first works on IM were elaborated by psychologists, highlighting the study by Schlenker (1980, p.6), which defined IM as the "stimulus to control projected images in real or imaginary social interactions" and reserved the self-presentation feature for cases where projected images are "self-relevant". Since then, IM has been studied in various financial and management contexts, including in the handling of gains (Tweedie & Whittington, 1990), in social and environmental accounting (Neu et al., 1998; Hooghiemstra, 2000) in the management of results (Steinbart, 1989), in the financial charts (Beattie & Jones, 2000) and in the photographs (Graves et al., 1996; Arndt & Bigelow, 2000; McKinstry, 1996).

However, there are recent studies that focus on IM in accounting narratives not only in annual reports but also in CS (Aerts, 1994, 2001; Brennan et al., 2009; Merkl-Davies et al., 2011; et al). Aerts (2005) characterized the annual report of companies under the "ex-post" conditions as giving rise to IM. But Merkl-Davis et al. (2011) also did so through the use of retrospective framing of organizational results.

The present study focuses on the adoption of IM strategies in the CS. However, there are already some studies in this field. In Portugal, Oliveira et al. (2016) analyzed the CS of Portuguese non-financial companies in 2010. In our work, we will analyze the Portuguese financial companies between the years 2006 to 2012.

Schlenker et al. (1994, p.634) define accounting as "the condition of being accountable to the public for the achievement of certain standards, thus fulfilling responsibilities, duties, expectations and other charges." However, accounting reporting is composed either by quantitative and quantitative information. In qualitative information, narratives can be an instrument available to managers to manage the others impressions, because they want to "control how others see them" (Leary & Kowalski, 1990, p.35).

Frink and Ferris (1998) argue that in a context of accountability, individuals engage in IM strategies in order to obtain an assessment of their own behaviour. IM is thus a way of influencing the relevant impressions and decisions, in order to gain rewards and avoid penalties.

Hypothesis Development

Some studies on IM have examined different research settings: the manipulation of results (Tweedie & Whittington, 1990), social and environmental accounting (Hooghiemstra, 2000; Neu et al., 1998), changes in corporate structure (Arndt & Bigelow, 2000). This work focuses on the use of IM strategies in CS narratives. The narratives included in CS are considered voluntary information. Its purpose is to provide an overview company's activities and performance throughout the year. The present study intends to investigate the extent to which the information contained in the CS whether intends to distort stakeholders' perception of the company's performance or it tries to show the real image of the company, although in a more favourable way.

According to Allport (1954, p.5), social psychology is the discipline that uses scientific methods "to understand and explain how the thoughts, feelings, and behaviours of individuals are influenced by the actual, imagined or implicit presence of other human beings". Through these strategies, financial information preparers tend to manipulate the users of financial information. At the organizational level, IM provides a logical reasoning for financial reporting, which can be controlled, managed, influenced and persuasive, with mandatory psychological nuances. Merkl-Davies et al. (2011) have assumed that the concerns of preparers of financial information are expressed verbally based on the actions of the users of such information with respect to financial reporting.

Leary and Kowalski (1990, p. 36) state that IM "consists of two subprocesses", namely motivation (impression motivation) and construction (impression construction). The first process aims to create a specific impression in the opinion of others, while the second process involves not only choosing how to create an impression on others, but also deciding how they will achieve it.

The impression motivation process is supported by three factors (Leary & Kowalski, 1990), the relevance of the impression to be created, the value of the expected results and the discrepancy between the current image and the desired impression. In turn, the process of impression construction is affected by five factors that are the self-concept of the person, their intended or unwanted identities, the constraints of the role the individual is in, the target value and the perceptions of how the person is seen at the time (Leary & Kowalski, 1990). Managers have incentives to engage in IM strategies if the objectives to be achieved are relevant, such as: maximizing the social and material value of the enterprise; maintaining and increasing self-esteem; and the creation of identity. The higher the value associated with a given outcome, the greater the likelihood that the manager will apply IM strategies. Some studies have shown that manipulation is aimed at reaching people or things of greater interest or when something is very desirable (Merkl-Davies et al., 2011; Stanton et al., 2004). The construction of the IM strategy involves "choosing the type of print to create" and "deciding how to do it" (Leary & Kowalski, 1990, p. 36). In a context of financial reporting, managers involve the construction of public images about certain facts, which may or may not be a reflection of self-image or an unwanted image. In the case of consistency, we are faced with the true and true image contained in the annual accounts reports and accounting narratives. However, in the opposite case, we are faced with dissimulating impressions about reality and substance. This concept was termed "self-presentation dissimulation" (Leary & Kowalski, 1990, p.40).

Some authors (Pennebaker et al., 2003; Newman et al., 2003; Merkl-Davies et al., 2011) evaluated the level of self-presentation dissimulation through six verbal language markers using three strategies of IM: rhetorical manipulation (number of words, personal pronouns in the first person, and personal pronouns in the third person), thematic manipulation (words with positive emotion or words with negative emotion), and manipulation of readability (words related to cognitive complexity).

Verbal language is considered one of the psychological markers of behaviour because it is "based on the assumption that words used by people possess psychological information beyond their literal meaning and independent of their semantic context" (Pennebaker et al., 2003, p.550).

Some studies have shown that CS is one of the most widely read parts of the annual reports by investors (Bartlett & Chandler, 1997, Courtis, 1986, 2004, Jones, 1988, Smith & Taffler, 1992). It has also been proven that CS exists to try to influence stakeholder decision making (Abrahamson & Amir, 1996; Kaplan et al., 1990). Such narratives serve to enhance the company's image, builds investor's confidence, and give more credibility to management activities (Aerts, 2001, 2005), especially when companies are struggling with scarce resources. Consequently, managers may have incentives to adopt IM strategies in order to manage the perceptions of the relevant stakeholders about the company's image and thus guarantee access to those resources that are vital to the survival of the company.

H1: The adoption of printing management strategies in the President's Letter by Portuguese financial companies is significantly different over the period 2006-2012.

Merkl-Davies et al. (2011, p.324) state that when the company has positive results "the motivation of the financial information preparers to use such IM strategies has to do with the goal that managers want to achieve (such as maximizing social and materials, the maintenance and valorization of self-esteem and the creation of identity), the value of the desired results and the discrepancy between the desired and current social image. Hyland (1998, p.235-237) points out that "the credibility of the message is easily achieved in the face of organizational successes (…)".

H1a: The adoption of impression management strategies in the CS of Portuguese financial companies with positive organizational performance is significantly different over the period 2006-2012.

Obtaining negative organizational results usually generates conflicts of interest between managers and company shareholders (Merkl-Davies et al., 2011). This is one of the reasons why managers tend to "distort user perception" (Godfrey et al., 2003, p.96) through the manipulation of financial information. This concealment is made by obfuscating glitches and highlighting successes (Adelberg, 1979). Some studies have focused specifically on IM strategies used to hide negative organizational performance. The two main IM strategies used to conceal the company's real image are manipulation of readability and rhetorical manipulation (Merkl-Davis & Brennan, 2007).

H1b: The adoption of impression management strategies in the CS of Portuguese financial companies with negative organizational performance is significantly different over the period 2006-2012.

Most of the authors (Adelberg, 1979; Godfrey et al., 2003; Clatworthy & Jones, 2006; Merkl-Davis & Brennan, 2007; Merkl-Davis et al., 2011, etc.) consider that IM is more used by non-profitable companies than by profitable companies. However, some authors argue the opposite stating that "managers tend to attribute positive results to their own efforts in order to increase their own self-esteem and negative outcomes to external factors that are beyond their control (egocentric)" (Merkl-Davies & Brennan, 2007, p.426).

H2: The adoption of impression management strategies in the CS of Portuguese financial companies with positive and negative organizational performance is significantly different

When the company does not use IM strategies or uses them unconsciously, usually the content of the narrative documents present a true and fair view of the company and makes that information more valuable. However, these strategies can be used consciously so as to make the company more attractive to investors and stakeholders in it. Some authors (Abrahamson & Park, 1994; Clatworthy e Jones, 2006; Leary & Kowalski, 1990; Merkl-Davies et al., 2011) consider that companies with greater public visibility tend to use IM strategies more often.

H3: The adoption of impression management strategies in the CS of Portuguese financial companies is correlated with the size of the company (public visibility).

METHODOLOGY

Sample

The sample was selected according to the following criterion: Individual Annual Reports and Accounts of the Portuguese financial institutions published in the Bank of Portugal (Eurosystem) that had a CS. The period of time selected was 2006 up to 2012. Considering that during this period the world financial crisis occurred, it is interesting to assess if IM strategies are more often used during economic recessive periods.

Table 1 shows the composition of the sample. The breakdown of the Portuguese financial companies included in the sample is as follows: of 73 companies only 27 publish the CS in their annual report and accounts, which represents that 42% of Banks, 40% of Savings banks, 31% of SGPS and 25% of Factoring companies.

In the period under analysis (2006 - 2012), 128 CS were extracted from the 27 financial institutions annual reports, whose narrative text was subject to a content analysis (Table 2).

Linguistic Indicators, Public Visibility, and Financial Organizational Performance

The CS in the annual report is a document generally used in IM research (Jones, 1988; Smith e Taffler, 1992, 1995, 2000; Clatworthy e Jones, 2001, 2006; Syderff e Weetman, 2002; Courtis, 1998, 2004). In this study, the dependent variables used were based on the evaluation of the adoption of three IM strategies in the CS of the financial companies. These IM strategies that were identified through the use of content analysis of their narrative text are: rhetorical manipulation, thematic manipulation and selectivity.

Content analysis was performed manually. Following the methodology of Merkl-Davies et al. (2011) and Clatworthy and Jones (2006), for the three IM strategies, we extracted information on six linguistic indicators: number of words, self-references, references to third parties, words with positive emotion, words with negative emotion and reference to indicators performance, both qualitatively and quantitatively. For each of these indicators, a dictionary was created that served as a decision rule and served as a coding instrument pf the content analysis.

Table 1. Sample distribution

Banking industry	Total	N	(%)
Banks	45	19	42%
Cooperative banks	5	2	40%
SGPS	16	5	31%
Factoring Companies	4	1	25%
Total	**73**	**27**	**37%**

Table 2. Sample

Years	President's Letter
2006	18
2007	19
2008	22
2009	21
2010	19
2011	13
2012	16
	128

The first linguistic indicator "number of words" was evaluated by counting the number of words included in the CS (Clatworthy & Jones, 2006; Merkl-Davies et al., 2011).

The second language indicator "self-references" was evaluated by the percentage of the number of words relating to three categories considered in relation to the total number of words included in the CS: personal pronouns in the first plural person; reference to the Group; reference to the name of the company (Clatworthy & Jones, 2006; Merkl-Davies et al., 2011).

The third linguistic indicator "reference to third parties" was evaluated by the percentage of the number of words related to third entities in relation to the total number of words included in the CS (Merkl-Davies et al., 2011).

The fourth indicator language "words with positive emotions" was evaluated by the percentage of the number of words with positive emotion in relation to the total number of words included in the CS (Merkl-Davies et al., 2011). The words with positive emotion were measured through the words used by the author with the intention of transmitting a positive perception of the reality to be described.

The fifth linguistic indicator "words with negative emotion" was evaluated by the percentage of the number of words with negative emotion in relation to the total number of words included in the CS (Merkl-Davies et al., 2011).

The sixth linguistic indicator is divided into two proxies: "qualitative references to financial performance indicators" and "quantified benchmarks of financial performance indicators". In the "qualitative references to financial performance indicators" we evaluated the number of references to financial performance indicators included in the CS. In the "quantified benchmarks of financial performance indicators" the number of references to financial performance indicators was duly quantified (Clatworthy & Jones, 2006). In these financial performance indicators, both company and market indicators were collected because they also influenced, even indirectly, the company's performance.

We also extracted data of two variables: public visibility of the company and financial organizational performance. The public visibility was assessed through the company's size, which was evaluated through the total assets (Branco & Rodrigues, 2006, 2008; Merkl-Davies et al., 2011). The financial organizational performance variable was evaluated through the growth rate of pre-tax results, in order to determine if a given company had a positive or negative organizational performance. This variable is dichotomic, assuming 1 if the company has a positive organizational performance and 0, otherwise (Courtis, 2004; Merkl-Davies et al., 2011; Smith & Taffler, 1992; Subramanian et al., 1993).

RESULTS

Descriptive Analysis

Table 3 indicates that on average, over the period 2006 to 2012, the size of the CS of Portuguese financial companies contains 892 words. However, Portuguese financial companies use few self-references, references to third parties and references of financial performance as IM instruments, when compared to previous studies (Clatworthy & Jones, 2006; Merkl-Davis et al., 2011).

In 2011, there was an increase in the use of these strategies. Most companies (0.53) had a negative growth rate and the number of third-party references (0.036) was slightly higher than the use of self-references (0.031). Most companies (0.53) had a negative growth rate and some authors (Brennan et al., 2009; Clatworthy e Jones, 2006; Merkl-Davies e Brennan, 2007; Merkl-Davies et al., 2011) have argued that when the firm achieves negative performances, managers tend to blame external factors, not assuming that those bad performances could be a consequence of their bad management. However, managers will tend to value their good management when the company obtains positive results (Merkl-Davies et al., 2011).

Following the study of Clatworthy and Jones (2006) and Merkl-Davies et al. (2011), it was expected that companies with positive incomes would use more self-references than references to third parties. However, Table 3 indicates that the mean values of self-references and references to third parties are very low compared to those presented in the existing literature (Clatworthy & Jones, 2006; Merkl-Davies et al., 2011). Oliveira et al. (2016) also obtained low mean values for these indicators.

The results in Table 3 also indicate that on average companies use more words with positive emotions, than words with negative emotions. This finding is consistent with Merkl-Davis et al. (2011) and Oliveira et al. (2016), which indicate that UK companies and Portuguese non-financial corporations use IM strategies not as an instrument of self-presentation dissimulation, but as a way of presenting a more favourable image of the company.

But in 2011, the mean value of words with positive emotion (0.056) is the lowest during the analyzed period (from 2006 to 2012) and the mean value of words with a negative emotion (0.037) is the highest in that period. There is a contradiction this year, and it can be concluded that Portuguese financial companies tend to show in the CS a real image of the company. However, they will use IM strategies this year to try to mitigate the financial distress of the company. The opposite occurs in 2006, where the number of words with positive emotion is the highest and the number of words with negative emotion is the lowest.

Regarding the references to financial performance indicators, Table 3 indicates that some CS does not include a single reference to financial performance. However, there is CS that reach the maximum value of 33 references to financial performance indicators. The mean values are very close to those found by Oliveira et al. (2016).

It is again verified that in 2011 the financial performance indicators the highest mean value over the period of analysis. These factors, which occur in 2011, coupled with the use of words with positive emotion may be related to the fall of GDP in the order of 1.6% compared to the previous year (GDP, 2010, -1.4%). Portugal made use of international financial assistance, which was implemented in April 2011 by the European Union (EU), the International Monetary Fund and the European Central Bank (ECB). According to the Portuguese Central Bank, 2011 was a difficult year for Portuguese households and for non-financial companies, due to the fact that there was a slowdown in the economic activity, wage cuts, higher unemployment and greater restrictions on the access to credit. All these restrictions lead to liquidity shortages. At this point, interest rates on access to credit were uncertain and banks began to demand more guarantees from creditors in lending. This situation may have influenced the use of IM strategies in CS in 2011.

Hypothesis Testing

Table 4 indicates the results of the Friedman test for the dependent and independent variables of seven banks that had all CS in their accounts reports over the period 2006 to 2012. Impression Management strategies, namely the number of words, self-references, words with positive emotion and reference to financial performance indicators are not significantly different over the period from 2006 to 2012. However, in the variables "references to third parties" and "words with negative emotion" there is a significant difference for a significance level of 5% over the period from 2006 to 2012. But, overall the results do not support hypothesis 1.

Table 5 presents the results of the Mann-Whitney U tests for differences in the adoption of IM strategies among companies with positive and negative organizational performance. The tests were performed for the entire study sample. The results indicate that in the variables "self-references", "references to third parties", "words with negative emotions and" financial performance indicators "there are no significant differences in the adoption of IM strategies for Portuguese financial companies with positive and negative organizational performance, over the period 2006 to 2012. Hypothesis 2 is not supported. These results corroborate the study by Merkl-Davies et al. (2011) when they consider that the adoption of words with positive and negative emotion is not significantly different between companies with negative performance and companies with a positive performance.

According to the social psychology theory of IM, managers of Portuguese financial companies adopt strategies of IM unconsciously, because the objective is not the management of the perceptions that the stakeholders have of the organizational performance, but rather as a way of favouring the corporate image.

However, there were only significant differences in two variables: "number of words" (there is a significant difference in the year 2011) and "words with positive emotion" (both in 2008 and 2010 there were significant differences).

Table 6 presents the non-parametric correlation tests between the adoption of IM strategies and the relevance of the company's public visibility. A negative correlation (-0.61) was found statistically significant (p-value <0.05) in 2011, between the number of words contained in the CP and the size of the company. This was also one of the years, where there were fewer CP publications from the companies in their reports. This may be related to the worsening of the economic crisis in Portugal and the restrictions imposed on the banking sector.

Table 3. Descriptive statistics

		2006		2007		2008		2009		2010		2011		2012	
Number of Words	Average	930.78		862.47		926.32		843.80		855.80		950.31		872.24	
	Median	805.50		986.00		911.00		942.00		735.50		891.00		746.00	
	Standard deviation	499.29		335.85		560.37		457.58		693.17		552.50		525.45	
	Minimum	181.00		218.00		227.00		124.00		242.00		239.00		175.00	
	Maximum	2,064.00		1,477.00		2,562.00		1,766.00		3,312.00		1,971.00		1,925.00	
Self Reference	Average	0.03		0.03		0.04		0.03		0.04		0.03		0.04	
	Median	0.03		0.03		0.03		0.03		0.03		0.03		0.03	
	Standard deviation	0.02		0.02		0.02		0.02		0.02		0.02		0.02	
	Minimum	0.01		0.01		0.01		0.01		0.01		0.01		0.01	
	Maximum	0.08		0.09		0.12		0.10		0.10		0.08		0.08	
Reference to Third Parties	Average	0.02		0.03		0.03		0.03		0.04		0.04		0.03	
	Median	0.02		0.02		0.03		0.03		0.03		0.04		0.03	
	Standard deviation	0.01		0.01		0.02		0.02		0.02		0.01		0.02	
	Minimum	0.00		0.01		0.01		0.00		0.02		0.01		0.01	
	Maximum	0.05		0.05		0.07		0.08		0.08		0.06		0.09	
Words with positive emotion	Average	0.08		0.07		0.06		0.06		0.07		0.06		0.07	
	Median	0.07		0.07		0.07		0.07		0.06		0.06		0.07	
	Standard deviation	0.02		0.02		0.02		0.01		0.02		0.02		0.02	
	Minimum	0.05		0.04		0.02		0.04		0.02		0.03		0.04	
	Maximum	0.12		0.11		0.10		0.08		0.12		0.09		0.09	
Words with negative emotion	Average	0.01		0.02		0.03		0.03		0.03		0.04		0.03	
	Median	0.01		0.02		0.03		0.02		0.03		0.03		0.03	
	Standard deviation	0.01		0.02		0.02		0.01		0.02		0.02		0.02	
	Minimum	0.00		0.00		0.00		0.01		0.00		0.01		0.00	
	Maximum	0.05		0.07		0.06		0.05		0.07		0.07		0.06	
Reference to Financial Performance Indicators	Average	8.13		6.57		8.22		8.81		7.80		8.92		6.67	
	Median	4.50		4.50		5.00		7.00		7.00		4.50		3.00	
	Standard deviation	8.44		4.27		8.76		7.14		6.22		11.36		7.42	
	Minimum	1.00		2.00		2.00		1.00		0.00		0.00		0.00	
	Maximum	32.00		15.00		32.00		31.00		22.00		40.00		23.00	
Growth Rate		N	%	N	%	N	%	N	%	N	%	N	%	N	%
Dummy	=1	15	83%	11	58%	7	32%	9	43%	4	21%	7	47%	5	31%
	=0	3	17%	8	42%	15	68%	12	57%	15	79%	8	53%	11	69%

Definition of variables: growth rate = 1, if the company had a positive RAI growth rate; 0, otherwise

Table 4. Friedman test for paired sample

	N	2006	2007	2008	2009	2010	2011	2012	Chi-square test	P-value (bilateral)
Number of words	7	1,098.57	960.14	1,124.57	1,108.14	1,078.71	1,277.14	1,231.71	10.22	0.12
		(3.29)	(2.71)	(3.71)	(3.43)	(4.00)	(5.14)	(5.71)		
Self-references	7	0.03	0.03	0.03	0.03	0.03	0.03	0.03	3.40	0.76
		(3.71)	(4.29)	(4.07)	(3.29)	(4.43)	(3.29)	(4.93)		
References to third parties	7	0.03	0.03	0.03	0.03	0.04	0.04	0.04	14.43	0.03
		(2.57)	(3.57)	(2.93)	(3.07)	(4.79)	(5.57)	(5.50)		
Words with positive emotion	7	0.07	0.07	0.06	0.07	0.06	0.06	0.06	6.75	0.34
		(4.86)	(5.14)	(4.14)	(4.14)	(3.79)	(2.71)	(3.21)		
Words with negative emotion	7	0.01	0.02	0.04	0.03	0.04	0.03	0.03	19.14	0.00
		(1.71)	(2.43)	(5.07)	(4.14)	(5.71)	(4.93)	(4.00)		
Reference to Financial Performance Indicators	7	12.43	7.57	10.00	10.00	7.86	10.71	7.71	6.08	0.41
		(5.64)	(4.29)	(3.21)	(3.71)	(3.50)	(4.07)	(3.57)		
Values of the means / year and mean ranks within the parentheses.										

The results also show a positive correlation (0.56), statistically significant (p-value <0.01) between words with negative emotion and company size in 2006. This result contradicts the results of Oliveira et al. (2016) and does not fully support hypothesis 3.

CONCLUSION

In this study, it was assessed whether, in a particularly difficult and demanding economic environment, financial firms feel more motivated to use IM strategies. According to agency theory, information asymmetry encourages managers to adopt opportunistic behaviours, as some authors (Adelberg, 1979) argue that managers tend to overshadow failures and highlight successes. However, from the perspective of social psychology, IM results from the social interaction between the parties. Therefore, there are other factors besides economic ones that lead managers to use IM strategies.

However, Portugal is undergoing a financial crisis, which presents important imbalances in the world economy and in the Portuguese financial market. Some of the Portuguese financial companies under study have presented great economic difficulties in recent years. Their accounts were subject to a number of audits to try to understand how these companies were able to move on to insolvency proceedings, such as the case of Banco Espirito Santo (BES) which reached historical losses of over 3.6 million Euros[1] and was recently subject to a resolution by the Portuguese Central Bank. Another example was the Banco Portugês de Negócios (BPN), which was nationalized due to the fact that parliamentary debates considered it to be the best solution because if the Bank went into insolvency, it would probably aggravate the economic crisis with impacts on the Portuguese financial system (Correia & Pereira, 2011).

Table 5. Mann-Whitney U test for independent samples

		2006	2007	2008	2009	2010	2011	2012
Nunber of words	Performance > 0	12.33	10.44	12.67	11.64	10.00	8.86	7.68
	Performance < 0	8.93	9.68	9.00	9.11	10.00	4.83	10.30
	Mann-Whitney U	14.00	40.50	35.00	37.00	30.00	8.00	18.50
	Wilcoxon W	134.00	106.50	63.00	82.00	150.00	29.00	84.50
	Z	-1.01	-0.29	-1.23	-0.95	0.00	-1.86	-1.02
	Asymp. Sig. (2-tailed)	0.31	0.77	0.22	0.34	1.00	0.06	0.31
	Exact Sig. [2*(1-tailed Sig.)]	0.36	0.78	0.24	0.37	1.00	0.07	0.32
Self-references	Performance > 0	11.33	12.13	10.67	10.27	9.87	7.57	8.59
	Performance < 0	9.13	8.45	13.29	10.78	10.50	6.33	8.30
	Mann-Whitney U	17.00	27.00	40.00	47.00	28.00	17.00	26.50
	Wilcoxon W	137.00	93.00	160.00	113.00	148.00	38.00	41.50
	Z	-0.65	-1.40	-0.88	-0.19	-0.20	-0.57	-0.11
	Asymp. Sig. (2-tailed)	0.51	0.16	0.38	0.85	0.84	0.57	0.91
	Exact Sig. [2*(1-tailed Sig.)]	0.57	0.18	0.41	0.88	0.89	0.63	0.91
References to third partie	Performance > 0	7.00	11.25	10.13	10.45	10.33	7.86	8.77
	Performance< 0	10.00	9.09	14.43	10.56	8.75	6.00	7.90
	Mann-Whitney U	15.00	34.00	32.00	49.00	25.00	15.00	24.50
	Wilcoxon W	21.00	100.00	152.00	115.00	35.00	36.00	39.50
	Z	-0.89	-0.83	-1.45	-0.04	-0.50	-0.86	-0.34
	Asymp. Sig. (2-tailed)	0.37	0.41	0.15	0.97	0.62	0.39	0.73
	Exact Sig. [2*(1-tailed Sig.)]	0.43	0.44	0.16	1.00	0.67	0.45	0.74
Words with positive emo	Performance > 0	7.67	8.38	9.53	10.73	8.80	6.43	8.68
	Performance < 0	9.87	11.18	15.71	10.22	14.50	7.67	8.10
	Mann-Whitney U	17.00	31.00	23.00	47.00	12.00	17.00	25.50
	Wilcoxon W	23.00	67.00	143.00	92.00	132.00	45.00	40.50
	Z	-0.65	-1.07	-2.08	-0.19	-1.80	-0.57	-0.23
	Asymp. Sig. (2-tailed)	0.51	0.28	0.04	0.85	0.07	0.57	0.82
	Exact Sig. [2*(1-tailed Sig.)]	0.57	0.31	0.04	0.88	0.08	0.63	0.83
Words with negative emo	Performance > 0	6.33	9.50	11.80	11.27	9.53	6.86	7.59
	Performance < 0	9.57	10.36	10.86	9.56	11.75	7.17	10.50
	Mann-Whitney U	13.00	40.00	48.00	41.00	23.00	20.00	17.50
	Wilcoxon W	19.00	76.00	76.00	86.00	143.00	48.00	83.50
	Z	-1.01	-0.33	-0.32	-0.65	-0.70	-0.14	-1.13
	Asymp. Sig. (2-tailed)	0.31	0.74	0.75	0.52	0.48	0.89	0.26
	Exact Sig. [2*(1-tailed Sig.)]	0.36	0.78	0.78	0.55	0.53	0.95	0.27
Reference To Financial Performance Indicators	Performance > 0	10.50	7.71	9.67	8.22	8.58	6.29	6.50
	Performance < 0	8.04	7.29	9.17	7.67	5.67	6.80	9.30
	Mann-Whitney U	13.50	23.00	34.00	25.00	11.00	16.00	13.50
	Wilcoxon W	104.50	51.00	55.00	46.00	17.00	44.00	58.50
	Z	-0.81	-0.19	-0.19	-0.24	-1.01	-0.25	-1.21
	Asymp. Sig. (2-tailed)	0.42	0.85	0.85	0.81	0.31	0.81	0.23
	Exact Sig. [2*(1-tailed Sig.)]	0.44	0.90	0.89	0.86	0.37	0.88	0.24

Table 6. Matrix of correlations

	2006	2007	2008	2009	2010	2011	2012
Nunber of words	-0.33	-0.33	-0.16	0.04	0.15	-0.61 *	-0.12
Self-references	-0.02	-0.09	-0.14	0.04	-0.27	0.11	-0.35
References to third parties	-0.05	0.26	0.06	0.01	-0.16	-0.11	0.10
Words with positive emotion	0.14	0.11	0.30	0.22	-0.13	0.27	-0.12
Words with negative emotion	0.56 *	0.33	0.38	0.41	0.26	0.02	0.31
Reference To Financial Performance Indicators	-0.16	0.11	0.10	0.25	0.20	-0.40	0.26

Significant correlations at a level of: **0,01; *0,05

The results indicate that Portuguese financial companies do not adopt IM strategies significantly in order to present a dissimulation of the business reality, that is, inconsistent with the theoretical arguments of the economic perspective. Organizational performance levels, measured by the growth rate of pre-tax results, do not affect the adoption of IM strategies. However, we have seen that in some years, there have been some exceptions. The variables "references to third parties" and "words with negative emotion" had a significant impact on their use over the period from 2006 to 2012. This may be related to the financial crisis experienced in this period. In the course of this study, some authors (Aerts, 1994; Clatworthy & Jones, 2003) argue that when a company achieves poor organizational performance, it tends to defend itself from attribution to the occurrence of external circumstances.

In this study, we analyzed a difficult economic period, especially the year 2011, where the Portuguese economy was greatly affected by the financial crisis. Future studies may analyze the extent to which the use of IM strategies in the CP of Portuguese financial companies varies according to other institutional and firm characteristics.

Some of the limitations of this study are related to the use of content analysis. In the present study, we only analyzed one particular aspect of the annual report: the Chairman's Statement. Future studies may consider other documents in order to assess the adoption of IM strategies.

REFERENCES

Abrahamson, E., & Amir, E. (1996). The information content of the president's letter to shareholders. *Journal of Business Finance & Accounting*, *23*(8), 1157–1182. doi:10.1111/j.1468-5957.1996.tb01163.x

Abrahamson, E., & Park, C. (1994). Concealment of negative organizational outcomes: An agency theory perspective. *Academy of Management Journal*, *37*(5), 1302–1334.

Adelberg, A. H. (1979). Narrative disclosures contained in financial reports: Means of communication or manipulation. *Accounting and Business Research*, *10*, 179–184. doi:10.1080/00014788.1979.9729157

Aerts, W. (1994). On the of accounting logic as an explanatory category in narrative accounting disclosures. *Accounting, Organizations and Society*, *19*(4/5), 337–353. doi:10.1016/0361-3682(94)90001-9

Aerts, W. (2001). Inertia in the attributional content of annual accounting narratives. *European Accounting Review*, *10*(1), 3–32. doi:10.1080/09638180122562

Aerts, W. (2005). Picking up the pieces: Impression management in the retrospective attributional framing of accounting outcomes. *Accounting, Organizations and Society*, *30*(6), 493–517. doi:10.1016/j.aos.2004.07.001

Allport, G. W. (1954). The historical background of social psychology. In G. Lindzey & E. Aronson (Eds.), *Handbook of social psychology* (pp. 1–46). New York: Random House.

Arndt, M., & Bigelow, B. (2000). Presenting structural innovation in an institutional environment: Hospitals' use of impression management. *Administrative Science Quarterly*, *45*(3), 494–522. doi:10.2307/2667107

Bartlett, S. A., & Chandler, R. A. (1997). The corporate report and the private shareholder: Lee and Tweedie twenty years on. *The British Accounting Review*, *29*(3), 245–261. doi:10.1006/bare.1996.0044

Beattie, V., & Jones, M. (2000). Impression management: The case of inter-country financial graphs. *Journal of International Accounting, Auditing & Taxation*, *9*(2), 159–183. doi:10.1016/S1061-9518(00)00030-6

Branco, M. C., & Rodrigues, L. L. (2006). Communication of corporate social responsibility by Portuguese banks: A legitimacy theory perspective. *Corporate Communications*, *11*(3), 232–248. doi:10.1108/13563280610680821

Branco, M. C., & Rodrigues, L. L. (2008). Factors influencing social responsibility disclosure by Portuguese companies. *Journal of Business Ethics*, *83*(4), 685–701. doi:10.100710551-007-9658-z

Brennan, N. M., Guillamon-Saorin, E., & Pierce, A. (2009). Impression management: Developing and illustrating a scheme of analysis for narrative disclosures – a methodological note. *Accounting, Auditing & Accountability Journal*, *22*(5), 789–832. doi:10.1108/09513570910966379

Clatworthy, M. A., & Jones, M. J. (2001). The effect of thematic structure on the variability of annual report readability. *Accounting, Auditing & Accountability Journal*, *14*(3), 311–326. doi:10.1108/09513570110399890

Clatworthy, M. A., & Jones, M. J. (2003). Financial reporting of good news and bad news: Evidence from accounting narratives. *Accounting and Business Research*, *33*(3), 171–185. doi:10.1080/00014788.2003.9729645

Clatworthy, M. A., & Jones, M. J. (2006). Differential patterns of textual characteristics and company performance in the chairman's statement. *Accounting, Auditing & Accountability Journal*, *19*(4), 493–511. doi:10.1108/09513570610679100

Correia, C., & Pereira, H. (2011). Nacionalizações e Privatizações: o regime das nacionalizações em Portugal, dos tempos da revolução ao caso BPN. Trabalho apresentado em Direito da Economia, Faculdade de direito da Universidade Nova de Lisboa, Lisboa, Portugal.

Costa, G. A., Oliveira, L. C., & Rodrigues, L. L. (2011). Factors associated with the publication of CEO letter. *Corporate Communication: An International Journal*, *18*(4), 432–450. doi:10.1108/CCIJ-07-2012-0045

Courtis, J. K. (1986). An investigation into annual report readability and corporate risk-return relationships. *Accounting and Business Research*, *16*, 285–294. doi:10.1080/00014788.1986.9729329

Courtis, J. K. (1998). Annual report readability variability: Tests of the obfuscation hypothesis. *Accounting, Auditing & Accountability Journal*, *11*(4), 459–471. doi:10.1108/09513579810231457

Courtis, J. K. (2004). Corporate report obfuscation: Artefact or phenomenon? *The British Accounting Review*, *36*(3), 291–312. doi:10.1016/j.bar.2004.03.005

Frink, D. D., & Ferris, G. R. (1998). Accountability, impression management, and goal setting in the performance evaluation process. *Human Relations*, *51*(10), 1259–1283. doi:10.1177/001872679805101003

Gardner, W. L., & Martinko, M. J. (1988). Impression management: An observational study linking audience characteristics with verbal self-presentations. *Academy of Management Journal*, *31*(1), 42–65.

Godfrey, J., Mather, P., & Ramsay, A. (2003). Earnings and impression management in financial reports: The case of CEO changes. *Abacus*, *39*(1), 95–123. doi:10.1111/1467-6281.00122

Graves, O. F., Flesher, D. L., & Jordon, R. E. (1996). Pictures and the bottom line: The television epistemology of US annual reports. *Accounting, Organizations and Society*, *21*(1), 57–88. doi:10.1016/0361-3682(94)00026-R

Hooghiemstra, R. (2000). Corporate communication and impression management – new perspectives on why companies engage in social reporting. *Journal of Business Ethics*, *27*(1/2), 55–68. doi:10.1023/A:1006400707757

Hyland, K. (1998). Exploring corporate rhetoric met discourse in the CEO's letter. *Journal of Business Communication*, *35*(2), 224–245. doi:10.1177/002194369803500203

Jones, M. J. (1988). A longitudinal study of the readability of the chairman's narratives in the corporate reports of a UK company. *Accounting and Business Research*, *18*(72), 297–306. doi:10.1080/00014788.1988.9729377

Kaplan, S. E., Pourciau, S., & Reckers, P. M. J. (1990). An examination of the effect of the corporate reports of a UK company. *Accounting and Business Research*, *18*(72), 297–305.

Leary, M. R., & Kowalski, R. M. (1990). Impression management: A literature review and two component model. *Psychological Bulletin*, *107*(1), 34–47. doi:10.1037/0033-2909.107.1.34

McKinstry, S. (1996). Designing the annual reports of Burton PLC from 1930 to 1994. *Accounting, Organizations and Society*, *21*(1), 89–111. doi:10.1016/0361-3682(95)00016-3

Merkl-Davies, D. M., & Brennan, N. M. (2007). Discretionary disclosure strategies in corporate narratives: Incremental information or impression management? *Journal of Accounting Literature*, *26*, 116–194.

Merkl-Davies, D. M., Brennan, N. M., & McLeay, S. J. (2011). Impression management and retrospective sense-making in corporate narratives: A social psychology perspective. *Accounting, Auditing & Accountability Journal*, *24*(3), 315–344. doi:10.1108/09513571111124036

Neu, D., Warsame, H., & Pedwell, K. (1998). Managing public impressions: Environmental disclosures in annual reports. *Accounting, Organizations and Society*, *23*(3), 265–282. doi:10.1016/S0361-3682(97)00008-1

Newman, M. L., Pennebaker, J. W., Berry, D. S., & Richards, J. M. (2003). Lying words: Predicting deception from linguistic styles. *Personality and Social Psychology Bulletin*, *29*(5), 665–675. doi:10.1177/0146167203029005010 PMID:15272998

Oliveira, J., Azevedo, G., & Borges, M. F. R. (2016). Impression Management and self-presentational dissimulation in Portuguese Chairmen's Statements. *Corporate Communication. International Journal (Toronto, Ont.)*.

Pennebaker, J. W., Mehl, M. R., & Niederhoffer, K. (2003). Psychological aspects of natural language use: Our words, our selves. *Annual Review of Psychology*, *54*, 547–577.

Porter, E. (1913). *Pollyanna*. Colonial Press.

Schlenker, B.R. (1980). *Impression management: the self-concept, social identity, and interpersonal relation*. Brooks/Cole Publishing Company.

Schlenker, B. R., Pennigton, J., Murphy, R., & Doherty, K. (1994). The triangle model of responsibility. *Psychological Review*, *101*(4), 632–625. doi:10.1037/0033-295X.101.4.632 PMID:7984709

Smith, M., & Taffler, R. J. (1992). The chairman's report and corporate financial performance. *Accounting and Finance*, *32*(2), 75–90. doi:10.1111/j.1467-629X.1992.tb00187.x

Smith, M., & Taffler, R. J. (1995). The incremental effect of narrative accounting information in corporate annual reports. *Journal of Business Finance & Accounting*, *22*(8), 1195–1216. doi:10.1111/j.1468-5957.1995.tb00901.x

Smith, M., & Taffler, R. J. (2000). The chairman's statement: A content analysis of discretionary narrative disclosures. *Accounting, Auditing & Accountability Journal*, *13*(5), 624–646. doi:10.1108/09513570010353738

Stanton, P., Stanton, J., & Pires, G. (2004). Impressions of an annual report: An experimental study. *Corporate Communications*, *9*(1), 57–69. doi:10.1108/13563280410516500

Staw, B. M., McKechnie, P. I., & Puffer, S. M. (1983). The justification of organizational performance. *Administrative Science Quarterly*, *28*(4), 582–600. doi:10.2307/2393010

Steinbart, P. J. (1989, September). The auditor's responsibility for the accuracy of graphs in annual reports: Some evidence of the need for additional guidelines. *Accounting Horizons*, 60–70.

Subramanian, R., Insley, R., & Blackwell, R. D. (1993). performance and readability: A comparison of annual reports of profitable and unprofitable corporations. *Journal of Business Communication*, *30*(1), 49–60. doi:10.1177/002194369303000103

Syderff, R., & Weetman, P. (2002). Development in content analysis: A transitivity index and DICTION scores. *Accounting, Auditing & Accountability Journal*, *15*(4), 523–545. doi:10.1108/09513570210440586

Tweedie, D. P., & Whittington, G. (1990). Financial reporting: Current problems and their implications for systematic reform. *Accounting and Business Research*, *21*, 87–102. doi:10.1080/00014788.1990.9729407

KEY TERMS AND DEFINITIONS

Chairman's Statement: A letter from the chairman of the board to shareholders reporting on the company's condition usually made part of the annual report. The report, typically no longer than two pages, includes a summary of initiatives, activities of the board, and personal perspective of the company's future.

Financial Reporting: Financial reporting is the process of producing statements that disclose an organization's financial status to management, investors, and the government.

Impression Management: Is an effort to control or influence other people's perceptions. This could be their perception of a certain person (including you), a material possession, or an event.

Performance: Is the completion of a task with the application of knowledge, skills, and abilities.

Social Psychology: The study of the manner in which the personality, attitudes, motivations, and behavior of the individual influence and are influenced by social groups.

ENDNOTE

1 http://www.dn.pt/inicio/economia/interior.aspx?content_id=4062112&page=-1consulted9/29/2014 at 7:30 p.m.

Chapter 10
Determinants of the Readability and Comprehensibility of Risk Disclosures:
Evidence From Portuguese Listed Companies

Jonas da Silva Oliveira
https://orcid.org/0000-0001-5374-1062
Instituto Universitário de Lisboa (ISCTE-IUL), Portugal

Graça Maria do Carmo Azevedo
https://orcid.org/0000-0002-6346-4035
University of Aveiro, Portugal

Augusta da Conceição Santos Ferreira
https://orcid.org/0000-0003-1659-3309
University of Aveiro, Portugal

Susana Patrícia Henriques Martins
University of Aveiro, Portugal

Cláudia Roberta de Araújo Alves Pinto
Polytechnic Institute of Viana do Castelo, Portugal

ABSTRACT

The chapter intends to determine if managers make use of impression management strategies to hide or obfuscate risk disclosures through the analyses of the risk information disclosed by Portuguese non-financial listed companies. A content analysis of the management reports, notes to the financial statements, and corporate governance reports of companies listed at Euronext Lisbon, in the years 2007, 2010, and 2013 was carried out. Findings indicate that the understandability of the risk information is positively associated with the company's size. Results also indicate that there is a negative association between the readability of risk information disclosed and the company's size and industry.

DOI: 10.4018/978-1-5225-7817-8.ch010

INTRODUCTION

Portuguese companies listed at Lisbon stock exchange have to comply with the legal obligations required either by accounting standards and corporate governance recommendations issued by the Securities Market Commission. More importantly, aligned with these requirements they have to disclose, in the management report, their main risks and uncertainties.

Companies are constantly subject to risks that result from their own decisions, but also from the decisions of their stakeholders. Although risk and uncertainty may be positive or negative, they tend to be perceived as negative. For this reason, sometimes the disclosure of risk information is planned in order to adopt the form considered less harmful to the company. Such planning may be justified by the fact that risk information is commerciallysensitive and therefore its reporting through the use of narratives may include specific communication strategies (such as obfuscation through the manipulation of readability), to pursue opportunistic purposes.

Narrative documents are then used as vehicles to influence stakeholders' perception on the company's performance. These manipulation techniques of narratives are called Impression Management (IM).

This topic has been studied by several researchers (Godfrey et al., 2003, Ogden and Clarke, 2005, Merkl-Davis and Brennan, 2007 and Cho et al., 2010). But so far the literature on the readabaility of risk-related disclosures has been scant. Consequently, this paper seeks to answer the following following research questions:

1. What is the level of readability/comprehensibility of risk information disclosed by Portuguese non-financial companies listed at Euronext Lisbon?
2. What factors affect the level of readability/comprehensibility of risk information?

The main objective of this work is to analyze the information disclosure on risk and to identify if there are IM practices and, as a secondary objective, to categorize the types of risk reported by the companies, to relate the level of disclosure (dependent variable) with factors that can influence the amount of information disclosed by the company, and to identify the communication strategies followed by the managers.

To this end, the management reports, the notes to financial statements, and the corporate governance reports for 2007 of a sample of 37 Porttuguese non-finance companies will be analyzed.

Findings show that risk reporting comprehensibility (readability) is associated positively (negatively) with size. In addition, the results also show that there is a negative association between risk reporting readability and company's industry. Regarding the different risk categories disclosed, both financial risk and operational risk are those with greater level of disclosure.

The present study contributes to the perceived understanding of the information disclosure on risk, namely in what concerns to the use of IM strategies. In addition, it is also the purpose of this empirical study identify which factors determine the comprehensibility and readability of risk reporting. Thus, the paper contributes to the existing literature on risk reporting and IM.

To achieve our objectives the chapter is divided into four sections. In the first section, there is a literature review where the contributions of the literature on IM are evidenced. Then, the methodology is described. In a third moment, the results are discussed. Finally, the main conclusions and limitations are presented.

LITERATURE REVIEW

According to Deumes (2008), managers, for the most part, attribute the word risk to various internal and external factors that affect the company's future performance. Normally, a risk is associated with a future event with negative consequences. But the risk does not have to be negative. Positive risks can also be found. Positive risk occurs when it creates opportunities, gains or creates value for the company, and according to the financial theory, namely, the financial equilibrium model, the greater is the risk, the greater is the return.

When talking about risk, it is necessary to differentiate this concept from the concept of uncertainty. If the event in question allows quantification, it is called risk. Otherwise, it will be a situation of uncertainty.

Risk information is disclosed by companies through the risk reports that should contain relevant aspects of organization, scrutiny, control, quantification, graduation and monitoring. These reports are considereds to be drawn up by risk managers or the equivalent function.

Risk reports may contain various disclosure items. Beretta and Bozzolan (2004) analyzed the companies listed on the Italian Stock Exchange and concluded that the companies disclose on average 75 different risk items in the Management Discussion & Analysis section and that the main areas of risk disclosed are: strategic, financial structure and business processes. They found that companies voluntarily disclose some information about future strategies but avoid communicating the results or quantifying the expected impacts. The authors state that the disclosures tend to be self-justifying in relation to the expectation of negative impacts.

Linsley and Shrives (2006), categorize the types of risk that UK companies may be subject to (financial risk, operational risk, environmental risk, strategic risk, regulatory risk and internal control risk). The authors concluded that the number of financial risk disclosures was significantly lower compared to operational risk disclosures. Linsley and Shrives (2006) also observed companies' willingness to disclose about future risks.

Abraham and Cox (2007) analyzed a sample of companies listed on the London Stock Exchange belonging to the FTSE 100 Index, to assess in which way the ownership structure affected the amount of risk reporting. They concluded that ownership structure affect risk reporting differently. The authors also noted that executive directors and independent managers had an influence on risk reports. On the other hand, the number of non-executive dependent managers was not related to the level of risk reporting. The authors found that in the 71 reports analyzed all contained information on internal control risk and financial risk, but not all published information on business risk. It is needed to take into account, that the reports analyzed were for the year 2002, the year following the significant fall in stocks, which may denounce that companies would be more likely to disclose more about risk.

Oliveira et al. (2011b) also verified that the existence of independent managers influences the risk disclosure. Oliveira et al. (2011c) in a study on Portuguese banks concluded that voluntary risk reporting appears to meet institutional pressures since it increases legitimacy and manages stakeholders' view of the bank. Oliveira et al. (2011a) observed that in the voluntary reporting there was a lack of transparency in issues related to operational risk, capital structure and capital adequacy.

Oliveira et al. (2013) verified that stakeholders' monitoring is an important factor to explain the risk disclosure by Portuguese credit institutions. The same authors report that there is a statistically significant relationship between credit risk disclosures and bank's public visibility. This behaviour may be due to a strategy to gain or maintain legitimacy and reputation. In previous studies, the same authors, when analyzing Portuguese companies in the non-financial sector, had already concluded that public visibility appeared to be an influence on risk disclosure (Oliveira et al., 2011b). The companies appeared to attempt to monitor their reputation by disclosing information of this nature.

While the information disclosed by companies about risk is important, it is also certain that their level of importance of this kind of information is determined by its readability and comprehensibility.

Smith and Smith (1971), Schroeder and Gibson (1990), Linsley and Lawrence (2007), Silva and Fernandes (2009) and Courtis (2011) studied these aspects having concluded that readability and comprehensibility of narratives is very low. Linsley and Lawrence (2007), concluded that of risk disclosures are difficult or very difficult to read.

Linsley and Shrives (2006) stated that statements of ownership of risk management policies coupled with a lack of consistency in narratives lead to information gaps, which may lead to stakeholders failing to assess the company's risk profile.

The study of readability and comprehensibility of corporate reporting narratives is associated with the so called IM communication strategies. The IM has its origins in the literature on social psychology (Schlenker, 1980). Leary and Kowalski (1990) define IM as interpersonal behaviour, in which people control the impressions that others form of them. Neu et al. (1998) report that in the context of corporate communication IM occurs when managers select the information to be disclosed and present it in a way that distorts the users' perception. According to Brennan et al. (2009), IM occurs more frequently in less regulated narrative disclosures and usually focuses on the interpretation of financial results. Merkl-Davies et al. (2011) concluded that when organizational results are negative, managers rush to construct retrospective processes rather than organizational performance.

Regarding the quality of financial reporting, Merkl-Davies and Brennan (2007) point out that the use of IM strategies can take the form of subconscious messages with the intent to manipulate the content and the presentation of financial information.

Courtis (2004) reports that managers have incentives through monetary compensations to adopt IM strategies, in order to influence the perception others have on the company's performance and, consequently, influence share prices. Most of the literature studied IM from an economic perspective, in which if IM strategies are related to negative organizational performance, they are seen as opportunistic and conscious behaviour from managers, to persuade the investors' perception on company's performance (Merkl-Davies and Brennan, 2007, 2011).

Among the explanatory theories use to justify the adoption of IM strategies are: agency theory, signalling theory, legitimacy theory, stakeholder theory, attribution theory, and institutional theory.

In the scope of agency theory, Courtis (1998) developed the so-called obfuscation hypothesis in which managers opportunistically convey a good view of the company, regardless of their performance, thus avoiding conflicts of interest. Merkl-Davies et al. (2011) concluded that in order to obfuscate negative outcomes managers introduce a positive bias in performance. Brennan et al. (2009) also observed the use of IM strategies in order to increase positive information and to ignore or underestimate negative information.

Consequently, managers are not neutral in the presentation of their accounting narratives (Sydserff and Weetman, 1999). They tend to overshadow failures and emphasize their successes (Adelberg, 1979).

Smith and Taffler (1992) and Rutherford (2003) used signalling theory to justify the glare hypothesis. In signalling theory, glare focuses on the behaviour of managers. When faced with well-performing companies, managers try to signal this superiority to other companies through greater transparency in the disclosure and presentation of company information. Morris (1987) also points out that companies with positive performances have a higher level of transparency. These information management and disclosure practices aim to signal their superiority to other companies and attract more investment.

The legitimacy theory is considered one of the dominant theories in information disclosure research. It is a theory that explains communication practices and through which one can change the perception about the legitimacy of the company (Merkl-Davies and Brennan, 2007).

Gray et al. (1996) argue that the legitimacy theory and stakeholder theory are correlated. While stakeholder theory focuses on the economic theory of motivations, the legitimacy theory focuses on the social motivations of the organization to provide information. Merkl-Davies and Brennan (2007) consider that companies manipulate the perception of stakeholders about the company through the use of IM strategies.

According to the attribution theory managers attribute good performance to internal causes related to management skills. When performance is bad or bad, managers tend to justify it with causes outside the company, against which managers could do nothing to counteract (Clatworthy and Jones, 2003).

The IM literature identifies seven communication strategies: manipulation of readability, rhetorical manipulation, thematic manipulation, visual and structural manipulation, performance comparisons, the choice of performance indicators and the attribution of organizational performance. Out of the seven strategies, six are used to conceal information. Within these six strategies, two (the manipulation of readability and rhetorical manipulation) are used to obfuscate bad news through verbal manipulation of information. The remaining four strategies are attributed to the emphasis on good news: thematic manipulation, visual and structural manipulation, performance comparisons and the choice of performance indicators. The last strategy refers to the attribution of organizational performance: This is a defensive technique, in which managers tend to excuse poor performance through factors external to the company (Brennan et al., 2009, Merkl-Davies and Brennan, 2007, 2011).

The present study will focus on the study of only two IM strategies: the manipulation of readability and the rhetorical manipulation.

Table 1 summarizes the studies on readability manipulation. These studies consider the manipulation of the reading facility as a means to obfuscate bad news. This complexity turns narratives difficult to read.

Table 2 presents the studies on rhetoric manipulation that are portrayed by the use of a persuasive language, in which there are linguistic choices and rhetorical devices used to obfuscate information to users.

Table 1. Summary of studies on readability manipulation

Study	Country	Findings
Adelberg (1979)	US	Narratives difficult to read. Negative association between readability and company's performance
Courtis (1986)	Canada	Readability is not associated with company's performance.
Courtis (1995)	Hong Kong	Readability is not associated with company's charateristics.
Courtis (1998)	Hong Kong	Readability negatively associated with company's exposure to press.
Rutherford (2003)	UK	Readability is not associated with company's characteristics.
Courtis (2004)	Hong Kong	Readability is associated with bad news.
Merkl-Davies (2007)	UK	Readability is negatively associated with company's size.

Source: Based on Merkl-Davies and Brennan (2007, pp. 134-138)

Table 2. Summary of studies on rhetoric manipulation

Study	Country	Rhetoric Observation Method	Results
Thomas (1997)	US	Passive construction, start of sentences, Relationship between the first and last paragraph, Euphemisms	Bad news is an objective fact and not attributable to individuals thought to be responsible.
Sydserff and Weetman (2002)	UK	Transitivity index, diction	The transitivity index is weighted but does not overlap the use of readability scores.
Yuthas et al. (2002)	US	Comprehensibility, veracity, legitimacy, sincerity, diction.	Very positive and very negative performances are more communicated.

Source: Based on Merkl-Davies and Brennan (2007, p. 140)

Managers can manipulate their rhetorical speech through the use of pronouns and passive voice basically to try to hide the negative performance of the company (Brennan et al., 2009; Merkel-Davies and Brennan, 2007).

The general evidence for rhetorical manipulation seems to suggest that firms do not use persuasive language in narrative documents in order to obfuscate negative outcomes (Merkl-Davies and Brennan, 2007).

HYPOTHESIS DEVELOPMENT

The present work focuses on the use of readability and rhetorical manipulation strategies in risk disclosures included in the management report, notes to the financial statements, and corporate governance report. More specifically, the present work intends to analyze the explanatory factors of readability/comprehensibility of risk disclosures. According to the previous literature, the explanatory factors are related to the size, profitability, leverage and industry.

Size

According to agency theory, larger firms are more reliant on external capital to finance themselves and face more agency costs due to information asymmetries (Jensen and Meckling, 1976). To increase investor's confidence managers reduce information asymmetries through the more risk disclosures.

Previous literature has concluded that risk information disclosure is associated with firms size as a way of reducing agency costs and managing corporate reputation, both at the level of non-financial (Oliveira et al., 2011b) and financial companies (Oliveira et al., 2013).

However, risk information is commercially sensitive. Therefore, it is expected that the managers of larger companies and, therefore, more easily scrutinized by their relevant stakeholders,, use communication strategies that allow them to manage the company's reputation. Acting this way, they try to construct a certain public image about the facts and/or events they are reporting that may or may not be consistent with how management sees these facts and/or events (Merkl-Davies et al., 2011).

H_{1a}: *The level of comprehensibility of risk information is associated with the company's size.*
H_{1b}: *The level of readability of risk information is associated with the company's size.*

Profitability

There are several studies that advocate a positive relationship between company performance and information disclosure (Debreceny and Rahman, 2005; Ousama et al., 2012; Raffournier, B., 1995). Verrecchia (1983) states that companies set a profitability threshold from which they must disclose. However, there are studies that find inverse relationships between disclosure and profitability (Cooke, 1989 and Garcia-Meca et al., 2005).

According to signalling theory, the most profitable companies are encouraged to advertise in greater quantity to distinguish themselves from the others in the market (Morris, 1987; Smith and Taffler, 1992 and Rutherford, 2003). On the other way, according to agency theory, information asymmetry encourages managers to adopt opportunistic behaviour. Adelberg (1979) argues that managers tend to overshadow their failures and highlight their successes. In fact, during financial crisis resources are even scarcer. Consequently, managers have incentives to manipulate stakeholder's perceptions on company's performance in order to attract those scarce resources that are vital to the survival of the company (Merkl-Davies, 2007).

H_{2a}: *The level of comprehensibility of risk information is associated with the company's profitability.*
H_{2b}: *The level of readability risk information is associated with the company's profitability.*

Leverage

The higher the level of a company's debt more information will be required by the lenders. According to agency theory, firms tend to disclose more information in order to reduce asymmetries and their agency costs (Jensen and Meckling, 1976).

On the other hand, according to the signalling theory, less indebted companies can disclose more information in order to show their superiority and viability to the market (Akerlof, 1970).

Previous literature has concluded that well-performing companies tend to signal this superiority to other companies through greater transparency in the disclosure and presentation of company information (Morris, 1987; Smith and Taffler, 1992; Rutherford, 2003). Since risk information is commercially sensitive, managers tend to describe positive organizational outcomes with more detail than negative outcomes in order to improve the perception that third-parties have about their performance (Merkl-Davies et al., 2011). To achieve this goal they may use IM strategies.

H_{3a}: *The level of comprehensibility of risk information is associated with company's leverage.*
H_{3b}: *The level of readability the risk information is associated with the company's leverage.*

Industry

Some studies found an association between corporate disclosure and the company's industry (Branco et al., 2011; Ousama et al., 2012). There are other studies that did not find any association between these two variables (Beretta and Bozzolan, 2004, Debreceny and Rahman, 2005, Garcia-meca et al., 2005). However, risk reporting is industry specific. Usually, companies tend to follow a model of company disclosure and that is usually related to their activity sector. From a legitimacy theory prespective, risk reporting can follow a model that commonly used within an industry, for example, those more environmentally sensitive. According to legitimacy theory, risk reporting can be used as a legitimation process to manage reputational risks. As a result, managers may feel the need to manage how risk information is disclosed to their stakeholders.

H_{4a}: *The level of comprehensibility of information about risk is associated with the company's industry.*
H_{4b}: *The readability level of risk information is associated with the company's industry.*

RESEARCH DESIGN

Sample

In the present study, a population of companies with securities listed on the regulated stock exchange market of Euronext Lisbon over a three-year period was used: 2007, 2010 and 2013.

In order to determine the explanatory factors of the levels of comprehensibility and readability of the risk reporting, a paired sample was extracted for each of the years under analysis. For this purpose, only companies with risk and risk management sections included in their management reports, notes to the financial statements and corporate governance reports were included in each sample year. All financial and insurer companies have been excluded for reasons related to their business models that subject them to a specific set of risks and regulations. The final sample includes a total of 37 non-financial companies, totaling 111 firm-year observations.

Dependent Variables

All documents were subject to a content analysis. The content analysis technique is widely used in business analysis studies. Jones and Shoemaker (1994) report that content analysis is a research method that allows conclusions to be drawn from the characteristics of information reporting. Moraes (1999) states that content analysis, as well as a research methodology used to interpret document content, is also used to understand and interpret messages that may not be interpreted in a common reading. In this way, the content analysis was used to quantify the disclosure of narrative information about risk disclosed in the annual reports.

The content analysis was carried out in three phases. In a first phase, the documents that within the Annual Report *i* at year *t* contained information about risk were selected. To this end, the sections of the management report, notes to the financial statements and corporate governance dealing with risk and risk management topics were selected.

This choice was based in accordance to the article 66, paragraph 1, of the Portuguese Commercial Companies Code, which states, "the management report shall contain (...) a description of the main risks and uncertainties with which it is faced." In addition, in accordance with article 66-A, paragraph 1, of the same Commercial Companies Code, "companies must provide information in the notes to the accounts: a) (...) disclosure of (...) risks (...) for the purpose of assessing the financial position of the company". In its turn, the Corporate Governance Report has on its structure a section for internal control and risk management.

In a second phase, the narratives of each document were selected. These texts were edited on Microsoft Word software and graphics, images or tables were deleted. Later, in a subsequent phase, these texts were introduced in the TextMeter software to calculate the following metrics: number of words, number of sentences and the Flesch Readability Index.

The metrics "number of words" was used by some studies (Abraham and Cox, 2007; Clatworthy and Jones, 2006; Fernandes and Silva, 2007; Merkl-Davies et al., 2011; Schroeder and Gibson, 1992). According to Zéghal and Ahmed (1990), this method presents consistency in determining the volume of disclosure because it is a smaller unit of measure for analysis. On the other hand, the metric "number of sentences" is also widely used (Abraham and Cox, 2007; Hackston and Milne, 1996; Linsley and Shrives, 2006; Linsley and Lawrence, 2007 and Schroeder and Gibson, 1992) because is measured globally and allows a better understanding.

According to Courtis (1998), Flesch Readability Index has been the preferred tool of researchers because of the easy access of this tool by computers, and the ease of interpretation and comparison with other studies (Schroeder and Gibson, 1992; Smith and Smith, 1971; Courtis, 1998; Linsley and Lawrence, 2007).

The results of the Flesch Readability formula (Flesch, 1948) fall in the range of 0 to 100. The value of 0 indicates a low readability, while the value of 100 indicates that the text has a high readability. The expression is based on the average length of the sentence and on the average number of syllables per word. So, the metric is calculated as follows:

Flesch Readability Index = 206,835 – (1,015 x CMF) – (84,6 x MSF)

where:

CMF = average length of the sentence (number of words divided by the number of sentences)

MSF = average length of syllables per words (the number of syllables divided by the number of words)

Although Flesch Readability formula has been developed and studied for the English language, according to Cavique (2008, p.62) "since it is not dependent on a dictionary, it can perfectly be used in Portuguese". However, the present work follows the methodology of Porto *et al.*, (2014). The authors, for the analysis of the readability of texts in Portuguese, used the Flesch Readability formula provided by the TextMeter software adjusted to measure the indexes correctly implemented for the Portuguese language. For this purpose, TextMeter software automatically makes available the remaining metrics used in this study: the number of words and number of sentences.

Thus, the present study attempts to analyze the explanatory factors of the use of IM strategies in the narrative texts of risk information disclosed by Portuguese listed non-financial companies in the period 2007-2013. The IM strategies analyzed are: rhetorical manipulation and readability manipulation. Table 3 presents the way in which these two strategies were evaluated.

Rhetorical manipulation is put into practice to make it difficult to understand narratives or to omit or distort certain information such as company performance. In this way, it is associated with the manipulation of comprehensibility. According to the previous literature the rhetorical manipulation was measured through the following proxies: the sum of the number of words and sum of the number of sentences.

Table 3. IM strategies definition

IM Strategies	Measurement
Rhetorical Manipulation	Sum of number of words
	Sum of number of sentences
Readability Manipulation	Flesch Readability Index

Regarding the readability manipulation, this was measured through the Flesch Readability Index. Merkl-Davies and Brennan (2007) point out that language is a powerful tool through which managers can make dominant discourses to show their power to stakeholders and thereby enhance the company's results in their favour.

There are several methods to measure readability. The most used features to analyze the readability in texts is the extension of the sentences or the number of syllables. However, according to Brennan et al. (2009), there are algorithms that, using these two metrics, calculate the readability of a text: Fog, Flesch, Kwolek, Date-Chall, Lix, Fry, Cloze, Texture Index and Diction. However, Flesch's ease-of-readability index, which counts the language variables in a text, thus measuring the likely reading difficulty for information users, is commonly used in previous literature.

In order to calculate the comprehensibility index and readability index, the procedures of Merkl-Davies et al. (2011) were applied. The original variables (number of words, number of sentences and Flesch readability index) were previously standardized. Subsequently, the comprehensibility/readability indices of company j in period t were calculated.

$$\text{Comprehensibility Index}_{jt} = Z\,(\text{Number of words}_{jit}) + Z\,(\text{Number of sentences}_{jit})$$

$$\text{Readability Index}_{jt} = Z\,(\text{Flesch Readability Index}_{jit})$$

where:

$j = 1,2,\ldots, n = 37$

$t = \{2007, 2010, 2013\}$

i = {management report, notes to the financial statements, corporate governance report}

Independent Variables

The independent variables were taken from the annual reports. Table 4 presents the independent variables, the way they were measured and the expected sign.

The size variable, according to Cooke (1992) can be determined by total assets, social capital, turnover, number of shareholders, among others. There are other studies that have studied the size through total assets (Borges, 2011; Linsley and Shrives, 2006; Merkl-Davies et al., 2011; Oliveira et al., 2011b). In the present study, the size variable was evaluated through the total assets.

Table 4. Independent Variables

Independent Variables	Measurement	Predicted Sign
Size	Total Assets (millions of euros)	?
Profitability	Return on Assets = Net Income / Total Assets	?
Leverage	Leverage = Total Liabilities / Total Assets	?
Industry	Dummy Variable = 1 if it is a manufacturing company and 0 otherwise	?

The profitability variable was measured by the asset return ratio calculated by the pre-tax result (EBIT) to the total asset. The profitability has been analyzed in several studies (Beretta and Bozzolan, 2004; Merkl-Davies and Brennan, 2007; Merkl-Davies et al., 2011; Smith and Smith, 1971).

The leverage variable was measured by the ratio total liabilities to the total assets. This method of calculation has been used in other studies (Abraham and Cox, 2007; Amran et al., 2009; Deumes and Knechel, 2008; Hassan, 2009 and Oliveira et al., 2011b).

The industry variable was measured through a dummy variable that assumes the value 1 if the company is a manufacturing company and the value 0 otherwise.

Estimation Model

The estimation model will analyze the determinants that affected the level of comprehensibility and readability of risk information. For this purpose, the following estimation models:

$$\text{Comprehensibility Index}_{jt} = \alpha_0 + \beta_1 \text{ Size}_{jt} + \beta_2 \text{ Profitability}_{jt} + \beta_3 \text{ Leverage}_{jt} + \beta_4 \text{ Industry}_{jt} + \ldots + \mu_{jt}$$

$$\text{Readability Index}_{jt} = \alpha_0 + \beta_1 \text{ Size}_{jt} + \beta_2 \text{ Profitability}_{jt} + \beta_3 \text{ Leverage}_{jt} + \beta_4 \text{ Industry}_{jt} + \ldots + \mu_{jt}$$

where,

$t = \{2007, 2010, 2013\}$ e $j = 1, 2, \ldots, n = 37$.

EMPIRICAL RESULTS AND DISCUSSION

Table 5 presents the results of the disclosures of the different risk categories, by type of disclosure, document and year. In general, the risk disclosure increased over the years studied, and from 2007 to 2010 the increase was more noticeable. This can easily be justified by the fact that the country plunged in the crisis in 2008, causing managers to feel the need to disclose more information to reassure investors.

In terms of risk categories, it is concluded that the two most publicized risk categories are financial risk (probably due to indebtedness in times of crisis and the need to show confidence), and operational risk (due to the fact that the company's operational activity is monitored thus showing a sense of stability to stakeholders). However, environmental risk is rarely mentioned, as companies are more likely to be concerned about holding and raising more capital than with their social responsibility.

In general, we have been able to find out about the evolution of the disclosure of all types of risk, with the only exception being the strategic risk that increases from 2007 to 2010 but decreases again in 2013. One possible justification for this variation may be changes in the economic environment that were felt in 2008. During the periods of financial distress companies felt a need to convey more risk reporting to investors. Finally, the disclosure of the risk is higher in the notes to the financial statements in 2007, but in later years companies have chosen to disclose more in the corporate governance report, perhaps because it is more targeted to corporate shareholders.

In turn, table 6 presents the mean values of the original dependent variables associated with the comprehensibility and readability of risk information.

Findings indicate that the year of 2010 is the year with lower mean values and the year of 2013 has highest mean values. By analyzing the number of words and sentences it can be verified that the corporate governance report is the place with the greatest level of risk information. However, the mean values of the Flesch readability index are very low, indicating that narratives are difficult to read. The mean values of the three analyzed variables (number of words, number of sentences and Flesch readability índex) in each year among the three different documents, were significantly different (p-value <0.01).

However, taking into account each disclosure document, considered individually, over the three years, only in the Corporate Governance Report there are statistically significant differences (p-value <0.01). Over the three years the amount of disclosures increases (number of words, number of sentences), improving the comprehensibility of texts. Readability also increases and therefore improves.

Table 7 presents the descriptive statistics of dependent variables and independent variables.

Taking into account the number of words and the number of sentences, the notes to the financial statements and the corporate governance report are on average documents where disclosure about risk is more difficult to understand, but easier to read, compared to the management report. The notes to the financial statements and the corporate governance report need to follow speficic regulation that may impact on langague turn it more complex and less understandable.

Since management reportt is a document that complements financial statements, has a voluntary nature, and managers have more discretionary freedom it is more propitious to evidence a message with better understanding. On average, company's profitability is very low and their level of leverage is very high. This is consistent with the characteristics of the Portuguese companies.

Table 5. Risk categories

Risk Categories	2007			2010			2013		
	Management Report	Notes	Corporate Governance	Management Report	Notes	Corporate Governance	Management Report	Notes	Corporate Governance
Financial Risk	9	32	11	15	36	25	13	37	31
Operational Risk	6	6	11	13	6	25	15	7	29
Environmental Risk	0	1	2	1	1	7	3	2	9
Strategic Risk	1	10	4	5	9	11	1	10	9
Regulatory Risk	0	3	4	7	3	17	6	3	27
Internal Control Risk	2	0	13	4	0	25	3	0	33

Table 6. Risk disclosure per type of document

	2007	2010	2013	Kruskal-Wallis Statistic	
Management Report					
- Number of words	259.514	828.806	816.895	3.717	
- Number of sentences	7.270	26.556	24.289	4.174	
- Flesch Index	6.432	10.500	9.421	2.856	
Notes					
- Number of words	981.703	1 297.639	1,397.816	3.349	
- Number of sentences	34.243	44.306	48.658	2.742	
- Flesch Index	25.649	26.278	28.053	0.684	
Corporate Governance					
- Number of words	524.081	1,553.278	2,470.105	32.203	***
- Number of sentences	15.297	50.833	77.342	33.901	***
- Flesch Index	7.730	13.528	15.921	15.232	***
Kruskal-Wallis Statistic					
- Number of words	24.159***	14.808***	30.875***		
- Number of sentences	29.098***	16.863***	33.671***		
- Flesch Index	35.877***	25.655***	39.515***		
Statistically significant differences at significance levels of: ***0.01; **0.05; *0.1					

Finally, about 35% of the companies included in the sample are manufacturing companies. Table 8 shows the analysis of whether dependent and independent variables follow a normal distribution.

The results of Table 8 show that, with an exception for the variables "readability index" (p-value > 0.05) and "indebtedness" (p-value > 0.05), none of the other dependent and independent variables follow a normal distribution (p-value < 0.05).

Table 9 shows the correlation matrix between the dependent variables "comprehensibility index" (Panel A), "readability index" (Panel B), and the other independent variables. Regarding comprehensibility, the results of Table 9 (panel A) show the existence of a statistically significant positive correlation between the comprehensibility index and size (p-value < 0.01) and profitability (p-value < 0.1). These results corroborate the hypotheses H_{1a} and H_{2a}. In turn, the results also show a negative correlation between the comprehensibility index and leverage (p-value < 0.01), corroborating the hypothesis H_{3a}. Between the comprehensibility index and industry, there is no correlation, not supporting the hypothesis H_{4a}.

Regarding readability, the results of Table 9 (panel B) show the existence of a statistically significant negative correlation between the readability index and size (p-value < 0,.1) and industry (p-value < 0.05). These results corroborate the hypotheses H_{1b} and H_{4b}. Between the variable readability index and the remaining dependent variables (profitability and leverage), there is no correlation, not supporting the hypotheses H_{2b} and H_{3b}.

The analysis of the correlation matrix also shows, among the several independent variables, very low correlation levels, evidencing the non-existence of multicollinearity problems between them.

Table 7. Descriptive statistics (original variables)

Variables	Measurement	N	Minimum	Maximum	Average	Standard Deviation	Skewness
Management Report							
Number of words	Sum	111	0.000	9,914.000	634.964	1,459.407	4.568
Number of sentences	Sum	111	0.000	339.000	19.351	46.275	4.961
Flesch Index	Index	111	0.000	38.000	8.775	11.525	0.899
Notes							
Number of words	Sum	111	0.000	5,150.000	1,226.622	1,068.562	2.101
Number of sentences	Sum	111	0.000	199.000	42.441	35.574	2.230
Flesch Index	Index	111	0.000	57.000	26.676	13.440	-0.300
Corporate Governance							
Number of words	Sum	111	0.000	6,940.000	1,524.081	1,628.595	1.201
Number of sentences	Sum	111	0.000	226.000	48.063	51.099	1.182
Flesch Index	Index	111	0.000	42.000	12.414	10.140	0.318
Size	Millions Euros	111	26.310	42,649.900	3,081.525	6,635.595	4.471
Profitability	Ratio	111	-0.140	1.570	0.043	0.154	9.063
Leverage	Ratio	111	0.070	1.440	0.723	0.189	0.428
					Sum	Percentage	
Industry	*Dummy* Variable	1 = manufacturing company			39	35%	
		0 = not manufacturing company			72	65%	

REGRESSION ANALYSIS

To be able to conclude on the confirmation or not of the hypotheses formulated a multiple linear regression model was used. The regression model was estimated using the ordinal least squares method, bearing in mind that we are dealing with balanced panel data (the Least Square Dummy Variables –LSDV- model was used). For this purpose, a model for pooled data was used, but the hypotheses of fixed effects and random effects were also checked.

The Kolmogorov-Smirnov (KS) and Shapiro-Wilk tests, for the dependent variables and for the independent variables (Table 8), may have relevant consequences in the inferences about these same variables, when worked on in the model, which required the prior normalization procedure of all, through the transformation of Blom, as suggested by Cooke (1988).

The assumptions of the model were verified for outliers, autocorrelation, multicollinearity, heteroscedasticity and normal distribution of residuals. Table 11 presents the results of the regression model. To test the existence of multicollinearity the Value Inflated Factors were calculated. The largest of these values (Model 1: VIF = 1,357; Model 2: VIF = 1,357) suggests that the problem of multicollinearity is minimal. White's heteroscedasticity test was performed to test the homogeneity of residue variances. Table 10 shows that the results in both models do not show heteroscedasticity (p-value > 0,05). The Kolmogorov-Smirnov test (with Lillefors correction) was used to test the normality of the residuals,

Table 8. Normality tests of dependent and independent variables

Variables	Kolmogorov-Smirnov[a]			Shapiro-Wilk		
	Statistic	df	p-value	Statistic	df	p-value
Panel A: Dependent Variables						
Management Report						
Number of words	0.332	111	0.000	0.466	111	0.000
Number of sentences	0.338	111	0.000	0.443	111	0.000
Flesch Index	0.344	111	0.000	0.754	111	0.000
Notes						
Number of words	0.164	111	0.000	0.783	111	0.000
Number of sentences	0.176	111	0.000	0.785	111	0.000
Flesch Index	0.086	111	0.043	0.969	111	0.010
Corporate Governance						
Number of words	0.175	111	0.000	0.853	111	0.000
Number of sentences	0.173	111	0.000	0.856	111	0.000
Flesch Index	0.160	111	0.000	0.925	111	0.000
Panel B: Dependent Variables (comprehensibility/readability index)						
Comprehensibility Index	0.142	111	0.000	0.892	111	0.000
Readability Index	0.069	111	0.200*	0.975	111	0.034
Panel C: Independent Variable						
Size	0.323	111	0.000	0.453	111	0.000
Profitabilty	0.335	111	0.000	0.286	111	0.000
Leverage	0.080	111	0.078	0.950	111	0.000
a. Lilliefors Significance Correction						

and the results show that in both models, residuals follow a normal distribution (p-value > 0,05). To test autocorrelation levels, the Durbin-Watson statistic was used, showing values (Model 1: DW = 1,450; Model 2: DW = 2,307) that suggest that the autocorrelation problem is minimal.

Table 10 shows that the regression models are valid globally, meaning that they are in general statistically significant to explain the levels of comprehensibility and readability of risk disclosures (Model 1: F = 27.856 with a p-value < 0.01; Model 2: F = 3.406 with p-value < 0.01).

Obtaining an adjusted R^2 of 0.594 in Model 1 and an adjusted R^2 of 0.116 in Model 2 shows that the explanatory power of the independent variables in the range of comprehensibility and readability index is 59.40% and 11.60%, respectively. As the data under analysis were panel data (balanced) the OLS models were used for pooled data. To analyze whether the OLS models for pooled data were appropriate, we evaluated the hypotheses of fixed effects using the F statistic (Model 1: F = 0.101 with a p-value> 0.05; Model 2 F = 0.005 with a p-value < 0.05), as well as the hypothesis of random effects using the Breusch-Pagan statistic (Model 1: LM = 1.530 with a p-value > 0.05; Model 2: LM = 1.541 with a p-value > 0.05). These results suggest that OLS models for pooled data are appropriate because they validate neither the hypothesis of fixed effects nor the existence of random effects.

Table 9. Correlations matrix

Variables		(1)		(2)		(3)		(4)		(5)
Panel A: Comprehensibility Level										
(1)	Comprehensibility Index	1.000								
(2)	Size	0.577	***	1.000						
(3)	Profitabilty	0.150	*	0.253	***	1.000				
(4)	Leverage	-0.166	**	-0.123		-0.202	**	1.000		
(5)	Industry	-0.116		-0.029		-0.059		0.263	***	1.000
Panel B: Readability Level										
(1)	Readability Index	1.000								
(2)	Size	-0.128	*	1.000						
(3)	Profitabilty	-0.006		0.253	***	1.000				
(4)	Leverage	-0.046		-0.123		-0.202	**	1.000		
(5)	Industry	-0.216	**	-0.029		-0.059		0.263	***	1.000
Statistically significant correlations at significance levels of: ***0.01; **0.05; *0.1										

Comprehensibility Index

The results of Table 10 show that the comprehensibility index is positively associated with firm size (p-value < 0,01) suggesting that the H_{1a} hypothesis is supported. This result is consistent with the arguments put forward by Oliveira *et al.*, (2011a) e Oliveira *et al.*, (2013). In addition, these results meet the assumptions of the agency theory. Larger companies disclose more risk information with less comprehensibility.

The comprehensility index is not associated with profitability, leverage and industry. In this case, is not possible to support the hypotheses H_{2a}, H_{3a} and H_{4a}.

Readability Index

The results of Table 10 show that the readability index is negatively associated with size (p-value < 0,1) and industry (p-value < 0,05), suggesting that the hypotheses H_{1b} and H_{4b} are supported. These results are consistent with the arguments put forward by Branco et al. (2011), Oliveira *et al.*, (2011a), Ousama et al. (2012) e Oliveira *et al.* (2013). The results are also consistent with the arguments used by the signalling and legitimacy theories.

So, it is possible to refer that larger companies, usually in the manufacturing sector, disclose risk information with less readability (difficult to read). On the other hand, the readability index is not associated with profitability and leverage. Therefore the hypotheses H_{2b}, H_{3b} is not supported.

CONCLUSION

This study analyzed the risk disclosure of Portuguese non-financial companies listed at Euronext Lisbon in the years 2007, 2010 and 2013. The risk and risk management sections of the Management Reports,

Table 10. OLS Regression results for the comprehensibility and readability of financial reporting on risk

	Predicted Sign	Model 1 Comprehensibility Index (N = 111)				Model 2 Readability Index (N = 111)			
		Pooled Model - LSDV				Pooled Model - LSDV			
		Coefficients	**T Statistic**	**p-value**	**VIF**	**Coefficients**	**T Statistic**	**p-value**	**VIF**
Constant		-0.633	-5.552	0.000		-0.272	-1.617	0.109	
Size	?	0.541	8.584	0.000	1.078	-0.156	-1.677	0.097	1.078
Profitabilty	?	0.058	0.895	0.373	1.123	0.059	0.623	0.534	1.123
Indebtedness	?	-0.076	-1.173	0.243	1.123	-0.001	-0.015	0.988	1.123
Activity Sector	?	-0.170	-1.307	0.194	1.076	-0.451	-2.350	0.021	1.076
Year of 2010	?	0.840	5.670	0.000	1.344	0.552	2.525	0.013	1.344
Year of 2013	?	1.227	8.350	0.000	1.357	0.735	3.388	0.001	1.357
Model Adjustment:									
R^2			0.616				0.164		
Adjusted R^2			0.594				0.116		
F Statistic			27.856	0.000			3.406	0.004	
Durbin-Watson			1.450				2.307		
Residues Heteroscedasticity									
White Test			1.318	0.237			0.674	0.731	
Residues Normality									
Kolmogorov-Smirnov Test			0.053	0.200			0.039	0.200	
Fixed Effects Hypothesis:									
F Test			0.101	0.904			0.005	0.883	
Random Effects Hypothesis:									
Breusch-Pagan Test			1.530	0.216			1.541	0.214	

Notes to the Financial Statements and Corporate Governance Reports were analyzed. Based on the content analysis technique applied to these documents it was possible to construct a Readability Index and a Comprehensibility Index. For the quantification of the comprehensibility level, we evaluated both the metrics "number of words" and "number of sentences". In turn, the readability index was quantified using Flesch's Readability Index, which measures the readability of risk reports.

Based on the previous literature on risk reporting and its relationship with IM strategies and resorting to the assumptions of the agency, signalling, legitimacy and stakeholders theories the development of the hypotheses were made.

Results indicate a lack of comparability of the disclosures made by the companies in the annual reports. There was no standard for disclosure of the various types of risk, which also shows subjectivity in the way risk information disclosure was made. The companies disclosed risk information in the way they think it was the most correct and it may be different from the other companies.

The results from regression model show that the variable "size" is the only variable with a positive influence on the comprehensibility index. In this way, it can be said that larger companies disclose more risk information but with less comprehensibility. On the other hand, the variables "size" and "industry" have a negative association with the readability index. Thus, larger companies, usually in the manufacturing sector, disclose more risk information but with less readability.

However, some limitations must be emphazised. First, the size of the sample may not be representative of the entire population due to the absence of information. Second, we only analyzed three years. Third, there may be other explanatory factors that were not considered in the empirical study. Finally, the last limitation takes into account the data dispersion which may lead us to think that the selection of years may have influenced our sample in some way.

The development of this study has a purpose to contribute to the perceived understanding of the information disclosure on risk, namely in what concerns the use of IM strategies. In addition, since the purpose of this study is the identification of the factors that determine the comprehensibility and readability of risk reportingwe hope to contribute to the existing literature risk reporting and IM. Further research should extend the sample and the number of years is order to better capture the economic effects of the recent financial crisis or even the effects of the recent economic and financial assistance to Portugal.

REFERENCES

Abraham, S., & Cox, P. (2007). Analysing the determinants of narrative risk information in UK FTSE 100 annual reports. *The British Accounting Review*, *39*(3), 227–248. doi:10.1016/j.bar.2007.06.002

Adelberg, A. H. (1979). Narrative disclosures contained in financial reports: Means of communication or manipulation. *Accounting and Business Research*, *10*, 179–184. doi:10.1080/00014788.1979.9729157

Aerts, W. (1994). On the of accounting logic as an explanatory category in narrative accounting disclosures. *Accounting, Organizations and Society*, *19*(4/5), 337–353. doi:10.1016/0361-3682(94)90001-9

Aerts, W. (2005). Picking up the pieces: Impression management in the retrospective attributional framing of accounting outcomes. *Accounting, Organizations and Society*, *30*(6), 493–517. doi:10.1016/j.aos.2004.07.001

Akerlof G. A. (1970). The Market for Lemons. *Quarterly Journal of Economics, 89*(3), 488-500.

Almedina, E. (2013). Legislação Comercial e das Sociedades Comerciais (4th ed.). Coimbra: Almedina Editora.

Amran, A., Bin, A. M. R., & Hassan, B. C. H. M. (2009). Risk reporting: An exploratory study on risk management disclosure in Malaysian annual reports. *Managerial Auditing Journal*, *24*(1), 39–57. doi:10.1108/02686900910919893

Bansal, P., & Clelland, I. (2004). Talking trash: Legitimacy, impression management, and unsystematic risk in the context of the natural environment. *Academy of Management Journal*, *47*(1), 93–103.

Basel Committee on Banking Supervision (BCBS). (n.d.). Retrieved from https://www.bis.org/publ/bcbsca07.pdf

Beretta, S., & Bozzolan, S. (2004). A framework for the analysis of firm risk communication. *The International Journal of Accounting*, *39*(3), 265–288. doi:10.1016/j.intacc.2004.06.006

Borges, M. F. R. (2011). *Impression Management e desempenho organizacional: o caso Português*. Aveiro: Universidade de Aveiro.

Branco, M. C., Delgado, C., Sousa, C., & Sá, M. (2011). Intellectual capital disclosure media in Portugal. *Corporate Communications*, *16*(1), 38–52. doi:10.1108/13563281111100962

Brennan, N. M., Guillamon-Saorin, E., & Pierce, A. (2009). Methodological insights: impression management: developing and illustrating a scheme of analysis for narrative disclosures-a methodological note. *Accounting, Auditing & Accountability Journal*, *22*(5), 789–832. doi:10.1108/09513570910966379

Cavique, L. (2008). Legibilidade de artigos científicos: Análise de dados da RCC. *Revista de Ciências da Computação*, *3*(3), 59–65.

Cho, C. H., Roberts, R. W., & Patten, D. M. (2010). The language of US corporate environmental disclosure. *Accounting, Organizations and Society*, *35*(4), 431–443. doi:10.1016/j.aos.2009.10.002

Clatworthy, M., & Jones, M. J. (2003). Financial reporting of good news and bad news: Evidence from accounting narratives. *Accounting and Business Research*, *33*(3), 171–185. doi:10.1080/00014788.2003.9729645

Clatworthy, M. A., & Jones, M. J. (2006). Differential patterns of textual characteristics and company performance in the chairman's statement. *Accounting, Auditing & Accountability Journal*, *19*(4), 493–511. doi:10.1108/09513570610679100

Cooke, T. E. (1989). Disclosure In The Corporate Annual Reports Of Swedish Companies. *Accounting and Business Research*, *19*(74), 113–124. doi:10.1080/00014788.1989.9728841

Cooke, T. E. (1992). The Impact of Size, Stock Market Listing and Industry Type on Disclosure in the Annual Reports of Japanese Listed Corporations. *Accounting & Business Research (Wolters Kluwer UK)*, *22*(87), 229–237. doi:10.1080/00014788.1992.9729440

Courtis, J. K. (1995). Readability of annual reports: Western versus Asian evidence. *Accounting, Auditing & Accountability Journal*, *8*(2), 4–17. doi:10.1108/09513579510086795

Courtis, J. K. (1998). Annual report readability variability: Tests of the obfuscation hypothesis. *Accounting, Auditing & Accountability Journal*, *11*(4), 459–472. doi:10.1108/09513579810231457

Courtis, J. K. (2004). Corporate report obfuscation: Artefact or phenomenon? *The British Accounting Review*, *36*(3), 291–312. doi:10.1016/j.bar.2004.03.005

Cristina, N., & Ioana, M. (2013). The Communication Process Of The Financial Reporting. *Annals of Faculty of Economics*, *1*(1), 1266–1272.

Debreceny, R., & Rahman, A. (2005). Firm-specific determinants of continuous corporate disclosures. *The International Journal of Accounting*, *40*(3), 249–278. doi:10.1016/j.intacc.2005.06.002

Deumes, R. (2008). Corporate risk reporting a content analysis of narrative risk disclosures in prospectuses. *Journal of Business Communication*, *45*(2), 120–157. doi:10.1177/0021943607313992

Deumes, R., & Knechel, R. W. (2008). Economic incentives for voluntary reporting on internal risk management and control systems. *Auditing*, *27*(1), 35–66. doi:10.2308/aud.2008.27.1.35

Ereira, S. M. (2007). *O relato do risco: uma análise no contexto das empresas cotadas na Euronext Lisbon (Dissertação de mestrado)*. Coimbra: Escola Superior de Tecnologias e Gestão de Leiria.

Fernandes, J. L. T., & Silva, C. A. T. (2007). Análise da legibilidade dos textos narrativos dos fatos relevantes divulgados pelas empresas brasileiras de capital aberto nos anos de 2002 a 2006. In Congresso USP de Iniciação Científica (Vol. 4, No. 2007, pp. 142-158). Academic Press.

Flesch, R. (1948). A new readability yardstick. *The Journal of Applied Psychology*, *32*(3), 221–233. doi:10.1037/h0057532

García-meca, E., Parra, I., Larrán, M., & Martínez, I. (2005). The explanatory factors of intellectual capital disclosure to financial analysts. *European Accounting Review*, *14*(1), 63–94. doi:10.1080/0963818042000279713

Godfrey, J., Mather, P., & Ramsay, A. (2003). Earnings and Impression Management in Financial Reports: The Case of CEO Changes. *Abacus*, *39*(1), 95–123. doi:10.1111/1467-6281.00122

Gray, R., Owen, D., & Adams, C. (1996). *Accounting & accountability: changes and challenges in corporate social and environmental reporting*. Prentice Hall.

Hackston, D., & Milne, M. J. (1996). Some Determinants of Social and Environmental Disclosures in New Zeland Companies. *Journal Auditing & Accountability*, *1*(9), 77–108. doi:10.1108/09513579610109987

Hassan, M. K. (2009). UAE corporations-specific characteristics and level of risk disclosure. *Managerial Auditing Journal*, *24*(7), 668–687. doi:10.1108/02686900910975378

Hooghiemstra, R. (2000). *Corporate communication and impression management—New perspectives why companies engage in corporate social reporting*. Springer Netherlands. doi:10.1007/978-94-011-4311-0_7

Jensen, M. C., & Meckling, W. H. (1976). Theory of the Firm: Managerial Behavior, Agency Costs and Ownership Structure. *Journal of Financial Economics*, *3*(4), 305–360. doi:10.1016/0304-405X(76)90026-X

Jones, M., & Shoemaker, P. (1994). Accounting Narratives: A Review of Empirical Studies of Content and Readability. *Journal of Accounting Literature, 13*, 142.

Jorion, P. (1997). *Value at Risk: The New Benchmark for Controlling Market Risk*. Chicago: Irwin.

Knight F. (1972). *Risco Incerteza e Lucro*. Edição expressão e cultura.

Leary, M. R., & Kowalski, R. M. (1990). Impression management: A literature review and two-component model. *Psychological Bulletin, 107*(1), 34–47. doi:10.1037/0033-2909.107.1.34

Linsley, P. M., & Lawrence, M. J. (2007). Risk reporting by the largest UK companies: Readability and lack of obfuscation. *Accounting, Auditing & Accountability Journal, 20*(4), 620–627. doi:10.1108/09513570710762601

Linsley, P. M., & Shrives, P. J. (2006). Risk reporting: A study of risk disclosures in the annual reports of UK companies. *The British Accounting Review, 38*(4), 387–404. doi:10.1016/j.bar.2006.05.002

Maroco, J. (2007). *Análise Estatística com utilização do SPSS. 3ª Edição.* Lisboa: Edições Sílabo.

Merkl-Davies, D. M., & Brennan, N. M. (2007). Discretionary disclosure strategies in corporate narratives: incremental information or impression management? *Journal of Accounting Literature, 27*, 116-196.

Merkl-Davies, D. M., & Brennan, N. M. (2011). A conceptual framework of impression management: New insights from psychology, sociology and critical perspectives. *Accounting and Business Research, 41*(5), 415–437. doi:10.1080/00014788.2011.574222

Merkl-Davies, D. M., Brennan, N. M., & McLeay, S. J. (2011). Impression management and retrospective sense-making in corporate narratives: A social psychology perspective. *Accounting, Auditing & Accountability Journal, 24*(3), 315–344. doi:10.1108/09513571111124036

Moraes, R. (1999). Análise de conteúdo. *Revista Educação, Porto Alegre, 22*(37), 7–32.

Morris, R. D. (1987). Signalling, agency theory and accounting policy choice. *Accounting and Business Research, 18*(69), 47–56. doi:10.1080/00014788.1987.9729347

Neu, D., Warsame, H., & Pedwell, K. (1998). Managing public impressions: Environmental disclosures in annual reports. *Accounting, Organizations and Society, 23*(3), 265–282. doi:10.1016/S0361-3682(97)00008-1

Oliveira, J., Rodrigues, L. L., & Craig, R. (2011). Risk-related disclosures by non-finance companies: Portuguese practices and disclosure characteristics. *Managerial Auditing Journal, 26*(9), 817–839. doi:10.1108/02686901111171466

Oliveira, J., Rodrigues, L. L., & Craig, R. (2011). Risk-related disclosure practices in the annual reports of Portuguese credit institutions: An exploratory study. *Journal of Banking Regulation, 12*(2), 100–118. doi:10.1057/jbr.2010.20

Oliveira, J., Rodrigues, L. L., & Craig, R. (2011). Voluntary risk reporting to enhance institutional and organizational legitimacy: Evidence from Portuguese banks. *Journal of Financial Regulation and Compliance, 19*(3), 271–289. doi:10.1108/13581981111147892

Oliveira, J., Rodrigues, L. L., & Craig, R. (2013). Public visibility and risk-related disclosures in Portuguese credit institutions. *The Journal of Risk, 15*(4), 57–90. doi:10.21314/JOR.2013.264

Oliveira, J., Rodrigues, L. L., & Craig, R. (2013). Technical note: company risk-related disclosures in a code law country: a synopsis. *Australasian Accounting. Business and Finance Journal, 7*(1), 123–130.

Ousama, A. A., Fatima, A.-H., & Hafiz-Majdi, A. R. (2012). Determinants of intellectual capital reporting Evidence from annual reports of Malaysian listed companies. *Journal of Accounting in Emerging Economies*, *2*(2), 119–139. doi:10.1108/20421161211229808

Pinheiro, S. F. (2014). A utilização de estratégias de impression management na carta do presidente: evidência nas empresas financeiras Portuguesas. Universidade de Aveiro.

Porto, J. S., Paiva, T. S. S., Amaral, C. L. F., Rebouças, T. N. H., & Silva, R. A. (2014). Legibilidade de artigos de um periódico nacional na área de melhoramento vegetal. *Cultivando o. Saber (Cumaná)*, *7*(2), 205–211.

Puga, J. F. R. (2012). *Relato dos riscos empresariais nas empresas da Euronext Lisbon (Dissertação de mestrado)*. Aveiro: Universidade de Aveiro.

Raffournier, B. (1995). The determinants of voluntary financial disclosure by Swiss listed companies. *European Accounting Review*, *4*(2), 261–280. doi:10.1080/09638189500000016

Rutherford, B. A. (2003). Obfuscation, textual complexity and the role of regulated narrative accounting disclosure in corporate governance. *The Journal of Management and Governance*, *7*(2), 187–210. doi:10.1023/A:1023647615279

Schlenker, B. R. (1980). *Impression management: The self-concept, social identity, and interpersonal relations*. Monterey, CA: Brooks/Cole Publishing Company.

Schroeder, N., & Gibson, C. (1992). Are summary annual reports successful? *Accounting Horizons*, *6*(2), 28.

Serrasqueiro, R. (2009). *A divulgação da informação sobre os riscos empresariais. XIV Encontro AECA*. Coimbra: AECA.

Smith, J. E., & Smith, N. P. (1971). Readability: A measure of the performance of the communication function of financial reporting. *The Accounting Review*, 552–561.

Smith, M., & Taffler, R. (1992). The chairman's statement and corporate financial performance. *Accounting and Finance*, *32*(2), 75–90. doi:10.1111/j.1467-629X.1992.tb00187.x

Solomon, J. F., Solomon, A., Norton, S. D., & Joseph, N. L. (2000). A Conceptual Framework for Corporate Risk Disclosure Emerging from the Agenda for Corporate Governance Reform. *The British Accounting Review*, *32*(4), 447–478. doi:10.1006/bare.2000.0145

Syderff, R., & Weetman, P. (1999). A texture index for evaluating accounting narratives: An alternative to readability formula. *Accounting, Auditing & Accountability Journal*, *12*(4), 459–488. doi:10.1108/09513579910283503

Syderff, R., & Weetman, P. (2002). Development in content analysis: A transitivity index and DICTION scores. *Accounting, Auditing & Accountability Journal*, *15*(4), 523–545. doi:10.1108/09513570210440586

Thomas, J. (1997). Discourse in the marketplace: The making of meaning in annual reports. *Journal of Business Communication*, *34*(1), 47–66. doi:10.1177/002194369703400103

Tirado, J. M., & Cabedo, J. D. (2003). The Disclosure of Risk in Financial Statements. *Accounting Forum, 28*, 181-200.

Yuthas, K., Rogers, R., & Dillard, J. F. (2002). Communicative action and corporate annual reports. *Journal of Business Ethics*, *41*(1/2), 141–157. doi:10.1023/A:1021314626311

Zéghal, D., & Ahmed, S. (1990). Comparisons of Social Responsibility Information Disclosure Media Used by Canadian Firms. *Accounting, Auditing & Accountability Journal*, *3*(1), 38–53. doi:10.1108/09513579010136343

KEY TERMS AND DEFINITIONS

Accounting Information: Information on accounting nature produced and disclosed to investors/stakeholders.

Comprehensibility: The quality of comprehensible language or thought.

Impression Management: Is the effort to control or influence other people's perceptions.

Readability: The quality of written language that makes it easy to read and understand.

Risk: Is the potential of gaining or losing something of value.

Transparency: Disclosure of legal, economic, financial, and other information that is relevant for citizens to understand the use of public resources.

Chapter 11
The Use of Financial Graphics as an Impression Management Tool:
Evidence of Portuguese Listed Companies

Graça Maria do Carmo Azevedo
https://orcid.org/0000-0002-6346-4035
University of Aveiro, Portugal

Jonas da Silva Oliveira
https://orcid.org/0000-0001-5374-1062
Instituto Universitário de Lisboa (ISCTE-IUL), Portugal

Augusta da Conceição Santos Ferreira
https://orcid.org/0000-0003-1659-3309
University of Aveiro, Portugal

Sara Raquel Pinto Marcelino Dias
University of Aveiro, Portugal

ABSTRACT

The main objective of this chapter is to determine the graph discrepancy index and to analyze which factors can actually influence the graphical discrepancy index, based on the strategies of impression management. For this particular purpose, a content analysis of management and financial reports was made, from 2010 to 2015, of Portuguese companies with securities admitted to trading in Euronext Lisbon. Findings indicate that companies tend to engage in printing management practices, but it was not possible to identify the determinants of such practices since all the hypotheses were rejected.

DOI: 10.4018/978-1-5225-7817-8.ch011

INTRODUCTION

Prior literature has identified specific communication strategies of financial information followed by managers to influence the stakeholders' decision-making process. These practices can be considered as manipulations and are designated in the accounting literature as impression management strategies (IM). According to Schlenker (1980), IM consists in trying to control, consciously or unconsciously, the perceptions of others, determining the consequences at the social level. To Hooghiemstra, (2000) it is a branch of social psychology that studies how individuals present themselves to others by giving them a favorable image.

When applied to financial reporting, IM strategies are seen as the set of procedures implemented by individuals (managers) in order to manipulate the perceptions others may have of the financial information disclosed, namely through specific legitimacy strategies (Carter & Dukerich, 1998). IM strategies are carried out because managers are aware of the relevance of financial information for the decision-making process of several stakeholders (Penrose, 2008).

In addition, IM strategies are enhanced by the fact that some reports are not subject to any kind of regulation requiring a consistent presentation by all companies. Thus, companies in an attempt to improve the external perception of financial information change the quantity as well as the type of information presented on a voluntary basis.

This voluntary information is commonly represented graphically. However, as graphics are not audited, there is room for IM actions. Thus, it is important to analyze whether companies use IM strategies in graphic representation to intentionally manipulate the stakeholder's perception of organizational outcomes.

Grounded on legitimacy theory and attribution theory, we intend to evaluate the levels of IM strategies adoption through graphic representations and address the following research problem: *do Portuguese listed companies use IM practices with graphic representation?*

The study is based on a content analysis of the annual reports and accounts of 36 Portuguese companies listed on the Euronext Lisbon stock exchange regulated market during the period from 2010 to 2015. A qualitative methodology was used to calculate the graphical discrepancy index (GDI) together with quantitative methodology, specifically the multiple regression model for the analysis of IM determinants, and consequently the following research questions:

1. Is there a graphics distortion in the annual reports and accounts of Portuguese companies listed on Euronext Lisbon stock exchange regulated market?
2. How relevant is the graphical distortion found in these companies?
3. Does company performance influence graphical distortion?
4. What are the determinants of graphical distortion?

Findings allow the identification of IM practices through graphic representation. However, they do not allow corroborating the hypotheses developed.

This study aims to contribute to the increasing literature in the field, alerting users of financial information to the existence of IM strategies that can lead to wrong perceptions and decisions.

The present chapter is organized as follows: in the next background section we present a literature and develop hypotheses; then, we describe the research design, discuss the main results and finalize with conclusions, limitations, and further research pathways.

BACKGROUND

The concept of IM, also called "self-presentation, is an Anglo-Saxon expression, originating in the literature on psychology that: refers to the process by which individuals attempt to control the impressions others form of them. Because the impressions people make on others have implications for how others perceive, evaluate, and treat them, as well as for their own views of themselves, people sometimes behave in ways that will create certain impressions in others' eyes". (Leary e Kowalski, 1990, p.1)

Despite its origin in psychology, IM began to be studied in the corporate reporting context as a potential explanation for managers' self-serving behaviors, to either positively influence the stakeholder's perception about the organizational outcomes to maximize expected returns and minimize punishments, or to adjust the company's public image to its social role. (Leary e Kowalski, 1990)

Some annual reports, such as management reports, contain a huge amount of voluntary disclosures and are not subject to regulation regarding visual information. Therefore, they are more likely to include IM practices (Niamh et al., 2009). According to Merkl-Davies and Brennan (2007), IM strategies can assume three types of manipulation: rhetorical manipulation that is based on persuasive language; thematic manipulation, which consists in the fact that managers hide the bad news by not reporting them; and visual and structural manipulation, which is reflected in the way documents are presented. The present study focuses on this last strategy.

Disclosures are the best tool to legitimize companies, since managers can influence the perceptions of outsiders, anticipating changes in expectations and preferences of the organizational environment.

There are several studies in the literature that attempt to determine the extent to which distortion of annual reports and company's performance can influence IM strategies. These studies are divided into different kinds of research: IM related to the performance of organizations (Borges, 2011), strategies and motivations that lead to the use of IM (Rahman, 2012), analysis of incremental information narratives (Niamh et al., 2009; Merkl-Davies & Brennan, 2007); IM focused on corporate and social reporting (Hooghiemstra, 2000); the use of financing strategies (Bastardo, 2015; Falschlunger et al., 2015; Uyar, 2009; Beattie & Jones, 2008; Mather et al., 2005; Beattie & Jones, 2001; Steinbart, 1989); and IM through graphic communication (Penteado, 2013; Cho et al., 2012b; Cho et al., 2012a; Jones, 2011; Pennington & Tuttle, 2009; Hill & Milner, 2003; Plumlee, 2002; Frownfelter-Lohrke & Fulkerson, 2001; Beattie & Jones, 2000a; Beattie & Jones, 2000b Mather et al., 2000; Beattie & Jones, 1999; Beattie & Jones, 1997; Mather et al., 1996; Beattie & Jones, 1992).

According to Beattie and Jones (2002, p.546), "graphs have been used in many technical and everyday contexts to communicate information effectively", and according to the same authors, the advantages of graphic communication are related to the ability of graphics to grasp users' attention. If the use of graphs is a graphic distortion, stakeholders are led to draw the wrong conclusions about performance (usually more favorable than it would be without distortion), influencing subsequent decisions (Pennington & Tuttle, 2009). The quality of graphic presentation depends on each individual's own technology and educational skills (Hill & Milner, 2003).

On the IM and the graphic distortion research field, there are several studies that corroborate these findings (Bastardo, 2015; Penteado, 2013; Cho et al., 2012b; Rahman, 2012; Uyar, 2009; Beattie & Jones, 2008; Beattie & Jones, 2002; Beattie & Jones, 2000[a]; Mather et al., 2000; Beattie & Jones, 1999; Beattie & Jones, 1997; Mather et al., 1996; Beattie & Jones, 1992), stating that such distortion positively affects the perception of stakeholders about the company. Beattie and Jones (1999) studied the top 100 listed companies on the Australian Stock Exchange and concluded graphical manipulation is due to measurement distortion, orientation distortion, and selectivity distortion issues. They also concluded that sales, profits, dividends per share and earnings per share were the most commonly used financial variables.

Most studies on graphical distortion use the graphical distortion index (GDI) to identify the incidence of measurement distortion (Beattie & Jones, 1999, D. Mather et al., 2005), developed by Tufte (1983) and improved by Taylor and Anderson (1986).

Beattie and Jones, (1992) identify three forms of graphic manipulation, such as selectivity, measurement distortion and presentation enhancement. Beattie and Jones (2008; 1997) also identify distortion guidance as a form of graphic manipulation.

Managers highlights graphical characteristics through graphical shape, three-dimensional effects with the intention of stimulating optical illusions, the use of several vertical axes with different scales without values and without data inverting time series, and inconsistent use of color, using colors in such a way that labels and markers are difficult to combine (Uyar, 2009).

Regarding graphic design, Beattie and Jones (1997) have found that UK companies tend to highlight the company's latest performance using different colors and fonts.

As already mentioned, the annual reports and accounts are used as mechanisms to manipulate financial information through IM, influencing the stakeholders' perception of the company's performance. This behavior can be supported by the assumptions of the theory of legitimacy that, according to Deegan (2002), focuses on how the organization presents itself to the society where it operates, and how it is understood by that same society, focusing on communication as a tool for changing perceptions. Companies seek legitimacy in order to obtain support from stakeholders. In this sense, the legitimacy theory makes it possible to study the means used by managers to report information to external stakeholders, as well as the reasons that can determine such behavior.

According to agency theory, larger companies are more dependent on external financial resources, determining that they have more agency costs related to higher information asymmetries (Jensen & Meckling, 1976). According to Watts and Zimmerman (1978), larger companies have higher political costs and by disclosing more financial information they increase the confidence of stakeholders in the company reducing those costs. Wallace et al. (1994) concluded that the size of the company is an important variable associated with the level of disclosure.

With regard to IM, Merkl Davies et al., (2011), emphasize that larger companies are more likely to use communication strategies as a way of manipulating the company's image over periods of crisis to build a positive public image that may not correspond to the real one.

H_1: The graphical discrepancy index is associated positively with the dimension of the company.

The debt ratio is crucial in assessing companies' financial health (El-Gazzar et al., 1999; Murphy, 1999; Zarzeski, 1996).

According to Watts and Zimmerman (1990), within the scope of positive accounting theory, the higher the level of indebtedness, the greater the need to transmit information that does not increase the risk associated with that same indebtedness. Considering agency theory, firms tend to disclose more information by reducing agency asymmetries and costs (Jensen e Meckling, 1976). If so, it is considered that indebted companies can view graphic distortion as a strategy for improving agency relationships between creditors and debtholders. However, viewed through a signaling theory lens, the less indebted companies can present more information to emphasize their financial and economic viability.

Thus, it can be assumed that companies with a higher debt ratio are more likely to use data manipulation strategies through graphic distortion than companies who are able to finance themselves through their own financial resources.

H_2: The graph discrepancy index is associated positively with the level of indebtedness.

According to signaling theory, companies with higher incomes have more incentives to disclose more information in order to distinguish themselves from others in the market (Morris, 1987). In addition, there are stakeholders interested in the success of the organization, so when companies cross periods of crisis there is a tendency to manipulate the information disclosed forging the perception of stakeholders (Merkl-Davies & Brennan, 2007). On the other hand, according to agency theory, information asymmetry encourages companies to adopt opportunistic behaviors.

From the perspective of Watts and Zimmerman (1978), high levels of profitability are associated with large political costs, so when companies have high returns there is a need to emphasize the credibility of this information. Thus, it is anticipated that companies have incentives to use IM, namely, graphic distortion to influence the perception of stakeholders about the company's performance. Hence, the following hypothesis is put forward:

H_3: The graph discrepancy index is associated positively with profitability.

Companies have an image and a reputation to maintain, and auditors are an essential part in achieving this objective, since they ensure the information disclosed by companies complies with the qualitative characteristics of financial information.

According to Chalmers and Godfrey (2004), multinational audit firms require more disclosure of financial information as a way to reduce bad reputation. In this way, companies audited by large audit firms, Big-Four, will tend to disclose more financial information and, due to the strong need to create a good reputation, they will tend to adopt IM practices, such as graphic distortion.

H_4: The graphical discrepancy index is associated positively with the type of audit firm.

The signaling theory states that companies that have positive performances tend to have a higher level of transparency, signaling their practices in order to attract those interested in the investment (Morris, 1987). In this sense, companies tend to present more positive information than negative information, as a way of showing a more favorable image.

Based on signaling theory, the information disclosed by companies contributes to the reduction of asymmetries (Ross, 1977). Moreover, since different industries present specific characteristics, there is a tendency for companies in the same industry to disclose the same type of information in order to become more competitive and more recognized in the market. Nonetheless, their competitiveness suggests that they may incur in IM practices by manipulating the graphical information in their annual reports and accounts. Hence, the following hypothesis is put forward:

H_5: The level of graphical discrepancy is associated with the activity sector.

RESEARCH DESIGN

Sample

This study analyzes the graphics presented in the consolidated management reports as well as the data disclosed in annual reports and accounts. Our sample includes all the Portuguese companies listed on the Lisbon stock exchange on the regulated securities market by Euronext Lisbon over a 6-year timeframe: 2010 to 2015.

Given the heterogeneity of these companies, non-financial companies with quoted values were considered in the sample. However, non-financial companies with insufficient information for analysis were excluded. Sports companies were also excluded because of the specificity of the activity they perform.

The final sample includes a total of 36 companies which corresponds to a total of 252 company-year observations.

Dependent Variable

The dependent variable studied was the GDI. The calculation of this variable was carried out with the objective of verifying that companies manipulate the financial information reflected in the graphics over the period of analysis.

The GDI is calculated based on the lie factor of Tufte (1983) and the methodology of Beattie and Jones (1992), through the following equation:

$$\mathrm{IDG} = \left[\left(\frac{\mathrm{a}}{\mathrm{b}}\right) - 1\right]$$

where:

$$a = \frac{height\,of\,the\,last\,column - height\,of\,the\,1st\,column}{height\,of\,1st\,column} * 100\%$$

$$b = \frac{value\,of\,the\,last\,column - value\,of\,the\,1st\,column}{value\,of\,the\,1st\,column} * 100\%$$

Based on prior literature review, the items studied include sales and turnover, earnings before interest, taxes, depreciation and amortization (EBITDA), earnings before interest and taxes (EBIT), earnings per share, share and net income for the period (RLP).

The GDI will be negative when the measure of the last period is less distant from the measure of the first period. On the contrary, the GDI will be positive when the measure of the last period is more distant than the one of the first period.

According to Beattie and Jones (2002), when the GDI equals zero, there is no distortion. When the GDI is positive the graph exaggerates its trend of values and, when the GDI is negative the graph underestimates the trend of values. Therefore, on the one hand, a positive GDI by increasing favorable results or reducing unfavorable results leads to a better representation of the company's performance, and, on the other hand, a negative GDI by increasing the unfavorable result or reducing the favorable outcome determines a worse performance of the company.

The GDI was calculated based on the content analysis methodology. According to Jones and Shoemaker (1994), this is a research method that facilitates the analysis of the characteristics of information dissemination. In a previous analysis of the visual information contained in the management reports, each type of graphic was considered per company.

The content analysis was done manually, using a ruler, considering centimeter as the unit of measure, and the collected data inserted in an excel file. This tool was used to calculate GDI.

Table 1 summarizes the interpretation of the GDI obtained for the sample.

Independent Variables and Econometric Model

The independent variables were collected from the annual reports and accounts of the sampled companies in each of the periods analyzed.

For each independent variable, a proxy identified in the literature review was considered and is presented in Table 2,

In order to analyze whether the independent variables are related to the GDI, a quantitative analysis was performed through a multiple linear regression model.

The econometric model will analyze the factors that influence GDI.

Table 1. Interpretation of the GDI

Type	Distortion for better	Distortion for worse
Increased favorable results	GDI Positive	GDI Negative
Reduction of unfavorable results	GDI Positive	GDI Negative
Increased unfavorable results	GDI Negative	GDI Positive
Reduction of favorable results	GDI Negative	GDI Positive

Table 2. Independent variables

Independent variables	Measurement	Predicted Sign
Dimension	Total Assets	+
Indebtedness	Total liabilities / Total assets	+
Yield	Net income for the period / Total assets	+
Auditor type	1 = Company audited by Big-Four; 0 = Company not audited by Big-Four	?
Activity sector	1 = Basic Materials; 2 = Manufacturing; 3 = Consumer Goods; 4 = Services; 5 = Telecommunications; 6 = Utilities; 7 = Financial; 8 = Technologies; 9 = Oil and Gas; 10 = Medical Assistance	?

$$GDIjt = \alpha 0 + \beta 1\,Dimension\,jt + \beta 2\,Profitability\,jt + \beta 3\,Indebtedness\,jt + \beta 4\,Activity\,Sector\,jt + \beta 5\,Auditor\,Type\,jt + \beta 6\,YEAR\,FIXED\,EFFECTS + \mu jt$$

where t = {2010,…,2015} and j=1,2,…,n (n=balanced sample)

RESULTS

Descriptive Analysis

Table 3 reflects the number of graphics presented for each financial performance indicator in a given year.

It can be seen that graphical representation has been decreasing over the analyzed period. In 2010, 248 graphs were found in annual reports and accounts, and in 2015 only 178 graphs. This finding is consistent with Bastardo (2015) and Uyar (2009). Regardless of the type of graphic presented, most companies bet on graphical representation, although the tendency to use it has decreased.

The item sales and turnover is the most represented graphically (585 graphs) followed by the variable EBITDA (378 graphs). These results contradict in part the study of Uyar (2009), who concluded that not only sales but also profits are the variables most used by companies in graphical representation.

The least represented items are dividends per share, with only 17 charts, followed by earnings per share, with 20 charts.

The dividends per share variable is the least represented graphically and also shows a tendency to decrease. In 2015 and 2014 only one graph was identified for this variable.

For firms with quoted values in Australia, Beattie and Jones (1999), concluded that the financial variables of sales and turnover, profits, dividends per share and earnings per share are the most represented graphically. The results of Beattie and Jones (1997), showed that the variables most used by listed companies in Australia are also the most used variables in the US and UK companies. These results are not consistent with those found among Portuguese listed companies.

Table 4 presents the average of the GDI, per year, for each financial performance indicator.

Table 3. Number of charts

Chart Type	Year						Total
	2010	2011	2012	2013	2014	2015	
Sales and Turnover	123	109	86	88	88	91	**585**
EBIT	7	6	6	5	6	8	**38**
EBITDA	81	74	54	64	52	53	**378**
Profits	5	6	9	7	11	6	**44**
Earnings per share	3	3	4	3	4	3	**20**
Earnings per share	4	4	3	4	1	1	**17**
Net Income	25	20	15	13	12	16	**101**
Total	**248**	**222**	**177**	**184**	**174**	**178**	**1183**

Table 4. Mean values of GDI for each financial performance indicator per year

Financial performance indicator	Year					
	2010	2011	2012	2013	2014	2015
Sales and Turnover	36.449%	22.616%	81.851%	50.207%	24.327%	72.793%
EBIT	67.124%	53.276%	46.524%	-17.686%	-2.033%	239.313%
EBITDA	23.286%	8.345%	14.144%	15.848%	44.035%	-0.046%
Profits	913.173%	-5.573%	247.653%	70.375%	27.900%	25.001%
Earnings per share	32.656%	-36.634%	13.700%	-119.478%	-68.711%	71.310%
Earnings per share	4,292.023%	4,079.583%	-1.807%	1,365.107%	-253.659%	-72.646%
Net income	66.888%	98.324%	-40.986%	-0.531%	-7.591%	40.624%

The sales and turnover variable is the only one that presents a positive GDI average in the entire period. The earnings variable also shows a positive GDI average for the whole period, except for 2011. This shows that there is a tendency to exaggerate the values reflected in the graphics.

On average, the earnings per share variable has a negative GDI. There is a tendency to underestimate the values reflected in the graphics.

The highest positive average of GDI is shown in the dividends per share variable in 2010 and the highest negative average is represented in the same variable but in the year 2014. It is also verified that the year 2010 presents a positive average GDI for all variables. Jones (2011) has also achieved similar results for UK companies.

Table 5 shows the number of graphics that exist in each sector, by type of chart. Bar charts are the most used in the reports and annual accounts of Portuguese companies with quoted values, followed by line graphs. Also according to the study of Bastardo (2015), Portuguese companies with quoted values make greater use of bar graphs. However, Uyar (2009) concluded that in Turkey the trend is no longer just the bar graph, but also pie charts and lines.

It is also concluded that the manufacturing industry is the one that uses graphical representation more frequently in annual reports, and the healthcare sector is the one with the lowest number of graphs. Jones (2011) concluded that UK manufacturing companies use graphs particularly to represent their financial information.

Table 6 shows the number of graphics per financial performance indicator in each industry. These data served as a basis for the computation of GDI.

Sales and turnover are the most representative in the annual reports. These results are possibly justified by the fact that sales and turnover are one of the main factors influencing investment by stakeholders.

Dividends per share and earnings per share are the least represented variables in most industries.

The manufacturing industry is the one that presents the most graphs in its annual reports and accounts, contrary to the telecommunications industry, with the least graphs, although these results are influenced by the number of companies included in each of the categories, as the manufacturing industry is represented by 13 companies and the telecommunications sector by 3 companies only.

It is important to point out that the basic materials industry has a great graphic representation since in this industry there are only 4 companies.

Table 7 shows the average of the GDI per financial performance indicator according to each industry.

Table 5. Number of existing graphics per industry for different types of graphics

Industry	Number of graphs				
	Bars	*Lines*	*Bars and Lines*	*Circular*	*Other*
Basic Materials	213	55	9	23	11
Manufacturing	582	170	78	168	22
Consumer goods	127	38	55	30	1
Services	238	25	77	46	-
Telecommunications	99	74	14	13	-
Utilities	366	77	87	95	14
Financial sector	79	59	8	15	-
Technology	144	29	7	32	14
Oil and Gas	141	34	15	70	7
Health care	59	2	1	25	1

Table 6. Number of graphics per financial performance indicator in a given industry

Chart Type	Industry									
	Basic Materials	Manufacturing	Consumer goods	Services	Telecommunications	Utilities	Financial sector	Technology	Oil and gas	Health care
Sales and volume of business	108	199	66	107	3	3	14	49	29	7
EBIT	19	1	1	4	-	-	2	7	2	2
EBITDA	85	128	57	23	3	11	17	46	1	7
Profits	-	11	-	20	-	4	-	7	-	1
Earnings per share	-	-	-	5	-	4	-	6	6	-
Dividends per share	-	2	-	-	2	3	-	-	10	-
Net Income	5	22	11	11	3	10	7	23	5	4

Table 7. Average of the GDI of each financial performance indicator per industry

Chart Type	Industry									
	Basic Materials	Manufacturing	Consumer goods	Services	Telecommunications	Utilities	Financial sector	Technology	Oil and gas	Health care
Sales and volume of business	64.870%	16.674%	101.805%	53.188%	219.015%	-32.677%	-5.421%	78.314%	5.594%	31.350%
EBIT	23.474%	141.667%	30.385%	477.001%	-	-	-1.496%	62.550%	-14.538%	-1.665%
EBITDA	7.359%	18.484%	1.388%	-11.667%	295.947%	227.182%	1.501%	3.506%	-35.746%	-14.927%
Profits	-	623.215%	-	3.171%	-	3.415%	-	196.099%	-	0.078%
Earnings per share	-	-	-	-33.267%	-	-29.687%	-	-13.030%	-3.718%	-
Dividends per share	-	89.351%	-	-	-5.556%	12,969.75%	-	-	-65.668%	-
Net income	-10.811%	51.704%	-10.749%	7.414%	53.492%	122.963%	-7.015%	-13.541%	8.421%	6.075%

In some industries, it was not possible to calculate the GDI due to the lack of graphical representation for some variables.

It is apparent that net income, sales and turnover have a positive and negative GDI in all sectors of activity. However, on average, the trend is positive, which means that companies tend to exaggerate the values reflected in the graphics.

As mentioned previously, the item sales and turnover has a strong influence on the stakeholder's decision, such as net income, so it is easy to associate the trend of negative and positive GDI, determined by the need to show a more favorable economic image for the company.

The highest GDI average is located in dividends per share for the Telecommunications, Utilities and Oil and Gas industries. These results are justified by the need these industries have to show more favorable results and returns to shareholders regarding their investments.

Table 8 presents the descriptive analysis of both the dependent variable and the independent variables. It can be verified that the GDI varies from -2.13 to 55.44, with a positive mean value. This result indicates that companies seek, through graphic representation, to give a more favorable image of their performance. Companies' profitability varies from -2.24 to 1.41, and companies' indebtedness varies from 0.03 to 5.36, with a mean value of 0.83. It can also be verified that 75.5% of the companies in the sample are not audited by the Big-Four, that is, most of the companies in the sample.

As for the type of industry, it is concluded that the Manufacturing sector is the most represented, comprising 27.8% of the companies in the sample, followed by Services, 13.9% of the companies in the sample. However, it is also verified that the less represented is the Oil and Gas industry with 2.8% of the companies in the sample.

Table 9 shows the correlation matrix between the dependent variables (IDG) and the independent variables.

The results show that there is no statistically significant positive correlation or negative correlation between the dependent variable and the independent variables. Therefore, all the hypotheses formulated (H1, H2, H3, H4, and H5) may not be supported. It is also verified that the independent variables present low levels of correlation among themselves, which may indicate that potential problems of multicollinearity are minimal.

Table 8. Descriptive analysis

	N	Minimum	Maximum	Mean	Standard Deviation
Dependent variable					
GDI	216	-2.13	55.44	1.26	6.37
Independent variables					
Dimension (T Assets)	216	725.06	42,873,017.00	4,335,622.67	7,980,470.71
Indebtedness	216	0.03	5.36	0.83	0.64
Profitability (ROA)	216	-2.24	1.41	0.00	0.20

		N	Percentage
Independent variables			
Auditor type	Big4	53	24.5%
	NBig4	163	75.5%
Sector	Basic Materials	24	11.1%
	Industrial	60	27.8%
	Consumer goods	18	8.3%
	Services	30	13.9%
	Telecommunications	12	5.6%
	Utilities	18	8.3%
	Financial sector	12	5.6%
	Technology	24	11.1%
	Oil and Gas	6	2.8%
	Health care	12	5.6%

Table 9. Matrix of correlations

	GDI	Dimension	Indebtedness	Profitability	Auditor type	Industry
GDI	1					
Dimension	-.015	1				
Indebtedness	-.012	-.075	1			
Profitability	.040	.070	-,158*	1		
Auditor type	-.055	.044	-,336**	,221**	1	
Industry	.012	,150*	-.084	-.038	-,179**	1

**. Significant correlation at a level of 0,01 (bilateral).
*. Significant correlation at a level of 0,05 (bilateral).

Regression Analysis

We have used an OLS regression analysis to test our hypothesis. The Kolmogorov-Smirnov (K-S) and Shapiro-Wilk tests were performed to analyze whether independent variables and dependent variables follow a normal distribution. Non-compliance with the normality of distribution has serious consequences on the conclusions drawn from these variables, especially when studied from the regression model. Thus, it was necessary to perform a normalization procedure of the continuous variables through the Blom transformation.

The assumptions of the model were verified with regard to autocorrelation, multicollinearity, heteroscedasticity, normal distribution of residues, and outliers. After the elimination of several outliers, we computed a new dependent variable GDI1 that was also normalized through the Blom transformation. The existence of multicollinearity was tested by calculating Value Inflated Factors (VIF). The VIF values are less than 10 indicating that there are no multicollinearity problems. The homogeneity of the residual variances was tested by a White's heteroskedasticity test. The normality of the residuals was tested through the Kolmogorov-Smirnov test (with Lillefors correlation). The autocorrelation levels were tested using the Durbin-Watson statistic.

The results obtained from the regression for each of the dependent variables (IDG and IDG1) are shown in Table 10.

In both models, none of the regression models were statistically significant. Furthermore, the adjusted R^2 is low - 0.001 and 0.035, respectively, for the model in which the dependent variable is GDI and where the dependent variable is GDI1 - which shows that the explanatory power of the independent variables in the variation of the discrepancy index does not allow conclusions to be drawn. Despite the different variation discussed in the descriptive analysis section, it seems that companies do not have specific incentives to manipulate graphics representation. Moreover, potential discrepancies found can be explained from an IM perspective. potentially these discrepancies are performed to present the true picture of the financial performance of the company, however in a more favorable way.

CONCLUSION

The present study focused on IM practices through graphic representation, used in the annual reports and accounts of a sample of 36 Portuguese listed companies on the Lisbon stock exchange.

Table 10. Results of the regression model

Variables	IDG			IDG1		
	Coefficients	Sig.	VIF	Coeficients	Sig.	VIF
(Constant)	0.429	0.104		0.348	0.227	
Dimension (T Assets)	-0.067	0.504	2.153	-0.148	0.262	2.675
Indebtedness	0.011	0.897	1.511	0.105	0.321	1.459
Profitability (ROA)	-0.038	0.650	1.512	-0.012	0.908	1.456
Auditor Type	-0.018	0.929	1.682	-0.003	0.989	1.798
Basic Material	-0.170	0.517	1.501	-0.112	0.712	1.391
Consumer goods	-0.346	0.212	1.281	-0.304	0.302	1.383
services	-0.296	0.206	1.432	-0.460	0.081	1.473
Telecommunications	-0.021	0.952	1.342	0.620	0.246	1.164
Utilities	-0.187	0.536	1.538	0.047	0.889	1.548
Financial	-0.574	0.086	1.278	-0.589	0.143	1.279
Technology	0.020	0.948	2.079	-0.281	0.416	2.562
Oil and Gas	-0.464	0.302	1.195	-0.438	0.340	1.273
Health care	-0.697	0.033	1.213	-1.061	0.012	1.240
Year 2011	-0.239	0.314	1.719	-0.015	0.954	1.706
Year 2012	-0.155	0.513	1.716	-0.052	0.845	1.759
Year 2013	-0.404	0.086	1.673	-0.282	0.281	1.713
Year 2014	-0.446	0.060	1.705	-0.440	0.097	1.701
Year 2015	-0.119	0.612	1.686	0.103	0.702	1.663
Adjusting the model:						
R^2	0.084				0.140	
R^2 adjusted	0.001				0.035	
F	1.007	0.454			1.331	0.177
Durbin-Watson	1.891				1.849	

It was concluded that Portuguese listed companies have relevant GDI. In general, these indices have allowed us to infer that manipulation is used to present financial information in a way that the company's performance seems more favorable. It should be noted that the period of analysis coincides with a period of crisis in which the performance of companies tended to decrease, and to that extent, the results obtained regarding the practice of MI were as expected.

Although IM practices were identified, it was not possible to identify the determinants of such practices, since all regression models were not statistically significant. The results of the regression model show that none of the independent variables has an influence on the GDI. In other words, the distortions in graphics contained in the management reports are not influenced by profitability, indebtedness, size, type of auditor or industry.

However, the inconclusive results of this work should take into account the limitations of the empirical analysis. Firstly, the size of the sample may not be representative, since several listed companies have been excluded due to lack of information, making the sample smaller. In addition, the study only contemplates a time frame of 6 years.

This study contributes to the increase of existing literature on the subject, alerting users of financial information to the existence of IM strategies that can lead stakeholders to have misperceptions and, ultimately, make decisions which could be different if there was no IM practice.

However, considering the several limitations identified, it would be interesting to develop other studies in which it would be possible to analyze other independent variables, other companies, over a larger period of time. It would still be interesting to make a comparison among other countries, as well as the reasons that determine the distortion of the information represented graphically.

It is still important to carry out future research, in order to elucidate the implementation of requirements regarding graphic construction, to assure that companies convey a reliable image of their financial information.

REFERENCES

Bastardo, A. (2015). *Graph Usage in Financial Reports: Evidence from Portuguese Listed Companies*. Dissertação de mestrado.

Beattie, V., & Jones, M. J. (1992). The use and abuse of graphs in annual reports: A theoretical framework and an empirical study. *Accounting and Business Research*, *22*(88), 291–303. doi:10.1080/00014788.1992.9729446

Beattie, V., & Jones, M. J. (1997). *A Comparative Study of the Use of Financial Graphs in the Corporate Annual Reports of Major U. S. and U. K. Companies*. Academic Press.

Beattie, V., & Jones, M. J. (1999). Australian Financial Graphs: An Empirical Study. *Abacus*, *35*(1), 46–76. doi:10.1111/1467-6281.00034

Beattie, V., & Jones, M. J. (2001). A six-country comparison of the use of graphs in annual reports. *The International Journal of Accounting*, *36*(2), 195–222. doi:10.1016/S0020-7063(01)00094-2

Beattie, V., & Jones, M. J. (2002). Measurement distortion of graphs in corporate reports: An experimental study. *Accounting, Auditing & Accountability Journal*, *15*(4), 546–564. doi:10.1108/09513570210440595

Beattie, V., & Jones, M. J. (2008). Corporate Reporting Using Graphs: A Review and Synthesis. *Jal*, *27*(June), 71–110.

Beattie, V. A., & Jones, M. J. (2000a). Changing Graph Use in Corporate Annual Reports: A Time-Series Analysis. *Contemporary Accounting Research*, *17*(2), 213–226. doi:10.1506/AAT8-3CGL-3J94-PH4F

Beattie, V. A., & Jones, M. J. (2000b). Impression management: The case of inter-country financial graphs. *Journal of International Accounting, Auditing & Taxation*, *9*(2), 159–183. doi:10.1016/S1061-9518(00)00030-6

Borges, M. F. (2011). *Impression Management e Desempenho Organizacional : o caso Português (Dissertação de mestrado)*. Instituto Superior de Contabilidade e Administração- Universidade de Aveiro.

Carter, M. S., & Dukerich, J. M. (1998). Corporate Responses to Changes in Reputation. *Corporate Reputation Review*, *1*(3), 250–270. doi:10.1057/palgrave.crr.1540047

Chalmers, K., & Godfrey, J. M. (2004). Reputation costs : The impetus for voluntary derivative financial instrument reporting. *Accounting, Organizations and Society*, *29*(2), 95–125. doi:10.1016/S0361-3682(02)00034-X

Cho, C. H., Michelon, G., & Patten, D. M. (2012a). Enhancement and obfuscation through the use of graphs in sustainability reports: Na international comparison. Sustainability Accounting. *Management and Policy Journal*, *3*(1), 74–88.

Cho, C. H., Michelon, G., & Patten, D. M. (2012b). Impression management in sustainability reports: An empirical investigation of the use of graphs. *Accounting and the Public Interest*, *12*(1), 16–37. doi:10.2308/apin-10249

Deegan, C. (2002). Introduction: The legitimising effect of social and environmental disclosures – a theoretical foundation. *Accounting, Auditing & Accountability Journal*, *15*(3), 282–311. doi:10.1108/09513570210435852

El-gazzar, S. M., Finn, P. M., & Jacob, R. (1999). *An Empirical Investigation of Multinational Firms â€TM Compliance with International Accounting Standards*. Academic Press.

Falschlunger, L. M., Eisl, C., Losbichler, H., & Greil, A. M. (2015). Impression management in annual reports of the largest European companies: A longitudinal study on graphical representations. *Journal of Applied Accounting Research*, *16*(3), 383–399. doi:10.1108/JAAR-10-2014-0109

Frownfelter-Lohrke, C., & Fulkerson, C. L. (2001). The Incidence and Quality of Graphics in Annual Reports: An International Comparison. *Journal of Business Communication*, *38*(3), 337–357. doi:10.1177/002194360103800308

Hill, W. Y., & Milner, M. (2003). Guidelines for graphical displays in financial reporting. *Accounting Education*, *12*(2), 135–157. doi:10.1080/0963928032000091747

Hooghiemstra, R. (2000). Corporate communication and impression management–new perspectives why companies engage in corporate social reporting. *Journal of Business Ethics*, *28*(1/2), 55–68. doi:10.1023/A:1006400707757

Jensen, M. C., & Meckling, W. H. (1976). Theory of the Firm : Managerial Behavior, Agency Costs and Ownership Structure. *Journal of Financial Economics*, *3*(4), 305–360. doi:10.1016/0304-405X(76)90026-X

Jones, M., & Shoemaker, P. (1994). Accounting Narratives: A Review of Empirical Studies of Content and Readability. *Journal of Accounting Literature, 13*.

Jones, M. J. (2011). The nature, use and impression management of graphs in social and environmental accounting. *Accounting Forum*, *35*(2), 75–89. doi:10.1016/j.accfor.2011.03.002

Leary, M. R., & Kowalski, R. M. (1990). Impression management: A literature review and two-component model. *Psychological Bulletin*, *107*(I), 34–47. doi:10.1037/0033-2909.107.1.34

Mather, D., Mather, P., & Ramsay, A. (2005). An investigation into the measurement of graph distortion in financial reports. *Accounting and Business Research*, *35*(2), 147–159. doi:10.1080/00014788.2005.9729670

Mather, P., Ramsay, A., & Serry, A. (1996). The use and representational faithfulness of graphs in annual reports: Australian Evidence. *Australian Accounting Review*, *6*(2).

Mather, P., Ramsay, A., & Steen, A. (2000). The use and representational faithfulness of graphs in Australian IPO prospectuses. *Accounting, Auditing & Accountability Journal*, *13*(1), 65–83. doi:10.1108/09513570010316144

Merkl-Davies, D. M., & Brennan, N. M. (2007). Discretionary disclosure strategies in corporate narratives : Incremental information or impression management? *Journal of Accounting Literature*, *26*, 116–196. Retrieved from http://hdl.handle.net/10197/2907

Morris, R. D. (1987). Signaling, Agency Theory and Accounting Policy Choice. *Accounting and Business Research*, *18*(69), 47–56. doi:10.1080/00014788.1987.9729347

Murphy, A. B. (1999). Firm Characteristics of Swiss Companies that Utilize International Accounting Standards. *The International Journal of Accounting*, *34*(1), 121–131. doi:10.1016/S0020-7063(99)80006-5

Niamh, B., Encarna, G.-S., & Aileen, P. (2009). Impression management: Developing and illustrating a scheme of analysis for narrative disclosures- a methodological note. *Accounting, Auditing & Accountability Journal*, *22*(5), 789–832. doi:10.1108/09513570910966379

Pennington, R., & Tuttle, B. (2009). Managing impressions using distorted graphs of income and earnings per share: The role of memory. *International Journal of Accounting Information Systems*, *10*(1), 25–45. doi:10.1016/j.accinf.2008.10.001

Penrose, J. M. (2008). Annual Report Graphic Use A Review of the Literature. *Journal of Business Communication*, *45*(2), 158–180. doi:10.1177/0021943607313990

Penteado, I. A. de M. (2013). *Gerenciamento de impressão em relatórios de sustentabilidade no Brasil: Uma análise do uso de gráficos (Programa de pós-graduação)*. Faculdade de Economia, Administração e Contabilidade de Ribeirão Preto-Universidade de São Paulo.

Plumlee, R. D. (2002). Impression Management with Graphs: Effects on Choices. *Journal of Information Systems*, *16*(2), 183–202. doi:10.2308/jis.2002.16.2.203

Rahman, S. (2012). Impression Management Motivations, Strategies and Disclosure Credibility of Corporate Narratives. *Journal of Management Research*, *4*(3), 1–14. doi:10.5296/jmr.v4i3.1576

Ross, S. A. (1977). The Determination of Financial Structure: The Incentive-Signaling Approach. *The Bell Journal of Economics*, *8*(1), 23–40. doi:10.2307/3003485

Schlenker, B. R. (1980). *Impression Management: The Self-concept, Social Identity, and Interpersonal Relations*. B. P. Company.

Schrand, C. M., & Walther, B. R. (2000). Strategic Benchmarks in Earnings Announcements: The Selective Disclosure of Prior-Period Earnings Components. *The Accounting Review*, *75*(2), 151–177. doi:10.2308/accr.2000.75.2.151

Steinbart, P. J. (1989). The Auditor's Responsibility for the Accuracy of Graphs in Annual Reports: Some Evidence of the Need for Additional Guidance. *Accounting Horizons*, *3*(3), 60–70.

Tufte, E. R. (1983). *The Visual Display of Quantitative Information*. C. G. Press.

Uyar, A. (2009). An analysis of graphic disclosure in annual reports: The case of Turkey. *Managerial Auditing Journal*, *24*(5), 423–444. doi:10.1108/02686900910956793

Wallace, R. S. O., Mora, A., & Naser, K. (1994). The relationship between the comprehensiveness of corporate annual reports and firm characteristics in Spain. *Accounting and Business Research*, *25*(97), 41–53. doi:10.1080/00014788.1994.9729927

Watts, R. L., & Zimmerman, J. L. (1978). Towards a Positive Theory of the Determination of Accounting Standards. *The Accounting Review*, *53*(1), 112–134.

Zarzeski, T. (1996). Spontaneous Harmonization Effects of Culture and Market Forces on Accounting Disclosures Practices. *Accounting Horizons*, *10*, 18–37.

KEY TERMS AND DEFINITIONS

Accounting Information: Information on accounting nature produced and disseminated by public or private entities.

Comprehensibility: The quality of comprehensible language or thought.

Impression Management: A process whereby someone tries to influence the observations and opinions of others about something. In a typical impression management process within a business, a manager might attempt to regulate and control information in their interactions with staff or the general public to give them the most favorable impression about their company and its objectives.

Reporting: Activity related to the practice of the report.

Stakeholders: Institutions or persons affected by reform.

Chapter 12
Convergence of Accounting Standards to International Standards and Earnings Management in Brazilian Companies

Caio Eduardo Silva Mulatinho
Federal Rural University of Pernambuco, Brazil

Laura Araújo Leal
Group Moura, Brazil

Dimmitre Morant Vieira Gonçalves Pereira
Federal University of Paraíba, Brazil

Marcleide Maria Macêdo Pederneiras
Federal University of Paraíba, Brazil

José Augusto de Medeiros Monteiro
Federal University of Alagoas, Brazil

Marcelo Victor José de Barros Ribeiro
Federal University of Pernambuco, Brazil

Rodrigo G. Amaro
Federal Rural University of Pernambuco, Brazil

ABSTRACT

This chapter sought to highlight the main challenges of the initial adoption of accounting standards converged to international standards applied to public companies and treasury-dependent companies and how the results of economic agents in public and private companies in Brazil are managed. Relevant legislation, norms, pronouncements, interpretations, and guidelines of competent bodies were analyzed through bibliographical and documentary research. The results demonstrated that between the two processes of accounting convergence to which such entities must submit, there are conflicts of terms and technical accounting procedures to assist these entities to the process of accounting convergence. Regarding earnings management, it was found that there is an earnings management in both sectors; however, the public sector reaches a high number of citizens, while the private sector is limited to stakeholders; however, both sectors, in some cases, multiplicity of components of the public sector, resembles the private sector.

DOI: 10.4018/978-1-5225-7817-8.ch012

INTRODUCTION

International accounting standards aim to standardize accounting practices, providing a universal business language that can serve as a basis for negotiations between markets (Navaes, 2010).

The process of convergence to the international accounting standards that have occurred in Brazil, both in the scope of corporate accounting, headed by the Accounting Pronouncements Committee (CPC), following the International Financial Reporting Standard (IFRS) and International Financial Reporting Interpretations (IFRICs) of the International Accounting Standards Board (IASB), and in the scope of public accounting, directed in Brazil by the National Treasury Secretariat (STN), observing the standards issued by the International Federation of Accountants (IFAC), had to adopt the new accounting and public accounting standards.

The deadline for the adoption of corporate accounting standards converging to the international standard for corporations, companies regulated by the Central Bank (BACEN) or the Superintendency of Private Insurance (SUSEP) and large companies, in 2010, according to Federal Accounting Council (CFC) Resolutions 1.255/09 and Brazilian Securities Commission (CVM) n. 457/07 and n. 485/10.

The deadline for the convergence of public accounting was set forth in Administrative Ordinance STN n. 634 of November 2013, and the Public Sector Accounting Plan (PCASP) and the Accounting Statements Applied to the Public Sector (DCASP) in accordance with the Manual of Applied Accounting to the Public Sector (MCASP) were adopted by all entities of the Federation until the end of 2014.

The need for convergence of international accounting standards for Santos, Cia and Cia (2011), arose from divergences found in the accounting results of companies, due to the lack of a single set of accounting standards, which was used by all countries, making it possible for the various companies to increase transparency, comparability and comprehensibility of the financial statements. The conflicting results in different markets made it difficult to exchange information (Suetugui & Cia, 2011).

The results presented by accounting in the financial statements of companies in different markets are important for economic agents and those interested in the financial situation of companies. With these results evidenced in the statements, market decisions are influenced (Trapp, 2009) and these data can be altered, intentionally, by the economic agents aiming at particular motivation, which Martinez (2001) called earnings management.

Earnings management happens when managers decide to change the financial statements to influence any of the parties involved in the company's performance (Bar-Yosef; Prencipe, 2009). The practice of this management for Paulo (2007) does not constitute fraud, as long as they use the power of judgment based on the legal limits.

Therefore, with the convergence of Brazilian accounting to international standards, where the main feature is the primacy of essence over form, the possibility of judgment becomes more evident (Baptista, 2009), that is, with the greatest discretion, the professional will be more likely to apply the techniques earnings management (Marra, Mazzola, & Prencipe, 2011).

Considering the divergence of deadlines and requirements between the referred accounting processes of convergence that apply jointly to public companies and public companies dependent on public treasury and the effects of this convergence in the earnings management, the present study proposes to answer the following problem: What are the main challenges of the initial adoption of accounting standards converged to international standards applied to public companies and treasury-dependent companies and how is the earnings management practiced by economic agents in public and private companies in Brazil?

ACCOUNTING CONVERGENCE

With the intensification of operations in global level after the second World War, due to regulatory differences in accounting between countries, companies now have the need to reconcile the different accounting information elaborated in the different countries where they operate with the accounting standards adopted by the headquarters of the controlling company (Schroede, Clark, & Cathey, 2005).

Due to this difficulty, according to Niyama (2005) studies began in this same period, around 1950 and 1960, to approach the international accounting, being from 1962 that the publications of research on international accounting harmonization began (Baker & Barabu, 2007). According to Baker and Barabu (2007), this process of harmonization was driven by the need to institutionalize accounting practices organized for the rise of capitalism and the current hegemony of global capital.

Faced with this need internationally converged standards, not only the accounting for private companies went through this process, but also accounting applied to the public sector, because, according to Vicente, Morais and Platt Neto (2012), although originated with a focus on the private sector, the movement of accounting convergence extended to the sector with a view to comparability and improvement in public accounting disclosure, common needs of both sectors.

CONVERGENCE OF ACCOUNTING APPLIED TO THE PRIVATE SECTOR

In order to promote a convergence of accounting standards at the international level, the International Accounting Standards Committee (IASC) was created in 1973, but progress towards a convergence of accounting standards was still slow, until in 1989 the IASC released the Framework for the Preparation and Presentation of Financial Statements, fortifying the process and increasing the interest on the theme (Baker & Barabu, 2007).

Promoting this process, in 2001 the IASC created the International Accounting Standards Board (IASB), which assumed the functions previously assigned to the IASC (Zeff, 2012). One year after this event, the European Commission determined through EC Regulation n. 1.606/02 that companies operating in European capital markets began to disclose their consolidated financial statements in accordance with international standards issued by the IASB from 2005.

The International Financial Reporting Standard (IFRS) has a committee inherited from the IASC responsible for issuing interpretations, the International Financial Reporting Interpretations Committee (IFRIC).

In the United States, the Securities and Exchange Commission (SEC) has permitted foreign companies operating on US stock exchanges to prepare their statements under IFRS since 2007, while continue to follow US GAAP (Generally Accepted Accounting Principles States) standards issued by the Financial Accounting Standards Board (FASB). (SEC, 2007).

In Brazil, this process of convergence culminated in the promulgation of Law n. 11.638/07, which established that the rules issued by the CVM should be in line with international accounting standards, and legitimized the Accounting Pronouncements Committee (CPC) as the entity responsible for the process in the country.

Currently, the CPC has 48 pronouncements, issued and approved by the CFC and the CVM. These pronouncements, interpretations and guidelines, except for PMEs, are mandatory since 2010, not only for publicly traded companies and for companies regulated by BACEN or SUSEP, but also for large companies, since Law 11.638 / 07 extended the applicability of Law 6.404/76 to companies that have a total asset in excess of R $ 240 million or gross annual revenue exceeding R$ 300 million.

The PMEs should comply with the technical pronouncement CPC PME, issued based on the IFRS for Small and Medium Entities (SME), which was transformed into the technical standard NBC TG 1.000 through Resolution CFC n.1.255/09, coming into force from the year 2010 on. However, recognizing the difficulty for small and medium-sized enterprises to fully adopt the provisions of NBC TG 1.000, the CFC issued the technical communicated CTG 1.000 in August 2013, providing for the full adoption of NBC TG 1.000, allowing PMEs not yet fully compliant with this norm to make full adoption from the years beginning in January 1, 2013.

CONVERGENCE OF ACCOUNTING APPLIED TO THE PUBLIC SECTOR

Accounting applied to the public sector, as well as in the private sector, underwent a broad process of convergence, which brought about changes in its conceptual framework. This process was formalized in November 2008, when the Federal Accounting Council (CFC) published the 11 (eleven) Brazilian Accounting Standards Applied to the Public Sector (NBCASP), aligning its conceptual framework with good international accounting practices. In addition, the 31 (thirty-one) International Public Sector Accounting Standards (IPSAS) were translated into Portuguese, serving as a subsidy for the construction of a new conceptual model of public accounting.

Also in this context, the National Treasury Secretariat (STN), as the maximum organ of the process of public accounting convergence, authorized by item I of art. 6 of Decree n.6.976, of October 7, 2009, and in item I of art. 17 of Law n.10.180 of February 6, 2001, issued Ordinance n. 109 of February 21, 2011 on the Technical Group for Standardization of Accounting Procedures (GTCON), responsible for the analysis of international regulations for convergence to the Brazilian reality. The products of this group's work were materialized in the publication of the Manual of Applied Accounting for the Public Sector (MCASP), which addresses, among other matters, the mandatory deadlines for adoption of new accounting practices, which is updated annually.

Since the duration of Law 4.320/64, which deals with the general standards of financial law for the preparation and control of budgets and balance sheets of public administration, public accounting had never undergone an update of its concepts and norms. In its Accounting Manuals Applied to the Public Sector (II Part), the National Treasury Secretariat highlights the new moment that government accounting is going through:

The arrival of the new millennium has led to the implementation of new actions for the modernization and austerity of accounting and public finance, highlighting two major milestones: the promulgation of the Fiscal Responsibility Law-LRF and the convergence of the public sector to international standards applied to the public sector.

This process of convergence of the Brazilian norms of public accounting to the international standards raises several issues to be overcome, such as the emergence of problems of interpretation, language and accounting terminology (Zeff, 2007). The challenges of convergence have been set, and it is up to researchers, students, and public accounting professionals to seek alternatives for Brazilian accounting to fully converge to good international accounting practices.

THE EARNINGS MANAGEMENT

Some international papers have been published on earnings management, especially in the last decades (Jones (1991), Dechow, Sloan, Sweeney (1995), Leuz, Nanda, Wysocki (2003), Kothari, Leone, Wasley (2005), Tendeloo and Vanstraelen (2005), Jeanjean and Stolow (2005), Zéghal, Chtourou, Sellami (2011), Leventis, Dimitropoulos, Anandarajan (2011), Aubert, Grudnitski (2012), Iatridis (2012); Tsipouridou, Spathis (2012).

In Brazil, studies have also been published, for example: Matsumoto and Parreira (2007); Silva (2010); Klann (2011); Rezende and Nakao (2012); Grecco (2013); Martinez (2013); Costa and Gartner (2015); Favoretto, Corrêa, Grecco (2017).

In these national and international studies it is identified that the earnings management can be limited through accounting standardization and in particular by the regulatory bodies of the capital markets, with the aim of guaranteeing the quality and comparability of information, transparency and disclosure of the equity position and performance, however, the process of managing earnings from the adoption of IFRS is not yet conclusive and research needs to be deepened, especially in Brazilian literature (Martinez, 2013).

Martinez (2013), further states that the practice of earnings management is due to the change in accounting results by economic agents with the objective of obtaining particular benefits.

Thus, the earnings management can be understood as a deliberate intervention in the financial statements, with the purpose of acquiring private gains (Schipper, 1989). That is, there is the judgment of administrative managers in financial information and in the operational activities with the intention to change them, overvaluing the information of the economic performance of the companies for some users (Healy & Wahlen, 1999).

Matsumoto and Parreira (2007), on the earnings management, adds that this practice influences the transparency of the information contained in the financial statements, modifying the reality of the company and this can impact the confidence, safety and solidity of users, as well as in decisions published by companies.

The earnings management, in the cases presented by Enron and Worldcom, which led to bankruptcy companies, is seen as detrimental, on the other hand, some authors believe that management can bring benefits as it can improve the value of information through disclosure shareholders and the public.

In this sense, Grecco (2013) asserts that the earnings management can be restricted from the accounting standards, with the purpose of assuring the quality and acomparability of the information, emphasizing that even though changes in accounting standards, improvements in quality accounting information are preserved, greatly reducing the manipulation of results.

MOTIVATIONAL FACTORS IN THE EARNINGS MANAGEMENT FROM THE ACCOUNTING INFORMATION

The results manipulation studies according to Costa and Gartner (2015) from the accounting information include motivational factors that stimulate this practice in both the public and private sectors.

The Table 1 shows the applicability of the reasons for manipulating information in the public sector.

In some cases, the public manager tends to manipulate the results in order to prevent or minimize the publication of unsatisfactory performance. For this, one should avoid disclosing accounting losses (item 1 of table 1), as well as adjusting results to the forecasts of financial analysts (item 4 of Table 1).

Table 1. Reasons for manipulating accounting information in the private sector and applicability to the public sector

Reasons to manipulate accounting information in the private sector	Applicability to the public sector
1.Avoid disclosure of accounting losses.	Fully
2.Minimize volatility of results over time.	Applicable to state-owned enterprises
3.Response based on performance, including stock options.	Applicable to state-owned enterprises
4.Adjust results to forecasts of financial analysts.	Fully
5.Loading securities on the capital Market.	Fully

Source: Costa and Gartner. (2015, p. 145).

When the manager aims to minimize the volatility of results over time (item 2 of table 1), and performance-based compensation, including stock options (item 3 of the table), the "public managers of direct management, local authorities and public foundations have remuneration tied to the constitutional ceiling, which makes it impossible to identify these motives "(Costa & Gartner, p.145,2015). This fact, it is evident that the manager is attached to the constitutional ceiling and that the Brazilian public service has no connection with the meritocracy, which evidences the inexistence of parameters of quality. The quantitative objectives in the public service overlap with the qualitative ones that base the said meritocracy.

When it comes to item 4 of Table 1, there is an obligation for the public sector to obtain fiscal fiscal targets set in the budget legislation, with Complementary Law n.101/2000, which determines that the Budgetary Guidelines Law (LDO) should annually contain the Fiscal Targets Annex (MFA) with the following elements: Revenues, Expenses, Primary Result, Nominal Result and Consolidated Debt. These goals guide the budget for the next three years. (Costa & Gartner, 2015, p.145).

In item 5 of Table 1, the public sector seeks to raise funds in the capital market according to the issuance of securities. Therefore, to ensure investor reliability, the public sector must demonstrate balance and fiscal strength. (Costa & Gartner, 2015, p.145). That is to say, the manager must demonstrate to the investor an organizational capacity in the financial system that shows all security effectiveness in relation to foreign and national investors, so you can get funding for the various operational activities of development.

When referring to the motives for common practice of manipulating information in the private sector, according to Paulo (2007, p. 68), there are three categories (shown in Table 2).

Table 2. Categories of manipulation of accounting information

Categories
1-Management of accounting results through accruals
2-Manipulation of the operational activities of the company
3- Classificatory manipulation of the elements of the financial statements

Source: Based on Paulo. (2007, p.59-60).

According to Costa and Gartner (2015, p.146), when referring to item 1 of table 2, earnings management happens when managers "use their judgment about accounting choices, in particular, about accruals to change the accounting reports with the purpose of modifying the performance evaluation and influencing the contractual relations of the company."

With regard to item 2 of the table 2, regarding the manipulation of the operational activities, it can be affirmed that the presence of the manipulation exists in function of the changes that may happen to be practiced with the objective of achieving significant results in the accounting information.

Regarding the classification manipulation of the elements of the statements (item 3 of Table 2), the author states that this "reclassification of the elements contained in the financial statements has an impact on the measurement of the components of assets, liabilities, shareholders' equity, income and expenses and, the liquidity, indebtedness, profitability and leverage of the company."(Costa & Gartner, 2015, p.146).

From the foregoing, it is evidenced that the existing constraints and delimitations, rigidly present in the legislations required by the management order, coupled with Brazilian constitutionality, causes a constant manipulation in the performance, forecasts and results presented in the publications of the financial statements.

There is no doubt that malleability, coupled with the volatility of a regime of secular foundations of a patrimonialism of non-meritocratic domination, is the facilitator so that performance may be the result of the commitment factor of the managers involved in every process.

METHOD OF RESEARCH

In order to answer the main challenges of the initial adoption of converged accounting standards, the international standards applied to public companies and treasury-dependent companies were analyzed, the relevant legislation, standards, pronouncements, interpretations and guidelines of the Accounting Pronouncements Committee (CPC), standards, interpretations and technical announcements of the Federal Accounting Council (CFC), standards and interpretations of the International Accounting Standards Board (IASB), the International Public Sector Accounting Standards (IPSAS), the Public Sector Accounting Manuals (MCASP) of the National Treasury Secretariat (STN) and the Brazilian Accounting Standards Applied to the Public Sector (NBCASP) of the Federal Accounting Council (CFC), Brazilian Accounting Standards (NBC) T 16.1 to 16.11.

Then, to identify and how the earnings management practiced by economic agents in public and private companies in Brazil, national and international articles published on the topic earnings management were mapped and analyzed. Firstly, a review of the literature on the main international studies on the topic was carried out. Then, a selection of thesis and dissertations on the subject was made in Brazil, which formed the basis for analysis, allowing the proposed objective to be achieved. Thus, considering the incipient number of empirical researches carried out, this study has an exploratory character, since it aims to examine a not much studied subject (Sampierre, 2006).

In this sense, the present research is characterized as bibliographical and documentary, based on elaborated materials, such as books and scientific articles, thus falling within the definition of bibliographic research as well as materials that have not yet received analytical treatment, thus characterizing itself as a documentary research.

ANALYSIS OF CHALLENGES OF THE INITIAL ADOPTION OF THE ACCOUNTING STANDARDS CONVERGED TO THE INTERNATIONAL STANDARDS BY PUBLIC UNDERTAKINGS AND SUBSIDIARY UNDERTAKINGS TREASURE

It can be seen from Law 4.320/64, that the field of application of Public Accounting comprehend the bodies of the Direct Administration and indirect administration entities, thus encompassing public companies and publicly-owned companies dependent on the public treasury. Supplementary Law nº. 101, May 4, 2000, which defines such treasury-dependent corporations as controlled companies that receive from a controlling entity, financial resources for the payment of personnel or general or capital expenses, last case, those arising from an increase in shareholding.

Ordinance n. 589 of the National Treasury Secretariat, in its art. 2, item II, reinforces the concept of state-owned companies:

II - dependent state enterprise: a company controlled by the Federal Government, the State, the Federal District or the Municipality, which has received financial resources from its controller in the preceding fiscal year, intended to pay personnel, general or capital expenses, excluding, in the latter case, those arising from an increase in equity interest and, in the current fiscal year, have budgetary authorization to receive financial resources with the same purpose.

Accordingly, companies that fall within the scope of accounting applied to the public sector must follow the guidelines for the Public Sector, including the use of the Plan of Accounts Applied to the Public Sector (new chart of accounts) and the elaboration of the new statements.

However, due to their legal nature, dependent state companies must also comply with the dictates of corporate accounting legislation.

Aligning the concepts of both public and private accounting, raises discussions about the difficulties highlighted in both convergence processes. While corporate accounting regulations conflict with the fiscal obligations acquired by public entities, the legislation applicable to the public sector is faced with budget concepts, which are often confused with accounting concepts applied to the public sector.

In addition, there are accounting procedures that the corporate legislation prohibits and that the norms of the public sector allow. An example is the reassessment, which, while corporate accounting legislation prohibits, public accounting allows such a procedure, as can be seen in Table 3.

This conflict occurs not because the international norms of public and private accounting differ, but because of the current brazilian legislation. The IFRS, which serve as a basis for the preparation of the pronouncements, interpretations and guidelines of the Accounting Pronouncements Committee (CPC), through the International Accounting Standards (IAS) 16 - Property, Plant and Equipment, evidence the permission to adopt the revaluation procedure of movable and immovable property:

Revaluation model: After recognition as an asset, an item of property, plant and equipment whose fair value can be reliably measured will be recognized at the revalued amount, its fair value at the revaluation date less any accumulated depreciation and accumulated impairment losses subsequent years. Revaluations will be made with sufficient regularity to ensure that the book value does not differ significantly from that which would be determined using the fair value at the end of the reporting period. (IASB, 2001). (Our Griffin).

Table 3. Equity revaluation procedure in accordance with corporate law and MCASP

LAW 6.404/76	MCASP
Article 6- The balances in the revaluation reserves shall be maintained until their actual realization or reversed until the end of the fiscal year in which this Law enters into force.	Several factors may cause the carrying amount of an asset to not correspond to its fair value. Thus, if the entity adopts this method of measurement after the initial recognition of a class of fixed assets or intangible assets, it is necessary that from time to time these goods go through a process aimed at adjusting their book value. The frequency with which the revaluations are carried out depends on the changes in the fair values of the asset items that will be revalued. When the fair value of an asset materially differs from its book value, a new revaluation is required. Asset items that undergo significant changes in fair value require annual revaluation [...].

Source: Adapted from Brazil. (1976, 2012).

CPC 27 - Fixed Assets, which was used for the technical interpretation of IAS 16 as a reference for the preparation of said pronouncement, makes a permissiveness of revaluation of fixed assets:

When the revaluation method is permitted by law, an entity shall choose either the cost method of item 30 or the revaluation method of the item as its accounting policy and apply that policy to an entire class of fixed assets. (CPC, 2009) (Our Griffin).

In fact, international accounting devices allow the revaluation of movable property. However, according to the text of CPC 27 it is necessary to observe the existence or not of legislation that makes use of this procedure.

Corporate law, however, predicting that many entities have their accounting balances from undervalued or unregistered fixed assets accounts allows a similar procedure, carried out only in the initial adoption of new accounting practices converged to international standards, attributed cost, which is not characterized as revaluation, but as an initial evaluation.

According to technical pronouncement CPC 13, Initial Adoption of Law n. 11.638/07 and Provisional Measure (MP) n. 449/08 (converted into Law 11.941/09), the initial framework for the adoption of brazilian accounting standards converged to international standards is at the time of the preparation of the opening balance sheet for the adoption of said standards.

Technical pronouncement CPC 37, Initial Adoption of International Accounting Standards, requires the entity to make the following changes to its opening balance sheet:

1. Recognize all assets and liabilities recognized by IFRSs;
2. Do not recognize items as assets and liabilities if such recognition is prohibited under IFRSs;
3. Reclassify items recognized in accordance with the set of accounting policies that had been following as a type of asset, liability or equity component but which are a different type of asset, liability or equity component under IFRSs; and
4. Apply IFRSs to the measurement of all recognized assets and liabilities.

Whereas dependent companies on the public treasury, on account of their legal compliance, in addition to the obligation to comply with corporate accounting standards, must comply with the precepts from the public sector regulations, STN through Administrative Ordinance n. 634 of November 19, 2013, provides for the mandatory deadlines for adoption of the Accounts Applied to the Public Sector (PCASP) and Financial Statements Applied to the Public Sector in its articles 4 and 8 by public entities dependent on the state treasury:

Parts IV (Plan of Accounts Applied to the Public Sector - PCASP) and V (Financial Statements Applied to the Public Sector - DCASP) shall be adopted by all entities of the Federation until the end of 2014.

Art. 4 From the national consolidation and by sphere of government of the accounts of 2014, to be carried out in 2015, shall be fully observed the parts IV (Plan of Accounts Applied to the Public Sector - PCASP) and V (Financial Statements Applied to the Public Sector - DCASP) of the Manual of Accounting Applied to the Public Sector - MCASP.

Single paragraph. The National Treasury Secretariat will not give discharge to the obligation set forth in paragraph 1 of art. 51 of Complementary Law Nº 101, dated May 4, 2000, if the accounts are submitted in breach of the provisions of the caput. "

According to the deadlines stipulated by the STN, when adopting the PCASP and entities that fall within the scope of public accountability (treasury dependent), which have not yet converged to the new public accounting practices, should prepare an initial Balance Sheet in accordance with the requirements of the Accounting Procedures Instructions (IPC 00), in item 15, prepared by STN:

Accordingly, all public sector entities must prepare an initial balance sheet to reflect the new accounting practices adopted for the public sector by December 31, 2014 (referred to as the "transition date"), as a starting point for accounting for them with the new standards for the sector. (Our Griffin).

There is another great challenge experienced by public companies and treasury-dependent companies: corporate law provides that the deadline for adopting Brazilian standards converged to international standards should have been started as of 2010. The deadline for adopting the standards related to the public sector has a deadline of December 31, 2014.

Receipt of accounting information of a corporate and public nature is another bottleneck to be overcome by these companies, since the systems used by them are the same as those used by legal entities governed by public law, which primarily observe the accounting procedures applied to the public sector. The non-use of a system for the storage of corporate accounting information may result in a material information loss, making the information registered, lacking reliability, above all, leading to treasury-dependent entities, in an effort to meet corporate obligations, outside the system.

Therefore, state-owned companies and treasury-dependent companies, because they fall within the scope of the accounting applied to the public sector, and because of their legal nature, should adopt fully the norms related to public accounting and maintain accounting control based on corporate accounting standards. It is suggested that the corporate information system of the federal government may have support for the receipt of accounting information of a corporate nature, so that there is no informational loss on the part of public entities.

Table 4. Summary table of accounting convergence in Brazil

	CORPORATE ACCOUNTING	PUBLIC ACCOUNTING
INTERNATIONAL ORGAN RESPONSIBLE	IASB	IFAC
THE BRAZILIAN ORGAN RESPONSIBLE	CPC	STN
APPLICABLE LEGISLATIO	Law 6.404/76 and its amendments CFC Resolutions Applicable to the private sector	Law 4.320/76 MCASP CFC Resolutions Applicable to the Public sector
APPLICATION	Private Law Organizations	Direct public administration, Indirect public administration, including public enterprises and mixed economy companies dependent on the treasury
DEADLINE FOR ADOPTION	2010	2014
INFORMATION SYSTEM CORPORATE	Basead on accountig standards corporate converged to the standards International.	Based on accounting standards applied to the public sector.
PROCEDURE OF ASSET REVALUATION	Fenced by legislation. Allows only, at initial adoption, the valuation by the assigned cost of the fixed assets, which does not characterized as a reassessment, but rather as an initial assessment.	Permitted by legislation.

Source: Prepared by the authors. (2015).

After reviewing all the literature proposed and referenced in the article, a summary is given in Table 4 containing the main divergences between the process in accounting applied to the private sector and the public sector.

ANALYSIS OF EARNINGS MANAGEMENT PRACTICED BY ECONOMIC AGENTS IN PUBLIC AND PRIVATE COMPANIES

When it comes to private sector companies, studies by Zéghal, Chtourou and Sellami (2011), states that the adoption of international accounting standards has reduced the practice of earnings management. These studies showed that due to the adoption of IFRS, it is possible to obtain a higher level of disclosure and transparency of the accounting information, allowing monitoring of earnings management.

In the studies conducted by Jeanjean and Stolowy (2008) in companies in Australia, France and the United Kingdom, it was found that the adoption of international accounting standards promoted a significant increase in earnings management in France. When analyzing German companies Tendeloo and Vanstraelen (2005), they also showed that the adoption of IFRS allowed a better earnings management.

When it comes to earnings management in the public sector, there is a shortage in the income, unlike the private sector.

In the study conducted by Costa and Gartner (2015) in ten public sector cases where earnings management was present, it was verified that this practice is not restricted to the private sector. In the result of the research it was evidenced that there is management in four categories: real management; management of accounting choices; classification of financial statements manipulation; and image management, that is, management reflects the relations between the Executive and Legislative Branches, as well as Government-Society relations; Government-Investors. Government-Economic Sector and Government-State.

Costa and Gartner (2015) in their published work, affirm that the earning management of information in the public sector impacts a high number of users compared to the private sector, considering that this sector is limited to the company stakeholders (investors, auditors, employees, creditors and suppliers). In some cases, such as the Caixa Economica Federal and Petrobras, a multiplicity of components was identified, matching the public sector to the private sector in terms of earnings management.

The lack of reach of standardization in all situations whether public or private sector companies and the existence of economic-financial incentives leads managers to use earnings management (Matsumoto and Parreira, 2007).

FUTURE RESEARCH DIRECTIONS

For future publications, considering that there is limited research on the earning management in the Brazilian public sector, it is necessary to develop new research in this area, before reaching any conclusion, because both the causes and the consequences directly affect the stakeholders in obtain information generated in the financial statements.

CONCLUSION

Regarding the adoption of the standards, it was evidenced that the corporate accounting and that applied to the public sector went through a process of convergence of Brazilian accounting standards to international standards. Both processes adopted different procedures and deadlines for the adoption of the respective regulations.

The companies dependent on the public treasury, due to their legal nature, must comply with both laws. The analysis of the regulations made it possible to observe that there is a convergence between public and private sector considerations, such as the procedure for the revaluation of fixed assets, which should be followed by entities dependent on the treasury. However, given the Brazilian reality, such procedure is forbidden by Federal Law.

The deadlines for initial adoption of the respective accounting standards are different. The corporate law required compliance with the new accounting standards as of January 1, 2010 and the public regulations had the deadline for December 31, 2014.

In addition, the corporate information systems used by the municipal, state and federal governments are parameterized according to the public accounting standards and do not cover corporate accounting procedures, which may cause loss of reliability of the corporate accounting reports evidenced by companies and mixed-income companies dependent on the treasury.

With regard to the earnings management practiced by private sector companies pointed out in the literature, for some authors, the practice of adopting international accounting standards points to an increase in the practice of earnings management in the private sector. This practice allows a greater level of disclosure and transparency of the information contained in the financial statements, allowing greater monitoring of results, however, the earnings management in some cases may be detrimental to the company.

The earnings management in the public sector, despite the shortage of literature, for some authors, it is evident that there is the manipulation of accounting information and this can be considered as "essential" in controlling inflation and meeting targets.

Earnings management occurs in both sectors. However, the public sector reaches a large number of citizens, while the private sector is limited to stakeholders, but the two sectors, in some cases, by the multiplicity of components of the public sector, resembles the private sector.

REFERENCES

Accounting Pronouncements Committee. (2009). *Technical Pronouncement CPC 27 - Ativo Imobilizado*. Brasília: CPC.

Accounting Pronouncements Committee. *A busca da convergência aos padrões internacionais: programa de trabalho - 2008 a 2010*. Retrieved from http://www.cpc.org.br/pdf/CPCplano%20de%20converg%C3%AAncia%20_%20junho_2008.pdf

Accounting Pronouncements Committee. (2008). *Technical Pronouncement CPC 13 - Adoção Inicial da Lei nº 11.638/07 e da Medida Provisória 449/08*. Brasília: CPC. Retrieved from http://www.cpc.org.br/pdf/CPC_13.pdf

Aubert, F., & Grudnitski, G. (2012). Analysts' estimates: What they could be telling us about the impact of IFRS on earnings manipulation in Europe. *Review of Accounting and Finance*, *11*(1), 53–72. doi:10.1108/14757701211201821

Baker, C. R., & Barabu, E. M. (2007). Evolution of research on international accounting harmonization: A historical and institutional perspective. *Socio-Economic Review, Oxford*, *5*(4), 603–632. doi:10.1093er/mwm014

Baptista, E. (2009). Ganhos em Transparencia Versus Novos Instrumentos de Manipulacao: o Paradoxo das Modificacoes Trazidas pela Lei no 11.638. *RAE- Revista de Administração de Empresas, 49*, 234-239. Disponível em https://rae.fgv.br/sites/rae.fgv.br/files/artigos/10.1590_S0034-75902009000200009.pdf

Bar-Yosef, S., & Prencipe, A. (2009). *Corporate governance and earnings management in familycontrolled companies*. Disponivel em: http://papers.ssrn.com/sol3/papers.cfm?abstract_id=1367543

Brazilian Securities Commission *n. 457* of July 13, 2007. Dispõe sobre a elaboração e divulgação das demonstrações financeiras consolidadas, com base no padrão contábil internacional emitido pelo International Accounting Standards Board (IASB).

Brazilian Securities Commission *n. 485* of September 01,2010. Altera a Instrução CVM nº 457, de 13 de julho de 2007, que dispõe sobre a elaboração e divulgação das demonstrações financeiras consolidadas, com base no padrão contábil internacional emitido pelo *International Accounting Standards Board* (IASB).

Costa, G. P. C. L., & Gartner, I. R. (2015). Manipulação de informações no setor público brasileiro: Evidências em dez casos pesquisados. *Revista Contemporânea de Contabilidade*, *12*(26), 141–162. doi:10.5007/2175-8069.2015v12n26p141

Dechow, P. M., Sloan, R. G., & Sweeney, A. P. (1995). Detecting earnings management. *The Accounting Review*, *70*(2), 193–225.

Favoretto, A. B., Corrêa, F. P., Silva, F. L. & Grecco, M. C. P. (2017). O Gerenciamento de Resultados Contábeis e o Controle de Provisões. *Redeca, 4*(2), 113-125.

Federal Accounting Council. *Comunicado Técnico CTG 1.000* of August 30, 2013. Dispõe sobre a adoção plena da NBC TG 1.000.

Federal Accounting Council. *Resolutions* n.1.255 of December 10, 2009. Aprova a NBC TG 1000 – Contabilidade para Pequenas e Médias Empresas. Disponível em: http://www.crcsp.org.br/portal_novo/legislacao_contabil/resolucoes/Res1255.htm

Grecco, M. C. P. (2013). Efeito da convergência brasileira às IFRS no gerenciamento de resultados das empresas abertas brasileiras não financeiras. *Brazilian Business Review*, *10*(4), 117–140.

Healy, P. M., & Wahlen, J. M. (1999). A review of the earnings management literature and its implications for standard setting. *Accounting Horizons*, *13*(4), 365–383. doi:10.2308/acch.1999.13.4.365

Iatridis, G. (2012). Audit quality in common-law and code-law emerging markets: Evidence on earnings conservatism, agency costs and cost of equity. *Emerging Markets Review*, *13*(2), 101–117. doi:10.1016/j.ememar.2012.01.001

International Accounting Standards Board (IASB) (2001). *International Accounting Standard 16 - Property, Plant and Equipament*. London: IASB.

Jeanjean, T., & Stolowy, H. (2008). Do accounting standards matter? An exploratory analysis of earnings management before and after IFRS adoption. *Journal of Accounting and Public Policy*, *27*(6), 480–494. doi:10.1016/j.jaccpubpol.2008.09.008

Jones, J. J. (1991). Earnings management during import relief investigations. *Journal of Accounting Research*, *29*(2), 193–228.

Klann, R. C. (2011). *Gerenciamento de resultados: Análise comparativa de Empresas Brasileiras e Inglesas antes e após a adoção das IFRS*. Tese de Doutorado da Universidade Regional de Blumenau – FURB, Programa de Pós Graduação em Ciências Contábeis, Blumenau, SC, Brasil.

Kothari, S. P., Leone, A. J., & Wasley, C. E. (2005). Performance matched discretionary accrual measures. *Journal of Accounting and Economics*, *39*(1), 163–197.

Law n. 10.180 of February 6, 2001. Organiza e disciplina os Sistemas de Planejamento e de Orçamento Federal, de Administração Financeira Federal, de Contabilidade Federal e de Controle Interno do Poder Executivo Federal, e dá outras providências. Disponível em: http://www.planalto.gov.br/ccivil_03/leis/leis_2001/l10180.htm

Law n. 11.638 of December 28, 2007. Altera e revoga dispositivos da Lei nº 6.404, de 15 de dezembro de 1976, e estende às sociedades de grande porte disposições relativas à elaboração e divulgação de demonstrações financeiras. Disponível em: http://www.planalto.gov.br/ccivil_03/_ato2007-2010/2007/lei/l11638.htm

Law n. 11.941 of May 27, 2009. Altera a legislação tributária federal relativa ao parcelamento ordinário de débitos tributários; institui o regime tributário de transição [...], e dá outras providências. Disponível em: http://www.planalto.gov.br/ccivil_03/_ato2007-2010/2009/lei/l11941.htm

Law n. 4.320 of March 17, 1964. Estatui Normas Gerais de Direito Financeiro para elaboração e controle dos orçamentos e balanços da União, dos Estados, dos Municípios e do Distrito Federal. Disponível em: www.planalto.gov.br/ccivil_03/leis/l4320.htm

Law n. 6.404 of December 15, 1976. Dispõe sobre as Sociedades por Ações. Disponível em: http://www.planalto.gov.br/ccivil_03/leis/l6404consol.htm

Law Supplementary n. 101 of May 4, 2000. Estabelece normas de finanças públicas voltadas para a responsabilidade na gestão fiscal e dá outras providências.

Leuz, C., Nanda, D., & Wysocki, P. D. (2003). Earnings management and investor protection: Na international comparison. *Journal of Financial Economics*, *69*(3), 505–527. doi:10.1016/S0304-405X(03)00121-1

Leventis, S., Dimitropoulos, P. E., & Anandarajan, A. (2011). Loan loss provisions, earnings management and capital management under IFRS: The case of EU Commerial Banks. *Journal of Financial Services Research*, *40*(1), 103–122. doi:10.100710693-010-0096-1

Manual de Contabilidade Aplicada ao Setor Público (MCASP) (2013). 5ª Edição - Brasília: Secretaria do Tesouro Nacional, Subsecretaria de Contabilidade Pública. Coordenação-Geral de Normas de Contabilidade Aplicadas à Federação.

Marra, A., Mazzola, P., & Prencipe, A. (2011). Board monitoring and earnings managementpre- and post-IFRS. *The International Journal of Accounting*, *46*(2), 205–230. doi:10.1016/j.intacc.2011.04.007

Martinez, A. L. (2001). *Gerenciamento dos resultados contábeis: estudo empírico das companhias abertas brasileiras. Tese de doutoramento em Ciências Contábeis.* São Paulo: FEA-USP.

Martinez, A. L. (2013). Gerenciamento de resultados no Brasil: um survey da literatura. *BBR-Brazilian Business Review, 10*(4).

Matsumoto, A. S., & Parreira, E. M. (2007). *Uma pesquisa sobre o gerenciamento de resultados contábeis: Causas e consequências.* Contabilidade. *Gestão e Governança, 10*(1), 141–157.

Navaes, B. M. P. L. (2010). *Harmonização das Normas Contábeis pela Aderência à Lei 11.639/2007 e a MP 449/2008 em Empresas Multinacionais e do Setor Público: Um Estudo de Multiplos Casos, 2010. Dissertacao (Mestrado em Engenharia da Producao).* Universidade Federal do Rio de Janeiro.

Niyama, J. K. (2005). Contabilidade internacional. São Paulo (Ed) Atlas.

Ordinance n. 109 of February 21, 2011. Dispõe sobre a composição e o funcionamento do Grupo Técnico de Padronização de Procedimentos Contábeis – GTCON. Disponível em: http://www3.tesouro.fazenda.gov.br/legislacao/download/contabilidade/Port_STN_109_2011_GTCON.pdf

Ordinance n. 589 of Dezembro 27, 2001, STN. Estabelece conceitos, regras e procedimentos contábeis para consolidação das empresas estatais dependentes nas contas públicas e dá outras providências.

Ordinance n. 634 of November 19, 2013, STN. Dispõe sobre regras gerais acerca das diretrizes, normas e procedimentos contábeis aplicáveis aos entes da Federação, com vistas à consolidação das contas públicas da União, dos Estados, do Distrito Federal e dos Municípios, sob a mesma base conceitual. Disponível em: https://www.tesouro.fazenda.gov.br/pt/responsabilidade-fiscal/contabilidadepublica/

Paulo, E. (2007). *Manipulação das informações contábeis: uma analise teorica e empirica sobre os modelos operacionais de deteccao de gerenciamento de resultados. 2007. Tese (Doutorado em Ciencias Contabeis).* Faculdade de Economia, Administracao e Contabilidade da Universidade de Sao Paulo.

Rezende, G. P., & Nakao, S. H. (2012). Gerenciamento de resultados e a relação com o lucro tributável das empresas brasileiras de capital aberto. *Universo Contábil, 8*(1), 6–21. doi:10.4270/ruc.2012101

Sampierre, R. H., Collado, C. F., & Lucio, P. B. (2006). *Metodologia de la investigación (4th ed.).* Iztapalapa: McGraw-Hill.

Santos, E. S., Cia, J. N. S., & Cia, J. C. (2011). US GAAP x normas brasileiras: Mensuracao do impacto das diferencas de normas no lucro duplamente reportado pelas empresas brasileiras emissoras de ADRS na NYSE. *Revista de Administração Mackenzie, Sao Paulo, 12*(1), 82–111. doi:10.1590/S1678-69712011000100004

Schipper, K. (1989). Earnings management. *Accounting Horizons, 3*(4), 91–102.

Schroeder, R. G., Clark, M. W., & Cathey, J. M. (2005). *Financial accounting theory and analysis (8th ed.).* John Wiley& Sons.

Securities and Exchange Commission (SEC). (2007). Acceptance From Foreign Private Issuers of Financial Statements Prepared in Accordance With International Financial Reporting Standards Without Reconciliation to U.S. GAAP. Disponível em: http://www.sec.gov/rules/final/2008/33-8879fr.pdf

Silva, J. O. (2010). *Relação entre a remuneração variável dos gestores e o gerenciamento de resultados nas empresas de capital aberto brasileiras. 2010. Dissertacao (Mestrado em Ciencias Contabeis).* Blumenau: Universidade Regional de Blumenau – FURB.

Suetugui, E., & Cia, J. N. S. (2011). Contabilidade no setor imobiliario residencial: Um estudo exploratorio da visao dos impactos da convergencia das normas brasileiras com normas internacionais – IFRS para alguns segmentos de mercado. In *Congresso USP de Iniciacao Cientifica em Contabilidade, 11, 2011*. Sao Paulo: USP.

Tendeloo, B. V., & Vanstraelen, A. (2005). Earnings Management under German GAAP versus IFRS. *European Accounting Review*, *14*(1), 155–180. doi:10.1080/0963818042000338988

Trapp, A. C. G. (2009). *A relação do conselho fiscal como componente de controle no gerenciamento de resultados contábeis. Tese (Doutorado em Ciencias Contabeis)*. Faculdade de Economia, Administracao e Contabilidade da Universidade de Sao Paulo.

Tsipouridou, M., & Spathis, C. (2012). Earnings management and the role of auditors in na unusual IFRS context: The case of Greece. *Journal of International Accounting, Auditing & Taxation*, *21*(1), 62–78. doi:10.1016/j.intaccaudtax.2012.01.005

Vicente, E.F.R., Morais, L.M., & Platt Neto, O.A. (2012). A Reforma na Contabilidade Pública Brasileira e o Processo de Convergência: implicações e perspectivas. *RIC – Revista de Informação Contábil*, *6*(2), 1-20.

Zeff, A. S. (2012). The Evolution of the IAS Cinto the IASB, and the Challenges it Faces. *The Accounting Review*, *87*(3), 807–837.

Zéghal, D., Chtourou, S., & Sellami, Y. M. (2011). An analysis of the effect of mandatory adoption of IAS/IFRS on earnings management. *Journal of International Accounting, Auditing & Taxation*, *20*(2), 61–72. doi:10.1016/j.intaccaudtax.2011.06.001

ADDITIONAL READING

Cavalier-Rosa, G., & Tiras, S. L. (2013). Brazil's adoption of IFRS: Fertile ground for examining earnings management. *Brazilian Business Review*, *10*(4), 133–146. doi:10.15728/bbr.2013.10.4.6

Ghosh, A., Marra, A., & Moon, D. (2010). Corporate boards, audit committees, and earnings management: Pre- and post-SOX evidence. *Journal of Business Finance & Accounting*, *37*(9), 1145–1176. doi:10.1111/j.1468-5957.2010.02218.x

Jiraporn, P., Miller, G. A., Yoon, S. S., & Kim, Y. S. (2008). Is earnings management opportunistic or beneficial? An agency theory perspective. *International Review of Financial Analysis*, *17*(3), 622–634. doi:10.1016/j.irfa.2006.10.005

Rodrigues, J. M. (2012). Convergência contábil internacional: uma análise da gqualidade da informação contábil em razão da adoção dos padrões internacionais de contabilidade editados pelo IASB. Tese submetida ao Programa de Multiinstitucional e Inter-Regional de Pós- Graduação em Ciências Contábeis. UnB/UFPB/UFRN.

KEY TERMS AND DEFINITIONS

Convergence: Point of agreement between several related objectives.

Deliberate: It is the act of deciding through reflexive actions.

Earnings Management: Act to manage actions that seek results confuences.

Intervention: It is mediation as a preponderant factor in solving problems.

Manipulation: Specific control of actions and results within public and/or private organizations.

Private Sector: Entity that retains all the initiatives and practices not sponsored by the government.

Public Sector: A certain part of the state that performs the work of delivering goods and services to the population that contributes its taxes.

Chapter 13
Developments in Earnings Management Practices in the IFRS Perspective:
An Application in a Public Company

Oguzhan Carikci
Suleyman Demirel University, Turkey

Mahmut Sami Ozturk
https://orcid.org/0000-0002-7657-3150
Suleyman Demirel University, Turkey

ABSTRACT

Financial statements are an important tool when it comes to determining the level of success of a company's management and setting its market value. Nevertheless, company managers may sometimes try to reflect the company's financial results differently. Strategic methods, used by the company to deliberately change the earnings they gain by using the flexibility provided by the accounting system, are called earnings management practices. This chapter examines the examples of a public company that is traded on the Istanbul Stock Exchange for the purpose of determining earnings management practices under International Financial Reporting Standards (IFRS). Given the results of the study, it is possible to say from the earnings management practices that the company only benefited from those in the legal framework.

INTRODUCTION

Profit or loss is an indicator of the overall financial performance of an enterprise. Profit can be defined as the surplus remaining after total costs are deducted from total revenue. It is the best-known measure of success in a firm. Companies must obtain profit to sustain their operations, to gain competitive advantage, to produce goods or services related with their operation subjects, to carry on with their commercial

DOI: 10.4018/978-1-5225-7817-8.ch013

activities, and to, eventually, ensure the continuity of the company. Profitability is both a fundamental criterion and the ultimate goal in strategic and forward-looking decisions to be taken in companies. In terms of legislation, the concept of profit has critical importance in the calculation of the tax payable. Regarding the sales strategy and pricing decisions, the expectations of business partners, profit distributions to the shareholders, and profitability of the company should be well managed. In addition, the profitability of the company has a decisive influence in determining the performance of the enterprise, employees, and managers.

As a result of changes in the existing strategies and accounting practices in the company, the operating results of the entity, as well as the obtained profit or loss amount in the current period, can change. However, it is possible to estimate the profit or loss expected to be achieved in future periods by examining the accounting data and activity results of the previous periods. The profit expected in the future can further be estimated by the profits obtained in the previous periods. Therefore, monitoring the profitability that varies over periods has a strategic importance for enterprises.

Earnings management is a key business policy that, in recent years, has increasingly come into prominence. Earnings management has more than one definition in the literature. Briefly, earnings management is defined as the interventions to financial reporting processes in order to obtain certain specific benefits. As can be understood from this definition, the results of operations can be manipulated to create a different impression on the company's operational results, especially in the case of public companies, where this policy is very much seen in practice.

The purpose of this study is to examine the earnings management practices of a company. In line with this, accounting practices of the company are evaluated under the determined headings within the framework of earnings management.

This study is important in terms of expressing the real earnings management practices of a company with numerical examples.

BACKGROUND

When studies on earnings management under the IFRS are examined in the literature, several stand out. In Callao and others' (2007) paper, the adaption of IFRS, and the effect on the comparability and relevance of financial reporting in Spain, are studied. Jeanjean and Stolowy (2008) made an exploratory analysis of earnings management before and after IFRS adoption. Barth and others (2008) mentioned earnings management according to International Accounting Standards (IAS). Callao and Jarne (2010) investigated the effect of IFRS to earnings management in the European Union. Rudra and Bhattacharjee (2012) explored whether or not IFRS influences earnings management in India. According to Tort's study (2013), the earnings management is clarified under IFRS. Hastuti and others (2016) examined the effect of IFRS on the real earnings management and internal control structure as a moderating variable. Rathke and others (2016) analyzed the level of earnings management in Latin America after the adoption of the IFRS and the role of cross-listing in the United States. Phetruen (2016) examines the effect of IFRS and the Sarbanes-Oxley Act (SOX)-like regulations on earnings management in East Asian countries.

When related studies in the literature are searched, it appears that the number of studies that include earnings management practices with numeral examples, according to IFRS in companies, is small. This study includes earnings management practices in a company subject to IFRS applications. In practice, applications are shown numerically and a better understanding of earnings management practices is provided. Therefore, it is considered that this study will contribute to the literature significantly.

EARNINGS MANAGEMENT AND APPLICATION EXAMPLES

Earnings Management and IFRS

Earnings Management

It is important for the enterprise to achieve its goals to ensure the success of the management and to maintain the competitiveness of the enterprise. Therefore, it is necessary, to evaluate periodically generated income in the most appropriate way. In this context, it can be said that one of the tools used by the management to ensure that the related targets can be achieved is the earnings management practices. So, company management can manipulate the earnings management (Phetruen, 2016).

Examples of the related earnings management applications can be seen all over the world, especially in recent years (Hastuti et al., 2016). It is known that accounting information users are benefiting from financial statements in investment decisions, strategic plans, resource generation, taxation operations, and other similar accounting processes. However, it is critical issue that financial statements are regulated in a fair manner, particularly for information users.

Earnings management practices have an impact on the reliability of the financial statements. When this effect is evaluated in terms of generally accepted accounting principles, the concept of earnings management has begun to be discussed, especially in comparison with the concept of accounting ethics in recent times. While some studies claim that earnings management is not in line with business ethics, it is also seen that the changes made in the financial reports of the company are actually carried out according to the legal basis. In short, when earnings management practices are evaluated, they can be implemented according to legal and illegal methods (Rudra and Bhattacharjee, 2012).

When the reasons why earnings management is used by companies are examined in detail, the application purposes of companies can be listed as follows. These include creating a positive image for the company in the market, reducing the investors' negative thoughts about the company, reducing the risks arising from existing regulations, increasing the credibility of the company, and obtaining the tax advantages.

The concept of earnings management has begun to be studied in the literature in the last few years, and some definitions used to explain earnings management are given below.

Earnings management is defined by Walker as: "The use of administrative discretion over (within Generally Accepted Accounting Principles) accounting and earnings reporting choices, and real economic decisions to influence how underlying economic events are reflected in one or more measures of earnings" (Phetruen, 2016). According to Scott, earnings management is also defined as "a management choice upon accounting policy, or a real activity that affects earnings as such that multiple objectives of the specific earnings reporting can be obtained" (Hastuti et al., 2016).

Methods emerged regarding the implementation of earnings management in enterprises, and these are generally gathered in two groups. These are given in the following sections.

Real Earnings Management

Real earnings management is implemented by the business management to manage the obtained income. Earnings management applications are carried out in accordance with the objectives determined by the business management, as a result of the adjustment of general business activities. Roychowdhury defines the real earnings management as: "Real activities manipulation is a departure from normal operational practices, motivated by managers' desire to mislead at least some stakeholders into believing that certain financial reporting goals have been met in the normal course of operations" (Tirkkonen, 2013). According to Cohen and others, there are three basic manipulation methods within the framework of real earnings management. These are (Cohen et al., 2008):

- The flexibility of credit conditions or augmentation of sales by lowering prices.
- The reduction of production costs and the cost of goods sold by increasing production. Managers are increasing their profits by increasing production to a higher level if necessary.
- The reduction of the optional expenses that include advertising, research and development, selling, and general and administrative expenses.

Accrual Based Earnings Management

The major purpose of accruals is to indicate the real performance of the firm by recording revenues and expenses to the period in which they are incurred, instead of presenting the cash inflows and outflows.

According to previous studies, firm managers prefer real earnings management activities compared to accrual-based earnings management. This is because real management activities can be indistinctive from optimal business decisions, and thus more difficult to detect, even though the costs involved in such activities can be economically important for the firm (Cohen and Zarowin, 2010).

Impacts of IFRS on Earnings Management

IFRS is the set of criteria established for the harmonization of accounting practices in different countries. By means of IFRS, financial statements prepared by companies in different countries can be compared easily. Further, transparency and accountability can be improved, foreign investments can be developed, all parties can be monitored in a transparent manner, and the quality and reliability of the financial results provided by the accounting information system can be increased.

While the IFRS in the developed economies adds value to the financial reports, the benefits of the standards in the emerging economies do not come into prominence very much (Rudra and Bhattacharjee, 2012).

In addition, IFRS reduces information asymmetry and cost of capital, and increases capital flows in a global context. As the cultural and economic structure of each country affects the local accounting system, IFRS contains some discrepancies for each country. For this reason, the local characteristics of the countries influence adaptation to IFRS implementations (Rathke et al., 2016).

IFRS have encouraged discretionary accounting and opportunistic behavior in some countries, likely because of certain country's specific characteristics and institutional and environmental conditions (Callao and Jarne, 2010; Tort, 2013).

IFRS is commonly considered principles-based by accounting standards. A process has been conducted to develop the standards in upcoming years by the International Accounting Standards Board (IASB). Adapting to the IAS\IFRS may improve earnings management (Phetruen, 2016).

Along with the publication of the IFRS, many changes have also been made in earnings management practices. IFRS presents the most appropriate accounting option for the presentation of a company's existing financial statements. However, by means of accounting choices, companies may choose different accounting transactions to reflect similar economic phenomena. Theoretically, across world, the IFRS applications are the same for all countries. However, each country has different incentive policies and applications affecting accounting operations. So, according to IFRS applications, earnings management practices differ for each country (Rathke et al., 2016).

Some IFRS standards that can be considered in the framework of earnings management are as follows (Tort, 2013):

- **IAS 39:** Financial assets should be measured at their fair values (except loans and receivables, held-to-maturity investments, and some investments in equity). Financial liabilities should be measured at amortized cost, using the effective interest method.
- **IAS 17:** The leased assets should be depreciated over the shorter of the lease term or the life of the asset where subsequent ownership of the asset is not guaranteed.
- **IAS 38:** Research expenditure shall be recognized as expense when they are incurred and intangible assets do not arise.
- **IAS 1:** There is no distinction between extraordinary and ordinary income and expenses.
- **IAS 12:** This requires an entity to account for deferred tax using the balance sheet liability method.
- **IAS 16 and IAS 38:** Property, plant and equipment should be valued at acquisition cost, or fair value.

Earnings Management Application on a Company

Information About the Research

The research question in this study is what companies do in the framework of earnings management practices. Therefore, within the scope of IFRS, earnings management applications of a company are examined. The interview technique was used to obtain data. Interviews were made with department managers to identify the company's earnings management practices. In addition, the documents obtained from the company and the published financial statements were examined.

This study selected the company to acquire detailed information about its earnings management practices. Moreover, the fact that the company is large-scale, and that its shares are traded in Borsa Istanbul, are additional the reasons for its election.

The company's name and private information are concealed due to ethical principles. The selected company is a manufacturing company operating in the manufacturing and electricity sectors. It sells products domestically and abroad, and has over 1,120 employees.

According to the interviews, information about the company is as follows:

The company performs all accounting transactions on the Enterprise Resource Planning (ERP) program. Transactions cannot be changed on the system because there are LOG records in the ERP program. Therefore, manipulation and modification of records are not permitted. In addition, since the company is subject to the Electronic-book (E-book) application, all journal entries are uploaded to the E-book system via the Internet. All uploaded journal entries can be instantly seen and controlled by the government. Therefore, the journal entries cannot be changed. The company does not refer to illegal earnings management practices because, according to the researches, there are no illegal interventions or changes in the made records. By means of these applications, the transparency and accountability of the company is increased. So, the trust of both the investors and all external information users is increased.

Earnings Management Practices of the Company

In this section, the company's earnings management practices are classified according to their purposes into the following headings. The subheadings in the application are determined according to the areas of the financial statements. The tables included in the applications are the result of information obtained from the company.

Earnings Management Practices for Assets

- Various precautions are taken against the fluctuations in the exchange rate. The loss that may arise in the exchange rate difference is partially prevented. For example, with regard to all of the machines, products and equipment purchased from abroad, discounts are provided for purchases made over a certain amount. This is due to agreements made with vendors. In the case of purchases made in the future, the discount rate can be arranged in favor of the company. The following table shows how the company benefited from discounts on the purchase of raw materials from abroad. The company managers consider this application as an earnings management application. However, this application can be also considered as a purchasing policy of the company.

In the context of the application in Table 1, the company has made an agreement with the seller company about raw material purchasing. Under the terms of the agreement, the company paid 4 US Dollar per unit by purchasing 100,000 items instead of paying 5 US Dollar per unit. The company will pay 1,720,000 US Dollar, not 2,150,000 US Dollar. So, as seen above, company obtained 430,000 TL profit advantage.

Table 1. Quantity discount due to the raw material purchase

	Quantity	Price (US Dollar)	Exchange Rate (US Dollar/Turkish Lira)	Total Amount (Turkish Lira)
Before Discount	100,000	5	4.3	2,150,000
After Discount	100,000	4	4.3	1,720,000
Difference (Quantity Discount Amount)				430,000

Source: (Obtained information in the purchasing department of the company)

- The company does not make rediscount transactions within the scope of earnings management in some interim periods determined by the business management. For the first three months of the year, the rediscount of receivables amount to be recorded is 2,500,000 TL. The company did not make the rediscount of receivables entry in the first 3 months period and did not recognize the rediscount amount of 2,500,000 TL. Therefore, as a direct result of this application, in the first 3 months of the company, the amount of 2,500,000 TL profit is increased. The company uses this policy to affect the company's stocks, share price, and risks.
- Depending on the preference, some fixtures can be recorded as expense. There is a limit determined by the government to record a fixture as expense. Fixtures that are recorded as assets are added to the cost of the investment. Due to the fixtures that are recorded as expense, the profit of the period decreases. So, the company recorded 53,000 TL fixtures as expense. The expenditure amount is lower than the annual profit of the company.
- In some periods when the profits need to be high, some fixed assets that are still in use (even though the useful economic life is over) can be sold and profit can be increased. The company can also benefit from this practice in some periods.

Earnings Management Practices for Liabilities

- As in the rediscount of receivables, same application can be made for rediscount of notes payables. However, if this practice is implemented, profit can be reduced because the rediscount income is not recorded. The company does not use the rediscount of notes payables application because it does not prefer to have a reduced profit.
- As a result of the good relations established with creditors and lenders, the interest rate applied by the banks to the company is lower than the current rate. Thus, the profit of the company is increased because the interest on the loan is reduced and the interest rate is reduced. As a result of the good relationship with the bank for the year, the loan interest rate is applied as 15.5% instead of 16.5%. With this application, the interest rate of the company decreased by 1%. This application is used to reduce the interest payable.
- In some periods, the capital structure of the company is changing by increasing capital. Due to the capital increase, the shareholders' equity is increasing, the financial ratios are changing, the credibility is increasing, the borrowing capacity is increasing and the risk is decreasing. Within the scope of legal earnings management, the capital is increased by the company. Permission is obtained from the Capital Markets Board (CMB) for this application. The capital increase limit is determined by CMB and this limit cannot be exceeded.
- The company can distribute more dividends higher than the current period profit by utilizing the previous years' profits. In relation to this, the profit distribution of the company is shown in Table 2.

Earnings Management Practices for Revenues

- Sales and profits are increased through the development of trust-based relationships with customers and dealers. The 'upper risk limit for each customer' application, determined by the company in order to carry out its business activities in a healthy way, is being implemented. In this application, a risk limit is determined for each customer by examining their current credit account,

Table 2. Planned profit distribution according to earnings management

1.	**Paid Capital**	**175,000,000**
2.	**General Legal Reserve**	**950,000,000**
	The information about the privilege: there is no privilege in profit distribution.	
3.	**Profit / Loss for the Period**	50,000,000
4.	**Tax**	6,345,000
5.	**Net Profit for the Period**	43,655,000
6.	**Loss for the Previous Periods**	0.00
7.	**General Legal Reserve (-)**	0.00
8.	**Distribution from Previous Years Profit**	95,350,000
9.	Donations made during year (+)	
10.	**Donations Added Net Distributable Profit for the Period**	
11.	First Profit Distribution to the Partners	95,350,000
	- Cash	
	- Bonus	
	- Total	
12.	Profit Distribution to Privileged Shareholders	
13.	Other Distributed Profit	
	- Members of the Board of Directors,	
	- Employees,	
	- Except Shareholders,	
14.	Profit Distribution to Redeemed Shares Owners	
15.	Second Profit Distribution to the Partners	
16.	General Legal Reserve Fund	
17.	Statuary Reserves	
18.	Special Backups	
19.	EXTRAORDINARY RESERVE	95,350,000
20.	Other Resources to be Distributed	

Source: (Obtained information in the accounting department of the company)

amount of cash sale, amount of unexpired cheques, amount of group cheques, and amount of overdue cheques. In addition, it examines whether there are mortgages and warrants that the customers can give against the risks determined for the customers. In short, with this application, the business has created a system to prevent future loss from collection transactions. Table 3 shows the risk status for different customer operations.

As seen in Table 3, the total risk of each business is determined by combining the credit account amount, unexpired cheques, overdue cheques, and unbilled services by a specific calculation method. For these risks, the mortgages and warrants that the customers can give to the company are recorded in the system.

Table 3. Determination of customers' risk limits

Name	Credit Account	Unexpired Cheque	Overdue Cheque	Unbilled	Total Risk	Mortgage	Warrant	Current Risk	Limit
Company A	121,500	0	0	0	121,500	0	0	121,500	150,000
Company B	224,200	50,000	20,000	30,000	324,200	0	0	324,200	350,000

Source: (Obtained information in the marketing department of the company)

- The company's future performance is expected to be positive in the annual reports. To accomplish this, its most efficient activities are presented periodically on the Internet and in social networks. Therefore, the company aims to increase the profit and the number of investors in the future.
- The company is able to obtain tax advantage within the legal limits. For example, investment incentives are being taken for the construction of waste facilities. Therefore, corporate tax is paid at a 15% discount. In export activities, the Value Added Tax (VAT) of the exports is deducted from the tax. Since the Social Security Institution (SSI) payments are made regularly, special discounts are made by SSI administration. In addition, severance pay incentives are obtained. As a result of all these sample applications, net profit is increased with the tax reduction provided by government. In some periods, the company reduces its production costs according to its policy. At the same time, some costs are reduced according to the cash flow budget. Thus, the obtained profit is increased. There is an application to calculate the investment contribution amount in Table 4.
- The company has received a 6 million TL export VAT return from the government for the 72 million TL exports. As a result of this discount, a tax benefit of 6 million TL was generated. The reason of the advantage is to support the companies' export activities by the government.

Table 4. Total investment contribution amount

1	Tax Discount Rate	80%
2	Building	8,250,000
3	Machines	32,500,000
4	Others	15,000,000
5 (=1+2+3+4)	Total	55,750,000
6	Investment Contribution Rate	40%
7 (=5*6)	Investment Contribution Amount	22,300,000
8	Benefit From Contribution Amount in Previous Year	4,500,000
9	Benefit From Contribution Amount in Current Year	0
10 (=7-8-9)	Benefit From Contribution Amount in Next Years	17,800,000
	Revaluation Rate	12%
	Indexation Amount	2,136,000
	Total Outstanding Investment Contribution Amount	15,664,000

Source: (Obtained information in the accounting department of the company)

- It may be ensured that profit is increased by making out the sales invoice before the goods are shipped. If there is VAT to be transferred, a sales invoice can be made in cash up to the transferred VAT amount. The collective cash sales invoice can be made for the intermittent shipments to be made in the export transactions. Thus, profit can be increased in the related month.

Earnings Management Practices for Expenses

- If necessary, changes and arrangements can be made in budget items in some periods. The reason for this is that the exchange rate is constantly changing, meaning it is necessary to revise the budgets. For example, the budget can be revised if the prices of spare parts to be bought from abroad are above the exchange rate determined at the beginning of the year.
- As a result of decisions made in the general assembly, research, development and advertisement expenses that were planned to be made in the future are determined in advance. Usually, these expenditures are determined as a percentage of the turnover. However, these expenditures can be increased or decreased in some specific periods. In the same way, general administrative expenses can be similarly reduced and shifted. In some periods, during which the company cannot reach its target profit according to its financial status, the donations to be made can be reduced or delayed.
- The company makes new technological and environmental investments to reduce its costs. It is planned that an investment will be made to produce electricity from waste heat after a decision taken in a previous year's general assembly. Therefore, a total investment of 120 million TL has been made for the aforementioned technology. As a result of this investment, the electricity cost of the company decreased by 25%. 40 million TL electricity expense is required before electricity is generated, but 30 million TL electricity expense has been generated during the year, as a result of the investment and the electricity produced. Therefore, the company reduced its cost by 10 million TL, resulting in a total of 10 million TL profit. In other words, the company obtained 50 million TL profit instead of 40 million TL. In addition, the investment will have amortized itself in 12 years. This example is shown in Table 5.
- In some cases, the company reduces the depreciation expense by extending the useful economic life of the assets over a period of time. The useful economic life of assets determined by the Treasury can be increased once by the companies. The useful economic life of a machine purchased by the company for 3,650,000 TL in 2013 has been determined as ten years. The company has extended the useful economic life of the machine from ten years to twenty years. Therefore, the depreciation expense of the company for the asset has also changed. Depreciation calculations made for this example are shown in Table 6 and Table 7.

Table 5. Increase in profit because of the investment and reduction in electricity expense

	Investment Amount (TL)	Electricity Expense (TL)	Profit
Before Investment	-	40,000,000	40,000,000
After Investment	120,000,000	30,000,000	50,000,000
Difference		10,000,000	10,000,000

Source: (Obtained information in the accounting department of the company)

Table 6. Calculation of depreciation before extension of machine's useful economic life

Years	Gross Value of Machine	Depreciation	Accumulated Depreciation	Net Value
2013	3,650,000	365,000	365,000	3,285,000
2014	3,650,000	365,000	730,000	2,920,000
2015	3,650,000	365,000	1,095,000	2,555,000
2016	3,650,000	365,000	1,460,000	2,190,000
2017	3,650,000	365,000	1,825,000	1,825,000
2018	3,650,000	365,000	2,190,000	1,460,000
2019	3,650,000	365,000	2,555,000	1,095,000
2020	3,650,000	365,000	2,920,000	730,000
2021	3,650,000	365,000	3,285,000	365,000
2022	3,650,000	365,000	3,650,000	0

Source: (Obtained information in the accounting department of the company)

Table 7. Calculation of depreciation after extension of machine's useful economic life

Years	Gross Value of Machine	Depreciation	Accumulated Depreciation	Net Value
2013	3,650,000	182,500	182,500	3467,500
2014	3,650,000	182,500	365,000	3285,000
2015	3,650,000	182,500	547,500	3102,500
2016	3,650,000	182,500	730,000	2920,000
2017	3,650,000	182,500	912,500	2737,500
2018	3,650,000	182,500	1,095,000	2555,000
2019	3,650,000	182,500	1,277,500	2372,500
2020	3,650,000	182,500	1,460,000	2190,000
2021	3,650,000	182,500	1,642,500	2007,500
2022	3,650,000	182,500	1,825,000	1825,000
2023	3,650,000	182,500	2,007,500	1642,500
2024	3,650,000	182,500	2,190,000	1460,000
2025	3,650,000	182,500	2,372,500	1277,500
2026	3,650,000	182,500	2,555,000	1095,000
2027	3,650,000	182,500	2,737,500	912,500
2028	3,650,000	182,500	2,920,000	730,000
2029	3,650,000	182,500	3,102,500	547,500
2030	3,650,000	182,500	3,285,000	365,000
2031	3,650,000	182,500	3,467,500	182,500
2032	3,650,000	182,500	3,650,000	0

Source: (Obtained information in the accounting department of the company)

As seen in Table 6 and Table 7, the company calculates depreciation expense as 365,000 TL for the related machine in 2017, before extension of machine's useful economic life. However, consequence of determining the useful economic life of the machine as twenty years, 182,500 TL depreciation expense has arisen for the machine in 2017. As a result, the depreciation expense of the machinery decreased by 182,500 TL in 2017. Also, for the asset, the depreciation expense of the company has decreased and, therefore, the profit has increased by 182,500 TL.

- Various audits, such as environmental controls and occupational health and safety inspections, are regularly carried out within the company to prevent penalties that may arise from laws, policies, and procedures. With these inspections, the company will be able to pre-empt the penalty that may be incurred.
- SSI premiums are paid 5% less due to the payments made by the company regularly to the SSI. As a result of this discount, the company pays a total of 9.5 million TL per year.
- If necessary, the profit of the company is affected by the method of changing the salaries of company managers. This application is not preferred because the company is registered to the SSI system. However, according to the profitability in the current period, when the premiums given to the managers are changed, the profit or loss of the company can also change.

CONCLUSION

In this study, earnings management practices in a manufacturing company applying IFRS were analyzed with numerical examples.

Although earnings management practices are widely used in companies, it is very difficult to document these applications in practice. Therefore, this study contributes to the literature, since examples and advantages of a company's earnings management practices are examined numerically here.

When the earnings management practices of the company are examined, it is seen that the company performs these applications within the legal limits. Some of the indications that the company fulfils legal obligations are as follows. It is seen that the tax and other legal liabilities that have to be paid are paid in due time by the company. It has been determined that the transparency and accountability of the business are at a high level through applications such as the ERP program used by the company and E-Book application.

The following evaluations were obtained by comparing the company's earnings management practices with case studies in the literature.

Mard and Vigneron (2014) concluded that public companies frequently use earnings management practices to reduce tax payments. In the study of Wijaya (2013), it is observed that some companies have obtained tax incentives through tax planning and net deferred tax liabilities. Further, Gasteratos et al., (2016) notes that there are also earnings management applications to provide tax advantage due to the indication of lower profit. Similarly, in order to obtain tax advantage, the company obtains tax discount through investment incentives and exports.

Sudaryati (2012) stated that the change in assets affects the company's profitability. Further, in the application, the company applies for earnings management practices related to assets. These include, for example, obtainment of quantity discount due to the raw material purchase, rediscount of receivables, and recording the fixtures as expense.

According to the study of Jie and Yan (2014), which is included in the case studies in the literature, firms use contract of executive compensation within the scope of earnings management practices. However, in this study, there is no earnings management practice related to the managers.

Apart from these, some of the earnings management practices applied in the company are as follows. By making technological investments in production, the company reduces expenses and increases profit. If necessary, the company reduces the depreciation expense and increases its profit by extending the useful economic life of the assets once. The interest rates and interest expense are reduced by means of the relationships established with the credit institutions.

Other earnings management examples that are not detected in the application, but which can be applied in the enterprises, are as follows:

- Enterprises can make provisions to the doubtful trade receivables at a high amount. Therefore, obtained profit can be decreased.
- The profit or loss of the enterprises can be changed by changing the stock valuation methods and unit costs of the products.
- Classification changes can be made between the interim accounts included in the financial statements of the enterprises.
- In the periods when the government gives tax amnesty, enterprises can benefit from this practice within the framework of earnings management.

REFERENCES

Barth, M. E., Landsman, W. R., & Lang, M. H. (2008). International accounting standards and accounting quality. *Journal of Accounting Research*, *46*(3), 467–498. doi:10.1111/j.1475-679X.2008.00287.x

Callao, S., & Jarne, J. I. (2010). Have IFRS affected earnings management in the European Union? *Accounting in Europe*, *7*(2), 159–189. doi:10.1080/17449480.2010.511896

Callao, S., Jarne, J. I., & Laínez, J. A. (2007). Adoption of IFRS in Spain: Effect on the comparability and relevance of financial reporting. *Journal of International Accounting, Auditing & Taxation*, *16*(2), 148–178. doi:10.1016/j.intaccaudtax.2007.06.002

Cohen, D. A., Dey, A., & Lys, T. Z. (2008). Real and accrual-based earnings management in the pre- and post-sarbanes-oxley periods. *The Accounting Review*, *83*(3), 757–787. doi:10.2308/accr.2008.83.3.757

Cohen, D. A., & Zarowin, P. (2010). Accrual-based and real earnings management activities around seasoned equity offerings. *Journal of Accounting and Economics*, *50*(1), 2–19. doi:10.1016/j.jacceco.2010.01.002

Gasteratos, I., Karamalis, M., Koutoupis, A., & Filos, I. (2016). Earning management in Greece: A case study in construction sector using Jones Model. *International Journal of Economics and Business Administration*, *6*(4), 3–16.

Hastuti, T. D., Ghozali, I., & Yuyetta, E. N. (2016). The effect of international financial reporting standards on the real earnings management and internal control structure as a moderating variable. *International Journal of Economics and Financial Issues*, *6*(4), 1807–1814.

Jeanjean, T., & Stolowy, H. (2008). Do accounting standards matter? An exploratory analysis of earnings management before and after IFRS adoption. *Journal of Accounting and Public Policy*, *27*(6), 480–494. doi:10.1016/j.jaccpubpol.2008.09.008

Jie, Z., & Yan, Z.L. (2014). Executive compensation and earnings management: Empirical study in china's listed companies. *Advances in Management, 7*(6).

Mard, Y., & Vigneron, L. (2014). *Does public/private status affect small and medium enterprises' earnings management practices? A study on French case.* Retrieved April 18, 2018, from http://www.crm-toulouse.fr/files/Documents/Mard.pdf

Phetruen, W. (2016). *The Effect of IFRS and sox-like regulations on earnings management in East Asian countries* (Unpublished doctoral dissertation). University of Essex.

Rathke, A. A. T., Santana, V. T., Lourenço, I. M. E. C., & Dalmácio, F. Z. (2016). International financial reporting standards and earnings management in Latin America. *Revista de Administração Contemporânea*, *20*(3), 368–388. doi:10.1590/1982-7849rac2016140035

Rudra, T., & Bhattacharjee, D. (2012). Does IFRS influence earnings management? Evidence from India. *Journal of Management Research*, *4*, 1–13.

Sakin, T. (2016). Kâr yönetimi ve Türkiye'deki kâr yönetimi çalışmalarının değerlendirilmesi. In Seçmeler 2016 (pp. 181-192). İstanbul: İstanbul Üniversitesi İşletme Fakültesi Muhasebe Enstitüsü.

Sudaryati, D. (2012). The balance sheet as an earnings management constraint. *Jurnal Akuntansi & Investasi*, *13*(1), 1–14.

Tirkkonen, M. (2013). *Earnings management as a scope of art-empirical analysis of accrual-based and real earnings management in Finnish listed companies during 2001-2010* (Unpublished master's thesis). Aalto University School of Business.

Tort, L. P. (2013). Earnings management under IFRS and PGC. *Revista de Comptabilitat i Direcció*, *16*, 161–185.

Wijaya, M. H. (2013). Effect of corporate tax rate reduction on earnings management practices: A case study in Indonesia. *Finance and Banking Journal*, *15*(2), 206–222.

KEY TERMS AND DEFINITIONS

Assets: Values that can be converted into cash and used to realize the activities of the enterprise.

Balance Sheet: A financial statement containing the assets that the entity owns and the liabilities that show how assets are acquired.

Expense: Monetary amount of goods and services consumed to obtain benefit.

Income Statement: A financial statement indicating the results of the operations of the enterprise.

Liabilities: Balance sheet component that shows how the assets are obtained.

Loss: Negative difference that is generated as a result of the deduction of expense from income.
Profit: Positive difference that is generated as a result of the deduction of expense from income.
Profit Distribution: Profit distribution obtained from business to the partners.
Revenue: Income that an enterprise has from business activities.

Compilation of References

Aabo, T., Pantzalis, C., & Park, J. (2017). Idiosyncratic Volatility: An Indicator of Noise Trading? *Journal of Banking & Finance*, *75*, 136–151. doi:10.1016/j.jbankfin.2016.11.003

Aaker, H., & Gjesdal, F. (2010). *Do Models of Discretionary Accruals Detect Actual Earnings Management via Inventory? A Comparison of General and Specific Models*. Academic Press.

Abdullah, S. N., & Ku, I. N. (2016). Women directors, family ownership and earnings management in Malaysia. *Asian Review of Accounting*, *24*(4), 525–550. doi:10.1108/ARA-07-2015-0067

Abeyratna, G., & Power, D. (2002). The post-announcement performance of dividend-changing companies: The dividend-signalling hypothesis revisited. *Accounting and Finance*, *42*(2), 131–151. doi:10.1111/1467-629X.00071

Abraham, S., & Cox, P. (2007). Analysing the determinants of narrative risk information in UK FTSE 100 annual reports. *The British Accounting Review*, *39*(3), 227–248. doi:10.1016/j.bar.2007.06.002

Abrahamson, E., & Amir, E. (1996). The information content of the president's letter to shareholders. *Journal of Business Finance & Accounting*, *23*(8), 1157–1182. doi:10.1111/j.1468-5957.1996.tb01163.x

Abrahamson, E., & Park, C. (1994). Concealment of negative organizational outcomes: An agency theory perspective. *Academy of Management Journal*, *37*(5), 1302–1334.

Accounting Pronouncements Committee. (2008). *Technical Pronouncement CPC 13 - Adoção Inicial da Lei nº 11.638/07 e da Medida Provisória 449/08*. Brasília: CPC. Retrieved from http://www.cpc.org.br/pdf/CPC_13.pdf

Accounting Pronouncements Committee. (2009). *Technical Pronouncement CPC 27 - Ativo Imobilizado*. Brasília: CPC.

Accounting Pronouncements Committee. *A busca da convergência aos padrões internacionais: programa de trabalho - 2008 a 2010*. Retrieved from http://www.cpc.org.br/pdf/CPCplano%20de%20converg%C3%AAncia%20_%20junho_2008.pdf

Achleitner, A., Günther, N., Kaserer, C., & Siciliano, G. (2014). Real earnings management and accrual based earnings management in family firms. *European Accounting Review*, *23*(3), 431–461. doi:10.1080/09638180.2014.895620

Acker, D., Stalker, M., & Tonks, I. (2002). Daily Closing Inside Spreads and Trading Volumes Around Earnings Announcements. *Journal of Business Finance & Accounting*, *29*(9/10), 1149–1179. doi:10.1111/1468-5957.00465

Adelberg, A. H. (1979). Narrative disclosures contained in financial reports: Means of communication or manipulation. *Accounting and Business Research*, *10*, 179–184. doi:10.1080/00014788.1979.9729157

AEP (Portuguese Entrepreneurial Association) (2011). *Livro Branco da Sucessão Empresarial. O desafio da sucessão empresarial em Portugal*. Associação Empresarial de Portugal.

Aerts, W. (1994). On the of accounting logic as an explanatory category in narrative accounting disclosures. *Accounting, Organizations and Society*, *19*(4/5), 337–353. doi:10.1016/0361-3682(94)90001-9

Aerts, W. (2001). Inertia in the attributional content of annual accounting narratives. *European Accounting Review*, *10*(1), 3–32. doi:10.1080/09638180122562

Aerts, W. (2005). Picking up the pieces: Impression management in the retrospective attributional framing of accounting outcomes. *Accounting, Organizations and Society*, *30*(6), 493–517. doi:10.1016/j.aos.2004.07.001

Afshartous, D., & Preston, R. (2011). Key result of interaction models with centering. *Journal of Statistics Education: An International Journal on the Teaching and Learning of Statistics*, *19*(3), 1–24. doi:10.1080/10691898.2011.11889620

Agoglia, C., Doupnik, T., & Tsakumis, G. (2011). Principles-Based versus Rules-Based Accounting Standards: The Influence of Standard Precision and Audit Committee Strength on Financial Reporting Decisions. *The Accounting Review*, *86*(3), 747–767. doi:10.2308/accr.00000045

Agrawal, A., & Cooper, T. (2015). Insider Trading before Accounting Scandals. *Journal of Corporate Finance*, *34*, 169–190. doi:10.1016/j.jcorpfin.2015.07.005

Aharony, J., Lin, C., & Loeb, M. (1993). Initial public offerings, accounting choices, and earnings management. *Contemporary Accounting Research*, *10*(1), 61–81. doi:10.1111/j.1911-3846.1993.tb00382.x

Ahmed, A. S., Lobo, G. J., & Zhou, J. (2000). Job security and income smoothing: An empirical test of the Fudenberg and Tirole (1995) model. *SSRN Working Paper Series*, October version.

Ahmed, A., Billings, B., & Morton, R. (2004). *Extreme Accruals, Earnings Quality, and Investor Mispricing.* Working paper, Florida State University.

Akerlof G. A. (1970). The Market for Lemons. *Quarterly Journal of Economics, 89*(3), 488-500.

Albornoz, B. G. (2003). *Alisamiento del beneficio y manipulación de ajustes por devengo: Análisis empírico en el contexto español. In Accounting Research Award "José M.ª Fernández Pirla" (XI Edition).* Madrid: ICAC.

Albornoz, B. G., & Alcarria, J. J. (2003). Analysis and diagnosis of income smoothing in Spain. *European Accounting Review*, *12*(3), 443–463. doi:10.1080/0963818022000001154

Alcidi, C., Belke, A., Giovannini, A., & Gros, D. (2016). Macroeconomic adjustment programmes in the euro area: An overall assessment. *International Economics and Economic Policy*, *13*(3), 345–358. doi:10.100710368-016-0350-6

Ali, A., Akbar, S., Ormrod, P., & Shah, S. Z. A. (2016). The impact and implications of international financial reporting standards in the United Kingdom: Evidence from the alternative investment market. *Australian Accounting Review*, *26*(4), 360–375. doi:10.1111/auar.12140

Ali, A., Chen, T. Y., & Radhakrishnan, S. (2007). Corporate disclosures by family firms. *Journal of Accounting and Economics*, *44*(1-2), 238–286. doi:10.1016/j.jacceco.2007.01.006

Allayannis, G., & Weston, J. P. (2006). *Earnings volatility, cash Flow volatility, and Firm value*. American Accounting Association, Annual Meeting.

Allee, K. D., & Yohn, T. L. (2009). The demand for financial statements in an unregulated environment: An examination of the production and use of financial statements by privately held small businesses. *The Accounting Review*, *84*(1), 1–25. doi:10.2308/accr.2009.84.1.1

Allport, G. W. (1954). The historical background of social psychology. In G. Lindzey & E. Aronson (Eds.), *Handbook of social psychology* (pp. 1–46). New York: Random House.

Almedina, E. (2013). Legislação Comercial e das Sociedades Comerciais (4th ed.). Coimbra: Almedina Editora.

Al-Najjar, B. (2018). Corporate governance and audit features: SMEs evidence. *Journal of Small Business and Enterprise Development*, *25*(1), 163–179. doi:10.1108/JSBED-08-2017-0243

Alp, A., & Ustundag, S. (2009). Financial reporting transformation: The experience of Turkey. *Critical Perspectives on Accounting*, *20*(5), 680–699. doi:10.1016/j.cpa.2007.12.005

Altinta, Ş. A. T., Sari, E. S., & OtluoĞlu, E. (2017). The impact of earnings management on the value relevance of earnings: empirical evidence from Turkey. *The Journal of International Social Research, 10*(51), 885–891.

Alves, M. do C. G., Saraiva, H. I. B., & Gabriel, V. M. de S. (2015). Normalização contabilística em Portugal : a sua evolução e situação atual. In *V Congresso dos TOC* (pp. 1–19). Retrieved from http://www.occ.pt/news/trabalhoscongv/pdf/32.pdf

Alves, S. (2014). The Effect of Board Independence on the Earnings Quality: Evidence from Portuguese Listed Companies. *Australasian Accounting. Business and Finance Journal*, *8*(3), 23–44.

Amaral, C. X. (2001). Processo de harmonização contabilística internacional : Tendências actuais. *Gestao e Desenvolvimento*, *10*, 33–58.

Amat Salas, O. (2010). Fiabilidad de la nueva normativa contable (PGC y NIIF) y detección de maquillajes contables. *Boletin de Estudios Economicos*, *65*(199), 93–105.

Amat, O., & Blake, J. (1996). Contabilidad creativa. *Gestion.*

Amat, O., & Gowthorpe, C. (2004). Creative accounting: Nature, incidence and ethical issues. *Journal of Economic Literature*, 1–19. doi:10.2139srn.563364

Ames, D. (2013). IFRS adoption and accounting quality: The case of South Africa. *Journal of Applied Economics & Business Research*, *3*(3), 154–165. doi:10.2308/accr-50494

Amihud, Y. (2002). Illiquidity and Stock Returns: Cross-Section and Time-Series Effects. *Journal of Financial Markets*, *5*(1), 31–56. doi:10.1016/S1386-4181(01)00024-6

Amihud, Y., Kamin, J. Y., & Ronen, J. (1983). 'Managerialism', 'ownerism' and risk. *Journal of Banking & Finance*, *7*(2), 189–196. doi:10.1016/0378-4266(83)90031-6

Amran, A., Bin, A. M. R., & Hassan, B. C. H. M. (2009). Risk reporting: An exploratory study on risk management disclosure in Malaysian annual reports. *Managerial Auditing Journal*, *24*(1), 39–57. doi:10.1108/02686900910919893

Anderson, R. C., Mansi, S. A., & Reeb, D. M. (2003). Founding family ownership and the agency cost of debt. *Journal of Financial Economics*, *68*(2), 263–285. doi:10.1016/S0304-405X(03)00067-9

Anderson, R. C., & Reeb, D. M. (2003). Founding family ownership and firm performance: Evidence from the S&P 500. *The Journal of Finance*, *58*(3), 1301–1328. doi:10.1111/1540-6261.00567

Anderson, R. C., & Reeb, D. M. (2004). Board composition: Balancing family influence in S&P 500 Firms. *Administrative Science Quarterly*, *49*, 1301–1328.

Angelidis, T., & Tessaromatis, N. (2008). Idiosyncratic Volatility and Equity Returns: UK Evidence. *International Review of Financial Analysis*, *17*(3), 539–556. doi:10.1016/j.irfa.2006.10.006

Archibald, T. R. (1967). The return to straight-line depreciation: An analysis of a change in accounting method. *Journal of Accounting Research*, *5*(Supplement), 164–180. doi:10.2307/2489918

Argilés-Bosch, J. M., García-Blandón, J., & Martínez-Blasco, M. (2012). Earnings management behaviour under the recent economic downturn in Spain. *International Finance Review*, *13*, 231–255. doi:10.1108/S1569-3767(2012)0000013011

Arletta, C., Coda Negozio, E., Di Diego, S., Fantoni, M., Fici, L., Imparato, A., …Zucca M. (2015). *PMI e M&A in Italia. Una strada sicura per la crescita.* Economia & Management, Milano, FrancoAngeli.

Armstrong, C., Core, J., Taylor, D., & Verrecchia, R. (2011). When Does Information Asymmetry Affect the Cost of Capital? *Journal of Accounting Research*, *49*(1), 1–40. doi:10.1111/j.1475-679X.2010.00391.x

Arndt, M., & Bigelow, B. (2000). Presenting structural innovation in an institutional environment: Hospitals' use of impression management. *Administrative Science Quarterly*, *45*(3), 494–522. doi:10.2307/2667107

Arnedo, L., Lizarraga, F., & Sánchez, S. (2007). Does public/private status affect the level of earnings management in code-law contexts outside the United States? a study based on the Spanish case. *The International Journal of Accounting*, *42*(3), 305–328. doi:10.1016/j.intacc.2007.06.004

Arthur, N., Tang, Q., & Lin, Z. (2015). Corporate accruals quality during the 2008–2010 global financial crisis. *Journal of International Accounting, Auditing & Taxation*, *25*, 1–15. doi:10.1016/j.intaccaudtax.2015.10.004

Ashari, N., Koh, H. C., Tan, S. L., & Wong, W. H. (1994). Factors affecting income smoothing among listed companies in Singapore. *Accounting and Business Research*, *24*(96), 291–301. doi:10.1080/00014788.1994.9729488

Aubert, F., & Grudnitski, G. (2012). Analysts' estimates: What they could be telling us about the impact of IFRS on earnings manipulation in Europe. *Review of Accounting and Finance*, *11*(1), 53–72. doi:10.1108/14757701211201821

Badolato, P. G., Donelson, D. C., & Ege, M. (2014). Audit committee financial expertise and earnings management: The role of status. *Journal of Accounting and Economics*, *58*(2–3), 208–230. doi:10.1016/j.jacceco.2014.08.006

Bagnoli, M., & Watts, S. (2010). Oligopoly, disclosure, and earnings management. *The Accounting Review*, *85*(4), 1191–1214. doi:10.2308/accr.2010.85.4.1191

Bahri, M., St-Pierre, J., & Sakka, O. (2017). Performance measurement and management for manufacturing SMEs: A financial statement-based system. *Measuring Business Excellence*, *21*(1), 17–36. doi:10.1108/MBE-06-2015-0034

Baker, C. R., & Barabu, E. M. (2007). Evolution of research on international accounting harmonization: A historical and institutional perspective. *Socio-Economic Review, Oxford*, *5*(4), 603–632. doi:10.1093er/mwm014

Baker, M., & Wurgler, J. (2002). Market Timing and Capital Structure. *The Journal of Finance*, *57*(1), 1–32. doi:10.1111/1540-6261.00414

Balakrishnan, K., & Cohen, D. A. (2009). *Product market competition, financial accounting misreporting and corporate governance: Evidence from accounting restatements* (Working Paper). New York University.

Ball, R. (2006). *International Financial Reporting Standards (IFRS): Pros and Cons for Investors*. Accounting and Business Research, International Accounting Policy Forum. 10.1080/00014788.2006.9730040

Ball, R. (2013). Accounting informs investors and earnings management is rife: Two questionable beliefs. *Accounting Horizons*, *27*(4), 847–853. doi:10.2308/acch-10366

Ball, R., Kothari, S., & Robin, A. (2000). The Effect of International Institutional Factors on Properties of Accounting Earnings. *Journal of Accounting and Economics*, *29*(1), 1–51. doi:10.1016/S0165-4101(00)00012-4

Ball, R., Robin, A., & Wu, J. (2003). Incentives versus standards: Properties of accounting income in four East Asian countries. *Journal of Accounting and Economics*, *36*(1-3), 235–270. doi:10.1016/j.jacceco.2003.10.003

Ball, R., & Shivakumar, L. (2005). Earnings Quality in UK Private Firms: Comparative Loss Recognition Timeliness. *Journal of Accounting and Economics*, *39*(1), 83–128. doi:10.1016/j.jacceco.2004.04.001

Ball, R., & Shivakumar, L. (2006). The role of accruals in asymmetrically timely gain and loss recognition. *Journal of Accounting Research*, *44*(2), 207–242. doi:10.1111/j.1475-679X.2006.00198.x

Ball, R., & Shivakumar, L. (2008). Earnings Quality at Initial Public Offerings. *Journal of Accounting and Economics*, *45*(2-3), 324–349. doi:10.1016/j.jacceco.2007.12.001

Balsam, S., Krishnan, J., & Yang, J. S. (2003). Auditor industry specialization and earnings quality. *Auditing*, *22*(2), 71–97. doi:10.2308/aud.2003.22.2.71

Bansal, P., & Clelland, I. (2004). Talking trash: Legitimacy, impression management, and unsystematic risk in the context of the natural environment. *Academy of Management Journal*, *47*(1), 93–103.

Baptista, E. (2009). Ganhos em Transparencia Versus Novos Instrumentos de Manipulacao: o Paradoxo das Modificacoes Trazidas pela Lei no 11.638. *RAE- Revista de Administração de Empresas, 49*, 234-239. Disponível em https://rae.fgv.br/sites/rae.fgv.br/files/artigos/10.1590_S0034-75902009000200009.pdf

Baralexis, S. (2004). Creative accounting in small advancing countries. *Managerial Auditing Journal*, *19*(3), 440–461. doi:10.1108/02686900410524427

Barghathi, Y., Collison, D., & Crawford, L. (2018). Earnings management and audit quality: Stakeholders' perceptions. *The Journal of Management and Governance*, *22*(3), 629–659. doi:10.100710997-017-9396-2

Barnea, A., Ronen, J., & Sadan, S. (1976). Classificatory smoothing of income with extraordinary items. *The Accounting Review*, *51*(1), 110–122.

Barth, M. E. (2018). The future of financial reporting: Insights from research. *Abacus*, *54*(1), 66–78. doi:10.1111/abac.12124

Barth, M. E., Landsman, W. R., & Lang, M. H. (2008). International accounting standards and accounting quality. *Journal of Accounting Research*, *46*(3), 467–498. doi:10.1111/j.1475-679X.2008.00287.x

Barth, M., Beaver, W., Hand, J., & Landsman, W. (1999). Accruals, Cash Flows and Equity Values. *Review of Accounting Studies*, *3*(3/4), 205–229. doi:10.1023/A:1009630100586

Barth, M., Beaver, W., Hand, J., & Landsman, W. (2005). Accruals, Accounting-Based Valuation Models, and the Prediction of Equity Values. *Journal of Accounting, Auditing & Finance*, *3*(4), 311–345. doi:10.1177/0148558X0502000401

Barth, M., Beaver, W., & Landsman, W. (1992). The Market Valuations Implications of Net Periodic Pension Costs. *Journal of Accounting and Economics*, *15*(1), 27–62. doi:10.1016/0165-4101(92)90011-P

Barth, M., Cram, D., & Nelson, K. (2001b). Accruals and Prediction of Future Cash Flows. *The Accounting Review*, *76*(1), 27–58. doi:10.2308/accr.2001.76.1.27

Bartlett, S. A., & Chandler, R. A. (1997). The corporate report and the private shareholder: Lee and Tweedie twenty years on. *The British Accounting Review*, *29*(3), 245–261. doi:10.1006/bare.1996.0044

Bar-Yosef, S., & Prencipe, A. (2009). *Corporate governance and earnings management in familycontrolled companies*. Disponivel em: http://papers.ssrn.com/sol3/papers.cfm?abstract_id=1367543

Basel Committee on Banking Supervision (BCBS). (n.d.). Retrieved from https://www.bis.org/publ/bcbsca07.pdf

Bastardo, A. (2015). *Graph Usage in Financial Reports: Evidence from Portuguese Listed Companies*. Dissertação de mestrado.

Basu, N., & Wang, X. (2011). Evidence on the Relation Between Inventory Changes, Earnings, and Firm value. *The International Journal of Business and Finance Research*, *5*(3), 1–14.

Basu, S. (1997). The Conservatism Principle and the Asymmetric Timeliness of Earnings. *Journal of Accounting and Economics*, *24*(2-3), 3–37. doi:10.1016/S0165-4101(97)00014-1

Beasley, M. (1996). An empirical analysis of the relation between the board of director composition and financial statement fraud. *The Accounting Review*, *71*(4), 443–464.

Beattie, V., & Jones, M. J. (1997). *A Comparative Study of the Use of Financial Graphs in the Corporate Annual Reports of Major U. S. and U. K. Companies*. Academic Press.

Beattie, V. A., & Jones, M. J. (2000a). Changing Graph Use in Corporate Annual Reports: A Time-Series Analysis. *Contemporary Accounting Research*, *17*(2), 213–226. doi:10.1506/AAT8-3CGL-3J94-PH4F

Beattie, V., Brown, S., Ewers, D., John, B., Manson, S., Thomas, D., & Turner, M. (1994). Extraordinary items and income smoothing: A positive accounting approach. *Journal of Business Finance & Accounting*, *21*(6), 791–811. doi:10.1111/j.1468-5957.1994.tb00349.x

Beattie, V., & Jones, M. (2000). Impression management: The case of inter-country financial graphs. *Journal of International Accounting, Auditing & Taxation*, *9*(2), 159–183. doi:10.1016/S1061-9518(00)00030-6

Beattie, V., & Jones, M. J. (1992). The use and abuse of graphs in annual reports: A theoretical framework and an empirical study. *Accounting and Business Research*, *22*(88), 291–303. doi:10.1080/00014788.1992.9729446

Beattie, V., & Jones, M. J. (1999). Australian Financial Graphs: An Empirical Study. *Abacus*, *35*(1), 46–76. doi:10.1111/1467-6281.00034

Beattie, V., & Jones, M. J. (2001). A six-country comparison of the use of graphs in annual reports. *The International Journal of Accounting*, *36*(2), 195–222. doi:10.1016/S0020-7063(01)00094-2

Beattie, V., & Jones, M. J. (2002). Measurement distortion of graphs in corporate reports: An experimental study. *Accounting, Auditing & Accountability Journal*, *15*(4), 546–564. doi:10.1108/09513570210440595

Beattie, V., & Jones, M. J. (2008). Corporate Reporting Using Graphs: A Review and Synthesis. *Jal*, *27*(June), 71–110.

Beatty, A., & Weber, J. (2003). The effects of debt contracting on voluntary accounting method changes. *The Accounting Review*, *78*(1), 119–142. doi:10.2308/accr.2003.78.1.119

Beaver, W. (1998). *Financial Reporting: An Accounting Revolution* (3rd ed.). Prentice Hall.

Beaver, W. (1999). Comments on "An Empirical Assessment of the Residual Income Valuation Model". *Journal of Accounting and Economics*, *26*(1-3), 35–42. doi:10.1016/S0165-4101(98)00042-1

Beaver, W. (2002). Perspectives on Recent Capital Research. *The Accounting Review*, *77*(2), 453–474. doi:10.2308/accr.2002.77.2.453

Beaver, W., & Demski, J. (1979, January). The Nature of Income Measurement. *The Accounting Review*, 38–46.

Beck, N., & Katz, J. N. (1995). What to do (and not to do) with time series cross-section data. *The American Political Science Review*, *89*(03), 634–647. doi:10.2307/2082979

Begley, J. (1990). Debt covenants and accounting choice. *Journal of Accounting and Economics*, *12*(1-3), 125–139. doi:10.1016/0165-4101(90)90044-5

Beidleman, C. R. (1973). Income smoothing: The role of management. *The Accounting Review*, *48*(4), 653–667.

Belke, A., & Schnabl, G. (2013). Four Generations of Global Imbalances. *Review of International Economics*, *21*(1), 1–5. doi:10.1111/roie.12015

Belot, F., & Serve, S. (2018). Earnings quality in private SMEs: do CEO demographics matter? *Journal of Small Business Management, 56*, 323–344. doi:10.1111/jsbm.12375

Ben Othman, H., & Zeghal, D. (2006). A study of earnings-management motives in the Anglo-American and Euro-Continental accounting models: The Canadian and French cases. *The International Journal of Accounting*, *41*(4), 406–435. doi:10.1016/j.intacc.2006.09.004

Beneish, D., & Vargus, E. (2002). Insider trading, earnings quality, and accrual mispricing. *The Accounting Review*, *77*(4), 755–791. doi:10.2308/accr.2002.77.4.755

Beneish, M. D. (1997). Detecting GAAP violation: Implications for assessing earnings management among firms with extreme financial performance. *Journal of Accounting and Public Policy*, *16*(3), 271–309. doi:10.1016/S0278-4254(97)00023-9

Beneish, M. D. (1999). Incentives Earnings and Penalties Related to Overstatements that Violate. *The Accounting Review*, *74*(4), 425–457. doi:10.2308/accr.1999.74.4.425

Beneish, M. D. (2001). Earnings management: A perspective. *Managerial Finance*, *27*(12), 3–17. doi:10.1108/03074350110767411

Bens, D. A., Goodman, T. H., & Neamtiu, M. (2012). Does investment-related pressure lead to misreporting? An analysis of reporting following M&A transactions. *The Accounting Review*, *87*(3), 839–865. doi:10.2308/accr-10210

Benston, G., & Krasney, M. (1978). The economic consequences of financial accounting statements. In *Economic Consequences of Financial Standards: Selected Papers* (pp. 159–252). Financial Accounting Standards Board.

Beretta, S., & Bozzolan, S. (2004). A framework for the analysis of firm risk communication. *The International Journal of Accounting*, *39*(3), 265–288. doi:10.1016/j.intacc.2004.06.006

Berger, A. N., Klapper, L. F., & Turk-Ariss, R. (2008). *Bank competition and financial stability*. Policy Research Working Paper No. 4696. World Bank.

Bergstresser, D., Desai, M., & Rauh, J. (2003). *The Gerstner Effect: managerial motivations and earnings manipulations*. Working Paper, Harvard Business School.

Bernard, V. (1995). The Feltham–Ohlson Framework: Implications for Empiricists. *Contemporary Accounting Research*, *11*(2), 733–747. doi:10.1111/j.1911-3846.1995.tb00463.x

Bernard, V., & Noel, J. (1991). Do Inventory Disclosures Predict Sales and Earnings? *Journal of Accounting, Auditing & Finance*, *6*(2), 145–181. doi:10.1177/0148558X9100600202

Bernard, V., & Stober, T. (1989). The Nature and Amount of Information in Cash Flows and Accruals. *The Accounting Review*, *64*(4), 624–652.

Bernstein, L. (1996). *Análisis de Estados Financeiros. Teoría, Aplicación e Interpretación*. Madrid: Ed. IRWIN.

Bernstein, L., & Siegel, J. (1979). The Concept of Earnings Quality. *Financial Analysts Journal*, *35*, 72–75. doi:10.2469/faj.v35.n4.72

Betz, M., O'Connell, L., & Shepard, J. M. (1989). Gender differences in proclivity for unethical behavior. *Journal of Business Ethics*, *8*(5), 321–324. doi:10.1007/BF00381722

Bharath, S., Sunder, J., & Sunder, S. (2008). Accounting quality and debt contracting. *The Accounting Review*, *83*(1), 1–28. doi:10.2308/accr.2008.83.1.1

Bhattacharya, D., Guner, N., & Ventura, G. (2012). Distortions, endogenous managerial skills and productivity differences. *Review of Economic Dynamics*, *13*, 11–25.

Bhattacharya, N., Desai, H., & Venkataraman, K. (2013). Does Earnings Quality Affect Information Asymmetry? Evidence from Trading Costs. *Contemporary Accounting Research*, *30*(2), 482–516. doi:10.1111/j.1911-3846.2012.01161.x

Bhattacharya, N., Ecker, F., Olsson, P., & Schipper, K. (2012). Direct and Mediated Associations among Earnings Quality, Information Asymmetry, and the Cost of Equity. *The Accounting Review*, *87*(2), 449–482. doi:10.2308/accr-10200

Bhat, V. N. (1996). Banks and income smoothing: An empirical analysis. *Applied Financial Economics*, *6*(6), 505–510. doi:10.1080/096031096333953

Black, F. (1980). The Magic in Earnings: Economic Earnings versus Accounting Earnings. *Financial Analysts Journal*, *36*(6), 19–24. doi:10.2469/faj.v36.n6.19

Bollen, N., Smith, T., & Whaley, R. (2004). Modeling the Bid/Ask Spread: Measuring the Inventory-Holding Premium. *Journal of Financial Economics*, *72*(1), 97–141. doi:10.1016/S0304-405X(03)00169-7

Bonito, A., & Pais, C. (2018). *The macroeconomic determinants of the adoption of IFRS for SMEs*. Revista de Contabilidad. doi:10.1016/j.rcsar.2018.03.001

Booth, G. G., Kallunki, J. P., & Martikainen, T. (1996). Post-announcement drift and income smoothing: Finnish evidence. *Journal of Business Finance & Accounting*, *23*(8), 1197–1211. doi:10.1111/j.1468-5957.1996.tb01165.x

Borges, M. F. (2011). *Impression Management e Desempenho Organizacional : o caso Português (Dissertação de mestrado)*. Instituto Superior de Contabilidade e Administração- Universidade de Aveiro.

Borges, M. F. R. (2011). *Impression Management e desempenho organizacional: o caso Português*. Aveiro: Universidade de Aveiro.

Bouchareb, M., Ajina, A., & Souid, S. (2014). Does the adoption of ias/ifrs with a strong governance mechanism can deter earnings management? *International Journal of Academic Research in Economics and Management Sciences*, *3*(1), 264–282. doi:10.6007/IJAREMS/v3-i1/645

Bowen, R. M., Rajgopal, S., & Venkatachalam, M. (2008). Accounting Discretion, Corporate Governance, and Firm Performance. *Contemporary Accounting Research*, *25*(2), 351–405. doi:10.1506/car.25.2.3

Bradley, M., Jarrell, G., & Kim, H. (1984). On the Existence of an Optimal Capital Structure: Theory and Evidence. *The Journal of Finance*, *39*(3), 857–878. doi:10.1111/j.1540-6261.1984.tb03680.x

Branco, M. C., Delgado, C., Sousa, C., & Sá, M. (2011). Intellectual capital disclosure media in Portugal. *Corporate Communications*, *16*(1), 38–52. doi:10.1108/13563281111100962

Branco, M. C., & Rodrigues, L. L. (2006). Communication of corporate social responsibility by Portuguese banks: A legitimacy theory perspective. *Corporate Communications*, *11*(3), 232–248. doi:10.1108/13563280610680821

Branco, M. C., & Rodrigues, L. L. (2008). Factors influencing social responsibility disclosure by Portuguese companies. *Journal of Business Ethics*, *83*(4), 685–701. doi:10.100710551-007-9658-z

Brazilian Securities Commission *n. 457* of July 13, 2007. Dispõe sobre a elaboração e divulgação das demonstrações financeiras consolidadas, com base no padrão contábil internacional emitido pelo International Accounting Standards Board (IASB).

Brazilian Securities Commission *n. 485* of September 01,2010. Altera a Instrução CVM nº 457, de 13 de julho de 2007, que dispõe sobre a elaboração e divulgação das demonstrações financeiras consolidadas, com base no padrão contábil internacional emitido pelo *International Accounting Standards Board* (IASB).

Brealey, R. A., & Myers, S. C. (1998). *Princípios de finanças empresariais*. Lisbon: McGraw-Hill.

Brennan, M. J., & Schwartz, E. S. (1978). Corporate Income Taxes, Valuation, and the Problem of Optimal Capital Structure. *The Journal of Business*, *51*(1), 103–114. doi:10.1086/295987

Brennan, N. M., Guillamon-Saorin, E., & Pierce, A. (2009). Impression management: Developing and illustrating a scheme of analysis for narrative disclosures – a methodological note. *Accounting, Auditing & Accountability Journal*, *22*(5), 789–832. doi:10.1108/09513570910966379

Bricker, R., Previts, G., Robinson, T., & Young, S. (1995). Financial analyst assessment of company earnings quality. *Journal of Accounting, Auditing & Finance*, *10*(3), 541–544. doi:10.1177/0148558X9501000307

Brown, L. (1996). Influencial Accounting Articles, Individuals, Ph.D. Granting Institutions and Faculties: A Citation Analysis. *Accounting, Organizations and Society*, *21*(7-8), 723–754. doi:10.1016/0361-3682(96)00012-8

Brown, S., & Hillegeist, S. (2007). How Disclosure Quality Affects the Level of Information Asymmetry. *Review of Accounting Studies*, *12*(2/3), 443–477. doi:10.100711142-007-9032-5

Buckmaster, D. (2001). *Development of the income smoothing literature 1893-1998: A focus on the United States*. JAI.

Burgstahler, D., Hail, L., & Leuz, C. (2004). *The importance of reporting incentives: Earnings management in European private and public firms* (Working Paper). Wharton Financial Institutions Center.

Burgstahler, D. C., Hail, L., & Leuz, C. (2006). The importance of reporting incentives: Earnings management in european private and public firms. *The Accounting Review*, *81*(5), 983–1016. doi:10.2308/accr.2006.81.5.983

Burgstahler, D., & Dichev, I. (1997). Earnings management to avoid earnings decreases and losses. *Journal of Accounting and Economics*, *24*(1), 99–126. doi:10.1016/S0165-4101(97)00017-7

Burgstahler, D., & Eames, M. J. (2003). Earnings Management to Avoid Losses and Earnings Decreases: Are Analysts Fooled? *Contemporary Accounting Research*, *20*(2), 253–294. doi:10.1506/BXXP-RGTD-H0PM-9XAL

Burkart, M., Panunzi, F., & Shleifer, A. (2003). Family firms. *The Journal of Finance*, *58*(5), 2167–2201. doi:10.1111/1540-6261.00601

Bushman, R. D., & Piotroski, J. D. (2006). Financial reporting incentives for conservative accounting: The influence of legal and political institutions. *Journal of Accounting and Economics*, *42*(1–2), 107–148. doi:10.1016/j.jacceco.2005.10.005

Bushman, R., Dai, Z., & Wang, X. (2010). Risk and CEO turnover. *Journal of Financial Economics*, *96*(3), 381–398. doi:10.1016/j.jfineco.2010.03.001

Cahan, S. F. (1992). The Effect of Antitrust Investigations on Discretionary Accruals: A Refined Test of the Political-Cost Hypothesis. *The Accounting Review*, *67*(1), 77–95.

Callao Gastón, S., & Jarne Jarne, J. I. (1995). La informacion financiera en el contexto internacional: analisis descriptivo. *Revista Espanola de Financiacion y Contabilidad1*, *24*(85), 937–969.

Callao Gastón, S., Ferrer García, C., Jarne Jarne, J. I., & Laínez Gadea, J. A. (2010). IFRS adoption in Spain and the United Kingdom : Effects on accounting numbers and relevance. *Advances in Accounting*. doi:10.1016/j.adiac.2010.08.003

Callao Gastón, S., & Jarne Jarne, J. I. (2011). El impacto de la crisis en la manipulación contable. *Revista de Contabilidad, 14*(2), 59–85. doi:10.1016/S1138-4891(11)70028-0

Callao, S., & Jarne, J. I. (2010). Have IFRS Affected Earnings Management in the European Union? *Accounting in Europe, 7*(2), 159–189. doi:10.1080/17449480.2010.511896

Callao, S., Jarne, J. I., & Laínez, J. A. (2007). Adoption of IFRS in Spain: Effect on the comparability and relevance of financial reporting. *Journal of International Accounting, Auditing & Taxation, 16*(2), 148–178. doi:10.1016/j.intacaudtax.2007.06.002

Campa, D., & Hajbaba, A. (2016). Do Targets Grab the Cash in Takeovers: The Role of Earnings Management. *JInternational Review of Financial Analysis, 44*, 56–64. doi:10.1016/j.irfa.2016.01.008

Campbell, J., Lettau, M., Malkiel, B., & Xu, Y. (2001). Have Individual Stocks Become More Volatile? An Empirical Exploration of Idiosyncratic Risk. *The Journal of Finance, 56*(1), 1–43. doi:10.1111/0022-1082.00318

Canadas, N. (2004). *Um Modelo Dual de Análise, Avaliação e Relato do Valor Intangível: O Caso das Telecomunicações Móveis em Portugal. Tese de doutoramento.* Universidade do Minho.

Canning, J. (1929). *The Economics of Accountancy*. New York: The Ronald Press Company.

Cannon, A. R. (2008). Inventory improvement and financial performance. *International Journal of Production Economics, 115*(2), 581–593. doi:10.1016/j.ijpe.2008.07.006

Cano-Rodriguez, M. (2010). Big Auditors, Private Firms and Accounting Conservatism: Spanish evidence. *European Accounting Review, 19*(1), 131–159. doi:10.1080/09638180902989426

Capkun, V., Collins, D., & Jeanjean, T. (2016). The effect of IAS/IFRS adoption on earnings management (smoothing): A closer look at competing explanations. *Journal of Accounting and Public Policy, 35*(4), 352–394. doi:10.1016/j.jaccpubpol.2016.04.002

Carlson, S. J., & Bathala, C. T. (1997). Ownership differences and firms' income smoothing behaviour. *Journal of Business Finance & Accounting, 24*(2), 179–196. doi:10.1111/1468-5957.00101

Carter, M. S., & Dukerich, J. M. (1998). Corporate Responses to Changes in Reputation. *Corporate Reputation Review, 1*(3), 250–270. doi:10.1057/palgrave.crr.1540047

Caruso, G. D., Ferrari, E. R., & Pisano, V. (2016). Earnings management and goodwill impairment: An empirical analysis in the Italian M&A context. *Journal of Intellectual Capital, 17*(1), 120–147. doi:10.1108/JIC-09-2015-0081

Cascino, S., Pugliese, A., Mussolino, D., & Sansone, C. (2010). The influence of family ownership on the quality of accounting information. *Family Business Review, 23*(3), 246–265. doi:10.1177/0894486510374302

Caves, R. E. (1980). Industrial organization, corporate strategy and structure. *Journal of Economic Literature, 18*(1), 64–92.

Cavique, L. (2008). Legibilidade de artigos científicos: Análise de dados da RCC. *Revista de Ciências da Computação, 3*(3), 59–65.

Cenni, S., Monferrà, S., Salotti, V., Sangiorgi, M., & Torluccio, G. (2015). Credit rationing and relationship lending. Does firm size matter? *Journal of Banking & Finance, 53*, 249–265. doi:10.1016/j.jbankfin.2014.12.010

Cerqueira, A., & Pereira, C. (2015). Accounting Accruals and Information Asymmetry in Europe. *Prague Economic Papers, 24*(6), 638–661. doi:10.18267/j.pep.528

Cerqueira, A., & Pereira, C. (2017). Accruals Quality, Managers' Incentives and Stock Market Reaction: Evidence from Europe. *Applied Economics*, *49*(16), 1606–1626. doi:10.1080/00036846.2016.1221047

Chalayer, S. (1994). *Identification et motivations des pratiques de lissage des résultats comptables des entreprises françaises cotées en Bourse* (Doctoral dissertation). Saint-Etienne University, France.

Chalmers, K., & Godfrey, J. M. (2004). Reputation costs : The impetus for voluntary derivative financial instrument reporting. *Accounting, Organizations and Society*, *29*(2), 95–125. doi:10.1016/S0361-3682(02)00034-X

Chaney, P. K., Jeter, D. C., & Lewis, C. M. (1998). The use of accruals in income smoothing: A permanent earnings hypothesis. *Advances in Quantitative Analysis of Finance and Accounting*, *6*, 103–135.

Chaney, P. K., & Lewis, C. M. (1995). Earnings management and firm valuation under asymmetric information. *Journal of Corporate Finance*, *1*(1), 319–345. doi:10.1016/0929-1199(94)00008-I

Chaney, P. K., & Lewis, C. M. (1995). Earnings management and firm valuation under asymmetric information. *Journal of Corporate Finance: Contracting. Governance and Organization*, *1*(3–4), 319–345.

Chaney, P. K., & Lewis, C. M. (1998). Income smoothing and underperformance in initial public offerings. *Journal of Corporate Finance*, *4*(1), 1–29. doi:10.1016/S0929-1199(97)00007-2

Chan, K., Chan, L., Jegadeesh, N., & Lakonishok, J. (2006). Earnings Quality and Stock Returns. *The Journal of Business*, *79*(3), 1041–1082. doi:10.1086/500669

Chen, C., Huang, A., & Jha, R. (2012). Idiosyncratic Return Volatility and the Information Quality Underlying Managerial Discretion. *Journal of Financial and Quantitative Analysis*, *47*(4), 873–899. doi:10.1017/S002210901200018X

Cheng, P., Man, P., & Yi, C. H. (2013). The impact of product market competition on earnings quality. *Accounting and Finance*, *53*(1), 4. doi:10.1111/j.1467-629X.2011.00457.x

Cheng, Q., & Warfield, T. (2005). Equity incentives and earnings management. *The Accounting Review*, *80*(2), 441–476. doi:10.2308/accr.2005.80.2.441

Chen, H., Tang, Q., Jiang, Y., & Lin, Z. (2010). The role of international financial reporting standards in accounting quality : Evidence from the European Union. *Journal of International Financial Management & Accounting*, *21*(3), 220–278. doi:10.1111/j.1467-646X.2010.01041.x

Chen, J. C., & Roberts, R. W. (2010). Toward a more coherent understanding of the organization-society relationship: A theoretical consideration for social and environmental accounting research. *Journal of Business Ethics*, *97*(4), 651–665. doi:10.100710551-010-0531-0

Chen, L., Firth, M., Gao, D. N., & Rui, O. M. (2006). Ownership structure, corporate governance, and fraud: Evidence from China. *Journal of Corporate Finance*, *12*(3), 424–448. doi:10.1016/j.jcorpfin.2005.09.002

Chen, L., & Zhao, X. (2006). On the relation between the market-to-book ratio, growth opportunity, and leverage ratio. *Finance Research Letters*, *3*(4), 254. doi:10.1016/j.frl.2006.06.003

Cheong, P. C., Teh, B. H., Ong, T. S., & Hong, Y. H. (2015). The relationship among audit quality, earnings management and financial performance of Malaysian Public Listed companies. *International Journal of Economics and Management*, *9*(1), 209–229.

Cheung, Y. L., Rau, P. R., & Stouraitis, A. (2006). Tunneling, propping, and expropriation: Evidence from connected party transactions in Hong Kong. *Journal of Financial Economics*, *82*(2), 341–386. doi:10.1016/j.jfineco.2004.08.012

Chia, Y., Lapsley, I., & Lee, H. (2007). Choice of auditors and earn-ings management during the Asian financial crisis. *Managerial Auditing Journal*, *22*(2), 177–196. doi:10.1108/02686900710718672

Chi, W., Lisic, L., & Pevzner, M. (2011). Is Enhanced Audit Quality Associated with Greater Real Earnings Management? *Accounting Horizons*, *25*(2), 315–335. doi:10.2308/acch-10025

Cho, C. H., Michelon, G., & Patten, D. M. (2012a). Enhancement and obfuscation through the use of graphs in sustainability reports: Na international comparison. Sustainability Accounting. *Management and Policy Journal*, *3*(1), 74–88.

Cho, C. H., Michelon, G., & Patten, D. M. (2012b). Impression management in sustainability reports: An empirical investigation of the use of graphs. *Accounting and the Public Interest*, *12*(1), 16–37. doi:10.2308/apin-10249

Cho, C. H., Roberts, R. W., & Patten, D. M. (2010). The language of US corporate environmental disclosure. *Accounting, Organizations and Society*, *35*(4), 431–443. doi:10.1016/j.aos.2009.10.002

Choi, J. H., Kim, J. B., & Zang, Y. (2010). Do abnormally high audit fees impair audit quality? *Auditing*, *29*(2), 115–140. doi:10.2308/aud.2010.29.2.115

Choi, J., Kim, J., & Lee, J. (2011). Value relevance of discretionary accruals in the Asian financial crisis of 1997–1998. *Journal of Accounting and Public Policy*, *30*(2), 166–187. doi:10.1016/j.jaccpubpol.2010.09.002

Christensen, H. B., Lee, E., Walker, M., & Zeng, C. (2015). Incentives or standards: What determines accounting quality changes around IFRS adoption? *European Accounting Review*, *24*(1), 31–61. doi:10.1080/09638180.2015.1009144

Christie, A. A. (1990). Aggregation of test statistics. *Journal of Accounting and Economics*, *12*(1–3), 15–36. doi:10.1016/0165-4101(90)90039-7

Christie, A., Joye, M., & Watts, R. L. (1989). *Organization of the firm: Theory and evidence*. Rochester, NY: Simon Graduate School of Business Administration. University of Rochester.

Christie, A., & Zimmerman, J. L. (1994). Efficient and Opportunistic Choices of Accounting Procedures: Corporate Control Contests. *The Accounting Review*, *69*(4), 539–566.

Cimini, R. (2015). How has the financial crisis affected earnings management? a European study. *Applied Economics*, *47*(3), 302–317. doi:10.1080/00036846.2014.969828

Clatworthy, M. A., & Jones, M. J. (2001). The effect of thematic structure on the variability of annual report readability. *Accounting, Auditing & Accountability Journal*, *14*(3), 311–326. doi:10.1108/09513570110399890

Clatworthy, M. A., & Jones, M. J. (2003). Financial reporting of good news and bad news: Evidence from accounting narratives. *Accounting and Business Research*, *33*(3), 171–185. doi:10.1080/00014788.2003.9729645

Clatworthy, M. A., & Jones, M. J. (2006). Differential patterns of textual characteristics and company performance in the chairman's statement. *Accounting, Auditing & Accountability Journal*, *19*(4), 493–511. doi:10.1108/09513570610679100

CMVM. (1999). *Recommendations of CMVM about corporate governance of Portuguese listed companies*. Available at www.cmvm.pt

CMVM. (2013). *CMVM corporate governance code*. Available at www.cmvm.pt

CMVM. (2014). *Report on corporate governance of Portuguese listed companies*. Annual Report. Available at www.cmvm.pt

Cohen, D. A., & Zarowin, P. (2008). *Economic Consequences of Real and Accrual-Based Earnings Management Activities*. Working Paper, New York University.

Cohen, L. J., Cornett, M. M., Marcus, A., & Tehranian, H. (2014). Bank Earnings Management and Tail Risk during the Financial Crisis. *Journal of Money, Credit & Banking, 46*(1), 171–197.

Cohen, D. A., Dey, A., & Lys, T. Z. (2008). Real and accrual-based earnings management in the pre- and post-sarbanes-oxley periods. *The Accounting Review*, *83*(3), 757–787. doi:10.2308/accr.2008.83.3.757

Cohen, D., & Zarowin, P. (2010). Accrual-based and Real Earnings Management Activities around Seasoned Equity Offerings. *Journal of Accounting and Economics*, *50*(1), 2–19. doi:10.1016/j.jacceco.2010.01.002

Cohen, J., Krishnamoorthy, G., & Peytchevaand, M. (2013). How Does the Strength of the Financial Regulatory Regime Influence Auditors' Judgments to Constrain Aggressive Reporting in a Principles-Based Versus Rules-Based Accounting Environment? *Accounting Horizons*, *27*(3), 579–601. doi:10.2308/acch-50502

Cohen, L., & Frazzini, A. (2008). Economic links and predictable returns. *The Journal of Finance*, *63*(4), 1977–2011. doi:10.1111/j.1540-6261.2008.01379.x

Commerford, B. P., Hermanson, D. R., Houston, R. W., & Peters, M. F. (2014). *Real Earnings Management: A Threat to Auditor Comfort?* Academic Press.

Cook, K. A., Huston, G. R., & Kinney, M. R. (2012). *Managing earnings by manipulating inventory: The effects of cost structure and valuation method.* Available at https://Ssrn.Com/Abstract=997437

Cooke, T. E. (1989). Disclosure In The Corporate Annual Reports Of Swedish Companies. *Accounting and Business Research*, *19*(74), 113–124. doi:10.1080/00014788.1989.9728841

Cooke, T. E. (1992). The Impact of Size, Stock Market Listing and Industry Type on Disclosure in the Annual Reports of Japanese Listed Corporations. *Accounting & Business Research (Wolters Kluwer UK)*, *22*(87), 229–237. doi:10.1080/00014788.1992.9729440

Copeland, R. M. (1968). Income smoothing. *Journal of Accounting Research*, *6*, 101–116. doi:10.2307/2490073

Copeland, R. M., & Wojdak, J. F. (1969). Income manipulation and the purchase-pooling choice. *Journal of Accounting Research*, *7*(2), 188–195. doi:10.2307/2489964

Coppens, L., & Peek, E. (2005). An analysis of earnings management by European private firms. *Journal of International Accounting, Auditing & Taxation*, *14*(1), 1–17. doi:10.1016/j.intaccaudtax.2005.01.002

Correia, C., & Pereira, H. (2011). Nacionalizações e Privatizações: o regime das nacionalizações em Portugal, dos tempos da revolução ao caso BPN. Trabalho apresentado em Direito da Economia, Faculdade de direito da Universidade Nova de Lisboa, Lisboa, Portugal.

Corwin, S., & Schultz, P. (2012). A Simple Way to Estimate Bid-Ask Spreads from Daily High and Low Prices. *The Journal of Finance*, *67*(2), 719–759. doi:10.1111/j.1540-6261.2012.01729.x

Costa, M., & Moreira, J. A. (2010). A experiência do auditor como determinante da qualidade da auditoria: uma análise para o caso português. *Contabilidade & Gestão*, (9).

Costa, G. A., Oliveira, L. C., & Rodrigues, L. L. (2011). Factors associated with the publication of CEO letter. *Corporate Communication: An International Journal*, *18*(4), 432–450. doi:10.1108/CCIJ-07-2012-0045

Costa, G. P. C. L., & Gartner, I. R. (2015). Manipulação de informações no setor público brasileiro: Evidências em dez casos pesquisados. *Revista Contemporânea de Contabilidade*, *12*(26), 141–162. doi:10.5007/2175-8069.2015v12n26p141

Courtis, J. K. (1986). An investigation into annual report readability and corporate risk-return relationships. *Accounting and Business Research*, *16*, 285–294. doi:10.1080/00014788.1986.9729329

Courtis, J. K. (1995). Readability of annual reports: Western versus Asian evidence. *Accounting, Auditing & Accountability Journal*, *8*(2), 4–17. doi:10.1108/09513579510086795

Courtis, J. K. (1998). Annual report readability variability: Tests of the obfuscation hypothesis. *Accounting, Auditing & Accountability Journal*, *11*(4), 459–471. doi:10.1108/09513579810231457

Courtis, J. K. (2004). Corporate report obfuscation: Artefact or phenomenon? *The British Accounting Review*, *36*(3), 291–312. doi:10.1016/j.bar.2004.03.005

Craig, R., & Walsh, P. (1989). Adjustments for 'extraordinary items' in smoothing reported profits of listed Australian companies: Some empirical evidence. *Journal of Business Finance & Accounting*, *16*(2), 229–245. doi:10.1111/j.1468-5957.1989.tb00015.x

Cristina, N., & Ioana, M. (2013). The Communication Process Of The Financial Reporting. *Annals of Faculty of Economics*, *1*(1), 1266–1272.

Cruz, S. N. da S. R. A., Azevedo, G. M. do C., & Pinheiro, C. F. R. (2013). Do POC ao SNC : evolução e aspetos diferenciadores. *Revista Portuguesa de Contabilidade, 3*(10).

Cummins, J. G., & Nyman, I. (2005). The dark side of competitive pressure. *The Rand Journal of Economics*, *36*(2), 361–377.

Custodio, C. (2014). Mergers and Acquisitions Accounting and the Diversification Discount. *The Journal of Finance*, *69*(1), 219–240. doi:10.1111/jofi.12108

d'Italia, B. (2018). *Relazione annuale 2017.* Retrieved from http://www.bancaditalia.it/pubblicazioni/relazione-annuale/2017/rel_2017.pdf

da Costa, S. F. (2007). *A Ley 16/2007, de 4 de Julho e a reforma do direito contabilístico Espanhol* (pp. 29–34). Revista TOC.

Dai, R. (2012). *International Accounting Databases on WRDS: Comparative Analysis.* Wharton Research Data Services. University of Pennsylvania.

Datta, S., Iskandar-Datta, M., & Singh, V. (2013). Product market power, industry structure, and corporate earnings management. *Journal of Banking & Finance*, *37*(8), 3273–3285. doi:10.1016/j.jbankfin.2013.03.012

Davis-Friday, P., Eng, L., & Liu, C. (2006). The effects of the Asian crisis, corporate governance and accounting system on the valuation of book value and earnings. *The International Journal of Accounting*, *41*(1), 22–40. doi:10.1016/j.intacc.2005.12.002

Davis, J., Schoorman, R., & Donaldson, L. (1997). Towards a stewardship theory of management. *Academy of Management Review*, *22*(1), 20–47. doi:10.5465/amr.1997.9707180258

Dayanandan, A., Donker, H., Ivanof, M., & Karahan, G. (2016). IFRS and accounting quality: Legal origin, regional, and disclosure impacts. *International Journal of Accounting & Information Management*, *24*(3), 296–316. doi:10.1108/IJAIM-11-2015-0075

de las Heras, E., Cañibano, L., & Moreira, J. A. (2012). The Impact of the Spanish financial act on audit quality. *Revista Española de Financiación y Contabilidad*, *41*(156), 521–546. doi:10.1080/02102412.2012.10779734

de Noguer, B. G., & Munõz, M. (2007). La calidad de los ajustes por devengo no afecta al coste de la deuda de las PYMES españolas. *Investigacion Economica*, *31*(1), 79–117.

de Sousa, A. S. N., Góis, C. M. G. G., & Viseu, C. M. P. (2017). A relação dos impostos com as necessidades de financiamento na manipulação de resultados. *XVI Congresso Internacional de Contabilidade e Auditoria.*

DeAngelo, H., & DeAngelo, L. (2000). Controlling stockholders and the disciplinary role of corporate payout policy: A study of the time mirror company. *Journal of Financial Economics*, *56*(2), 153–207. doi:10.1016/S0304-405X(00)00039-8

Debreceny, R., & Rahman, A. (2005). Firm-specific determinants of continuous corporate disclosures. *The International Journal of Accounting*, *40*(3), 249–278. doi:10.1016/j.intacc.2005.06.002

Dechow, P. (1994). Accounting Earnings and Cash Flows as Measure of Firm Performance: The Role of Accounting Accruals. *Journal of Accounting and Economics*, *18*, 3–42. doi:10.1016/0165-4101(94)90016-7

Dechow, P. M., Ge, W., Larson, C. R., & Sloan, R. G. (2011). Predicting Material Accounting Misstatements. *Contemporary Accounting Research*, *28*(1), 17–82. doi:10.1111/j.1911-3846.2010.01041.x

Dechow, P. M., Richardson, S., & Tuna, I. (2003). Why are earnings kinky? An examination of the earnings management explanation. *Review of Accounting Studies*, *8*(2–3), 355–384. doi:10.1023/A:1024481916719

Dechow, P. M., & Sloan, R. G. (1991). Executive incentives and the horizon problem: An empirical investigation. *Journal of Accounting and Economics*, *14*(1), 51–89. doi:10.1016/0167-7187(91)90058-S

Dechow, P. M., Sloan, R. G., & Sweeney, A. P. (1995). Detecting Earnings Management. *The Accounting Review*, *70*(2), 193–225.

Dechow, P. M., Sloan, R. G., & Sweeney, A. P. (1995). Detecting earnings management. *The Accounting Review*, *70*(2), 199.

Dechow, P., & Dichev, I. (2002). The Quality of Accruals and Earnings: The Role of Accrual Estimation Errors. *The Accounting Review*, *77*(s-1), 35–59. doi:10.2308/accr.2002.77.s-1.35

Dechow, P., Ge, W., & Schrand, C. (2010). Understanding Earnings Quality: A Review of the Proxies, their Determinants and their Consequences. *Journal of Accounting and Economics*, *50*(2-3), 344–401. doi:10.1016/j.jacceco.2010.09.001

Dechow, P., Hutton, A., & Sloan, R. (1999). An Empirical Assessment of the Residual Income Valuation Model. *Journal of Accounting and Economics*, *26*(1-3), 1–34. doi:10.1016/S0165-4101(98)00049-4

Dechow, P., Kothari, S., & Watts, R. (1998). The Relation Between Earnings and Cash Flows. *Journal of Accounting and Economics*, *25*, 133–168. doi:10.1016/S0165-4101(98)00020-2

Dechow, P., & Schrand, C. (2004). *Earnings quality*. Charlottesville, VA: CFA Institute Research Foundation.

Dechow, P., & Schrand, C. (2004). *Earnings Quality*. Research Foundation of CFA Institute.

Dechow, P., Sloan, R., & Sweeney, A. (1995). Detecting Earnings Management. *The Accounting Review*, *70*(2), 193–225.

Dechow, P., Sloan, R., & Sweeney, A. (1995). Detecting earnings management. *The Accounting Review*, *70*, 193–225.

Dechow, P., Sloan, R., & Sweeney, A. (1996). Causes and consequences of earnings manipulation: An analysis of firms subject to enforcement actions by the SEC. *Contemporary Accounting Research*, *13*(1), 1–36. doi:10.1111/j.1911-3846.1996.tb00489.x

Deegan, C. (2002). Introduction: The legitimising effect of social and environmental disclosures – a theoretical foundation. *Accounting, Auditing & Accountability Journal*, *15*(3), 282–311. doi:10.1108/09513570210435852

DeFond, M. L., & Jiambalvo, J. (1994). Debt covenant violation and manipulation of accruals. *Journal of Accounting and Economics*, *17*(1–2), 145–176. doi:10.1016/0165-4101(94)90008-6

DeFond, M. L., & Park, C. W. (1997). Smoothing income in anticipation of future earnings. *Journal of Accounting and Economics*, *23*(2), 115–139. doi:10.1016/S0165-4101(97)00004-9

DeFond, M., Hu, X., Hung, M., & Li, S. (2011). The impact of mandatory IFRS adoption on foreign mutual fund ownership: The role of comparability. *Journal of Accounting and Economics*, *51*(3), 240–258. doi:10.1016/j.jacceco.2011.02.001

DeFond, M., Hu, X., Hung, M., & Li, S. (2012). Has the widespread adoption of IFRS reduced US firms' attractiveness to foreign investors? *Journal of International Accounting Research*, *11*(2), 27–55. doi:10.2308/jiar-50205

Demerjian, P. R., Donovan, J., & Lewis-Western, M. F. (2018). Income smoothing and the usefulness of earnings for monitoring in debt. *SSRN Working Paper Series*, April version.

Desai, M. (2005). The Degradation of Reported Corporate Profits. *The Journal of Economic Perspectives*, *19*(4), 171–192. doi:10.1257/089533005775196705

Detzen, D., & Zulch, H. (2012). Executive compensation and goodwill recognition under IFRS: Evidence from European mergers. *Journal of International Accounting, Auditing & Taxation*, *21*(2), 106–126. doi:10.1016/j.intaccaudtax.2012.07.002

Deumes, R. (2008). Corporate risk reporting a content analysis of narrative risk disclosures in prospectuses. *Journal of Business Communication*, *45*(2), 120–157. doi:10.1177/0021943607313992

Deumes, R., & Knechel, R. W. (2008). Economic incentives for voluntary reporting on internal risk management and control systems. *Auditing*, *27*(1), 35–66. doi:10.2308/aud.2008.27.1.35

Dhaliwal, D. S. (1980). The Effect of the Firm's Capital Structure on the Choice of Accounting Methods. *The Accounting Review*, *55*(1), 78–84.

Dhaliwal, D. S. (1980). The effect of the firm's capital structure on the choice of accounting methods. *The Accounting Review*, *55*(1), 78–85.

Dhaliwal, D. S., Frankel, M., & Trezevant, R. (1994). The taxable and book income motivation for a LIFO layer liquidation. *Journal of Accounting Research*, *32*(2), 278–289. doi:10.2307/2491286

Dias, P. (2015). *As diferenças entre o resultado contabilístico e o fiscal e a gestão dos resultados Evidência empírica de empresas privadas portuguesas (Tese de Doutoramento)*. Lisboa: ISCTE-IUL.

Dichev, I. D., Graham, J., Harvey, C. R., & Rajgopal, S. (2013). Earnings Quality: Evidence from the Field. *Journal of Accounting and Economics*, *56*(2–3), 1–33. doi:10.1016/j.jacceco.2013.05.004

Dichev, I. D., & Skinner, D. J. (2002). Large-sample evidence on the debt covenant hypothesis. *Journal of Accounting Research*, *40*(4), 1091–1123. doi:10.1111/1475-679X.00083

Dichev, I. D., & Tang, W. (2009). Earnings volatility and earnings predictability. *Journal of Accounting and Economics*, *47*(1-2), 160–181. doi:10.1016/j.jacceco.2008.09.005

Dimitras, A. I., Kyriakou, M. I., & Iatridis, G. (2015). Financial crisis, GDP variation and earnings management in Europe. *Research in International Business and Finance*, *34*, 338–354. doi:10.1016/j.ribaf.2015.02.017

Dimitropoulos, E., Asteriou, P., Dimitrios Kousenidis, D., & Leventis, S. (2013). The impact of IFRS on accounting quality: Evidence from Greece. *Advances in Accounting*, *29*(1), 108–123. doi:10.1016/j.adiac.2013.03.004

Ding, R., & Jia, Y. (2012). Auditor mergers, audit quality and audit fees: Evidence from the PricewaterhouseCoopers merger in the UK. *Journal of Accounting and Public Policy*, *31*(1), 69–85. doi:10.1016/j.jaccpubpol.2011.08.002

do Carmo, C. R., Moreira, J. A., & Miranda, M. C. (2010). A qualidade dos accruals e o custo do financiamento nas empresas portuguesas: uma análise por grupos de dimensão. In XVI Encuentro AECA (pp. 1–31). Leiria.

do Carmo, C. R., Moreira, J. A., & Miranda, M. C. (2016). Earnings quality and cost of debt: Evidence from Portuguese private companies. *Journal of Financial Reporting and Accounting*, *14*(2), 178–197. doi:10.1108/JFRA-08-2014-0065

Doadrio, L., Alvarado, M., & Carrera, N. (2015). Reforma de la normativa contable española: Análisis de su entramado institucional. *Spanish Accounting Review*, *18*(2), 200–216. doi:10.1016/j.rcsar.2015.02.002

Dos Santos, A., & Paulo, E. (2006). Diferimento das perdas cambiais como instrumento de gerenciamento de resultados. *Brazilian Business Review*, *3*(1), 15–31.

Dou, Y., Hope, O., & Thomas, W. (2013). Relationship-specificity, contract enforceability, and income smoothing. *The Accounting Review*, *88*(5), 1629–1656. doi:10.2308/accr-50489

Doyle, J., Ge, W., & McVay, S. (2007). Accruals and internal control over financial reporting. *The Accounting Review*, *82*(5), 1141–1170. doi:10.2308/accr.2007.82.5.1141

DuCharme, L. L., Malatesta, P. H., & Sefcik, S. E. (2001). Earnings Management: IPO Valuation and Subsequent Performance. *Journal of Accounting, Auditing & Finance*, *16*(4), 369–396. doi:10.1177/0148558X0101600409

Duffy, D., Fitzgerald, J., Byrne, D., & Timoney, K. (2013). *Quarterly Economic Commentary, Winter*. Dublin: ESRI.

Duke, J., & Hunt, H. III. (1990). An empirical examination of debt covenant restrictions and accounting-related debt proxies. *Journal of Accounting and Economics*, *12*(1-3), 43–63. doi:10.1016/0165-4101(90)90041-2

Dye, R. A. (1985). Disclosure of nonproprietary information. *Journal of Accounting Research*, *23*(1), 123–145. doi:10.2307/2490910

Easley, D., Hvidkjaer, S., & O'Hara, M. (2002). Is Information Risk a Determinant of Asset Returns? *The Journal of Finance*, *57*(5), 2185–2221. doi:10.1111/1540-6261.00493

Easley, D., & O'Hara, M. (2004). Information and the Cost of Capital. *The Journal of Finance*, *59*(4), 1553–1583. doi:10.1111/j.1540-6261.2004.00672.x

Easterwood, C. M. (1998). Takeovers and incentives for earnings management: An empirical analysis. *Journal of Applied Business Research*, *14*(1), 29–47. doi:10.19030/jabr.v14i1.5726

Easton, P. D., & Zmijewski, M. E. (1989). Cross-sectional variation in the stock market response to accounting earnings announcements. *Journal of Accounting and Economics*, *11*(2-3), 117–141. doi:10.1016/0165-4101(89)90003-7

Edey, H. (1957, January). Business Valuation, Goodwill and the Super-Profit Method. *Accountancy*.

Edwards and Bell (1961). *The Theory and Measurement of Business Income*. Author.

Eilifsen, A. (1996). The relationship between accounting and taxation in Norway. *European Accounting Review*, *5*(sup1), 835–844. doi:10.1080/09638189600000061

Eilifsen, A., Knivsfla, K. H. IV, & Saettem, F. (1999). Earnings manipulation : Cost of capital versus tax. *European Accounting Review*, *8*(3), 481–491. doi:10.1080/096381899335899

El-gazzar, S. M., Finn, P. M., & Jacob, R. (1999). *An Empirical Investigation of Multinational Firms â€TM Compliance with International Accounting Standards*. Academic Press.

Elgers, P. T., Pfeiffer, R. J. Jr, & Porter, S. L. (2003). Anticipatory income smoothing: A re-examination. *Journal of Accounting and Economics*, *35*(3), 405–422. doi:10.1016/S0165-4101(03)00039-9

Elliot, J., & Hanna, J. D. (1996). Repeated Accounting Write-Offs and the Information Content of Earnings. *Journal of Accounting Research*, *34*(Supplement), 135–155. doi:10.2307/2491430

Ereira, S. M. (2007). *O relato do risco: uma análise no contexto das empresas cotadas na Euronext Lisbon (Dissertação de mestrado)*. Coimbra: Escola Superior de Tecnologias e Gestão de Leiria.

Erickson, M., & Wang, S. (1999). Earnings Management by Acquiring Firms in Stock for Stock Mergers. *Journal of Accounting and Economics*, *27*(2), 149–176. doi:10.1016/S0165-4101(99)00008-7

European Central Bank. (2009). *Does it pay to have the Euro? Italy's politics and financial markets under the Lira and the Euro*. Working Paper Series, No. 1064, 1–41.

European Central Bank. (2017). *Business investment developments in the euro area since the crisis*. Retrieved from https://www.ecb.europa.eu/pub/pdf/other/eb201607_article02.en.pdf?e917ba5e5156495c3a382abf942e9e53

European Commission. (2003). Commission Recommendation of 6 May 2003 concerning the definition of micro, small and medium-sized enterprises. *Official Journal of the European Union*, 36–41. Retrieved from https://eur-lex.europa.eu/legal-content/EN/TXT/PDF/?uri=CELEX:32003H0361&from=EN

European Commission. (2009). *Final Report of the Expert Group – Overview of Family-Business-Relevant Issues: Research, Networks, Policy Measures and Existing Studies*. Directorate-Generale for Entreprise and Industry. Available online at: http://ec.europa.eu/entreprise/policies/sms/index_en.htm

European Commission. (2017a). *2017 SBA fact sheet Portugal*. Author.

European Commission. (2017b). *2017 SBA fact sheet Spain*. Author.

European Stability Mechanism. (2014). *European Stability Mechanism Annual Report -2014*. Author.

Ewert, R., & Wagenhofer, A. (2011). *Earnings Quality Metrics and What They Measure*. Working Paper, August. University of Graz.

Ewert, R., & Wagenhofer, A. (2015). Economic Relations Among Earnings Quality Measures. *Abacus*, *51*(3), 311–355. doi:10.1111/abac.12054

Faccio, M., & Lang, L. (2002). The ultimate ownership of Western European corporations. *Journal of Financial Economics*, *65*(3), 365–395. doi:10.1016/S0304-405X(02)00146-0

Falschlunger, L. M., Eisl, C., Losbichler, H., & Greil, A. M. (2015). Impression management in annual reports of the largest European companies: A longitudinal study on graphical representations. *Journal of Applied Accounting Research*, *16*(3), 383–399. doi:10.1108/JAAR-10-2014-0109

Fama, E., & French, K. (1997). Industry Costs of Equity. *Journal of Financial Economics*, *43*(2), 153–193. doi:10.1016/S0304-405X(96)00896-3

Fama, E., & Jensen, M. (1983). Separation of ownership and control. *The Journal of Law & Economics*, *26*(2), 301–325. doi:10.1086/467037

Fama, E., & Miller, M. (1972). *The Theory of Finance*. New York: Rinehand S. Winston.

FASB. (1978). *Statements of Financial Accounting Concepts, n.º 1, Objectives of Financial Reporting by Business Enterprises*. Stanford, CT: Financial Accounting Standard Board (FASB).

Favoretto, A. B., Corrêa, F. P., Silva, F. L. & Grecco, M. C. P. (2017). O Gerenciamento de Resultados Contábeis e o Controle de Provisões. *Redeca*, *4*(2), 113-125.

Federal Accounting Council. *Comunicado Técnico CTG 1.000* of August 30, 2013. Dispõe sobre a adoção plena da NBC TG 1.000.

Federal Accounting Council. *Resolutions* n.1.255 of December 10, 2009. Aprova a NBC TG 1000 – Contabilidade para Pequenas e Médias Empresas. Disponível em: http://www.crcsp.org.br/portal_novo/legislacao_contabil/resolucoes/Res1255.htm

Feltham, G., & Ohlson, J. (1995). Valuation and Clean Surplus Accounting for Operating and Financial Activities. *Contemporary Accounting Research*, *11*(2), 689–732. doi:10.1111/j.1911-3846.1995.tb00462.x

Feltham, G., & Ohlson, J. (1996). Uncertainty Resolution and the Theory of Depreciation Measurement. *Journal of Accounting Research*, *34*(2), 209–234. doi:10.2307/2491500

Fernandes, J. L. T., & Silva, C. A. T. (2007). Análise da legibilidade dos textos narrativos dos fatos relevantes divulgados pelas empresas brasileiras de capital aberto nos anos de 2002 a 2006. In Congresso USP de Iniciação Científica (Vol. 4, No. 2007, pp. 142-158). Academic Press.

Fernández-Rodríguez, E., & Martínez-Arias, A. (2015). La discrecionalidad en las diferencias temporarias entre Contabilidad y Fiscalidad. *Spanish Journal of Finance and Accounting*, *44*(2), 180–207. doi:10.1080/02102412.2015.1006427

Ferramosca, S., & Allegrini, M. (2018). The complex role of family involvement in earnings management. *Journal of Family Business Strategy*, *9*(2), 128–141. doi:10.1016/j.jfbs.2018.01.001

Ferreira, M., & Laux, P. (2007). Corporate Governance, Idiosyncratic Risk, and Information Flow. *The Journal of Finance*, *62*(2), 951–989. doi:10.1111/j.1540-6261.2007.01228.x

Ferrer, R. C., & Ferrer, G. J. (2016). Earnings management indicators and their impact on inventory turnover under food, beverage and tobacco sector: A thorough study using simultaneous equations model. *Academy of Accounting and Financial Studies Journal*, *20*(2), 93–103.

Filip, A., & Raffournier, B. (2014). Financial crisis and earnings management: The European evidence. *The International Journal of Accounting*, *49*(4), 455–478. doi:10.1016/j.intacc.2014.10.004

Fischer, E. O., Heinkel, R., & Zechner, J. (1989). Dynamic Capital Structure Choice : Theory and Tests. *The Journal of Finance*, *44*(1), 19–40. doi:10.1111/j.1540-6261.1989.tb02402.x

Fitzgerald, J. (2012). Financial Crisis, Economic Adjustment and a Return to Growth in the EU. *Revue de l'OFCE, Debates and Policies*, 127.

Flesch, R. (1948). A new readability yardstick. *The Journal of Applied Psychology*, *32*(3), 221–233. doi:10.1037/h0057532

Foster, G. (1986). *Financial statement analysis*. Prentice-Hall, Inc.

Fosu, S. (2013). Capital structure, product market competition, and firm performance: Evidence from South Africa. *The Quarterly Review of Economics and Finance*, *53*(2), 140–151. doi:10.1016/j.qref.2013.02.004

Francis, J. R., Khurana, I. K., & Pereira, R. (2005). Disclosure incentives and effects on cost of capital around the world. *The Accounting Review*, *80*(4), 1125–1162. doi:10.2308/accr.2005.80.4.1125

Francis, J. R., Maydew, E. L., & Spark, H. C. (1999). The role of Big 6 auditors in the credible reporting of accruals. *Auditing*, *18*(2), 17–34. doi:10.2308/aud.1999.18.2.17

Francis, J., Hanna, J. D., & Vincent, L. (1996). Causes and Effects of Discretionary Asset Write-Offs. *Journal of Accounting Research*, *34*, 117–134. doi:10.2307/2491429

Francis, J., LaFond, R., Olsson, P., & Schipper, K. (2004). Cost of Equity and Earnings Attributes. *The Accounting Review*, *79*(4), 967–1010. doi:10.2308/accr.2004.79.4.967

Francis, J., LaFond, R., Olsson, P., & Schipper, K. (2005). The Market Pricing of Accruals Quality. *Journal of Accounting and Economics*, *39*(2), 295–327. doi:10.1016/j.jacceco.2004.06.003

Frankel, R., & Li, X. (2004). Characteristics of a firm's information environment and the information asymmetry between insiders and outsiders. *Journal of Accounting and Economics*, *37*(2), 229–259. doi:10.1016/j.jacceco.2003.09.004

Frank, M. M., Lynch, L. J., & Rego, S. O. (2009). Tax reporting aggressiveness to aggressive and its relation financial reporting. *The Accounting Review*, *84*(2), 467–496. doi:10.2308/accr.2009.84.2.467

Frank, M. Z., & Goyal, V. K. (2009). Capital Structure Decisions around the World: Which Factors Are Reliably Important? *Financial Management*, *38*(1), 1–37. doi:10.1111/j.1755-053X.2009.01026.x

Frink, D. D., & Ferris, G. R. (1998). Accountability, impression management, and goal setting in the performance evaluation process. *Human Relations*, *51*(10), 1259–1283. doi:10.1177/001872679805101003

Froot, K., Scharfstein, D., & Stein, J. (1993). Risk management Coordinating corporate investment and Financing Policies. *The Journal of Finance*, *48*(5), 1624–1658. doi:10.1111/j.1540-6261.1993.tb05123.x

Frownfelter-Lohrke, C., & Fulkerson, C. L. (2001). The Incidence and Quality of Graphics in Annual Reports: An International Comparison. *Journal of Business Communication*, *38*(3), 337–357. doi:10.1177/002194360103800308

Fudenberg, D., & Tirole, J. (1995). A theory of income and dividend smoothing based on incumbency rents. *Journal of Political Economy*, *103*(1), 75–93. doi:10.1086/261976

Gabrielsen, G. J., Gramlich, J., & Plenborg, T. (2002). Managerial ownership, information content of earnings, and discretionary accruals in a non-US setting. *Journal of Business Finance & Accounting*, *29*(7/8), 967–988. doi:10.1111/1468-5957.00457

Gaio, C. (2010). The relative importance of firm and country characteristics for earnings quality around the world. *European Accounting Review*, *19*(4), 693–738. doi:10.1080/09638180903384643

Gao, J., Gao, B., & Wang, X. (2017). Trade-off between real activities earnings management and accrual-based manipulation-evidence from China. *Journal of International Accounting, Auditing & Taxation*, *29*, 66–80. doi:10.1016/j.intaccaudtax.2017.08.001

Gao, L., & Zhan, J. (2015). Firms' earnings smoothing, corporate social responsibility, and valuation. *Journal of Corporate Finance*, *32*, 108–127. doi:10.1016/j.jcorpfin.2015.03.004

García-meca, E., Parra, I., Larrán, M., & Martínez, I. (2005). The explanatory factors of intellectual capital disclosure to financial analysts. *European Accounting Review*, *14*(1), 63–94. doi:10.1080/0963818042000279713

Gardner, W. L., & Martinko, M. J. (1988). Impression management: An observational study linking audience characteristics with verbal self-presentations. *Academy of Management Journal*, *31*(1), 42–65.

Gassen, J., & Fuelbier, R. U. (2015). Do Creditors prefer smooth earnings? Evidence from European Private Firms. *Journal of International Accounting Research*, *14*(2), 151–180. doi:10.2308/jiar-51130

Gasteratos, I., Karamalis, M., Koutoupis, A., & Filos, I. (2016). Earning management in Greece: A case study in construction sector using Jones Model. *International Journal of Economics and Business Administration*, *6*(4), 3–16.

Gaver, J. J., Gaver, K. M., & Austin, J. R. (1995). Additional evidence on bonus plans and income management. *Journal of Accounting and Economics*, *19*(1), 3–28. doi:10.1016/0165-4101(94)00358-C

Ge, V., & McVay, S. (2005). The diclosure of material weaknesses in internal control after the Sarbanes -Oxley Act. *Accounting Horizons*, *19*(3), 137–158. doi:10.2308/acch.2005.19.3.137

Ghabdian, B., Attaran, N., & Froutan, O. (2012). Ownership structure and earnings management: Evidence from Iran. *International Journal of Business and Management*, *7*(15), 88–97. doi:10.5539/ijbm.v7n15p88

Ghosh, A., Gu, Z., & Jain, P. (2005). Sustained Earnings and Revenue Growth, Earnings Quality, and Earnings Response Coefficients. *Review of Accounting Studies*, *10*(1), 33–57. doi:10.100711142-004-6339-3

Giavazzi, F., & Spaventa, L. (2010). *Why the current account matters in a monetary union Lessons from the financial crisis in the Euro area*. Author.

Gibbins, M., Richardson, A., & Waterhouse, J. (1990). The management of corporate financial disclosure: Opportunism, ritualism, policies, and process. *Journal of Accounting Research*, *28*(1), 121–143. doi:10.2307/2491219

Godfrey, J. M., & Jones, K. L. (1999). Political cost influences on income smoothing via extraordinary item classification. *Accounting and Finance*, *39*(3), 229–254. doi:10.1111/1467-629X.00025

Godfrey, J., Mather, P., & Ramsay, A. (2003). Earnings and impression management in financial reports: The case of CEO changes. *Abacus*, *39*(1), 95–123. doi:10.1111/1467-6281.00122

Goncharov, I., & Zimmermann, J. (2006). Earnings management when incentives compete: The role of tax accounting in Russia. *Journal of International Accounting Research*, *5*(1), 41–65. doi:10.2308/jiar.2006.5.1.41

Gong, G., Louis, H., & Sun, X. (2008). Earnings Management, Lawsuits, and Stock-for-Stock Acquirers' Market Performance. *Journal of Accounting and Economics*, *46*(1), 62–77. doi:10.1016/j.jacceco.2008.03.001

González, J. S., & García-Meca, E. (2013). Does corporate governance influence earnings management in Latin American markets? *Journal of Business Ethics*, *121*(3), 419–440. doi:10.100710551-013-1700-8

Gonzalo Angulo, J. A. (2014). La reforma contable española de 2007: Um balance. *Revista de Contabilidad: Spanish Accounting Review*, *17*(2), 183–200. doi:10.1016/j.rcsar.2014.09.001

Gordon, M. J. (1964). Postulates, principles and research in accounting. *The Accounting Review*, *39*(2), 251–263.

Gordon, M., & Shapiro, E. (1956). Capital Equipment Analysis: The Required Rate of Profit. *Management Science*, *3*(1), 102–110. doi:10.1287/mnsc.3.1.102

Gorgan, C., Gorgan, V., Dumitru, V. F., & Pitulice, I. C. (2012). The Evolution of the Accounting Practices During the Recent Economic Crisis : Empirical Survey Regarding the Earning Management. *The Amfiteatru Economics Journal*, *14*(32), 550–563.

Gottardo, P., & Moisello, A. M. (2019). Earnings Management, Issues and Firm Market Value. In *Capital Structure, Earnings Management, and Risk of Financial Distress*. Cham: Springer. doi:10.1007/978-3-030-00344-9_5

Gracia-Sarubbi, F., San Juan-Pajares, C. A., & Rodríguez-López, Á. (2014). Evolución del proceso de armonización contable en España y Brasil en el período 1973-2013. *Cuadernos de Contabilidad*, *15*(38), 397–425. doi:10.11144/Javeriana.cc15-38.epac

Graham, J., Harvey, C., & Rajgopal, S. (2005). The Economic Implications of Corporate Financial Reporting. *Journal of Accounting and Economics*, *40*(1–3), 3–73. doi:10.1016/j.jacceco.2005.01.002

Graves, O. F., Flesher, D. L., & Jordon, R. E. (1996). Pictures and the bottom line: The television epistemology of US annual reports. *Accounting, Organizations and Society*, *21*(1), 57–88. doi:10.1016/0361-3682(94)00026-R

Gray, R., Owen, D., & Adams, C. (1996). *Accounting & accountability: changes and challenges in corporate social and environmental reporting*. Prentice Hall.

Grecco, M. C. P. (2013). Efeito da convergência brasileira às IFRS no gerenciamento de resultados das empresas abertas brasileiras não financeiras. *Brazilian Business Review*, *10*(4), 117–140.

Green, A., & Mayes, D. (1991). Technical inefficiency in manufacturing industries. *Economic Journal (London)*, *101*(406), 523–538. doi:10.2307/2233557

Greene, W. H. (2008). *Econometric Analysis*. Pearson.

Grullon, G., & Michaely, R. (2007). *Corporate payout policy and product market competition*. Working Paper. Retrieved from http://ssrn.com/abstract=972221

Guadalupe, M., & Perez-Gonzalez, F. (2010). *Competition and private benefits of control*. Working Paper. Retrieved from http://ssrn.com/abstract=890814

Guenther, D. A. (1994). The relation between tax rates and pre-tax returns direct evidence from the 1981 and 1986 tax rate reductions. *Journal of Accounting and Economics*, *18*(3), 379–393. doi:10.1016/0165-4101(94)90027-2

Guidry, F., Leone, A. J., Rock, S., Simon, W. E., Beneish, D., Billings, B., & Stuart, N. (1999). Earnings-based bonus plans and earnings management by business-unit managers. *Journal of Accounting and Economics*, *26*, 113–142. doi:10.1016/S0165-4101(98)00037-8

Guimarães, R., Lima, L., Ocejo, J. L. S., & Gonçalves, P. (1998). Alternativas contabilísticas: estudo comparativo entre Portugal e Espanha. VII Jornadas de Contabilidade e Auditoria.

Guimarães, J. (2010). Reflexões sobre o SNC. *Contabilidade & Empresas*, *2*, 22–27.

Gul, F., Srinidhi, B., & Ng, A. (2011). Does board gender diversity improve the in formativeness of stock prices. *Journal of Accounting and Economics*, *51*(3), 314–338. doi:10.1016/j.jacceco.2011.01.005

Gull, A. A., Nekhili, M., Nagati, H., & Chtioui, T. (2018). Beyond gender diversity: How specific attributes of female directors affect earnings management. *The British Accounting Review*, *50*(3), 255–274. doi:10.1016/j.bar.2017.09.001

Gunny, K. (2005). *What Are the Consequences of Real Earnings Management?* Working Paper, University of Colorado at Boulder.

Gunny, K. A., Jacob, J., & Jorgensen, B. N. (2013). Implications of the integral approach and earnings management for alternate annual reporting periods. *Review of Accounting Studies*, *18*(3), 868–891. doi:10.100711142-013-9235-x

Gupta, M., Pevzner, M., & Seethamraju, C. (2010). The implications of absorption cost accounting and prodution decisions for future firm performance and valuation. *Contemporary Accounting Research*, *27*(3), 889–922. doi:10.1111/j.1911-3846.2010.01030.x

Gu, Z., Lee, C. W. J., & Rosett, J. G. (2005). What determines the variability of accounting accruals? *Review of Quantitative Finance and Accounting*, *24*(3), 313–334. doi:10.100711156-005-6869-1

Habib, A. (2005). Firm-specific determinants of income smoothing in Bangladesh: An empirical evaluation. *Advances in International Accounting*, *18*, 53–71. doi:10.1016/S0897-3660(05)18003-9

Habib, A., Uddin, B. B., & Islam, A. (2013). Financial distress, earnings management and market pricing of accruals during the global financial crisis. *Managerial Finance*, *39*(2), 155–180. doi:10.1108/03074351311294007

Hackston, D., & Milne, M. J. (1996). Some Determinants of Social and Environmental Disclosures in New Zeland Companies. *Journal Auditing & Accountability*, *1*(9), 77–108. doi:10.1108/09513579610109987

Hagerman, R. L., & Zmijewski, M. E. (1979). Some economic determinants of accounting policy choice. *Journal of Accounting and Economics*, *1*(2), 141–161. doi:10.1016/0165-4101(79)90004-1

Hand, J. (2001). Discussion of Earnings, Book Values, and Dividends in Equity Valuation: An Empirical Perspective. *Contemporary Accounting Research*, *18*(1), 121–130. doi:10.1506/6A7C-74ML-TGBD-DYBW

Harris, M., & Raviv, A. (1991). The Theory of Capital Structure. *The Journal of Finance*, *46*(1), 297–355. doi:10.1111/j.1540-6261.1991.tb03753.x

Hasbrouck, J. (2009). Trading Costs and Returns for U.S. Equities: Estimating Effective Costs from Daily Data. *The Journal of Finance*, *64*(3), 1445–1477. doi:10.1111/j.1540-6261.2009.01469.x

Hassan, M. K. (2009). UAE corporations-specific characteristics and level of risk disclosure. *Managerial Auditing Journal*, *24*(7), 668–687. doi:10.1108/02686900910975378

Hastuti, T. D., Ghozali, I., & Yuyetta, E. N. (2016). The effect of international financial reporting standards on the real earnings management and internal control structure as a moderating variable. *International Journal of Economics and Financial Issues*, *6*(4), 1807–1814.

Hayn, C., & Hughes, P. J. (2006). Leading indicators of goodwill impairment. *Journal of Accounting, Auditing & Finance*, , *21*(3), 223–265. doi:10.1177/0148558X0602100303

Healy, P. M. (1985). The effect of bonus schemes on accounting decisions. *Journal of Accounting and Economics*, *7*(1-3), 85–107. doi:10.1016/0165-4101(85)90029-1

Healy, P. M., & Palepu, K. G. (2001). Information asymmetry, corporate disclosure, and the capital markets: A review of the empirical disclosure literature. *Journal of Accounting and Economics*, *31*(1–3), 405–440. doi:10.1016/S0165-4101(01)00018-0

Healy, P., & Wahlen, J. (1999). A Review of the Earnings Management Literature and Its Implications for Standard Setting. *Accounting Horizons*, *13*(4), 365–383. doi:10.2308/acch.1999.13.4.365

Hepworth, S. R. (1953). periodic income smoothing. *The Accounting Review*, *28*(1), 32–39.

Hepworth, S. R. (1953). Smoothing periodic income. *The Accounting Review*, *28*(1), 32–39.

Herath, H. S. B., & Lu, X. (2017, September). Inference of economic truth from financial statements for detecting earnings management: Inventory costing methods from an information economics perspective. *Managerial and Decision Economics*, 1–14. doi:10.1002/mde.2912

Hermalin, B., & Weisback, M. (2007). *Transparency and corporate governance*. NBER working paper No. 12875.

Hermanns, S. (2006). *Financial Information and Earnings Quality*. Working paper, Facultes Universitaires Notre-Dame de la Paix.

Hicks, J. (1939). *Value and Capital*. Oxford University Press.

Hill, W. Y., & Milner, M. (2003). Guidelines for graphical displays in financial reporting. *Accounting Education*, *12*(2), 135–157. doi:10.1080/0963928032000091747

Höglund, H., & Sundvik, D. (2016). Outsourcing of accounting tasks and tax management: Evidence from a corporate tax rate change. *Applied Economics Letters*, *23*(7), 482–485. doi:10.1080/13504851.2015.1083074

Höglund, H., & Sundvik, D. (2018). Do auditors constrain intertemporal income shifting in private companies? *Accounting and Business Research*, 1–26. doi:10.1080/00014788.2018.1490166

Ho, L. J., & Kang, F. (2013). Auditor Choice and Audit Fees in Family Firms: Evidence from the S&P 1500. *Auditing*, *32*(4), 71–93. doi:10.2308/ajpt-50533

Holthausen, R. W., Larcker, D. F., & Sloan, R. G. (1995). Annual bonus schemes and the manipulation of earnings. *Journal of Accounting and Economics*, *19*(1), 29–74. doi:10.1016/0165-4101(94)00376-G

Hooghiemstra, R. (2000). Corporate communication and impression management – new perspectives on why companies engage in social reporting. *Journal of Business Ethics*, *27*(1/2), 55–68. doi:10.1023/A:1006400707757

Hooghiemstra, R. (2000). *Corporate communication and impression management—New perspectives why companies engage in corporate social reporting*. Springer Netherlands. doi:10.1007/978-94-011-4311-0_7

Houqe, M. N., Dunstan, K., Waresul, A., & Van, Z. (2010). *Board ethics and auditor choice: International evidence.* Working Paper n.º 72, Centre for Accounting, Governance and Taxation Research.

Howard, M. (1996). Downsizing to destruction. *Management Accounting: Magazine for Chartered Management Accountants*, *74*, 66.

Hsiao, C. (2004). *Analysis of panel data* (Vol. 47). Computers & Mathematics with Applications; doi:10.1016/S0898-1221(04)90099-5

Huguet, D., & Gandía, J. L. (2016). Audit and earnings management in Spanish SMEs. *BRQ Business Research Quarterly*, *19*(3), 171–187. doi:10.1016/j.brq.2015.12.001

Huili, Z., Ran, Z., & Jingyi, L. (2010). Does female senior management affect earnings quality: A large sample analysis of Chinese listed firms. *The Theory and Practice of Finance and Economics*, *6*, 62–66.

Hunt, H. (1985). Potential determinants of corporate inventory accounting decisions. *Journal of Accounting Research*, *23*(2), 448–467. doi:10.2307/2490820

Hunt, H. (1986). The separation of corporate ownership and control: Theory, evidence and implications. *Journal of Accounting Literature*, *5*, 85–124.

Hutton, A., Marcus, A., & Tehranian, H. (2009). Opaque Financial Reports R^2. *Journal of Financial Economics*, *49*(1), 67–86. doi:10.1016/j.jfineco.2008.10.003

Hyland, K. (1998). Exploring corporate rhetoric met discourse in the CEO's letter. *Journal of Business Communication*, *35*(2), 224–245. doi:10.1177/002194369803500203

Iatridis, G. (2012). Audit quality in common-law and code-law emerging markets: Evidence on earnings conservatism, agency costs and cost of equity. *Emerging Markets Review*, *13*(2), 101–117. doi:10.1016/j.ememar.2012.01.001

Iatridis, G., & Dimitras, A. I. (2013). Financial crisis and accounting quality: Evidence from five European countries. *Advances in Accounting*, *29*(1), 154–160. doi:10.1016/j.adiac.2013.03.001

IFRS. (2015). *Post-implementation Review of Review of IFRS 3 Business Combinations. Report and Feedback Statement.* IFRS.

Imhoff, E. A. (1981). Income smoothing: An analysis of critical issues. *The Quarterly Review of Economics and Business*, *21*(3), 23–42.

Iñiguez, R., & Poveda, F. (2004). Long-run abnormal returns and income smoothing in the spanish stock market. *European Accounting Review*, *13*(1), 105–130. doi:10.1080/0963818032000138224

International Accounting Standards Board (IASB) (2001). *International Accounting Standard 16 - Property, Plant and Equipament*. London: IASB.

Irvine, P., & Pontiff, J. (2009). Idiosyncratic return volatility, cash flows, and product market competition. *Review of Financial Studies*, *22*(3), 1149–1177. doi:10.1093/rfs/hhn039

Jackson, A. B. (2017). Discretionary Accruals: Earnings Management ... or Not? *Abacus*, *54*(2), 136–153. doi:10.1111/abac.12117

Jaffer, M. J., & Sohail, S. B. (2007). *Corporate Governance Issues in Family-Owned Enterprises*. Center for International Private Enterprise (CIPE), Economic Reform Feature Service. Available at http://www.cipe.org/publications/fs/pdf/042007.pdf

Jaggi, B., Leung, S., & Gul, F. (2009). Family control, board independence and earnings management: Evidence based on Hong Kong firms. *Journal of Accounting and Public Policy*, *28*(4), 281–300. doi:10.1016/j.jaccpubpol.2009.06.002

Jaggi, B., & Sannella, A. (1995). The association between the accuracy of management earnings forecasts and discretionary accounting changes. *Journal of Accounting, Auditing & Finance*, *10*(1), 1–21. doi:10.1177/0148558X9501000101

Jarne Jarne, J. I. (2000). *Clasificación y evolución internacional de los sistemas contables*. Associación Española de Contabilidad y Administración de Empresas.

Jayaraman, S. (2008). Earnings Volatility, Cash Flow Volatility and Informed Trading. *Journal of Accounting Research*, *46*(4), 809–851. doi:10.1111/j.1475-679X.2008.00293.x

Jeanjean, T., & Stolowy, H. (2008). Do accounting standards matter? An exploratory analysis of earnings management before and after IFRS adoption. *Journal of Accounting and Public Policy*, *27*(6), 480–494. doi:10.1016/j.jaccpubpol.2008.09.008

Jelinek, K. (2007). The effect of leverage increases on real earnings management. *The Journal of Business and Economic Studies*, *13*(Fall), 24–46.

Jenkins, D. S., Kane, G. D., & Velury, U. (2006). Earnings quality decline and the effect of industry specialist auditors: An analysis of the late 1990s. *Journal of Accounting and Public Policy*, *25*(1), 71–90. doi:10.1016/j.jaccpubpol.2005.11.003

Jensen, M. C., & Meckling, W. H. (1976). Theory of the firm: Managerial behavior, agency costs and ownership structure. *Journal of Financial Economics*, *3*(4), 305–360. doi:10.1016/0304-405X(76)90026-X

Jiang, F., Zhu, B., & Huang, J. (2013). CEO's financial experience and earnings management. *Journal of Multinational Financial Management*, *23*(3), 134–145. doi:10.1016/j.mulfin.2013.03.005

Jie, Z., & Yan, Z.L. (2014). Executive compensation and earnings management: Empirical study in china's listed companies. *Advances in Management, 7*(6).

Jiraporn, P., & DaDalt, P. (2009). Does founding family control affect earnings management? *Applied Economics Letters*, *16*(2), 113–119. doi:10.1080/17446540701720592

Johnson, M. F. (1999). Business cycles and the relation between security returns and earnings. *Review of Accounting Studies*, *14*(2), 93–117. doi:10.1023/A:1009649018325

Jones, M., & Shoemaker, P. (1994). Accounting Narratives: A Review of Empirical Studies of Content and Readability. *Journal of Accounting Literature, 13*, 142.

Jones, M., & Shoemaker, P. (1994). Accounting Narratives: A Review of Empirical Studies of Content and Readability. *Journal of Accounting Literature, 13.*

Jones, J. (1991). Earnings Management During Import Relief Investigation. *Journal of Accounting Research, 29*(2), 193–228. doi:10.2307/2491047

Jones, J. J. (1991). Earnings management during import relief investigations. *Journal of Accounting Research, 29*(2), 193–228.

Jones, M. J. (1988). A longitudinal study of the readability of the chairman's narratives in the corporate reports of a UK company. *Accounting and Business Research, 18*(72), 297–306. doi:10.1080/00014788.1988.9729377

Jones, M. J. (2011). *Creative accounting, fraud and international accounting scandals.* John Wiley & Sons.

Jones, M. J. (2011). The nature, use and impression management of graphs in social and environmental accounting. *Accounting Forum, 35*(2), 75–89. doi:10.1016/j.accfor.2011.03.002

Jorion, P. (1997). *Value at Risk: The New Benchmark for Controlling Market Risk.* Chicago: Irwin.

Kamin, J. Y., & Ronen, J. (1978). The smoothing of income numbers: Some empirical evidence on systematic differences among management-controlled and owner-controlled firms. *Accounting, Organizations and Society, 3*(2), 141–157. doi:10.1016/0361-3682(78)90022-3

Kanagaretnam, K., Lobo, G. J., & Mathieu, R. (2003). Managerial incentives for income smoothing through bank loan loss provisions. *Review of Quantitative Finance and Accounting, 20*(1), 63–80. doi:10.1023/A:1022187622780

Kane, G. D., Richardson, F., & Graybeal, P. (1996). Recession-induced stress and the prediction of corporate failure. *Contemporary Accounting Research, 13*(2), 631–650. doi:10.1111/j.1911-3846.1996.tb00517.x

Kaplan, S. E., Pourciau, S., & Reckers, P. M. J. (1990). An examination of the effect of the corporate reports of a UK company. *Accounting and Business Research, 18*(72), 297–305.

Karampinis, N. I., & Hevas, D. L. (2013). Effects of IFRS adoption on tax-induced incentives for financial earnings management: Evidence from Greece. *The International Journal of Accounting, 48*(2), 218–247. doi:10.1016/j.intacc.2013.04.003

Karuna, C., Subramanyam, K. R., & Tian, F. (2012). *Industry product market competition and earnings management.* Paper presented at American Accounting Association Financial Accounting and Reporting Section Mid-Year Conference.

Karuna, C., Subramanyam, K. R., & Tian, F. (2015). *Competition and earnings management.* Working Paper.

Karuna, C. (2007). Industry product market competition and managerial incentives. *Journal of Accounting and Economics, 43*(2–3), 275–297. doi:10.1016/j.jacceco.2007.02.004

Kasznik, R. (1997). *On the association between voluntary disclosure and earnings management.* Research Paper No. 1401, University of Stanford.

Kasznik, R. (1999). On the association between voluntary disclosure and earnings management. *Journal of Accounting Research, 37*(1), 57–81. doi:10.2307/2491396

Kelly, P. (2014). Information Efficiency and Firm-Specific Return Variation. *Quarterly Journal of Finance, 4*(4), 1–44. doi:. doi:10.1142/S2010139214500189

Kesavan, S., & Mani, V. (2010). *The predictive power of abnormal inventory growth : Application to earnings forecasting for retailers.* North.

Kim, Y., & Yi, C. (2006). Ownership structure, business group affiliation, listing status, and earnings management: Evidence from Korea. *Contemporary Accounting Research*, *23*(2), 427–464. doi:10.1506/7T5B-72FV-MHJV-E697

Kirschenheiter, M., & Melumad, N. D. (2002). Can 'big bath' and earnings smoothing co-exist as equilibrium financial reporting strategies? *Journal of Accounting Research*, *40*(3), 761–796. doi:10.1111/1475-679X.00070

Klann, R. C. (2011). *Gerenciamento de resultados: Análise comparativa de Empresas Brasileiras e Inglesas antes e após a adoção das IFRS.* Tese de Doutorado da Universidade Regional de Blumenau – FURB, Programa de Pós Graduação em Ciências Contábeis, Blumenau, SC, Brasil.

Klann, R. C., & Beuren, I. M. (2018). Earnings management IFRS adoption in Brazilian and British companies. *International Journal of Disclosure and Governance*, *15*(1), 13–28. doi:10.105741310-018-0032-4

Knight F. (1972). *Risco Incerteza e Lucro*. Edição expressão e cultura.

Koch, B. S. (1981). Income smoothing: An experiment. *The Accounting Review*, *56*(3), 574–586.

Kordestani, G. R., & Mohammadi, M. R. (2016). A study of the relationship between product market competition and earnings management. *Procedia Economics and Finance*, *36*, 266–273. doi:10.1016/S2212-5671(16)30037-5

Kormendi, R., & Lipe, R. (1987). Earnings Innovations, Earnings Persistence, and Stock Returns. *The Journal of Business*, *60*(3), 323–345. doi:10.1086/296400

Kothari, S. (1992). Price-Earnings Regressions in the Presence of Prices Leading Earnings. *Journal of Accounting and Economics*, *15*(2-3), 173–202. doi:10.1016/0165-4101(92)90017-V

Kothari, S. P. (2001). Capital markets research in accounting. *Journal of Accounting and Economics*, *31*(1–3), 105–231. doi:10.1016/S0165-4101(01)00030-1

Kothari, S. P., Leone, A. J., & Wasley, C. E. (2005). Performance matched discretionary accrual measures. *Journal of Accounting and Economics*, *39*(1), 163–197.

Kothari, S., Leone, A., & Wasley, C. (2005). Performance Matched Discretionary Accrual Measures. *Journal of Accounting and Economics*, *39*(1), 163–197. doi:10.1016/j.jacceco.2004.11.002

Kothari, S., Mizik, N., & Roychowdhury, S. (2016). Managing for the Moment: The Role of Earnings Management via Real Activities versus Accruals in SEO Valuation. *The Accounting Review*, *91*(2), 559–586. doi:10.2308/accr-51153

Koumanakos, E., Siriopoulos, C., & Georgopoulos, A. (2005). Firm acquisitions and earnings management: Evidence from Greece. *Managerial Auditing Journal*, *20*(7), 663–678. doi:10.1108/02686900510611212

Kousenidis, D. V., Ladas, A. C., & Negakis, C. I. (2013). The effects of the European debt crisis on earnings quality. *International Review of Financial Analysis*, *30*, 351–362. doi:10.1016/j.irfa.2013.03.004

KPMG. (2017). *Mercato M&A in Italia: nei primi 9 mesi chiuse operazioni per 27 miliardi di euro*. Retrieved from: https://home.kpmg.com/it/it/home/media/press-releases/2017/10/m-a-in-italia-primi-9-mesi-2017.html

KPMG. (2018). *Continuing to climb. Global Banking M&A trends 2018.* Retrieved from https://assets.kpmg.com/content/dam/kpmg/xx/pdf/2018/04/2018-banking-m-and-a-trends.pdf

Kraus, A., & Litzenberger, R. H. (1973). A State-Preference Model of Optimal Financial Leverage. *The Journal of Finance*, *28*(1), 911–922. doi:10.1111/j.1540-6261.1973.tb01415.x

Krishman, G. V., & Parsons, L. M. (2007). Getting to the bottom line: An exploration of gender and earnings quality. *Journal of Business Ethics*, *78*(1-2), 65–76. doi:10.100710551-006-9314-z

Kvaal, P., & Nobes, C. (2010). International Differences in IFRS Policy Choice: A Research Note. *Accounting and Business Research*, *40*(2), 173–187. doi:10.1080/00014788.2010.9663390

La Porta, R., Lopes-de-Silanes, F., Shleifer, A., & Vishny, R. (1998). Law and Finance. *Journal of Political Economy*, *106*(6), 1113–1155. doi:10.1086/250042

La Porta, R., Lopez-de-Silanes, F., & Shleifer, A. (1999). Corporate ownership around the World. *The Journal of Finance*, *LIV*(2), 471–517. doi:10.1111/0022-1082.00115

La Porta, R., Lopez-de-Silanes, F., Shleifer, A., & Vishny, R. W. (2000). Agency problems and dividend policies around the World. *The Journal of Finance*, *55*(1), 1–33. doi:10.1111/0022-1082.00199

Laksmana, I., & Yang, Y. (2014). Product market competition and earnings management: Evidence from discretionary accruals and real activity manipulation. *Advances in Accounting*, *30*(2), 264. doi:10.1016/j.adiac.2014.09.003

Lambert, R. A. (1984). Income smoothing as rational equilibrium behaviour. *The Accounting Review*, *59*(4), 604–618.

Lambert, R., Leuz, C., & Verrecchia, R. (2007). Accounting Information, Disclosure, and the Cost of Capital. *Journal of Accounting Research*, *45*(2), 385–420. doi:10.1111/j.1475-679X.2007.00238.x

Lambert, R., Leuz, C., & Verrecchia, R. (2012). Information Asymmetry, Information Precision, and the Cost of Capital. *Review of Finance*, *16*(1), 1–29. doi:10.1093/rof/rfr014

Landsman, W. R. (2007). Is fair value accounting information relevant and reliable? Evidence from capital market research. *Accounting and Business Research*, *37*(SI), 19–30. doi:10.1080/00014788.2007.9730081

Lang, M. H., & Lundholm, R. J. (1996). Corporate disclosure policy and analyst behavior. *The Accounting Review*, *71*(4), 467–492.

Lara, J., Grambovas, C., & Walker, M. (2009). *On the Development of an Efficient Deflator for the Estimation of Accounting-Based Valuation Models*. Working paper.

Law n. 10.180 of February 6, 2001. Organiza e disciplina os Sistemas de Planejamento e de Orçamento Federal, de Administração Financeira Federal, de Contabilidade Federal e de Controle Interno do Poder Executivo Federal, e dá outras providências. Disponível em: http://www.planalto.gov.br/ccivil_03/leis/leis_2001/l10180.htm

Law n. 11.638 of December 28, 2007. Altera e revoga dispositivos da Lei nº 6.404, de 15 de dezembro de 1976, e estende às sociedades de grande porte disposições relativas à elaboração e divulgação de demonstrações financeiras. Disponível em: http://www.planalto.gov.br/ccivil_03/_ato2007-2010/2007/lei/l11638.htm

Law n. 11.941 of May 27, 2009. Altera a legislação tributária federal relativa ao parcelamento ordinário de débitos tributários; institui o regime tributário de transição [...], e dá outras providências. Disponível em: http://www.planalto.gov.br/ccivil_03/_ato2007-2010/2009/lei/l11941.htm

Law n. 4.320 of March 17, 1964. Estatui Normas Gerais de Direito Financeiro para elaboração e controle dos orçamentos e balanços da União, dos Estados, dos Municípios e do Distrito Federal. Disponível em: www.planalto.gov.br/ccivil_03/leis/l4320.htm

Law n. 6.404 of December 15, 1976. Dispõe sobre as Sociedades por Ações. Disponível em: http://www.planalto.gov.br/ccivil_03/leis/l6404consol.htm

Law Supplementary n. 101 of May 4, 2000. Estabelece normas de finanças públicas voltadas para a responsabilidade na gestão fiscal e dá outras providências.

Leary, M. R., & Kowalski, R. M. (1990). Impression management: A literature review and two component model. *Psychological Bulletin, 107*(1), 34–47. doi:10.1037/0033-2909.107.1.34

Lee, B. B., & Choi, B. (2002). Company size, auditor type, and earnings management. *Journal of Forensic Accounting, III*, 27–50.

Lee, C., Myers, J., & Swaminathan, B. (1999). What Is the Intrinsic Value of the Dow? *The Journal of Finance, 54*(5), 1693–1741. doi:10.1111/0022-1082.00164

Lee, H. Y., & Mande, V. (2002). The Effect of the Private Securities Litigation Reform Act of 1995 on Accounting Discretion of Client Managers of Big 6 and Non-Big 6 Auditors. *Auditing, 22*(1), 93–108. doi:10.2308/aud.2003.22.1.93

Leland, H. E. (1994). Corporate Debt Value, Bond Covenants, and Optimal Capital Structure. *The Journal of Finance, 49*(4), 1213–1252. doi:10.1111/j.1540-6261.1994.tb02452.x

Leland, H. E., & Pyle, D. H. (1977). Informational Asymmetries, Financial Structure, and Financial Intermediation. *The Journal of Finance, 32*(2), 371–387. doi:10.2307/2326770

Leuz, C., Nanda, D., & Wisocki, P. (2003). Investor Protection and Earnings Management: An International Comparison. *Journal of Financial Economics, 69*, 505–527. doi:10.1016/S0304-405X(03)00121-1

Leuz, C., & Verrecchia, R. (2000). The Economic Consequences of Increased Disclosure: Evidence from International Cross-Listings. *Studies on Accounting Information and the Economics of the Firm. Supplement to the Journal of Accounting Research, 38*, 91–124. doi:10.2307/2672910

Lev, B., & Kunitzky, S. (1974). On the association between smoothing measures and the risk of common stocks. *The Accounting Review, 49*(2), 259–270.

Lev, B., & Ohlson, J. (1982). Market-based empirical research in accounting: A review, interpretations and extension. *Journal of Accounting Research, 20*(Supplement), 249–331. doi:10.2307/2674685

Leventis, S., Dimitropoulos, P. E., & Anandarajan, A. (2011). Loan loss provisions, earnings management and capital management under IFRS: The case of EU Commerial Banks. *Journal of Financial Services Research, 40*(1), 103–122. doi:10.100710693-010-0096-1

Levitt, A. (1998). The importance of high quality accounting standards. *Accounting Horizons, 12*(2), 79–82.

Liberty, S. E., & Zimmerman, J. L. (1986). Labor union, contract negotiations and accounting choices. *The Accounting Review, 61*(4), 692–712.

Licerán-Gutiérrez, A., & Cano-Rodríguez, M. (2017). A Review on the multidimensional analysis of earnings quality. In *XIX Congresso AECA. Santiago de Compostela, Espanha.* (pp. 1–24). Academic Press. 10.2139srn.2998134

Linsley, P. M., & Lawrence, M. J. (2007). Risk reporting by the largest UK companies: Readability and lack of obfuscation. *Accounting, Auditing & Accountability Journal, 20*(4), 620–627. doi:10.1108/09513570710762601

Linsley, P. M., & Shrives, P. J. (2006). Risk reporting: A study of risk disclosures in the annual reports of UK companies. *The British Accounting Review, 38*(4), 387–404. doi:10.1016/j.bar.2006.05.002

Lipe, R. (1990). The Relation Between Stock Returns and Accounting Earnings Given Alternative Information. *The Accounting Review, 65*, 49–71.

Li, S., & Richie, N. (2016). Income smoothing and the cost of debt. *China Journal of Accounting Research, 9*(3), 175–190. doi:10.1016/j.cjar.2016.03.001

Lisboa, I. (2017). Impact of financial crisis and family control on earning management of Portuguese listed firms. *European Journal of Family Business*, *6*(2), 118–131. doi:10.1016/j.ejfb.2017.06.002

Lisboa, I., & Kacharava, A. (2018). Does financial crisis impact earnings management: Evidence from Portuguese and UK. *European Journal of Applied Business and Management*, *4*(1), 80–100.

Liu, J., Nissim, D., & Thomas, J. (2002). Equity Valuation Using Multiples. *Journal of Accounting Research*, *40*(1), 135–172. doi:10.1111/1475-679X.00042

Liu, M., Shi, Y., Wilson, C., & Wu, Z. (2017). Does family involvement explain why corporate social responsibility affects earnings management? *Journal of Business Research*, *75*, 8–16. doi:10.1016/j.jbusres.2017.02.001

Liu, S., & Skerratt, L. (2018). Earnings quality across different reporting regimes: Listed, large private, medium-sized, small and micro companies in the UK. *Journal of Applied Accounting Research*, *19*(1), 2–19. doi:10.1108/JAAR-02-2015-0009

Li, X. (2010). The impacts of product market competition on the quantity and quality of voluntary disclosures. *Review of Accounting Studies*, *15*(3), 663–711. doi:10.100711142-010-9129-0

Lobo, G., Song, M., & Stanford, M. (2012). Accruals Quality and Analyst Coverage. *Journal of Banking & Finance*, *36*(2), 497–508. doi:10.1016/j.jbankfin.2011.08.006

Lo, K., & Lys, T. (2001). The Ohlson Model: Contribution to Valuation Theory, Limitations, and Empirical Applications. *Journal of Accounting, Auditing & Finance*, *15*(3), 337–367. doi:10.1177/0148558X0001500311

Lopes, C., Cerqueira, A., & Brandão, E. (2010). Impact of IFRS adoption on accounting quality in European firms. *Journal of Modern Accounting and Auditing*, *6*(9), 20–31.

Louis, H. (2004). Earnings Management and the Market Performance of Acquiring Firms. *Journal of Financial Economics*, *74*(1), 121–148. doi:10.1016/j.jfineco.2003.08.004

Manual de Contabilidade Aplicada ao Setor Público (MCASP) (2013). 5ª Edição - Brasília: Secretaria do Tesouro Nacional, Subsecretaria de Contabilidade Pública. Coordenação-Geral de Normas de Contabilidade Aplicadas à Federação.

Marciukaityte, D., & Park, J. C. (2009). *Market competition and earnings management.* Retrieved from https://papers.ssrn.com/sol3/papers.cfm?abstract_id=1361905

Mard, Y., & Vigneron, L. (2014). *Does public/private status affect small and medium enterprises' earnings management practices? A study on French case.* Retrieved April 18, 2018, from http://www.crm-toulouse.fr/files/Documents/Mard.pdf

Markarian, G., & Gill, B. (2012). Income smoothing and idiosyncratic volatility, *SSRN Working Paper Series*, February version.

Markarian, G., & Santalò, J. (2014). Product market competition, information and earnings management. *Journal of Business Finance & Accounting*, *41*(5–6), 574.

Maroco, J. (2007). *Análise Estatística com utilização do SPSS. 3ª Edição*. Lisboa: Edições Sílabo.

Marquardt, C., & Zur, E. (2015). The Role of Accounting Quality in the M&A Market. *Management Science*, *61*(3), 604–623. doi:10.1287/mnsc.2013.1873

Marques, A., & Silva, N. (2010). A contabilidade criativa e o Sistema de Normalização Contabilística. Sistema de Normalização Contabilística - Jornadas de Contabilidade e Fiscalidade.

Marques, A. P., & Couto, A. I. (2017). SMEs and Family Smes: Specificities from the Portuguese Socio-Business Context. *European Journal of Economics and Business Studies*, *3*(2), 190–199. doi:10.26417/ejes.v8i1.p190-199

Marques, M., Rodrigues, L. L., & Craig, R. (2011). Earnings management induced by tax planning: The case of Portuguese private firms. *Journal of International Accounting, Auditing & Taxation*, *20*(2), 83–96. doi:10.1016/j.intaccaudtax.2011.06.003

Marra, A., Mazzola, P., & Prencipe, A. (2011). Board monitoring and earnings managementpre- and post-IFRS. *The International Journal of Accounting*, *46*(2), 205–230. doi:10.1016/j.intacc.2011.04.007

Martinez, A. L. (2013). Gerenciamento de resultados no Brasil: um survey da literatura. *BBR-Brazilian Business Review*, *10*(4).

Martinez, A. L. (2001). *Gerenciamento dos resultados contábeis: estudo empírico das companhias abertas brasileiras. Tese de doutoramento em Ciências Contábeis*. São Paulo: FEA-USP.

Martins, O., & Moreira, J. A. (2009). Endividamento bancário e qualidade da informação financeira: um estudo para o caso Português. *Jornal de Contabilidade, 388*, 217–231.

Mather, D., Mather, P., & Ramsay, A. (2005). An investigation into the measurement of graph distortion in financial reports. *Accounting and Business Research*, *35*(2), 147–159. doi:10.1080/00014788.2005.9729670

Mather, P., Ramsay, A., & Serry, A. (1996). The use and representational faithfulness of graphs in annual reports: Australian Evidence. *Australian Accounting Review*, *6*(2).

Mather, P., Ramsay, A., & Steen, A. (2000). The use and representational faithfulness of graphs in Australian IPO prospectuses. *Accounting, Auditing & Accountability Journal*, *13*(1), 65–83. doi:10.1108/09513570010316144

Matsumoto, A. S., & Parreira, E. M. (2007). *Uma pesquisa sobre o gerenciamento de resultados contábeis: Causas e consequências*. Contabilidade. *Gestão e Governança*, *10*(1), 141–157.

Maydew, E. L. (1997). Tax-induced earnings management by firms with net operating losses. *Journal of Accounting Research*, *35*(1), 83–96. doi:10.2307/2491468

Mayer-Sommer, A. (1979). Understanding and acceptance of the efficient markets hypothesis and its accounting implications. *The Accounting Review*, *54*(1), 88–106.

McKinstry, S. (1996). Designing the annual reports of Burton PLC from 1930 to 1994. *Accounting, Organizations and Society*, *21*(1), 89–111. doi:10.1016/0361-3682(95)00016-3

McNichols, M. (2002). Discussion of the Quality of Accruals and Earnings: The Role of Accrual Estimation Errors. *The Accounting Review*, *77*(s-1), 61–69. doi:10.2308/accr.2002.77.s-1.61

McNichols, M. F. (2000). Research design issues in earnings management studies. *Journal of Accounting and Public Policy*, *19*(4-5), 313–345. doi:10.1016/S0278-4254(00)00018-1

Mendes, C. A., & Rodrigues, L. L. (2007). Determinantes da manipulação contabilística. *Revista de Estudos Politécnicos*, *4*(7), 189–210.

Mendes, C. A., & Rodrigues, L. L. (2007). Determinantes da Manipulação Contabilística. *Revista de Estudos Politécnicos*, *IV*(7), 189–210.

Merkl-Davies, D. M., & Brennan, N. M. (2007). Discretionary disclosure strategies in corporate narratives: incremental information or impression management? *Journal of Accounting Literature, 27*, 116-196.

Merkl-Davies, D. M., & Brennan, N. M. (2007). Discretionary disclosure strategies in corporate narratives : Incremental information or impression management? *Journal of Accounting Literature*, *26*, 116–196. Retrieved from http://hdl.handle.net/10197/2907

Merkl-Davies, D. M., & Brennan, N. M. (2007). Discretionary disclosure strategies in corporate narratives: Incremental information or impression management? *Journal of Accounting Literature*, *26*, 116–194.

Merkl-Davies, D. M., & Brennan, N. M. (2011). A conceptual framework of impression management: New insights from psychology, sociology and critical perspectives. *Accounting and Business Research*, *41*(5), 415–437. doi:10.1080/00014788.2011.574222

Merkl-Davies, D. M., Brennan, N. M., & McLeay, S. J. (2011). Impression management and retrospective sense-making in corporate narratives: A social psychology perspective. *Accounting, Auditing & Accountability Journal*, *24*(3), 315–344. doi:10.1108/09513571111124036

Michelson, S. E., Jordan-Wagner, J., & Wootton, C. W. (1995). A market based analysis of income smoothing. *Journal of Business Finance & Accounting*, *22*(8), 1179–1193. doi:10.1111/j.1468-5957.1995.tb00900.x

Michelson, S. E., Jordan-Wagner, J., & Wootton, C. W. (2000). The relationship between the smoothing of reported income and risk-adjusted returns. *Journal of Economics and Finance*, *24*(2), 141–159. doi:10.1007/BF02752709

Milgrom, P., & Roberts, J. (1992). *Economics, organization and management*. Englewood Cliffs, NJ: Prentice Hall.

Miller, M., & Modigliani, F. (1961). Dividend Policy, Growth and the Valuation of Shares. *The Journal of Business*, *34*(4), 411–433. doi:10.1086/294442

Minton, B. A., & Schrand, C. (1999). The impact of cash flow volatility on discretionary investment and the costs of debt and equity financing. *Journal of Financial Economics*, *54*(3), 423–460. doi:10.1016/S0304-405X(99)00042-2

Miralles-Marcelo, J. L., Miralles-Quirós, M. del M., & Lisboa, I. (2014). The impact of family control on firm performance: Evidence from Portugal and Spain. *Journal of Family Business Strategy*, *5*(2), 156–168. doi:10.1016/j.jfbs.2014.03.002

Missonier-Piera, F. (2004). Economic determinants of multiple accounting method choices in a Swiss context. *Journal of International Financial Management & Accounting*, *15*(2), 118–144. doi:10.1111/j.1467-646X.2004.00104.x

Modigliani, F., & Miller, M. (1958). The Cost of Capital, Corporate Finance and the Theory of Investment. *The American Economic Review*, *48*(3), 261–297.

Modigliani, F., & Miller, M. H. (1963). Corporate Income Taxes and the Cost of Capital: A Correction. *The American Economic Review*, *53*(3), 433–443.

Monsen, R. J., Chiu, J. S., & Cooley, D. E. (1968). The effect of separation of ownership and control on the performance of the large firm. *The Quarterly Journal of Economics*, *82*(3), 435–451. doi:10.2307/1879516

Monsen, R. J. Jr, & Downs, A. (1965). A theory of large managerial firms. *Journal of Political Economy*, *73*(3), 221–236. doi:10.1086/259012

Monterrey Mayoral, J., & Sánchez-Segura, A. (2006). Las características socioeconómicas como incentivos para la información financiera: evidencia empírica Española. *Investigaciones Economicas, 30*(3), 611–634. Retrieved from http://www.scopus.com/inward/record.url?eid=2-s2.0-38849199573&partnerID=tZOtx3y1

Monterrey Mayoral, J., & Sánchez-Segura, A. (2017). Los impuestos como determinantes de la inversión empresarial. evidencia empírica en empresas españolas que no cotizan en bolsa. *Spanish Accounting Review*, 1–15. doi:10.1016/j.rcsar.2017.04.001

Monterrey Mayoral, J., & Sánchez Segura, A. (2010). Diferencias en agresividad fiscal entre empresas familiares y no familiares. *Revista Española de Financiación y Contabilidad, 39*(145), 65–97. doi:10.1080/02102412.2010.10779679

Monterrey Mayoral, J., & Sánchez-Segura, A. (2009). Como afectan los impuestos a la calidad del resultado? evidencia empirica en las empresas españolas no cotizadas. *Spanish Accounting Review, 12*, 117–138. doi:10.1016/S1138-4891(09)70004-4

Monterrey, J. (1998). Un recorrido por la contabilidad positiva. *Revista Española de Financiación y Contabilidad, 27*(95), 427–467.

Moraes, R. (1999). Análise de conteúdo. *Revista Educação, Porto Alegre, 22*(37), 7–32.

Morais, A. I., & Curto, J. D. (2008). Accounting quality and the adoption of IASB standards – Portuguese evidence. *Revista Contabilidade & Finanças, 19*(48), 103–111. doi:10.1590/S1519-70772008000300009

Morck, R., Yeung, B. & Yu, W. (2000). The Information Content of Stock Markets: Why Do Emerging Markets Have Synchronous Stock Price Movements? *Journal of Financial Economics, 58d*(1-2), 215-260. doi:. doi:10.1016/S0304-405X(00)0007d1-d4

Moreira, J. (2006). *Are financing needs a constraint to earnings management? evidence for private Portuguese firms* (Working paper). Porto.

Moreira, J. A. (2009). O PEC e outros "sinais" fiscais: impacto sobre a manipulação dos resultados. *Jornal de Contabilidade, 386*, 155–169.

Moreira, J. A. (2010). O SNC – Sistema de Normalização Contabilística e a qualidade da informação financeira: consequências (esperadas) do uso do justo valor. Sistema de Normalização Contabilística - Jornadas de Contabilidade e Fiscalidade.

Moreira, J. A. C. (2008). *A Manipulação dos Resultados das Empresas: um contributo para o estudo do caso português*. Academic Press.

Morris, R. D. (1987). Signalling, agency theory and accounting policy choice. *Accounting and Business Research, 18*(69), 47–56. doi:10.1080/00014788.1987.9729347

Moses, O. D. (1987). Income smoothing and incentives: Empirical tests using accounting changes. *The Accounting Review, 62*(2), 358–377.

Mota, G., Nunes, J., & Ferreira, M. (2004). *Finanças Empresariais – Teoria e Prática*. Team.

Mulford, C. W., & Comiskey, E. E. (2011). *The Financial Numbers Game : Detecting Creative Accounting Practices*. John Wiley & Sons.

Muritala, T. A. (2012). An Empirical Analysis of Capital Structure on Firms' Performance in Nigeria. *International Journal of Advances in Management and Economics, 1*(5), 116–124.

Murphy, A. B. (1999). Firm Characteristics of Swiss Companies that Utilize International Accounting Standards. *The International Journal of Accounting, 34*(1), 121–131. doi:10.1016/S0020-7063(99)80006-5

Myers, J. (1999). Implementing Residual Income Valuation with Linear Information Dynamics. *The Accounting Review, 74*(1), 1–28. doi:10.2308/accr.1999.74.1.1

Myers, S. (2001). Capital Structure. *The Journal of Economic Perspectives, 15*(2), 81–102. doi:10.1257/jep.15.2.81

Myers, S., & Majluf, N. (1984). Corporate financing and investment decisions when firms have information that investors do not have. *Journal of Financial Economics*, *13*(2), 187–221. doi:10.1016/0304-405X(84)90023-0

Na, K., & Hong, J. (2017). CEO gender and earnings management. *Journal of Applied Business Research*, *33*(2), 297–308. doi:10.19030/jabr.v33i2.9902

Nardi, P. C. C., & Nakao, S. H. (2009). Gerenciamento de resultados e a relação com o custo da dívida das empresas brasileiras abertas. *Revista Contabilidade & Finanças*, *20*(51), 77–100. doi:10.1590/S1519-70772009000300006

Naser, K. (1993). *Creative Financial Accounting: Its Nature and Use*. Prentice Hall.

Navaes, B. M. P. L. (2010). *Harmonização das Normas Contábeis pela Aderência à Lei 11.639/2007 e a MP 449/2008 em Empresas Multinacionais e do Setor Público: Um Estudo de Multiplos Casos, 2010. Dissertacao (Mestrado em Engenharia da Producao)*. Universidade Federal do Rio de Janeiro.

Nelson, M. W., Elliott, J. A., & Tarpley, R. L. (2003). How are earnings managed: Example from auditors. *Accounting Horizons*, *17*(Supplement), 17–35. doi:10.2308/acch.2003.17.s-1.17

Neu, D., Warsame, H., & Pedwell, K. (1998). Managing public impressions: Environmental disclosures in annual reports. *Accounting, Organizations and Society*, *23*(3), 265–282. doi:10.1016/S0361-3682(97)00008-1

Newman, M. L., Pennebaker, J. W., Berry, D. S., & Richards, J. M. (2003). Lying words: Predicting deception from linguistic styles. *Personality and Social Psychology Bulletin*, *29*(5), 665–675. doi:10.1177/0146167203029005010 PMID:15272998

Nickell, S. J. (1996). Competition and corporate performance. *Journal of Political Economy*, *104*(4), 724–746. doi:10.1086/262040

Niskanen, M., Karjalainen, J., & Niskanen, J. (2010). The role of auditing in Small, Private Family Firms: Is it about Quality and Crebility? *Family Business Review*, *23*(3), 230–245. doi:10.1177/0894486510374456

Nissim, D. (2017). *Overproduction and EBITDA*. Columbia Business School Research Paper, No. 17-102. doi:10.2139srn.3054282

Niyama, J. K. (2005). Contabilidade internacional. São Paulo (Ed) Atlas.

Niyama, J., Rodrigues, A. M., & Rodrigues, J. (2015). Some thoughts on creative accounting and international accounting standards. *Revista Universo Contábil*, (1), 69–87. doi:10.4270/ruc.2015104

Nobes, C. (2006). The Survival of International Differences under IFRS: Towards a Research Agenda. *Accounting and Business Research*, *36*(3), 233–245. doi:10.1080/00014788.2006.9730023

Ohlson, J. (1988). *Accounting Earnings, Book Value and Dividends. The Theory of the Clean Surplus Equation*. Working paper, Columbia University.

Ohlson, J. (1995). Earnings, Book Values and Dividends in Equity Valuation. *Contemporary Accounting Research*, *11*(2), 661–687. doi:10.1111/j.1911-3846.1995.tb00461.x

Ohlson, J. (1999). On Transitory Earnings. *Review of Accounting Studies*, *3*(3/4), 145–162. doi:10.1023/A:1009653114699

Ohlson, J. (2001). Earnings, Book Values and Dividends in Equity Valuation: An Empirical Perspective. *Contemporary Accounting Research*, *3*(1), 107–120. doi:10.1506/7TPJ-RXQN-TQC7-FFAE

Ohlson, J., & Zhang, X. (1998). Accrual Accounting and Equity Valuation. *Journal of Accounting Research*, *36*(Supplement), 85–111. doi:10.2307/2491308

Oliveira, J., Azevedo, G., & Borges, M. F. R. (2016). Impression Management and self-presentational dissimulation in Portuguese Chairmen's Statements. *Corporate Communication. International Journal (Toronto, Ont.).*

Oliveira, J., Rodrigues, L. L., & Craig, R. (2011). Risk-related disclosure practices in the annual reports of Portuguese credit institutions: An exploratory study. *Journal of Banking Regulation, 12*(2), 100–118. doi:10.1057/jbr.2010.20

Oliveira, J., Rodrigues, L. L., & Craig, R. (2011). Risk-related disclosures by non-finance companies: Portuguese practices and disclosure characteristics. *Managerial Auditing Journal, 26*(9), 817–839. doi:10.1108/02686901111171466

Oliveira, J., Rodrigues, L. L., & Craig, R. (2011). Voluntary risk reporting to enhance institutional and organizational legitimacy: Evidence from Portuguese banks. *Journal of Financial Regulation and Compliance, 19*(3), 271–289. doi:10.1108/13581981111147892

Oliveira, J., Rodrigues, L. L., & Craig, R. (2013). Public visibility and risk-related disclosures in Portuguese credit institutions. *The Journal of Risk, 15*(4), 57–90. doi:10.21314/JOR.2013.264

Oliveira, J., Rodrigues, L. L., & Craig, R. (2013). Technical note: company risk-related disclosures in a code law country: a synopsis. *Australasian Accounting. Business and Finance Journal, 7*(1), 123–130.

Onesti, T., & Romano, M. (2012). *Earnings Management and Goodwill Accounting: Implication on Dividend Policy in Italian Listed Companies*. Retrieved from https://ssrn.com/abstract=2179159

Ordinance n. 109 of February 21, 2011. Dispõe sobre a composição e o funcionamento do Grupo Técnico de Padronização de Procedimentos Contábeis – GTCON. Disponível em: http://www3.tesouro.fazenda.gov.br/legislacao/download/contabilidade/Port_STN_109_2011_GTCON.pdf

Ordinance n. 589 of Dezembro 27, 2001, STN. Estabelece conceitos, regras e procedimentos contábeis para consolidação das empresas estatais dependentes nas contas públicas e dá outras providências.

Ordinance n. 634 of November 19, 2013, STN. Dispõe sobre regras gerais acerca das diretrizes, normas e procedimentos contábeis aplicáveis aos entes da Federação, com vistas à consolidação das contas públicas da União, dos Estados, do Distrito Federal e dos Municípios, sob a mesma base conceitual. Disponível em: https://www.tesouro.fazenda.gov.br/pt/responsabilidade-fiscal/contabilidadepublica/

Ousama, A. A., Fatima, A.-H., & Hafiz-Majdi, A. R. (2012). Determinants of intellectual capital reporting Evidence from annual reports of Malaysian listed companies. *Journal of Accounting in Emerging Economies, 2*(2), 119–139. doi:10.1108/20421161211229808

Pagano, M., Roelle, A., & Zechner, J. (2002). The geography of equity listing: Why do companies list abroad? *The Journal of Finance, 57*(6), 2651–2694. doi:10.1111/1540-6261.00509

Palmer, J. (1973). The profit performance effects of the separation of ownership from control in large U.S. industrial corporations. *The Bell Journal of Economics and Management Science, 4*(1), 293–303. doi:10.2307/3003151

Parker, R., & Nobes, C. (2004). *Comparative international accounting*. Pearson.

Parte-Esteban, L., & Ferrer García, C. (2014). The influence of firm characteristics on earnings quality. *International Journal of Hospitality Management, 42*, 50–60. doi:10.1016/j.ijhm.2014.06.008

Păşcan, I.-D. (2015). Measuring the effects of IFRS adoption on accounting quality: A review. *Procedia Economics and Finance, 32*(15), 580–587. doi:10.1016/S2212-5671(15)01435-5

Pastor, L., & Veronesi, P. (2003). Stock valuation and learning about profitability. *The Journal of Finance, 58*(5), 1749–1789. doi:10.1111/1540-6261.00587

Patelli, L., & Pedrini, M. (2015). Is tone at the top associated with financial reporting aggressiveness? *Journal of Business Ethics, 126*(1), 3–19. doi:10.100710551-013-1994-6

Paulo, E. (2007). *Manipulação das informações contábeis: uma analise teorica e empirica sobre os modelos operacionais de deteccao de gerenciamento de resultados. 2007. Tese (Doutorado em Ciencias Contabeis).* Faculdade de Economia, Administracao e Contabilidade da Universidade de Sao Paulo.

Peasnell, K. V., Pope, P. F., & Young, S. (2000). Detecting earnings management using cross-sectional abnormal accruals models. *Accounting and Business Research, 30*(4), 313–326. doi:10.1080/00014788.2000.9728949

Pellicer, M. J. A., & Blasco, M. A. V. (2004). Actuación discrecional sobre el resultado ante un cambio en la normativa fiscal. *Revista Española de Financiación y Contabilidad, 33*(122), 603–636. doi:10.1080/02102412.2004.10779527

Peni, E., & Vähämaa, S. (2010). Female executives and earnings management. *Managerial Finance, 36*(7), 629–645. doi:10.1108/03074351011050343

Penman, S. (1998). Combining Earnings and Book Value in Equity Valuation. *Contemporary Accounting Research, 15*(3), 291–324. doi:10.1111/j.1911-3846.1998.tb00562.x

Penman, S. (2001). *Financial Statement Analysis and Security Valuation.* New York: McGraw Hill/Irwin.

Penman, S., & Zhang, X. (2002). Accounting Conservatism, the Quality of Earnings, and Stock Returns. *The Accounting Review, 77*(2), 237–264. doi:10.2308/accr.2002.77.2.237

Pennebaker, J. W., Mehl, M. R., & Niederhoffer, K. (2003). Psychological aspects of natural language use: Our words, our selves. *Annual Review of Psychology, 54*, 547–577.

Pennington, R., & Tuttle, B. (2009). Managing impressions using distorted graphs of income and earnings per share: The role of memory. *International Journal of Accounting Information Systems, 10*(1), 25–45. doi:10.1016/j.accinf.2008.10.001

Penrose, J. M. (2008). Annual Report Graphic Use A Review of the Literature. *Journal of Business Communication, 45*(2), 158–180. doi:10.1177/0021943607313990

Penteado, I. A. de M. (2013). *Gerenciamento de impressão em relatórios de sustentabilidade no Brasil: Uma análise do uso de gráficos (Programa de pós-graduação).* Faculdade de Economia, Administração e Contabilidade de Ribeirão Preto-Universidade de São Paulo.

Pereira, A., & Alves, M. do C. G. (2017). Earnings management and European Regulation 1606/2002: Evidence from non-financial Portuguese companies listed in Euronext. *Spanish Accounting Review, 20*(2), 107–117. doi:10.1016/j.rcsar.2017.05.002

Perera, D., & Chand, P. (2015). Issues in the adoption of international financial reporting standards (IFRS) for small and medium-sized enterprises (SMES). *Advances in Accounting, 31*(1), 165–178. doi:10.1016/j.adiac.2015.03.012

Perry, S. E., & Williams, T. H. (1994). Earnings management preceding management buyout offers. *Journal of Accounting and Economics, 18*(2), 157–179. doi:10.1016/0165-4101(94)00362-9

Persakis, A., & Iatridis, G. (2016). Audit quality, investor protectionand earnings management during the financial crisis of 2008: An international perspective. *Journal of International Financial Markets, Institutions and Money, 41*, 73–101. doi:10.1016/j.intfin.2015.12.006

Persakis, A., & Iatridis, G. E. (2015). Earnings quality under financial crisis: A global empirical investigation. *Journal of Multinational Financial Management, 30*(c), 1–35. doi:10.1016/j.mulfin.2014.12.002

Pestana, M. H., & Gageiro, J. N. (2014). *Análise de dados para as ciências sociais* (6th ed.). Edições Sílabo.

Phetruen, W. (2016). *The Effect of IFRS and sox-like regulations on earnings management in East Asian countries* (Unpublished doctoral dissertation). University of Essex.

Pineda González, C. (2000). Determinantes de la calidad del resultado. *Revista de Contabilidad, 3*(5), 149–182.

Pinheiro, S. F. (2014). A utilização de estratégias de impression management na carta do presidente: evidência nas empresas financeiras Portuguesas. Universidade de Aveiro.

Plumlee, R. D. (2002). Impression Management with Graphs: Effects on Choices. *Journal of Information Systems, 16*(2), 183–202. doi:10.2308/jis.2002.16.2.203

Pope, P. F., & McLeay, S. J. (2011). The European IFRS experiment: Objectives, research challenges and some early evidence. *Accounting and Business Research, 41*(3), 233–266. doi:10.1080/00014788.2011.575002

Porciau, S. (1993). Earnings management and non-routine executive changes. *Journal of Accounting and Economics, 16*(1-3), 317–336. doi:10.1016/0165-4101(93)90015-8

Porter, E. (1913). *Pollyanna*. Colonial Press.

Porter, M. E. (1990). The competitive advantage of nations. *Harvard Business Review*, 77–93.

Porto, J. S., Paiva, T. S. S., Amaral, C. L. F., Rebouças, T. N. H., & Silva, R. A. (2014). Legibilidade de artigos de um periódico nacional na área de melhoramento vegetal. *Cultivando o. Saber (Cumaná), 7*(2), 205–211.

Preinreich, G. (1938). Annual Survey of Economic Theory: The Theory of Depreciation. *Econometrica, 6*(3), 219–231. doi:10.2307/1907053

Prencipe, A., Bar-Yosef, S., & Dekker, H. (2014). Accounting research in family firms: Theoretical and empirical challenges. *European Accounting Review, 23*(3), 361–385. doi:10.1080/09638180.2014.895621

Prencipe, A., Bar-Yosef, S., Mazzola, P., & Pozza, L. (2011). Income smoothing in family-controlled companies: Evidence from Italy. *Corporate Governance, 19*(6), 529–546. doi:10.1111/j.1467-8683.2011.00856.x

Prencipe, A., Markarian, G., & Pozza, L. (2008). Earnings management in family-firms: Evidence from R&D cost capitalization in Italy. *Family Business Review, 21*(1), 71–88. doi:10.1111/j.1741-6248.2007.00112.x

Puga, J. F. R. (2012). *Relato dos riscos empresariais nas empresas da Euronext Lisbon (Dissertação de mestrado).* Aveiro: Universidade de Aveiro.

Pustylnick, I., Temchenko, O., & Gubarkov, S. (2017). Estimating the influence of accounting variables change on earnings management detection. *Journal of International Studies, 10*(1), 110–122. doi:10.14254/2071-8330.2017/10-1/7

Raffournier, B. (1995). The determinants of voluntary financial disclosure by Swiss listed companies. *European Accounting Review, 4*(2), 261–280. doi:10.1080/09638189500000016

Rahman, S. (2012). Impression Management Motivations, Strategies and Disclosure Credibility of Corporate Narratives. *Journal of Management Research, 4*(3), 1–14. doi:10.5296/jmr.v4i3.1576

Rajan, R. G., & Zingales, L. (1995). What Do We Know about Capital Structure? Some Evidence from International Data. *The Journal of Finance, 50*(5), 1421–1460. doi:10.1111/j.1540-6261.1995.tb05184.x

Rajgopal, S., & Venkatachalam, M. (2011). Financial Reporting Quality and Idiosyncratic Return Volatility. *Journal of Accounting and Economics, 51*(1-2), 1–20. doi:10.1016/j.jacceco.2010.06.001

Raman, K., Shivakumar, L., & Tamayo, A. (2013). Target's Earnings Quality and Bidders' Takeover Decisions. *Review of Accounting Studies, 18*(4), 1050–1087. doi:10.100711142-013-9224-0

Ramanna, K., & Watts, R. (2012). Evidence on the effects of unverifiable fair-value accounting. *Review of Accounting Studies*, *17*, 749–780. doi:10.100711142-012-9188-5

Rangan, S. (1998). Earnings management and the performance of seasoned equity offerings. *Journal of Financial Economics*, *50*(1), 101–122. doi:10.1016/S0304-405X(98)00033-6

Rathke, A. A. T., Santana, V. T., Lourenço, I. M. E. C., & Dalmácio, F. Z. (2016). International financial reporting standards and earnings management in Latin America. *Revista de Administração Contemporânea*, *20*(3), 368–388. doi:10.1590/1982-7849rac2016140035

Razzaque, R. M., Ali, M. J., & Mather, P. R. (2016). Real earnings management in family firms: Evidence from an emerging economy. *Pacific-Basin Finance Journal*, *40*, 237–250. doi:10.1016/j.pacfin.2015.12.005

Reed, W., & Ye, H. (2009). Which panel data estimator should I use? *Applied Economics*, *43*(8), 985–1000. doi:10.1080/00036840802600087

Reese, W., & Weisback, M. (2002). Protection of minority shareholder interests, cross-listing in the United States, and subsequent equity offerings. *Journal of Financial Economics*, *66*(1), 65–104. doi:10.1016/S0304-405X(02)00151-4

Reguera Alvarado, N., Laffarga Briones, J., & Fuentes Ruiz, P. de. (2012). Afecta la crisis a la gestión de reultados? *Revista de La Asociación Española de Contabilidad y Administración de Empresas*, (97), 22–23.

Rezaee, Z. (2002). The Three Cs of Fraudulent Financial Reporting. *Internal Auditor*, 56–61. doi:10.3102/00346543067001043

Rezende, G. P., & Nakao, S. H. (2012). Gerenciamento de resultados e a relação com o lucro tributável das empresas brasileiras de capital aberto. *Universo Contábil*, *8*(1), 6–21. doi:10.4270/ruc.2012101

Richardson, F. M., Kane, G. D., & Lobinger, P. (1998). The impact of recession on the prediction of corporate failure. *Journal of Business Finance & Accounting*, *25*(1/2), 167–186. doi:10.1111/1468-5957.00182

Richardson, S., Sloan, R., Soliman, M., & Tuna, I. (2005). Accrual Reliability, Earnings Persistence and Stock Prices. *Journal of Accounting and Economics*, *39*(3), 437–485. doi:10.1016/j.jacceco.2005.04.005

Richardson, S., Sloan, R., Soliman, M., & Tuna, I. (2006). The Implications of Accounting Distortions and Growth for Accruals and Profitability. *The Accounting Review*, *81*(3), 713–743. doi:10.2308/accr.2006.81.3.713

Roberts, R., & Mahoney, L. (2004). Stakeholder Conceptions of the Corporation: Their Meaning and Influence in Accounting Research. *Business Ethics Quarterly*, *14*(3), 339–431. doi:10.5840/beq200414326

Rodrigues, L. L. (2013). Manipulação de contas ou marketing das percepções? In A. M. Rodrigues & T. Tavares (Eds.), *O SNC e os juízos de valor: uma perspectiva crítica e multidisciplinar* (pp. 265–285). Almedina.

Ronen, J., & Sadan, S. (1981). *Smoothing income numbers: Objectives, means, and implications*. Addison-Wesley Publishing Company.

Rossi, S., & Volpin, P. F. (2004). Cross-country determinants of mergers and acquisitions. *Journal of Financial Economics*, *74*(2), 277–304. doi:10.1016/j.jfineco.2003.10.001

Ross, S. A. (1977). The Determination of Financial Structure: The Incentive Signalling Approach. *The Bell Journal of Economics*, *8*(1), 23–40. doi:10.2307/3003485

Roychowdhury, S. (2006). Earnings management through real activities manipulation. *Journal of Accounting and Economics*, *42*(3), 335–370. doi:10.1016/j.jacceco.2006.01.002

Roychowdhury, S., Kothari, S. P., & Mizik, N. (2012). *Managing for the Moment: The Role of Real Activity Versus Accruals Earnings Management in SEO Valuation*. SSRN Electronic Journal. doi:10.2139srn.1982826

Rudra, T., & Bhattacharjee, D. (2012). Does IFRS influence earnings management? Evidence from India. *Journal of Management Research*, *4*, 1–13.

Rutherford, B. A. (2003). Obfuscation, textual complexity and the role of regulated narrative accounting disclosure in corporate governance. *The Journal of Management and Governance*, *7*(2), 187–210. doi:10.1023/A:1023647615279

Sakin, T. (2016). Kâr yönetimi ve Türkiye'deki kâr yönetimi çalışmalarının değerlendirilmesi. In Seçmeler 2016 (pp. 181-192). İstanbul: İstanbul Üniversitesi İşletme Fakültesi Muhasebe Enstitüsü.

Salamon, G. L., & Smith, E. D. (1979). Corporate control and managerial misrepresentation of firm performance. *The Bell Journal of Economics*, *10*(1), 319–328. doi:10.2307/3003333

Sampierre, R. H., Collado, C. F., & Lucio, P. B. (2006). *Metodologia de la investigación (4th ed.)*. Iztapalapa: McGraw-Hill.

Santos, E. S., Cia, J. N. S., & Cia, J. C. (2011). US GAAP x normas brasileiras: Mensuracao do impacto das diferencas de normas no lucro duplamente reportado pelas empresas brasileiras emissoras de ADRS na NYSE. *Revista de Administração Mackenzie, Sao Paulo*, *12*(1), 82–111. doi:10.1590/S1678-69712011000100004

Schipper, K. (1989). Commentary on Earnings Management. *Accounting Horizons*, *3*, 91–102.

Schipper, K. (1989). Commentary on earnings management. *Accounting Horizons*, 91–102. doi:10.1016/0361-3682(86)90013-9

Schipper, K. (1989). Earnings management. *Accounting Horizons*, *3*(4), 91–102.

Schipper, K., & Vincent, L. (2003). Earnings Quality. *Accounting Horizons*, *17*(s-1supplement), 97–110. doi:10.2308/acch.2003.17.s-1.97

Schlenker, B.R. (1980). *Impression management: the self-concept, social identity, and interpersonal relation*. Brooks/Cole Publishing Company.

Schlenker, B. R. (1980). *Impression Management: The Self-concept, Social Identity, and Interpersonal Relations*. B. P. Company.

Schlenker, B. R. (1980). *Impression management: The self-concept, social identity, and interpersonal relations*. Monterey, CA: Brooks/Cole Publishing Company.

Schlenker, B. R., Pennigton, J., Murphy, R., & Doherty, K. (1994). The triangle model of responsibility. *Psychological Review*, *101*(4), 632–625. doi:10.1037/0033-295X.101.4.632 PMID:7984709

Schrand, C. M., & Walther, B. R. (2000). Strategic Benchmarks in Earnings Announcements: The Selective Disclosure of Prior-Period Earnings Components. *The Accounting Review*, *75*(2), 151–177. doi:10.2308/accr.2000.75.2.151

Schroeder, N., & Gibson, C. (1992). Are summary annual reports successful? *Accounting Horizons*, *6*(2), 28.

Schroeder, R. G., Clark, M. W., & Cathey, J. M. (2005). *Financial accounting theory and analysis (8th ed.)*. John Wiley& Sons.

Securities and Exchange Commission (SEC). (2007). Acceptance From Foreign Private Issuers of Financial Statements Prepared in Accordance With International Financial Reporting Standards Without Reconciliation to U.S. GAAP. Disponível em: http://www.sec.gov/rules/final/2008/33-8879fr.pdf

Serrasqueiro, R. (2009). *A divulgação da informação sobre os riscos empresariais. XIV Encontro AECA*. Coimbra: AECA.

Setia-Atmaja, L. S., Tanewski, G. A., & Skully, M. (2009). The role of dividends, debt and board structure in the governance of family-controlled firms. *Journal of Business Finance & Accounting*, *36*(7&8), 863–898. doi:10.1111/j.1468-5957.2009.02151.x

Shalev, R. (2009). The information content of business combination disclosure level. *The Accounting Review*, *84*(1), 240. doi:10.2308/accr.2009.84.1.239

Shalev, R., Zhang, I. X., & Zhang, Y. (2013). CEO compensation and fair value accounting: Evidence from purchase price allocation. *Journal of Accounting Research*, *51*(4), 819–854. doi:10.1111/1475-679X.12015

Shi, G., Sun, J., & Zhang, L. (2017). Product market competition and earnings management: A firm-level analysis. *Journal of Business Finance & Accounting*, 1–21.

Shivakumar, L. (2000). Do firms mislead investors by overstating earnings before seasoned equity offerings? *Journal of Accounting and Economics*, *29*(3), 339–371. doi:10.1016/S0165-4101(00)00026-4

Shleiefer, A., & Vishny, R. (1997). A survey of corporate governance. *The Journal of Finance*, *52*(2), 737–783. doi:10.1111/j.1540-6261.1997.tb04820.x

Shleifer, A. (2004). Does competition destroy ethical behavior? *The American Economic Review*, *92*(2), 414–418. doi:10.1257/0002828041301498

Shleifer, A., & Vishny, R. W. (2003). Stock market driven acquisitions. *Journal of Financial Economics*, *70*(3), 295–311. doi:10.1016/S0304-405X(03)00211-3

Shukeri, S. N., Shin, O. W., & Shaari, M. S. (2012). Does board of director's characteristics affect firm performance? Evidence from Malaysian public listed companies. *International Business Research*, *5*(9), 120–127. doi:10.5539/ibr.v5n9p120

Siebels, J. F., & zu Knyphausen-Aufseß, D. (2012). A review of theory in family business research: The implications for corporate governance. *International Journal of Management Reviews*, *14*(3), 280–304. doi:10.1111/j.1468-2370.2011.00317.x

Silva, J. O. (2010). *Relação entre a remuneração variável dos gestores e o gerenciamento de resultados nas empresas de capital aberto brasileiras. 2010. Dissertacao (Mestrado em Ciencias Contabeis)*. Blumenau: Universidade Regional de Blumenau – FURB.

Siregar, S. V., & Utama, S. (2008). Type of earnings management and the effect of ownership structure, firm size, and corporate-governance practices: Evidence from Indonesia. *The International Journal of Accounting*, *43*(1), 1–27. doi:10.1016/j.intacc.2008.01.001

Skinner, D. J., & Dechow, P. M. (2000). Earnings management: Reconciling the Views of accounting academics, practitioners, and regulators. *Accounting Horizons*, *14*(2), 235–250. doi:10.2308/acch.2000.14.2.235

Skinner, D. J., & Sloan, R. G. (2002). Earnings surprises, growth expectations and stock returns or don't let an earnings torpedo sink your portfolio. *Review of Accounting Studies*, *7*(2-3), 289–310. doi:10.1023/A:1020294523516

Sloan, R. (1996). Do Stock Prices Fully Reflect Information in Accruals and Cash Flows about Future Earnings? *The Accounting Review*, *71*, 289–315.

Smith, E. D. (1976). The effect of the separation of ownership from control on accounting policy decisions. *The Accounting Review*, *51*(4), 707–723.

Smith, J. E., & Smith, N. P. (1971). Readability: A measure of the performance of the communication function of financial reporting. *The Accounting Review*, 552–561.

Smith, M., & Taffler, R. J. (1992). The chairman's report and corporate financial performance. *Accounting and Finance*, *32*(2), 75–90. doi:10.1111/j.1467-629X.1992.tb00187.x

Smith, M., & Taffler, R. J. (1995). The incremental effect of narrative accounting information in corporate annual reports. *Journal of Business Finance & Accounting*, *22*(8), 1195–1216. doi:10.1111/j.1468-5957.1995.tb00901.x

Smith, M., & Taffler, R. J. (2000). The chairman's statement: A content analysis of discretionary narrative disclosures. *Accounting, Auditing & Accountability Journal*, *13*(5), 624–646. doi:10.1108/09513570010353738

Soderstrom, N. S., & Sun, K. J. (2007). IFRS adoption and accounting quality: A review. *European Accounting Review*, *16*(4), 675–702. doi:10.1080/09638180701706732

Solomon, J. F., Solomon, A., Norton, S. D., & Joseph, N. L. (2000). A Conceptual Framework for Corporate Risk Disclosure Emerging from the Agenda for Corporate Governance Reform. *The British Accounting Review*, *32*(4), 447–478. doi:10.1006/bare.2000.0145

Srinidhi, B., Gul, F. A., & Tsui, J. (2011). Female directors and earnings quality. *Contemporary Accounting Research*, *28*(5), 1610–1644. doi:10.1111/j.1911-3846.2011.01071.x

Stanton, P., Stanton, J., & Pires, G. (2004). Impressions of an annual report: An experimental study. *Corporate Communications*, *9*(1), 57–69. doi:10.1108/13563280410516500

Staw, B. M., McKechnie, P. I., & Puffer, S. M. (1983). The justification of organizational performance. *Administrative Science Quarterly*, *28*(4), 582–600. doi:10.2307/2393010

Steinbart, P. J. (1989). The Auditor's Responsibility for the Accuracy of Graphs in Annual Reports: Some Evidence of the Need for Additional Guidance. *Accounting Horizons*, *3*(3), 60–70.

Steinbart, P. J. (1989, September). The auditor's responsibility for the accuracy of graphs in annual reports: Some evidence of the need for additional guidelines. *Accounting Horizons*, 60–70.

Stenheim, T., & Madsen, D. O. (2016). Goodwill Impairment Losses, Economic Impairment, Earnings Management and Corporate Governance. *Journal of Accounting and Finance*, *16*(2), 11–30.

Stolowy, H., & Breton, G. (2000). *A framework for the classification of accounts manipulations*. Working paper.

Stolowy, H., & Breton, G. (2003). La gestion des donnés comptables: une revue de la littérature. *Comptabilité-Contrôle-Audit, 9*(1), 125–152.

Stubben, S. R. (2010). Discretionary revenues as a measure of earnings management. *The Accounting Review*, *85*(2), 695–717. doi:10.2308/accr.2010.85.2.695

Subramanian, R., Insley, R., & Blackwell, R. D. (1993). performance and readability: A comparison of annual reports of profitable and unprofitable corporations. *Journal of Business Communication*, *30*(1), 49–60. doi:10.1177/002194369303000103

Subramanyam, K. R. (1996). The pricing of discretionary accruals. *Journal of Accounting and Economics*, *22*(1-3), 249–281. doi:10.1016/S0165-4101(96)00434-X

Sudaryati, D. (2012). The balance sheet as an earnings management constraint. *Jurnal Akuntansi & Investasi*, *13*(1), 1–14.

Suetugui, E., & Cia, J. N. S. (2011). Contabilidade no setor imobiliario residencial: Um estudo exploratorio da visao dos impactos da convergencia das normas brasileiras com normas internacionais – IFRS para alguns segmentos de mercado. In *Congresso USP de Iniciacao Cientifica em Contabilidade, 11, 2011*. Sao Paulo: USP.

Sundvik, D. (2017). Book-tax conformity and earnings management in response to tax rate cuts. *Journal of International Accounting, Auditing & Taxation, 28*, 31–42. doi:10.1016/j.intaccaudtax.2016.12.003

Sweeney, A. P. (1994). Debt-covenant violations and managers' accounting responses. *Journal of Accounting and Economics, 17*(3), 281–308. doi:10.1016/0165-4101(94)90030-2

Syderff, R., & Weetman, P. (1999). A texture index for evaluating accounting narratives: An alternative to readability formula. *Accounting, Auditing & Accountability Journal, 12*(4), 459–488. doi:10.1108/09513579910283503

Syderff, R., & Weetman, P. (2002). Development in content analysis: A transitivity index and DICTION scores. *Accounting, Auditing & Accountability Journal, 15*(4), 523–545. doi:10.1108/09513570210440586

Tendeloo, B. V., & Vanstraelen, A. (2005). Earnings Management under German GAAP versus IFRS. *European Accounting Review, 14*(1), 155–180. doi:10.1080/0963818042000338988

Teoh, S. H., Welch, I., & Wong, T. J. (1998). Earnings Management and the Underperformance of Seasoned Equity Offerings. *Journal of Financial Economics, 50*(1), 63–99. doi:10.1016/S0304-405X(98)00032-4

Teoh, S., Welch, I., & Wong, T. (1998). Earnings Management and the Long-run Market Performance of Initial Public Offerings. *The Journal of Finance, 53*(6), 1935–1974. doi:10.1111/0022-1082.00079

Teoh, S., & Wong, T. (2002). Why new issues and high-accrual firms underperform: The role of analysts' credulity. *Review of Financial Studies, 15*(3), 869–900. doi:10.1093/rfs/15.3.869

Thomas, J. (1997). Discourse in the marketplace: The making of meaning in annual reports. *Journal of Business Communication, 34*(1), 47–66. doi:10.1177/002194369703400103

Tirado, J. M., & Cabedo, J. D. (2003). The Disclosure of Risk in Financial Statements. *Accounting Forum, 28*, 181-200.

Tirkkonen, M. (2013). *Earnings management as a scope of art-empirical analysis of accrual-based and real earnings management in Finnish listed companies during 2001-2010* (Unpublished master's thesis). Aalto University School of Business.

Titman, S., & Wessels, R. (1988). The Determinants of Capital Structure. *The Journal of Finance, 43*(1), 1–19. doi:10.1111/j.1540-6261.1988.tb02585.x

Tort, L. P. (2013). Earnings management under IFRS and PGC. *Revista de Comptabilitat i Direcció, 16*, 161–185.

Trapp, A. C. G. (2009). *A relação do conselho fiscal como componente de controle no gerenciamento de resultados contábeis. Tese (Doutorado em Ciencias Contabeis).* Faculdade de Economia, Administracao e Contabilidade da Universidade de Sao Paulo.

Trueman, B., & Titman, S. (1988). An explanation for accounting income smoothing. *Journal of Accounting Research, 26*, 127–139. doi:10.2307/2491184

Tseng, L. J., & Lai, C. W. (2007). The relationship between income smoothing and company profitability: An empirical study. *International Journal of Management, 24*(4), 727–733.

Tsipouridou, M., & Spathis, C. (2012). Earnings management and the role of auditors in na unusual IFRS context: The case of Greece. *Journal of International Accounting, Auditing & Taxation, 21*(1), 62–78. doi:10.1016/j.intaccaudtax.2012.01.005

Tucker, J. W., & Zarowin, P. A. (2006). Does income smoothing improve earnings informativeness? *The Accounting Review, 81*(1), 251–270. doi:10.2308/accr.2006.81.1.251

Tufte, E. R. (1983). *The Visual Display of Quantitative Information*. C. G. Press.

Turner, L., Dietrich, J. R., Anderson, K., & Bailey, A. (2001). *Accounting restatements.* Working paper, United States Securities and Exchange Commission.

Tweedie, D. P., & Whittington, G. (1990). Financial reporting: Current problems and their implications for systematic reform. *Accounting and Business Research, 21*, 87–102. doi:10.1080/00014788.1990.9729407

Ussman, A. M. (2004). *Empresas Familiares* [Family business]. Lisboa: Edições Sílabo. (in Portuguese)

Uyar, A. (2009). An analysis of graphic disclosure in annual reports: The case of Turkey. *Managerial Auditing Journal, 24*(5), 423–444. doi:10.1108/02686900910956793

Vähämma, E. (2014). Executive turnover, gender, and earnings management: An exploratory analysis. *Accounting Perspectives, 13*(2), 103–122. doi:10.1111/1911-3838.12029

Van Hulle, K. (2004). From accounting directives to International Accounting Standards. In C. Leuz, D. Pfaff, & A. Hopwood (Eds.), *International perspectives on research trends, policy and practices.* Oxford, UK: Oxford University Press. doi:10.1093/0199260621.003.0014

Verrecchia, R. E. (1983). Discretionary disclosure. *Journal of Accounting and Economics, 5*(1), 179–194. doi:10.1016/0165-4101(83)90011-3

Vicente, E.F.R., Morais, L.M., & Platt Neto, O.A. (2012). A Reforma na Contabilidade Pública Brasileira e o Processo de Convergência: implicações e perspectivas. *RIC – Revista de Informação Contábil, 6*(2), 1-20.

Vieira, E. S. (2016). Earnings management in public family firms under economic adversity. *Australian Accounting Review, 26*(2), 190–207. doi:10.1111/auar.12096

Villalonga, B., & Amit, R. (2006). How do family ownership, control and management affect firms value? *Journal of Financial Economics, 80*(2), 385–417. doi:10.1016/j.jfineco.2004.12.005

Wallace, R. S. O., Mora, A., & Naser, K. (1994). The relationship between the comprehensiveness of corporate annual reports and firm characteristics in Spain. *Accounting and Business Research, 25*(97), 41–53. doi:10.1080/00014788.1994.9729927

Wang, D. (2006). Founding family ownership and earnings quality. *Journal of Accounting Research, 44*(3), 19–656. doi:10.1111/j.1475-679X.2006.00213.x

Wang, Z., & Williams, T. H. (1994). Accounting income smoothing and stockholder wealth. *Journal of Applied Business Research, 10*(3), 96–110. doi:10.19030/jabr.v10i3.5929

Warfield, T., Wild, J., & Wild, K. (1995). Managerial Ownership, Accounting Choices, and Informativeness of Earnings. *Journal of Accounting and Economics, 20*(1), 61–91. doi:10.1016/0165-4101(94)00393-J

Watrin, C., Ebert, N., & Thomsen, M. (2014). Book-Tax Conformity and Earnings Management: Insights from European One-and Two-Book Systems. *The Journal of the American Taxation Association, 36*(2), 55–89. doi:10.2308/atax-50769

Watts, R. L., & Zimmerman, J. L. (1978). Towards a Positive Theory of Determination of Accounting Standards. *The Accounting Review.* doi:10.2307/245729

Watts, R. L., & Zimmerman, J. L. (1978). Towards a positive theory of the determination of accounting standards. *The Accounting Review, 53*(1), 112–134.

Watts, R. L., & Zimmerman, J. L. (1978). Towards a Positive Theory of the Determination of Accounting Standards. *The Accounting Review, 53*(1), 112–134.

Watts, R. L., & Zimmerman, J. L. (1990). Positive Accounting Theory: A ten year perspective. *The Accounting Review*, *65*(1), 131–156.

Waweru, N. M., & Prot, N. P. (2018). Corporate governance compliance and accrual earnings management is eastern Africa: Evidence from Kenya and Tanzania. *Managerial Auditing Journal*, *33*(2), 171–191. doi:10.1108/MAJ-09-2016-1438

Welch, I. (2011). Two common problems in capital structure research: The financial-debt-to-asset ratio and issuing activity versus leverage changes. *International Review of Finance*, *11*(1), 1–17. doi:10.1111/j.1468-2443.2010.01125.x

Whelan, C., & Mcnamara, R. (2004). *The Impact of Earnings Management on the Value-relevance of Financial Statement Information*. Academic Press.

White, G. E. (1970). Discretionary accounting decisions and income normalization. *Journal of Accounting Research*, *8*, 260–273. doi:10.2307/2490111

White, H. (1980). A Heteroskedasticity-Consistent Covariance Matrix Estimator and a Direct Test for Heteroskedasticity. *Econometrica*, *48*(4), 817. doi:10.2307/1912934

Wijaya, M. H. (2013). Effect of corporate tax rate reduction on earnings management practices: A case study in Indonesia. *Finance and Banking Journal*, *15*(2), 206–222.

Xie, B., Davidson, W. N. III, & DaDalt, P. J. (2003). Earnings management and corporate governance: The roles of the board and the audit committee. *Journal of Corporate Finance*, *9*(3), 295–316. doi:10.1016/S0929-1199(02)00006-8

Xingqiang, D., Shaoyuan, L., & Hongmei, P. (2017). Do women top managers always mitigate earnings management? Evidence from China. *Accountability in Research*, *1*, 39–45.

Xu, Y., & Malkiel, B. (2003). Investigating the Behavior of Idiosyncratic Volatility. *The Journal of Business*, *76*(4), 613–644. doi:10.1086/377033

Yang, C. Y., Lai, H. N., & Tan, B. L. (2008). Managerial ownership structure and earnings management. *Journal of Financial Reporting and Accounting*, *6*(1), 35–53. doi:10.1108/19852510880000634

Yuthas, K., Rogers, R., & Dillard, J. F. (2002). Communicative action and corporate annual reports. *Journal of Business Ethics*, *41*(1/2), 141–157. doi:10.1023/A:1021314626311

Zalata, A. M., Tauringana, V., & Tingbani, I. (2018). Audit committee financial expertise, gender, and earnings management: Does gender of the financial expert matter? *International Review of Financial Analysis*, *55*, 170–183. doi:10.1016/j.irfa.2017.11.002

Zang, A. (2012). Evidence on the Trade-Off between Real Activities Manipulation and Accrual-Based Earnings Management. *The Accounting Review*, *87*(2), 675–703. doi:10.2308/accr-10196

Zarzeski, T. (1996). Spontaneous Harmonization Effects of Culture and Market Forces on Accounting Disclosures Practices. *Accounting Horizons*, *10*, 18–37.

Zeff, A. S. (2012). The Evolution of the IAS Cinto the IASB, and the Challenges it Faces. *The Accounting Review*, *87*(3), 807–837.

Zéghal, D., & Ahmed, S. (1990). Comparisons of Social Responsibility Information Disclosure Media Used by Canadian Firms. *Accounting, Auditing & Accountability Journal*, *3*(1), 38–53. doi:10.1108/09513579010136343

Zeghal, D., Chtourou, S. M., & Fourati, Y. M. (2012). The effect of mandatory adoption of ifrs on earnings quality: Evidence from the European Union. *Journal of International Accounting Research*, *11*(2), 1–25. doi:10.2308/jiar-10221

Zéghal, D., Chtourou, S., & Sellami, Y. M. (2011). An analysis of the effect of mandatory adoption of IAS/IFRS on earnings management. *Journal of International Accounting, Auditing & Taxation*, *20*(2), 61–72. doi:10.1016/j.intaccaudtax.2011.06.001

Zhao, Y., & Chen, K. (2008). The influence of takeover protection on earnings management. *Journal of Business Finance & Accounting*, *35*(3), 347–375. doi:10.1111/j.1468-5957.2008.02081.x

Zimmer, I. (1986). Accounting for interest by real estate developers. *Journal of Accounting and Economics*, *8*(1), 37–51. doi:10.1016/0165-4101(86)90009-1

Zimmerman, J. L. (1983). Taxes and firm size. *Journal of Accounting and Economics*, *5*(C), 119–149. doi:10.1016/0165-4101(83)90008-3

Zmijewski, M. E., & Hagerman, R. L. (1981). An income strategy approach to the positive theory of accounting standard setting/choice. *Journal of Accounting and Economics*, *3*(2), 129–149. doi:10.1016/0165-4101(81)90010-0

About the Contributors

Jonas Oliveira, PhD in Accounting from the School of Economics and Management, University of Minho, Portugal. He is an Assistant Professor of Accounting at ISCTE-IUL Business School, Lisbon. He has previously worked at the University of Aveiro as an Adjunct Professor of Accounting. His research interests are corporate risk reporting, corporate governance mechanisms, impression management strategies used corporate reporting, sustainability and integrated reporting. He publishes academic articles in some well-recognized journals such as the Managerial Auditing Journal, Australian Accounting Review, Corporate Communications: an International Journal, Meditari Accountancy Research, European Business Review, and Journal of Risk. He is a member of the Editorial Board of the Accounting and Finance Research. He has own some best papers awards. Recently, he has researched on topics related to corporate social responsibility and integrated reporting. Currently, he supervises PhD students on integrated reporting, corporate social responsibility and risk reporting (enterprise risk management).

Graca Azevedo has a PhD in Management (scientific field: Accounting) at the Institute of Higher Labor and Enterprise – ISCTE. She has published and presented several articles in national and international journals and conferences as well. She is a member of the Editorial Board of international journal "Accounting and Finance Research". She currently teaches courses in scientific field of Financial Accounting at the Institute of Higher Learning in Accounting and Administration of the University of Aveiro. Her research interests are related to financial reporting, impression management strategies and international accounting standards.

Augusta Ferreira completed her first degree at the Higher Institute of Accounting and Administration of Aveiro. She has got her Masters Degree in Business Management Specialization in Corporate Finance at Minho University and she holds a PhD in Accounting at Aveiro University and Minho University. Currently she teaches Accounting within the accounting scientific area at Higher Institute Accounting and Administration of Aveiro (Aveiro University) and she is interested in researching public accounting, accounting information systems, disclosure of financial information and accountability. She has presented and published many articles in national and international journals and conferences.

* * *

Rodrigo G. Amaro, Master in Accounting from UFPE (2010) and holds a degree in Administration from the same institution (2007). Composes the permanent staff of the Federal Rural University of Pernambuco (UFRPE). He currently serves as the Internal Ministerial Controller (CMI) of the Public Ministry of Pernambuco (MPPE). He was the Chief Executive Officer of Pernambuco Participações e Investimentos S / A (Perpart - Sociedade de Economia Mista, linked to the State Administration Department of Pernambuco) from 2011 to 2014 and was responsible for designing and implementing the "Minha Imóvel Legal" regularization program legal land ownership of social interest. From 2015 until the beginning of 2016, he held the position of Secretary of State Comptroller's Office (SCGE) and General Ombudsman of the State of Pernambuco, during which he implemented the "Contingency Plan for Expenses" to confront the economic crisis in Pernambuco, in this year the State obtained the largest reduction of costs of costing in Brazil. Until January 2017, he held the position of Executive Secretary for Project Development (SEPROJ) of the Special Adviser to the Governor of Pernambuco (AESP), where he led the analysis of the economic and financial viability of the securitization project for the public assets of the State. In the scope of the research, the study focuses on the analysis of the control mechanisms required by Public Sector Governance (GSP). He works in the undergraduate and postgraduate teaching in the areas of Administration and Accounting Sciences. In 2009, he coordinated the Working Groups of the National Council of Internal Control Organs of the States and the Federal District (Conaci) for the elaboration of "Guidelines for internal control in the public sector". He was University Council (Consuni) of UFPE for two terms, Research and Extension Education Counselor (CEPE) in 2005 and Board Member in 2009. He also held the position of President of the Fiscal Council of the Pension and Pensions Foundation of the State Pernambuco (FUNAPE) between 2011 and 2015 and member of the Board of Directors of the Agronomic Research Institute (IPA) from 2011 to 2014.

Cláudia Roberta de Araújo Alves Pinto is a PhD Student at the University of Aveiro and a Lecturer at the Polytechnic Institute of Viana do Castelo. Her research interest is risk reporting.

Laura Araújo Leal is Accounting Supervisor and Accounting Professor. Graduated in Tax Planning from the Federal University of Pernambuco (UFPE), and graduated in Accounting from Mauritius University of Nassau - Recife. Worked in the Working Group on Accounting Procedures of Public Companies and State Mixed Economy Societies (GTCon Estatais), created through State Decree No. 39,594, of July 15, 2013, with the objective of facilitating the accounting convergence of Public Companies and Mixed Economy Societies of the State of Pernambuco.

Marcelo Victor José de Barros Ribeiro, PhD student in Accounting and Master in Public Management from the Federal University of Pernambuco (UFPE). Specialist in Financial Mathematics and Statistics from Cândido Mendes University - Rio de Janeiro (UCAM / RJ). Contador, Bachelor of Science in Accounting from Universidade Católica de Pernambuco (UNICAP). He is currently a professor at the Frassinetti Faculty in Recife (Fafire), permanent staff accountant at the Foundation for Science and Technology Support of the State of Pernambuco (FACEPE), Instructor at the School of Treasury Administration (Esaf) and Instructor and Lecturer at the Regional Accounting Council in Pernambuco (CRC/PE), Ad Hoc Evaluator of Public Management and Citizenship Papers (FGV / EAESP). He was a professor at the Federal University of Pernambuco of the accounting sciences course, Coordination of the Superintendency of Patrimony and Chairman of the Permanent Inventory Committee of Pernambuco Participações e Investimentos S/A (Perpart), Technical Advisor of the Working Group on Accounting

Procedures of Companies State University of Pernambuco (GTCon State), Professor of the Faculty of Santa Helena (FSH), Professor of the Faculty of Applied Sciences of Limoeiro (Facal), Guest Professor of the Postgraduate Program in Public Management at the Faculdade Joaquim Nabuco, Professor of the Specialization Course in Public Management at the Federal Institute of Pernambuco (IFPE) and Consultant and Accounting Analyst at the company Ferreira & Associados Auditores Independentes He is interested in the following areas: Public Management, Applied Accounting to the Public Sector, Financial and Budgetary Administration, Accounting International.

Adele Caldarelli is Full Professor of Accounting and Head of the Department of Economics, Management, Institutions of the University of Naples Federico II. She has managed as principal author a number of research projects on Accounting and Management Accounting, as well as on Business Ethics, co-authored with both Italian and international researchers, published in national and international peer reviewed journals, and accepted to international conferences.

Raffaela Casciello is Ph.D. Student in Management at the Department of Economics, Management, Institutions of the University of Naples Federico II. Her main area of research and publication regards Accounting, Management Accounting and IAS/IFRS.

Stéphanie Fernandes Pinheiro was a Master student in Accounting at the University of Aveiro. Her research interests are impression management strategies related to corporate reporting.

Maria Filipa Nogueira, PhD Student in Accounting at the University of Aveiro since 2018. Management PhD student at the University of Évora from 2010 to 2017. Degree of Master in Technological Innovation and Industrial Management, business finance business, with defense of dissertation entitled "Design of a management panel at a school of polytechnic higher Education", at the Technical Superior Institute of the Technical University of Lisbon, in 01/03/2007. Degree in business management, the Superior Institute of Languages and Administration of Santarém, completed in the school year 1992/93. Bachelor's degree in business management, by the Superior School of Management of Santarém, completed in the school year of 1988/89. The professional activity is divided into two parts. In the initial phase your activity developed in companies of the manufacturing sector, having played a role in the administrative and financial sector of the companies where he worked. Since 1995 started teaching at Polytechnic Institutes. Non-teaching activity Head of the Administrative/financial Department of the firm Prebesan, Lda, in the period from 01/09/1991 to 30/09/95. Accountant at Friedlander Portugal-Industrial Assemblies, Lda, from 03/09/1990 to 31/08/1991. Head of financial department of RIBACAL – the record-keeping agricultural cooperative from 23/02/1990 to 20/08/1990. Analysis and execution of general and Cost Accounting with focus on the internal audit and with the objective of being the quantitative control of the production and consumptions carried out at Companhia Nacional de Fiação e Tecidos de Torres Novas, SA, from 22/11/1989 to 22/02/1990. Teaching Activity Professor at the Superior School of Management and Technology of Santarém integrated in the Polytechnic Institute of Santarém since 21/02/2000. Professor at the School of Technology, Management, Art and Design (ESTGAD) of Caldas da Rainha, inserted at the Polytechnic Institute of Leiria from 01/09/1999 to 21/02/2000. Professor at School of Social Communication at the Polytechnic Institute of Lisbon, from 2/01/1998 to 31/08/1999. Professor at the School of Technology, Management, Art and Design (ESTGAD) of Caldas da Rainha, inserted at the Polytechnic Institute of Leiria from 13/10/1995 to 22/12/1997.

Cristina Gonçalves Góis is Coordinator Professor in Accounting in the Coimbra Business School ISCAC (Portugal). PhD in accounting from the University of Extremadura (Spain). Master in Accounting and Corporate Finance. Director of the Bachelor in Accounting and Audit. Research topics include corporate governance, financial reporting, integrated reporting and corporate social responsibility.

Dimmitre Morant Vieira Gonçalves Pereira, Master in Accounting Sciences from the Graduate Program in Accounting Sciences of University of Brasilia (UnB), graduated in Accounting Sciences from the Federal University of Pernambuco (UFPE) and Assistant Professor at the Federal University of Paraíba (UFPB). He acted as project manager of accounting convergence of the Working Group on Accounting Procedures of Public Companies and Mixed Economy Societies of Pernambuco (State GTCon).

Susana Patrícia Henriques Martins was a Master student at the University of Aveiro. Her research interest is risk reporting.

Susana Jorge is a Tenured Professor with accreditation at the Faculty of Economics, University of Coimbra, Portugal. Research affiliations: Affiliated researcher of CICP – Centro de Investigação em Ciência Política (Research Centre in Political Science), University of Minho, (Braga) Portugal. Collaborator researcher at the CeBER – Center for Business and Economics Research, University of Coimbra, (Coimbra) Portugal. Collaborator researcher at the CICF – Centro de Investigação em Contabilidade e Fiscalidade (Research Centre in Accounting and Taxation), Instituto Politécnico do Cávado e do Ave, (Barcelos) Portugal. Teaching and research expertise: Lecturer in Business Financial Accounting and Public Sector Accounting at undergraduate and Master levels respectively. Researcher in Public Sector Accounting and Management, especially focusing on financial reporting and in Local Government. Other: Board Member of the CIGAR Network. Associated with the SIG on Accounting and Accountability of the IRSPM. Associated with the Panel XII on Public Sector Financial Management of EGPA. Between February 2013 and October 2018 was member of the Public Sector Accounting Standards Committee (CNCP) of the Portuguese Accounting Standard-Setting Commission, where worked on the adaptation of IPSAS to Portugal. Member of the Scientific Commission of the Portuguese Municipal Transparency Index (ITM), annually published by Transparência e Integridade – Transparency International Portugal. Co-author of the Portuguese Municipalities Financial Yearbook (Anuário Financeiro dos Municípios), currently in its 13th edition.

Lúcia Lima Rodrigues is a Full Professor of Accounting at the University of Minho, Braga, Portugal. Her main research areas include international accounting, accounting history, corporate social responsibility, risk reporting, and accounting for intellectual capital and intangible assets. She has published eight books, several book chapters and over 80 refereed articles in international journals, including Accounting, Organizations and Society, Accounting, Auditing and Accountability Journal, European Accounting Review, Business History, Journal of Business Ethics, Accounting Forum and Critical Perspectives on Accounting. She is the Editor of the refereed Portuguese Journal of Accounting and Management, member of the Editorial Board of several international journals, and Book review Editor of the European Accounting Association (EAA). She is a member of the Academic panel of the European Financial Reporting Advisory Group (EFRAG). She is the representative of Portugal at the Accounting Regulatory Committee (ARC) and at the European Financial Reporting Advisory Group (EFRAG - CFSS). Since she is at the moment the leader of this Portuguese accounting standards setting body (Comissão de Normalização Contabilística-CNC) and the President of Financial Accounting Group of the Portuguese Chartered Accountants Association, her research aims to develop theory but also to support practitioners.

Marcleide Maria Macêdo Pederneiras, PhD, Professor at the Federal University of Paraíba - UFPB and Master's Program in Public Administration - PROFIAP / UFCG / CCJS. He holds a Master's degree in Accounting and a PhD in Administration / PROPAD / UFPE. Post-Doctorate at the University of Minho at EEG- School of Economics and Management / Braga- Portugal. Author of several chapters of books. Has publications in the area of Accounting Education, Public Administration and Performance Measurement / Management in Hospitality Companies.

Mara Madaleno is Auxiliar Professor and Coordinator of the Master Degree in Economics at DEGEIT, University of Aveiro. She is researcher at the Research Unit on Governance, Competitiveness and Public Policies (GOVCOPP), being Vice Coordinator of the System for Decisions Support Research Group.

Marco Maffei is Associate Professor of Accounting at the Department of Economics, Management, Institutions of the University of Naples Federico II. His main area of research and publications regards risk disclosure, performance measurement, financial instruments, IAS/IFRS and going concern. Moreover, he is Professor of accounting for financial instruments at Toulouse Business School. He is also coordinator of the project #empl-oi funded by the European Union.

Liliana Marques Pimentel is Adjunct Professor in the Department of Management and Economics of the School of Technology and Management of the Polytechnic Institute of Leiria and Assistant Professor in the Faculty of Economics of the University of Coimbra. Deputy Mayor of Condeixa-a-Nova from 2013 to the present. PhD in Business Management, specializing in Accounting and Finance, Faculty of Economics, University of Coimbra. The research areas of interest are Financial Accounting and Public Accounting.

José Augusto de Medeiros Monteiro, Master in Accounting Sciences from the Graduate Program in Accounting Sciences (PPGCC) of the Federal University of Pernambuco (UFPE) and graduated in Accounting Sciences from the Federal University of Paraíba (UFPB). He is currently an Assistant Professor at the Federal University of Alagoas (UFAL - Campus Sertão/Santana do Ipanema Unit). He was Professor of the Joaquim Nabuco Faculty (2014-2015) and Advisor in the MBA in Public Management of the Federal Institute of Pernambuco (IFPE) (2014). He acted as technical advisor (2013-2014) and as technical coordinator (2014-2015) of accounting convergence of the Working Group on Accounting Procedures of Public Companies and Mixed Economy Societies of Pernambuco (State GTCon).

Sara Raquel Pinto Marcelino Dias was a Master student at the University of Aveiro. Her research interest is impression management strategies related to corporate reporting.

Maria Fátima Ribeiro Borges is a PhD student in Accounting at the University of Aveiro. Her research interests are impression management strategies related to corporate reporting. She has published in the international journal *Corporate Communications: An International Journal*.

Inna Sousa Paiva held a PhD in Accounting in Instituto Universitário de Lisboa (ISCTE-IUL) – Portugal. Professor of Accounting on Department of Accounting – Instituto Universitário de Lisboa. Guest professor in international universities teaches in courses of master programs. Research interests are International Financial Reporting Standards, Accounting Quality and Corporate Social Responsibility. Author of several publications in national and international journals, books and book chapters.

Laura Parte is an Associate professor of Accounting at the Universidad Nacional de Educación a Distancia (UNED), Madrid (Spain). Her main research areas are financial reporting, earnings management, financial statements analysis, accounting education and tourism management. She has published several book chapters and articles in international peer reviewed journals, including Spanish Accounting Review, Spanish Journal of Finance and Accounting, European Research on Management and Business Economics, International Journal of Accounting and Information Management, Benchmarking: an International Journal, Tourism Management, International Journal of Hospitality Management, International Journal of Contemporary Hospitality Management and Tourism Economics. She has been involved in different competitive projects related to these research areas.

Andreia Sousa, PhD student in Accounting at the University of Aveiro, Master Degree in Accounting and Business Taxation at Coimbra Business School and Licenciate Degree in Accounting and Auditing at the same Institute. She has published and presented some academic articles in national and international conferences and congresses. Also, she is Certified Accountant. Her research interests are earnings management, quality of financial information, materiality in financial reporting and business taxation.

Paulo Varela Dias, PhD in Accounting and MBA in Management, by ISCTE-IUL, Post-Graduate in Finance, by CEMAF-ISCTE and Graduate in Management, by UML. He is coordinator of Courses of Taxation, Business Taxation, Company Tax Management, Principles and Procedures of Tax Litigation and Taxation of Non-Residents. He is Executive Director of the Executive MBA and Director of Post-Graduation in Tax Management at INDEG-ISCTE.

Elisabete Vieira is Coordinator Professor and Coordinator of the Master Degree in Finance at ISCA, University of Aveiro. She is researcher at the Research Unit on Governance, Competitiveness and Public Policies (GOVCOPP), being Vice Coordinator of the Competitiveness, Innovation and Sustainability (CIS) Research Group.

Clara Viseu is Adjunct Professor at Coimbra Business School I ISCAC, Polytechnic Institute of Coimbra, Portugal. PhD in Mathematics from the University of Beira Interior. Master in Probability and Statistics from the University of Lisbon. Collaborator researcher at the CICF – Centro de Investigação em Contabilidade e Fiscalidade (Research Centre in Accounting and Taxation), IPCA, Portugal. Research topics include econometrics, multivariate statistical analysis, extreme value theory.

Index

A

B

C

D

E

F

G

H

I

L

M

N

O

P

Q

R

S

T

www.ingramcontent.com/pod-product-compliance
Lightning Source LLC
LaVergne TN
LVHW080636011026
849160LV00014B/1237